Lecture Notes in Artificial Intelligence 660

Subseries of Lecture Notes in Computer Science
Edited by J. Siekmann

Lecture Notes in Computer Science
Edited by G. Goos and J. Hartmanis

E. Lamma P. Mello (Eds.)

Extensions of Logic Programming

Third International Workshop, ELP '92
Bologna, Italy, February 26-28, 1992
Proceedings

Springer-Verlag
Berlin Heidelberg New York
London Paris Tokyo
Hong Kong Barcelona
Budapest

Series Editor

Jörg Siekmann
University of Saarland
German Research Center for Artificial Intelligence (DFKI)
Stuhlsatzenhausweg 3, W-6600 Saarbrücken 11, FRG

Volume Editors

Evelina Lamma
Paola Mello
DEIS University of Bologna
Viale Risorgimento 2, I-40136 Bologna, Italy

CR Subject Classification (1991): D.1.6, I.2.3

ISBN 3-540-56454-3 Springer-Verlag Berlin Heidelberg New York
ISBN 0-387-56454-3 Springer-Verlag New York Berlin Heidelberg

Printed in Germany

Typesetting: Camera ready by author
Printing and binding: Druckhaus Beltz, Hemsbach/Bergstr.
45/3140-543210 - Printed on acid-free paper

Preface

This volume contains papers presented at the third international workshop on extensions of logic programming, which was held at the Dipartimento di Elettronica, Informatica e Sistemistica of the University of Bologna, February 26–28, 1992.

The two previous workshops were held at the University of Tübingen, Germany, in December 1989 and at the Swedish Institute of Computer Science (SICS) in Kista, Sweden, in January 1991. Proceedings of these previous meetings have been published as Vol. 475 (P. Schroeder-Heister, ed.) and Vol. 596 (L.-H. Eriksson, L. Hallnäs, P. Schroeder-Heister, eds.) respectively, in the Lecture Notes in Artificial Intelligence series.

The main goal of the workshop was to discuss extensions of logic programming towards the artificial intelligence and software engineering areas, providing an opportunity to demonstrate implemented systems.

The papers presented here cover both theoretical and practical aspects. Some papers investigate topics such as abductive reasoning and negation. Some works discuss how to enhance the expressive power of logic programming by introducing constraints, sets and integration with functional programming. Other papers deal with the structuring of knowledge into modules, taxonomies and objects with the aim of extending logic programming towards software engineering applications. A section is devoted to papers concentrating on proof theory and inspired by Gentzen-style sequent or natural deduction systems. Moreover, topics such as concurrency are considered to enhance the expressive power of logic languages. Finally, some papers mainly concern techniques for implementing some of these logic programming extensions.

We would like to thank the authors and the reviewers for their contributions. We thank also the following institutions for their sponsorship and patronage:

DEIS (Dipartimento di Elettronica, Informatica e Sistemistica);
AI*IA (Associazione Italiana per l'Intelligenza Artificiale);
CIOC (Centro Interazione Operatore Calcolatore, CNR Bologna);
CNR (Consiglio Nazionale delle Ricerche);
Direzione Progetto Finalizzato CNR Sistemi Informatici e Calcolo Parallelo;
GULP (Gruppo Utenti e Ricercatori Logic Programming).

We extend special thanks to the people in Bologna, working at the Dipartimento di Elettronica, Informatica e Sistemistica whose help made the workshop possible. Finally, we would like to thank Jörg Siekmann and Springer-Verlag for publishing these proceedings in their Lecture Notes series.

Bologna, November 1992 — Evelina Lamma, Paola Mello

Contents

Negation

Constraints, Functions and Sets

Modules, Objects and Inheritance

Concurrency

Proof Theory

Implementation Issues

SLWV - A Theorem Prover for Logic Programming

Luís Moniz Pereira, Luis Caires and José Alferes

AI Centre, Uninova and DCS, U.Nova de Lisboa+
2825 Monte da Caparica, Portugal

Abstract. The purpose of this work is to define a theorem prover that retains the procedural aspects of logic programing. The proof system we propose (SLWV-resolution, for Selected Linear Without contrapositive clause Variants)) is defined for a set of clauses in the implicational form (keeping to the form of logic programs), not requiring contrapositives, and has an execution method that respects the execution order of literals in a clause, preserving the procedural flavor of logic programming. SLWV-resolution can be seen as a combination of SL-resolution and case-analysis, which admits a form of linear derivation. We show its soundness and completeness by establishing a one-to-one mapping between SLWV and SL derivations which also clarifies the motivation and the method.Our work can be seen as an extension to logic programs that goes beyond normal programs, and thus beyond (positive) definite clause programming, by allowing also definite negative heads. Thus we admit program clauses with both positive and (classically) negated atoms conjoined in the body, and at most one literal as its head (clauses with disjunctions of literals in the head are transformed into a single clause of that form). As this approach does not require clause contrapositives and admits a leftmost selection function, the implementation can and does preserve the pragmatic procedural reading explicitly provided by the programmer. The implementation, not described here, relies on the source program being preprocessed into directly executable Prolog. Preprocessing keeps the overall program structure untouched, and thus a directly recognizable execution pattern that mimics Prolog is obtained: this is useful in debugging. Additionally, the preprocessing is such that Prolog programs run with negligible overhead. Various program examples and attending derivations are proffered.

Introduction

The purpose of this work is to define a theorem prover that retains the procedural aspects of logic programing. It can be seen as an extension to logic programs that goes beyond normal programs, as defined in [4], and thus beyond (positive) definite clause programming, by allowing also definite negative heads. In order to keep to the clausal form of logic programs, the proof system we define (SLWV resolution) applies, without loss of generality, to sets of clauses in the implicational form, though not requiring any contrapositive variants.Clauses with negative literals in the head are transformed into a single contrapositive clause with $\perp$ there, where this new symbol denotes falsehood. Accordingly, refuting a top goal G is equivalent to adding the clause $\perp \leftarrow G$ and finding a derivation for $\perp$. In order to preserve the procedural aspects of the language, it is our aim to maintain the execution order of literals in a clause. So we can't use contrapositives. The proof system we propose can be seen as a combination of SL-resolution [3] and case-analysis that admits a form of linear

+ E-mail: {lmp,lxc,jja}@fct.unl.pt Ph: +351-1-2953156 Telex:14542 FCTUNL P

derivation. As an example let us consider a procedural-like representation of a SL-resolution (Fig. 1.) for the program:

```
(1) arrested(X) :- ¬ paytaxes(X).
(2) sad(X):- ¬ drunk(X), nomoney(X).
(3) ¬ drunk( john ).
(4) drunk(X) :- sad(X).
(5) nomoney(X) :- paytaxes(X).
```

and query `?- arrested(john).`

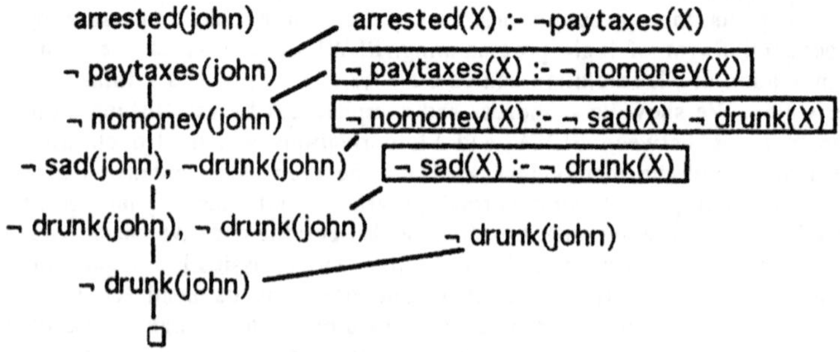

Fig. 1. SL derivation

Clauses inside boxes show where a contrapositive was used to resolve a literal. In such cases, our method, instead of relying on contrapositives, tries alternative reduction branches for the ancestors of the literal in order to find a matching complementary literal, and then resolves both using case-analysis. Figure 2 illustrates in a simple way how our method proceeds in this example (following the arrows reveals the execution trace).

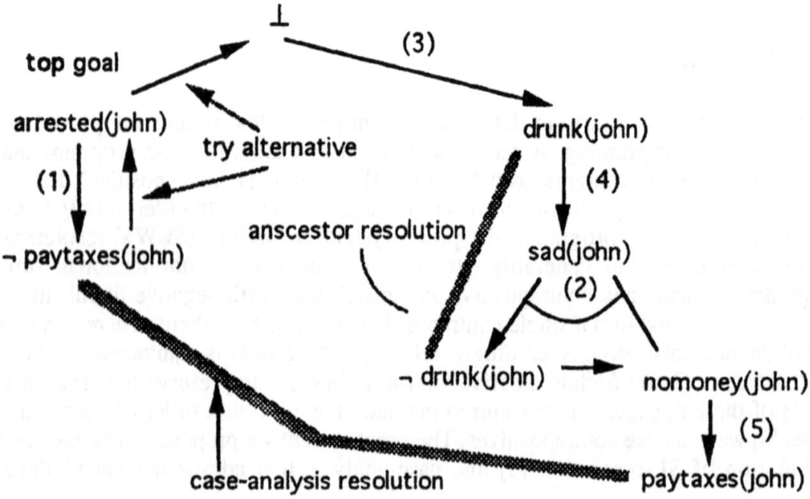

Fig. 2. SLWV intuition

Labeled arrows show resolutions with a program clause (whose number is given). Note how clause (3) is used as ⊥ ← drunk(john), ⊥ being a symbol for "false", which is also the root ancestor of the top goal , ⊥ ← arrested(john).
The "try alternative step" corresponds to the choice of an alternative clause for some ancestor (in this case only available for ⊥). Here we can also see that the case-analysis resolution step corresponds to the use of a contrapositive[1].
The preceding example illustrates the basic intuition behind SLWV: that the use of contrapositives (as required by SL) can be replaced by a case analysis rule that resolves literals by cancellation with complementary ones to be found on disjunctive branches for a common ancestor. This is akin to Loveland's nH-Prolog [6], but there are significant differences in the way of attaining it. This will be examined in section 6, comparing the two methods.

The organization of this paper is as follows: in sections 1 and 2 we define the proof system used for normal programs by giving a complete set of inference rules. In section 3 we examine the connection with resolution proofs and, prove its equivalence to SL-resolution (thus showing soundness and completeness). Section 4 explains how we extend the method for clauses with negative heads. In Section 5 we define disjunctive answers and explain how the theorem prover handles such answers. In section 6 we compare our method with Loveland's nH-Prolog [6]. Section 7 describes a simple executor for the method. Finally, in section 8, we draw some conclusions.

1. Language and Proofs

The class of programs we consider initially are finite sets of clauses of the implicative form $H \leftarrow B_1, B_2, \ldots B_n$ (or H ← **B** for short) where H is an atom and the B_j for all j are literals. n may be 0, in which case we write H ← T, where T stands for truth (an atom satisfied by all models). Similarly, ⊥ stands for falsehood (i.e. it is an atom false in all models). In the metalanguage, for a literal A, we will use the notation -A for expressing the complementary literal of A. In section 4 we show the translation of clauses with a negative head into this form.

1.1. Basic Definitions

Labels are finite sets of literals. &-clauses are conjunctions of literals. L-Clauses are pairs L#G, where L is a label and G a &-clause. L-Resolvents are finite sequences of L-Clauses. ❑ denotes the empty L-Clause. If C is a L-Clause and σ a substitution, then (C)σ denotes the L-Clause obtained by application of σ to C.

The intended meaning of a L-Clause PN#F is the disjunction $F \vee A_1 \vee A_2 \vee \ldots \vee A_n$, for $A_i \in$ PN. Thus F is logically equivalent to ø#F.

Now, let Π be a program, PN a label, σ,τ substitutions, and ε the empty substitution.

1 The equivalence between our method and SL-resolution, specially in what concerns the use of contrapositives, is discussed in section 3 herein.

2. Inference Rules

These rules are the basic inferences of the system, and state the deducibility relation between formulae (which are L-Clauses).

2.1. ❑-Rules

The empty L-Clause is derivable with empty substitution.

$$\frac{}{\square\ [\varepsilon]} \qquad [R1]$$

The T atom is derivable with empty substitution.

$$\frac{\square}{PN\#T\ [\varepsilon]} \qquad [R2]$$

A cancellable L-clause is derivable.

$$\frac{\square}{PN\#A\ [\sigma]} \quad \text{if } \sigma = mgu(A,A_i) \text{ and } A \text{ is } \text{-}A_i \text{ for some } A_i \in PN \qquad [R3]$$

2.2. &-Rule

$$\frac{PN\#g\ [\sigma]\ (PN\#G)\sigma\ [\tau]}{PN\#(g,G)\ [\sigma\tau]} \qquad [R4]$$

A conjunction is derivable by deriving each conjunct in sequence.

2.3. ←-Rule

$$\frac{(PN \cup \{g\}\#B)\sigma\ [\tau]}{PN\#g\ [\sigma\tau]} \text{ for some } A \in PN \cup \{g\}, \text{ if } H \leftarrow B \in \Pi \text{ and } \sigma = mgu(A,H) \quad [R5]$$

This rule embodies the usual resolution step of SL, but allows, besides the current goal, any ancestor to be expanded.

Any A verifying the above stated condition is called a *reducible* literal. The actual A used is said to be *reduced* by the clause H ← B upon application of R5.

2.4. Proofs

Derivations in this system are tree-shaped, since there is a rule (namely R4) involving more than one premise. As usual, we say that a literal F is deducible if there is a derivation for ø#F such that every branch terminates with ❑. However, we can devise a linear refutation scheme, by allowing formulae to be sequences of L-Clauses (L-Resolvents). So, we start off with ø#F, and apply the rules backwards. Application of R4 then always introduces a nonsingular L-Resolvent. When applying any rule to the latest L-Resolvent in the sequence, we select a L-Clause in it and proceed. As stated above, the inference rules above are sound and complete for the class of formulas in consideration, this fact being shown herein by a construction that maps a SLWV proof into a SL proof and conversely.

3. SLWV-Resolution and SL-Resolution Proofs

In this section, we define SLWV resolution and reveal a connection between SLWV-resolution and SL resolution proofs, showing soundness and completeness by establishing correspondence between SLWV and SL derivations, which also clarifies the motivation for introducing SLWV and its derivation method.We start by defining the general shape of a (linear) SLWV derivation. Then we will show a convenient representation of SL and SLWV derivations using trees. Afterwards, a pair of mappings between SL and SLWV trees will be defined, providing a way of showing completeness and soundness for our method, by reducing it to SL soundness and completeness [3]. The existence of the mappings also shows that any selection function adopted by SL carries over to SLWV. Without loss of generality, in the sequel we will assume a leftmost selection function.

3.1. SLWV linear derivations

We now consider the linear refutation method over L-Resolvents suggested above (assuming that the selected literal is always the leftmost one). Let $\mathcal{R}$ be a L-Resolvent. Then, the following defines a left to right SLWV linear derivation $\mathcal{G}$ for a literal G.

D1. F_1 is ø # G.

D2. If F_n is ❑, then F_n is the last L-Resolvent of $\mathcal{G}$.

D2'. If F_n is PN # T $\mathcal{R}$ then F_{n+1} is $\mathcal{R}$.

D3. If F_n is PN # (g, G) $\mathcal{R}$, then F_{n+1} is PN # g PN # G $\mathcal{R}$.

D4. If F_n is PN # A $\mathcal{R}$, with A a literal, then

D4.1 If $A\sigma$ is complementary of $AL_j\sigma$ for some $AL_j \in$ PN and σ = mgu(A,AL_j),then F_{n+1} is $\mathcal{R}\sigma$.

D4.2 If there is a clause H ← **B**, and mgu σ such that $A\sigma = H\sigma$, then F_{n+1} is (PN ∪ {A} #B)σ $\mathcal{R}\sigma$.

D4.3 Otherwise, let D ∈ PN be an atom for which there exists both a clause H ← **B**, and a mgu σ such that $D\sigma = H\sigma$. In this case, let F_{n+1} be (PN ∪ {A} #B)σ $\mathcal{R}\sigma$.

A SLWV refutation for a literal A is a SLWV derivation constructed using the above stated rules, such that its last L-Resolvent is ❑. Note that there is non-determinism in D4, both in the choice of a matching literal (D4.1) and in the choice of a program clause (D4.2 and D4.3). As usual, we are interested in fair derivations (eg. finite or every L-clause is eventually selected).

Example 3.1.1. Let us consider now an example similar to the one in the Introduction. For brevity we use shortened predicate names.
Π = {arr(X) ← ¬pay(X), sad(X)← ¬dr(X); nom(X) ; arr(X)← dr(j); dr(X)← sad(X); nom(X) ← pay(X)}.

A SLWV refutation of arr(j) is:

{ }#arr(j)	by D1
{arr(j)}# ¬pay(j)	by D4.2
{arr(j), ¬pay(j)}# dr(j)	by D4.3
{arr(j), ¬pay(j), dr(j)}# sad(j)	by D4.2
{arr(j),¬pay(j),dr(j),sad(j)}# (¬dr(j), nom(j))	by D4.2
{arr(j),¬pay(j),dr(j),sad(j)}# ¬dr(j) {arr(j),¬pay(j),dr(j),sad(j)}# nom(j)	by D3
{arr(j),¬pay(j),dr(j),sad(j)}# nom(j)	by D4.1
{arr(j), ¬pay(j), dr(j), sad(j), nom(j)}# pay(j)	by D4.2
☐	by D4.1

Example 3.1.2. Let Π = { p ← a,b ; p ← ¬a, b ; p ← ¬b }.
Then the following constitutes a proof of p:

1.	{ }#p by D1	
2.	{p}#a{p}#b	by D4.2 & D3
3.	{p,a}#¬a{p,a}#b{p}#b	by D4.3 & D3
4.	{p,a}#b{p}#b	by D4.1
5.	{p,a,b}#¬b{p}#b	by D4.3
6.	{p}#b	by D4.1
7.	{p,b}#¬a{p,b}#b	by D4.3 & D3
8.	{p,b,¬a}#¬b{p,b}#b	by D4.3
9.	{p,b}#¬b	by D4.1
10	☐	by D4.1

For the program of example 3.1.2, we display in figure 3 a partial search tree (choices points are related to the way in which the clauses were chosen). The path shown highlighted is the one actually chosen by the leftmost/ancestor-order strategy used by the operative implementation (for the presented clause order).

This strategy always selects the leftmost literal, following the ancestor chain "upwards" when looking for disjunctive branches.

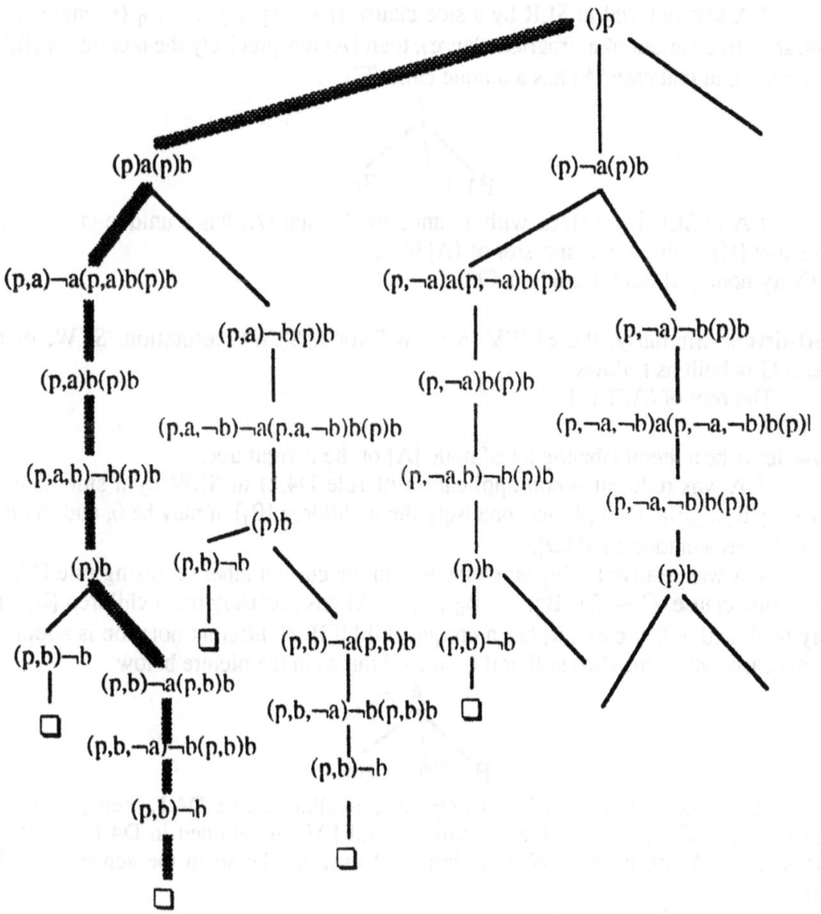

Fig. 3. Partial search tree for example .

3.2. SL and SLWV Derivation Trees

We now briefly introduce a tree notation for both SL and SLWV refutations. Both types of trees have their nodes labeled by literals (e.g. [A] is a node labeled by the literal A). For simplicity's sake we assume that variables have been removed from the SL and SLWV refutations through instantiation, so we can restrict this presentation to the propositional case.

Definition: The SL-tree SLT for a SL refutation SLR of a literal G is constructed as follows (from root to leaf nodes):

a) The root of SLT is [G].

Now, let A be a literal labeling a leaf node [A] of the current tree.

b) If A was reduced in SLR by a side clause $H \leftarrow B_1, B_2, \ldots, B_n$ (eventually a contrapositive variant of a program clause), then [A] has precisely the n children [B_i]. n may be 0; in that case [A] has a unique child [□].

c) If A in SLR is resolved with an ancestor H then [A] has a unique child [□]. Note that [H] is also a tree-ancestor of [A] in SLT.
d) Every node [□] has no children. □

Definition: Similarly, the SLWV-tree SWT for a SLWV refutation, SLW, of a literal G is built as follows:
a) The root of SWT is [G].

Now, let A be a literal labeling a leaf node [A] of the current tree.
b) If A was reduced (upon application of rule D4.2) in SLW by a side clause $A \leftarrow B_1, B_2, \ldots, B_n$, then [A] has precisely the n children [B_i]. n may be 0, and in that case [A] has a unique child [□].
c) If A was resolved using an element C in the current label set (using rule D4.3) and a side clause $C \leftarrow B_1, B_2, \ldots, B_n$, then [A] has precisely the n children [B_i]. n may be 0, and in that case [A] has a unique child [□]. A different notation is adopted in this case, where the chosen literal is singled out as in the picture below

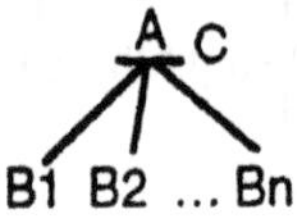

d) If A was resolved in SLW using the cancellation rule D4.1, then [A] has a unique child [□]. Note that the matching literal [AL] mentioned in D4.1 is a tree-ancestor of [A] in the tree SWT (although it may not be so in the sense of a SL proof).
d) Every node [□] has no children.

Note that in an SLWV-tree no contrapositive variants of the given clauses are ever used.

We can now state:

I) Every SLWV tree can be translated into an equivalent SL-tree (where contrapositives are eventually used).

II) Every SL-tree can be translated into an equivalent SLWV-tree (using the case-analysis rule).

The proof of the existence of the translation SL into SLWV goes as follows. We first present a result concerning allowed inversions of proof chains. Then, starting with a pure SL-tree, we proceed by removing the edges where contrapositive clause variants are used, substituting them by legitimate SLWV steps (involving the case analysis rule), until no such edge remains. Note that during the translation process there is a need to consider a mixed SL-SLWV tree (because of the use of contrapositives and of SLWV steps *both* may be present).

We start to state and prove:

Lemma 3.2: Let -A be the complementary of a literal A. Let [A] be a node in a SL-tree, and T[A] its subtree rooted in [A]. Let [A] → [A_1] → ... → [A_k] → [❑] be a path A on T[A].
Then, T[A] can be inverted on path A to yield a tree T* with subtrees identical to their occurrences in T[A], except the ones containing some [A_j]. The path corresponding to A in T* will appear as [-A_k] → [-A_{k-1}] → ... → [A]. Furthermore, all steps used on T[A] will remain valid in T*.

Proof. (by induction on the depth of T[A]).
Induction base: suppose that T[A] is (L0) from figure 4.
Then A was resolved upon by a clause A ← R, A_k. Consider the contrapositive variant -A_k ← R, -A. Forthwith, T* is obtained, namely (L1). Otherwise, T[A] has the form (L2). So, consider the contrapositive variant clause A_k ←R, -A_{k-1}, and the inversion (L3), that exists by induction hypothesis. Let then T* be (L4).

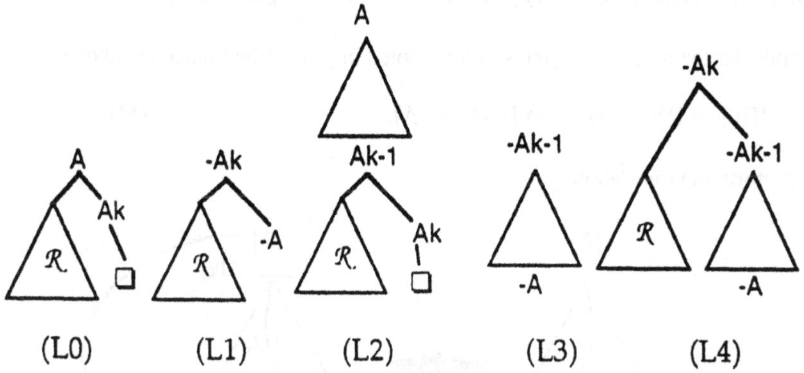

Fig. 4. Tree transformations.

An issue arises regarding steps involving ancestor cancelation with some A_i in the path considered, for they are no longer available in the inverted tree. However, every such particular ancestor used must have been resolved with a program clause in the inversion and now appears as -A_i, so the problem is fixed by duplicating the proof for -A_i where a cancelation with A_i occurred before. ❑

Now, the announced translation method is given.

We proceed by removing the edges where contrapositive variants are used, substituting them by legitimate SLWV steps. At each removal step a number of uses of contrapositive variants are removed and none is introduced. Since the original tree is finite, we will end up with a pure SLWV-tree. Note that during the translation process there is a need to consider a mixed SL-SLWV tree (because of the use of contrapositives and of SLWV steps both may be present).

Step 1: If there are no edges where contrapositives of the original clause set are used, the translation is finished. Otherwise,

Step 2: Locate a node [A] closest to the root expanded by the use of a contrapositive $A \leftarrow B_1, \neg H_1, \ldots, B_n$ of a program clause whose given form is $H_1 \leftarrow B_1, \ldots, B_n$. Now $[\neg H_1]$ must be resolved by either ancestor resolution (with a positive ancestor) or by a side clause $\neg H_1 \leftarrow B$ that must also be a contrapositive variant since there are no clauses with negative heads in the original clause set. Inductively, a path on the subtree rooted in [A]

$$[A] \rightarrow [\neg H_1] \rightarrow \ldots \rightarrow [\neg H_k] \rightarrow [\square] \qquad (*)$$

can be identified.

Below [A], this path is constituted uniquely by (the negation of) heads of clauses in the form given in the original clause set such that the last one ($[\neg H_k]$) must be resolved with some (necessarily positive) ancestor $X = H_k$ of $[\neg H_1]$.

So, consider the inversion of the sub-tree rooted in [A] on the branch (*) above

$$[H_k] \rightarrow [H_{k-1}] \rightarrow \ldots \rightarrow [H_1] \rightarrow [\text{-}A]. \qquad (**)$$

and perform the translation

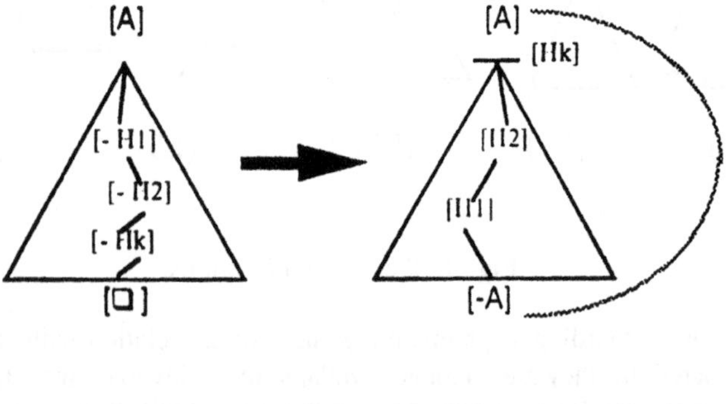

Fig. 5. Sub tree inversion.

Note that all remaining steps in the translated subtree remain valid by Lemma 3.2. In particular, the first step is justified by D4.3.

Next, go to step 1. □

Now a compreensive example.

Example 3.3. Let Π =

$$\{ \quad p \leftarrow a,b \;;\; p \leftarrow q1,c \;;\; a \leftarrow \neg q, a2 \;;\; a \leftarrow \neg d \;;$$
$$q1 \leftarrow x \;;\; x \leftarrow q, d \;;\; c \leftarrow x \;;\; p \leftarrow \neg b \;;$$
$$d \leftarrow \;;\; a2 \leftarrow \quad \},$$

and the following SL-tree for Π.

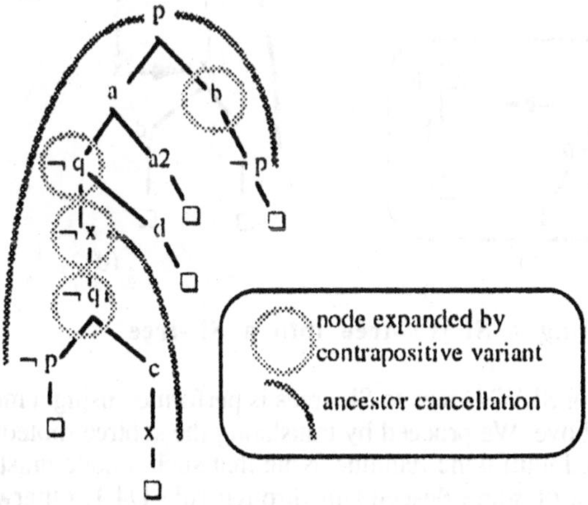

Now (step 2), inverting the subtree rooted in $\neg q$ as displayed in (a), we get the mixed SL/SLWV tree of (b).

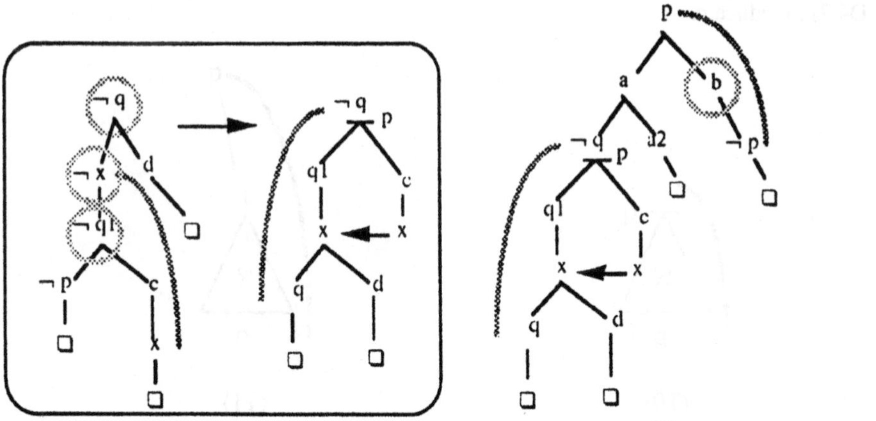

(a) (b)

Note that the atom x was resolved by cancellation with its ancestor $\neg x$ in the original SL tree, this being no longer possible in the translation. As suggested above, instead of duplicating the subtree below x (in the translated tree), we simply indicate the possible merge of the identical occurrences of x (that they are identical results from their former cancellation in the SL tree). Finally, the inversion (c) will yield the final pure SLWV-tree displayed in fig. (d).

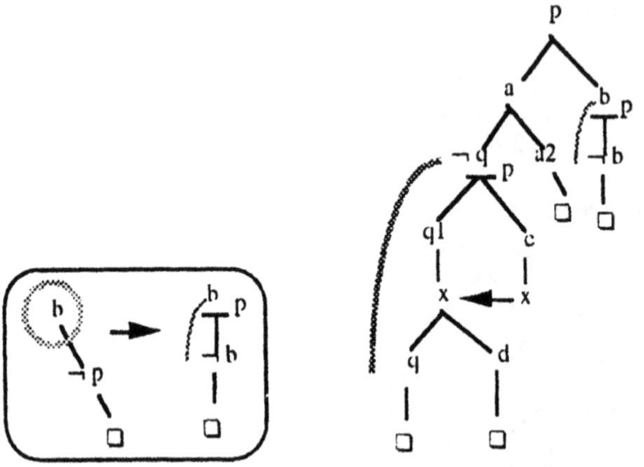

(c) (d)

3.3. Translating a SLWV-tree into a SL-tree

The translation of SLWV-trees to SL-trees is performed using a method similar to the one described above. We proceed by translating the subtree rooted at the nodes where D4.3 was applied until none remains. Note that such a node must always participate in the resolution of some descendant through rule D4.1, otherwise the mentioned subtree will be redundant. So consider the subtree (T0), and perform the inversion (T1) of (T0) on [q] → ... → [¬p], resolving -q with the ancestor q of p used in (T0) (via D4.3) to reduce p.

(T0) (T1)

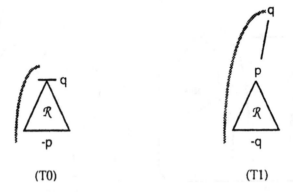

Fig.6. Translation step for SLWV to SL.

Note that R will now involve the use of contrapositive variants, as would be expected.

4. Defining Negative Definite Program Clauses

Up to now we have considered only progran clauses with positive head literals. However, a clause $\neg H \leftarrow \mathbf{B}$ can be soundly rewritten as $\bot \leftarrow H, \mathbf{B}$ where $\bot$ is the logical constant standing for 'false'. This suggests the translation of every negative definite clause in a corresponding clause for $\bot$. Now $\Pi \vdash g$ iff $\vdash \Pi \rightarrow g$ iff $\vdash (\Pi \,\&\, \neg g) \rightarrow \bot$.

Thus $\Pi \vdash g$ iff $\vdash \Pi \cup \{\bot \leftarrow g\} \rightarrow \bot$, so $\Pi \vdash g$ iff $\Pi \cup \{\bot \leftarrow g\} \vdash \bot$. Now, a proof of $\bot$ in this setting has as first two lines

1. $\bot$
2. $\{\bot\}\ g$

Thus, whenever programs with negative definite clauses are defined, in establishing a derivation we can start as usual from the relevant literal to be proved (such literal can now freely be either positive or negative), but considering $\bot$ as a root ancestor.

Note however that a tradeoff exists when this approach is applied for the leftmost/ancestor-order. For when a clause $\neg p \leftarrow \mathbf{B}$ is written, it will not be used for reducing $\neg p$ until the search space related to all ancestors below $\bot$ is exhausted.

5. Disjunctive Answers

The intuitive desired meaning of a disjunctive answer is readily shown with an example. Suppose we have the program:
Π = { nomoney(john) $\leftarrow$ $\neg$nomoney(mary), nopay(father); nopay(father) },

meaning that john or mary (or both) have no money if their father is not paid, and their father is not paid. The query $\leftarrow$nomoney(X) intends to ask about who has no money. As there is no X such that nomoney(X) can be derived, the answer such a query is no. But we know that one of john or mary have no money; more generally, there may be a set of terms such that at least one of them has some property or obeys some relation. A disjunctive answer to the (disjunctive) query "$\vee\!\leftarrow$ nomoney(X)" in Π should be X=john or X=mary, denoting that nomoney(john) $\vee$ nomoney(mary) is a logical consequence of Π.

Our purpose in this section is first to present a definition of answers and of disjunctive answers. We will then argue that SLWV, due to its logic programing like strategy, is suitable to capture the concept of disjunctive answer by describing how it can provide such answers.

5.1. Definition 5.1.:
An answer to a query $\leftarrow$P(X) in a program Π is a substitution σ (for the variables of P(X)) such that $\Pi \cup \neg P(X)\sigma$ is inconsistent.

This is the usual definition of an answer to a query. We now extend this definition to disjunctive answers.

5.2. Definition 5.2.:
A disjunctive answer to a disjunctive query $\vee\leftarrow P(X)$ is a finite set of substitutions Σ such that $\Pi \cup \bigcup_{\sigma\in\Sigma} \neg P(X)\sigma$ is inconsistent.

In other words, Σ is a disjunctive answer to a query $\vee\leftarrow P(X)$ such that

$$\bigvee_{\sigma\in\Sigma} P(X)\sigma \text{ is a logical consequence of } \Pi.$$

To solve the problem of how to find such answers we prove a proposition that states when there exists a disjunctive answer to a query.

5.3. Proposition 5.3.:
There exists a disjunctive answer Σ to a query $\vee\leftarrow P(X)$ in Π iff *tg* (top goal) is a logical consequence of $\Pi \cup \{tg \leftarrow P(X)\}$ (*tg* being a new predicate symbol, not occurring elsewhere in Π).

Proof: According to Herbrand's theorem [1], $\Pi_1 = \Pi \cup tg \leftarrow P(X)$ derives *tg* iff there exists a finite subset of $\Pi_2 = \text{ground}(\Pi)^2 \cup tg \leftarrow P(X)\sigma_1 \cup ... \cup tg \leftarrow P(X)\sigma_n \cup ...$ ($\sigma_1, ..., \sigma_n, ...$ being all the possible Herbrand Universe substitutions for P(X)) deriving *tg* (regarding that the top goal *tg* does not introduce new symbols on Π_1). Let S be the finite subset S of $\{ P(X)\sigma_1, ..., P(X)\sigma_n, ... \}$ made out from the bodies of clauses with head *tg* from the finite subset of Π_2 that derives it. As *tg* does not occur in Π, for it to be derived from Π_2, according to the resolution principle, the disjunction of the elements of S must logically follow from Π_2. Thus the set of substitutions applied to P(X) on S is, by definition, a disjunctive answer Σ to a query $\vee\leftarrow P(X)$ in Π.

Based on this proposition, for answering a query $\vee\leftarrow P(X)$ in SLWV we implicitly add to the program the clause $tg \leftarrow P(X)$ and consider the new query $\leftarrow tg$, keeping track of the substitutions for P(X) every time the system *uses* this special clause. Given the procedural aspects of SLWV execution, memory of such substitutions can be easily kept.

Example 5.4. Reconsider the program given at the beginning of this section and the query $\vee\leftarrow$nomoney(X). A derivation for this query, based on SLWV plus the additional (rightmost) set shown that keeps track of the substitutions performed on nomoney whenever the special clause tg $\leftarrow$ nomoney(X) is used, is[3]:

1. {}#tg % {}

2ground(Π) denotes the program obtained from Π by replacing all clauses by all their ground instances.
3 For the sake brevity, in this derivation nm stands for nomoney, np for nopay, j for john, m for mary and f for father.

2. {tg}# nm(X) % {nm(X)}
3. {tg, nm(j)}# ¬nm(m) {tg, nm(j)}# np(f) % {nm(j)}
4. {tg, nm(j), ¬nm(m)}# nm(X) {tg, nm(j)}# np(f) % {nm(j),nm(X)}
5. {tg, nm(j), ¬nm(m)}# nm(m) {tg, nm(j)}# np(f) % {nm(j),nm(m)}
6. {tg, nm(j),np(f)} # δ % {nm(j),nm(m)}
7. ❑ % {nm(j),nm(m)}

As expected, a disjunctive answer for the query is {X/john,X/mary}.

6. Comparison with Near-Horn Prolog [6]

A similar theorem prover is the one described in [6] as nH-Prolog. In this section we compare our method with that one, focussing on the most significant differences.

The proof procedure described in [6] does not allow for the use of selection functions. Adopting in SLWV a selection function that only uses rule D4.3 for negative literals, and expands first the conjunctive branches with positive literals to solve, mimics nH-Prolog derivations. Thus we argue that our proof system is more general than the one of nH-Prolog.

Example 6.1. Consider the following program taken from [6].

```
q :- a,b.
a :- c.
b :- e.
a :- d.
b :- f.
c ; d.
e ; f.
```

where the last two clauses are in a form such that only one literal is in the head, say:

```
c :- ¬d.
e :- ¬f.
```

Figure 7 below shows a partial search tree for SLWV derivations, where a SLWV path with a selection function that mimics the nH-Prolog derivation given in fig.6 of [6] is highlighted; the other path highlighted is the one chosen by our SLWV executor according to its own selection function.

Let us look closely at the nH-Prolog derivation, and contrast it with the corresponding non mimicking SLWV derivation:

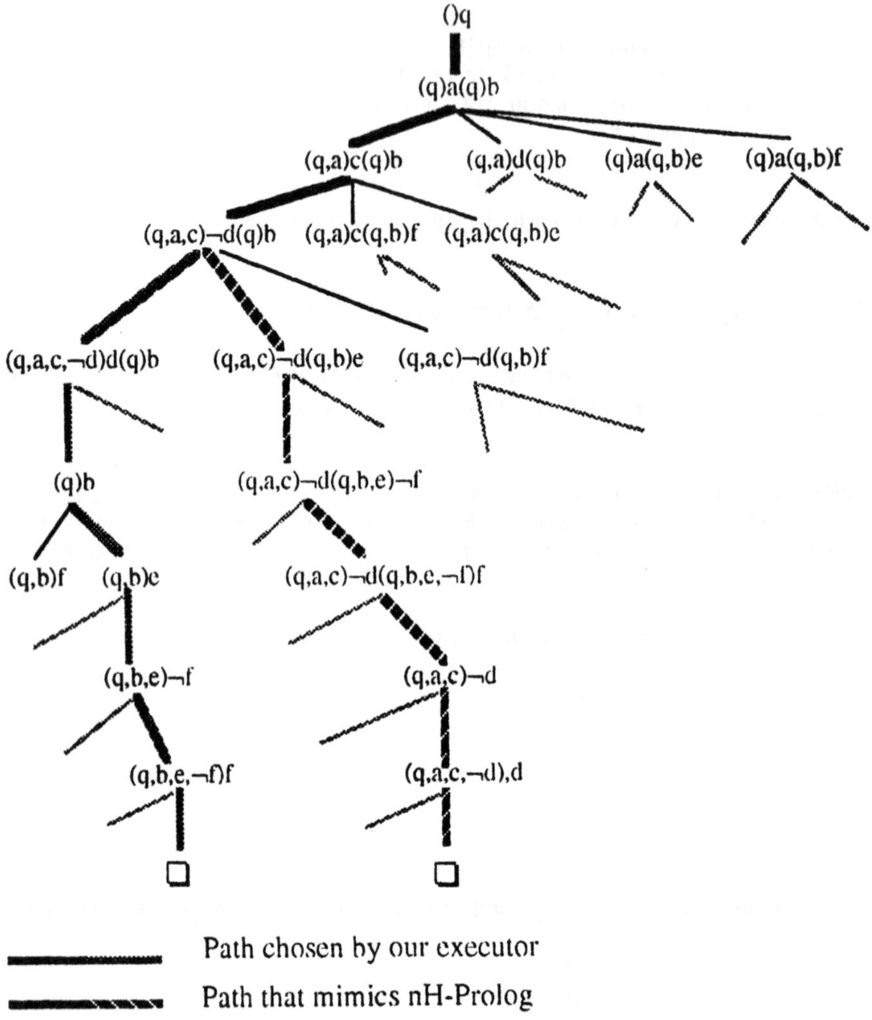

Fig.7. Comparing nH-Prolog with SLWV.

?- q.	The top goal	()q
:- a,b.	First clause for q	(q)a (q)b
:- c,b.	First clause for a	(q,a)c (q)b
:- b#[d]	Clause for c; d is deferred / ¬d is suspended	(q,a,c)¬d (q)b
:- e#[d]	First clause for b	(q,a,c)¬d (q,b)e
:- #[f,d]	Clause for e; f is deferred	(q,a,c)¬d (q,b,e)¬f
:- b#f[d]	Restart using ancestor b / by rule D4.3 b is chosen	
:- f#f[d]	Second clause for b	(q,a,c)¬d (q,b,e,¬f)f
:- #f[d]	Cancellation	(q,a,c)¬d
:- a#d	Restart using ancestor a / by rule D4.3 a is chosen	
:- d#d	Second clause for a	(q,a,c,¬d)d
:- #d	Cancellation	☐

In order to use logic as a programming language, SLWV with the selection function used by our executor (c.f. section 7) has some properties, not common to nH-Prolog, that are important:

→ In a conjunction, like in Prolog, literals are solved one by one from left to right (i.e. no resolution of a literal starts before the resolution of the previous). As in Prolog this is important to impart a procedural reading to programs. In contrast in nH-Prolog, even for clauses with only one literal at the head, the resolution of a literal can start before the end of the resolution of the previous one (in the example above, on clause *q :- a,b* literal *b* is solved before the resolution of *a* is completed).

→ We need not use various contrapositive variants of a clause, as in happens nH-Prolog for clauses with multiple heads. This, combined with the property above, gives the programer the chance of imposing an order on literals, and so the chance of pragmatically choosing among various possible derivations. Like in Prolog the order of literals in the body of clauses can heavily influence on the efficiency of the program. It is up to the programer to choose the most efficient one.

Another point where our system compares favorably with nH-Prolog is the one concerning answers. The disjunctive form of answers in nH-Prolog implies that when answers with only one literal are wanted, possible failure is only detected a posterior, i.e. only after the complete disjunctive answer is calculated and the bidings are found incompatible. In our system these failures are detected on the fly.

nH-Prolog syntax, and its use of contrapositive variants for clauses with disjunctive conclusions, precludes the need for ancestor resolution. In order to be complete, SLWV has to use both case analysis and ancestor resolution. However this does not represent an additional complexity, since case analysis and ancestor resolution are dealt with in a single implementation mechanism (note, below, that cancellation is performed with elements of a single label set, independently of the fact of their being ancestors or members of an alternative disjunctive branch).

For *near Horn problems* our theoretical approach apparently compares unfavorably with nH-Prolog. This is due to the fact that every literal, in order to solve, has available not only clauses with it at the head, but also clauses with any of its ancestors at the head, thus enlarging the search space even for cases where it is unnecessary. This problem is easily improved with the help of some static analysis of the program.

7. On the Implementation of SLWV

Next we present the outline of a simple Prolog executor for the method above, relying on the preprocessing of clauses and on the addition of a few specific kernel predicates written in Prolog[4]. For simplicity we won't consider the kind of answers described in

4 The complete code is available on request.

section 5. The goal of the implementation presented here is not efficiency, but rather to illustrate the additional mechanism needed.

We begin with a description of the external syntax of programs. Afterwards we describe the preprocessor and internal syntax. Then we present two new mechanisms to execute preprocessed programs, cancel and climb, their implementation in Prolog, and give some ideas on how the executor can be thought of in terms of a low level implementation, comparing the two new mechanisms with existing ones in Prolog. Finally we add some hints on how to improve the executor.

7.1. External syntax

A program is a set of clauses of the form *head :- body* where *head* is a literal and *body* is a literal or a conjunction of literals. *head :- true* can also be represented as *head*.
This syntax extends Horn clauses to allow negative literals anywhere and subsumes normal programs.

7.2. Preprocessing

In order to have a single positive literal in the head, each clause ¬ L :- Body is transformed into **false** :- L, Body. Introducing a top goal :- G is equivalent to introducing the clause **false**:-G, as explained in section 5 above.

According to our method, calls for a goal must be associated with a label set. As no clauses have a negative head, to achieve greater efficiency in applying clauses by rule D4.3 and also for faster application of D4.1, we represent the label set PN by two lists, P and N, where P comprises the positive and N the negative literals.

In order to ensure completeness of the executor (for finite derivation spaces), one has to be sure that in the non-deterministic rule (D4) all possibilities are tried. So an execution order is introduced:

→ A called goal first checks for cancellation with elements of the label set (rule D4.1). This is taken care of by the cancel mechanism described in section 7.3.

→ After that all clauses for the goal are tried (rule D4.2), in the order expressed by the program. This is guaranteed by the Prolog implementation.

→ Finally the climb mechanism (described in section 7.4) is activated to ensure the application of rule D4.3. This mechanism is responsible for choosing ancestors in turn (the most recent first) and, for each one, for knowing which clauses for it to use next. In order to make the latter possible, we introduce in each goal, additionally to P and N, a further parameter C, specifying the clauses it can use in a particular call. When C is unbound every clause is to be considered.

Consequently, each clause is augmented by the preprocessor with the three argument variables P, N and C. Hence, a clause with p(X) as head

$p(X)$:- $b_p(Y)$, ¬ $b_n(Z)$, ... is transformed into

```
p(X,P,N,index) :- bp(Y,[x-p(X)|P],N,_), $neg( bn(Z,[x-p(X)|P],N,_)),...
```

where *index* is the number of this clause, starting with 0, in the sequence of clauses for p.

In all goals, `x-p(X)` is fronted to `p`: the tag x is used to state that literal `p` has been reduced. Suspended literals[5] contain a free variable parameter instead; this parameter is used to check whether their reduction occurred by cancellation with complementary ones, either in P or in N (cf. 7.3 below), by binding the parameter to x when cancellation occurs.

$neg is a kernel predicate enveloping the atom of each negated goal, to be explained later.

In order to enable access to the underlying Prolog in our programs, literals of the form `call(Goal)` are preprocessed simply to `Goal`.

The splitting of proof branches (D3) is guaranteed by Prolog's execution of a conjunction.

7.3. The "cancel" mechanism

To ensure application of rule D4.1, when trying to solve a goal one has, first of all, to check for a cancellation in PN. This mechanism can be seen as if achieving a match of a suspended literal with the head of a clause contrapositive with the negation of the goal at the head.

So for each predicate p(Y), the preprocessor adds, as first clause for p:

```
p(Y,_,N,_) :- member(x-p(Y),N).                                  [CR]
```

where the symbol x serves to indicate, by binding within the list element, that a cancellation has occurred.

For negative goals we add as first clause for **$neg** a clause similar to [CR].

7.4. The "climb" mechanism

When solving a goal p(Y), after trying all clauses with this literal at the head, and to ensure the complete application of rule D4.3, the executor must try alternative clauses for the ancestors, in order to find an alternative disjunctive branch containing a literal ¬p(Z). We call this the climb mechanism. To invoke this mechanism, the preprocessor adds, as the last clause for every p(X):

```
p(X,P,N,_) :- climb(P,N,p(X)).                                   [CC]
```

5 By a suspended literal we mean a non-ancestor literal that was introduced in the label set, according to D4.1.2.

where **climb** is a kernel predicate, that in turn chooses an element of the P label set (as we don't have preprocessed negated heads N is ignored) and reconsiders it on its alternative clauses.

```
climb(P,N,G) :-
      choose_one(P,AnsPred,ClauseNumber,NewP),
      translate(AnsPred,[X-G|NewP],N,ClauseNumber,AnsGoal),
      AnsGoal,
      X == x.
```

To ensure that in the present derivation the original goal actually cancels, as explained before in 7.2, a check for the binding of X with x is performed.

translate is a fact predicate with an instance introduced for each program predicate by the preprocessor. It transforms elements of P or N into the form of preprocessed predicate calls (i.e. p(X,P,N,C)) given P,N, and C, and vice-versa. p(X) introduces:

```
translate(p(X), P, N, C, p(X,P,N,C)) :- !.
```

As this problem is the same for negative literals, we have as last clause for **$neg**, similar to [CC].

The predicate `choose_one(P,AnsPred,ClauseNumber,NewP)` chooses from `P` the ancestor alternative clause with `AnsPred` at the head and number `ClauseNumber`, and builds for it the new `P` list `NewP`. Here various search strategies can apply. The simplest one is to choose the next clause for the closest ancestor, and if no more clauses exist, choose the next unused clause for the ancestor before (backtracking is used to implement this order). To ensure completeness, when the last clause is reached for the root ancestor predicate $\perp$ (which has no ancestors) wraparound is allowed and its first clause is chosen again (contrast this with [6] page 14 where wraparound is eventually needed at every ancestor). When initiating a wraparound possible looping is detected and avoided by failing (implementation details not disclosed here).

An improvement is to choose only ancestor clauses that may lead to the complementary literal. This alternative is much more efficient, but has to keep information about the call graph, which may be worth considering if a low level implementation is produced.

We can view the climb mechanism as an elaboration of standard Prolog backtracking that keeps information about the failed branches. This information is mainly about ancestor goals, variable bindings and failed goals (corresponding here to suspended literals). This fact, plus the similarity between the cancel mechanism and the matching of goals with clause heads, suggests a unifying low level implementation (possibly based on the modification of a Prolog virtual machine).

7.5. Improving the executor

The climb mechanism, jointly with backtracking, introduces undesired repeated solutions. For example, consider the program:

```
(1) p :- q.
(2) p :- ¬q.
```

with the top goal ?- p. In the first solution p calls q using (1), q invokes the climb mechanism and succeeds by cancelling with ¬q of (2). By backtracking, p calls ¬q using (2), q invokes the climb mechanism and succeeds by cancelling with q of (1), reaching this way the second solution. In fact this solution is exactly the one reached at the beginning.

Another way to characterize this problem is to say that it happens because both negative and positive literals can invoke the climb mechanism. If only one type of literals could invoke the climbing, no such problem could arise. Note that completeness would not be lost. Suppose we disable the climb mechanism for, say, positive literals. If a positive literal was to succeed by climbing, then there exists a complementary literals that by climbing will cancel with it. This is so because we may eventually reuse clauses for any predicate, given that we may perform a wraparound at the root ancestor of any derivation.

However, if we only allow climbing on the negative literals, there is no need for these literals to attempt to cancel, because there won't exist positive suspended literals. It is the positive literals that should attempt to cancel with the suspended negative ones. We can be more flexible by stipulating, for each predicate name, that the climb mechanism is invoked by positive literals and the cancel mechanism by negative ones, or vice-versa. For each predicate name, according to a static analysis of the problem (not described here), we can choose the alternative that seems the most efficient.

Other easy static analysis of the program can be made in order to improve efficiency. For example, if a literal L does not appear in the body of any clause then there is no need to climb nor cancel either on goals L or ¬L (and so clauses [CR] and [CC] can be omitted altogether). In particular, for a Horn program, no attempt is made to cancel nor climb on any literal, and consequently no significant time and space overheads occur.

8. Conclusions

We've defined a new (resolution) theorem proving method, and proved its correctness, which allows for procedural logic programing with classical negation. We also showed how it is adequate for producing disjunctive answers.

For its simplicity and Prolog-like strategy, our method turns out to be attractive for programming in clausal logic, being well suited to extend logic programming with

classical negation. Furthermore, the procedural information of clause and goal order is complied with, which is still a desirable feature in (present) logic programing.
In particular, Horn program derivations map directly into SLD ones. In our implementation, based on preprocessing into Prolog, their runtime is comparable to that under Prolog.

Because of its similarity, a detailed comparison with [6] is made separately in section 6, where we favour our method.

Comparing it with the ones presented in [12,13], we find that it has the advantage of not needing contrapositive variants and retaining the procedural pragmatics of a program. The same considerations apply to the MESON strategy [5]; additionally SLWV differs from this strategy because in our case one can restart from any ancestor.

Another method for logic programming with negation that doesn't make use of contrapositives is that of [10]. This method builds for each problem a deduction system where the rules and axioms depend on the clause set. This approach seems to be conceptually more complex, and in contrast to ours has an execution trace difficult to relate to the source program. Moreover it presents a significant overhead in the execution of Horn programs.

The method described in [7] has the advantage of being both very simple and efficient (at least for a certain class of programs) though, as it is based on model generation, the user has no control over the execution order.

We do not make any efficiency comparisons as we do not have available any of the other implementations.

Acknowledgements

We thank ESPRIT Basic Research Project COMPULOG (no. 3012), Instituto Nacional de Investigação Científica, and Gabinete de Filosofia do Conhecimento for their support.

References

1. Chang C. and R. Lee.: Symbolic Logic and Mechanical Theorem Proving, Academic Press, New York, 1973.
2. Eshghi, K. and R. Kowalski.: Abduction Compared with Negation as Failure, Logic Programming: Proceedings of the Sixth International Conference, (Levi and Martelli eds.), MIT Press, 1989.
3. Kowalski, R. : Linear Resolution with Selection Function, Artificial Intelligence, vol 2, pp 227-260, 1971.
4. Lloyd, J.: Foundations of Logic Programming , second edition, Springer-Verlag, 1987.
5. Loveland, D.W.: Automated Deduction , North Holland, 1978.

6. Loveland, D.W.: Near-Horn Prolog and Beyond. In Journal of Automated Reasoning, vol 7, nº 1, pp 1-26, 1991.

7. Manthey, R. and F. Bry: SATCHMO: a theorem prover implemented in Prolog. In Proceedings of CADE 88 (9th Conference on Automated Deduction), Argonne, Illinois, pp 23-26 May, LNCS, Springer Verlag.

8. Pelletier, F. J.: Seventy-five Problems for testing Automatic Theorem Provers. Journal of Automated Reasoning 2 (1986) pp 191-216.

9. Pereira L., L. Caires and J. Alferes: Classical Negation in Logic Programs. In Proceedings of the Seventh "Seminário Brasileiro de Inteligência Artificial" , Campina Grande PB, Brazil, Nov. 90, UFPB/CCT - Departamento de Sistemas e Computação, 7º SBIA, Caixa Postal 10106, 58100 - Campina Grande -PB, Brazil.

10. Plaisted, D. A.: Non-Horn clause logic Programing without Contrapositives. Journal of Automated Reasoning 4 (1988) pp 287-325.

11. Smith, B.T. and Loveland, D. W.: A Simple near-Horn Prolog Interpreter. In Logic Programming: Proceedings of the Fifth International Conference, pp 794-804, Seattle, 1988.

12. Stickel, M.E. et al: An Analysis of Consecutively Bounded Depth-First Search with Applications in Automated Deduction, Proceedings of the Ninth International Joint Conference of Artificial Intelligence, Los Angeles California, August 85.

13. Stickel, M.E.: A Prolog Technology Theorem Prover: Implementation by an extended Prolog Compiler, Proceedings of the Eight International Conference in Automated Deduction, Oxford, England, July 86.

A Correct Goal-directed Proof Procedure for a General Logic Program with Integrity Constraints

Ken Satoh, Noboru Iwayama

Institute for New Generation Computer Technology
1-4-28 Mita, Minato-ku, Tokyo 108, Japan
email:ksatoh@icot.or.jp, iwayama@icot.or.jp

Abstract. We present a correct goal-directed procedure for consistent logic program with integrity constraints in stable model semantics [5]. Although there are correct bottom-up procedures for every general logic program [13, 4, 15, 7] to compute stable models, there are no proposed correct goal-directed procedure for every general logic program. Our proposed procedure is correct not only for successful derivation but also for finite failure. This procedure is an extension of Eshghi's procedure [3] which is correct for every call-consistent logic program, and can be regarded as a combination of the model elimination procedure [10] and consistency checking in updates of implicit deletions [14].

1 Introduction

Recently, stable model semantics was proposed for an alternate semantics of general logic programs [5]. The semantics reflects epistemic character of negation in logic programming and is related to the existing systems of nonmonotonic reasoning such as Default Logic and Autoepistemic Logic. Moreover, the semantics can be used as a formal basis of abduction in logic programming [3, 8]. So, the semantics is very useful for representing various non-deductive reasoning in terms of logic programming.

However, there is a problem of computation for stable model semantics. Although some have proposed bottom-up procedures which compute stable models for every logic program [13, 4, 15, 7], only Eshghi and Kowalski [3] proposed a goal-directed procedure which is not correct for every logic program but a call-consistent logic programs. Major difficulty of goal-directed procedure comes from its locality whereas stable model semantics has a global property. In general, we must search every rule in a logic program to obtain a stable model. goal-directed procedure, however, searches only rules relevant for a query.

To solve the problem, some people are working on a modification of semantics which fits to Eshghi and Kowalski's procedure [1, 9]. Although this approach seems interesting, there are still arguments which semantics is best. In stead of this approach, this paper goes into the other direction. That is, we stick to the original stable model semantics and try to fix Eshghi's procedure.

A solution from this approach is as follows. Firstly, we guarantee that a considered logic program has always a stable model by checking consistency in accordance with addition of rules. Secondly, we pursue a procedure which answers "yes" (if stopped) if there is a stable model which satisfies a query and answers "no" (if stopped) if there is no stable model which satisfies a query. In our opinion, Eshghi's procedure has the problem on correctness because it does not search rules which are actually relevant to query.

Consider the following example in [3].

$$p \leftarrow \sim q \qquad (1)$$
$$q \leftarrow \sim p \qquad (2)$$
$$r \leftarrow q \qquad (3)$$
$$r \leftarrow \sim r \qquad (4)$$

If we ask ?-*p* then Eshghi's procedure answers "yes" since the procedure only considers rules (1) and (2). However, if *p* is true, then *q* must be false and the rule (3) is no longer applicable and it leads to inconsistency by the rule (4). As far as we know, this phenomenon was firstly observed by Sadri and Kowalski [14] and called "implicit deletion". They also gave a procedure which checks integrity constraints by implicit deletion and proved its correctness. We use their idea to infer that rules (3) and (4) are also relevant to the query ?-*p*.

Then, our procedure becomes a combination of model elimination procedure [10] and consistency check adapted from [14]. Concerning model elimination procedure, we use it in a different manner and for a different purpose. We use model elimination procedure in a different manner because rules (clauses) in a logic program is directed and we do not consider its contrapositives. We use model elimination procedure for a different purpose because we want to detect consistency instead of inconsistency.

Moreover, by obtaining this procedure, we automatically obtain a procedure for our first purpose, to check consistency for added rules. It is because this procedure contains a subprocedure which checks consistency for rules relevant to query.

The structure of the paper is as follows. Firstly, we give definitions necessary for our procedure and then we show a goal-directed procedure of evaluating a query for a general logic program with integrity constraints. Finally, we compare it with related researches. For proofs of the theorems, see Appendix.

2 Goal-Directed Procedure

We restrict ourselves to considering a propositional case. If we consider predicate case, we change it into a ground logic program by instantiating every variable to an element of Herbrand universe of considered logic program to obtain a propositional program.

A literal is a proposition or negated proposition of the form $\sim l$.

Definition 1. Let l be a literal. We denote the *inverse* of the literal as $\bar{l}$ and define it as follows.

1. If l is a positive literal, then $\bar{l} = \sim l$.
2. If l is a negative literal of the form $\sim l'$, then $\bar{l} = l'$.

We use a special literal $\bot$ which expresses inconsistency.

Then, we define a general logic program and integrity constraints.

Definition 2. Let A be a propositional symbol, and $L_1, ..., L_m (m \geq 0)$ be propositional literals. A *general logic program* consists of (possibly countably infinite) rules of the form:

$$A \leftarrow L_1, L_2, ..., L_m.$$

We call A the *head* of the rule and $L_1, ..., L_m$ the *body* of the rule. Let R be a rule. We denote the head of R as $head(R)$ and the set of literals in the body of R as $body(R)$ and the set of positive literals in the body of R as $pos(R)$ and $neg(R) = \{p | \sim p \in body(R)\}$

Definition 3. Let $L_1, ..., L_m (m \geq 0)$ be propositional literals. A set of *integrity constraints* consists of (possibly countably infinite) formulas of the form:

$$\bot \leftarrow L_1, L_2, ..., L_m.$$

$\bot$ means inconsistency and we write integrity constraints as the above form for notational convenience so that we do not have to distinguish integrity constraints and rules. So, from this point, we call the above set of rules and integrity constraints *a logic program*.

Definition 4. A *stable model* for a logic program is a set of propositions M if $\bot \notin M$ and M is equal to the minimal model of T^M where

$$T^M = \{H \leftarrow B_1, ..., B_k | H \leftarrow B_1, ..., B_k, \sim A_1, ..., \sim A_m \text{ is a rule in } T \text{ and } A_i \notin M \text{ for each } i = 1, ..., m.\}$$

This definition gives a stable model of T which satisfies all integrity constraints. We say that T is *consistent* if there exists a stable model for T.

Before showing a procedure, we need the following definitions.

Definition 5. Let T be a logic program.

1. A set of resolvents w.r.t. a positive literal p and T, $resolve(p, T)$ is the following set of rules:

   $$resolve(p, T) = \{H \leftarrow L_1, ..., L_{i-1}, L_{i+1}, ..., L_k | H \leftarrow L_1, ..., L_k \in T \text{ and } p = L_i\}$$

2. A set of resolvents w.r.t. a negative literal $\sim p$ and T, $resolve(\sim p, T)$ is the following set of rules:

   $$resolve(\sim p, T) = \{\bot \leftarrow L_1, ..., L_k | H \leftarrow L_1, ..., L_k \in T \text{ and } p = H\} \cup \{H \leftarrow L_1, ..., L_{i-1}, L_{i+1}, ..., L_k | H \leftarrow L_1, ..., L_k \in T \text{ and } \sim p = L_i\}$$

The second definition of a resolvent for a negative literal corresponds with a resolvent obtained by "extended" resolution introduced in [14]. This extended resolution and the resolution for a positive literal express "forward" evaluation of the rule.

Example 1. Consider the following program T:

$$p \leftarrow \sim q \tag{1}$$
$$q \leftarrow \sim p \tag{2}$$
$$r \leftarrow q \tag{3}$$
$$r \leftarrow \sim r \tag{4}$$

Then, $resolve(q, T)$ is a set of the following rule:

$r \leftarrow$ from (3)

And, $resolve(\sim p, T)$ is a set of the following rules:

$\perp \leftarrow \sim q$ from (1)
$q \leftarrow$ from (2)

Definition 6. Let l be a literal and T be a logic program. Then, a set of deleted rules, $del(l, T)$, w.r.t. l and T is the following set of rules:
$del(l, T) = \{H \leftarrow L_1, ..., L_k|$
$H \leftarrow L_1, ..., L_k \in T$ and there exists some $L_i (1 \leq i \leq k)$ such that $\bar{l} = L_i\}$

Example 2. Consider the program in Example 1. Then, $del(q, T)$ is a set of the following rule:

$p \leftarrow \sim q$ from (1)

And, $del(\sim q, T)$ is a set of the following rule:

$r \leftarrow q$ from (3)

Now, we give a derivation procedure. The procedure consists of 4 subprocedures, $derive(p, \Delta)$, $literal\_con(l, \Delta)$, $rule\_con(R, \Delta)$ and $deleted\_con(R, \Delta)$ where p is a proposition and Δ is a set of literals which have already been assumed and l is a literal and R is a rule.

Each subprocedure returns a set of literals which is a union of Δ and literals which are newly found to be assumed during the execution of subprocedure.

In subprocedures, there is a select operation and **fail** operation. A select operation expresses a nondeterministic choice among alternatives and a **fail** operation expresses an immediately failure of the execution. So, a subprocedure succeeds if calls of subprocedures in the subprocedure is successful. We say *a subprocedure succeeds with* Δ if the subprocedure successfully returns Δ.

An informal specification of 4 procedures as follows.

1. $derive(p, \Delta)$ mainly searches a rule of p whose body is true. Intuitively speaking, if this procedure succeeds, there exists a stable model which satisfies such a rule.

2. *literal_con*(l, Δ) checks consistency of l. Intuitively speaking, if this procedure succeeds, there exists a stable model which satisfies l. In this procedure, we assume l for ancestor resolution in model elimination procedure.
3. *rule_con*(R, Δ) checks consistency of a rule R. Intuitively speaking, if this procedure succeeds, there exists a stable model which satisfies R. This procedure can be used also for checking integrity constraints for addition of a rule.
4. *deleted_con*(R, Δ) checks consistency of implicit deletion of rule R.

Figure 1 and Figure 2 describe the procedures in detail. If we remove *deleted_con* and do not consider resolvents obtained by the "forward" evaluation of the rule, then this procedure coincides with Eshghi's procedure [3]. In other words, our procedure is obtained by augmenting Eshghi's procedure by an integrity constraint checking in a bottom-up manner and an implicit deletion checking.

We can show the following theorems.

Theorem 7. *Let T be a consistent logic program. If derive$(p, \{\})$ succeeds, then there exists a stable model M for T such that $M \models p$.*

This theorem means that if the procedure *derive*$(p, \{\})$ answers "yes", then there is a stable model which satisfies a query ?-p.

We need the consistency of a program for correctness since there might be a rule such as $p \leftarrow \sim p$ which leads to inconsistency for the whole program and we cannot detect such rule if the rule is irrelevant to a query.

The following theorem expresses an integrity constraint check for an added rule.

Theorem 8. *Let T be a consistent logic program and R be a rule. If rule_con$(R, \{\})$ succeeds, then $T \cup \{R\}$ is consistent.*

So, by this theorem, we can use the above procedure to check consistency in accordance with addition of rules.

The following are theorems related to the correctness for finite failure.

Theorem 9. *Let T be a logic program. Suppose that every selection of rules terminates for derive$(p, \{\})$. If there exists a model M for T such that $M \models p$, then there is a selection of rules such that derive$(p, \{\})$ succeeds.*

This theorem means that if we can do an exhaustive search for selection of rules and there is a stable model which satisfies a query, then the procedure always answers "yes".

From the above theorem, we obtain the following corollary for a finite failure.

Corollary 10. *Let T be a logic program. If derive$(p, \{\})$ fails, then for every stable model M for T, $M \not\models p$.*

```
derive(p, Δ) p: a proposition; Δ: a set of literals
begin
  if p ∈ Δ then return Δ
  elseif ~p ∈ Δ then fail
  else
  begin
    select R ∈ T such that head(R) = p
    if such a rule is not found then fail
    Δ0 := Δ, i := 0
    for every l ∈ body(R) do
    begin
      if l ∈ pos(R) and derive(l, Δi) succeeds with Δi+1
        then i := i + 1 and continue
      elseif l ∈ neg(R) and literal_con(l, Δi) succeeds with Δi+1
        then i := i + 1 and continue
    end
    if literal_con(p, Δi) succeeds with Δ' then return Δ'
  end
end (derive)

literal_con(l, Δ) l: a literal; Δ: a set of literals
begin
  if l ∈ Δ then return Δ
  elseif l = ⊥ or l̄ ∈ Δ then fail
  else
  begin
    Δ0 := {l} ∪ Δ, i := 0
    for every R ∈ resolve(l, T) do
      if rule_con(R, Δi) succeeds with Δi+1
        then i := i + 1 and continue
    for every R ∈ del(l, T) do
      if deleted_con(R, Δi) succeeds with Δi+1
        then i := i + 1 and continue
  end
  return Δi
end (literal_con)
```

Fig. 1. The definition of *derive* and *literal_con*

The procedure *derive*$(p, \{\})$ answers "no", then there is no stable model which satisfies the query. Moreover, the above corollary means that we can use a finite failure to check if a literal is true in all stable models since finite failure of *derive*$(p, \{\})$ means that every stable model satisfies $\sim p$. Similarly, a finite failure of *literal_con*$(\sim p, \{\})$ means that every stable model satisfies p.

From the above correctness for a finite failure, we can say completeness result for a finite program provided that we can check a loop of the same call of *derive*(p, Δ) to make the execution fail.

Corollary 11. *Let T be a finite logic program. If there exists a stable model M*

rule_con(R, Δ) R: a rule; Δ: a set of literals
begin
  select (a) or (b)
  (a) **select** $l \in body(R)$
    if $l \in pos(R)$ **and** *literal_con*$(\bar{l}, \Delta)$ succeeds with Δ'
      then return Δ'
    elseif $l \in neg(R)$ **and** *derive*$(\bar{l}, \Delta)$ succeeds with Δ'
      then return Δ'
  (b) $\Delta_0 = \Delta$, $i := 0$
    for every $l \in body(R)$ **do**
    begin
      if $l \in pos(R)$ **and** *derive*(l, Δ_i) succeeds with Δ_{i+1}
        then $i := i + 1$ **and continue**
      elseif $l \in neg(R)$ **and** *literal_con*(l, Δ_i) succeeds with Δ_{i+1}
        then $i := i + 1$ **and continue**
    end
    if *literal_con*$(head(R), \Delta_i)$ succeeds with Δ' **then return** Δ'
end (*rule_con*)

deleted_con(R, Δ) R:a rule; Δ: a set of literals
begin
  select (a) or (b)
  (a) **if** *derive*$(head(R), \Delta)$ succeeds with Δ' **then return** Δ'
  (b) **if** *literal_con*$(\sim head(R), \Delta)$ succeeds with Δ' **then return** Δ'
end (*deleted_con*)

Fig. 2. The definition of *rule_con* and *deleted_con*

for T *such that* $M \models p$, *derive*$(p, \{\})$ *(with loop check) succeeds.*

Corollary 12. *Let* T *be a finite consistent logic program. If there exists a stable model* M *for* T *such that* $M \models R$, *there is a selection of rules such that* *rule_con*$(R, \{\})$ *(with loop check) succeeds.*

3 Examples

Example 3. Consider the program in Example 1. Then, Figure 3 shows a sequence of calling procedures obtained for *derive*$(q, \{\})$.

In Figure 3, during the execution of *derive*$(q, \{\})$, rule (2) is selected. Then, *literal_con*$(\sim p, \{\})$ is invoked to make the body of (2) to be true. To show that $\sim p$ is consistent with the program, we check two resolvents for $\sim p$. They are $(\bot \leftarrow \sim q)$ and $(q \leftarrow)$.

1. To show $(\bot \leftarrow \sim q)$ is consistent with the program, we invoke *derive*$(q, \{\sim p\})$. Note that $\sim p$ is assumed in this call since *literal_con*$(\sim p, \{\})$ has been invoked. Then, we invoke *literal_con*$(\sim p, \{\sim p\})$ to show that the body of (2) to be true and this time, this check succeeds since $\sim p$ is already assumed.

Since the body of (2) is true, we check the consistency of the head of (2) by checking its resolvent ($r \leftarrow$) and implicit deletion for rule (1).

(a) To show that ($r \leftarrow$) is consistent with the program, we check if r is consistent with the program. It is consistent since $derive(r, \{r, q, \sim p\})$ succeeds for implicit deletion check of rule (4).

(b) To show consistency of implicit deletion for (1), we invoke $literal\_con(\sim p, \{r, q, \sim p\})$ and the call succeeds.

2. For the consistency check for ($q \leftarrow$), $rule\_con((q \leftarrow), \{r, q, \sim p\})$ succeeds since q has been assumed.

Finally, we invoke $literal\_con(q, \{r, q, \sim p\})$ and this call succeeds since q has been assumed.

Example 4. Figure 4 shows a sequence of calling procedures obtained for $derive(p, \{\})$ for the above program by depth-first search.

In Figure 4, during the execution of $derive(p, \{\})$, rule (1) is selected. Then, $literal\_con(\sim q, \{\})$ is invoked to make the body of (1) to be true. To show $\sim q$ is consistent with the program, we check two resolvents for $\sim q$, that is ($p \leftarrow$) and ($\bot \leftarrow \sim p$), and implicit deletion of (3)

The consistency check for two resolvents for $\sim q$ succeeds and we invoke $deleted\_con((r \leftarrow q), \{p, \sim q\})$. To show $deleted\_con((r \leftarrow q), \{p, \sim q\})$, we must show either $derive(r, \{p, \sim q\})$ or $literal\_con(\sim r, \{p, \sim q\})$. Unfortunately, neither possibility can be shown to be true due to rule (4) and therefore, we cannot derive p.

4 Related Work

4.1 Eshghi's procedure

As we have said in Section 2, if we remove *deleted_con* and *literal_con* for positive literals from the procedure and do not consider resolvents obtained by the "forward" evaluation of the rule, it is identical with Eshghi's procedure. Although *literal_con* for positive literals and "forward" evaluation of the rule is mainly used for a forward checking of integrity constraints, we cannot omit them even if there are no integrity constraints as the following example shows.

Consider the following program and the query $derive(q, \{\})$.

$$p \leftarrow \sim q \qquad (1)$$

$$q \leftarrow \sim p \qquad (2)$$

$$s \leftarrow q \qquad (3)$$

$$r \leftarrow s, \sim r \qquad (4)$$

Then, without forward evaluation of positive literals q and s to infer that $r \leftarrow \sim r$ emerges from (4), we cannot detect inconsistency.

Also consider the following program and the query $derive(q, \{\})$.

$$p \leftarrow \sim q \qquad (1)$$

$$q \leftarrow \sim p \qquad (2)$$

```
derive(q, {})
  select (2)
    literal_con(~p, {})
      rule_con((⊥ ← ~q), {~p}) (resolvent with (1))
        derive(q, {~p})
          select (2)
            literal_con(~p, {~p})
            succeeds with {~p} (literal_con(~p, {~p}))
            literal_con(q, {~p})
              rule_con((r ←), {q, ~p}) (resolvent with (3))
                literal_con(r, {q, ~p})
                  deleted_con((r ← ~r), {r, q, ~p}) (for (4))
                    derive(r, {r, q, ~p})
                    succeeds with {r, q, ~p} (derive(r, {q, ~p}))
                  succeeds with {r, q, ~p} (deleted_con((r ← ~r), {r, q, ~p}))
                succeeds with {r, q, ~p} (literal_con(r, {q, ~p}))
              succeeds with {r, q, ~p} (rule_con((r ←), {q, ~p}))
                deleted_con((p ← ~q), {r, q, ~p}) (for (1))
                literal_con(~p, {r, q, ~p}) (for (1))
                succeeds with {r, q, ~p} (literal_con(~p, {r, q, ~p}))
              succeeds with {r, q, ~p} (deleted_con((p ← ~q), {r, q, ~p}))
            succeeds with {r, q, ~p} (literal_con(q, {~p}))
        succeeds with {r, q, ~p} (derive(q, {~p}))
      succeeds with {r, q, ~p} (rule_con((⊥ ← ~q), {~p}))
      rule_con((q ←), {r, q, ~p}) (resolvent with (2))
        literal_con(q, {r, q, ~p})
        succeeds with {r, q, ~p} (literal_con(q, {r, q, ~p}))
      succeeds with {r, q, ~p} (rule_con((q ←), {r, q, ~p}))
    succeeds with {r, q, ~p} (literal_con(~p, {}))
    literal_con(q, {r, q, ~p})
    succeeds with {r, q, ~p} (literal_con(q, {r, q, ~p}))
succeeds with {r, q, ~p} (derive(q, {}))
```

Fig. 3. Calling Sequence for *derive*$(q, \{\})$

$$s \leftarrow q \tag{3}$$
$$r \leftarrow \sim s \tag{5}$$
$$r \leftarrow \sim r \tag{6}$$

In this case, the forward evaluation of positive literals q and s is necessary to infer that (5) is implicitly deleted and it leads to inconsistency by (6).

4.2 Model Elimination Procedure

literal_con actually corresponds with model elimination procedure [10] in the sense that *literal_con* firstly searches to check if there is the checked literal in the assumed literals and then, to check if the checked literal is inconsistent with the checked literal being added to a set of the assumed literals.

$derive(p, \{\})$
select (1)
$literal\_con(\sim q, \{\})$
$rule\_con((p \leftarrow), \{\sim q\})$ **(resolvent with (1))**
$literal\_con(p, \{\sim q\})$
$deleted\_con((q \leftarrow \sim p), \{p, \sim q\})$ **(for (2))**
$literal\_con(\sim q, \{p, \sim q\})$ **(for (2))**
$rule\_con((\bot \leftarrow \sim p), \{p, \sim q\})$ **(resolvent with (2))**
$derive(p, \{p, \sim q\})$
$deleted\_con((r \leftarrow q), \{p, \sim q\})$ **(for (3))**
$derive(r, \{p, \sim q\})$
select (3)
$derive(q, \{p, \sim q\})$
fail $(derive(q, \{p, \sim q\}))$
select (4)
$literal\_con(\sim r, \{p, \sim q\})$
$rule\_con((\bot \leftarrow q), \{\sim r, p, \sim q\})$ **(resolvent with (3))**
$literal\_con(\sim q, \{\sim r, p, \sim q\})$
$rule\_con((\bot \leftarrow \sim r), \{\sim r, p, \sim q\})$ **(resolvent with (4))**
$derive(r, \{\sim r, p, \sim q\})$
fail $(derive(r, \{\sim r, p, \sim q\}))$
$literal\_con(\sim r, \{\sim r, p, \sim q\})$
$literal\_con(\bot, \{\sim r, p, \sim q\})$
fail $(literal\_con(\bot, \{\sim r, p, \sim q\}))$
fail $(rule\_con((\bot \leftarrow \sim r), \{\sim r, p, \sim q\}))$
fail $(literal\_con(\sim r, \{p, \sim q\}))$
fail $(derive(r, \{p, \sim q\}))$
$literal\_con(\sim r, \{p, \sim q\})$
$rule\_con((\bot \leftarrow q), \{\sim r, p, \sim q\})$ **(resolvent with (3))**
$literal\_con(\sim q, \{\sim r, p, \sim q\})$
$rule\_con((\bot \leftarrow \sim r), \{\sim r, p, \sim q\})$ **(resolvent with (4))**
$derive(r, \{\sim r, p, \sim q\})$
fail $(derive(r, \{\sim r, p, \sim q\}))$
$literal\_con(\sim r, \{\sim r, p, \sim q\})$
$literal\_con(\bot, \{\sim r, p, \sim q\})$
fail $(literal\_con(\bot, \{\sim r, p, \sim q\}))$
fail $(rule\_con((\bot \leftarrow \sim r), \{\sim r, p, \sim q\}))$
fail $(literal\_con(\sim r, \{p, \sim q\}))$
fail $(deleted\_con((r \leftarrow q), \{p, \sim q\}))$
fail $(literal\_con(\sim q, \{\}))$
fail $(derive(p, \{\}))$

Fig. 4. Calling Sequence for $derive(p, \{\})$

However, there are three main differences between model elimination procedure and *literal_con*.

1. We do not want inconsistency which is the original goal for model elimination procedure, but we want consistency to assume the checked literal.
2. In model elimination procedure, a contrapositive form of a rule is logically equivalent to the original form, but in logic programming, it is not the case. Consider the following three rules.

   $r \leftarrow \sim p$ (1)
   $p \leftarrow \sim q$ (2)
   $q \leftarrow \sim p$ (3)

   If we consider a program $T_1 = \{(1),(2)\}$ and a query ?-r for T_1, then we check consistency for $\sim p$ and then fails since p is derived by the rule (2). On the other hand, if we consider a program $T_2 = \{(1),(3)\}$ and a query ?-r for T_2, then we check consistency for $\sim p$ and then succeeds. This example shows that if we use a contrapositive form, the result might be different. So, we can say that we have a *directed* model elimination procedure in our procedure.
3. In model elimination procedure, we discard assumed literals in a branch of an AND-tree if we detect inconsistency. On the other hand, we accumulate assumed literals in Δ in our procedure so that coherence of assumed literals maintains over branches of an AND-tree.

4.3 Sadri's Integrity Constraint Checker

Sadri and Kowalski propose an integrity constraint check by augmenting SLDNF procedure with "forward" evaluation of rules and an inconsistency check for implicit deletions [14]. Although they show correctness for their procedure to find inconsistency of a update for any logic program with integrity constraints, they only show completeness to find inconsistency of a update for a subclass of a logic program with integrity constraints such that the body of each rule contains no negative literals. This means that they do not guarantee consistency for an addition of a rule for every general logic program. On the other hand, if *rule_con*$(R, \{\})$ succeeds, we can guarantee that R is consistent with the current program even if it contains negative literals in the body.

Moreover, since we accumulate assumed literals, we can prove consistency for addition of rules for a wider class of logic programs. For example, consider the following program:

$p \leftarrow \sim q$ (1)
$q \leftarrow \sim p$ (2)

For a check of consistency for addition of a rule, $(p \leftarrow)$, in Sadri's system, we firstly check whether q is implicitly deleted or not sicnce rule (2) is deleted by p. However, to do so, they invoke a query ?-q to the original program and the execution enters an infinite loop.

On the other hand, in our procedure, *rule_con*$((p \leftarrow), \{\})$ succeeds in showing consistency for the addition as Figure 5 shows.

rule_con$((p \leftarrow), \{\})$
  literal_con$(p, \{\})$
    deleted_con$((q \leftarrow \sim p), \{p\})$ (for (2))
      literal_con$(\sim q, \{p\})$
        rule_con$((p \leftarrow), \{p, \sim q\})$ (resolvent with (1))
        succeeds with $\{p, \sim q\}$ (*rule_con*$((p \leftarrow), \{p, \sim q\})$)
        rule_con$((\perp \leftarrow \sim p), \{p, \sim q\})$ (resolvent with (2))
        succeeds with $\{p, \sim q\}$ (*rule_con*$((\perp \leftarrow \sim p), \{p, \sim q\})$)
      succeeds with $\{p, \sim q\}$ (*literal_con*$(\sim q, \{p\})$)
    succeeds with $\{p, \sim q\}$ *deleted_con*$((q \leftarrow \sim p), \{p\})$
  succeeds with $\{p, \sim q\}$ (*literal_con*$(p, \{\})$)
succeeds with $\{p, \sim q\}$ (*rule_con*$((p \leftarrow), \{\})$)

Fig. 5. Calling Sequence for *rule_con*$((p \leftarrow), \{\})$

4.4 Poole's System

Poole [11] develops default and abductive reasoning system called *Theorist*. Since our procedure uses assumptions, his work is also related. However, there are two major differences.

1. The basic language for *Theorist* is a first-order language whereas we use a logic program. So, in *Theorist*, a contrapositive form of a rule is needed whereas in our setting, we do not have to consider the contrapositive form.
2. Assumptions in *Theorist* correspond with normal defaults without prerequisites in Default Logic [12] which of the form

$$\frac{: w}{w}.$$

So, their system can be regarded as a subclass of Default Logic which consists of proper axioms and the above form of defaults.
On the other hand, from the relationship between an extension of Default Logic and a stable model of logic programs [6], our system can be regarded as a subclass of Default Logic which consists of no proper axioms and any arbitrary form of defaults by the following translation.

$$H \leftarrow B_1, ..., B_k, \sim A_1, ..., \sim A_m \Rightarrow \frac{B_1 \wedge ... \wedge B_k : \neg A_1, ..., \neg A_m}{H}$$

5 Conclusion

In this paper, we propose a goal-directed procedure for a general logic program with integrity constraints. This procedure can be regarded as a combination of a modified model elimination procedure and checking of consistency by an implicit deletion. As a further study, we think that the following are needed.

1. Negations in general logic programs are "negation as ignorance". However, in nonmonotonic reasoning, we use not only negation as ignorance but also a logical negation. So, we should handle these logical negations as well in our procedure.
2. We should compare with bottom-up procedures to compute stable models [13, 4, 15, 7] in terms of computational complexity.

Appendix

We need the following definitions and lemmas to prove Theorems.

Definition 13. Let Δ be a set of literals. $\mathcal{F}(\Delta)$ is the following set of rules:

$$\{p \leftarrow |p \in \Delta\} \cup \{\bot \leftarrow p| {\sim} p \in \Delta\}$$

Definition 14. Let T be a logic program. A set of propositions M is a *finite grounded model* for T if the following are satisfied.

1. M is a model of T.
2. M can be written as a sequence of propositions $\langle p_1, p_2, ..., p_n\rangle$ such that each p_j has at least one rule R_j such that $head(R_j) = p_j$ and $pos(R_j) \subseteq \{p_1, ..., p_{j-1}\}$ where $p_1, ..., p_{j-1}$ are the element of the sequence up to $j-1$ and $(neg(R_j) \cap M) = \emptyset$. We say a sequence of such rules for proposition p_j is *a sequence of supporting rules* for p_j and especially a sequence of supporting rules for p_n, $\langle R_1, R_2, ...R_n\rangle$, is *a sequence of supporting rules* for M.

We can prove the following lemma by extending [2, Theorem 3.8].

Lemma 15. *Let T be a logic program. A set of propositions M is a finite grounded model for T if and only if M is a finite stable model for T.*

Lemma 16. *Let T be a logic program and Δ be a set of literals such that $\bot \notin \Delta$ and for every $l \in \Delta$, $\bar{l} \notin \Delta$.*

1. *Suppose derive(p, Δ) succeeds with Δ' and let $\mathcal{R}$ be a set of rules in T which are checked during the execution. Then, $pos(\Delta')$ (a set of positive literals in Δ') is a stable model for $\mathcal{R} \cup \mathcal{F}(\Delta)$.*
2. *Suppose literal_con(l, Δ) succeeds with Δ' and let $\mathcal{R}$ be a set of rules in T which are checked during the execution. Then, $pos(\Delta')$ is a stable model for $\mathcal{R} \cup \mathcal{F}(\{l\} \cup \Delta)$.*

3. *Suppose rule_con(R, Δ) succeeds with Δ' and let $\mathcal{R}$ be a union of $\{R\}$ and a set of rules in T which are checked during the execution. Then, pos(Δ') is a stable model for $\mathcal{R} \cup \mathcal{F}(\Delta)$.*
4. *Suppose deleted_con(R, Δ) succeeds with Δ' and let $\mathcal{R}$ be a set of rules in T which are checked during the execution. Then, pos(Δ') is a stable model for $\mathcal{R} \cup \mathcal{F}(\Delta)$.*

Proof of Lemma: We prove the lemma by induction of the number of calls of subprocedures during the execution.

Suppose that we have only one call of subprocedure to succeed. In this case, *derive(p, Δ)* or *literal_con(l, Δ)* has been invoked only once. The both cases confirm the statements in the lemma.

Suppose that if we have n calls ($n \geq 1$) of subprocedures to succeed, then the statements in the lemma are true.

(1) Suppose *derive(p, Δ)* checks a set of hypotheses $\mathcal{R}$ and returns Δ' by $n+1$ calls of subprocedures. Since $n+1 \geq 2$, we enter **else** part in *derive*. Let R be the selected rule in **select**.

Let i be the number of **for** loops and $\mathcal{R}_{k-1} (1 \leq k \leq i)$ be a set of rules checked during the k-th **for** loop and Δ_{k-1} be the initial set of hypotheses at the k-th **for** loop.

We firstly show that for every $\Delta_k (1 \leq k \leq i)$, *pos*($\Delta_k$) is a stable model for $\mathcal{R}_0 \cup .. \cup \mathcal{R}_{k-1} \cup \mathcal{F}(\Delta)$ by induction of the number of the **for** loop.

For the first loop, we have the following two cases.

1. Suppose the call of subprocedure in the first loop is *derive*(l, Δ_0). Then, *derive*(l, Δ_0) checks $\mathcal{R}_0$ and outputs Δ_1. By the inductive hypothesis for number of the calls of subprocedures, *pos*(Δ_1) is a stable model for $\mathcal{R}_0 \cup \mathcal{F}(\Delta_0)$, that is, $\mathcal{R}_0 \cup \mathcal{F}(\Delta)$ and the above statement is proved.
2. Suppose the call of subprocedure in the first loop is *literal_con*(l, Δ_0). Then, *literal_con*(l, Δ_0) checks $\mathcal{R}_0$ and outputs Δ_1. By the inductive hypothesis for number of the calls of subprocedures, *pos*(Δ_1) is a stable model for $\mathcal{R}_0 \cup \mathcal{F}(\Delta_0 \cup \{l\})$. Since l is a negative literal, *pos*(Δ_1) is also a stable model for $\mathcal{R}_0 \cup \mathcal{F}(\Delta)$ and the above statement is proved.

We assume that for every $\Delta_k (1 \leq k)$, *pos*(Δ_k) is a stable model for $\mathcal{R}_0 \cup .. \cup \mathcal{R}_{k-1} \cup \mathcal{F}(\Delta)$. Then, we prove the above statement for $k+1$-th loop.

1. Suppose the call of the subprocedure in the $k+1$-th loop is *derive*(l, Δ_k). Then, *derive*(l, Δ_k) checks $\mathcal{R}_k$ and outputs Δ_{k+1}. By the inductive hypothesis for number of the calls of subprocedures, *pos*(Δ_{k+1}) is a stable model for $\mathcal{R}_k \cup \mathcal{F}(\Delta_k)$.
   Since *pos*(Δ_k) is a model for $\mathcal{R}_0 \cup .. \cup \mathcal{R}_{k-1} \cup \mathcal{F}(\Delta)$ and we can easily see *pos*(Δ_k) $\subseteq$ *pos*(Δ_{k+1}) and *neg*(Δ_k) $\cap$ *pos*(Δ_{k+1}) $= \emptyset$, *pos*(Δ_{k+1}) is at least a model for $\mathcal{R}_0 \cup .. \cup \mathcal{R}_k \cup \mathcal{F}(\Delta)$.

Since $pos(\Delta_{k+1})$ is a stable model for $\mathcal{R}_k \cup \mathcal{F}(\Delta_k)$, for every $p' \in pos(\Delta_{k+1})$, we have a sequence of supporting rules in $\mathcal{R}_k \cup \mathcal{F}(\Delta_k)$ by Lemma 15. Moreover, for every $p' \in pos(\Delta_k)$, there is a sequence of supporting rules $\mathcal{R}_0 \cup .. \cup \mathcal{R}_{k-1} \cup \mathcal{F}(\Delta)$.
Therefore, for every $p' \in pos(\Delta_{k+1})$, if its sequence of supporting rules in $\mathcal{R}_k \cup \mathcal{F}(\Delta_k)$ contains a rule, $(p'' \leftarrow)$, in $\mathcal{F}(\Delta_k)$, we can replace it by the sequence of supporting rules for p'' in $\mathcal{R}_0 \cup .. \cup \mathcal{R}_{k-1} \cup \mathcal{F}(\Delta)$. Thus, for every $p' \in pos(\Delta_{k+1})$, there is a sequence of supporting rules in $\mathcal{R}_0 \cup .. \cup \mathcal{R}_k \cup \mathcal{F}(\Delta)$ and the above statement is proved.

2. Suppose the call of the subprocedure in the $k+1$-th loop is *literal_con*(l, Δ_k). We can prove the above statement in a similar way to the previous case.

Therefore, the above statement for the **for** loop is true and especially, $pos(\Delta_i)$ is a stable model for $\mathcal{R}_0 \cup .. \cup \mathcal{R}_{i-1} \cup \mathcal{F}(\Delta)$

Let $\mathcal{R}'$ be a set of rules checked during the last *literal_con*(p, Δ_i) and Δ' be an output of the last *literal_con*(p, Δ_i). Then, $\mathcal{R} = \{R\} \cup \mathcal{R}_0 \cup ... \cup \mathcal{R}_{i-1} \cup \mathcal{R}'$.

Now, we prove that $pos(\Delta')$ is a stable model for $\{R\} \cup \mathcal{R}_0 \cup .. \cup \mathcal{R}_{i-1} \cup \mathcal{R}' \cup \mathcal{F}(\Delta)$, that is, $\mathcal{R} \cup \mathcal{F}(\Delta)$. By the inductive hypothesis for number of the calls of subprocedures, $pos(\Delta')$ is a stable model for $\mathcal{R}' \cup \mathcal{F}(\Delta_i \cup \{p\})$.

We can easily check that $pos(\Delta')$ is at least a model for $\mathcal{R} \cup \mathcal{F}(\Delta)$. Thus, it is sufficient to show that there is a sequence of supporting rules for every $p' \in pos(\Delta')$ in $\mathcal{R} \cup \mathcal{F}(\Delta)$. If the sequence of supporting rules of p' in $\mathcal{R}' \cup \mathcal{F}(\Delta_i \cup \{p\})$ contains a rule, $(p'' \leftarrow)$, in $\mathcal{F}(\Delta_i \cup \{p\})$, we can replace it by the sequence of supporting rules for p'' in $\{R\} \cup \mathcal{R}_0 \cup .. \cup \mathcal{R}_{i-1} \cup \mathcal{F}(\Delta)$. Thus, for every $p' \in pos(\Delta')$, there is a sequence of supporting rules in $\{R\} \cup \mathcal{R}_0 \cup .. \cup \mathcal{R}_{i-1} \cup \mathcal{R}' \cup \mathcal{F}(\Delta)$, that is, $\mathcal{R} \cup \mathcal{F}(\Delta)$.

Therefore, $pos(\Delta')$ is a stable model for $\mathcal{R} \cup \mathcal{F}(\Delta)$ and case 1 in the lemma is proved.

(2) Suppose *literal_con*(l, Δ) checks a set of hypotheses $\mathcal{R}$ and returns Δ' by $n+1$ calls of subprocedures. Since $n + 1 \geq 2$, we enter **else** part in *literal_con*.

Let j be the number of **for** loops for *rule_con* and $R_{k-1} (1 \leq k \leq j)$ be a resolvent for the k-th **for** loop and $\mathcal{R}_{k-1}$ be a set of rules checked during the k-th **for** loop and Δ_{k-1} be the initial set of hypotheses at the k-th **for** loop.

We firstly show that for every $\Delta_k (1 \leq k \leq j)$, $pos(\Delta_k)$ is a stable model for $\mathcal{R}_0 \cup .. \cup \mathcal{R}_{k-1} \cup \{R_0, ..., R_{k-1}\} \cup \mathcal{F}(\Delta \cup \{l\})$ by induction of the number of the **for** loop.

Suppose the call of the first loop is *rule_con*(R_0, Δ_0). Then, *rule_con*(R_0, Δ_0) checks $\mathcal{R}_0$ and outputs Δ_1. By the inductive hypothesis for number of the calls of subprocedures, $pos(\Delta_1)$ is a stable model for $\mathcal{R}_0 \cup \{R_0\} \cup \mathcal{F}(\Delta_0)$, that is, $\mathcal{R}_0 \cup \{R_0\} \cup \mathcal{F}(\Delta \cup \{l\})$.

Now, we assume that for every $\Delta_k (1 \leq k)$, $pos(\Delta_k)$ is a stable model for $\mathcal{R}_0 \cup .. \cup \mathcal{R}_{k-1} \cup \{R_0, ..., R_{k-1}\} \cup \mathcal{F}(\Delta \cup \{l\})$ and prove the above statement for $k+1$-th loop.

Suppose the call of the subprocedure in the $k+1$-th loop is *rule_con*(R_k, Δ_k). Then, *rule_con*(R_k, Δ_k) checks $\mathcal{R}_k$ and outputs Δ_{k+1}. By the inductive hypothesis for number of the calls of subprocedures, $pos(\Delta_{k+1})$ is a stable model for $\mathcal{R}_k \cup \{R_k\} \cup \mathcal{F}(\Delta_k)$.

We can easily see that $pos(\Delta_{k+1})$ is at least a model for $\mathcal{R}_0 \cup .. \cup \mathcal{R}_k \cup \{R_0, ..., R_k\} \cup \mathcal{F}(\Delta \cup \{l\})$. Thus, it is sufficient to prove that there is a sequence of supporting rules for every $p \in pos(\Delta_{k+1})$ in $\mathcal{R}_0 \cup .. \cup \mathcal{R}_k \cup \{R_0, ..., R_k\} \cup \mathcal{F}(\Delta \cup \{l\})$.

If the sequence of supporting rules of p in $\mathcal{R}_k \cup \{R_k\} \cup \mathcal{F}(\Delta_k)$ contains a rule, $(p' \leftarrow)$, in $\mathcal{F}(\Delta_k)$, we can replace it by the sequence of supporting rules for p' in $\mathcal{R}_0 \cup .. \cup \mathcal{R}_{k-1} \cup \{R_0, ..., R_{k-1}\} \cup \mathcal{F}(\Delta \cup \{l\})$. Thus, for every $p \in pos(\Delta_{k+1})$, there is a sequence of supporting rules in $\mathcal{R}_0 \cup .. \cup \mathcal{R}_k \cup \{R_0, ..., R_k\} \cup \mathcal{F}(\Delta \cup \{l\})$ and the above statement is proved.

However, each $R_k (0 \leq k \leq j-1)$ is not a rule in T but a resolvent for l and a rule R'_k in T. Therefore, to prove case 2 in the lemma, we must show that $pos(\Delta_j)$ is a stable model for $\mathcal{R}_0 \cup .. \cup \mathcal{R}_{j-1} \cup \{R'_0, ..., R'_{j-1}\} \cup \mathcal{F}(\Delta \cup \{l\})$.

We can easily check that $pos(\Delta_j)$ is a model for $\mathcal{R}_0 \cup .. \cup \mathcal{R}_{j-1} \cup \{R'_0, ..., R'_{j-1}\} \cup \mathcal{F}(\Delta \cup \{l\})$. Therefore, it is sufficient to show that there is a sequence of supporting rules for every $p \in pos(\Delta_j)$ in $\mathcal{R}_0 \cup .. \cup \mathcal{R}_{j-1} \cup \{R'_0, ..., R'_{j-1}\} \cup \mathcal{F}(\Delta \cup \{l\})$. If l is negative, we can replace every occurrence of R_k in every sequence of supporting rules by R'_k. Else if l is positive, we can replace every occurrence of R_k in every sequence of supporting rules by $\langle (l \leftarrow), R'_k \rangle$. Therefore, $pos(\Delta_j)$ is a stable model for $\mathcal{R}_0 \cup .. \cup \mathcal{R}_{j-1} \cup \{R'_0, ..., R'_{j-1}\} \cup \mathcal{F}(\Delta \cup \{l\})$.

Let $\mathcal{R}'$ be $\mathcal{R}_0 \cup .. \cup \mathcal{R}_{j-1} \cup \{R'_0, ..., R'_{j-1}\}$ and $i - j$ be the number of for loops for *deleted_con* and $R_{k-1} (j+1 \leq k \leq i)$ be a deleted rule for $k-j$-th for loop for *deleted_con* and $\mathcal{R}_{k-1}$ be a set of rules checked during $k-j$-th for loop and Δ_{k-1} be the initial set of hypotheses at the $k-j$-th for loop. Then, $\mathcal{R} = \mathcal{R}' \cup \mathcal{R}_j \cup .. \cup \mathcal{R}_{i-1} \cup \{R_j, ..., R_{i-1}\}$.

We can prove in a similar way to the proof for the statement about for loop of *rule_con* that $pos(\Delta_i)$ is a stable model for $\mathcal{R}' \cup \mathcal{R}_j \cup .. \cup \mathcal{R}_{i-1} \cup \{R_j, ..., R_{i-1}\} \cup \mathcal{F}(\Delta \cup \{l\})$.

Since $\Delta' = \Delta_i$ and $\mathcal{R} = \mathcal{R}' \cup \mathcal{R}_j \cup .. \cup \mathcal{R}_{i-1} \cup \{R_j, ..., R_{i-1}\}$, $pos(\Delta')$ is a stable model for $\mathcal{R} \cup \mathcal{F}(\Delta \cup \{l\})$. Thus, case 2 in the lemma is proved.

(3) Suppose *rule_con*(R, Δ) returns Δ' with $n+1$ calls of subprocedures.

1. Suppose we select (a) and we select a positive literal p from *body*(R). Then, *literal_con*$(\sim p, \Delta)$ is invoked. Let $\mathcal{R}'$ be a set of rules checked during *literal_con*$(\sim p, \Delta)$. Then, by the inductive hypothesis for number of the calls of subprocedures, $pos(\Delta')$ is a stable model for $\mathcal{R}' \cup \mathcal{F}(\Delta \cup \{\sim p\})$. Since $pos(\Delta')$ satisfies $\sim p$, it also satisfies R and $\mathcal{F}(\Delta)$. Therefore, $pos(\Delta')$ is a stable model for $\mathcal{R}' \cup \{R\} \cup \mathcal{F}(\Delta)$.
2. Suppose we select (a) and we select a negative literal $\sim p$ from *body*(R). Then, *derive*(p, Δ) is invoked. Let $\mathcal{R}'$ be a set of rules checked during *derive*(p, Δ). Then, by the inductive hypothesis for number of the calls of subprocedures, $pos(\Delta')$ is a stable model for $\mathcal{R}' \cup \mathcal{F}(\Delta)$. Since $pos(\Delta')$ satisfies p, it also satisfies R. Therefore, $pos(\Delta')$ is a stable model for $\mathcal{R}' \cup \{R\} \cup \mathcal{F}(\Delta)$.
3. Suppose we select (b). Let $\mathcal{R}'$ be a set of rules checked before returning Δ'. Then, in a similar way to (1), we can show that $pos(\Delta')$ is a stable model

for $\mathcal{R}' \cup \mathcal{F}(\Delta)$. Since $pos(\Delta')$ also satisfies R and there is a sequence of supporting rules of $head(R)$, $pos(\Delta')$ is a stable model for $\mathcal{R}' \cup \{R\} \cup \mathcal{F}(\Delta)$.

Therefore, $pos(\Delta')$ is a stable model for $\mathcal{R}' \cup \{R\} \cup \mathcal{F}(\Delta)$ and case 3 in the lemma is proved.

(4) Suppose *deleted_con*(R, Δ) checks a set of hypotheses $\mathcal{R}$ and returns Δ' with $n+1$ calls of subprocedures. In both selections of (a) and (b), we can show that $pos(\Delta')$ is a stable model for $\mathcal{R} \cup \mathcal{F}(\Delta)$ by inductive hypothesis for number of the calls of subprocedures. Therefore, case 4 in the lemma is proved. □

Proof of Theorem 7: Suppose *derive*$(p, \{\})$ succeeds with Δ but for every stable model M for T, $M \not\models \mathcal{F}(\Delta)$. Let $\mathcal{R}$ be a set of checked rules during *derive*$(p, \{\})$. Let $\mathcal{R}_1$ be a set of rules in $\mathcal{R}$ with a literal l such that $l \notin \Delta$ and $\bar{l} \notin \Delta$ and let $\mathcal{R}_2$ be $\mathcal{R} - \mathcal{R}_1$. Then, every rule R in $\mathcal{R}_1$ satisfies the following conditions.

1. There exists a literal $l \in body(R)$ such that $\bar{l} \in \Delta$.
2. Then, $head(R) \in \Delta$ or $\sim head(R) \in \Delta$ since *deleted_con* for R has been invoked.

Let T_1 be a set of rules in $T - \mathcal{R}$ with a literal l such that $l \in \Delta$ or $\bar{l} \in \Delta$ and let T_2 be $T - \mathcal{R} - T_1$. Then, every rule R in T_1 satisfies the following conditions.

1. For every literal $l \in body(R)$, $l \notin \Delta$ and $\bar{l} \notin \Delta$ since otherwise, the rule has been checked.
2. $head(R) \in \Delta$ since if $\sim head(R) \in \Delta$, *rule_con* for the resolvent of R and $\sim head(R)$ has been invoked.

Let M' be a stable model for $\mathcal{R}$. From the assumption, there is no stable model for T which subsumes M'.

This means that there is no stable model for $\mathcal{R}_2 \cup T_2$ which subsumes M' since if there is such a model, every rule in $\mathcal{R}_1 \cup T_1$ is satisfied by the stable model and this contradicts the assumption.

Suppose there is a stable model for T_2 then there is a stable model for $\mathcal{R}_2 \cup T_2$ since there is no common proposition between $\mathcal{R}_2$ and T_2, and $\mathcal{R}_2$ itself has the stable model M'. This contradicts the above result. Therefore, there is no stable model for T_2.

Then, any rule in $T - T_2$ cannot save inconsistency for T_2 even if it is added since any rule in $T - T_2$ does not have a proposition in T_2 as its head. Therefore, there is no stable model for T and this contradicts the consistency of T. □.

Proof of Theorem 8: In a similar way to the proof above. □

Proof of Theorem 9: It is sufficient to show the following. □

Lemma 17. *Let T be a logic program and Δ be a set of literals such that $\perp \notin \Delta$ and for every $l \in \Delta, \bar{l} \notin \Delta$.*

1. *Suppose that derive(p, Δ) terminates for every selection. If there exists a stable model M for $T \cup \mathcal{F}(\Delta)$ such that $M \models p$, then there is a selection of rules for which derive(p, Δ) succeeds with Δ' and M is a stable model for $T \cup \mathcal{F}(\Delta')$.*
2. *Suppose that literal_con(l, Δ) terminates for every selection. If there exists a stable model M for $T \cup \mathcal{F}(\Delta)$ such that $M \models l$, then there is a selection of rules for which literal_con(l, Δ) succeeds with Δ' and M is a stable model for $T \cup \mathcal{F}(\Delta')$.*
3. *Suppose that rule_con(R, Δ) terminates for every selection. If there exists a stable model M for $T \cup \mathcal{F}(\Delta)$ such that $M \models R$, then there is a selection of rules for which rule_con(R, Δ) succeeds with Δ' and M is a stable model for $T \cup \mathcal{F}(\Delta')$.*
4. *Suppose that deleted_con(R, Δ) terminates for every selection. If there exists a stable model M for $T \cup \mathcal{F}(\Delta)$, then there is a selection of rules for which deleted_con(R, Δ) succeeds with Δ' and M is a stable model for $T \cup \mathcal{F}(\Delta')$.*

Proof of Lemma: We prove by induction of number of the longest calls of subprocedures among selections.

Suppose that number of the longest calls of subprocedures is one. In this case, *derive*(p, Δ) or *literal_con*(l, Δ) has been invoked only once. The both cases confirm the statements in the lemma.

Suppose that the lemma is satisfied if number of the longest calls is at most n.

(1) Suppose that $T \cup \mathcal{F}(\Delta)$ has a stable model M s.t. $M \models p$ and *derive*(p, Δ) terminates with $n+1$ calls as the longest calls of the subprocedures. Since M satisfies p, $\sim p \notin \Delta$. Therefore, it does not fail at **elseif** part in *derive* and we enter **else** part.

Since M satisfies p, there is a sequence of supporting rules for p. We can use a rule R in the tail of its sequence as a selected rule at **select** operation.

Then, we enter **for** loop. We check every literal in *body*(R) in an arbitrary order. We show that for each k-th **for** loop, Δ_k can be returned and M is a stable model for $T \cup \mathcal{F}(\Delta_k)$ by induction of the number of the loop.

For the first loop, we have the following two cases.

1. Suppose the first checked literal is a positive literal p'. Then, we invoke *derive*(p', Δ_0). M is a stable model for $T \cup \Delta_0$. And since R is an element of the sequence of supporting rules and $p' \in$ *body*(R), $M \models p'$. Therefore, by the inductive hypothesis for number of the longest calls of subprocedures, *derive*(p', Δ_0) succeeds with Δ_1 and M is a stable model for $T \cup \mathcal{F}(\Delta_1)$.
2. Suppose the first checked literal is a negative literal $\sim p'$. Then, we invoke *literal_con*($\sim p', \Delta_0$). M is a stable model for $T \cup \Delta_0$. And since R is an element of the sequence of supporting rules and $\sim p' \in$ *body*(R), $M \models \sim p'$. Therefore, by the inductive hypothesis for number of the longest calls of subprocedures, *literal_con*($\sim p', \Delta_0$) succeeds with Δ_1 and M is a stable model for $T \cup \mathcal{F}(\Delta_1)$.

We assume that for each k-th loop, Δ_k can be returned and M is a stable model for $T \cup \mathcal{F}(\Delta_k)$. Then, in a similar way to the proof for the first loop, we can prove that Δ_{k+1} can be returned and M is a stable model for $T \cup \mathcal{F}(\Delta_{k+1})$.

Since $derive(p, \Delta)$ terminates, the iteration eventually terminates. Let i be a number of calls.

Finally, we call $literal\_con(p, \Delta_i)$. Since M is a stable model for $T \cup \mathcal{F}(\Delta_i)$ and $M \models p$, Δ' can be returned and M is a stable model for $T \cup \mathcal{F}(\Delta')$ by the inductive hypothesis for number of the longest calls of subprocedures.

Therefore, $derive(p, \Delta)$ succeeds with Δ' and M is a stable model for $T \cup \mathcal{F}(\Delta')$ and case 1 in the lemma is proved.

(2) Suppose that $T \cup \mathcal{F}(\Delta)$ has a stable model M s.t. $M \models l$ and $literal\_con(l, \Delta)$ terminates with $n+1$ calls as the longest calls of the subprocedures. Since M satisfies l, $\bar{l} \notin \Delta$. Therefore, it does not fail at **elseif** part in $literal\_con$ and we enter **else** part.

We show that for each k-th **for** loop for $rule\_con$, Δ_k can be returned and M is a stable model for $T \cup \mathcal{F}(\Delta_k)$ by induction of the number of the loop.

Let us consider the first loop of $rule\_con(R, \Delta_0)$. Since M is a stable model for $T \cup \Delta_0$ and $M \models l$ and $R \in resolve(l, T)$, M also satisfies R. Therefore, by the inductive hypothesis for number of the longest calls of subprocedures, $rule\_con(R, \Delta_0)$ succeeds with Δ_1 and M is a stable model for $T \cup \mathcal{F}(\Delta_1)$.

We assume that for each k-th loop, Δ_k can be returned and M is a stable model for $T \cup \mathcal{F}(\Delta_k)$. Then, in a similar way to the proof for the first loop, we can prove that Δ_{k+1} can be returned and M is a stable model for $T \cup \mathcal{F}(\Delta_{k+1})$.

Similarly, we can show that for each k-th loop for $deleted\_con$, Δ_k can be returned and M is a stable model for $T \cup \mathcal{F}(\Delta_k)$.

Since $literal\_con(l, \Delta)$ terminates, these iterations eventually terminate.

Therefore, $literal\_con(l, \Delta)$ succeeds with Δ' and M is a stable model for $T \cup \mathcal{F}(\Delta')$ and case 2 in the lemma is proved.

(3) Suppose that $T \cup \mathcal{F}(\Delta)$ has a stable model M s.t. $M \models R$ and $rule\_con(R, \Delta)$ terminates with $n+1$ calls as longest calls of the subprocedures. $M \models R$ means the following cases.

1. There is a positive literal $p \in body(R)$ such that $M \models \sim p$. Then, we select (a) and call $literal\_con(\sim p, \Delta)$. Since $M \models \sim p$, we can use inductive hypothesis for number of the longest calls of subprocedures to show that $literal\_con(\sim p, \Delta)$ succeeds with Δ' and M is a stable model for $T \cup \mathcal{F}(\Delta')$.
2. There is a negative literal $\sim p \in body(R)$ such that $M \models p$. Then, we select (a) and call $derive(p, \Delta)$. Since $M \models p$, we can use inductive hypothesis for number of the longest calls of subprocedures to show that $derive(p, \Delta)$ succeeds with Δ' and M is a stable model for $T \cup \mathcal{F}(\Delta')$.
3. For every $l \in body(R)$, $M \models l$ and $M \models head(R)$. In this case, we select (b). Then, in a similar way to (1), we can prove that Δ' is returned and M is a stable model for $T \cup \mathcal{F}(\Delta')$.

Therefore, the case 3 in the lemma is proved.

(4) Suppose that $T \cup \mathcal{F}(\Delta)$ has a stable model M and *deleted_con*(R, Δ) terminates with $n+1$ calls as the longest calls of the subprocedures. Since M is a stable models, either $M \models$ *head*(R) or $M \models\sim$*head*(R).

1. Suppose $M \models$ *head*(R). Then, we select (a). We can use inductive hypothesis for number of the longest calls of subprocedures to show that *derive*(*head*$(R), \Delta)$ succeeds with Δ' and M is a stable model for $T \cup \mathcal{F}(\Delta')$.
2. Suppose $M \models\sim$ *head*(R). Then, we select (b). We can use inductive hypothesis for number of the longest calls of subprocedures to show that *literal_con*$(\sim$ *head*$(R), \Delta)$ succeeds with Δ' and M is a stable model for $T \cup \mathcal{F}(\Delta')$.

For both cases, the case 4 in the lemma is proved. □

Proof of Corollary 10: By the contrapositive of Theorem 9. □

Proof of Corollary 11: *derive*$(p, \{\})$ for a finite program always terminates if we check the same call of *derive*. Then use Theorem 9. □.

Proof of Corollary 12: In a similar way to Corollary 11. □

Acknowledgments

We thank Bob Kowalski, Francesca Toni and Fariba Sadri from Imperial College, Laura Giordano and Maria Luisa Sapino from University of Turin, Phan Minh Dung from AIT, Paolo Mancarella from University of Pisa, François Bry from ECRC for instructive comments. Special thanks must go to Evelina Lamma and Paola Mello from University of Bologna for inviting Ken Satoh to the stimulating and fruitful workshop, 3rd Workshop on Extensions of Logic Programming at Bologna.

References

1. Dung, P. M., Negations as Hypotheses: An Abductive Foundation for Logic Programming, *Proc. of ICLP'91*, pp. 3 – 18 (1991).
2. Elkan, C., A Rational Reconstruction of Nonmonotonic Truth Maintenance Systems, *Artificial Intelligence*, **43**, pp. 219 – 234 (1990).
3. Eshghi, K., Kowalski, R. A., Abduction Compared with Negation by Failure, *Proc. of ICLP'89*, pp. 234 – 254 (1989).
4. Fages, F., A New Fixpoint Semantics for General Logic Programs Compared with the Well-Founded and the Stable Model Semantics, *Proc. of ICLP'90*, pp. 442 – 458 (1990).
5. Gelfond, M., Lifschitz, V., The Stable Model Semantics for Logic Programming, *Proc. of LP'88*, pp. 1070 – 1080 (1988).
6. Gelfond, M., Lifschitz, V., Logic Programs with Classical Negation, *Proc. of ICLP'90*, pp. 579 – 597 (1990).
7. Inoue, K., Koshimura, M., Hasegawa, R., Embedding Negation as Failure into a Model Generation Theorem Prover, *Proc. of CADE-11*, LNAI607, pp. 400 – 415 (1992).

8. Kakas, A. C., Mancarella, P., Generalized Stable Models: A Semantics for Abduction, *Proc. of ECAI'90*, pp. 385 - 391 (1990).
9. Kakas, A. C., Mancarella, P., Stable Theories for Logic Programs, *Proc. of ILPS'91*, pp. 85 - 100 (1991).
10. Loveland, D. W., *Automated Theorem Proving: A Logical Basis*, North-Holland (1978).
11. Poole, D., Compiling a Default Reasoning System into Prolog, *New Generation Computing*, Vol. 9, No. 1, pp. 3 - 38 (1991).
12. Reiter, R., A Logic for Default Reasoning, *Artificial Intelligence*, **13**, pp. 81 - 132 (1980).
13. Saccà, D., Zaniolo, C., Stable Models and Non-Determinism in Logic Programs with Negation, *Proc. of PODS'90*, pp. 205 - 217 (1990).
14. Sadri, F., Kowalski, R., A Theorem-Proving Approach to Database Integrity, *Foundations of Deductive Database and Logic Programming*, (J. Minker, Ed.), Morgan Kaufmann Publishers, pp. 313 - 362 (1988).
15. Satoh, K., Iwayama, N., Computing Abduction Using the TMS, *Proc. of ICLP'91*, pp. 505 - 518 (1991).

DECLARATIVE SEMANTICS OF HYPOTHETICAL LOGIC PROGRAMMING WITH NEGATION AS FAILURE

Phan Minh Dung
Division of Computer Science
Asian Institute of Technology
GPO Box 2754, Bangkok 10501, Thailand
E-mail: dung@cs.ait.ac.th

Abstract

We define the stable semantics for general hypothetical logic programs. We consider resolving a hypothetical goal (G : R) in a context P as consisting of two steps: (i) Updating the context by inserting the clauses in R into it, and (ii) Resolving the goal G wrt the new context P U R. The consequence of viewing the assumptions R in a hypothetical goal (G : R) as an update request imposes a kind of update semantics on the semantics of P. We study this problem and introduce the rational semantics for hypothetical programs.

0. Introduction

We assume the existence of a fixed language with a finite alphabet (with at least one constant symbol), big enough to contain each program considered in this paper. The Herbrand base of this language is denoted by **HB**.

The programs, clauses and goals considered in this paper build a subset of the following syntax.

$$C ::= A \mid A <\!\!- G \mid \neg A <\!\!- G \mid (x)C$$

$$P ::= C \mid P_1 \,\&\, P_2$$

$$G ::= A \mid \neg A \mid G_1 \,\&\, G_2 \mid G : P$$

A clause is a C-expression. A program is a closed P-expression. A goal is a G-expression. Goals of the form G : P are called hypothetical goals. A normal program is a program not containing hypothetical goals.

---

[1]x is universally quantified in C.

Incorporating hypothetical reasoning into logic programming has made it suited for a wide range of applications, especially in knowledge representation. One example is the formalization of the British Nationality Act [5]. The Act, for example, rules that a child born in the Kingdom after the commencement can become a British citizen if his father who is dead at the time of his birth, would have been entitled to register as a British citizen, had he been alive at that time. This rule can be formalized as the following hypothetical clause:

become-citizen(X) <- born-in-UK(X) &
[become-citizen(father(X)) : alive(father(X))]

Hypothetical logic programming provides also an useful tool to build structured knowledge base. For example, if we want to build a knowledge base about birds then it is convenient to build a main module containing only general rules and facts like the rule "birds can fly". Specific knowledge about specific kind of birds like the rule "penguin can not fly" is contained in specific modules. When, for example, a question about penguin is asked, the specific knowledge about penguin is added into the main module and is removed again afterwards. Formally, this can be realized in hypothetical logic programming as follows:

Main module P: fly(X) <- bird(X)

Specific module R: bird(X) <- penguin(X)
¬ fly(X) <- penguin(X)
penguin(Tweety)

The question "Can Tweety fly" is represented by the hypothetical goal (fly(Tweety) : R). Resolving this goal in the context P is defined as resolving fly(Tweety) in the context P U R. The conflict between the general clause and the second clause in R is solved by an overriding rule giving a specific information higher priority than the more general one.

In the same spirit, Miller [11] has showed that goal of the form (G : R) can be interpreted as a request to load the code in R prior to attempting G and unload that code after G succeeds or fails. In that way, hypothetical logic programming provides an logical explanation of parametric modules and abstract datatypes. Further hypothetical logic programming provides also an unified framework for object-level- and metaprogramming [5,2].

to view R as representing a request to update the context before resolving G.

Updating a knowledge base will lead to a revision of the current beliefs drawn from the knowledge base. It is rational and widely accepted that only those beliefs, against them new evidences emerge from the update, need to be revised. Thus, the beliefs of the updated knowledge base must represent a "minimal change" of the current beliefs. This "minimal change" condition is the most characteristic feature of any update semantics [4].

The appearance of hypothetical goals in a hypothetical programs lends a dynamic aspect to it: A hypothetical program can be viewed as representing a collection of (hypothetical) processes consisting of a series of successive (hypothetical) update operations.

So, any semantics for hypothetical logic programming should satisfy the following three conditions: (i) it should be a semantics of justified beliefs, (ii) it should be a kind of "process"-semantics, and (iii) it should capture the "minimal change" semantics of knowledge base updates.

The second condition suggests that the semantics should be Kripke-like while the first one suggests a generalization of stable semantics. The last condition suggests that the expected semantics is a kind of rational stable Kripke-like semantics.

There are at least three different calling methods for hypothetical goals (G : R) [2,12,11]. The first method requires the insertion of the clauses in R into the calling context P and then resolving G in the context P U R. In the second method, G is resolved in the context R, independent of the context in which (G : R) is called. This corresponds very much to the way modules are called in classical imperative languages like Pascal or Algol. The third method allows an overriding of specific information against more general one in the case of conflict. As this paper studied only the first calling method, we will restrict our study to normal hypothetical programs, i.e. programs without explicit negation, whose syntax is specified in the following:

$$C ::= A \mid A \leftarrow G \mid (x)C$$

$$P ::= C \mid P_1 \,\&\, P_2$$

$$G ::= A \mid \neg A \mid G_1 \,\&\, G_2 \mid G : P$$

The paper is organized in two major parts: In the first part, we will

Negation as failure is an important concept in logic programming. It plays a crucial role in applications of logic programming in knowledge representation [6,3,7,13]. But until now, the semantics of negation as failure is studied almost exclusively in the framework of normal logic programming. Only few works have been done so far to study its semantics in hypothetical logic programming. An early paper of Gabbay et all [5] pointed out the difficulty of this enterprise. Other authors have studied the semantics of negation for special classes of hypothetical programs. Harland [8] generalized the Fitting semantics for a special class of hypothetical logic programs where practically, the negation is applied only on predicates defined by normal clauses. Bonner and McCarty [1] generalized the perfect model semantics for stratified hypothetical logic programs.

It is still an open question today as how to specify the intuitive semantics of general hypothetical logic programs with negation as failure.

So, this paper is devoted to this problem.

First, we give an example to demonstrate the need for non-stratified hypothetical logic programs.

Example 1[2] The following non-stratified program P determines the parity of a relation r.

```
P:    even <- ¬odd
      odd  <- select(X),[even : mark(X)]
      select(X) <- r(X), ¬mark(X)

R:    r(0) <-
      ...
      r(n) <-
```

The goal (even : R) succeeds wrt P if R contains an even number of entries, and fails otherwise.
//

To understand the semantics of negation in hypothetical logic programming, it is essential to give a clear intuitive interpretation of hypothetical goals. Procedurally, resolving a hypothetical goal (G : R) in context P is defined as resolving G in context P U R. So it is natural

---

[2].In [1], a stratified program for this problem is given. Our non-stratified version is more natural, easier to understand and also more efficient than that program.

generalize the stable model semantics of normal logic programs to stable Kripke-like model semantics for general hypothetical logic programming. Then we give examples and discuss its applications and relations to other approaches. In the second part, we introduce the rational semantics and discuss its problems. We conclude the paper with a discussion about possible extensions of this paper.

1. Preliminaries: Stable Model of Normal Logic Programs

Let M be a set of ground atoms and P be a normal logic program. The Gelfond-Lifschitz transformation of P wrt M, written P_M is obtained from G_P, the set of ground instances of clauses in P, by (i) deleting each clause in G_P whose body contains a negative literal $\neg A$ with $A \in M$, and (ii) deleting all the negative literals from the remaining clauses. M is a stable model of P if M is the least Herbrand model of P_M [6].

The following lemma gives a characterization of stable model which will be used later to generalize the stable semantics for general hypothetical logic programming.

Lemma 1 Let M be a set of ground atoms and P be a normal logic program. An operator T_M: $2^{HB} \rightarrow 2^{HB}$ is defined by

$$T_M(N) = \{ A \mid \text{ there is } A \leftarrow A_1,..,A_n, \neg B_1,..,\neg B_m \text{ in } G_P \text{ s.t. } \{A_1,..,A_n\} \subseteq N \text{ and } \{B_1,..,B_m\} \cap M = \emptyset \}$$

Then M is stable iff M is the least fixed point of T_M
//

2. Stable Kripke-Like Model Semantics

For the sake of convenience, a program is often considered as a set of closed clauses. A variable which is bound at the outermost of a clause is called a global variable of it. The set of ground instantiations of clauses of a hypothetical program P, denoted by G_P, is obtained by instantiating all the global variables of clauses in P with ground terms in all possible ways.

Let P be a program. W_P is defined as the smallest set satisfying (i) $P \in W_P$, and (ii) if $Q \in W_P$ and (G : R) is a goal appearing in G_Q then $Q \cup R \in W_P$. It is clear that if P is a normal program then $W_P = \{P\}$.

A Kripke-like model of P is a mapping from W_P into 2^{HB}. The set of all Kripke-like models of P is denoted by KL_P. A partial order <<

between Kripke-like models of P is defined by I << J iff for each Q $\in W_P$: $I(Q) \subseteq J(Q)$. It is clear that $(KL_P, <<)$ is a complete lattice.

Definition Let $I,J \in KL_P$, A be an atom, and G be a goal. Define $J,I,P \models G$ inductively as follows:

$J,I,P \models A$	if	$A \in J(P)$
$J,I,P \models \neg A$	if	$A \notin I(P)$
$J,I,P \models G_1 \,\&\, G_2$	if	$J,I,P \models G_1$ and $J,I,P \models G_2$
$J,I,P \models (G : Q)$	if	$J,I,P \cup Q \models G$

//

Let $I \in KL_P$. A transformation T_I: $KL_P \rightarrow KL_P$ is defined as follows:

$$T_I(J)(Q) = \{ A \mid \text{there is a clause } A \leftarrow G \text{ in } G_Q \text{ s.t. } J,I,Q \models G \}$$

Theorem 2 T_I is monotonic and 'omega'-continuous.

Proof The theorem follows directly from the following two propositions.

Proposition 1 T_I is monotonic

Proof: Let $J,J' \in KL_P$ with $J \le J'$. We need to show $T_I(J)(Q) \subseteq T_I(J')(Q)$ for any arbitrary $Q \in W_P$. Let $A \in T_I(J)(Q)$. Thus there is a clause $A \leftarrow G$ in Q s.t. $J,I,Q \models G$. By induction on the size of G, it is easy to see that $J',I,Q \models G$ holds. Thus $A \in T_I(J')(Q)$.

Proposition 2 Let $J_0 \le J_1 \le \ldots \le J_n \le ..$ be a sequence of Kripke-like models of P, and $J = lub(J_i)_i$. Further let $I \in KL_P$. Then $T_I(J) = lub(T_I(J_i))_i$

Proof: Let $Q \in W_P$ and $A \in T_I(J)(Q)$. Thus there is a clause $A \leftarrow G$ s.t. $J,I,Q \models G$. By induction on the size of G, it is easy to show that there is an i s.t. $J_i,I,Q \models G$. That means that $A \in T_I(J_i)(Q)$. The proposition follows directly from the monotonicity of T_I.

//

DEFINITION *Let I be a Kripke-like model of P. Then I is a stable model of P iff I is the least fixpoint of T*

//

Example 2 P: $p <- \neg r$
$s <- (p : \{r<-\})$

$W_P = \{P,Q\}$ with $Q = P \cup \{r<-\}$.

Let I: $I(P) = \{p\}$, $I(Q) = \{r\}$.

Let $I_1 = T_I(\emptyset)$. So $I_1(P) = \{p\}$, $I_1(Q) = \{r\}$
$I_2 = T_I(I_1)$. So $I_2(P) = \{p\}$, $I_2(Q) = \{r\}$

Thus I is the least fixed point of T_I. So I is a stable Kripke-like model of P.
//

That our notion of stable Kripke-like models is a generalization of Gelfond and Lifschitz's notion of stable models of normal logic programs follows directly from the lemma 1.

In [1], Bonner and McCarty has extended the concept of stratification for hypothetical logic programs and generalized the perfect model semantics [P] for this class of programs. The following lemma shows that for Bonner and McCarty's stratified hypothetical programs, stable Kripke-like semantics, and perfect model semantics coincide.

Theorem 3 Let P be a stratified hypothetical program. Then P has an unique stable Kripke-like model I such that for each ground atom A, $A \in I(P)$ iff A is true wrt perfect model semantics of P.
//

3. Rational Semantics: Assumptions as Updates

Resolving a ground hypothetical goal (G : R) in the context of a program P is interpreted in this chapter as consisting of two steps: First updating the context P by inserting the clauses in R into it, and then resolving the goal G wrt the new context.

The semantics of update and belief revision has attracted attention of many researchers lately [4,14]. In general, it is widely accepted that any update semantics should satisfy the "minimal change" condition which intuitively means that only those of the current beliefs of a knowledge base need to be revised if new evidences against them emerge from the update.

We have defined the stable Kripke-like semantics. As we interpret the assumptions R in a hypothetical goal (G : R) as a request to update the calling context, it is interesting to ask the important question as whether or not this semantics satisfies the "minimal change" condition. Let us elaborate on it through an example.

Let I be a stable Kripke-like model of P. As we basically are only interested in the conclusions we could draw from P, I(P) can be viewed as the set of current beliefs drawn from the knowledge base P. If I satisfies the "minimal change" condition then for any P U R $\in W_P$, I(P U R) must represent a minimal change of I(P). But unfortunately, the following example shows that not every stable Kripke-like model satisfies this rational condition.

Example 3 Let P be

d <- (a : {c<-})
a <- ¬b
b <- ¬a

W_P = {P,Q} with Q = P U {c<-}.

Let I(P) = {a}, I(Q) = {b,c}

It is not difficult to see that I is a stable Kripke-like model of P. I(P)={a} can be viewed as the set of current beliefs drawn from P. As c has no connections, what so ever, to a and b, we expect that inserting the unit clause c<- into P would have no effect on a. In other words, we expect that a continues to be believed after inserting c<- into P, i.e. a is expected to be true wrt I(Q). But this is apparently not the case with I. It is easy to see that I(Q) does not represent a minimal change of I(P). To satisfy the minimal change condition, I(Q) should be {a,c,d}.
//

In the following, we will define a rational semantics for hypothetical programs satisfying the "minimal change" condition.

To do so, it is necessary to specify which part of the current beliefs can be kept and which part has to be given up after inserting a new set of clauses into a program P. The partial Kripke-like models is introduced for this purpose.

For each set S of atoms, let ¬.S = { ¬p | p $\in$ S }.

A <u>partial Kripke-like model</u> of P is a mapping I: W_P --> $2^{HB} \times 2^{\neg.HB}$ such that for each Q $\in W_P$, S U S' is consistent where I(Q) = (S,S').

For each partial Kripke-like model I of P, the positive and negative parts of I are denoted by I^+,I^-, respectively, i.e. I^+: W_P --> 2^{HB}, and I^-:

$W_P \rightarrow 2^{\neg.HB}$ such that for each $Q \in W_P$, $I(Q) = (I^+(Q), I^-(Q))$.

Remark From now on, a Kripke-like model $I \in KL_P$ is considered as a (total) Kripke-like model $<I^+, I^->$ with $I^+(Q) = I(Q)$ and $I^-(Q) = \neg.(HB \backslash I(Q))$ for each $Q \in W_P$.

A partial order between partial Kripke-like models of P is defined by: $I << J$ iff for each $Q \in W_P$, $I^-(Q)$ (resp. $I^+(Q)$) is a subset of $J^-(Q)$ (resp. $J^+(Q)$). I is said to be a <u>submodel</u> of J.

Let I be a partial Kripke-like model of P, A be an atom, and G be a goal. Define $I^+, I^-, P \models G$, and $I^+, I^-, P \models \neg G$ inductively as follows:

$I^+, I^-, P \models A$	if	$A \in I^+(P)$
$I^+, I^-, P \models \neg A$	if	$A \in I^-(P)$
$I^+, I^-, P \models G_1 \,\&\, G_2$	if	$I^+, I^-, P \models G_1$ and $I^+, I^-, P \models G_2$
$I^+, I^-, P \models \neg(G_1 \,\&\, G_2)$	if	$I^+, I^-, P \models \neg G_1$ or $I^+, I^-, P \models \neg G_2$
$I^+, I^-, P \models (G : Q)$	if	$I^+, I^-, P \cup Q \models G$
$I^+, I^-, P \models \neg(G : Q)$	if	$I^+, I^-, P \cup Q \models \neg G$

//

The operator T_I is adapted for a partial Kripke-like model I as follows:

T_I: $[W_P \rightarrow 2^{HB}] \rightarrow [W_P \rightarrow 2^{HB}]$[3]

$T_I(J)(Q) = \{ A \mid$ there is $A \leftarrow G$ in G_P s.t. $J, I^-, Q \models G \}$

Definition A partial Kripke-like model I of P is **justified** if

(1) I^+ is the least fixed point of T_I.

(2) For each $Q \in W_P$, for each $\neg A \in I^-(Q)$, for each $A \leftarrow G$ in G_Q: $I^+, I^-, Q \models \neg G$

//

It is easy to see that a (total) Kripke-like model is justified iff it is stable.

---

[3]. [X --> Y] denotes the set of all mappings from X into Y.

Definition Let R be a program. A justified partial Kripke-like model I of P is <u>invariant</u> wrt the update R if for each A <- G in G_R, if $\neg A \in I^-(P)$ then $I^+, I^-, P \not\models \neg G$

//

Intuitively, a justified partial Kripke-like model I is invariant wrt R if adding R into P, I will not be changed.

Let I be a partial Kripke-like model of P and $Q \in W_P$. Then the restriction of I on W_Q is a partial Kripke-like model of Q and is denoted by $I|_Q$.

DEFINITION Let I be a stable Kripke-like model of P.

I is **rational at P** if for each justified partial Kripke-like submodel J of I, for each R such that $P \cup R \in W_P$, the following condition is satisfied: If J is invariant wrt R then $J^i(P) \subseteq I^i(P \cup R)$ for $i \in \{+,-\}$.

I is **rational** if $I|_Q$ is rational at Q for each $Q \in W_P$.

Example 4 P:

d <- (a : {c<-})
a <- $\neg$b
b <- $\neg$a

$W_P = \{P,Q\}$ with $Q = P \cup \{c<-\}$

Let I: $I(P) = <\{a\},\{\neg b,\neg c,\neg d\}>$, $I(Q) = <\{b,c\},\{\neg a,\neg d\}>$
J: $J(P) = <\{a\},\{\neg b\}>$, $J(Q) = <\{c\},\emptyset>$

It is clear that J is justified and invariant wrt {c<-}. Since $J^-(P) = \{\neg b\}$ is not a subset of $I^-(Q) = \{\neg a,\neg d\}$, I is not rational (as expected) though it is stable.

It is not difficult to see that I' with $I'(P) = <\{a,d\},\{\neg b,\neg c\}>$ and $I'(Q) = <\{a,c,d\},\{\neg b\}>$ is a rational stable Kripke-like model of P which clearly captures the intuitive semantics of P.

//

The <u>rational semantics</u> of a hypothetical logic program is defined as the collection of all of its rational (total) stable Kripke-like models of P. Since not every normal logic program has a stable model, it is clear that the rational semantics is not defined for every hypothetical logic program, either. Even in the case P does have an unique stable Kripke-like model, the rational semantics can be undefined as the following example shows.

Example 5 This example is to show that the existence of a stable Kripke-like model does not guarantee the existence of a rational stable Kripke-like model.

P: p <- ¬q,e
q <- ¬p
r <- (p : {e<-})
s <- ¬s,¬r

W_P = {P,Q} with Q = P U {e<-}.

It is not difficult to see that I with I(P) = $<\{q,r\},\{\neg p,\neg e,\neg s\}>$ and I(Q) = $<\{e,p,r\},\{\neg q,\neg s\}>$ is the unique stable model of P. Further let J be a partial Kripke-like model of P with J(P) = $<\{q\},\{\neg p\}>$, and J(Q) = $<\{e\},\emptyset>$. J is clearly justified. It is not difficult to see that J is invariant wrt {e<-}. But $J^-(P)$ = {¬p} is not a subset of $I^-(Q)$ = {¬q,¬s}. So I is not rational. Since I is the only stable Kripke-like model of P, we can conclude that P has no rational semantics.
//

4. Discussion and Conclusion

The problem of stable semantics is that it is not defined for each logic program. There are different approaches to semantics of negation in normal logic programming which overcome this problem [7,3,10]. Two of them is the well-founded model approach [7], and the preferred extension approach [3,15]. It is not very difficult to generalize these two approaches for hypothetical logic programs. Of interest for us here is the questions as whether these two approaches can accommodate the idea of rational semantics. Let us consider the following example.

Example 6 (Well-Founded Semantics is not Rational)

P: a <- ¬b
c <- (a : {b <- ¬a})

W_P = {P,Q} with Q = P U {b <- ¬a}

Let us try to define a well-founded semantics for P. As c can in no way affect a and b, it is clear that a is true and b is false wrt well-founded semantics of P. The truth value of c wrt P depends on the truth value of a wrt Q. As Q contains the clause b <- ¬a, Q is clearly equivalent to the following normal program

R: a <- ¬b

b <- ¬a
c <- a

As the well-founded model of R is empty, i.e. each of a,b,c is undefined, c is also undefined wrt well-founded semantics of P. That means that the well-founded semantics of P is defined by the partial Kripke-like model I with I(P) = <{a},{¬b}> and I(Q) = <∅,∅>. It is easy to see that I is a justified submodel of I itself, and I is invariant wrt {b <- ¬a}. So we expect that I^{*}(P) is a subset of I^{*}(Q) which is apparently not the case. So the well-founded semantics of P is not rational.

//

Thus we can conclude that the well-founded semantics is not rational in the sense that it does not respect the "minimal change" condition. Supporter of the well-founded semantics can argue that this may not be harmful as the assumptions in the hypothetical goals need not be interpreted as update. But if not as that, then as what ?

So a generalization of well-founded semantics for hypothetical logic programming will not solve the problem that stable rational semantics is not defined for each hypothetical logic program. It is natural now to ask whether a generalization of the other approach, the preferred model semantics introduced by Dung in [3], can help.

In the full version of this paper, we will show that indeed, there exists for each hypothetical logic program a preferred Kripke-like model which can be considered as a kind of generalized rational stable Kripke-like semantics. The following examples illustrates this result.

Example 7 Let us take again a look at the following program

P:
p <- ¬q,e
q <- ¬p
r <- (p : {e<-})
s <- ¬s,¬r

W_r = {P,Q} with Q = P U {e<-}.

It is intuitively clear that the expected semantics of P is captured by the following partial Kripke-like model I:

I(P) = <{q},{¬p,¬e,¬r}> I(Q) = <{q,e},{¬p,¬r}>

I is also the unique preferred Kripke-like model of P.

//

Another natural way to generalize the rational stable semantics is to define a Kripke-like model of P as a partial mapping from W_P into 2^{HB}. This point is illustrated by the following example.

Example 8 P: p<- (a: {C1}),(b: {C2})

with C1: a<- ¬b, C2: b<- ¬a,

W_P = {P,P1,P2,P3} with P1 = P U {C1}, P2 = P U {C2}, P3 = P U {C1,C2}

P has no rational stable Kripke-like model.

Let I: W_P --> 2^{HB} with I(P) = {p}, I(P1) = {a}, I(P2) = {b} and I(P3) is undefined.

It is clear that I capture the intuitive semantics of P.
//

Acknowledgement

Many thanks to Evelina Lamma and Paola Mello for the invitation to attend the third workshop on Extension of Logic Programming. In fact, the invitation was the stimulation for me to write this paper. I would like also to thank Aravindan Chandrabose for his help in printing the paper. Last but not least, a lot of thanks also to the anonymous referees for the constructive comments.

References

[1] Bonner A.J., McCarty L.T.
'Adding negation as failure to intuitionistic logic programming'
In Proceedings of North American Conference on Logic programming, 1990, MIT Press

[2] Brogi A., Lamma E., Mello P.
'A general framework for structuring logic programs'
Technical report March 1990, DEIS, University of Bologna

[3] Dung P.M.
'Negations as hypotheses: An abductive foundation for logic programming'
In Proceedings of the Eighth International Conference on Logic programming, June 1991, Paris, France

[4] Fagin R., Kuper G.M., Ullman J.D., Vardi M.Y
'Updating logical databases'
Advances in Computing research, Vol 3, pp 1-18

[5] Gabbay D.M., Reyle U.
'N-Prolog: an extension of prolog with hypothetical implications'
J. logic programming 4, 1984

[6] Gelfond M., Lifschitz V.
'The stable model semantics for logic programs'
Proceedings of Fifth Int. Conf. and Symp. on LP, 1988

[7] Van Gelder A., Ross K., Schlipf J.S.
'Unfounded set and well-founded semantics for general logic programs'
in Proc. of PODS 1988

[8] Harland, J.
'Success and Failure for Hereditary Harrop Formulae'
Technical Report 91/17, Department of Computer Science, University of Melbourne

[9] Kowalski R.A.
'Logic for problem solving'
Elsevier North Holland, New York, 1979

[10] Kakas T., Mancarella P.
'Stable theories of logic programs'
Proc. of ILPS 1991, Nov 1991, USA, MIT Press

[11] Miller, D.
'Logical Analysis of Modules in Logic Programming'
J. Logic Programming, 1989: 79-108

[12] Monteiro L., Porto A.
'Contextual logic programming'
Proc. of Sixth ICLP, 1989, MIT Press

[13] Przymusinski T.C.
'On the declarative semantics of deductive databases and logic programs'
in Foundation of Deductive databases and Logic programming, J. Minker (ed.), 1988

[14] Pereira L.M., Alferes J.L., Aparicio J.N
'Contradiction Removal Within Well-founded Semantics'
Proc. of the first Intern. Workshop on Logic programming and Nonmonotonic Logic, Washington, June 1991, MIT Press

[15] Sacca D., Zaniolo C.
'Partial Models and three-Valued Models in Logic programs with Negation'
Proc. of the first Intern. Workshop on Logic programming and Nonmonotonic Logic, Washington, June 1991, MIT Press

Conditional Narrowing with Constructive Negation*

María José Ramírez[1], Moreno Falaschi[2]

[1] Departamento de Sistemas Informáticos y Computación,
Universidad Politécnica de Valencia,
Camino de Vera s/n, Apdo. 22012, 46020 Valencia, Spain.

[2] Dipartimento di Informatica,
Università di Pisa,
Corso Italia 40, 56125 Pisa, Italy

Abstract. In this paper we present a narrower for conditional equational theories whose clauses allow disequations in their bodies (*normal theories*). Our approach deals with disequations in a constructive manner and thus allows non ground negative queries. We give a formal operational semantics for normal theories and define the notion of *completion* and *stratification* of a normal theory. We show that there exists one minimal model for the completion of a stratified normal theory. Then we prove the correctness of the operational semantics with respect to the *completion* of a *stratified* normal theory.

Keywords: Equational logic programming, constructive negation, term rewriting systems, narrowing.

1 Introduction

In this paper we are concerned with an algorithm specialized in solving equations and negated equations (*disequations*) with respect to a *normal equational theory*, i.e. a conditional equational theory which allows disequations in the conditions of the clauses (but not in the head). The ability to deal with disequations is not only of theoretical interest but also desirable in practice. Different approaches for handling disequations have been proposed. For instance, in the framework of logic programming Colmerauer solves disequations in the algebra of rational trees for the semantic definition of Prolog II [14]. Lassez, Maher and Marriott prove the solvability of systems of equations and disequations on the Herbrand Universe [28]. In this paper we focus on conditional equations whose conditions

* The work of the first author has been partially supported by CICYT under grant TIC 92-0793. The work of the second author has been partially supported by "Progetto Finalizzato Sistemi Informatici e Calcolo Parallelo of C.N.R." under grant n.9100880.PF69

may contain disequations. We solve disequations with an algorithm which follows an idea similar to that defined by Stuckey in [40]. On the other hand, our approach is different since we refer to equational theories, while [40] focuses on the use of constructive negation in Constraint Logic Programming.

The introduction of negation has been widely investigated in the framework of logic programming [13,17,27,29] and has also been recently investigated in the framework of equational programming [5,6,26]. Negation as failure (NAF) is the mechanism traditionally used in logic programming to implement negation. However, NAF can only handle ground negative subgoals since it cannot generate any new bindings for query variables. ***Constructive Negation*** [11,12,40] can be used to find answers for negative subgoals in the same way as for positive ones. The basic idea is that the answer for a negative goal is simply the negation of the set of answers for its positive version. In order to evaluate $\sim Q$, a subderivation with Q as the top query is executed until it reduces to a simplified formula F. Then, a normalisation and negation procedure is applied to F to compute the simplified formula for $\sim Q$. This operational mechanism subsumes negation as failure. We propose to use this idea in the context of equational programming. This allows to solve negative non-ground queries as well as positive ones. Kaplan [26] investigates the algebraic properties of positive/negative conditional term rewriting systems and defines the class of *reducing* systems for which there exists an algebra of normal forms as *quasi-initial* model. Bachmair and Ganzinger [5,6] consider general equational clauses and give a criterion, based on a total ordering on ground terms, to prove that a consistent clause equality theory has a unique *perfect* model [36,37]. Moreover, [6] introduces the concept of saturation as an extension of the Knuth-Bendix completion method to transform a set of conditional equations with negative and positive conditions into a confluent system. All these approaches [5,6,26] consider ground systems and the results can be easily applied to negative ground queries. Our approach aims to deal with negative non-ground queries as well.

We aim to develop a system which may also be suitable for the integration of different programming paradigms, such as logic and equational programming, in a single framework. There have been several proposals [7,15,19,20,32] on this, but the treatment of negation has not been widely investigated in any of them. One way to the integration of equational and logic programming is the use of narrowing strategies, see e.g. [19,20,32]. Narrowing is a strategy to solve a system of equations within an equational theory $\mathcal{E}$: given an equational query, narrowing is able to find a complete set of $\mathcal{E}$-unifiers for it. However, narrowing does not handle systems which include negation.

We present an algorithm (*extended narrower*) which solves equations and disequations with respect to a normal equational theory. Equations and disequations are handled in a similar way, following the idea that a simplified form of a negated formula can be obtained from its complementary positive one. We show that the answer to a conjunction of equations and disequations in an equational theory with constructors is a complex system involving negation and quantifiers, where the symbols of equality and disequality can be syntactically interpreted.

We give a formal operational semantics for normal theories and define the notion of *completion* and *stratification* of a normal theory. These definitions have similarities with those for logic programming [3,4,13]. Roughly speaking, completion for us means that we replace the implications in a conditional equational theory with co-implications, so that the resulting completed theory allows negative logical consequences. Completed theories are not necessarily consistent. Thus, we introduce the concept of *stratified* theory, which essentially means introducing some syntactic restrictions to disallow recursion through negation. We show that there exists one minimal model for the completion of a stratified normal theory. Then we prove the correctness of the operational semantics with respect to the *completion* of a *stratified* normal theory. For reasons of space we omit some of the proofs, which can be found in [38].

The paper is organized as follows. Section 2 contains a short introduction to equations, conditional rewrite systems and universal unification. In Section 3, we define normal equational theories. In Section 4 we give a formal operational semantics for our algorithm. The notions of completion and stratification for normal equational theories are given in Sections 5 and 6, respectively. In Section 7 we prove the correctness of the operational semantics. Finally, Section 8 concludes and mentions further research.a

2 Preliminaries

In this section we briefly review some basic concepts about equations, conditional rewrite systems and $\mathcal{E}$-unification. For any concept which is not explicitly defined the reader may refer to [22,39].

We will use the symbols V, Σ and Π to denote the sets of variables, function symbols and predicate symbols respectively. $\tau(\Sigma)$ and $\tau(\Sigma \cup V)$ denote the sets of ground terms and terms built on Σ and V, respectively. $\tau(\Sigma)$ is usually called the Herbrand Universe ($\mathcal{H}_\Sigma$) over Σ and it will be denoted by $\mathcal{H}$. The set of variables occurring in a term t is denoted $Var(t)$. This notation extends naturally to other syntactic objects.

A ***substitution*** is defined as an almost identical mapping from the set of variables V into the set of terms $\tau(\Sigma \cup V)$.

Let θ be a substitution and let $W \subseteq V$ be a set of variables. We define the restriction of θ to W by $\theta \uparrow_W(x) = x\theta$ if $x \in W$, otherwise $\theta \uparrow_W(x) = x$.

A substitution $\theta = \{x_1/t_1, \ldots, x_n/t_n\}$ can be represented by a conjunction of equations $\hat{\theta} = (x_1 = t_1, \ldots, x_n = t_n)$, where x_i is a variable and t_i is a term over $\tau(\Sigma \cup V)$. $\hat{\theta}$ is called the equational representation of θ. The empty substitution is denoted by ϵ and its equational representation is $\emptyset$. The notions of application and composition are defined in the usual way [28,33].

A sequence of terms $t_1, \ldots, t_n$ will be denoted by $\tilde{t}$. By considering the usual representation of a term as a labelled tree, the occurrences are sequences of integers denoting an access path in a term. $O(t)$ and $\bar{O}(t)$ denote respectively the set of occurrences and non-variable occurrences of t. By $t[u \leftarrow t']$ we denote the replacement of the subterm of t at the occurrence u by the term t'. The definitions of occurrence sets, non-variable occurrence set, subterms and subterm replacement naturally extend to systems of equations [24].

A Σ-equation $s = t$ is a pair of terms s and t ($s, t \in \tau(\Sigma \cup V)$). A Horn equational Σ-theory $\mathcal{E}$ is a finite set of equational Horn clauses of the form $l = r \Leftarrow e_1, \ldots, e_n$. with $n \geq 0$ where e_i is a Σ-equation, $1 \leq i \leq n$.

The Σ-equation in the head is implicitely oriented from left to right and the literals e_i in the body are ordinary non-oriented Σ-equations. A Σ-disequation is a formula $s \neq t$ where s, t are terms. The prefix Σ will be usually dropped when clear from the context.

Each Horn equational theory $\mathcal{E}$ generates a smallest congruence ($=_\mathcal{E}$) over the set of terms $\tau(\Sigma \cup V)$. We will denote by $\mathcal{H}/\mathcal{E}$ the finest partition $\tau(\Sigma)/_{=\mathcal{E}}$ induced by $\mathcal{E}$ over the set of ground terms $\tau(\Sigma)$. A Horn equational theory $\mathcal{E}$ can be viewed as a conditional term rewriting system R, where the rules are the heads and the conditions are the respective bodies. If all clauses in $\mathcal{E}$ have an empty body then $\mathcal{E}$ and R are unconditional, otherwise they are conditional. The equational theory $\mathcal{E}$ is said to be canonical if the binary one-step rewriting relation $\rightarrow_R$ defined by R is noetherian and confluent. Confluence can be ensured by syntactical characterizations [8,10,32]. We now recall the concept of $\mathcal{E}$-unification, i.e. the problem of existence of a common instance of two terms under an equational theory $\mathcal{E}$.

Let $t = s$ be an equation. A substitution σ is called an $\mathcal{E}$-unifier of $t = s$ iff $\mathcal{E} \models t\sigma = s\sigma$, or equivalenty, $t\sigma =_\mathcal{E} s\sigma$. In this case, t and s are said $\mathcal{E}$-unifiable.

An $\mathcal{E}$-unification algorithm defines a procedure to solve an equation $t = s$ within the theory $\mathcal{E}$. A solution is represented by an $\mathcal{E}$-unifier. An $\mathcal{E}$-unification algorithm is complete if it generates a complete set of $\mathcal{E}$-unifiers for all $\mathcal{E}$-unifiable input terms. Complete unification algorithms are known for various theories. *Narrowing* is a complete unification algorithm for unconditional canonical theories [16,23] and conditional canonical theories satisfying different restrictions [21,31]. [39] presents a classification of equational theories from the point of view of the universal unification.

Let $\mathcal{E}$ be a Horn equational theory. A function symbol $f \in \Sigma$ is *irreducible* iff there is no clause $(l = r \Leftarrow e_1, \ldots, e_n) \in \mathcal{E}$ such that $l \in V$ or f occurs as the outermost function symbol in l. f is a *defined* function symbol if it is not irreducible.

In theories where the above distinction is made the signature Σ is partitioned as $\Sigma = C \uplus F$, where C is the set of irreducible symbols and F is the set of defined function symbols.

Let $\mathcal{E}$ be a Horn equational theory and f a defined function symbol. Then f is said to be completely defined (everywhere defined [9]) over its domain iff it does not occur in any ground term in normal form. $\mathcal{E}$ is said to be completely defined iff each defined function symbol is completely defined. In a completely defined theory the set of normal ground terms is the set of terms over C ($\tau(C)$).

A completely defined Horn equational theory $\mathcal{E}$ will be called a Horn equational theory with constructors iff a further condition is satisfied: each equation in the left hand side of the head of any clause is of the form $f(t_1, t_2, \ldots, t_n) = t$

where $f \in F$ and no defined symbols occur in any of $t_1, \ldots, t_n$.

3 Normal Equational Theories

In the following we consider conjunctions of equations and disequations whose solvability will be checked with respect to a normal equational theory $\mathcal{E}^{\sim}$. Roughly speaking, a normal equational theory is an equational theory whose clauses may contain negation in their body. Formally:

Definition 1. A normal equational clause is a clause of the form
$t = s \Leftarrow e_1, \ldots, e_m, d_1, \ldots, d_n.$
where the equation in the head is implicitely oriented from left to right, $e_1, \ldots, e_m$ are non-oriented equations, $d_1, \ldots, d_n$ are non-oriented disequations and $m, n \geq 0$.

Definition 2. A normal equational theory $\mathcal{E}^{\sim}$ is a finite set of normal equational clauses.

We notice that when the bodies of the clauses in the theory $\mathcal{E}^{\sim}$ do not contain disequations then $\mathcal{E}^{\sim}$ is a Horn equational theory.

Definition 3. A normal goal is a clause with no head.

Example 1. Let us consider a normal equational theory which defines the non-negative rational numbers represented as pairs of natural numbers [35]. $/, +, *$ are rational valued function symbols denoting division, addition and multiplication respectively, and $+_{\mathrm{N}}, *_{\mathrm{N}}$ are the natural valued addition and multiplication functions.

$$\begin{aligned} \mathcal{E}_1^{\sim} = \{\; & 0/m = 0 \Leftarrow m \neq 0. \\ & m/c = n/d \Leftarrow m *_{\mathrm{N}} d = c *_{\mathrm{N}} n, c \neq 0, d \neq 0. \\ & (m/c) + (n/d) = ((m *_{\mathrm{N}} d) +_{\mathrm{N}} (c *_{\mathrm{N}} n))/(c *_{\mathrm{N}} d). \\ & (m/c) * (n/d) = (m *_{\mathrm{N}} n)/(c *_{\mathrm{N}} d). \;\} \end{aligned}$$

A normal equational theory $\mathcal{E}^{\sim}$ can be viewed as a conditional term rewriting system R where the rules are the heads and the conditions (containing disequations) are the respective bodies. The basis for the treatment of these rewriting systems is provided by Kaplan in [26][3]. In particular, Kaplan has proved that in the case of reducing P/N systems[4] there exists a well-defined rewrite relation

[3] Such systems are called positive/negative systems (P/N systems) by Kaplan.

[4] A P/N system R is called reducing if there exists a reduction ordering $>$ such that if $t \rightarrow s \Leftarrow \tilde{B} \in R$ and σ is a substitution then $t\sigma > s\sigma, u\sigma, v\sigma, u'\sigma, v'\sigma$, for all $u = v, u' \neq v'$ in $\tilde{B}$.

which can be constructed as a limit. Some properties of reducing P/N systems are also discussed in [26]. Thus, these systems are proved to be finitely terminating and the question of confluence is addressed by providing a complete critical pair criterion a la Knuth-Bendix. Another characterization of the confluence of normal equational theories can also be stated following [8,34].

For the reasons we will state in the following section, throughout the paper we require normal equational theories to be theories with constructors.

4 Operational Semantics

In this section we present our approach to solve normal goals in a normal equational theory $\mathcal{E}^{\sim}$. Our operational mechanism, $\mathcal{C}$onditional $\mathcal{N}$arrowing with $\mathcal{C}$onstructive $\mathcal{N}$egation, is an adaptation of the innermost conditional narrowing algorithm to solve negated subgoals.

4.1 Conditional Narrowing Calculus

Let us briefly recall the conditional narrowing algorithm. A goal is an expression of the form (g *with* θ) where g is a set of equations and θ is a substitution which is assumed to be restricted to the variables of the initial goal. To solve g the algorithm starts with the goal (g *with* ϵ) and tries to derive goals (recording the applied substitutions in the *with*-parts) until a terminal goal ($\emptyset$ *with* θ) is reached. Each substitution θ in a terminal goal is an $\mathcal{E}$-unifier of g.

The children of a goal (g *with* θ) in a (narrowing) search tree are given by:

1. If g sintactically unifies with mgu σ then there is a unique child

$$\emptyset \textit{ with } \theta\sigma$$

2. Otherwise, if $u \in \bar{O}(g)$ then there is a child

$$(g[u \leftarrow r_k], \tilde{B}_k)\sigma \textit{ with } \theta\sigma$$

for each clause

$$l_k = r_k \Leftarrow \tilde{B}_k$$

from $\mathcal{E}$ such that $\sigma = mgu(g/u, l_k)$[5]. g/u is called a redex of g.

Finally, we introduce our concept of frontier of a search tree which will be used in the definition of the equational constructive negation rule.

Definition 4. [40] A *frontier* of a search tree for a goal G (or frontier of G) is the set of nodes at depth one in the search tree.

---

[5] The variables in g and in the clauses are assumed to be disjoint.

4.2 Equational Constructive Negation

We show that disequations in equational theories can be solved in a constructive way in equational theories, following a mechanism similar to that of [40], using a suitable conditional narrowing algorithm. This algorithm introduces negation and quantification in the constructed answer to a goal. The computed answer is a complex system involving elementary formulae. An *elementary formula* is either a (possibly quantified) equation ($x = t$ or $\tilde{\forall}\ x = t$) or a (possibly quantified) disequation ($x \neq t$ or $\tilde{\forall}\ x \neq t$) where x is a variable and t is a term distinct from x. A computed answer is a conjunction whose elements are elementary formulae or negated conjunctions of elementary formulae. Similarly, the goals involve throughout a computation a form which also includes negation and quantification. We extend the syntax of goals as follows:

Definition 5. An extended subgoal is recursively defined as either

- an equation,
- or $\sim \exists \tilde{Z}(g_1, \ldots, g_n \Box E)$, where every $g_i, i = 1, \ldots n$, is an extended subgoal, E is a complex system involving elementary formulae and $\tilde{Z}$ denotes some variables in $(g_1, \ldots, g_n \Box E)$. Notice that $(g_1, \ldots, g_n \Box E)$ is shorthand for $(g_1 \wedge \ldots \wedge g_n \wedge E)$.

The extended subgoals of the form $\sim \exists \tilde{Z}(g_1, \ldots, g_n \Box E)$ are referred to as *negated subgoals*. The rest of the subgoals, the equations, are called *non-negated subgoals*. We define the *complementary subgoal* for a negated subgoal $\sim \exists \tilde{Z}(g_1, \ldots, g_n \Box E)$ as $(g_1, \ldots, g_n \Box E)$.

Similarly to Constraint Logic Programming, we use the $\Box$ symbol in the extended subgoals since the system E will act as a constraint in our computational mechanism.

Definition 6. An extended goal is a conjunction of extended subgoals.

We can easily extend the syntax of a normal equational theory with bodies that are conjunctions of extended subgoals since a disequation, $t \neq s$, can be expressed as the extended subgoal $\sim (t = s \Box \emptyset)$. Similarly, a normal goal g can be represented as an extended goal g' where each disequation, $t \neq s$, of g has the form $\sim (t = s \Box \emptyset)$ in g'.

The conditional narrowing algorithm can be modified to solve negated subgoals in a constructive way. Roughly speaking, when a negated subgoal is selected to be solved, a sub-derivation for the complementary subgoal is invoked. Then the first level of the search tree is considered. The substitution applied in each derivation step (represented as a system of equations) is added to the node of this branch as a constraint. Thus, we consider the nodes of the search tree as containing a part which represents the subgoals yet to be solved and another one (the constraint) which represents a partial answer to the goal. Then, we define the search tree at depth one of the negated subgoal as a suitable transformation of these nodes. In what follows, $g \Box E$ denotes a node of the search tree, where g is an extended goal and E is a partial answer of the initial goal. To solve an extended goal g_0, the algorithm starts with the goal $g_0 \Box \emptyset$. We will often represent the set of nodes of a search tree as a disjunction. We will use $E \cdot E'$ to denote the conjunction of the systems E and E'.

Let us define the constructive negation algorithm to solve negated subgoals with respect to normal equational theories.

Definition 7. *Equational Constructive Negation Rule*
Let $s \equiv \sim \exists \tilde{Z}(g \Box E)$ be a selected negated subgoal to be solved. Then the frontier of the search tree for s is defined as follows:

- If g only contains equations and does not syntactically unify, then the frontier of the search tree for s is empty.
- If g only contains equations and syntactically unifies with mgu σ then the frontier of the search tree for s has as node $(\emptyset \Box \forall \tilde{Z} \sim E \cdot \hat{\sigma})$ if $\sim \exists \tilde{Z}\ E \cdot \hat{\sigma}$ is solvable.
- If g has redexes then let $(g_1 \Box E \cdot \hat{\theta}_1), \ldots, (g_m \Box E \cdot \hat{\theta}_m)$ be the frontier of the search tree for $g \Box E$, where every g_i is an extended goal and θ_i is the substitution applied in the reduction from g to g_i. Consider the disjunction:

$$\exists \tilde{Z}, \tilde{Y}_1(g_1 \Box E_1) \ \vee \ \ldots \ \vee \ \exists \tilde{Z}, \tilde{Y}_m(g_m \Box E_m)$$

where E_i is $E \cdot \theta_i$ and $\tilde{Y}_i$, $1 \leq i \leq m$, denotes the variables in $(g_i \Box E_i)$ which do not appear in $(g \Box E)$. Then apply the following rules [40]:

1. Negation of the disjunction. Apply the following De Morgan law:

$$\sim \bigvee_{j=1}^{m} \exists \tilde{Z}, \tilde{Y}_j\, (g_j \Box E_j) = \bigwedge_{j=1}^{m} \sim \exists \tilde{Z}, \tilde{Y}_j\, (g_j \Box E_j)$$

2. Transformation of each conjunction. Then, apply the rule of decomposition:

$$\sim \exists \tilde{Z}, \tilde{Y}_k\, (g_k \Box E_k) \leftrightarrow (\emptyset \Box \forall \tilde{Z}, \tilde{Y}_k \sim E_k) \ \vee \ (\sim \exists \tilde{Z}, \tilde{Y}_k\, (g_k \Box E_k))$$

Finally, take the disjunctive normal form of the formulae resulting from (2).

The general form of each node of the frontier of the search tree for a negated subgoal $\sim \exists \tilde{Z}(g \Box E)$, obtained applying the equational constructive negation rule to the frontier $\{g_1 \Box E_1, \ldots, g_m \Box E_m\}$ of its complementary subgoal, is a conjunction of extended subgoals yet to be solved. In the first node of this frontier, $\emptyset \Box \forall \tilde{Z}, \tilde{Y}_1 \sim E_1 \cdots \forall \tilde{Z}, \tilde{Y}_m \sim E_m$, the conjunction of subgoals to be solved is empty. Therefore, if the system $\forall \tilde{Z}, \tilde{Y}_1 \sim E_1 \cdots \forall \tilde{Z}, \tilde{Y}_m \sim E_m$ is solvable then this system is an answer for the negated subgoal. Indeed, for each application of the equational constructive negation rule, the system in the first node of this frontier is a possible answer to the negated subgoal. Thus, if a negated subgoal has a solution, then it is always found in a finite number of derivation steps. The other nodes of the frontier contain subgoals to be solved and (in their $\Box$ parts) information about the answers to the negated subgoal. Figure 1 shows the relationship between the frontiers of the search trees of a negated subgoal, $\sim \exists \tilde{Z}\, g \Box E$, and its complementary one, $g \Box E$, for the particular case $m = 2$. For the sake of readability, we use the concise notation $\tilde{\exists}$ *subgoal* and $\tilde{\forall}$ *subgoal* instead of the more precise $\exists\, \tilde{Z}$ *subgoal* and $\forall\, \tilde{Z}$ *subgoal*.

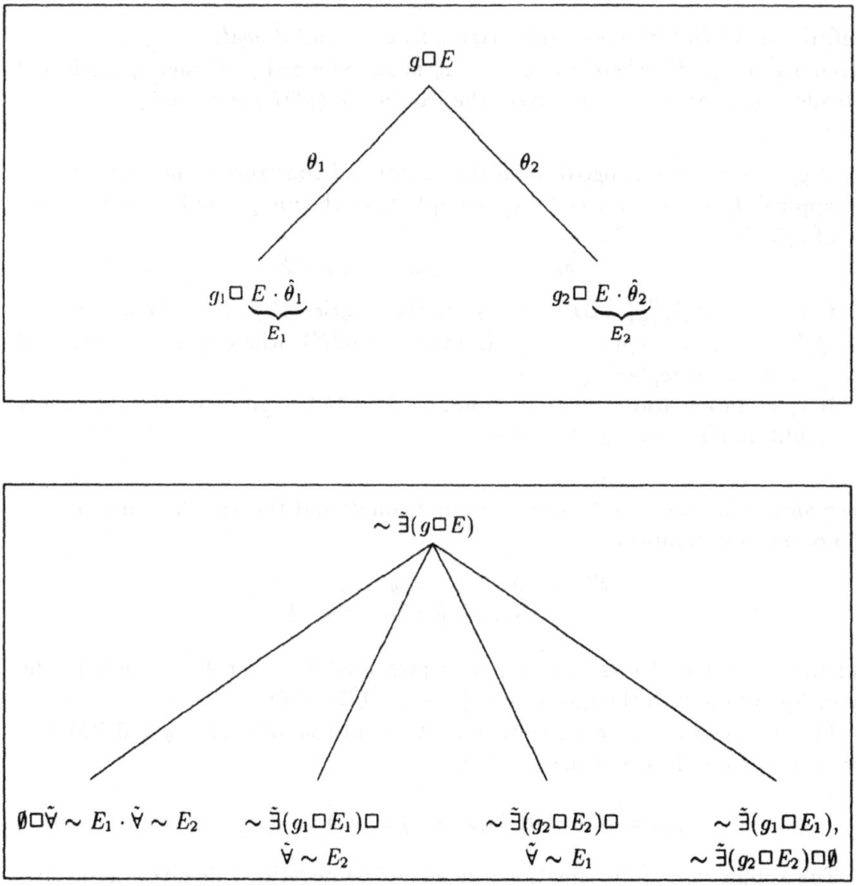

Fig. 1. Relationship between a negated subgoal and its complementary subgoal.

The transformation applied in the definition of the frontier of the search tree for a negated subgoal from the frontier of the search tree for its complementary subgoal introduces negation and quantification in the answer system. We are only interested in answer systems whose equations and disequations only involve variables and constructors terms, because answers of this form can be thought of as systems of syntactic equations and disequations whose solvability can be checked using well-known algorithms (such as [30]). If the narrowing algorithm uses a strategy which selects only innermost redexes and we consider equational theories with constructors then any answer is a system which satisfies the above requirement.[6]

Let us define the operational mechanism to solve extended goals wrt normal equational theories.

Definition 8. *Operational mechanism solving extended goals.*
Given a goal $(g \Box E)$ where $g = g_1, \ldots, g_n$ is an extended goal, and g_j a selected extended subgoal of g to be solved, the frontier of $(g \Box E)$ is given by:

- If g_j is a negated subgoal, then the equational constructive negation rule is applied. If the search tree for g_j is empty then the unique node of the frontier of $(g \Box E)$ is
$$g_1, \ldots, g_{j-1}, g_j+1, \ldots, g_n \Box E$$
Otherwise, if $(\bigvee_{i=1}^{p} f_i \Box E_i)$ represents the frontier of g_j, then the disjunction $\bigvee_{i=1}^{p} g'_i \Box E \cdot E_i$ represents the frontier of $(g \Box E)$, where g'_i is the extended goal obtained replacing g_j by f_i in g.
- If g_j is an equation, then the frontier of $(g \Box E)$ is given by the innermost conditional narrowing algorithm.

Example 2. Consider the following normal equational theory which defines the sum of natural numbers:

$$\begin{aligned} \mathcal{E}^{\sim} = \{\, 0 + y \quad &= y. \\ s(x) + y &= s(x + y).\, \} \end{aligned}$$

and the normal goal $c \equiv x + y \neq 0$, represented by $\sim (x + y = 0 \Box \emptyset)$. The algorithm starts with the goal $g_0 \equiv \sim (x + y = 0 \Box \emptyset) \Box \emptyset$.

The sub-derivation for the complementary subgoal of $\sim (x + y = 0 \Box \emptyset)$, has two nodes at depth one of the search tree

$$\{(y = 0 \Box x = 0), (s(x' + y) = 0 \Box x = s(x'))\}.$$

The application of the equational constructive negation rule gives the following frontier of the search tree of the negated subgoal $\sim (x + y = 0 \Box \emptyset)$:

6 Fribourg ([17]) has shown that for canonical Horn equational theories with constructors and using an innermost conditional narrowing algorithm, any computed answer is a substitution involving only terms formed solely from constructors and variables.

$$(\emptyset\Box x \neq 0 \cdot \forall x'\ x \neq s(x')) \vee$$
$$(\sim (y = 0\Box x = 0)\Box\forall x'\ x \neq s(x')) \vee$$
$$(\sim \exists x'(s(x' + y) = 0\Box x = s(x'))\Box x \neq 0\ ) \vee$$
$$(\sim (y = 0\Box x = 0),\ \sim \exists x'(s(x' + y) = 0\Box x = s(x'))\Box\emptyset)$$

The search tree at depth one for g_0 coincides with the frontier of the search tree of the negated subgoal $\sim (x + y = 0\Box\emptyset)$, where the first node is pruned since the system $x \neq 0, \forall x'\ x \neq s(x')$ is not solvable in the Herbrand universe over the signature of the natural numbers. Thus, the three nodes of the search tree for g_0 at depth one are

$$(i)\quad \sim (y = 0\Box x = 0)\Box\forall x'\ x \neq s(x')$$
$$(ii)\ \sim \exists x'(s(x' + y) = 0\Box x = s(x'))\Box x \neq 0$$
$$(iii) \sim (y = 0\Box x = 0),\ \sim \exists x'(s(x' + y) = 0\Box x = s(x'))\Box\emptyset$$

The next derivation step for the first node has $\sim (y = 0\Box x = 0)$ as goal to be solved. Its search tree has a unique node $\emptyset\Box \sim (x = 0, y = 0)$ since in the complementary subgoal, $y = 0\Box x = 0$, the equation $y = 0$ has no narrowable occurrences and syntactically unifies with mgu $\sigma = \{y/0\}$.

Hence, the node of the search tree of the selected goal (i) is

$$(i.1)\ \emptyset\Box\forall x'\ x \neq s(x') \cdot \sim (x = 0, y = 0)$$

whose system of equations and disequations is the first answer to $x + y \neq 0$. Let us notice that this system represents an infinite set of solutions of the form $x = 0, y = s(n)$ where $n \in N$.

4.3 Conditional $\mathcal{N}$arrowing with Constructive $\mathcal{N}$egation

In this section we present an innermost (conditional) narrowing algorithm to solve normal goals, which handles the negative subgoals following the approach presented in Section 4.2. The algorithm is presented as a transition system, called $\mathcal{I}$nnermost $\mathcal{C}$onditional $\mathcal{N}$arrowing with constructive $n$egation ($\mathcal{ICN}cn$).

Definition 9. An $\mathcal{ICN}cn$-state is a tuple $\langle S, L\rangle$, where S is a list of systems involving elementary formulae and L is a (possibly empty) list of goals $g\Box E$ where g is an extended goal and E is a complex system which represents a partial solution of the initial goal.

The first component of an $\mathcal{ICN}cn$-state represents the list of answers for the initial goal and the second component represents the list of the nodes of the search tree yet to be narrowed. This list is treated as a queue to emulate a breadth-first strategy.

Definition 10. Initial $\mathcal{ICN}cn$-state.
Let g be an extended goal. Then $\langle \emptyset, g\square\emptyset \rangle$ is an initial $\mathcal{ICN}cn$-state.

Definition 11. Terminal $\mathcal{ICN}cn$-states.
A terminal $\mathcal{ICN}cn$-state is a state of the form $\langle S, L\rangle$ where S is non-empty.

Roughly speaking, in order to solve an extended goal g, the algorithm selects an extended subgoal of g. If a non-negated subgoal is selected, then standard narrowing is performed at one innermost occurrence and the resulting list of the nodes of the frontier of the search tree is added to the current list of goals. If the selected subgoal is a negated subgoal then the equational constructive negation rule is applied to obtain its frontier which is represented as a list. Then, each element in this list replaces the selected negated subgoal in the actual goal, resulting in the new goals. The list of these goals is then added to the current list of goals. Finally, when a terminal state $\langle S, L\rangle$ is achieved, each system E of the list S is an answer for g. The $\mathcal{ICN}cn$ calculus is defined by means of a stratified transition system. $\rightarrow_{E\mathcal{CN}}$ formalizes the rules for the equational constructive negation. $\rightarrow_f$ is built over $\rightarrow_{E\mathcal{CN}}$ and formalizes the rules for the selection of subgoals and expansion of the frontier of the search tree. $\rightarrow_{\mathcal{ICN}cn}$ is built over $\rightarrow_f$, controls the expansion of the search tree (by means of $\rightarrow_f$, rule (9)) and returns the answers for the initial goal. Formally:

Definition 12. $\mathcal{ICN}cn$ transition relation[7].

Unification Rules for Constructive Negation

$$(1)\ \frac{\begin{array}{l} g \text{ only contains equations and} \\ \text{syntactically unifies with } \mathit{mgu}\ \sigma\ \wedge\ \mathit{solvable}(\sim \exists \tilde{Z}\ E\cdot\hat{\sigma}) \end{array}}{\sim \exists\ \tilde{Z}(g\square E) \rightarrow_{E\mathcal{CN}} [\emptyset\square\forall\tilde{Z}\ \sim(E\cdot\hat{\sigma})]}$$

$$(2)\ \frac{\begin{array}{l} g \text{ only contains equations and} \\ \text{syntactically unifies with } \mathit{mgu}\ \sigma\wedge\ \sim \mathit{solvable}(\sim \exists \tilde{Z}\ E\cdot\hat{\sigma}) \end{array}}{\sim \exists\ \tilde{Z}(g\square E) \rightarrow_{E\mathcal{CN}} [\emptyset\square \mathit{false}]}$$

Constructive Negation Rules

$$(3)\ \frac{\langle g\square E\rangle \rightarrow_f L\ \wedge\ e\_c\_n(L, \sim \exists\ \tilde{Z}(g\square E)) = L'}{\sim \exists\ \tilde{Z}(g\square E) \rightarrow_{E\mathcal{CN}} L'}$$

$$(4)\ \frac{(1),(2) \text{ and } (3) \text{ do not apply}}{\sim \exists\ \tilde{Z}(g\square E) \rightarrow_{E\mathcal{CN}} [\,]}$$

Frontier expansion Rules

$$(5)\ \frac{\begin{array}{l} e\in g\ \wedge\ u\in \mathit{Inner}(e)\wedge \\ s\_to\_l(\{\langle i,\sigma\rangle :\ \mathit{narred}(e,u,i,\sigma)\})\ = [\langle i_j,\sigma_j\rangle]_{j=1}^{n} \end{array}}{\langle g\square E\rangle \rightarrow_f\ [(g\setminus\{e\}\cup\{e[u\leftarrow r_{i_j}]\}\cup \tilde{B}_{i_j})\sigma_j\square E\cdot\hat{\sigma}_j]_{j=1}^{n}}$$

[7] We assume that in the following rules g is non-empty.

$$(6)\ \frac{\sim \exists \check{Z}(g'\Box E') \in g \wedge \sim \exists \check{Z}(g'\Box E') \rightarrow_{EC\mathcal{N}} [g'_i\Box E'_i]_{i=0}^n}{\langle g\Box E\rangle \rightarrow_f [g \setminus \{\sim \exists \check{Z}(g'\Box E')\} \cup \{g'_i\}\Box E \cdot E'_i]_{i=0}^n}$$

$$(7)\ \frac{\sim \exists \check{Z}(g'\Box E') \in g \wedge \sim \exists \check{Z}(g'\Box E') \rightarrow_{EC\mathcal{N}} [\emptyset\Box false]}{\langle g\Box E\rangle \rightarrow_f [\,]}$$

Unification Rule for Equations

$$(8)\ \frac{g \text{ only contains equations and syntactically unifies with } mgu\ \sigma \wedge solvable(E \cdot \hat{\sigma})}{\langle S, (g\Box E) \bullet L\rangle \rightarrow_{\mathcal{IC}\mathcal{N}cn} \langle E \cdot \hat{\sigma} \bullet S, L\rangle}$$

Narrowing Rules

$$(9)\ \frac{\langle g\Box E\rangle \rightarrow_f L'}{\langle S, (g\Box E) \bullet L\rangle \rightarrow_{\mathcal{IC}\mathcal{N}cn} \langle S,\ L \circ L'\rangle}$$

$$(10)\ \frac{(8) \text{ and } (9) \text{ do not apply}}{\langle S, (g\Box E) \bullet L\rangle \rightarrow_{\mathcal{IC}\mathcal{N}cn} \langle S, L\rangle}$$

where:

1. $Inner(e)$ is the set of innermost non-variable occurrences of e.
2. $narred(e, u, i, \sigma) \Leftrightarrow ((l_i = r_i \Leftarrow \check{B}_i) \in \mathcal{E}^{\sim} \ \wedge \ \sigma = mgu(e/u, l_i)\ )$, where e is an equation.
3. $solvable(E)$ is true if E is a solvable system involving elementary formulae. As we have mentioned, there exist known algorithms [30] checking the solvability of these systems.
4. $e\_c\_n(L, g)$ transforms the list L which represents the frontier of the search tree for the complementary subgoal of g into another list which represents the frontier of the search tree for g, following the process described in the equational constructive negation rule (Definition 7).
5. $\bullet$ (front and rear of a list), $\circ$ (concatenation of two lists) and s_to_l (list of elements of a set) are defined as usual.

5 Completion of Normal Equational Theories

One way to reason about negative information is by introducing the concept of completion [13]. In this section we define the completion of a normal equational theory which involves adding to the theory the only if halves of the definitions of the function symbols[8] together with an equality theory.

[8] If $f(t_1, \ldots, t_n) = r \Leftarrow \check{B}$. is a clause in an equational theory, then f is called the name of the clause. The set of all clauses with the same name f is called the definition of f.

Definition 13. *Completed definition of function symbol*

Let $\mathcal{E}^{\sim}$ be a normal equational theory. Consider the following sequence of transformations on the set of clauses in $\mathcal{E}^{\sim}$. Let

$$f(t_1, \ldots, t_n) = t \Leftarrow \tilde{B}.$$

be any clause in $\mathcal{E}^{\sim}$. We transform this clause into

$$\begin{aligned} f(x_1, \ldots, x_n) = w \Leftarrow \exists\, y_1, \ldots, y_k\ (\ (x_1 = t_1) \land \ldots \land (x_n = t_n) \land \\ (w = t) \land \tilde{B}\ ) \end{aligned}$$

where $y_1, \ldots, y_k$ are the variables of the original clause, and $x_1, \ldots, x_n, w$ are distinct variables that do not appear anywhere in $\mathcal{E}^{\sim}$. Now all formulas obtained in the previous step with a function symbol f on the left-hand side of the head

$$\begin{gathered} f(x_1, \ldots, x_n) = w \Leftarrow F_1 \\ \vdots \\ f(x_1, \ldots, x_n) = w \Leftarrow F_m \end{gathered}$$

are replaced by

$$f(x_1, \ldots, x_n) = w \Leftarrow F_1 \ \lor \ \ldots \ \lor \ F_m$$

The completed definition of f is then the formula

$$\forall\, x_1, \ldots, x_n, w\, (f(x_1, \ldots, x_n) = w \Leftrightarrow F_1 \ \lor \ \ldots \ \lor \ F_m)$$

Example 3. The completed definition of the function symbol $+$ from Example 2 is

$$\begin{aligned} \forall\, x_1, x_2, w\, (+(x_1, x_2) = w \Leftrightarrow\ & \exists\, y\, ((x_1 = 0) \land (x_2 = y) \land (w = y)) \lor \\ & \exists\, x, y\, ((x_1 = s(x)) \land (x_2 = y) \land \\ & (w = s(+(x, y))))) \end{aligned}$$

We now define the completion of a normal equational theory.

Definition 14. Let $\mathcal{E}^{\sim}$ be a normal equational theory. The completion of $\mathcal{E}^{\sim}$, denoted by $comp(\mathcal{E}^{\sim})$, is the collection of completed definitions of function symbols in $\mathcal{E}^{\sim}$ together with the Clark's equality theory (CET) where the free equality axioms are defined over irreducible function symbols.

The model theoretic semantics of a normal equational theory $\mathcal{E}^{\sim}$ is based on considering models of $comp(\mathcal{E}^{\sim})$ rather than models of $\mathcal{E}^{\sim}$ itself. Hence, the concept of a correct answer is defined as follows:

Definition 15. *Correct answer*

Let $\mathcal{E}^{\sim}$ be a normal equational theory, g a normal goal and E an answer system for g with respect to $\mathcal{E}^{\sim}$. We say that E is a correct answer for g with respect to $comp(\mathcal{E}^{\sim})$ if for all substitution θ such that $CET \models E\theta$ then $g\theta$ is a logical consequence of $comp(\mathcal{E}^{\sim})$.

The completion will play an important part in the soundness results for the equational constructive negation rule.l

6 Stratified Equational Theories

Hölldobler has developed a model theory for equational theories giving a fixpoint characterization ([21]). He shows that the least fixpoint of an operator T associated with an equational theory and defined as a mapping between interpretations is the least Herbrand E-model[9] of the theory. However, this result can not be generalized to normal equational theories since the operator T does not need to be monotonic in presence of negation. It has been shown ([26]) that normal equational theories may have minimal models but no least model. Still, only one of these minimal models correspond to the intended meaning of the theory[10].

On the other hand, even if every normal equational theory is consistent, its completion may not be consistent. Let us consider, e.g, the following normal equational theory: $\mathcal{E}^{\sim} = \{a = b \Leftarrow a \neq b\}$, which is inconsistent since $(a = b \Leftrightarrow a \neq b)$ is a formula of $comp(\mathcal{E}^{\sim})$.

For this reason we introduce some syntactic restrictions on the theory. Similarly to logic programming [3,4], we propose a treatment of negation which is based on the restriction of normal equational theories to be stratified. Informally, first some function symbols should be defined in terms of themselves without the use of negation and, next, some new function symbols can be defined in terms of themselves without the use of negation and in terms of the previous function symbols, possibly with the use of negation. Note that, with these restrictions, recursion by negation is not allowed. The theory $\mathcal{E}^{\sim}$ in the above example does not satisfy these conditions, hence it is not stratified.

Definition 16. *Stratified equational theories*

A normal equational theory $\mathcal{E}^{\sim}$ is called stratified if there exists a partition

$$\mathcal{E}^{\sim} = \mathcal{E}_1^{\sim} \dot{\cup} \ldots \dot{\cup} \mathcal{E}_n^{\sim}$$

such that the following two conditions hold for $i = 1, \ldots, n$:

---

[9] In this context, the Herbrand base of an equational theory is the set of ground equations that can be built from the elements of the Herbrand universe. An interpretation is a subset of the Herbrand base and an E-interpretation is an interpretation which obeys the axioms of equality (i.e. reflexivity, symmetry, etc.).

[10] This coincides with the concept of supported model in logic programming ([3,4]).

1. If an equation $u = v$ occurs in the head or in the body of a clause in $ground(\mathcal{E}_i^{\sim})$[11] and the outermost function symbol of u (v) is f then, if f is a defined function symbol then its definition is contained within $\bigcup_{j<i} \mathcal{E}_j^{\sim}$.
2. If a disequation $u \neq v$ occurs in the body of a clause in $ground(\mathcal{E}_i^{\sim})$ and the outermost function symbol of u (v) is f then, if f is a defined function symbol then its definition is contained within $\bigcup_{j<i} \mathcal{E}_j^{\sim}$.

We say that $\mathcal{E}^{\sim}$ is stratified by $\mathcal{E}_1^{\sim} \dot{\cup} \ldots \dot{\cup} \mathcal{E}_n^{\sim}$ and each $\mathcal{E}_i^{\sim}$ is called an *equational stratum* of $\mathcal{E}^{\sim}$. An equational stratum defines new function symbols in terms of themselves (positively) and in terms of the function symbols from the previous strata (possibly negatively).

Example 4. Let $\mathcal{E}^{\sim}$ be the following normal equational theory:

$$r = a.$$
$$q = b \Leftarrow r \neq b.$$
$$p = a \Leftarrow q \neq a.$$

Then $\mathcal{E}^{\sim}$ is stratified by $\mathcal{E}^{\sim} = \{r = a.\} \cup \{q = b \Leftarrow r \neq b.\} \cup \{p = a \Leftarrow q \neq a.\}$.

Example 5. The following normal equational theory is not stratified:

$$f(x) = a \Leftarrow x \neq a.$$

because there exist instances of this clause, e.g. $f(f(a)) = a \Leftarrow f(a) \neq a$, that do not satisfy condition 2.

Since we consider stratified equational theories we give a standard fixpoint characterization of them extending to the equational case the fixpoint theory of non-monotonic operators which is described in [3,4] for logic programming with negation.

For the sake of simplicity, in the following a normal equational clause will be denoted by $(t = s \Leftarrow \tilde{E}, \tilde{D})$, where $\tilde{E}$ and $\tilde{D}$ represent, respectively, the equations and disequations in the body of the clause. By $\bar{D}$ we denote $\{u_i' = v_i' \mid u_i' \neq v_i' \in \tilde{D}\}$. A Herbrand E-interpretation I satisfies a normal equational clause P of a normal equational theory $\mathcal{E}^{\sim}$ iff for each ground instance $t = s \Leftarrow \tilde{E}, \tilde{D}$ of P we have $t = s \in I$ whenever $\tilde{E} \subseteq I$ and $\bar{D} \not\subseteq I$. A Herbrand E-model for $\mathcal{E}^{\sim}$ is a Herbrand E-interpretation for $\mathcal{E}^{\sim}$ that satisfies each normal equational clause in $\mathcal{E}^{\sim}$.

We associate an operator $T_{\mathcal{E}^{\sim}}$ with a normal equational theory $\mathcal{E}^{\sim}$ as follows:

Definition 17. Let $\mathcal{E}^{\sim}$ be a normal equational theory and I an interpretation of $\mathcal{E}^{\sim}$. The mapping $T_{\mathcal{E}^{\sim}} : 2^{B(\mathcal{E}^{\sim})} \longrightarrow 2^{B(\mathcal{E}^{\sim})}$ is defined as:

[11] The set of all ground instances of the clauses in $\mathcal{E}_i^{\sim}$

$$T_{\mathcal{E}^\sim}(I) = \{t = t : t \text{ is a ground term}\} \cup \{e \in B(\mathcal{E}^\sim) : \text{there exists an } u \in O(e) \text{ and a ground instance } t \to s \Leftarrow \tilde{E}, \tilde{D} \text{ of a clause in } \mathcal{E}^\sim \text{ such that } e/u = t, \tilde{E} \cup \{e[u \leftarrow s]\} \subseteq I \text{ and } \tilde{D} \not\subseteq I\}$$

Definition 18. Given a canonical normal equational theory $\mathcal{E}^\sim$ stratified by $\mathcal{E}^\sim = \mathcal{E}_1^\sim \dot{\cup} \ldots \dot{\cup} \mathcal{E}_n^\sim$ we define a sequence of Herbrand E-interpretations by putting

$$M_1 = T_{\mathcal{E}_1^\sim} \Uparrow \omega(\emptyset)$$
$$M_2 = T_{\mathcal{E}_2^\sim} \Uparrow \omega(M_1)$$
$$\vdots$$
$$M_n = T_{\mathcal{E}_n^\sim} \Uparrow \omega(M_{n-1})$$

where clearly $M_1 \subseteq M_2 \subseteq \cdots \subseteq M_n$[12].

Let $M_{\mathcal{E}^\sim} = M_n$. The following theorem establishes the main result of this section.

Theorem 19. *Let $\mathcal{E}^\sim$ be a canonical normal equational theory stratified by $\mathcal{E}^\sim = \mathcal{E}_1^\sim \dot{\cup} \cdots \dot{\cup} \mathcal{E}_n^\sim$. Then*

1. *$M_{\mathcal{E}^\sim}$ is a Herbrand E-model of $\mathcal{E}^\sim$.*
2. *$M_{\mathcal{E}^\sim}$ is a minimal Herbrand E-model of $\mathcal{E}^\sim$.*
3. *$M_{\mathcal{E}^\sim}$ is a Herbrand E-model of $comp(\mathcal{E}^\sim)$.*

7 Soundness

In this section we give the soundness results of our equational constructive negation rule with respect to the completed program. Let us recall that the systems in the leaves of the search tree have a form which allows to test their solvability in *CET*.

First, we show that a canonical normal equational theory is a logical consequence of its completion.

[12] The cumulative powers of an operator T are defined in [3,4] as:

$$T \Uparrow 0(I) = I$$
$$T \Uparrow (n+1)(I) = T(T \Uparrow n(I)) \cup T \Uparrow n(I)$$
$$T \Uparrow \omega(I) = \bigcup_{n<\omega} T \Uparrow n(I)$$

Proposition 20. *Let $\mathcal{E}^{\sim}$ be a canonical normal equational theory. Then $\mathcal{E}^{\sim}$ is a logical consequence of $comp(\mathcal{E}^{\sim})$.*

To state the soundness results we need the following lemmata.

Lemma 21. *If $\mathcal{E}$ is a canonical Horn equational theory with constructors and $\{G_1, \ldots, G_n\}$ is a frontier of a goal G then*

$$comp(\mathcal{E}) \models G \longleftrightarrow (\exists\, Y_1\, G_1) \;\vee\; \ldots \;\vee\; (\exists\, Y_n\, G_n)$$

where Y_i is the set of variables in G_i not in G.

Proof. The lemma follows straightforwardly from proposition 20 and from the fact that if $\{G_1, \ldots, G_n\}$ is a frontier for G then every derivation for G passes through one frontier node since the operational mechanism which is used to build the search tree is correct and complete ([18]).

Lemma 22. *If $\mathcal{E}^{\sim}$ is a canonical stratified normal equational theory with constructors, G is a goal and $\{G_1, \ldots, G_n\}$ is a frontier of G then*

$$comp(\mathcal{E}^{\sim}) \models G \longleftrightarrow (\exists\, Y_1\, G_1) \;\vee\; \ldots \;\vee\; (\exists\, Y_n\, G_n)$$

where Y_i is the set of variables in G_i not in G.

Proof. We prove the lemma by induction on the number of calls to negative subderivations. In the base case, the selected subgoal of G is an equation and $\mathcal{E}^{\sim}$ is a canonical Horn equational theory with constructors, then the lemma holds by Lemma 21. For the induction step, the interesting case is if the selected subgoal of G is a negated subgoal $\sim \exists\, \tilde{Z}\, (g \Box E)$, then by the induction hypothesis the frontier $\{(g_1 \Box E_1), \ldots, (g_n \Box E_n)\}$ for the derivation of $(g \Box E)$ is such that

$$comp(\mathcal{E}^{\sim}) \models g \Box E \longleftrightarrow \exists\, Y_1'\, (g_1 \Box E_1) \;\vee\; \ldots \;\vee\; \exists\, Y_n'\, (g_n \Box E_n)$$

Now, if $F_1, \ldots, F_p$ are the goals returned after negating the frontier, we have

$$comp(\mathcal{E}^{\sim}) \models \sim \exists\, \tilde{Z}\, (g \Box E) \longleftrightarrow F_1 \;\vee\; \ldots \;\vee\; F_p$$

Therefore,

$$comp(\mathcal{E}^{\sim}) \models G \longleftrightarrow (\exists\, Y_1\, G_1) \;\vee\; \ldots \;\vee\; (\exists\, Y_n\, G_n)$$

since every $\exists\, Y_i\, G_i$ is obtained from G by replacing $\sim \exists\, \tilde{Z}\, (g \Box E)$ by F_i. So that, in the general case the lemma holds by building the frontier iteratively.

Theorem 23. Soundness

Let $\mathcal{E}^{\sim}$ be a canonical stratified normal equational theory with constructors and g a normal goal represented by the extended goal g_0. If $\langle [\,], [g_0 \Box \emptyset] \rangle \rightarrow_{\mathcal{ICN}cn} \langle S, L \rangle$ then every system E_i in S is a correct answer for g_0.

Proof. If $\langle [\,], [g_0 \Box \emptyset] \rangle \rightarrow_{\mathcal{ICN}cn} \langle S, L \rangle$ then for every system $E_i \in S$ there exists a narrowing derivation in the search tree for $g_0 \Box \emptyset$

$$g_0 \Box \emptyset, \exists Y_1 (g_1 \Box E'_1), \ldots, \exists Y_n (g_n \Box E'_n)$$

such that every $\exists Y_k (g_k \Box E'_k)$ belongs to the frontier of $\exists Y_{k-1}(g_{k-1} \Box E'_{k-1})$ and $\exists Y_n (g_n \Box E'_n)$ has a frontier $\{G_1, \ldots, G_p\}$ such that G_j is of the form $\emptyset \Box E_i$. Then by Lemma 22

$$comp(\mathcal{E}^{\sim}) \models g_0 \Box \emptyset \longleftrightarrow F_0$$
$$comp(\mathcal{E}^{\sim}) \models \exists Y_1 (g_1 \Box E'_1) \longleftrightarrow F_1$$
$$\vdots$$
$$comp(\mathcal{E}^{\sim}) \models \exists Y_n (g_n \Box E'_n) \longleftrightarrow G_1 \vee \ldots \vee \exists Y_j (\emptyset \Box E_i) \vee \ldots \vee G_p$$

Now, E_i is solvable since $E_i \in S$. Thus, for all substitution θ such that $CET \models \exists Y_j E_i\theta$, the last disjuntion is true and hence, by the above co-implications, each computed answer $E_i \in S$ is a correct answer for $g_0 \Box \emptyset$.

8 Conclusion and Further Research

We have presented an algorithm based on constructive negation which extends narrowing to deal with systems of equations and disequations. We have then defined the notions of *completion* and *stratified* normal equational theories and have proved the soundness of the operational semantics with respect to the completion. We are currently investigating the completeness of our computation rule and how to use the extended narrower as a kernel for a language which integrates equational and logic programming as an instance of the Constraint Logic Programming Scheme [1,2,25].

References

1. M. Alpuente and M. Falaschi. Narrowing as an Incremental Constraint Satisfaction Algorithm. In J. Maluszyński and M. Wirsing, editors, *Proc. of PLILP'91*, volume 528 of *Lecture Notes in Computer Science*, pages 111–122. Springer-Verlag, Berlin, 1991.
2. M. Alpuente, M. Falaschi, and G. Levi. Incremental Constraint Satisfaction for Equational Logic Programming. Technical report, Dipartimento di Informatica, Università di Pisa, 1991. To appear in *Theoretical Computer Science*.
3. K. R. Apt. Introduction to Logic Programming. In J. van Leeuwen, editor, *Handbook of Theoretical Computer Science*, volume B: Formal Models and Semantics. Elsevier, Amsterdam and The MIT Press, Cambridge, 1990.
4. K. R. Apt, H. Blair, and A. Walker. Towards a Theory of Declarative Knowledge. In J. Minker, editor, *Foundations of Deductive Databases and Logic Programming*, pages 89–148. Morgan Kaufmann, Los Altos, Ca., 1988.
5. L. Bachmair and H. Ganzinger. On restrictions of ordered paramodulation with simplification. In E. Y. Shapiro, editor, *Proc. 10th Int'l Conf. on Automated Deduction*, volume 449 of *Lecture Notes in Computer Science*, pages 427–441, 1990.

6. L. Bachmair and H. Ganzinger. Perfect Model Semantics for Logic Programs with Equality. In K. Furukawa, editor, *Proc. Eighth Int'l Conf. on Logic Programming*, pages 645–659. The MIT Press, Cambridge, Mass., 1991.
7. M. Bellia and G. Levi. The relation between logic and functional languages. *Journal of Logic Programming*, 3:217–236, 1986.
8. J.A. Bergstra and J.W. Klop. Conditional Rewrite Rules: confluence and termination. *Journal of Computer and System Sciences*, 32:323–362, 1986.
9. P. Bosco, E. Giovannetti, and C. Moiso. Narrowing vs. SLD-resolution. *Theoretical Computer Science*, 59:3–23, 1988.
10. P. G. Bosco, E. Giovannetti, G. Levi, C. Moiso, and C. Palamidessi. A complete semantic characterization of K-LEAF, a logic language with partial functions. In *Proc. of the Fourth IEEE Symposium on Logic Programming*, pages 318 - 327, San Francisco, 1987. IEEE Computer Society Press, N.W., Washington.
11. D. Chan. Constructive Negation Based on the Completed Database. In R. A. Kowalski and K. A. Bowen, editors, *Proc. Fifth Int'l Conf. on Logic Programming*, pages 111–125. The MIT Press, Cambridge, Mass., 1988.
12. D. Chan. An Extension of Constructive Negation and its Application in Coroutining. In E. Lusk and R. Overbeck, editors, *Proc. North American Conf. on Logic Programming'89*, pages 477–493. The MIT Press, Cambridge, Mass., 1989.
13. K.L. Clark. Negation as Failure. In H. Gallaire and J. Minker, editors, *Logic and data bases*. Plenum Press, New York, 1978.
14. A. Colmerauer. Equations and Inequations on Finite and Infinite Trees. In *Proc. Int'l Conf. on Fifth Generation Computer Systems*, pages 85–99. ICOT, Tokio, 1984.
15. N. Dershowitz and A. Plaisted. Logic Programming cum Applicative Programming. In *Proc. First IEEE Int'l Symp. on Logic Programming*, pages 54–66. IEEE, 1984.
16. M. Fay. First Order Unification in an Equational Theory. In *4th Int'l Conf. on Automated Deduction*, pages 161–167, 1979.
17. M. Fitting. A Kripke-Kleene semantics for logic programs. In *Journal of Logic Programming*, volume 2, pages 295–312, 1985.
18. L. Fribourg. Slog: a logic programming language interpreter based on clausal superposition and rewriting. In *Proc. Second IEEE Int'l Symp. on Logic Programming*, pages 172–185. IEEE, 1985.
19. E. Giovannetti, G. Levi, C. Moiso, and C. Palamidessi. Kernel Leaf: A Logic plus Functional Language. *Journal of Computer and System Sciences*, 42, 1991.
20. J. Goguen and J. Meseguer. Eqlog: Equality, Types and Generic Modules for Logic Programming. In D. de Groot and G. Lindstrom, editors, *Logic Programming, Functions, Relations and Equations*, pages 295–363. Prentice-Hall, 1986.
21. S. Hölldobler. *Foundations of Equational Logic Programming*, volume 353 of *Lecture Notes in Artificial Intelligence*. Springer-Verlag, Berlin, 1989.
22. G. Huet and D.C. Oppen. Equations and Rewrite Rules: a Survey. In *Formal Languages: perspectives and open problems*, pages 349–405. Academic Press, 1980.
23. J.M. Hullot. Canonical Forms and Unification. In *5th Int'l Conf. on Automated Deduction*, volume 87 of *Lecture Notes in Computer Science*, pages 318–334. Springer-Verlag, Berlin, 1980.
24. H. Hussman. Unification in conditional-equational theories. Technical report, Fakultät für Mathematik und Informatik, Universität Passau, 1986.

25. J. Jaffar, J.-L. Lassez, and M.J. Maher. A logic programming language scheme. In D. de Groot and G. Lindstrom, editors, *Logic Programming, Functions, Relations and Equations*, pages 441–468. Prentice Hall, Englewood Cliffs, NJ, 1986.
26. S. Kaplan. Positive/negative conditional rewriting. In S.Kaplan and J.-P. Jouannaud, editors, *Conditional Term Rewriting Systems*, volume 308 of *Lecture Notes in Computer Science*, pages 129–143. Springer-Verlag, Berlin, 1987.
27. K. Kunen. Negation in logic programming. *Journal of Logic Programming*, 4:289–308, 1987.
28. J.-L. Lassez, M. J. Maher, and K. Marriott. Unification Revisited. In J. Minker, editor, *Foundations of Deductive Databases and Logic Programming*, pages 587–625. Morgan Kaufmann, Los Altos, Ca., 1988.
29. J. W. Lloyd. *Foundations of Logic Programming*. Springer-Verlag, Berlin, 1987. Second edition.
30. M. J. Maher. Complete Axiomatizations of the Algebras of Finite, Rational and Infinite Trees. In *Proc. Third IEEE Symp. on Logic In Computer Science*, pages 348–357. Computer Science Press, New York, 1988.
31. A. Middeldorp and E. Hamoen. Counterexamples to completeness results for basic narrowing. In H. Kirchner and G. Levi, editors, *Proc. Third Int'l Conf. on Algebraic and Logic Programming*, volume 632 of *Lecture Notes in Computer Science*, pages 244–258. Springer-Verlag, Berlin, 1992.
32. J.J. Moreno and M. Rodriguez-Artalejo. BABEL: A Functional and Logic Programming Language based on a constructor discipline and narrowing. In I. Grabowski, P. Lescanne, and W. Wechler, editors, *Algebraic and Logic Programming*, volume 343 of *Lecture Notes in Computer Science*, pages 223–232. Springer-Verlag, Berlin, 1988.
33. W. Nutt, P. Réty, and G. Smolka. Basic narrowing revisited. *Journal of Symbolic Computation*, 7:295–317, 1989.
34. M. O'Donnell. *Computing in Systems Described by Equations*, volume 58 of *Lecture Notes in Computer Science*. Springer-Verlag, Berlin, 1977.
35. P. Padawitz. *Computing in Horn Clause Theories*, volume 16 of *EATCS Monographs on Theoretical Computer Science*. Springer-Verlag, Berlin, 1988.
36. T. Przymusinski. On the Declarative Semantics of Deductive Databases and Logic Programs. In J. Minker, editor, *Foundations of Deductive Databases and Logic Programming*, pages 193–216. Morgan Kaufmann, Los Altos, Ca., 1988.
37. T. Przymusinski. On the Declarative and Procedural Semantics of Logic Programs. *Journal of Automated Reasoning*, 5(2):201–228, 1989.
38. M.J. Ramírez and M. Falaschi. Conditional narrowing with constructive negation. Technical report, Dipartimento di Informatica, Università di Pisa, 1992.
39. J.H. Siekmann. Universal unification. In *7th Int'l Conf. on Automated Deduction*, volume 170 of *Lecture Notes in Computer Science*, pages 1–42. Springer-Verlag, Berlin, 1984.
40. P. J. Stuckey. Constructive Negation for Constraint Logic Programming. In *Proc. Sixth IEEE Symp. on Logic In Computer Science*. IEEE Computer Society Press, 1991.

$CLP(\mathcal{AD})$ as a Deductive Database Language with Updates

Elisa Bertino[1], Maurizio Martelli[1], Danilo Montesi[2]

[1] Dipartimento di Informatica e Scienze dell'Informazione, Università di Genova, Viale Benedetto XV 3, 16132 Genova, Italia
{bertino,martelli}@cisi.unige.it
[2] Dipartimento di Informatica, Università di Pisa, Corso Italia 40, 56125 Pisa, Italia
montesi@di.unipi.it

Abstract. In this paper we propose a logic-based language, $CLP(\mathcal{AD})$ which is an instance of the Constraint Logic Programming schema and is a convenient semantic framework to be used for deductive database language with updates. $CLP(\mathcal{AD})$ can be seen as an extension of Datalog with base relations updates and the notion of transaction. The semantics of this language is given in two steps and is based on a notion of observable corresponding to the computed answer constraint. Moreover, some useful notions of equivalence between databases with respect to a transaction and between transactions with respect to a database are given.

1 Introduction

Logic languages are particularly suited to model data and deduction of information from the data. Unfortunately, such languages, as they were at the beginning of their development, lacked the ability to model dynamic aspects in database design and specification. For example the update problem has been addressed in several papers [1, 16, 15, 19]. The update language in deductive databases can be either separated or integrated with the query language. The most interesting database systems are those that allow to describe in a unique language queries and updates. Such systems allow to update the tuples for which a binding is provided by the query language. The proposals of deductive database languages with updates such us Glue-Nail [7], DatalogA [16] and $\mathcal{LDL}$ [17] approach the problem by giving ad-hoc solutions, and introducing updates in the language whose semantics was either lacking or given in a different formalism such as dynamic logic [15]. Using dynamic logic, in order to maintain the conventional meaning of conjuncts of updates, the Church-Rosser (CR) property of a database must be satisfied. The class of databases satisfying the CR property has only a theoretical interest. Thus, in $\mathcal{LDL}$ the meaning of a conjunct of updates in all the non-CR property databases is that of a sequence. Moreover, in DatalogA and $\mathcal{LDL}$ insertions and removals are immediately triggered, as soon as a rule body is satisfied. Thus, a single query can be evaluated on different states. Starting from the current database state s_1, the query fires the rules of the database.

While satisfying the rules the current database state s_1 becomes $s_2, s_3 \ldots$ ending in the final state s_n. Such a process leads to complex semantic issue. The model of such a database is a graph, with a starting state and an ending state. Due to the above evaluation model the transactional behavior is complex and is not defined.

In this paper we take a different approach, that is updates are not immediately triggered as soon as a rule body is satisfied. Therefore, a single query is evaluated in the same state, i.e., the current state, namely on the state prior to any change. Only after successful completion of the query such updates are executed. Such process leads to a simpler semantics. In addition we express the updates in a declarative style. The basic idea is to consider updates to a deductive database as constraints in constraint logic programming. Note that constraints are not integrity constraints. These constraints are interpreted as updates and are executed altogether at the end of a computation . In this way we model the transactional behavior of a query. Complex transactions can be expressed by means of sequences of goals. In [3] sequences of goals are also considered together with a single language to built complex transactions.

In our proposal a database state is a set of ground facts, that is the *extensional database* (EDB). The *intensional database* (IDB) is a set of rules. Each rule has in the body the constraints to express insertions and deletions. Updates are defined in the IDB and/or in the query. Such queries are called update queries. In the following we show how to merge updates expressed in declarative style in a declarative query language.

In order to merge update and query languages we consider a new proposal in the logic programming field which allows to integrate logic programming with different programming paradigms and specific problem solving techniques, namely, Constraint Logic Programming (shortly $CLP(X)$) [11, 12]. $CLP(X)$ is definitely one of the most important extensions of the logic programming paradigm and has been used to model the combination of the deductive power of logic programming and different kinds of computational aspects (from handling real numbers to concurrency). It is a schema which generalizes logic programming by including constraints. A nice property of logic programming such as equivalent model-theoretic, fixpoint and operational-semantics is maintained. In $CLP(X)$, various constraint logic programming languages can be accommodated according to the choice of the domain of constraints X. This integration allows, for example, to tackle problems having a numerical and/or logical character in a declarative way. Some existing proposals of $CLP(X)$ languages are $CLP(\Re)$ [13], CHIP [8] and Prolog III [6]. Aside from the Herbrand domain ($\mathcal{H}$), which all the above languages share, they have different domains to express constraints. For example, $CLP(\Re)$ only permits constraints on real terms, Prolog III on linear rational and on boolean terms and CHIP on linear rational, boolean and finite domain terms. Another relevant feature of $CLP(X)$ is the distinction between testing for solvability and computing a solution of a given constraint formula. In the logic programming case, this is combined into the unification process, which tests for solvability by computing a solution (a set of equations in normal form or a *most general unifier*). In $CLP(X)$, the computation of a solution of a constraint is left to a constraint solver, which does not affect the semantic definition of the language.

Let us first show how the $CLP(X)$ can be easily used as a deductive database language. As an example, we use $CLP(\mathcal{H})$ where $\mathcal{H}$ is the Herbrand universe built over a finite one sorted function free alphabet, and $=$ is the only predicate symbol for the constraint language and it is interpreted as syntactic equality over the domain $\mathcal{H}$.

Example 1.1 *Let us consider the following database* $DB = IDB \cup EDB_1$ *(where* $\cup$ *denoted the set union between sets of rules).*

$$
\begin{aligned}
EDB_1 = \{\; & \texttt{father(bob,tom).} \\
& \texttt{father(tom,john).} \\
& \texttt{father(tom,peter).} \;\}
\end{aligned}
$$

$$
\begin{aligned}
IDB = \{\; & \texttt{grandfather(X,Y)} \leftarrow \texttt{father(X,Z),father(Z,Y).} \\
& \texttt{grandfather(X,Y)} \leftarrow \texttt{father(X,Z),mother(Z,Y).} \;\}
\end{aligned}
$$

The query `grandfather(bob,X)`*, evaluated in* DB*, computes the constraints* $\{\texttt{X} = \texttt{john}\}$ *and* $\{\texttt{X} = \texttt{peter}\}$.

Remark
Indeed, the semantics of $CLP(\mathcal{H})$ does not model the *set oriented* behavior of Datalog [4], i.e. a set of answers. In Section 4 we define a semantics to model updates and the set oriented feature of deductive database languages starting from the semantics for $CLP(X)$.

The contribution of this paper is the definition of an instance of the $CLP(X)$ schema, named $CLP(\mathcal{AD})$ for database applications. $CLP(\mathcal{AD})$ is a deductive database language providing updates to base relations, that is to insert and delete ground facts from the current database state. The updates are constraints over a special constraint domain called $\mathcal{AD}$. The transactional behavior of update queries is also defined. The semantics of a transaction, that is an update query is given in two steps. We recall that a transaction is a set of update operations that form an *atomic unit execution* which can either commit, producing a new database state (EDB_{i+1}), or abort, leaving the database in its initial state (EDB_i).

The first step semantics is inherited from the semantics of $CLP(X)$ based on the observable corresponding to the computed answer constraint as presented in [10]. Thus, we have model-theoretic, fixpoint and operational semantics. The second step semantics provides the semantics of a transaction. $CLP(\mathcal{AD})$, can be used to model subsets of DatalogA [16], $\mathcal{LDL}$ [17] and Glue-Nail [7]. Note that in absence of updates our language and its semantics reduce to a different formalization of Datalog. Moreover, the query evaluation technique developed for deductive databases can be easily extended to our language. As a byproduct we have some equivalence notions between databases with respect to a transaction and between transactions with respect to a database. These equivalence notions can be used to optimize databases and transactions, using database and transaction transformation in addition to classic Datalog optimization techniques [4]. In the present work the words update, query and transaction are considered synonymous.

In the remainder of this section we recall the basic terminology of Datalog and $CLP(X)$. Section 2 introduces the $CLP(\mathcal{AD})$ language. Section 3 describes the semantics for $CLP(\mathcal{AD})$ programs modeling computed answer constraints. Section 4 defines the semantics of a transaction with respect to a database. Section 5 shows how some existing approaches for modeling updates can be mapped into $CLP(\mathcal{AD})$. Finally, some conclusions are given in Section 6.

1.1 Terminology of Datalog language

We recall the basic concepts of Datalog [5]. Datalog, is in many respects, a simplified version of a logic programming language [2, 14]. A logic program consists of a set of *facts* and *rules*. Note that a Datalog program is just a set of rules: in this paper it has also facts. Facts are assertions about an application domain, such us "John is the father of Harry". Rules are sentences which allow facts to be deduced from other facts. An example of a rule is: "If X is a parent of Y and Y is a parent of Z, then X is a grandparent of Z". Note that rules, in order to be general, usually contain *variables* (in our case, X, Y, and Z). In Datalog both facts (H) and rules ($H \leftarrow B_1, \ldots, B_n$) are represented as definite Horn clauses where H and each B_i are atoms of the form $p(t_1, \ldots, t_k)$ (shortly $p(\tilde{t})$) such that p is a *predicate symbol* and the $t_j's$ $(1 \leq j \leq k)$ are *terms*. The symbols "$\leftarrow$" and "," denote the logical implication and conjunction respectively. A term is either a *constant* or a *variable*. Any Datalog program consists of facts and rules and must satisfy the following *safety conditions*: each fact is *ground* and each variable which occurs in the head of a rule must also occur in the body of the same rule. These conditions guarantee that the set of all facts which can be derived from a Datalog program is a finite set of ground facts. The information in Datalog is subdivided into two components, the *Extensional Database (EDB)* and the *Intensional Database (IDB)*. The EDB is a set of ground facts, the IDB is a Datalog set of rules. The predicate symbols occurring in EDB and in IDB are divided into two disjoint sets: the *EDB-predicate symbols*, which are the ones occurring in the EDB and the *IDB-predicate symbols*, which occur in IDB but not in EDB. Moreover, it is required that the head predicate symbols of each rule in IDB are IDB-predicate symbols. EDB-predicate symbols may occur in IDB, but only in a rule body. The standard *Herbrand Universe* $\mathcal{H}$ is the set of constant symbols, i.e., $\{t_1 \ldots, t_k\}$ such that $t_i's$ $(1 \leq i \leq k)$ are constants. The *Herbrand Base*, $\mathcal{B}$ is the set of all facts that we can express in the language of Datalog, i.e. all atoms of the form $p(t_1, \ldots, t_k)$ such that the $t_i's$ $(1 \leq i \leq k)$

are constants. $\mathcal{B}^e$ denotes the extensional part of the Herbrand base, i.e., all the atoms of $\mathcal{B}$ whose predicate symbol is an EDB-predicate symbol and, similarly, $\mathcal{B}^i$ denotes the set of all the atoms of $\mathcal{B}$ whose predicate symbol is an IDB-predicate symbol. The semantics of a Datalog program IDB depends on the extensional part EDB. As in logic programming, the semantics of a Datalog program P is captured by three different notions, namely operational, fixpoint and model-theoretic semantics, which are proved equivalent [2, 5, 14]. In the following we consider a Datalog program DB as $IDB \cup EDB$. The operational semantics consists of all those ground atoms which have a successful derivation (denoted by the notation $A \longmapsto^* \Box$), i.e.

$$\mathcal{O}(DB) = \{A \mid A \in \mathcal{B}, A \longmapsto^* \Box\}$$

By $2^{\mathcal{B}}$ we denote the powerset of a set $\mathcal{B}$. The fixpoint semantics is defined as the least fixpoint of the operator $T_{DB} : 2^{\mathcal{B}} \longrightarrow 2^{\mathcal{B}}$, which is called the immediate consequence operator and which nicely characterizes the bottom-up style of computation. Recalling that $T_{DB} \uparrow n$ denotes the n-th iteration of an operator T_{DB} starting from $\emptyset$ and that T_{DB} is defined as follows (when $I \in 2^{\mathcal{B}}$)

$$\begin{aligned} T_{DB}(I) = \{A \mid A \in \mathcal{B}, \exists A \leftarrow B_1, \ldots, B_n \\ &\textit{ground instance of a rule in } DB, \\ &\{B_1, \ldots, B_n\} \subseteq I \;\; \}, \end{aligned}$$

the fixpoint semantics is $\mathcal{F}(DB) = T_{DB} \uparrow \omega$. In the case of Datalog programs since $\mathcal{H}$ is finite and function free the least fixpoint is reached in a finite number of iterations, i.e. $\mathcal{F}(DB) = T_{DB} \uparrow n$. Finally, the model-theoretic semantics of a program DB, i.e. the set of all ground atoms which are logical consequences of DB, is $\mathcal{M}(DB) = \bigcap$ *HMod(DB)*, where *HMod(DB)* is the set of Herbrand models of DB.

1.2 Terminology of Constraint Logic Programming

We recall the basic concepts as defined in [12]. The $CLP(X)$ framework is defined using a many-sorted first order language, where $SORT = \bigcup_i SORT_i$ denotes the finite set of sorts used. A *signature* of an n-ary function, predicate or variable symbol f is a sequence of respectively $n+1$, n, 1 elements of SORT. By *sort* of f we denote the last element in the signature of the function symbol f. Σ, Π and V (possibly subscripted) denote possibly denumerable collections of function symbols, predicate symbols and variables with their signatures. We make the assumption that there exists a denumerable set of variable symbols for each sort and that Σ, *the set of function symbols*, contains at least one symbol. A (Π, Σ, V)-atom is an element $p(t_1, \ldots, t_n)$ where $p \in \Pi$ is n-ary and $t_i \in \tau(\Sigma \cup V), i = 1, \ldots, n$. $\tau(\Sigma \cup V)$ is the set of terms constructed with Σ and V. A (Π, Σ, V)-constraint is a possibly empty or infinite conjunction of (Π, Σ, V)-atoms. In the following a tilde over a symbol t, i.e. $\tilde{t}$, will denote a finite sequence of symbols. For example, $\tilde{X}$ denotes a sequence of variables. $Var(E)$ and $Pred(E)$ denote respectively the variables and the predicate symbols of an expression E. All the following definitions are related to the condition that $\Pi = \Pi_c \cup \Pi_B$ and $\Pi_c \cap \Pi_B = \emptyset$.

Definition 1.1 *(CLP programs) A (Π, Σ, V)-program is a set of rules of the form*

$$H \leftarrow c_1, \ldots c_k \quad or \quad H \leftarrow c_1, \ldots c_k, B_1, \ldots, B_n$$

where $c_i, 0 \leq i \leq k$ are (Π_c, Σ, V)-atoms, H (the head) and $B_j, 0 \leq j \leq n$ are (Π_B, Σ, V)-atoms. The right part of the implication is called body. A goal is a program rule with no head.

Definition 1.2 *A (Π_B, Σ, V)-constrained atom is an expression of the form $p(\tilde{X}) \leftarrow c$, where c is a (Π_c, Σ, V)-constraint and $p(\tilde{X})$ is a (Π_B, Σ, V)-atom with distinct variables as arguments.*

In $CLP(X)$, X stands for a specific constraint domain over which the computation is performed. Then, let us introduce the notion of *structure* which gives the semantic interpretation of such a domain.

Definition 1.3 *A structure $\Re(\Pi, \Sigma)$ is defined over (sorted) alphabets Π and Σ of predicate and function symbols, where Π contains the equality symbol "=". $\Re(\Pi, \Sigma)$ consists of*

- *a collection $\mathcal{DR}$ of non-empty sets $\mathcal{DR}_s$ where s ranges over the sorts in SORT.*
- *an assignment to each n-ary function symbol $f \in \Sigma$ of a function $\mathcal{DR}_{s_1} \times \ldots \times \mathcal{DR}_{s_n} \rightarrow \mathcal{DR}_s$ where $(s_1, s_2, \ldots, s_n, s)$ is the signature of f.*
- *an assignment to each n-ary predicate symbol $p \in \Pi_c$, apart from = (which is interpreted as syntactic equality), of a function $\mathcal{DR}_{s_1} \times \ldots \times \mathcal{DR}_{s_n} \rightarrow \{True, False\}$ where $(s_1, s_2, \ldots, s_n)$ is the signature of p.*

An $\Re(\Pi, \Sigma)$-valuation for a (Π, Σ, V)-expression is a mapping $\theta : V \rightarrow \mathcal{DR}$, where $V = \bigcup_{s \in SORT} V_s$ is the set of all variables, $\theta(X_s) \in \mathcal{DR}_s$, and s is the sort of the variable X_s.

(Π, Σ, V)-programs, (Π_c, Σ, V)-constraints and (Π_B, Σ, V)-atoms will be called programs, constraints and atoms. Moreover $\Re(\Pi, \Sigma)$ will be denoted by $\Re$. The notion of $\Re$-valuation is extended in the obvious way to terms and constraints. If C is a finite set of atomic constraints, we write $\Re \models C\theta$ iff $\forall c \in C, \Re \models c\theta$ ($c\theta$ is $\Re$-equivalent to $True$) holds. Given an expression E and an $\Re$-valuation θ, $E\theta$ denotes the result of the application operation.

Definition 1.4 *(solvability) A constraint c is $\Re$-solvable iff there exists a $\Re$-valuation θ such that $\Re \models c\theta$. θ is called an $\Re$-solution of c. A constrained atom $p(\tilde{X}) \leftarrow c$ is $\Re$-solvable iff c is $\Re$-solvable.*

2 The $CLP(\mathcal{AD})$ Language

The $CLP(\mathcal{AD})$ language merges the update and the query languages. The name $\mathcal{AD}$ used for the domain was originally chosen to point out that the language treats both ***action*** (updates) and ***deduction*** (queries). The update language is defined as a constraint language. The answers to a query are also defined by means of constraints. Thus, the rules of our language have in the body the constraint language part which is split into the ***variable constraints*** and the ***update constraints***. Updates in DatalogA and $\mathcal{LDL}$ are modeled by some specials atoms of the form

$$\pm p(t_1, \ldots, t_n)$$

where p is an n-ary base relation, and $t_1, \ldots, t_n$ are ground terms. We also use the above notation to express updates. Intuitively, the meaning of $+p(\tilde{t})$ is to insert the tuple $\tilde{t}$ into the base relation p. Similarly, the meaning of $-p(\tilde{t})$ is to delete the tuple $\tilde{t}$ from the base relation p. Given an update, say $+p(a)$, on a database state EDB_i the desired result of the update is that $p(a)$ belongs to the database state EDB_{i+1}. Similarly, the absence of $p(a)$ from the database state EDB_{i+1} is the result of the update $-p(a)$. Thus, given the current database state and the updates the new database state can be easily computed. Roughly speaking there are two type of updates. Strong updates are updates which can be executed only if some preconditions are satisfied. Weak updates do not care about any precondition. In the following we consider strong updates due to the fact that most relational systems support strong updates. However, our approach is parametric with respect to the type of updates considered. The strong updates preconditions are such that to remove (insert) $p(a)$, it must (not) be present in EDB_i.

1. $EDB_i \cup \{p(a)\} = EDB_i$
2. $EDB_i \setminus \{p(a)\} = EDB_i$

The above equations respectively express the preconditions for $-p(a)$, that is $p(a) \in EDB_i$ and for $+p(a)$ that is $p(a) \notin EDB_i$. We could then say that the desired result of the update $-p(a)$ $(+p(a))$ is achieved by starting from a database state EDB_i and removing (adding) $p(a)$ to it to get the database state EDB_{i+1}. The updates $-p(a)$ and $+p(a)$ are not allowed together, due to the unsatisfiability of the above equations. Our constraint domain $\mathcal{AD}$ must be able to handle the above constraints, and in addition, constraints providing bindings for the variables of the queries, i.e., variable constraints, must also be considered (see Example 1.1). A deductive database with updates is made of three components: EDB, IDB and the update query Q. IDB and Q can contain updates.

Let us now define the language to specify our deductive database by means of its building blocks, that are EDB, IDB and Q.

Definition 2.1 *Let Σ, V and Π be sets of constant, variable and predicate symbols respectively. The set of predicate symbols Π is partitioned into Π_{EDB}, Π_{IDB} the predicate symbols of Datalog, $\Pi_{c^u} = \{+p, -p \mid p \in \Pi_{EDB}\}$ the predicate symbols of the update constraints and $\Pi_{c^v} = \{=\}$ the predicate symbol of variable constraints. We denote the atoms built from the set of predicate symbols (Π), constant symbols (Σ) and variable symbols (V) as (Π, Σ, V)-atoms. In a similar way we denote different kinds of sets of atoms as (Π_{EDB}, Σ)-atoms, $(\Pi_{IDB}, \Sigma \cup V)$-atoms, $(\Pi_{c^v}, \Sigma \cup V)$-atoms, $(\Pi_{c^u}, \Sigma \cup V)$-atoms.*

Definition 2.2 *(EDB) Let $\mathcal{B}^e$ be the Herbrand base built over Π_{EDB} and Σ, then a state or extensional database $EDB \in 2^{\mathcal{B}^e}$ is a (possibly empty) set of (Π_{EDB}, Σ)-atoms, i.e. ground base relations.*

In the following we denote with $EDB_i, i = 1, \ldots, n$ the possible extensional databases.

Definition 2.3 *(IDB) The intensional database IDB is a set of constrained rules of the form*

$$H \leftarrow c^v, c^u, B_1, \ldots, B_n$$

where B_i's are $(\Pi_{IDB} \cup \Pi_{EDB}, \Sigma \cup V)$-atoms and H is a $(\Pi_{IDB}, \Sigma \cup V)$-atom. $B_1, \ldots, B_n$ can be empty. c^v (c^u) denotes a set of variable (update) constraints $c_1^v, \ldots, c_k^v$ ($c_1^u, \ldots, c_s^u$) respectively. Each variable (update) constraint c_i^v, $i = 1, \ldots, s$ ($c_j^u, j = 1, \ldots, k$) is a $(\Pi_{c^v}, \Sigma \cup V)$-atom ($(\Pi_{c^u}, \Sigma \cup V)$- atom).

Definition 2.4 *(Q) An update query Q is a body of a constrained rule.*

To be consistent with the $CLP(\mathcal{AD})$ notation, a base relation **father(bob, tom)** should be written as **father(bob, tom)** $\leftarrow$. In the following we use the former notation. Note that the extensional and intensional databases are particular $CLP(\mathcal{AD})$ programs.

Let us give now a first example of a $CLP(\mathcal{AD})$ database (program) which shows an extensional database, an intensional database, update queries and which allows to informally describe the operational behavior of the language.

Example 2.1 *Let us consider the database of Example 1.1 with a constrained rule to change the name of the father. The sets of predicate symbols are:* $\Pi_{EDB} = \{$**father**, **mother**$\}$, $\Pi_{IDB} = \{$**grandfather**, **changefather**$\}$ *and* $\Sigma = \{$**bob**, **tom**, **john**, **peter**, **jack**, **pat**$\}$. $DB_1' = IDB' \cup EDB_1$ *and*

$EDB_1 = \{$ **father(bob, tom).**
father(tom, john).
father(tom, peter). $\}$

$$
\begin{aligned}
IDB' = \{\; & \texttt{grandfather(X,Y)} \leftarrow \texttt{father(X,Z),father(Z,Y).}\\
& \texttt{grandfather(X,Y)} \leftarrow \texttt{father(X,Z),mother(Z,Y).}\\
& \texttt{changefather(Y,Z)} \leftarrow \texttt{-father(Y,W),+father(Z,W),}\\
& \qquad\qquad\qquad\qquad \texttt{father(Y,W).}\;\; \}.
\end{aligned}
$$

The update query **changefather(tom,jack)** , *evaluated in* DB_1', *computes the new extensional database* EDB_2 *that is* {**father(bob,tom),father(jack,john), father(jack,peter)**}. *If* $EDB_3 =$ {**father(bob,tom),father(jack,john)**} *the update query* **grandfather(X,tom)** *evaluated in* $DB_3' = IDB' \cup EDB_3$, *fails and the extensional database remains* EDB_3.

3 The First Step Semantics: $DB = IDB \cup EDB$

The semantics of a $CLP(\mathcal{AD})$ program is given in terms of the semantics of $CLP(X)$ specialized over the constraint domain $\mathcal{AD}$. The semantics for $CLP(X)$ introduced in [10] is the one which has the richest information content, and which models the answer to a query, that is, the notion of computed answer constraints. In this section we outline this semantics for the $CLP(\mathcal{AD})$ language. This semantics characterizes the computed answer constraints, that is the answer variable constraints and the answer update constraints. The answer update constraints represent the updates which have to be performed to compute the new database state. Note that our approach does not require the database state to change in a monotone way. Other approaches, for example dealing with concurrency [18], consider the *store-as-valuation* and therefore allow only monotonic state evolutions. Let us introduce some notions about the constraint domain and the interpretation of the constraint language. The constraint domain for query-update is $\mathcal{AD} = \langle \mathcal{H}, EDB \rangle$ where $\mathcal{H}$ denotes the Herbrand universe, and $EDB \subseteq \mathcal{B}^e$ denotes a subset of the Herbrand base built over Π_{EDB} and Σ.

Definition 3.1 *A structure* $\Re$ *is defined over a (finite) one sort alphabet* Π *and* Σ *of predicate and constant symbols.* $\Re$ *consists of*

- *a pair* $\langle \mathcal{H}, EDB \rangle$
- *an assignment which maps each constant symbol* $c \in \Sigma$ *into itself in* $\mathcal{H}$
- *an assignment to each predicate symbol in* $\Pi_{c^v} \cup \Pi_{c^u}$ *such that*
  1. *(Equality)* $=$ *is interpreted as syntactic equality over* $\mathcal{H}$.
  2. *(Update)* $\forall p \in \Pi_{EDB}$
     (a) $+p(\tilde{t}) = True$ *iff* $p(\tilde{t}) \notin EDB$
     (b) $-p(\tilde{t}) = True$ *iff* $p(\tilde{t}) \in EDB$

An $\Re$*-valuation for a* (Π, Σ)*-expression is a mapping* $\theta : V \to \mathcal{H}$ *where* V *is the set of all variables, and* $\theta(X) \in \mathcal{H}$.

Note that the updates are only on base relations. The above interpretation of updates does not allow to insert (remove) ground atoms that were (not) in EDB, respectively. For example considering the extensional database $EDB = \{p(a)\}$ the update $+p(a)$ is not allowed.

Definition 3.2 *($\Re$-solvability) A constraint c^v, c^u is $\Re$-solvable iff there exists an $\Re$-valuation θ for c^v, c^u such that $\Re \models (c^v, c^u)\theta$ i.e., $\Re \models c^v$ and $\Re \models c^u$. θ is called the $\Re$-solution of c^v, c^u.*

Note that the consistency among update constraints is checked at each derivation step by means of the $\Re$-solvability, that is $\Re \models (c^v, c^u)\theta$. Thus, complementary updates are not solvable due to the fact that an atom cannot at the same time belong and not belong to the extensional database.

We now introduce the definition of derivation step, derivation and successful derivation.

Definition 3.3 *(derivation step) Let DB be a $CLP(\mathcal{AD})$ program. A derivation step of a query $Q = c^v, c^u, G_1, \ldots, G_t$ in DB results in a query of the form $c'^v, c'^u, \tilde{B}_1, \ldots, \tilde{B}_t$, and is denoted by $c^v, c^u, G_1, \ldots, G_t \overset{\Re}{\longmapsto} c'^v, c'^u, \tilde{B}_1, \ldots, \tilde{B}_t$ if there exist t variants of rules in DB, $H_j \leftarrow c_j^v, c_j^u, \tilde{B}_j$, $j = 1, \ldots, t$ with no variables in common with Q and with each other, such that c'^v, c'^u is $\Re$-solvable with $c'^v = c^v \cup c_1^v \cup \ldots \cup c_t^v \cup \{H_1 = G_1\} \cup \ldots \cup \{H_t = G_t\}$ and $c'^u = c^u \cup c_1^u \cup \ldots \cup c_t^u$.*

Definition 3.4 *(derivation) Let DB be a $CLP(\mathcal{AD})$ program. A derivation of a query Q is a finite or infinite sequence of queries such that every query, apart from Q is obtained from the previous one by means of a derivation step.*

Definition 3.5 *(successful derivation) Let DB be a $CLP(\mathcal{AD})$ program. A successful derivation of a query Q is a finite sequence whose last element is a query of the form c'^v, c'^u. c'^v, c'^u is the answer constraint of the derivation. All other finite derivations are finitely failed. The successful derivation of a query Q which yields the answer constraint c'^v, c'^u, is denoted by $Q \overset{\Re}{\longmapsto}{}^* c'^v, c'^u$.*

Note that the above notions are given with respect to a fixed solvability notion which is defined over the algebraic structure $\Re$. The successful derivation collects in the answer constraint c'^v, c'^u the bindings for the variables in the query together with the updates. The execution of such updates are modeled by the second step semantics.

In the following we introduce some preliminary notions of π-interpretations and π-models to define the operational, fixpoint and model-theoretic semantics. The semantics is an instantiation of the one given in [10] where $X = \mathcal{AD}$. Therefore, definitions, lemmas, theorems and proofs of this section are an instantiation over our constraint domain of definitions, lemmas, theorems and proofs given in [10]. Let us first introduce an operator which returns the set of "ground" instances. .

Definition 3.6 *The set of "domain instances" $[p(\tilde{X}) \leftarrow c^v, c^u]$ of a constrained atom $p(\tilde{X}) \leftarrow c^v, c^u$ is defined as*

$$[p(\tilde{X}) \leftarrow c^v, c^u] = \{(p(\tilde{X}) \leftarrow c^v, c^u)\theta \mid \theta \text{ is an } \Re\text{-solution of } c^v, c^u\}.$$

This definition can be extended to sets of constrained atoms. Let S be a set of constrained atoms. Then $[S] = \bigcup_{A \in S}[A]$.

Let us now define a preorder on constrained atoms representing the notion of "being more constrained".

Definition 3.7 *Let $a_1 = p(\tilde{X}) \leftarrow c_1^v, c_1^u$, $a_2 = p(\tilde{X}) \leftarrow c_2^v, c_2^u$. Then*

$$a_1 \sqsubseteq a_2 \ \ iff \ \ [a_1] \subseteq [a_2]$$

Lemma 3.1 *The relation $\sqsubseteq$ is a preorder.*

Definition 3.8 *We denote by $\equiv$ the equivalence induced by the preorder $\sqsubseteq$ on the set of constrained atoms, ($a_1 \equiv a_2$ iff $a_1 \sqsubseteq a_2$ and $a_2 \sqsubseteq a_1$).*

The following definitions introduce the notions of interpretations base, interpretations and models for $CLP(\mathcal{AD})$ databases.

Definition 3.9 (π-base) *Let DB be a (Π, Σ, V)-program and let $\mathcal{A}$ be the set of all $\Re$-solvable constrained atoms for DB. The π-base of interpretations $\mathcal{B}$ is the quotient set of $\mathcal{A}$ with respect to the equivalence relation $\equiv$.*

The ordering induced by $\sqsubseteq$ on $\mathcal{B}$ will still be denoted by $\sqsubseteq$. For the sake of simplicity A will represent the equivalence class of the constrained atom A.

Definition 3.10 (π-interpretation) *A π-interpretation is any subset of $\mathcal{B}$. $\mathcal{I}$ denotes the set of all the π-interpretations.*

Definition 3.11 (truth) *Let I be an interpretation. A constrained atom $p(\tilde{X}) \leftarrow c^v, c^u$ is true in I iff $[p(\tilde{X}) \leftarrow c^v, c^u] \subseteq [I]$. A rule $H \leftarrow c^v, c^u, B_1, \ldots, B_n$. is true in I iff for each $\Re$-valuation θ such that θ is an $\Re$-solution of c^v, c^u and $\{(H_1 \leftarrow c_1^v, c_1^u)\theta, \ldots, (H_n \leftarrow c_n^v, c_n^u)\theta\} \subseteq [I]$ implies $(H \leftarrow c^v, c_1^v, \ldots, c_n^v, H_1 = B_1, \ldots, H_n = B_n, c^u, c_1^u, \ldots, c_n^u)\theta \subseteq [I]$.*

Definition 3.12 (π-models) *A π-model of a $CLP(\mathcal{AD})$ database DB is any π-interpretation in which all the rules of DB are true.*

3.1 Operational semantics

Now we show the semantics which fully characterizes the operational behavior of a $CLP(\mathcal{AD})$ database. Note that now interpretations and models are based on constrained atoms modulo an equivalence relation which considers equivalent instances of constrained atoms representing the same set of solutions.

Definition 3.13 *Let DB be a $CLP(\mathcal{AD})$ program. Then*

$$\mathcal{O}(DB) = \{p(\tilde{X}) \leftarrow c^v, c^u \in \mathcal{B} \mid p(\tilde{X}) \overset{\Re}{\longmapsto}{}^{*} c^v, c^u \ \}$$

This operational semantics corresponds to SS_3 of [10], that is the set of successful constrained atoms (non-necessarily ground) that are effectively computed starting with a most general constrained atom. Let us now show the soundness and completeness result for $\mathcal{O}(DB)$. The proof of the following theorem is essentially the same of the proof of Theorem 4.11 in [10].

Theorem 3.1 *Let DB be a $CLP(\mathcal{AD})$ program and $Q = c^v, c^u, G_1, \ldots, G_t$ be any goal. Then $Q \overset{\Re}{\longmapsto}{}^{*} c'^v, c'^u$ iff there exist t constrained atoms $H_j \leftarrow c_j^v, c_j^u \in \mathcal{O}(DB), j = 1, \ldots, t$ which share no variables with Q and with each other, such that $c^v \cup c_1^v \cup \ldots \cup c_t^v \cup G_1 = H_1 \cup \ldots \cup G_t = H_t$ and c'^v have the same solutions for the variables in Q and $c^u \cup c_1^u \cup \ldots \cup c_t^u$ and c'^u are consistent and equivalent.*

Example 3.1 *Let us consider $\Pi_{EDB} = \{q, t\}$, $\Pi_{IDB} = \{p, r, s\}$, $\Sigma = \{a, b\}$ and $EDB_3 = \{\mathtt{q(a)}\}$. We denote the semantic domain in "roman" style and the syntactic domain in "*`typewriter`*" style.*

$$\begin{aligned} IDB = \{\ & \mathtt{p(X)} \leftarrow -\mathtt{q(X)}, \mathtt{q(X)} \\ & \mathtt{r(X)} \leftarrow +\mathtt{t(X)}, \mathtt{p(X)} \\ & \mathtt{s(X)} \leftarrow +\mathtt{q(X)}\ \} \end{aligned}$$

$$\begin{aligned} \mathcal{O}(DB_3) = \{\ & p(X) \leftarrow X = a, -q(X) \\ & r(X) \leftarrow X = a, +t(X), -q(X) \\ & s(X) \leftarrow +q(X) \\ & q(X) \leftarrow X = a\ \} \end{aligned}$$

Note that in $\mathcal{O}(DB_3)$ of the above example the query $\mathtt{r(X)}$ produces the answer constraint $\mathtt{X} = \mathtt{a}, +\mathtt{t(X)}, -\mathtt{q(X)}$. The semantics above induces an equivalence relation as shown below. The notion of observable behavior considered is the answer constraint c^v, c^u.

Definition 3.14 *Let DB_1 and DB_2 be $CLP(\mathcal{AD})$ programs. Then $DB_1 \cong DB_2$ iff $\mathcal{O}(DB_1) = \mathcal{O}(DB_2)$.*

3.2 Fixpoint semantics

The fixpoint semantics can also be defined instantiating the general schema for $CLP(X)$. Let us now introduce the immediate consequence operator.

Definition 3.15 *Let DB be a $CLP(\mathcal{AD})$ program and let $J \subseteq \mathcal{B}$.*

$$
\begin{array}{rl}
T_{DB}(J) = \{ & p(\tilde{X}) \leftarrow c'^{v}, c'^{u} \in \mathcal{B} \mid \\
& \exists \text{ a renamed rule } p(\tilde{t}) \leftarrow c_0^v, c_0^u, p_1(\tilde{t_1}), \ldots, p_n(\tilde{t_n}) \text{ in } DB \\
& \exists\, p_i(\tilde{X_i}) \leftarrow c_i^v, c_i^u \in J, 1 \leq i \leq n \text{ which share no variables} \\
& c'^{v} = c_0^v \cup \{\tilde{X_1} = \tilde{t_1}, \ldots, \tilde{X_n} = \tilde{t_n}\} \cup \{c_1^v, \ldots, c_n^v\} \cup \{\tilde{X} = \tilde{t}\} \\
& c'^{u} = c_0^u \cup \{c_1^u, \ldots, c_n^u\} \\
& c'^{v}, c'^{u} \text{ is } \Re\text{-solvable} \\
\} &
\end{array}
$$

The immediate consequence operator is continuous on the cpo $(\mathcal{I}, \subseteq)$ and $\mathcal{F}(DB)$ is the least fixpoint of T_{DB}.

Definition 3.16 *Let DB be a $CLP(\mathcal{AD})$ program. Then the fixpoint semantics $\mathcal{F}(DB)$ of DB is $\mathcal{F}(DB) = T_{DB} \uparrow n$.*

Note that the set Σ is finite and function free, then the least fixpoint is reached in a finite number of steps. In the following we consider the relation between the operational and the fixpoint semantics. The proof of the following lemma mimics the one of Lemma 5.7 in [10].

Lemma 3.2 *Let Q be a query and DB be a $CLP(\mathcal{AD})$ program. $Q \in \mathcal{O}(DB)$ iff there exists a finite n such that $G \in T_{DB} \uparrow n$.*

The proof of the following theorem is essentially the same of the one of Theorem 5.8 in [10].

Theorem 3.2 (equivalence of the operational and the fixpoint semantics) *Let DB be a $CLP(\mathcal{AD})$ program. Then $\mathcal{O}(DB) = \mathcal{F}(DB)$.*

3.3 Model-theoretic semantics

Note that since we are concerned with the algebraic semantics on the particular structure $\Re$ considered as domain of computation, the notion of $\models_{\Re}$ is considered instead of the standard notion of logical consequence $\models$. In the following $\mathcal{M}(DB)$ denotes the model-theoretic semantics of a program DB. It is easy to show that the intersection of a set of π-models is not always a π-model. Therefore in general there exists no least π-model with respect to set inclusion. In the following we will then introduce an ordering $\preceq$ and a lattice structure on π-interpretations which allows to restore the model intersection property. It is possible then to define the model theoretic semantics of a program DB as the greatest lower bound of the set of all π-models of DB.

Definition 3.17 *[10]* (ordering on π-interpretations) *We define a relation $\preceq$ on $\mathcal{I}$ as follows. Let $I_1, I_2 \in \mathcal{I}$. Then*
$I_1 \leq I_2$ *iff* $\forall A_1 \in I_1 \exists A_2 \in I_2$ *such that* $A_1 \sqsubseteq A_2$ *and*
$I_1 \preceq I_2$ *iff* $(I_1 \leq I_2)$ *and* $(I_2 \leq I_1$ *implies* $I_1 \subseteq I_2)$.

The previous definition and the following lemmata extend to the $CLP(X)$ case results given in [9] for logic programs.

Lemma 3.3 *[10] The relation $\preceq$ is an ordering on $\mathcal{I}$. Moreover $(\mathcal{I}, \preceq)$ is a complete lattice.*

Lemma 3.4 *[10] Let M be the set of π-models for a program DB. Then glb(M) (according to $\preceq$ ordering) is a π-model of DB.*

Definition 3.18 *Let DB be a $CLP(\mathcal{AD})$ program. Its* model theoretic semantics *$\mathcal{M}_{DB}$ is defined as $\mathcal{M}_{DB} = glb\{N \mid N$ is a π-model of $DB\}$.*

The proof of the following theorem is similar to the one of Lemma 6.12 in [10].

Theorem 3.3 *Let DB be a $CLP(\mathcal{AD})$ program. Then $\mathcal{O}(DB)$ is a π-model of DB.*

4 The Second Step Semantics

The semantics given in the previous subsection does not consider the information given by the query, the transactional behavior of the query and does not perform the updates computing the new database state. In order to capture those features we define the semantics of a query Q with respect to a database DB by means of $\mathcal{O}(DB)$. First we define the function which computes the new database state by means of the answer update constraints. Note that computing the new database state we change the structure which gives the semantic interpretation of the constraint language. Therefore if we have a sequence of database states $EDB_1; EDB_2; \ldots; EDB_n$ we also have a sequence of structures $\Re_1; \Re_2; \ldots; \Re_n$.

Definition 4.1 *Let EDB_i be the current database state and $c^u = c^u_1, \ldots, c^u_h$ be the answer update constraint. Then the new database state is computed by means of the function $\Delta : 2^{\mathcal{B}^e} \times 2^{C^u} \rightarrow 2^{\mathcal{B}^e}$ as follows:*

$$\Delta(EDB_i, c^u) = (EDB_i \setminus \{p(\tilde{t}) \mid -p(\tilde{t}) \in c^u\}) \cup \{p(\tilde{t}) \mid +p(\tilde{t}) \in c^u\}$$

where $2^{\mathcal{B}^e}$ is the set of possible database states and C^u is the set of possible updates.

Note that the above definition does not consider c^u as a sequence of ground updates but as a set of ground updates. Note that in the Example 3.1 the non-ground constrained atom $\mathtt{s(X)} \leftarrow +\mathtt{q(X)}$ is present in $\mathcal{O}(DB_3)$. Therefore, we use the assumption that our database is safe through invocation by a query. Such assumption ensures us that the updates are always ground. Before introducing the semantics with respect to a query note that in order to model the set of answers, we can consider

$$\mathcal{O}(Q, DB) = \{\langle c_j^v, c_j^u \rangle \mid Q \stackrel{\Re}{\longmapsto}{}^{*} \; c_j^v, c_j^u \;\; \}.$$

We choose the set of answers as semantics because this is the standard approach of the database field. However, once again, our approach is parametric with respect to the cardinality of solutions. In the following we define the semantics of a query Q with respect to the intensional database IDB evaluated in the database state EDB_i. The observable behavior of such semantics is: the set of answers, the (possibly) new state and the result of the query which behaves as a transaction and therefore can be Abort or Commit. Therefore, we define a function $\mathcal{S}$, which maps the query, the intensional database and the current state to the set of answers, the new state and the result of the transaction.

Definition 4.2 *Let $DB_i = IDB \cup EDB_i$ be the database, $Q = c^v, c^u, G_1, \ldots, G_t$ be a query. Then the semantics is defined by means of $\mathcal{S} : GOALS \times IDBS \times 2^{\mathcal{B}^e} \rightarrow 2^{C^v} \times 2^{\mathcal{B}^e} \times Result$. $Q \in GOALS$, $IDB \in IDBS$, $EDB_i \in 2^{\mathcal{B}^e}$, $\{c_1^v, \ldots, c_k^v\} \in 2^{C^v}$ and $Result = \{Abort, Commit\}$. $\mathcal{S}$ is defined as follow*

$$\mathcal{S}[\![Q, IDB]\!]_{EDB_i} = \begin{cases} \langle Answers, EDB_{i+1}, Commit \rangle & \text{if } OK \\ \\ \langle \emptyset, EDB_i, Abort \rangle & otherwise \end{cases}$$

where $Answers = \;\; c^v \; = c'^v \cup \{\tilde{X} = \tilde{t}\}$, EDB_{i+1} is computed by means of $\Delta(EDB_i, \bar{c}^u)$ and the condition OK expresses the fact that the set $\bar{c}^u = \bigcup_j c_j^u \hat{c}_j^v$ is consistent, that is, there are not complementary ground updates. By $c_j^u \hat{c}_j^v$ we denote the ground updates obtained by substituting the variables in c_j^u with the ground terms associated with the variables in c_j^v.

Note that the definition above provides the set of all possible answers to the update query Q and considers all possible updates in order to compute the new database state. This is effectively done only if the set of updates is consistent.

Example 4.1 *Let us consider the $EDB_1 = \{\mathtt{q(a)}, \mathtt{q(b)}\}$, and*

$$\begin{aligned} IDB = \{ \; & \mathtt{s(X)} \leftarrow -\mathtt{q(X)}, -\mathtt{t(X)} \\ & \mathtt{r(X)} \leftarrow +\mathtt{t(X)}, \mathtt{q(X)} \;\; \} \end{aligned}$$

then

$$\begin{aligned} \mathcal{O}(DB_1) = \{\ & s(X) \leftarrow -q(X), -t(X) \\ & r(X) \leftarrow X = a, +t(X) \\ & r(X) \leftarrow X = b, +t(X) \\ & q(X) \leftarrow X = a \\ & q(X) \leftarrow X = b\ \} \end{aligned}$$

Let us consider the query $Q_1 = \mathtt{r(X)}$*, then*

$$\mathcal{S}[\![G_1, IDB]\!]_{EDB_1} = \langle\{\{X = a\}, \{X = b\}\}, EDB_2, Commit\rangle$$

where $EDB_2 = \{\mathtt{q(a)}, \mathtt{q(b)}, \mathtt{t(a)}, \mathtt{t(b)}\}$.

$$\begin{aligned} \mathcal{O}(DB_2) = \{\ & s(X) \leftarrow -q(X), -t(X) \\ & r(X) \leftarrow X = a, +t(X) \\ & r(X) \leftarrow X = b, +t(X) \\ & q(X) \leftarrow X = a \\ & q(X) \leftarrow X = b \\ & t(X) \leftarrow X = a \\ & t(X) \leftarrow X = b\ \} \end{aligned}$$

Let us consider the query $Q_2 = \mathtt{X} = \mathtt{a}, \mathtt{s(X)}$*, then*

$$\mathcal{S}[\![Q_2, IDB]\!]_{EDB_2} = \langle\{X = a\}, EDB_3, Commit\rangle$$

where $EDB_3 = \{\mathtt{q(b)}, \mathtt{t(b)}\}$.

$$\begin{aligned} \mathcal{O}(DB_3) = \{\ & s(X) \leftarrow -q(X), -t(X) \\ & r(X) \leftarrow X = b, +t(X) \\ & q(X) \leftarrow X = b \\ & t(X) \leftarrow X = b\ \} \end{aligned}$$

Let us consider the query $Q_3 = \mathtt{X} = \mathtt{b}, \mathtt{r(X)}$*, then*

$$\mathcal{S}[\![Q_3, IDB]\!]_{EDB_3} = \langle\emptyset, EDB_3, Abort\rangle$$

Note that the set oriented behavior holds for queries and for updates as well. It is very useful with respect to updates to insert/delete a set of ground facts. This feature is present in $\mathcal{LDL}$. We consider two $CLP(\mathcal{AD})$ programs with respect to a query, its equivalence is a straightforward consequence of Definition 3.14 but also between queries with respect to a program. The notion of observable behavior considered in both cases is the set of variable constraints, the next database state and the result of the update query.

Definition 4.3 *Let IDB and IDB′ be CLP(AD) programs, EDB_i any database state and Q be any query. Then*

$$IDB \cong_Q IDB' \ iff \ \forall EDB_i, \mathcal{S}[\![Q, IDB]\!]_{EDB_i} = \mathcal{S}[\![Q, IDB']\!]_{EDB_i}$$

Note that with the above assumption the set of all possible database states is finite. Thus the set of possible answer constraints is finite and therefore it is possible to decide in a finite time the above equivalence.

Definition 4.4 *Let IDB be a CLP(AD) program, EDB_i any database state and Q_1, Q_2 be two queries. Then*

$$Q_1 \cong_{IDB} Q_2 \ iff \ \forall EDB_i, \mathcal{S}[\![Q_1, IDB]\!]_{EDB_i} = \mathcal{S}[\![Q_2, IDB]\!]_{EDB_i}$$

Note that the equivalence notion between programs can be used for optimizations based on program transformation, while the equivalence notion between queries can be useful for optimization based on query transformations, that is the query can be transformed into another one preserving its behavior.

5 Related work

In the following we consider some examples written in DatalogA, $\mathcal{LDL}$, Glue-Nail and we rewrite them in $CLP(\mathcal{AD})$ to show that they can be captured within our approach.

Example 5.1 *Let us consider the intensional database written in DatalogA and taken from [16]. The query* `fireEmp` *fires all the employees who earn more than their managers.*

```
mgr(X,Y) ← emp(X,M,S),mgr(M,Y)
mgr(X,Y) ← emp(X,Y,S)
fireEmp  ← emp(N,X,S1),mgr(N,M),emp(M,Y,S2),
           S1 > S2,−emp(N,M,S1)
```

the equivalent intensional database written in $CLP(\mathcal{AD})$ language is

```
mgr(X,Y) ← emp(X,M,S),mgr(M,Y)
mgr(X,Y) ← emp(X,Y,S)
fireEmp  ← −emp(N,M,S1),emp(N,X,S1),mgr(N,M)
           emp(M,Y,S2),S1 > S2
```

The query `fireEmp` *fires all the employees who earn more than their managers due to the set oriented feature.*

Example 5.2 *Let us consider the intensional database written in $\mathcal{LDL}$ and taken from [17]. The program calls for increasing salaries of employees in the database department by* 10%.

$$\begin{aligned}\texttt{raise(db)} \leftarrow\ & \texttt{eds(N, db, Sal)},\\ & \texttt{NewSal} = \texttt{Sal} * 1.1,\\ & -\texttt{eds(N, db, Sal)},\\ & +\texttt{eds(N, db, NewSal)}.\end{aligned}$$

the equivalent intensional database written in CLP($\mathcal{AD}$) language is

$$\begin{aligned}\texttt{raise(db)} \leftarrow\ & -\texttt{eds(N, db, Sal)}, +\texttt{eds(N, db, NewSal)}\\ & \texttt{eds(N, db, Sal)}, \texttt{NewSal} = \texttt{Sal} * 1.1\end{aligned}$$

where the insertions and deletions are unordered. The updates are related with the information in the body of the rule. For example `eds(N, db, Sal), NewSal= Sal* 1.1`, *provides the bindings for the various arguments of the delete and insert operations. This is close to the marking and updates phases of $\mathcal{LDL}$.*

In order to ensure that the execution order is immaterial for the meaning of the conjunct, $\mathcal{LDL}$ requires that the programs satisfy the Church-Rosser property, i.e., regardless of the order of evaluation for the atoms in the body of the rule the resulting state of the program must be the same. Indeed if the $\mathcal{LDL}$ programs satisfy this property then its semantics can be defined formally, otherwise the intended meaning is the left-to-right valuation of the atoms in the body of the rules. For example considering a left-to-right order of execution the final "observable" (the state, for $\mathcal{LDL}$) of +p(a), p(X), −p(b) is different from the observable of −p(b), +p(a), p(X). In our case there is no order among update atoms, (nor among the ordinary atoms) which are all evaluated in the new current state. CLP($\mathcal{AD}$) has no syntactic restrictions on the form of a program.

Example 5.3 *Let us consider the assignment statement written in Glue-Nail and taken from [7].*

$$\texttt{r(X, Y)+} = \texttt{s(X, W), t(f(W, X), Y)}$$

The effect of executing this statement is that the tuple (X, Y) has to be added to relation `r` *if there is a tuple* `(X,W)` *in relation* `s`, *and a tuple* `(f(W,X),Y)` *in relation* `t`. *All such* `(X,Y)` *tuples have to be added to relation* `r`. *Note that Glue assignment statements are not logical rules; rather, they are operational directives. The equivalent statement can be written in CLP($\mathcal{AD}$) as a query*

$$\texttt{+r(X, Y), s(X, W), t(f(W, X), Y)}$$

where the set of tuples are computed inside the body of the query, i.e. the relations `s(X,W), t(f(W,X),Y)`.

6 Conclusions

In this paper we have proposed an approach to formalize elementary updates in a logic-based language for database by means of an instance of the $CLP(X)$ schema. The semantics, modeling the computed answer constraints, represents the building block used to define the semantics of a query with respect to a program. This last semantics, based on a rich notion of observable, provides a unifying linguistic and semantic framework to model the set oriented features of deductive database languages, updates to the extensional database and the transactional behavior of a query. Some equivalence notions between programs and queries are considered. Our approach has several interesting properties.

- Provides a framework for querying and updating logic programs, characterizing the operational behavior, and inducing equivalence relations.
- Church-Rosser property or other syntactic restrictions are not needed for defining a clear semantics.
- Set oriented features, with respect to updates and queries are provided in a natural way.
- The close relationship with other deductive database languages shows that our framework can capture relevant features of these languages with a well founded semantics.

We are currently investigating the extension of the above language to introduce integrity constraints, the updates of intensional relations and the modular construction for large deductive databases.

References

1. S. Abiteboul. Updates, a New Frontier. In M. Gyssens, J.Paredaens, and D. Van Gucht, editors, *Proc. Second Int'l Conf. on Database Theory*, volume 326 of *Lecture Notes in Computer Science*, pages 1–18. Springer-Verlag, Berlin, 1988.
2. K.R. Apt. Introduction to Logic Programming. In J. Van Leeuwen, editor, *Handbook of Theoretical Computer Science*. Elsevier, Amsterdam and The MIT Press, Cambridge, 1990. Volume B: Formal Models and Semantics.
3. E. Bertino, M. Martelli, and D. Montesi. A Incremental Semantics for CLP(AD). To appear in *Fourth Italian Conference on Theoretical Computer Science*, 1992.
4. S. Ceri, G. Gottlob, and L. Tanca. *Logic Programming and Databases*. Springer-Verlag, Berlin, 1990.
5. S. Ceri, G. Gottlob, and L. Tanca. What You Always Wanted to Know About Datalog - And Never Dared to Ask. *IEEE Tran. on Knowledge and Data Eng.*, 1(1):146– 164, March 1989.
6. A. Colmerauer. Opening the Prolog-III universe. BYTE magazine, vol. 12, n. 9, 1987.
7. M. A. Derr, G. Phipps, and K. A. Ross. Glue-Nail: A Deductive Database System. In *Proc. Int'l Conf. ACM on Management of Data*, pages 308–317, 1991.
8. M. Dincbas et al. The Constraint Logic Programming Language CHIP. In *Proc. Int'l Conf. on Fifth Generation Computer Systems*. Institute for New Generation Computer Technology, 1988.

9. M. Falaschi, G. Levi, M. Martelli, and C. Palamidessi. A model-theoretic reconstruction of the operational semantics of logic programs. Technical Report TR 32/89, Dipartimento di Informatica, Università di Pisa, 1989. To appear in *Information and Computation*.
10. M. Gabbrielli and G. Levi. Modeling answer constraints in Contraint Logic Programs. In K. Furukawa, editor, *Proc. Eighth Int'l Conf. on Logic Programming*, pages 238–252. The MIT Press, Cambridge, Mass., 1991.
11. J. Jaffar and J.-L. Lassez. Constraint Logic Programming. In *Proc. Fourteenth Annual ACM Symp. on Principles of Programming Languages*, pages 111–119. ACM, New York, USA, 1987.
12. J. Jaffar and J.-L. Lassez. Constraint Logic Programming. Technical report, Department of Computer Science, Monash University, June 1986.
13. J. Lassez and S. Michaylor. Methdology and implementation of a CLP system. In J.-L. Lassez, editor, *Proc. Fourth Int'l Conf. on Logic Programming.* The MIT Press, Cambridge, Mass., 1987.
14. J.W. Lloyd. *Foundations of logic programming.* Springer-Verlag, Berlin, 1987. Second edition.
15. S. Manchanda and D. S. Warren. A Logic-based Language for Database Updates. In J. Minker, editor, *Foundation of Deductive Databases and Logic Programming*, pages 363–394. Morgan-Kaufmann, 1988.
16. S. Naqvi and R. Krishnamurthy. Database Updates in Logic Programming. In *Proc. of the ACM Symposium on Principles of Database Systems*, pages 251–262. ACM, New York, USA, 1988.
17. S. Naqvi and S. Tsur. *A Logic Language for Data and Knowledge Bases.* Computer Science Press, 1989.
18. V. A. Saraswat, M. Rinard, and P. Panangaden. Semantic foundations of concurrent constraint programming. In *Proc. Eighteenth Annual ACM Symp. on Principles of Programming Languages.* ACM, New York, USA, 1991.
19. M. Winslett. A Framework for Comparison of Updates Semantics. In *Proc. of the ACM Symposium on Principles of Database Systems*, pages 315–324. ACM, New York, USA, 1988.

Logic Programming with Functions over Order-Sorted Feature Terms

Hassan Aït-Kaci and Andreas Podelski

Digital Equipment Corporation, Paris Research Laboratory
85, avenue Victor Hugo, 92500 Rueil-Malmaison, France

{hak,podelski}@prl.dec.com

Abstract. LIFE is an experimental programming language proposing to integrate logic programming, functional programming, and object-oriented programming. It replaces first-order terms with ψ-terms, data structures which allow computing with partial information. These are approximation structures denoting sets of values. LIFE further enriches the expressiveness of ψ-terms with functional dependency constraints. Whereas LIFE's relations defined as Horn-clauses use ψ-term unification for parameter-passing, LIFE's functions use ψ-term matching (*i.e.*, one-way unification). We explain the meaning and use of functions in LIFE declaratively as solving partial information constraints. These constraints do not attempt to generate their solutions but behave as demons filtering out anything else. In this manner, LIFE functions act as declarative coroutines.

> The paradox of culture is that language [...] is too linear, not comprehensive enough, too slow, too limited, too constrained, too unnatural, too much a product of its own evolution, and too artificial. This means that [man] must constantly keep in mind the limitations language places upon him.
>
> EDWARD T. HALL, *Beyond Culture*.

1 Introduction

This paper is an informal, albeit precise and detailed, overview of the operational mechanism underlying functional reduction in the context of a logic programming framework. It is formulated using order-sorted feature terms as data structures seen as constraints. This mechanism and data structure are used in the language LIFE [5].

1.1 The task

LIFE extends the computational paradigm of Logic Programming in two essential ways:

- by using a data structure richer than that provided by first-order constructor terms; and,
- by allowing interpretable functional expressions as *bona fide* terms.

The first extension is based on ψ-terms which are attributed partially-ordered sorts denoting sets of objects [1, 2]. In particular, ψ-terms generalize first-order constructor terms in their rôle as data structures in that they are endowed with a unification operation denoting type intersection. This gives an elegant means to incorporate a calculus of multiple inheritance into symbolic programming. Importantly, the denotation-as-value of constructor terms is replaced by the denotation-as-approximation of ψ-terms. A consequence of this is that the notion of fully defined element, or ground term, is no longer available. Hence, such familiar tools as variable substitutions, instantiation, unification, *etc.*, must be reformulated in the new setting [5].

The second extension deals with building into the unification operation a means to reduce functional expressions using definitions of interpretable symbols over data patterns.[1] Our basic idea is that unification is no longer seen as an atomic operation by the resolution rule. Indeed, since unification amounts to normalizing a conjunction of equations, and since this normalization process commutes with resolution, these equations may be left in a normal form that is not a fully solved form. In particular, if an equation involves a functional expression whose arguments are not sufficiently instantiated to match a ***definiens*** of the function in question, it is simply left untouched. Resolution may proceed until the arguments are ***proven*** to match a definition from the accumulated constraints in the context [3]. This simple idea turns out invaluable in practice. Here are a few benefits.

- Such non-declarative heresies as the *is* predicate in Prolog and the *freeze* meta-predicate in some of its extensions [14, 10] are not needed.
- Functional computations are determinate and do not incur the overhead of the search strategy needed by logic programming.
- Higher-order functions are easy to return or pass as arguments since functional variables can be bound to partially applied functions.
- Functions can be called before the arguments are known, freeing the programmer from having to know what the data dependencies are.
- It provides a powerful search-space pruning facility by changing "generate-and-test" search into demon-controlled "test-and-generate" search.
- Communication with the external world is made simple and clean [9].
- More generally, it allows concurrent computation. Synchronization is obtained by checking entailment [13, 15].

There are two orthogonal dimensions to elucidate regarding the use of functions in LIFE:

- characterizing functions as approximation-driven coroutines; and,
- constructing a higher-order model of LIFE approximation structures.

This present article is concerned only with the first item, and therefore considers the case of first-order rules defining partial functions over ψ-terms.

1.2 The method

The most direct way to explain the issue is with an example. In LIFE, one can define functions as usual; say:

$$fact(0) \rightarrow 1.$$
$$fact(N : int) \rightarrow N * fact(N - 1).$$

[1] Several patterns specifying a same function may possibly have overlapping denotations and therefore the order of the specified patterns define an implicit priority, as is usual in functional programming using first-order patterns (*e.g.*, [12]).

More interesting is the possibility to compute with partial information. For example:

minus(*negint*) → *posint*.
minus(*posint*) → *negint*.
minus(*zero*) → *zero*.

Let us assume that the symbols *int*, *posint*, *negint*, and *zero* have been defined as sorts with the approximation ordering such that *posint*, *zero*, *negint* are pairwise incompatible subsorts of the sort *int* (*i.e.*, $posint \wedge zero = \bot, negint \wedge zero = \bot, posint \wedge negint = \bot$). This is declared in LIFE as $int := \{posint; zero; negint\}$. Furthermore, we assume the sort definition $posint := \{posodd; poseven\}$; *i.e.*, *posodd* and *poseven* are subsorts of *posint* and mutually incompatible.

The LIFE query $Y = minus(X : poseven)$? will return $Y = negint$. The sort *poseven* of the actual parameter is incompatible with the sort *negint* of the formal parameter of the first rule defining the function *minus*. Therefore, that rule is skipped. The sort *poseven* is more specific than the sort *posint* of the formal parameter of the second rule. Hence, that rule is applicable and yields the result $Y = negint$.

The LIFE query $Y = minus(X : string)$ will fail. Indeed, the sort *string* is incompatible with the sort of the formal parameter of every rule defining *minus*.

Thus, in order to determine which of the rules, if any, defining the function in a given functional expression will be applied, two tests are necessary:

- verify whether the actual parameter is more specific than or equal to the formal parameter;
- verify whether the actual parameter is at all compatible with the formal parameter.

What happens if both of these tests fail? Consider the query consisting of the conjunction:

$Y = minus(X : int), X = minus(zero)$?

for example. Like Prolog, LIFE follows a left-to-right resolution strategy and examines the equation $Y = minus(X : int)$ first. However, both foregoing tests fail and deciding which rule to use among those defining *minus* is inconclusive. Indeed, the sort *int* of the actual parameter in that call is neither more specific than, nor incompatible with, the sort *negint* of the first rule's formal parameter. Therefore, the function call will *residuate* on the variable X. This means that the functional evaluation is suspended pending more information on X. The second goal in the query is treated next. There, it is found that the actual parameter is incompatible with the first two rules and is the same as the last rule's. This allows reduction and binds X to *zero*. At this point, X has been instantiated and therefore the residual equation pending on X can be reexamined. Again, as before, a redex is found for the last rule and yields $Y = zero$.

The two tests above can in fact be worded in a more general setting. Viewing data structures as constraints, "more specific" is simply a particular case of constraint entailment. We will say that a constraint *disentails* another whenever their conjunction is unsatisfiable; or, equivalently, whenever it entails its negation. In particular, first-order matching is deciding entailment between constraints consisting of equations over first-order terms. Similarly, deciding unifiability of first-order terms amounts to deciding "compatibility" in the sense used informally above.

The suspension/resumption mechanism illustrated in our example is repeated each time a residuated actual parameter becomes more instantiated from the context; *i.e.*, solving other parts of the query. Therefore, it is most beneficial for a practical algorithm testing entailment and disentailment to be incremental. This means that, upon resumption, the test for the instantiated actual parameter builds upon partial results obtained by the previous test. One outcome of the results presented in this paper is that it is possible to build such a test; namely, an algorithm deciding simultaneously two problems in an incremental manner—entailment and disentailment. The technique that we have devised to do that is called *relative simplification* of constraints.

This technique is relevant in the general framework of concurrent constraint logic programming, represented by, *e.g.*, the guarded Horn-clause scheme of Maher [13], Concurrent Constraint Programming (CCP) [15], and Kernel Andorra Prolog (KAP) [11]. These schemes are parameterized with respect to an abstract class of constraint systems. An incremental test for entailment and disentailment between constraints is needed for advanced control mechanisms such as delaying, coroutining, synchronization, committed choice, and deep constraint propagation. LIFE is formally an instance of this scheme, namely a CLP language using a constraint system based on order-sorted feature structures [6]. It employs a related, but limited, suspension strategy to enforce deterministic functional application. Roughly, these systems are concurrent thanks to a new effective discipline for procedure parameter-passing that we could describe as "call-by-constraint-entailment" (as opposed to Prolog's call-by-unification).

In this paper, we recall the basic terminology and notation of LIFE, unification and matching, and we sketch the essence of relative simplification. Formal material rewording everything in rigorous terms can be found in [4]. Nevertheless, in the final section we include the formal version of the simplification rules specifying the algorithms discussed informally in this paper, and state the theoretical results proven in [4].

2 LIFE Data Structures

The data objects of LIFE are ψ-terms. They are structures built out of sorts and features. ψ-Terms are partially ordered as data descriptions to reflect more specific information content. A ψ-term is said to *match* another one if it is a more specific description. For first-order terms, a matching substitution is a variable binding which makes the more general term equal to the more specific one. This notion is not appropriate here. Unification is introduced as taking the greatest lower bound (GLB) with respect to this ordering.

2.1 Sorts and features

Sorts are symbols. They are meant to denote sets of values. Here are a few examples: *person*, *int*, *true*, 3.5, $\perp$, $\top$. Note that a value is assimilated to a singleton sort. We call S the set of all sorts. They come with a partial ordering $\leq$, meant to reflect set inclusion.[2] For example,

- $\perp \leq$ *john* $\leq$ *man* $\leq$ *person* $\leq \top$;
- $\perp \leq$ *true* $\leq$ *bool* $\leq \top$;
- $\perp \leq 2 \leq$ *poseven* $\leq$ *int* $\leq \top$.

[2] Sorts and their relative ordering are specified by the user.

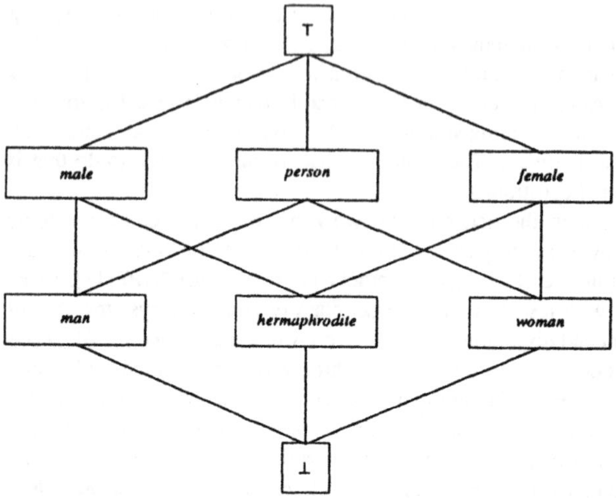

Fig. 1. A partial order of sorts

The sorts $\top$ (top) and $\bot$ (bottom) are respectively the greatest and the least sort in $\mathcal{S}$ and denote respectively the whole domain of interpretation and the empty set.

Sorts also come with a GLB operation $\wedge$. For example,

- $person \wedge male = man$;
- $male \wedge female = hermaphrodite$;
- $man \wedge woman = \bot$;

etc., which can be visualized as shown in Figure 1. We will refer back to this figure in several examples to come.

Features (or attribute labels) are also symbols and used to build ψ-terms by attaching attributes to sorts. The set of feature symbols is called $\mathcal{F}$. We will use words and natural numbers as features. The latter are handy to specify attributes by positions as subterms in first-order terms. Examples of feature symbols are *age*, *spouse*, 1, 2.

2.2 ψ-Terms

Basic ψ-terms are the simplest form of ψ-terms. They are:

- variables; *e.g.*, $X, Y, Z, \ldots$
- sorts; *e.g.*, *person*, *int*, *true*, 3.5, $\top$, …
- tagged sorts; *e.g.*, $X : \top,\; Y : person, \ldots$

Stand-alone variables are always implicitly sorted by $\top$, and stand-alone sorts are always implicitly tagged by some variable occurring nowhere else. Thus, one might say that a basic ψ-term is always of the form *variable* : *sort*.

Features are used to build up more complex ψ-terms. Thus, the following ψ-term is obtained from the ψ-term *person* by attaching the feature *age* typed by the ψ-term *int*:[3]

$$X : person(age \Rightarrow I : int).$$

The sort at the root of a ψ-term, here *person*, is called its *principal sort*. A ψ-term can be seen as a record structure. Features correspond to field identifiers, and fields are, in turn, associated to ψ-terms. These are flexible records in the sense that variably many fields may be attached to the principal sort. For example, we can augment the ψ-term above with another feature:

$$\begin{aligned} X : person(&age \Rightarrow I : int, \\ &spouse \Rightarrow Y : person(age \Rightarrow J : int)). \end{aligned}$$

This ψ-term denotes the set of all objects X of sort *person* (in the intended domain), whose value I under the function *age* is of sort *int*, whose value Y under the function *spouse* is of sort *person*, and the value J of Y under the function *age* is of sort *int*.

The following ψ-term is more specific, in the sense that the above set becomes smaller if one further requires that the values I and J coincide; namely, $age(X) = age(spouse(X))$:

$$\begin{aligned} X : person(&age \Rightarrow I : int, \\ &spouse \Rightarrow Y : person(age \Rightarrow I)). \end{aligned}$$

It denotes the subset of individuals in the previous set of *person*'s whose age is the same as their spouse's. This ψ-term uses a coreference thanks to sharing the variable I. The next ψ-term is even more specific, since it contains an additional (circular) coreference; namely, $X = spouse(spouse(X))$:

$$\begin{aligned} X : person(&age \Rightarrow I : int, \\ &spouse \Rightarrow Y : person(age \Rightarrow I, \\ &\qquad spouse \Rightarrow X)). \end{aligned}$$

It denotes the set of all individuals in the previous set whose spouse's spouse is the individual in question. Note that only variables that are used as coreference tags need to be put explicitly; *i.e.*, those that occur at least twice.

To be well-formed, the syntax of a ψ-term requires three conditions to be satisfied: (1) the sort $\perp$ may not occur; (2) at most one occurrence of each variable has a sort; (3) all the features attached to a sort are pairwise different. These conditions are necessary to ensure that a ψ-term expresses coherent information. For example, $X : man(friend \Rightarrow X : woman)$, violating Condition (2), is not a ψ-term, but $X : man(friend \Rightarrow X)$ is.

As for ordering, a ψ-term is made more specific through:

- sort refinement; *e.g.*, $X : int \leq U : \top$;
- adding features typed by ψ-terms; *e.g.*, $X : \top(age \Rightarrow int) \leq U : \top$;
- adding coreference; *e.g.*, $X : \top(likes \Rightarrow X) \leq U : \top(likes \Rightarrow V)$.

Note that, as record structures, ψ-terms are both record types and record instances. They, in addition, permit *mixing* type and value information. Finally, they also permit constraining records with equations on their parts.

[3] To illustrate the ψ-term ordering, we will give a decreasing matching sequence of ψ-terms going from more general to more specific ones.

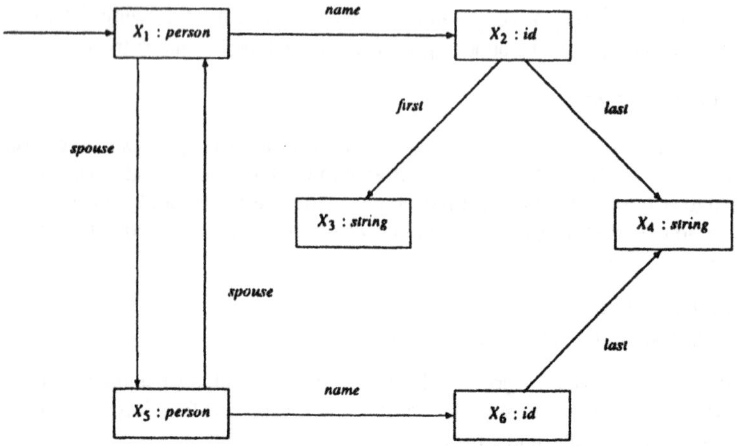

Fig. 2. An OSF-Graph

2.3 ψ-Terms as graphs

There is a straightforward representation of a ψ-term as a rooted directed graph. Let us assume that every variable is explicitly sorted (if necessary, by the sort $\top$) and every sort is explicitly tagged (if necessary, by a single-occurrence variable). The nodes of the graph are the variables, their labels are the corresponding sorts; for every feature mapping one variable X to another one Y there is an arc (X, Y) labeled by that feature. One node is marked as the root (whose label is called the root sort or the principal sort of the ψ-term).

For example, the ψ-term:

$$\begin{aligned} X_1 : person(name \Rightarrow X_2 : id(&first \Rightarrow X_3 : string, \\ &last \Rightarrow X_4 : string), \\ spouse \Rightarrow X_5 : person(&name \Rightarrow X_6 : id(last \Rightarrow X_4), \\ &spouse \Rightarrow X_1)). \end{aligned}$$

corresponds to the OSF-graph shown in Figure 2.

2.4 ψ-Terms as values

One particular interpretation is readily available for ψ-terms. Namely, the syntactic interpretation Ψ whose domain is the set of all ψ-terms. Note that ψ-terms have a dual personality. They are syntactic objects (graphs) representing the values of the domain of Ψ, *and* they also are types which denote sets. In the particular case of the interpretation Ψ, they denote subsets of the domain of Ψ; *i.e.*, sets of ψ-terms. We shall see this dual view does not lead to paradox, *au contraire*.

In the interpretation Ψ, a sort $s \in \mathcal{S}$ denotes the set of all ψ-terms whose root sort is a subsort of s. A feature $\ell \in \mathcal{F}$ denotes the function mapping a ψ-term to its sub-ψ-term under that feature, or to $\top$, if there is none.

Thus, a sort denotes the set of all ψ-term values which, as ψ-term types, are more specific than the basic ψ-term s. In fact, it is possible to show that in general a ψ-term denotes the set of all ψ-terms which are more specific than the ψ-term itself. This is the "ψ-terms as filters" principle established in [5]. It yields directly the fact that the partial ordering $\leq$ on ψ-terms is exactly set-inclusion of the sets denoted by the ψ-terms in the ψ-term domain.

2.5 Feature trees as values

We obtain two other examples of OSF-algebras when we "compress" the ψ-term domain by identifying values. In a first step, we say that two ψ-terms which are equal up to variable renaming represent the same value of the domain, or: two isomorphic graphs are identified. We call the OSF-algebra hereby obtained Ψ_0.

It is well known that a rooted directed graph represents a unique rational tree obtained by unfolding. Hence, unfolding an OSF-graph yields what we call a feature tree. Such a tree is one whose nodes are labeled with sorts and whose edges are labeled with features. Therefore, we can also identify ψ-terms which represent the same rational tree. The domain hereby obtained is essentially the feature tree structure $\mathcal{T}$ introduced first in [7] and [8].

2.6 Unification of ψ-terms

We say that ψ_1 is unifiable with ψ_2 if $\psi_1 \wedge \psi_2 \neq \bot$; *i.e.*, if there exist ψ-terms with non-empty denotations which are more specific than both ψ_1 and ψ_2. One can show that then there exists a unique (up to variable renaming) ψ-term ψ which is the most general of all these, the 'greatest lower bound' (GLB) of ψ_1 and ψ_2, written $\psi = \psi_1 \wedge \psi_2$.

For the set denotation of ψ-terms, $\wedge$ is exactly set intersection. An important result illustrating the significance of the ψ-term interpretation Ψ is that ψ_1 is unifiable with ψ_2 if and only if the intersection of the two sets denoted by ψ_1 and ψ_2 in the ψ-term domain is non-empty.

2.7 Constraints and ψ-terms

We also view a ψ-term logically as a constraint formula by flattening it into what we call its *dissolved form*. For ease of notation, we shall write $(X : \psi)$ to indicate that the root variable of the ψ-term ψ is X.

More precisely, the ψ-term $X : s(\ell_1 \Rightarrow (X_1 : \psi_1), \ldots, \ell_n \Rightarrow (X_n : \psi_n))$ corresponds to the conjunction of the constraint $X : s \;\&\; X.\ell_1 \doteq X_1 \;\&\; X.\ell_n \doteq X_n$ and of the constraints corresponding to $\psi_1, \ldots, \psi_n$. A basic ψ-term $X : s$ corresponds to the sort constraint $X : s$. For example, the ψ-term:

$$\begin{aligned} \psi \;\equiv\; X : person(&likes \Rightarrow X,\\ &age \Rightarrow Y : int) \end{aligned}$$

is identified with the constraint:

$$\psi \equiv X : person \;\&\; X.age \doteq Y \;\&\; Y : int \;\&\; X.likes \doteq X.$$

Thus, the constraint ψ is a conjunction of atomic sort constraints of the form $X : s$ and atomic feature constraints of the form $X.\ell \doteq Y$. The interpretation of the sort and feature constraints over the intended domain is straightforward, given that sorts are interpreted as subsets of the domain and features as unary functions over the domain.

A value lies in the set denoted by the ψ-term ψ in an interpretation $\mathcal{I}$ if and only if the constraint $X \doteq Z \;\&\; \psi$ is satisfiable in the interpretation $\mathcal{I}$, with that value assigned to the variable X, and Z being the root variable of ψ. All variables of ψ are implicitly existentially quantified. This reflects our view of ψ-terms as set-denoting types.

2.8 Rules for Unification

Unifying $(X_1 : \psi_1)$ and $(X_2 : \psi_2)$ amounts to deciding satisfiability of the conjunction $\psi_1 \;\&\; \psi_2 \;\&\; X_1 \doteq X_2$. Thus, the unification algorithm can be specified in terms of constraint normalization rules. A constraint containing the conjunction over the line is rewritten into an *equivalent* constraint by replacing this conjunction by the constraint under the line. We only need four rules that are illustrated schematically on an example below. (Refer to the sorts of Figure 1.)

Equality:

$$\frac{\ldots X : person \;\;\&\;\; U : male \;\;\&\;\; U \doteq X \;\ldots}{\ldots X : person \;\;\&\;\; X : male \;\;\&\;\; U \doteq X \;\ldots}$$

Sorts:

$$\frac{\ldots X : person \;\;\&\;\; X : male \;\ldots}{\ldots X : man \;\ldots}$$

Features:

$$\frac{\ldots X.likes \doteq Y \;\;\&\;\; X.likes \doteq V \;\ldots}{\ldots X.likes \doteq Y \;\;\&\;\; V \doteq Y \;\ldots}$$

Clash:

$$\frac{\ldots X : \bot \;\ldots}{\bot}$$

One can show that a constraint is satisfiable if and only if it is normalized to a constraint different from the *false* constraint $\bot$. If we identify every constraint containing a sort constraint of the form $X : \bot$ with the *false* constraint, we omit the the clash rule.

In particular, the ψ-terms $(X_1 : \psi_1)$ and $(X_2 : \psi_2)$ are unifiable if and only if $\psi_1 \;\&\; \psi_2 \;\&\; X_1 \doteq X_2$ is normalized into a constraint ψ different from $\bot$. This constraint ψ corresponds, apart from its equalities (between variables), to the ψ-term (unique up to variable renaming) $\psi_1 \wedge \psi_2$.

3 Relative Simplification

We use the framework of first-order logic to transform the combined entailment/disentailment problem into one that can be solved by the relative simplification algorithm.

3.1 Matching and entailment

In the remainder of this paper, when considering the matching problem $\psi_1 \leq \psi_2$, we will refer to ψ_1 as the actual parameter and its variables (named $X, Y, Z, \ldots$) as global, and to ψ_2 as the formal parameter and its variables (named $U, V, W, \ldots$) as local.

In the Concurrent Constraint Logic Programming framework, the matching problem generalizes to the entailment problem; namely, whether the actual constraint, also called context, entails the formal constraint, also called guard [13, 15].

First observe that, for example, the first-order term $t_1 = f(Z, f(Y, Y))$ matches the term $t_2 = f(W, V)$, and that the implication:

$$\forall X \forall Y \forall Z \; (X \doteq f(Z, f(Y, Y)) \rightarrow \exists U \exists V \exists W \; (X \doteq U \;\&\; U \doteq f(W, V)))$$

is valid. Generally, the term t_1 matches t_2 (noted $t_1 \leq t_2$) if and only the implication $X \doteq t_1 \rightarrow \exists U \exists V \; (X \doteq U \;\&\; U \doteq t_2)$ is valid, where V stands for all variables of t_2. More shortly, $X \doteq t_1$ entails $X \doteq U \;\&\; U \doteq t_2$.

Note, however, that there is an essential difference between ψ-term matching and first-order term matching. For example, the term $f(a, a)$ matches the term $f(V, V)$. This is true because first order terms denote individuals. This is no longer true in LIFE. For example, the ψ-term $X : f(1 \Rightarrow Y : int, 2 \Rightarrow Z : int)$ does not match the ψ-term $U : f(1 \Rightarrow V, 2 \Rightarrow V)$ as two occurrences of the same sort does not entail that the individuals in that sort be equal. Therefore, $X : s(1 \Rightarrow \psi_1, 2 \Rightarrow \psi_2)$ is less specific than the ψ-term $U : s(1 \Rightarrow V, 2 \Rightarrow V)$ only if the root variables of ψ_1 and ψ_2 are identical (or bound together).

This does *not* mean that values and operations on them are not available in LIFE.[4] What the above point illustrates is that to recognize that a sort is a fully determined value, and hence to enforce identity of all its distinct occurrences, one needs this information declared explicitly, in effect adding an axiom to the formalization of such sorts. So-declared *extensional* sorts can then be treated accordingly thanks to an additional inference rule (being a minimal non-bottom sort is not sufficient). Without this rule, however, equality of distinct occurrences cannot be entailed and the behavior illustrated is the only correct one. The point of this paper being independent if this issue, we shall omit this additional rule.

The fact that $(X : \psi_1) \leq (U : \psi_2)$, *i.e.*, the ψ-term $(X : \psi_1)$ matches the ψ-term $(U : \psi_2)$, translates into the fact that the corresponding constraint ψ_1 *entails* the constraint $\psi_2 \;\&\; U \doteq X$. This means that the implication $\psi_1 \rightarrow \exists U, V, W \ldots \; \psi_2 \;\&\; U \doteq X$ is valid. Here, $\exists U, V, W \ldots$ indicates that all local variables are existentially quantified. The global variables are universally quantified.

3.2 Entailment of general constraints

We will now give a precise explanation of a fact which is well-known for constructor terms. An actual parameter t_1 matches a formal parameter t_2 if and only if the unification of the two terms binds only variables of t_2, but no variable of t_1. In other words, only local, but no global, variables are instantiated.

[4] Of course, one can use actual values of sort *int*, *real*, or *string* in expressions with their usual operations as in most programming languages. In fact, LIFE provides the additional freedom to write such expressions mixing actual values or their sort approximations *int*, *real*, or *string*. Such expressions are either solved by local propagation or *residuate* pending further refinements of the non-value sorts into values.

The unification of the term $t_1 = f(Z, f(Y, Y))$ and the term $t_2 = f(W, V)$ yields the variable bindings $W \doteq Z$ and $V \doteq f(Y, Y)$. On the other hand, the conjunction:

$$X \doteq f(Z, f(Y, Y)) \ \& \ U \doteq X \ \& \ U \doteq f(W, V)$$

is equivalent to:

$$X \doteq f(Z, f(Y, Y)) \ \& \ (\, U \doteq X \ \& \ V \doteq f(Y, Y) \ \& \ W \doteq Z \,),$$

and the last part of this conjunction is valid if the local variables U, V, W are existentially quantified.

This is the general principle which underlies the relative simplification algorithm. Namely, the actual constraint ψ_1 entails $\psi_2 \ \& \ U \doteq X$ if and only if the following holds. Their conjunction $\psi_1 \ \& \ \psi_2 \ \& \ U \doteq X$ is equivalent to the conjunction $\psi_1 \ \& \ \psi_2'$ of the actual constraint ψ_1 and a constraint ψ_2' which is valid if existentially quantified over the local variables. In our case, ψ_2' will be a conjunction of equalities binding local to global variables. Formally,

$$\models \psi_1 \rightarrow \exists U, V, W, \ldots \ \psi_2 \ \& \ U \doteq X$$

if and only if there exists a formula ψ_2' such that

$$\models (\psi_1 \ \& \ \psi_2 \ \& \ U \doteq X) \leftrightarrow (\psi_1 \ \& \ \psi_2') \quad and \quad \models \exists U, V, W \ldots \ \psi_2'.$$

This statement is correct since validity of the implication $\psi_1 \rightarrow \exists U \ \psi_2 \ \& \ U \doteq X$ is the same as the validity of the equivalence $(\psi_1 \ \& \ (\exists U \ \psi_2 \ \& \ U \doteq X)) \leftrightarrow \psi_1$. This fact is analogous to the fact that a set is the subset of another one if and only if it is equal to the intersection of the two. The condition $\models \exists U, V, W \ldots \ \psi_2'$ in the statement expresses that $\psi_1 \ \& \ (\exists U, V, W, \ldots \ \psi_2')$ is equivalent to ψ_1.

3.3 Towards relative simplification

Operationally, in order to show that $(X : \psi_1) \leq (U : \psi_2)$ holds, it is sufficient to show that the conjunction $\psi_1 \ \& \ \psi_2 \ \& \ U \doteq X$ is equivalent to $\psi_1 \ \& \ \psi_2'$, where ψ_2' is some constraint which, existentially quantified over the variables of ψ_2, is valid. In our case, again, ψ_2' will be a conjunction of equalities binding variables of ψ_2 to variables of ψ_1.

Therefore, in order to test $(X : \psi_1) \leq (U : \psi_2)$, we will apply successively the unification rules on the constraint $\psi_1 \ \& \ \psi_2 \ \& \ U \doteq X$ if they do not modify ψ_1. We obtain three kinds of transformations which are illustrated schematically below. (Refer to the sorts of Figure 1.)

Equality:

$$\frac{\ldots X \doteq Y \ \ \& \ \ U \doteq X \ldots}{\ldots X \doteq Y \ \ \& \ \ U \doteq Y \ldots}$$

Sorts:

$$\frac{\ldots X : man \ \ \& \ \ U \doteq X \ \ \& \ \ U : person \ldots}{\ldots X : man \ \ \& \ \ U \doteq X \ldots}$$

Features:

$$\frac{\ldots X.likes \doteq Y \ \ \& \ \ U \doteq X \ \ \& \ \ U.likes \doteq V \ldots}{\ldots X.likes \doteq Y \ \ \& \ \ U \doteq X \ \ \& \ \ V \doteq Y \ldots}$$

The equality rule is derived from the corresponding unification rule, which has to be restricted to modify only the formal constraint. If the actual constraint contains an equality between two global variables, then occurrences of one of them may be eliminated for the other. A global variable is never eliminated for a local one.

The sort rule corresponds to two applications of unification rules, first the elimination of the local by the global variable, and then the reduction of two sort constraints on the same variable (here $X : man$ & $X : person$) to one sort constraint (namely $X : man \wedge person$). Clearly, if the "global sort" is a subsort of the "local sort" then this application does not modify the global constraint. The feature rule works quite similarly.

For example, the rules above can be used to show that the ψ-term:

$$\psi_1 \equiv X : man(likes \Rightarrow Y : person, age \Rightarrow I : int)$$

matches the ψ-term:

$$\psi_2 \equiv U : person(likes \Rightarrow V).$$

Namely, the constraint ψ_1 & ψ_2 & $U \doteq X$:

$$\begin{array}{l} X : man \;\; \& \; X.likes \doteq Y \; \& \; Y : person \; \& \; X.age \doteq I \; \& \; I : int \\ \& \; U : person \; \& \; U.likes \doteq V \\ \& \; U \doteq X \end{array}$$

is normalized into:

$$\begin{array}{l} X : man \; \& \; X.likes \doteq Y \; \& \; Y : person \; \& \; X.age \doteq I \; \& \; I : int \\ \& \; V \doteq Y \; \& \; U \doteq X; \end{array}$$

that is,

$$\psi_1 \;\&\; V \doteq Y \;\&\; U \doteq X.$$

Clearly, $\exists U \exists V \left(V \doteq Y \;\&\; U \doteq X\right)$ is valid. Therefore, the constraint ψ_1 entails the constraint ψ_2 & $U \doteq X$.

3.4 Relative simplification for entailment

The rules above are such that ψ_1 & ψ rewrites to ψ_1 & ψ'; *i.e.*, the global constraint ψ_1 is not modified by the simplification. In this case, we say that the constraint ψ simplifies to ψ' relatively to the actual constraint ψ_1. In other words, ψ_1 acts as a context relatively to which simplification of ψ is carried out. In general, this context formula may be any formula. Hence, we can reformulate the rules above as relative-simplification rules. We use the notation $\frac{\psi}{\psi'}\,[\phi]$ to mean that ψ is simplified into ψ' relatively to the context formula ϕ. Schematically,

Equality:

$$\frac{\ldots\; U \doteq X \;\ldots}{\ldots\; U \doteq Y \;\ldots} \; [\ldots X \doteq Y \ldots]$$

Sorts:

$$\frac{\ldots\; U \doteq X \;\&\; U : person \;\ldots}{\ldots\; U \doteq X \;\&\; \;\ldots} \; [\ldots X : man \ldots]$$

Features:

$$\frac{\ldots\ U \doteq X\ \&\ U.likes \doteq V\ \ldots}{\ldots\ U \doteq X\ \&\ V \doteq Y\ \ldots}\quad [\ldots\ X.likes \doteq Y\ \ldots]$$

Using these rules, the constraint $\psi_2 \equiv U \doteq X\ \&\ U : person\ \&\ U.likes \doteq V$ in the previous example simplifies to $\psi_2' \equiv U \doteq X\ \&\ V \doteq Y$ relatively to:

$$\psi_1 \equiv X : man\ \&\ X.likes \doteq Y\ \&\ Y : person\ \&\ X.age \doteq I\ \&\ I : int.$$

Invariance of relative simplification is the following property. If ψ simplifies to ψ' relatively to ϕ, then the conjunction of ψ with ϕ is equivalent to the conjunction of ψ' with ϕ.

This invariance justifies the correctness of the relative simplification algorithm with respect to entailment. Namely, if ψ simplifies to ψ' relatively to ϕ and ψ' consists only of equations binding local variables, then ϕ entails ψ.

Proof of completeness of the algorithm needs the assumption that the set $\mathcal{F}$ of features is infinite. Note that exactly thanks to the infiniteness of $\mathcal{F}$ our framework accounts for flexible records; *i.e.*, the indefinite capacity of adding fields to records.

3.5 Relative simplification for disentailment

If the result of the matching test $\psi_1 \leq \psi_2$ is negative, *i.e.*, the actual constraint does not entail the formal constraint, then we must know more; namely, whether the two terms are non-unifiable. Non-unifiability is equivalent to the fact that the actual parameter will not match the formal one even when further instantiated; *e.g.*, when further constraints are attached as conjuncts. Logically, this amounts to saying that a context formula ϕ *disentails* a guard constraint ψ if and only if the conjunction $\phi\ \&\ \psi$ is unsatisfiable. In terms of relative simplification, ϕ disentails ψ if and only if ψ simplifies to the *false* constraint $\perp$ relatively to ϕ.

For example, $X : male$ is non-unifiable with $U : woman$.[5] The constraint $U : woman\ \&\ U \doteq X$ simplifies to $\perp$ relatively to the constraint $X : male$, since $woman \wedge male = \perp$, using a rule of the form indicated below, and then the Clash rule.

Sorts:

$$\frac{\ldots\ U \doteq X\ \ \&\ \ U : woman\ \ldots}{\ldots\ U \doteq X\ \ \&\ \ U : woman \wedge male\ \ldots}\quad [\ldots X : male\ \ldots]$$

The following example shows that a sort clash cannot always be detected by comparing sorts in the formal constraint one by one with sorts in the actual constraint; *i.e.*, one needs several steps with intermediate sort intersections.

The ψ-term $Z : \top(likes \Rightarrow X : male, friend \Rightarrow Y : female)$ is non-unifiable with the ψ-term $W : \top(likes \Rightarrow U : person, friend \Rightarrow U)$. The constraint $\phi \equiv X : male\ \&\ Y : female$ disentails the constraint $\psi \equiv U \doteq X\ \&\ U \doteq Y\ \&\ U : person$. Operationally, the constraint ψ simplifies to $\perp$ relatively to the context ϕ. Here are the steps needed to determine this:

---

[5] Refer to the sorts of Figure 1.

$$\cfrac{\cfrac{\dots U \doteq X \,\&\, U \doteq Y \,\&\, U : person \dots}{\dots U \doteq X \,\&\, U \doteq Y \,\&\, U : person \wedge male \dots}}{\cfrac{\dots U \doteq X \,\&\, U \doteq Y \,\&\, U : man \wedge female \dots}{\bot}}$$

There is an issue regarding the enforcing of functionality of features in the simplification of a constraint ψ relatively to a context ϕ. This may be explained as follows. Let us suppose that two global variables X and Y become bound to the same local variable U. Then,

- the context ϕ entails the constraint ψ only if ϕ contains $X \doteq Y$; and,
- the context ϕ disentails the constraint ψ if the same path of features starting from X and Y, respectively, leads to variables X' and Y', respectively, whose sorts are incompatible.

There are essentially two cases, depending on whether a new local variable has to be introduced or not. Each case is illustrated in the next two examples.

The ψ-term:[6]

$$\begin{aligned}\phi \equiv Z : \top(&likes \Rightarrow X : \top(age \Rightarrow I_1 : poseven),\\ &friend \Rightarrow Y : \top(age \Rightarrow I_2 : posodd))\end{aligned}$$

is non-unifiable with the ψ-term:

$$\begin{aligned}\psi \equiv W : \top(&likes \Rightarrow U,\\ &friend \Rightarrow U)\end{aligned}$$

That is, the constraint ϕ disentails the constraint ψ. Operationally, with the context ϕ, the constraint ψ simplifies, in a first step, to:

$$W \doteq Z \,\&\, U \doteq X \,\&\, U \doteq Y.$$

Then, using the rule:

$$\frac{\dots U \doteq X \,\&\, U \doteq Y \dots}{\dots U \doteq X \,\&\, U \doteq Y \,\&\, J \doteq I_1 \,\&\, J \doteq I_2 \dots} \quad [\dots X.age \doteq I_1 \,\&\, Y.age \doteq I_2 \dots]$$

where J is a new variable, to:

$$W \doteq Z \,\&\, U \doteq X \,\&\, U \doteq Y \,\&\, J \doteq I_1 \,\&\, J \doteq I_2$$

and finally to $\bot$, since the sorts of I_1 and I_2 (*poseven* and *posodd*) are incompatible.

The rules enforce the following property: a global variable is never bound to more than one local variable. Therefore, if the variable X or the variable Y is already bound to a local variable, *no* new local variable must be introduced. This is illustrated by the second example.

The ψ-term:

$$\begin{aligned}\phi \equiv Z : \top(&likes \Rightarrow X : \top(age \Rightarrow I_1 : poseven),\\ &friend \Rightarrow Y : \top(age \Rightarrow I_2 : posodd),\\ &age \Rightarrow I_1)\end{aligned}$$

[6] We assume that $poseven \wedge posodd = \bot$.

is non-unifiable with the ψ-term:

$$\psi \equiv W : \top(\mathit{likes} \Rightarrow U,\ \mathit{friend} \Rightarrow U(\mathit{age} \Rightarrow J),\ \mathit{age} \Rightarrow J)$$

Operationally, with the context ϕ, the constraint ψ simplifies, in a first step, to:

$$W \doteq Z \;\&\; U \doteq X \;\&\; U \doteq Y \;\&\; J \doteq I_1.$$

Then, using the rule:

$$\frac{\ldots\ U \doteq X \;\&\; U \doteq Y \;\&\; J \doteq I_1\ \ldots}{\ldots\ U \doteq X \;\&\; U \doteq Y \;\&\; J \doteq I_1 \;\&\; J \doteq I_2\ \ldots}\quad [\ldots\ X.\mathit{age} \doteq I_1 \;\&\; Y.\mathit{age} \doteq I_2\ \ldots]$$

where J is a new variable, to:

$$W \doteq Z \;\&\; U \doteq X \;\&\; U \doteq Y \;\&\; J \doteq I_1 \;\&\; J \doteq I_2$$

and finally to $\perp$, for the same reason as above.

In order to be complete with respect to disentailment, the algorithm must keep track of all pairs of variables $(X, Y), \ldots, (X', Y')$ whose equality is induced by the binding of X and Y to the same local variable. That is, it must propagate equalities along features. In our presentation, it will be conceptually sufficient to refer explicitly to the actual equalities binding the global variables to a common local variable. Practically, this can of course be done more efficiently.

3.6 Specifying the relative simplification algorithm

If $\psi \;\&\; U \doteq X$ simplifies to ψ' relatively to ϕ and no relative-simplification rule can be applied further, then:

- ϕ entails $\psi \;\&\; U \doteq X$; formally,

  $$\models \phi \rightarrow \exists U, V, W \ldots (\psi \;\&\; U \doteq X),$$

  if and only if ψ', with the variables of ψ existentially quantified, is valid; formally:

  $$\models \exists U, V, W \ldots\ \psi'.$$

- ϕ disentails $\psi \;\&\; U \doteq X$; formally:

  $$\models \phi \rightarrow \neg\exists U, V, W \ldots (\psi \;\&\; U \doteq X),$$

  if and only if $\psi' = \perp$.

This test is *incremental*. Namely, every relative simplification of the constraint ψ to some constraint ψ' relatively to the context ϕ is also a relative simplification relatively to an incremented context $\phi \;\&\; \phi'$, for any constraint ϕ'.

Recapitulating, our original goal was a simultaneous test of matching and non-unifiability for two given ψ-terms ψ_1 and ψ_2. This test was recast as a test of entailment and disentailment for the constraints to which the ψ-terms dissolve. Namely, if X and U are the root variables of ψ_1 and ψ_2, respectively, the test whether ψ_1 entails or disentails $\psi_2 \;\&\; U \doteq X$.

In our setting, the entailment test succeeds if and only if ψ_2' is a conjunction of matching equations; *i.e.*, of the form $\psi_2' \equiv U \doteq X \;\&\; V \doteq Y \;\&\; W \doteq Z \ldots$, where the local variables $U, V, W, \ldots$ are all different.

Feature Decomposition:

$$(B.1)\quad \frac{\psi \;\&\; U.\ell \doteq V \;\&\; U.\ell \doteq W}{\psi \;\&\; U.\ell \doteq V \;\&\; W \doteq V}$$

Sort Intersection:

$$(B.2)\quad \frac{\psi \;\&\; U : s \;\&\; U : s'}{\psi \;\&\; U : s \wedge s'}$$

Variable Elimination:

$$(B.3)\quad \frac{\psi \;\&\; U \doteq V}{\psi[V/U] \;\&\; U \doteq V} \qquad \text{if } U \in Var(\psi) \text{ and } U \neq V$$

Inconsistent Sort:

$$(B.4)\quad \frac{\psi \;\&\; X : \bot}{\bot}$$

Variable Clean-up:

$$(B.5)\quad \frac{\psi \;\&\; U \doteq U}{\psi}$$

Fig. 3. Basic Simplification

4 Simplification Rules

We give now the formal version of the simplification rules specifying the algorithms discussed informally in this paper, and state the theoretical results proven in [4]. Here, OSF-constraints are conjunctions of atomic sort constraints of the form $X : s$, atomic feature constraints of the form $X.\ell \doteq Y$, and equations $X \doteq Y$. Their interpretations over OSF-algebras are straightforward (*cf.*, Section 2.7).

4.1 Unification–Satisfiability

The first algorithm, called basic simplification, determines whether a constraint ϕ is consistent; *i.e.*, if it is satisfiable in some OSF-algebra $\mathcal{A}$—and, therefore, in particular in Ψ. Unification of two ψ-terms reduces to this problem.

Given an OSF-constraint ϕ, it can be normalized by choosing non-deterministically and applying any applicable rule among the transformations rules shown in Figure 3 until none applies. A rule transforms the numerator into the denominator. The expression $\phi[X/Y]$ stands for the formula obtained from ϕ after replacing all occurrences of Y by X.

Feature Decomposition:

$$\text{(F.1)} \quad \frac{\psi \ \& \ U.\ell \doteq V \ \& \ U.\ell \doteq W}{\psi \ \& \ U.\ell \doteq V \ \& \ W \doteq V}$$

Relative Feature Decomposition:

$$\text{(F.2)} \quad \frac{\psi \ \& \ U \doteq X \ \& \ U.\ell \doteq V}{\psi \ \& \ U \doteq X \ \& \ V \doteq Y} \qquad \textit{if } X.\ell \doteq Y \in \phi$$

Relative Feature Equality:

$$\text{(F.3)} \quad \frac{\psi \ \& \ U \doteq X_1 \ \& \ U \doteq X_2 \ \& \ V \doteq Y_1}{\psi \ \& \ U \doteq X_1 \ \& \ U \doteq X_2 \ \& \ V \doteq Y_1 \ \& \ V \doteq Y_2} \qquad \begin{array}{l} \textit{if } X_1.\ell \doteq Y_1 \in \phi, X_2.\ell \doteq Y_2 \in \phi \\ \textit{and } V \doteq Y_2 \notin \psi \end{array}$$

Variable Introduction:

$$\text{(F.4)} \quad \frac{\psi \ \& \ U \doteq X_1 \ \& \ U \doteq X_2}{\psi \ \& \ U \doteq X_1 \ \& \ U \doteq X_2 \ \& \ V \doteq Y_1 \ \& \ V \doteq Y_2} \qquad \begin{array}{l} \textit{if } X_1.\ell \doteq Y_1 \in \phi, X_2.\ell \doteq Y_2 \in \phi \\ \textit{and } Y_1 \notin Var(\psi) \textit{ and } Y_2 \notin Var(\psi) \\ \textit{where } V \textit{ is a new variable} \end{array}$$

Fig. 4. Simplification relatively to ϕ : Features

The rules of Figure 3 are solution-preserving (*i.e.*, equivalence transformations), finite terminating, and confluent (modulo variable renaming).

The effectuality of the basic-simplification system is summed up in the following statement:

Effectuality of basic-simplification *The constraint ψ is satisfiable if and only if the normal form ψ' of ψ is different from the false constraint, i.e., $\psi' \neq \bot$.*

4.2 Matching–Entailment/Disentailment

The next algorithm, called relative simplification, determines whether a consistent constraint ϕ entails or disentails a constraint ψ which is the dissolved form of some ψ-term with root variable U. That is, it decides two problems simultaneously:

- the validity of the implication $\forall \mathcal{X} \ (\phi \rightarrow \exists \mathcal{U}. \ (\psi \ \& \ U \doteq X) \ )$;
- the unsatisfiability of the conjunction $\phi \ \& \ \psi \ \& \ U \doteq X$.

Matching of two ψ-terms reduces to the first of the two problems, non-unifiability to the second.

The *relative-simplification* system for OSF-constraints is given by the rules in Figures 4, 5, and 6. An OSF-constraint ψ simplifies to ψ' relatively to ϕ by a simplification rule ρ if $\frac{\psi}{\psi'}$ is an instance of ρ and the applicability condition (on ϕ and on ψ) is satisfied. We say that ψ simplifies to ψ' relatively to ϕ if it does so in a finite number of steps.

Relative Variable Elimination:

$$\text{(E.1)}\quad \frac{\psi \ \&\ U \doteq X \ \&\ V \doteq X}{\psi[U/V] \ \&\ U \doteq X \ \&\ V \doteq X} \qquad \textit{if } V \in Var(\psi),\ V \doteq X \notin \psi, \textit{ and } U \neq V$$

Equation Entailment:

$$\text{(E.2)}\quad \frac{\psi \ \&\ U \doteq X \ \&\ U \doteq Y}{\psi \ \&\ U \doteq X} \qquad \textit{if } X = Y \textit{ or if } X \doteq Y \in \phi.$$

Fig. 5. Simplification relatively to ϕ : Equations

The relative-simplification system preserves an important invariant property: the conjunction $\phi \ \&\ \psi$ is equivalent to the conjunction $\phi \ \&\ \psi'$. Again, the rules are finite terminating, and confluent (modulo variable renaming).

A set of bindings $U_i \doteq X_i$, $i = 1, \ldots, n$ is a *functional binding* if all the variables U_i are mutually distinct.

The effectuality of the relative-simplification system is summed up in the following statement:

Effectuality of relative-simplification *The solved* OSF*-constraint* ϕ *entails (resp., disentails) the* OSF*-constraint* $\exists U.\ (U \doteq X \ \&\ \psi)$ *if and only if the normal form* ψ' *of* $\psi \ \&\ U \doteq X$ *relatively to* ϕ *is a conjunction of equations making up a functional binding (resp., is the false constraint* $\psi' = \bot$*).*

5 Conclusion

We have presented informally the essence of LIFE that is relevant to functions and explained the gist of our method for deciding incrementally entailment and disentailment of constraints. We call this new technique relative simplification. Reading this paper will provide an elaborate intuition of the technical details reported formally in [4]. There, we expound the concept of relative simplification as a general proof-theoretic method for proving guards in concurrent constraint logic languages using guarded rules. The specific relative simplification rules for OSF-constraints are given and proven correct and complete. Then, residuation is naturally explained using relative simplification. Finally, the operational semantics of function reduction is shown to be congruent with the semantics of ψ-terms as approximation structures.

Sort Intersection:

(S.1) $$\frac{\psi \,\&\, U : s \,\&\, U : s'}{\psi \,\&\, U : s \wedge s'}$$

Sort Containment:

(S.2) $$\frac{\psi \,\&\, U \doteq X \,\&\, U : s}{\psi \,\&\, U \doteq X} \qquad \textit{if } X : s' \in \phi, \textit{ and } s' \leq s$$

Sort Refinement:

(S.3) $$\frac{\psi \,\&\, U \doteq X \,\&\, U : s}{\psi \,\&\, U \doteq X \,\&\, U : s \wedge s'} \qquad \textit{if } X : s' \in \phi, \textit{ and } s \wedge s' < s$$

Relative Sort Intersection:

(S.4) $$\frac{\psi \,\&\, U \doteq X \,\&\, U \doteq X'}{\psi \,\&\, U \doteq X \,\&\, U \doteq X' \,\&\, U : s \wedge s'} \qquad \begin{array}{l} \textit{if } X : s \in \phi, X' : s' \in \phi, \\ s \wedge s' < s, s \wedge s' < s', \\ \textit{and } U : s'' \notin \psi, \textit{ for any sort } s'' \end{array}$$

Sort Inconsistency:

(S.5) $$\frac{\psi \,\&\, U : \bot}{\bot}$$

Fig. 6. Simplification relatively to ϕ : Sorts

References

1. Hassan Aït-Kaci. An algebraic semantics approach to the effective resolution of type equations. *Theoretical Computer Science*, 45:293–351, 1986.
2. Hassan Aït-Kaci and Roger Nasr. LOGIN: A logic programming language with built-in inheritance. *Journal of Logic Programming*, 3:185–215, 1986.
3. Hassan Aït-Kaci and Roger Nasr. Integrating logic and functional programming. *Lisp and Symbolic Computation*, 2:51–89, 1989.
4. Hassan Aït-Kaci and Andreas Podelski. Functions as passive constraints in LIFE. PRL Research Report 13, Digital Equipment Corporation, Paris Research Laboratory, Rueil-Malmaison, France, June 1991. Revised, Novembre 1992.
5. Hassan Aït-Kaci and Andreas Podelski. Towards a meaning of LIFE. In Jan Maluszyński and Martin Wirsing, editors, *Proceedings of the 3rd International Symposium on Programming Language Implementation and Logic Programming (Passau, Germany)*, pages 255–274. Springer-Verlag, LNCS 528, August 1991.
6. Hassan Aït-Kaci and Andreas Podelski. Towards a meaning of LIFE. PRL Research Report 11, Digital Equipment Corporation, Paris Research Laboratory, Rueil-Malmaison, France, 1991. (Revised, October 1992; to appear in the Journal of Logic Programming).
7. Hassan Aït-Kaci, Andreas Podelski, and Gert Smolka. A feature-based constraint system for logic programming with entailment. In *Proceedings of the 5th International Conference on Fifth Generation Computer Systems*, pages 1012–1022, Tokyo, Japan, June 1992. ICOT.
8. Rolf Backofen and Gert Smolka. A complete and decidable feature theory. DFKI Research Report RR-30-92, German Research Center for Artificial Intelligence, Saarbrücken, Germany, 1992.
9. Staffan Bonnier and Jan Maluszyński. Towards a clean amalgamation of logic programs with external procedures. In Robert A. Kowalski and Kenneth A. Bowen, editors, *Logic Programming. Proceedings of the 5th International Conference and Symposium*, pages 311–326, Cambridge, MA, 1988. MIT Press.
10. Alain Colmerauer. Prolog II: Manuel de référence et modèle théorique. Rapport technique, Université de Marseille, Groupe d'Intelligence Artificielle, Faculté des Sciences de Luminy, Marseille, France, March 1982.
11. Seif Haridi and Sverker Janson. Kernel Andorra Prolog and its computation model. In David H. D. Warren and Peter Szeredi, editors, *Logic Programming, Proceedings of the 7th International Conference*, pages 31–46, Cambridge, MA, 1990. MIT Press.
12. Robert Harper, Robin Milner, and Mads Tofte. The definition of standard ML – Version 2. Report LFCS-88-62, University of Edinburgh, Edinburgh, UK, 1988.
13. Michael Maher. Logic semantics for a class of committed-choice programs. In Jean-Louis Lassez, editor, *Logic Programming, Proceedings of the Fourth International Conference*, pages 858–876, Cambridge, MA, 1987. MIT Press.
14. Lee Naish. *MU-Prolog 3.1db Reference Manual*. Computer Science Department, University of Melbourne, Melbourne, Australia, May 1984.
15. Vijay Saraswat. Concurrent constraint programming. In *Proceedings of the 7th Annual ACM Symposium on Principles of Programming Languages*, pages 232–245. ACM, January 1990.

A Direct Semantic Characterization of RELFUN*

Harold Boley
Deutsches Forschungszentrum für Künstliche Intelligenz
Box 2080, D-6750 Kaiserslautern, F. R. Germany
boley@informatik.uni-kl.de

Abstract

This paper attempts a direct semantic formalization of first-order relational-functional languages (the characteristic RELFUN subset) in terms of a generalized model concept. Function-defining conditional equations (or, footed clauses) and active call-by-value expressions (in clause premises) are integrated into first-order theories. Herbrand models are accomodated to relational-functional programs by not only containing ground atoms but also ground molecules, i.e. specific function applications paired with values. Extending SLD-resolution toward innermost conditional narrowing of relational-functional clauses, SLV-resolution is introduced, which, e.g., flattens active expressions. The T_P-operator is generalized analogously, e.g. by unnesting ground-clause premises. Soundness and completeness proofs for SLV-resolution naturally extend the corresponding results in logic programming.

1 Introduction

RELFUN is a logic language primarily extended by call-by-value (eager) functions that may be non-ground, non-deterministic, varying-arity, and higher-order. These functions are defined by extended Horn clauses having a 'foot' premise for value returning. This extension can also be viewed as (directed) conditional equations permitting 'extra' variables in conditions, which may accumulate partial results. It entails the following syntactic changes of PROLOG:

Footed clauses: Starting with DATALOG, "`:-`"-rules may be augmented by an ampersand infix, "`&`", between the normal body premises and the foot premise; facts (empty bodies), by a joined infix, "`:-&`".

Active expressions: Proceeding to PROLOG, passive structures are rewritten using square brackets, "`[...]`", reserving round parentheses, "`(...)`", for RELFUN's active call-by-value expressions (permitted in premises).

*This research was supported by the BMFT under Grant ITW 8902 C4.

As shown by the Fibonacci programs in example 1, RELFUN's function-defining footed clauses (e.g. for `fibfun`) can be developed from PROLOG-like relation-defining Horn clauses (e.g. for `fibrel`) via an intermediate footed-clause form using a generalized relational `is`-primitive in a functional, `let`-like manner (e.g. for `fibfis`). When reading such clauses we extend PROLOG's "... *if* ..." for "`... :- ...`" to "... *if* ... *returns* ..." for "`... :- ... & ...`" (or just "... *returns* ..." for "`... :-& ...`"). [1]

Example 1 *Recursive Fibonacci relations and functions in RELFUN.*

```
fibris(N,F) :- F is fibfun(N).

fibrel(0,s[0]).
fibrel(s[0],s[0]).
fibrel(s[s[N]],F) :-  fibrel(N,X), fibrel(s[N],Y), plusrel(X,Y,F).

fibfis(0)         :-& s[0].
fibfis(s[0])      :-& s[0].
fibfis(s[s[N]]) :-    X is fibfis(N), Y is fibfis(s[N]) & plusfun(X,Y).

fibfun(0)         :-& s[0].
fibfun(s[0])      :-& s[0].
fibfun(s[s[N]]) :-& plusfun(fibfun(N),fibfun(s[N])).


plusrel(0,N,N).
plusrel(s[M],N,P) :-  plusrel(M,s[N],P).

plusfun(0,N)      :-& N.
plusfun(s[M],N) :-& plusfun(M,s[N]).
```

Relation definitions in RELFUN employ generalized Horn clauses, namely 'hornish' clauses, which may again call arbitrary functions, either within any argument of a relation call or the right-hand side (rhs) of the `is`-primitive (e.g. in `fibris`). So the body premises of hornish clauses are relational on the **top-level** (just binding variables, like Horn-clause premises), but may **contain** functional applications (also returning values). Conversely, the head and foot of footed clauses can be regarded as the two sides of an equation, giving these clauses a principal functional flavor, although their body conditions are exactly like the relational top-level premises of hornish clauses. Altogether, RELFUN's clauses tightly integrate relational and functional characteristics. [2]

[1] While the infix "`:-&`" corresponds to a (directed, unconditional) " $=$ ", the mixfix "`:- ... &`" corresponds to a (directed, conditional) " $\dot{\dot{=}}$ ". However, we will not formalize functions using a logic with a distinguished (directed) equality predicate, but will 'build in' "`:-&`" and "`:- ... &`" even more deeply, as new connectives.

[2] Still, rather than indiscriminately speaking of 'relational-functional' language constructs, we will didactically distinguish 'relational' and 'functional' constructs on the basis of their principal characteristics.

The following functional version of J. W. Lloyd's relational slowsort example [7] shows the use of non-ground and non-deterministic subfunction calls for defining a deterministic main function.

Example 2 *A functional slowsort program in RELFUN.*

```
% Sort filters non-deterministic permutations through sorted:
sort(X) :-& sorted(perm(X)).

% Return sorted lists unchanged, fail for unsorted ones:
sorted([]) :-& [].
sorted([X]) :-& [X].
sorted([X,Y|Z]) :- lesseq(X,Y) & cons(X,sorted([Y|Z])).

% Permute by a non-ground delete call returning U-less lists
% and binding U for a cons call enclosing the perm recursion:
perm([]) :-& [].
perm([X|Y]) :-& cons(U,perm(delete(U,[X|Y]))).

% Non-deterministically delete X elements from list argument:
delete(X,[X|Y]) :-& Y.
delete(X,[Y|Z]) :-& cons(Y,delete(X,Z)).

% A less-or-equal relation over s-terms:
lesseq(0,X).
lesseq(s[X],s[Y]) :- lesseq(X,Y).

% cons(h,t) calls h and t by value, [h|t] only instantiates h and t:
cons(X,Y) :-& [X|Y].
```

Since programs for Fibonacci numbers, list sorting, and many other purposes are normally used in a deterministic mode, we think they should be formulated as functions rather than relations, indicating the preferred direction of computation. However, in RELFUN such functions still permit inverse calls (e.g. `s[0] is fibfun(W)` non-deterministically binds `W` to `0` or `s[0]`) and can make natural internal use of relations (e.g. `lesseq`) and non-deterministic functions (e.g. `perm` and `delete`).

A comprehensive overview of RELFUN and related work as well as pointers to its applications and to its original operational (interpretative), LISP-implemented semantics can be found in [3]. Among the tools of the RELFUN implementation there is a term-rewriting algorithm `relationalize` for transforming footed and hornish clauses into Horn clauses, thus indirectly characterizing their model-theoretic semantics. However, this semantic indirectness makes our understanding of functions totally dependent on our understanding of relations (inverting the dependency incurred by the LISP-based interpreter), whereas we work towards "equal declarative depth" for both of them.

The present paper thus attempts to directly characterize the semantics of 'basic' RELFUN, the pure-RELFUN subset exemplifying fixed-arity first-order relational-functional languages, in terms of a generalized model concept: RELFUN models contain both **atoms** (relations) and **directed unconditional equations** (functions). This would permit a common foundation of logic and functional programming, reducing the gap between these declarative paradigms. Through a model-theoretic foundation of relational-functional languages, the semantic characteristics available or lacking in either of these declarative-programming paradigms can be assessed in a way more neutral than via the indirection of mutual implementions of, and cross-translations between these paradigms. For instance, on the basis of our characterization we can study such questions as "How will functional call-by-value expressions enrich (and complicate) the semantics of relational languages?" or "How will the relational meaning of non-ground arguments carry over to the functional meaning of arguments and returned values?" Another important motivation of the present work is to make the many alternative relational-functional integration proposals (see, e.g., [1] and [4]) comparable on a common ground, revealing their deeper, non-syntactic differences. Finally, we think the model-theoretic treatment can provide us with a long-term yardstick for developing a 'minimal' integration of the essential concepts of relational and functional languages: in the multitude of integration proposals, only "Occam's razor" can help sorting out the **proper integration constructs** from other "nice features".

In fact, with basic RELFUN we have attempted to operationally explore a tight, minimum integration of the concepts of a relation and a function themselves. Among other things, the classical eager functional expressions (innermost reduction) have been extended to non-deterministic function nestings to accomodate relational non-determinism. Then, the semantic interpretation of functions just uses mappings to sets of domain individuals, and expressions are semantically evaluated using **expression assignments**, a natural, set-valued extension of relational term assignments. These semantic extensions are less complicated than the semantics of lazy expressions (outermost reduction) as a relational-functional integration concept, as introduced by other recent proposals (e.g., K-LEAF [6] and BABEL [8]): eagerness keeps the semantics strict and simple, whereas laziness accepts the non-strictness overhead to give a meaning to unifications involving non-terminating expressions. While basic RELFUN's operational integration concepts may be close to a minimum, its current model-theoretic characterization is still quite preliminary and will certainly need further simplification and improvement.

On the other hand, pure-RELFUN extensions of the present treatment could directly incorporate the semantics of varying-arity operations, which can also be reduced to unary ones over lists. Similarly, RELFUN's higher-order operations should not be too difficult to add, as they are restricted to those reducible to first-order operations using an `apply` dummy as introduced for corresponding PROLOG extensions by D. H. D. Warren [10]. While these two extensions have long existed in the implemented RELFUN system, further extensions such as finite domains will first require their own operational test phase before we can think of including them in the formal semantics. Finally, some aspects of our RELFUN extensions of SLD-resolution, Herbrand models, and T_P-operators will probably be transferable to other languages.

Our basic semantic treatment draws heavily on chapters 1 and 2 of J. W. Lloyd's book [7], construing a parallel between first-order relations and first-order functions, enabled by suitably generalizing the latter in a non-ground, non-deterministic fashion. This relational-functional parallel in the formal definitions given here derived from considerations in language design such as expressive power, orthogonality, and uniformity of constructs. But it also simplifies transferring foundation theorems of logic programming (as found, e.g., in J. W. Lloyd's book) to eager, non-ground, non-deterministic first-order functional programming and to unified relational-functional programming. We think that a fundament for functional programming should be 'grounded' on a level as deep as the (Herbrand-)model-theoretic fundament of relational programming. Specifically this means that we will try to establish function definitions as subsets $\{f(a_1, ..., a_n) \texttt{ :-\& } b, \ldots\}$ of so-called ground 'molecules' (directed unconditional equations) from the Herbrand 'cross' just like relation definitions are established as subsets $\{r(a_1, ..., a_n), \ldots\}$ of ground atoms from the Herbrand base. Intuitively, Herbrand cross models employ molecules for the 'pointwise' definition of a (discrete) function, akin to the familiar notion of the 'graph' (or 'extension') of a function as a set of pairs. Avoiding dependencies between the molecules of such a model which correspond to the usual 'functionality' restriction $f(a_1, ..., a_n) \texttt{ :-\& } b \wedge f(a_1, ..., a_n) \texttt{ :-\& } c \Longrightarrow b = c$, it will **simplify** this semantics that we permit $b \neq c$ i.e., non-deterministic functions. [3] Unaffected by non-determinism, the **directedness** of functional computation is expressed by the '$f(a_1, ..., a_n)$-to-b' order of each molecule $f(a_1, ..., a_n) \texttt{ :-\& } b$ in an Herbrand cross model.

On the basis of the unified pure-RELFUN constructs, the impure relational-functional features can also be introduced in a uniform manner. For instance, after proving results corresponding to the "independence of the computation rule" in [7], we could proceed from 'and-parallel' to 'and-sequential' relational-functional premise evaluation, which is the operational semantics actually implemented for RELFUN (just as for PROLOG). Similarly, the resolution/model-theoretic 'or-parallelism' of relational-functional clauses could be weakened toward the operational (but implementation-incomplete!) 'or-sequentialism' of backtracking. Finally, functions and relations can be forced to operate (more) deterministically using the same cut, `commit`, or substitute constructs; however, adapting our model-theoretic approach to such optional determinism specifications may be difficult because of the semantic problems with cut-like notions.

2 Extending First-Order Theories to First-Order Relational-Functional Theories

We now begin with the formal development of first-order relational-functional programming by 'functionally' extending the "Foundations of Logic Programming" [7], which should also be consulted for references to classical work.

[3](Re)specializing RELFUN to a sublanguage with only deterministic functions would cause semantic changes starting off from the interpretation concept. (While our non-deterministic function symbols are assigned mappings to the powerset of the domain, deterministic function symbols could be assigned constructor-like mappings to the domain itself.) Within models the 'deterministic-function' restriction could then be introduced as an axiom, but this would change Herbrand's sets to (non-free) **algebras**.

A *first-order relational-functional theory* consists of:

1. An alphabet.
2. A first-order relational-functional language (the well-formed formulas of the theory).
3. A set of axioms (a designated subset of the well-formed formulas).
4. A set of inference rules.

Definition 1 *The* alphabet *of a first-order relational-functional theory consists of nine classes of symbols (some notational conventions are given in parentheses, where all letters used may be subscripted):*

1. *Variables (normally denoted by the letters x, y, and z).* [4]
2. *Constants (normally denoted by the letters a, b, and c).*
3. *Constructors*[5] *(normally denoted by the letters j, k, and l).*
4. *Function symbols (normally denoted by the letters f, g, and h).*
5. *Relation symbols*[6] *(normally denoted by the letters p, q, and r).*
6. *Functional connectives (two binary infixes denoted by* `is` *and* `:-&` *and a ternary mixfix denoted by* `:-` *together with* `&`*).*
7. *Relational connectives (a unary prefix denoted by* $\neg$ *and binary infixes denoted by* $\wedge$, $\vee$, `:-` *, and* $\leftrightarrow$*).*[7]
8. *Quantifiers (denoted by* $\exists$ *and* $\forall$*).*
9. *Punctuation symbols ("[", "]", "(", ")", and ",").*

The union of the classes of function and relation symbols will be referred to as operation symbols *or, briefly,* operators.

Note that RELFUN's implemented operational semantics does not differentiate subclasses for constructor, function, and relation symbols but contextually distinguishes uses of symbols from a united class, even permitting a given symbol to have occurrences in more than one subclass (e.g., the main operator symbol of a body premise will act as a relation but may re-occur in a foot premise, where it will act as a function; also, meta-calls make operators from constructors).

[4] In larger examples we will capitalize variable names and use digit suffixes instead of subscripts, e.g. x_1 becoming $X1$, to conform to RELFUN's actual PROLOG-like naming conventions.

[5] Often called "functors" or even "function symbols" in the literature.

[6] Often called "predicate symbols" in the literature.

[7] Much like in PROLOG's program clauses, "`:-`" without a consecutive "`&`" plays the role of "$\leftarrow$".

Definition 2 *A* term *is defined inductively:*

1. *A variable is a term.*

2. *A constant is a term.*

3. *If k is an n-ary constructor and $t_1, \ldots, t_n$ are terms, then $k[t_1, \ldots, t_n]$ is a term, called a* structure.

The above use of square brackets for applying a constructor to arguments clearly sets off 'passive' structures from 'active' operator applications as defined below with the more usual round parentheses. In our semantic treatment of relational-functional languages the bracketing type serves readability but provides no information beyond that already implicit in the symbol classes, 'constructor' vs. 'operator'. In the implemented version of RELFUN, not distinguishing symbol classes, this information is exclusively conveyed by "[...]" vs. "(...)".

In RELFUN *cns* is employed as the binary list constructor (LISP's *cons* or "."), and *nil*, as usual, as the constant denoting the empty list. Externally, a *list term* having the right-recursively nested form $cns[t_1, cns[t_2, cns[\ldots, cns[t_n, t]\ldots]]]$ is written (PROLOG-like) as the linearized varying-arity term $[t_1, t_2, \ldots, t_n]$ for $t = nil$ or, $[t_1, t_2, \ldots, t_n|t]$ for t being a variable. However, we regard the varying-arity form as (passive) applications of a constructor *tup*, understood to precede unprefixed "[...]"-terms.

Definition 3 *An* expression *is defined inductively:*

1. *A term is an expression.*

2. *If f is an n-ary function symbol and $E_1, \ldots, E_n$ are expressions, then $f(E_1, \ldots, E_n)$ is an expression, called an* application; *if all of $E_1, \ldots, E_n$ are terms, $f(E_1, \ldots, E_n)$ is called a* flat application.

Such a notion of expressions is essential in functional programming, but lacks in non-extended logic programming (in [7], "expression" is given a different, peripheral meaning).

Definition 4 *A* (well-formed) formula *is defined inductively:*

1. *If r is an n-ary relation symbol and $E_1, \ldots, E_n$ are expressions, then $r(E_1, \ldots, E_n)$ is a formula, called a* relationship; *if all of $E_1, \ldots, E_n$ are terms, $r(E_1, \ldots, E_n)$ is called a* flat relationship *or, since this is the most basic kind of formula, an* atomic formula *or, simply, an* atom.

2. *If E is an expression and t is a term, then (t **is** E) is a formula, called a* setting formula *or, simply, a* setter; *if E is a flat application, (t **is** E) is called a* flat setter; *if E is a term, (t **is** E) is called a* term setter.

3. If e *is a flat application and* E *is an expression, then* (e :-& E) *is a formula; if* E *is a term,* (e :-& E) *is called a* molecular formula *or, simply, a* molecule.

4. If e *is a flat application,* E *is an expression, and* W *is a formula, then* (e :- W & E) *is a formula.*

5. If W_1 *and* W_2 *are formulas, then so are* $(\neg W_1), (W_1 \wedge W_2), (W_1 \vee W_2), (W_1$:- $W_2)$, *and* $(W_1 \leftrightarrow W_2)$.

6. If W *is a formula and* x *is a variable, then* $(\exists x W)$ *and* $(\forall x W)$ *are formulas.*

The restriction of e being a flat application in items *3.* and *4.* reflects the "constructor discipline" [9] of RELFUN's footed clauses. It could be dropped in a more general equational treatment of first-order relational-functional languages. Conversely, instead of letting W_1 be an arbitrary formula in $(W_1$:- $W_2)$ of item *5.*, it could be immediately restricted to an atomic formula (flat relationship), as required for RELFUN's hornish clauses.

Note that the parentheses employed to build applications and relationships are indispensible parts of the syntax. The parentheses around entire formulas, however, are just used for grouping and will frequently be omitted if no ambiguities arise under the following partial precedence order: "$\neg$", "$\forall$", "$\exists$" precede "is" precedes "$\wedge$" precedes "$\vee$" precedes ":-&", ":- ... &", ":-", "$\leftrightarrow$".

There is a close kinship between flat setters and molecules, which will be confirmed in definition 16. Thus, an operation that switches between both formula types will be convenient.

Definition 5 *The self-inverse setter/molecule swapping operation "$\otimes$" is defined as an exponentiation operator over sets of molecules, flat setters, and relationships (the u_i must be terms).*[8]

$$\begin{aligned} r(u_1,\ldots,u_m)^{\otimes} &= r(u_1,\ldots,u_m) \\ (t \texttt{ is } g(u_1,\ldots,u_m))^{\otimes} &= g(u_1,\ldots,u_m) \texttt{ :-\& } t \\ (g(u_1,\ldots,u_m) \texttt{ :-\& } t)^{\otimes} &= t \texttt{ is } g(u_1,\ldots,u_m) \\ \{F_1,\ldots,F_n\}^{\otimes} &= \{F_1^{\otimes},\ldots,F_n^{\otimes}\} \end{aligned}$$

Example 3 a, b, c, x, y, $k[a,x,b]$, $l[y,y]$, *and* $k[a,l[y,y],b]$ *are terms;* $f(y,k[a,l[y,y],b],c,l[y,y])$ *is a flat application;* $r(b,f(y,k[a,l[y,y],b],c,l[y,y]))$ *is a (non-flat) relationship.* $f(y,k[a,l[y,y],b],c,l[y,y])$:-& $k[a,x,b]$ *is a molecule;* $(f(y,k[a,l[y,y],b],c,l[y,y])$:-& $k[a,x,b])^{\otimes} = k[a,x,b]$ is $f(y,k[a,l[y,y],b],c,l[y,y])$ *is a flat setter.*

Definition 6 *The* first-order relational-functional language *given by an alphabet consists of the set of all formulas built from the symbols of the alphabet.*

[8] If "$\otimes$" is applicable to a formula F, then $(F^{\otimes})^{\otimes} = F$.

In the following we will focus special kinds of formulas, namely RELFUN's clauses. Unaffected by their Horn-clause extensions (expressions, setters, and foot premises), they are closed formulas by assuming all variables to have a prenex universal quantifier.

Definition 7 *A* (program) clause *is a hornish (program) clause or a footed (program) clause. If w is an atomic formula, e is a flat application, $V_1, \ldots, V_n$ are relationships or setters, and E is an expression, then w :- $V_1, \ldots, V_n$, abbreviating w :- $(V_1 \wedge \ldots \wedge V_n)$, is a* hornish (program) clause *and e :- $V_1, \ldots, V_n$ & E, abbreviating e :- $(V_1 \wedge \ldots \wedge V_n)$ & E, is a* footed (program) clause. *w or e is the* head, *$V_1, \ldots, V_n$ is the* body, *and E is the* foot *of the clause. If $V_1, \ldots, V_n$ are all atoms, the hornish (program) clause w :- $V_1, \ldots, V_n$ is also called a* Horn (program) clause. *For $n = 0$, i.e. with an empty body, a hornish (program) clause w :- , abbreviating w :- true, is written as w, while a footed (program) clause e :- & E, abbreviating e :- true & E, is written as e :-& E.*

Definition 8 *A* ((first-order) relational-functional) program P *is a finite set of program clauses $\{c_1, \ldots, c_n\}$. P is usually written (with "."-terminators) as:*

c_1.

...

c_n.

A program will play the role of the set of axioms of a first-order relational-functional theory.

Definition 9 *The* empty (hornish) clause, *denoted $\square$, is the hornish clause of the form* :- , *which abbreviates false :- true. A* terminal ((t-)footed) clause, *denoted $\Delta(t)$, t a term, is a footed clause of the form* :-& t, *which abbreviates $\square$ & t. The* trivial (hornish) clause, *denoted $\top$, is the hornish clause of the form true :- true.*

Definition 10 *A* relational goal *is a hornish clause of the form*

:- $V_1, \ldots, V_n$

that is, it has an empty head. A functional goal *is a footed clause of the form*

:- $V_1, \ldots, V_n$ & E

that is, it has an empty head.

It should be kept in mind that a relational goal is 'relational' in the usual sense only on the top-level: the V_i's need not be atoms but may be nested relationships or setters. Conversely, a functional goal may of course contain V_i's that are atoms.[9]

[9] Thus, "relational goal" should perhaps be renamed into "hornish goal", and "functional goal" into "footed goal". However, this would entail new words in the later definitions for "relational"/"functional" derivation, answer, etc.

3 Relational-Functional Interpretations and Models

First, we will consider general interpretations of full first-order relational-functional languages. Then, these will be restricted to Herbrand-like interpretations of RELFUN's clause programs. Since the basic RELFUN formalized here does not contain a negation construct, we will neglect RELFUN's three-valued open-world semantics and its differentiation of the truth values false and unknown [3].

Definition 11 *A* pre-interpretation *J of a first-order relational-functional language L consists of:*

1. *A non-empty set D, called the* domain *of the pre-interpretation.*
2. *For each constant in L, the assignment of an element in D.*
3. *For each n-ary constructor in L, the assignment of a mapping from D^n to D.*

Definition 12 *An* interpretation *I of a first-order relational-functional language L consists of a pre-interpretation J with domain D of L together with:*

1. *For each n-ary relation symbol in L, the assignment of a mapping from D^n into $\{true, false\}$ (or, equivalently, a relation on D^n).*
2. *For each n-ary function symbol in L, the assignment of a mapping from D^n to 2^D, the powerset of D.*

We say I is based on *J.*

Definition 13 *Let J be a pre-interpretation of a first-order relational-functional language L. A* variable assignment (wrt *J) is an assignment to each variable in L of an element in the domain of J.*

Definition 14 *Let J be a pre-interpretation with domain D of a first-order relational-functional language L and let V be a variable assignment. The* term assignment (wrt *J* and *V) of the terms in L is defined as follows:*

1. *Each variable is given its assignment according to V.*
2. *Each constant is given its assignment according to J.*
3. *If k' is the assignment of the n-ary constructor k according to J and $t'_1, \ldots, t'_n$ are the term assignments of $t_1, \ldots, t_n$, then $k'(t'_1, \ldots, t'_n) \in D$ is the term assignment of $k[t_1, \ldots, t_n]$.*

Definition 15 *Let I be an interpretation with domain D of a first-order relational-functional language L and let V be a variable assignment. The* expression assignment (wrt *I* and *V) of the expressions in L is defined as follows:*

1. *If t' is the term assignment of the term t wrt I and V, then $\{t'\}$ is the expression assignment of t.*

2. *If f' is the mapping assigned to the n-ary function symbol f by I and $E'_1, \ldots, E'_n$ are the expression assignments of $E_1, \ldots, E_n$, then the union of all $f'(t'_1, \ldots, t'_n) \in 2^D$ for each $t'_1 \in E'_1$, ..., $t'_n \in E'_n$ is the expression assignment of $f(E_1, \ldots, E_n)$.*

Definition 16 *Let I be an interpretation with domain D of a first-order relational-functional language L and let V be a variable assignment. Then a formula in L can be given a* truth value, *true or false, (wrt I and V) as follows (we let (a possibly embellished version of) t denote a term, of e, denote a flat application, of E, denote an expression, and of W, denote a formula):*

1. *If the formula has the form $r(E_1, \ldots, E_n)$, then the truth value of the formula is true if there exist $t'_1 \in E'_1$, ..., $t'_n \in E'_n$ such that $r'(t'_1, \ldots, t'_n)$ has truth value true, where r' is the mapping assigned to r by I and $E'_1, \ldots, E'_n$ are the expression assignments of $E_1, \ldots, E_n$ wrt I and V; otherwise, the formula's truth value is false.*

2. *If the formula has the form $f(t_1, \ldots, t_n)$:-& E, then the truth value of the formula is true if the expression assignment of E wrt I and V is E' and $E' \subseteq f'(t'_1, \ldots, t'_n)$, where f' is the mapping assigned to f by I, and $t'_1, \ldots, t'_n$ are the term assignments of $t_1, \ldots, t_n$ wrt I and V; otherwise, the formula's truth value is false.*

3. *If the formula has the form t* is *E, then its truth value is true if the expression assignment of E wrt I and V is E' and $t' \in E'$, where t' is the term assignment of t wrt I and V; otherwise, its truth value is false.* [10]

4. *If the formula has the form e :- false & E, then its truth value is true. If the formula has the form e :- true & E, then the truth value is that of e :-& E.* [11]

5. *If the formula has the form $\neg W$, $W_1 \wedge W_2$, $W_1 \vee W_2$, W_1 :- W_2, or $W_1 \leftrightarrow W_2$, then the truth value is given by the usual truth tables.*

6. *If the formula has the form $\forall x W$, then the truth value of the formula is true if for all $d \in D$ the subformula W has truth value true wrt I and $V(x/d)$, where $V(x/d)$ is V except that x is assigned d; otherwise, the formula's truth value is false.*

---

[10]Thus the instance t is $f(t_1, \ldots, t_n)$ has the same truth value as the instance $f(t_1, \ldots, t_n)$:-& t, defined through item 2. The different syntaxes are maintained even in these special cases for marking off the body-goal use of the former from the clause-definition use of the latter. Also, in RELFUN's implemented operational semantics, successful setters return their evaluated rhs, rather than just true.

[11]For formalizing RELFUN's "valued conjunctions", definition 3 could introduce a third class of expressions, co-inductively with the formulas of definition 4, making the symbol "&" a binary infix instead of its actual use as part of a ternary mixfix: If W is a formula and E is an expression, then (W & E) is an expression. This enables simulating formulas of the form e :- W & E by nestings of the form e :-& (W & E). For this, the expression (*true* & E) can be assigned the value of E. However, assigning *false* to (*false* & E), blurring the distinction between (2^D-valued) expressions and ({*true*, *false*}-valued) formulas, would, e.g., cause *fac*(N) :-& (*zerop*(N) & 1) to return *false* for *fac*(1) instead of signalling inapplicability. Therefore, in RELFUN (*false* & E) is actually assigned the failure-signalling truth value *unknown*, which can be regarded as the empty expression value $\{\} \in 2^D$.

7. *If the formula has the form $\exists xW$, then its truth value is true if there exists $d \in D$ such that W has truth value true wrt I and $V(x/d)$; otherwise, its truth value is false.*

This functionally extended truth concept directly transfers to the classical definitions of, e.g., *model, validity*, and *logical consequence*, for which we refer to [7].

Example 4 *Consider the formula $\forall x(x$ **is** $f(g(x), g(x)))$ and the following interpretation I. Let $D = \{1, 2, \ldots\}$ be the natural numbers, let f be assigned the function that maps two naturals to the singleton set of their product, and let g be assigned the function that maps a natural to the set of its divisors. Then I is a model of the formula because all naturals have at least themselves and 1 as divisors.*

The definitions of groundness and Herbrand universes and bases adapt the corresponding classical notions; the definitions of Herbrand crosses and crossbases extend the notion of Herbrand bases in order to define models of, respectively, functional and relational-functional programs, as motivated in section 1.

Definition 17 *A* ground term, ground atom, *or* ground molecule *is, respectively, a term, atom, or molecule not containing variables.*

Definition 18 *The* Herbrand universe U_P *of a program P is the set of all ground terms that can be formed out of the constants and constructors appearing in P.*

Definition 19 *The* Herbrand base B_P *of a program P is the set of all ground atoms that can be formed by using the relation symbols from P with ground terms from the Herbrand universe U_P as arguments.*

Definition 20 *The* Herbrand cross C_P *of a program P is the set of all ground molecules that can be formed by using the function symbols from P with ground terms from the Herbrand universe U_P as arguments and using ground terms from U_P as foots.*

Definition 21 *The* Herbrand crossbase X_P *of a program P is the union $B_P \cup C_P$ of its Herbrand base B_P and its Herbrand cross C_P.*

Example 5 *The (deterministic, extra-variables,* **is***-less) program P_1*

$f(X)$:- $p(X), q(Y)$ & $g(g(X,Y),Y)$.
$g(a,a)$:-& $k[X]$.
$g(k[X], l[X])$:-& $g(X,X)$.
$p(k[X])$.
$q(l[X])$.

uses the constructors k and l, and employs the operators f and g (as functions) as well as *p and q (as relations).*

The Herbrand universe U_{P_1} *of* P_1 *is*
$\{a, k[a], l[a], k[k[a]], k[l[a]], l[k[a]], l[l[a]], \ldots\}$.

The Herbrand base B_{P_1} *of* P_1 *is*
$\{p(a), q(a), p(k[a]), p(l[a]), q(k[a]), q(l[a]), \ldots\}$.

The Herbrand cross C_{P_1} *of* P_1 *is*
$\{f(a)$:-& $a, f(a)$:-& $k[a], f(a)$:-& $l[a], \ldots,$
$g(a,a)$:-& $a, g(a,a)$:-& $k[a], g(a,a)$:-& $l[a], \ldots,$
$\ldots\}$.

The Herbrand crossbase $X_{P_1} = B_{P_1} \cup C_{P_1}$ *of* P_1 *is*
$\{p(a), q(a), p(k[a]), p(l[a]), q(k[a]), q(l[a]), \ldots,$
$f(a)$:-& $a, f(a)$:-& $k[a], f(a)$:-& $l[a], \ldots,$
$g(a,a)$:-& $a, g(a,a)$:-& $k[a], g(a,a)$:-& $l[a], \ldots,$
$\ldots\}$.

Two generalized model concepts can now be defined, extending the usual Herbrand models for relational programs to models for functional and relational-functional programs.

Definition 22 *An* Herbrand (base), Herbrand cross, or Herbrand crossbase interpretation *is a subset of the Herbrand base, Herbrand cross, or Herbrand crossbase, respectively.*

Definition 23 *Let I be an Herbrand (base), Herbrand cross, or Herbrand crossbase interpretation and let P be a program. Then I is, respectively, an* Herbrand (base), Herbrand cross, or Herbrand crossbase model *for P if P is true wrt I.*

We concentrate the further development on relational-functional Herbrand crossbase models, which, however, constitute disjoint unions of Herbrand cross models and Herbrand (base) models.

The "model intersection" proposition 6.1 of [7] obviously also holds for the crossbase extension.

Proposition 1 (Model intersection property) *Let P be a relational-functional program and* $\{M_i\}_{i \in I}$ *be a non-empty set of Herbrand crossbase models for P. Then* $\bigcap_{i \in I} M_i$ *is an Herbrand crossbase model for P.*

Since every relational-functional program P has X_P as an Herbrand crossbase model, the set of all Herbrand crossbase models for P is non-empty, and proposition 1 permits the following definition.

Definition 24 *The* least Herbrand crossbase model M_P *for a relational-functional program P is the intersection of all Herbrand crossbase models for P.*

Example 6 *For u assuming all values from U_{P_1}, the following Herbrand crossbase interpretation I, contained in X_{P_1}, is an (the least) Herbrand crossbase model of P_1 (cf. example 5):*

$\{f(k[a])$:-& $k[u]$, $g(a,a)$:-& $k[u]$, $g(k[a], l[a])$:-& $k[u]$,
$p(k[u])$, $q(l[u])\}$.

Thus, while P_1 deterministically returns the non-ground term $k[X]$ for certain arguments of the functions f and g (failing for other ones), the model of P_1 contains infinitely non-deterministic molecules that let f and g return the ground terms $k[a], k[k[a]], k[l[a]], \ldots$ for the same argument combinations.

Proposition 2 *Let P be a relational-functional program and I an Herbrand crossbase model of P (in particular, the least one). Then there exist a Horn program $\tilde{P}$ and an Herbrand model $\tilde{I}$ of $\tilde{P}$ (in particular, the least one) such that there is a bijection between I and $\tilde{I}$.*

Example 7 *The relational-functional program P_1 of example 5 can be transformed into the following Horn program $\tilde{P}_1$ by flattening the g nesting and introducing result parameters for f and g (note that the g-molecule becomes an atom):*

$\tilde{f}(X,R)$:- $p(X), q(Y), \tilde{g}(X,Y,S), \tilde{g}(S,Y,R)$.
$\tilde{g}(a,a,k[X])$.
$\tilde{g}(k[X], l[X], R)$:- $\tilde{g}(X,X,R)$.
$p(k[X])$.
$q(l[X])$.

An (the least) Herbrand model $\tilde{I}$ of $\tilde{P}_1$ is (where $u \in U_{\tilde{P}_1} = U_{P_1}$):

$\{\tilde{f}(k[a], k[u])$, $\tilde{g}(a,a,k[u])$, $\tilde{g}(k[a], l[a], k[u])$,
$p(k[u])$, $q(l[u])\}$.

The bijection between I and $\tilde{I}$ is obvious: untilded (functional) molecules correspond to tilded (relational) atoms; untilded atoms remain unchanged.

While the above bijection, call it b_{LAST}, introduces the new parameter in position $n+1$, there is another bijection, b_{FIRST}, introducing it in position 1, as actually done by RELFUN's `relationalize` *algorithm [3]. That is, an Herbrand model such as $\tilde{I}$ alone does not carry the entire information of the original Herbrand crossbase model such as I: the type of bijection must be specified along with the Herbrand model in order to preserve in the relations the computation direction ('mode') of the original functions. For instance, while $(b_{LAST})^{-1} \circ b_{LAST}(I) = I$, the composition $(b_{FIRST})^{-1} \circ b_{LAST}$ would transform I to* *the Herbrand crossbase model*

$\{f(k[u])$:-& $k[a]$, $g(a, k[u])$:-& a, $g(l[a], k[u])$:-& $k[a]$,
$p(k[u])$, $q(l[u])\}$

which is not equivalent to I.

Let us now proceed to the generalized notions of relational-functional answers and their correctness.

Definition 25 *Let* P *be a relational-functional program and* G_r *and* G_f *be a relational and a functional goal, respectively. A* relational answer *for* $P \cup \{G_r\}$ *is a substitution for variables of* G_r*. A* functional answer *for* $P \cup \{G_f\}$ *is a term paired with a substitution for variables of* G_f.

It should be understood that the substitution does not necessarily contain a binding for every variable in G_r or G_f. Since RELFUN's operational semantics considers relations as true-valued functions, a relational answer operationally returns the term `true` along with yielding a substitution.

Definition 26 *Let* P *be a relational-functional program,* G_r *a relational goal* :- $B_1, \ldots, B_k$ *with* θ *an answer for* $P \cup \{G_r\}$*, and* G_f *a functional goal* :- $B_1, \ldots, B_k$ & F *with* (t, θ) *an answer for* $P \cup \{G_f\}$*. We say that* θ *is a* correct (relational) answer *for* $P \cup \{G_r\}$ *if* $\forall((B_1 \wedge \ldots \wedge B_k)\theta)$ *is a logical consequence of* P*. We say that* (t, θ) *is a* correct (functional) answer *for* $P \cup \{G_f\}$ *if* $\forall((B_1 \wedge \ldots \wedge B_k \wedge (t \texttt{ is } F))\theta)$ *is a logical consequence of* P.

The following lemma shows that functional answers, i.e. "value returning to the top-level", can be simulated by relational answers binding top-level return values to a special variable.

Lemma 1 *Let* P *be a relational-functional program,* G_f *a functional goal* :- $B_1, \ldots, B_k$ & F*, and* G_r *a relational goal* :- $B_1, \ldots, B_k, (x \texttt{ is } F)$ *with* x *a new variable. Then the following statements are equivalent:*

1. (t, θ) *is a correct functional answer for* $P \cup \{G_f\}$.
2. $\theta\{x/t\}$ *is a correct relational answer for* $P \cup \{G_r\}$.

Proof
(t, θ) *is a correct functional answer for* $P \cup \{G_f\}$
iff
$\forall((B_1 \wedge \ldots \wedge B_k \wedge (t \texttt{ is } F))\theta)$ *is a logical consequence of* P
iff
$\forall((B_1 \wedge \ldots \wedge B_k \wedge (x \texttt{ is } F))\theta\{x/t\})$ *is a logical consequence of* P
iff
$\theta\{x/t\}$ *is a correct relational answer for* $P \cup \{G_r\}$.

4 SLV-Resolution

We now extend SLD-resolution to first-order relational-functional clauses, where the SLD-case will be called *body resolution*. The extended resolution method, similar to innermost conditional narrowing [5], will be called *SLV-resolution* (SL-resolution for "Valued clauses" i.e., RELFUN's definite-clause extension). It provides the set of inference rules of a first-order relational-functional theory. The detailed example 8 at the end of this section will illustrate most SLV-resolution concepts.

Definition 27 *Let G_r be the relational goal* `:-` $B_1, \ldots, B_m, \ldots, B_k$*; further let C be the hornish clause d* `:-` $V_1, \ldots, V_v$ *or the footed clause e* `:-` $W_1, \ldots, W_w$ `&` E *or the trivial clause* T*. Then G'_r is* (relationally) derived *from G_r and C using mgu θ if one of the following five inference rules applies (we let t's or u's denote terms):*

Body resolution

1. B_m *is an atom, called the* selected atom, *in* G_r.
2. C *is the hornish clause* d `:-` $V_1, \ldots, V_v$ *and θ is the mgu of B_m and d.*
3. G'_r *is the relational goal* `:-` $(B_1, \ldots, B_{m-1}, V_1, \ldots, V_v, B_{m+1}, \ldots, B_k)\theta$.

is-rhs resolution

1. B_m *is a formula of the form t* `is` $g(u_1, \ldots, u_m)$*, called the* selected flat setter, *in* G_r.
2. C *is the footed clause* e `:-` $W_1, \ldots, W_w$ `&` E *and θ is the mgu of $g(u_1, \ldots, u_m)$ and e.*
3. G'_r *is the relational goal* `:-` $(B_1, \ldots, B_{m-1}, W_1, \ldots, W_w, t$ `is` $E, B_{m+1}, \ldots, B_k)\theta$.

Body flattening

1. B_m *in G_r is a formula of the form* $r(E_1, \ldots, E_{i-1}, h(E_{i,1}, \ldots, E_{i,n_i}), E_{i+1}, \ldots, E_m)$*, called the* selected nested relationship, *and $h(E_{i,1}, \ldots, E_{i,n_i})$ is an embedded application, called the* selected (relationship-)embedded application.
2. C *is the trivial clause* T *and θ is the identity substitution (hence, trivially, an mgu).*
3. x *is a new variable.*
4. G'_r *is the relational goal* `:-` $B_1, \ldots, B_{m-1}$, x `is` $h(E_{i,1}, \ldots, E_{i,n_i}), r(E_1, \ldots, E_{i-1}, x, E_{i+1}, \ldots, E_m), B_{m+1}, \ldots, B_k$.

is-rhs flattening

1. B_m *in G_r is a formula of the form t* `is` $g(E_1, \ldots, E_{i-1}, h(E_{i,1}, \ldots, E_{i,n_i}), E_{i+1}, \ldots, E_m)$*, called the* selected nested setter, *and $h(E_{i,1}, \ldots, E_{i,n_i})$ is an embedded application, called the* selected (`is`-)embedded application.

2. *C is the trivial clause* $\top$ *and* θ *is the identity substitution (hence, trivially, an mgu).*
3. x *is a new variable.*
4. G'_r *is the relational goal* :- $B_1, \ldots, B_{m-1}$, x **is** $h(E_{i,1}, \ldots, E_{i,n_i}), t$ **is** $g(E_1, \ldots, E_{i-1}, x, E_{i+1}, \ldots, E_m), B_{m+1}, \ldots, B_k$.

Term unification

1. B_m *is a formula of the form* t_1 **is** t_2*, called the* selected term setter, *in* G_r.
2. *C is the trivial clause* $\top$ *and* θ *is the mgu of* t_1 *and* t_2.
3. G'_r *is the relational goal* :- $(B_1, \ldots, B_{m-1}, B_{m+1}, \ldots, B_k)\theta$.

Definition 28 *Let* G_f *be the functional goal* :- $B_1, \ldots, B_k$ & F*; further let C be the hornish clause d* :- $V_1, \ldots, V_v$ *or the footed clause e* :- $W_1, \ldots, W_w$ & E *or the trivial clause* $\top$. *Then* G'_f *is* (functionally) derived *from* G_f *and C using mgu* θ *if one of the following three inference rules applies (we let u's denote terms):*

Relational subderivation (using one of the five rules of definition 27)

1. G_r *is* :- $B_1, \ldots, B_k$*, called the* selected relational subgoal *of* G_f.
2. G'_r *is relationally derived from* G_r *and C using mgu* θ.
3. G'_f *is the functional goal* :- G'_r & $F\theta$.

Foot resolution

1. F *is a formula of the form* $g(u_1, \ldots, u_m)$*, called the* selected flat application, *in* G_f.
2. *C is the footed clause e* :- $W_1, \ldots, W_w$ & E *and* θ *is the mgu of* $g(u_1, \ldots, u_m)$ *and e.*
3. G'_f *is the functional goal* :- $(B_1, \ldots, B_k, W_1, \ldots, W_w$ & $E)\theta$.

Foot flattening

1. F *in* G_f *is a formula of the form* $g(E_1, \ldots, E_{i-1}, h(E_{i,1}, \ldots, E_{i,n_i}), E_{i+1}, \ldots, E_m)$*, called the* selected nested application, *and* $h(E_{i,1}, \ldots, E_{i,n_i})$ *is an embedded application, called the* selected (application-)embedded application.
2. *C is the trivial clause* $\top$ *and* θ *is the identity substitution (hence, trivially, an mgu).*
3. x *is a new variable.*
4. G'_f *is the functional goal* :- $B_1, \ldots, B_k, x$ **is** $h(E_{i,1}, \ldots, E_{i,n_i})$ & $g(E_1, \ldots, E_{i-1}, x, E_{i+1}, \ldots, E_m)$.

Although we first presented relational goals (in definition 27) and then extended them to functional goals (in definition 28), the inference rules would not have to distinguish body and foot premises for their "selection function" (or, item *1.* of each rule), and they do not in the actual implementation: (relational) body resolution and (functional) foot resolution, as well as body and foot flattening, could be treated together. Similarly, inference rules operating in the top-level of premises and in is-rhs's have a common realization: (relational) body resolution and (functional) is-rhs resolution, as well as body flattening and is-rhs flattening, could be identified. However, our more discriminative presentation will clarify the case analysis of the soundness proof.

Definition 29 *Let P be a relational-functional program and G be a (relational or functional) goal. A* (relational resp. functional) SLV-derivation *of $P \cup \{G\}$ consists of a finite or infinite sequence $G_0 = G, G_1, G_2, \ldots$ of (relational resp. functional) goals, a sequence $C_1, C_2, \ldots$ of variants of program clauses of $P \cup \{\top\}$, $\top$ the trivial clause, and a sequence $\theta_1, \theta_2, \ldots$ of mgu's such that each G_{i+1} is derived from G_i and C_{i+1} using θ_{i+1}.*

Definition 30 *A* (relational) SLV-refutation *of $P \cup \{G_r\}$, G_r a relational goal, is a finite SLV-derivation of $P \cup \{G_r\}$ that has the empty hornish clause $\Box$ as the last goal in the derivation. A* (functional) SLV-refutation *of $P \cup \{G_f\}$, G_f a functional goal, is a finite SLV-derivation of $P \cup \{G_f\}$ that has the terminal footed clause $\Delta(t)$ as the last goal in the derivation. If $G_n = \Box$ or $G_n = \Delta(t)$, we say the refutation has* length n.

Definition 31 *An* unrestricted (relational or functional) SLV-refutation *is a (relational or functional) SLV-refutation, except that the substitutions θ_i are not required to be most general unifiers. They are only required to be unifiers.*

Definition 32 *Let P be a relational-functional program. The* relational success set *of P is the set of all ground atoms $a \in B_P$ such that $P \cup \{$:- $a\}$ has a relational SLV-refutation. The* functional success set *of P is the set of all ground molecules (e :-& t) $\in C_P$ such that $P \cup \{$:-& e$\}$ has a functional SLV-refutation with last goal $\Delta(t)$. The* success set *of P is the union of the relational and functional success sets of P.*

Proposition 3 *Let P be a relational-functional program. The* functional success set *of P is the set of all ground molecules (e :-& t) $\in C_P$ such that $P \cup \{$:- (t is e)$\}$ has a relational SLV-refutation.*

Proof

The ground flat setter (t is e) = (e :-& t)$^{\otimes}$ leads to a relational SLV-refutation iff e, also being the corresponding molecule's ground flat application, leads to a functional SLV-refutation with last goal $\Delta(t)$.

Definition 33 *Let P be a relational-functional program; further, let G_r be a relational goal. Suppose there is an SLV-refutation of $P \cup \{G_r\}$ and let $\theta_1, \ldots, \theta_n$ be its sequence of mgu's. A* computed (relational) answer *for $P \cup \{G_r\}$ is the substitution θ obtained by restricting the composition $\theta_1 \ldots \theta_n$ to the variables of G_r.*

Definition 34 *Let P be a relational-functional program; further, let G_f be a functional goal. Suppose there is an SLV-refutation of $P \cup \{G_f\}$ and let $\theta_1, \ldots, \theta_n$ be its sequence of mgu's and let $\Delta(t)$ be its last goal.* A computed (functional) answer *for $P \cup \{G_f\}$ is the pair $(t\theta_1 \ldots \theta_n, \theta)$, with the term t extracted from $\Delta(t)$ and the substitution θ obtained by restricting the composition $\theta_1 \ldots \theta_n$ to the variables of G_f.*

Lemma 2 *Let P be a relational-functional program, G_f a functional goal* `:-` *$B_1, \ldots, B_k$* `&` *F, and G_r a relational goal* `:-` *$B_1, \ldots, B_k$, (x* `is` *F) with x a new variable. Then the following statements are equivalent:*

1. *(t, θ) is a computed functional answer for $P \cup \{G_f\}$.*
2. *$\theta\{x/t\}$ is a computed relational answer for $P \cup \{G_r\}$.*

Proof
(t, θ) is a computed functional answer for $P \cup \{G_f\}$
iff
there is an SLV-refutation of $P \cup \{G_f\}$ with a sequence of mgu's $\theta_1, \ldots, \theta_n$ and last goal $\Delta(u)$ such that t is $u\theta_1 \ldots \theta_n$ and θ restricts the composition $\theta_1 \ldots \theta_n$ to the variables of G_f
iff
there is an SLV-refutation of $P \cup \{G_r\}$ with a sequence of mgu's $\theta_1, \ldots, \theta_n, \{x/t\}$ such that $\theta\{x/t\}$ restricts the composition $\theta_1 \ldots \theta_n\{x/t\}$ to the variables of G_r
iff
$\theta\{x/t\}$ is a computed relational answer for $P \cup \{G_r\}$.

Example 8 *The (non-deterministic, no-extra-variables,* `is`*-using) program P_2*

$f(X)$ `:-` $p(g(a), g(X))$ `&` $h(g(X))$.
$g(a)$ `:-&` c.
$g(a)$ `:-&` $h(c)$.
$h(X)$ `:-&` b.
$p(X, c)$ `:-` X `is` $h(a), q(h(X))$.
$q(b)$.

uses no constructors, hence belongs to the DATALOG-extending DATAFUN subset of RELFUN; it has the finite Herbrand universe $\{a, b, c\}$, hence a finite Herbrand crossbase.

A functional SLV-refutation of $P_2 \cup \{$ `:-&` *$f(Y)\}$ is:*

$G_0 = G =$ `:-&` $f(Y)$
Foot resolution of $f(Y)$ with $C_1 = f(X1)$ `:-` *$p(g(a), g(X1))$* `&` *$h(g(X1))$, $\theta_1 = \{Y/X1\}$:*
$G_1 =$ `:-` $p(g(a), g(X1))$ `&` $h(g(X1))$
Body flattening of $p(g(a), \ldots)$ with $C_2 = \top$, $\theta_2 = \{\}$:
$G_2 =$ `:-` $Z1$ `is` $g(a), p(Z1, g(X1))$ `&` $h(g(X1))$
`is`*-rhs resolution of $Z1$* `is` *$g(a)$ with $C_3 = g(a)$* `:-&` *$h(c)$, $\theta_3 = \{\}$:*

$G_3 =$:- $Z1$ **is** $h(c), p(Z1, g(X1))$ & $h(g(X1))$
is-*rhs resolution of* $Z1$ **is** $h(c)$ *with* $C_4 = h(X2)$:-& b, $\theta_4 = \{X2/c\}$:
$G_4 =$:- $Z1$ **is** $b, p(Z1, g(X1))$ & $h(g(X1))$
Term unification of $Z1$ **is** b *with* $C_5 = \top$, $\theta_5 = \{Z1/b\}$:
$G_5 =$:- $p(b, g(X1))$ & $h(g(X1))$
Body flattening of $p(\ldots, g(X1))$ *with* $C_6 = \top$, $\theta_6 = \{\}$:
$G_6 =$:- $Z2$ **is** $g(X1), p(b, Z2)$ & $h(g(X1))$
is-*rhs resolution of* $Z2$ **is** $g(X1)$ *with* $C_7 = g(a)$:-& c, $\theta_7 = \{X1/a\}$:
$G_7 =$:- $Z2$ **is** $c, p(b, Z2)$ & $h(g(X1))$
Term unification of $Z2$ **is** c *with* $C_8 = \top$, $\theta_8 = \{Z2/c\}$:
$G_8 =$:- $p(b, c)$ & $h(g(X1))$
Body resolution of $p(b, c)$ *with* $C_9 = p(X3, c)$:- $X3$ **is** $h(a), q(h(X3))$, $\theta_9 = \{X3/b\}$:
$G_9 =$:- b **is** $h(a), q(h(b))$ & $h(g(X1))$
is-*rhs resolution of* b **is** $h(a)$ *with* $C_{10} = h(X4)$:-& b, $\theta_{10} = \{X4/a\}$:
$G_{10} =$:- b **is** $b, q(h(b))$ & $h(g(X1))$
Term unification of b **is** b *with* $C_{11} = \top$, $\theta_{11} = \{\}$:
$G_{11} =$:- $q(h(b))$ & $h(g(X1))$
Body flattening of $q(h(b))$ *with* $C_{12} = \top$, $\theta_{12} = \{\}$:
$G_{12} =$:- $Z3$ **is** $h(b), q(Z3)$ & $h(g(X1))$
is-*rhs resolution of* $Z3$ **is** $h(b)$ *with* $C_{13} = h(X5)$:-& b, $\theta_{13} = \{X5/b\}$:
$G_{13} =$:- $Z3$ **is** $b, q(Z3)$ & $h(g(X1))$
Term unification of $Z3$ **is** b *with* $C_{14} = \top$, $\theta_{14} = \{Z3/b\}$:
$G_{14} =$:- $q(b)$ & $h(g(X1))$
Body resolution of $q(b)$ *with* $C_{15} = q(b)$, $\theta_{15} = \{\}$:
$G_{15} =$:-& $h(g(a))$[12]
Foot flattening of $h(g(a))$ *with* $C_{16} = \top$, $\theta_{16} = \{\}$:
$G_{16} =$:- $Z4$ **is** $g(a)$ & $h(Z4)$
is-*rhs resolution of* $Z4$ **is** $g(a)$ *with* $C_{17} = g(a)$:-& c, $\theta_{17} = \{\}$:
$G_{17} =$:- $Z4$ **is** c & $h(Z4)$
Term unification of $Z4$ **is** c *with* $C_{18} = \top$, $\theta_{18} = \{Z4/c\}$:
$G_{18} =$:-& $h(c)$
Foot resolution of $h(c)$ *with* $C_{19} = h(X6)$:-& b, $\theta_{19} = \{X6/b\}$:
$G_{19} =$:-& b

This length-19 refutation happens to use RELFUN's implemented PROLOG-like 'leftmost' computation rule (however, RELFUN implements flattening in a condensed 'and-parallel' fashion). Operationally speaking, "$f(Y)$ returns b and binds Y to a": The refutation has last goal $G_{19} = \Delta(b)$, and $\theta_1 \ldots \theta_{19}$ restricted to Y is $\{Y/a\}$; hence the computed functional answer is $(b, \{Y/a\})$.

*The equivalent computed relational answer for $P_2 \cup \{$:- Z **is** $f(Y)\}$ is $\{Y/a, Z/b\}$. Here, the refutation uses **is**-rhs resolutions and performs an **is**-rhs flattening instead of the corresponding rules operating on the foot, and it needs a final term unification. Functional computation is somewhat hidden in the auxiliary setter's rhs. However, the kernel*

[12]The binding $\theta_7 = \{X1/a\}$ from the relational subderivation $G_2, \ldots, G_{15}$ is applied here.

subderivations of the functional and relational refutations are essentially the same.

The success set of P_2 is (functional and relational partitions displayed in separate lines):[13]

$\{f(a)$:-& b, $g(a)$:-& b, $g(a)$:-& c, $h(a)$:-& b, $h(b)$:-& b, $h(c)$:-& b,
$q(b)$, $p(b,c)\}$

5 Soundness of SLV-Resolution

While the following result addresses relational goals, only the first of the five SLV-resolution rules to be considered corresponds to the classical case of logic programming as proved by K. L. Clark.

Theorem 1 (Soundness of relational SLV-resolution) *Let P be a relational-functional program and G_r a relational goal. Then every computed answer for $P \cup \{G_r\}$ is a correct answer for $P \cup \{G_r\}$.*

Proof
Let G_r be the relational goal :- $B_1, \ldots, B_k$ and $\theta_1, \ldots, \theta_n$ be the sequence of mgu's used in an SLV-refutation of $P \cup \{G_r\}$. We have to show that $\forall((B_1 \wedge \ldots \wedge B_k)\theta_1 \ldots \theta_n)$ is a logical consequence of P. The result is proved by induction on the length of the refutation.

Suppose first that $n = 1$. This means that G_r is a goal of the form :- B_1, to which either of two of the five SLV-resolution rules applies:

Body resolution *B_1 is an atom, the program has a unit clause of the form d :- , and $B_1\theta_1 = d\theta_1$. Since $B_1\theta_1$:- is an instance of a unit clause of P, it follows that $\forall(B_1\theta_1)$ is a logical consequence of P.*

is-rhs resolution *Cannot derive $\Box$ in one step.*

Body flattening *Cannot derive $\Box$ in one step.*

is-rhs flattening *Cannot derive $\Box$ in one step.*

Term unification *B_1 is a formula of the form t_1 **is** t_2 and θ_1 is the mgu of t_1 and t_2. Since $t_1\theta_1 = t_2\theta_1$, it follows that $\forall(B_1\theta_1)$ is valid, hence, trivially, is a logical consequence of P.*

Next suppose that the result holds for computed answers that come from SLV-refutations of length $n-1$. Suppose $\theta_1, \ldots, \theta_n$ is the sequence of mgu's used in a refutation of $P \cup \{G_r\}$ of length n. One of the five SLV-resolution rules applies:

[13] In higher-order RELFUN, this can be obtained from the computed answers of an operator-variable, varying-arity goal [3] such as :-& *Op*(|*Args*).

Body resolution *Let B_m be the selected atom of G_r and the hornish clause* d :- $V_1, \ldots, V_v$ *($v \geq 0$) be the first input clause. By the induction hypothesis,* $\forall((B_1 \wedge \ldots \wedge B_{m-1} \wedge V_1 \wedge \ldots \wedge V_v \wedge B_{m+1} \wedge \ldots \wedge B_k)\theta_1 \ldots \theta_n)$ *is a logical consequence of P. Thus, if $v > 0$, $\forall((V_1 \wedge \ldots \wedge V_v)\theta_1 \ldots \theta_n)$ is a logical consequence of P. In this case, as well as for $v = 0$, $\forall(B_m\theta_1 \ldots \theta_n)$, which is the same as $\forall(d\theta_1 \ldots \theta_n)$, is a logical consequence of P. Hence $\forall((B_1 \wedge \ldots \wedge B_k)\theta_1 \ldots \theta_n)$ is a logical consequence of P.*

is-rhs resolution *Let B_m be the selected flat setter* t **is** $g(u_1, \ldots, u_m)$ *of G_r and the footed clause* e :- $W_1, \ldots, W_w$ & E *($w \geq 0$) be the first input clause. By the induction hypothesis,* $\forall((B_1 \wedge \ldots \wedge B_{m-1} \wedge W_1 \wedge \ldots \wedge W_w \wedge t \text{ is } E \wedge B_{m+1} \wedge \ldots \wedge B_k)\theta_1 \ldots \theta_n)$ *is a logical consequence of P. Thus, for $w \geq 0$,* $\forall((W_1 \wedge \ldots \wedge W_w \wedge t \text{ is } E)\theta_1 \ldots \theta_n)$ *is a logical consequence of P. Consequently, $\forall(B_m\theta_1 \ldots \theta_n)$, which is the same as* $\forall((t \text{ is } e)\theta_1 \ldots \theta_n)$*, is a logical consequence of P. Hence $\forall((B_1 \wedge \ldots \wedge B_k)\theta_1 \ldots \theta_n)$ is a logical consequence of P.*

Body flattening *Let B_m be the selected nested relationship $r(E_1, \ldots, E_{i-1}, h(E_{i,1}, \ldots, E_{i,n_i}), E_{i+1}, \ldots, E_m)$ with the selected embedded application $h(E_{i,1}, \ldots, E_{i,n_i})$ of G_r. By the induction hypothesis,* $\forall((B_1 \wedge \ldots \wedge B_{m-1} \wedge (x \text{ is } h(E_{i,1}, \ldots, E_{i,n_i})) \wedge r(E_1, \ldots, E_{i-1}, x, E_{i+1}, \ldots, E_m) \wedge B_{m+1} \wedge \ldots \wedge B_k)\theta_1 \ldots, \theta_n)$*, x the new variable chosen by the SLV-refutation, is a logical consequence of P. Thus,* $\forall((x \text{ is } h(E_{i,1}, \ldots, E_{i,n_i}))\theta_1 \ldots \theta_n)$ *and* $\forall(r(E_1, \ldots, E_{i-1}, x, E_{i+1}, \ldots, E_m)\theta_1 \ldots \theta_n)$ *are logical consequences of P. Consequently, $\forall(B_m\theta_1 \ldots \theta_n)$ is a logical consequence of P. Hence $\forall((B_1 \wedge \ldots \wedge B_k)\theta_1 \ldots \theta_n)$ is a logical consequence of P.*

is-rhs flattening *Let B_m be the selected nested setter* t **is** $g(E_1, \ldots, E_{i-1}, h(E_{i,1}, \ldots, E_{i,n_i}), E_{i+1}, \ldots, E_m)$ *with the selected embedded application $h(E_{i,1}, \ldots, E_{i,n_i})$ of G_r. By the induction hypothesis,* $\forall((B_1 \wedge \ldots \wedge B_{m-1} \wedge (x \text{ is } h(E_{i,1}, \ldots, E_{i,n_i})) \wedge (t \text{ is } g(E_1, \ldots, E_{i-1}, x, E_{i+1}, \ldots, E_m)) \wedge B_{m+1} \wedge \ldots \wedge B_k)\theta_1 \ldots \theta_n)$*, x the new variable chosen by the SLV-refutation, is a logical consequence of P. Thus,* $\forall((x \text{ is } h(E_{i,1}, \ldots, E_{i,n_i}))\theta_1 \ldots \theta_n)$ *and* $\forall((t \text{ is } g(E_1, \ldots, E_{i-1}, x, E_{i+1}, \ldots, E_m))\theta_1 \ldots \theta_n)$ *are logical consequences of P. Consequently, $\forall(B_m\theta_1 \ldots \theta_n)$ is a logical consequence of P. Hence $\forall((B_1 \wedge \ldots \wedge B_k)\theta_1 \ldots \theta_n)$ is a logical consequence of P.*

Term unification *Let B_m be the selected term setter* t_1 **is** t_2 *of G_r. By the induction hypothesis, $\forall((B_1 \wedge \ldots \wedge B_{m-1} \wedge B_{m+1} \wedge \ldots \wedge B_k)\theta_1 \ldots \theta_n)$ is a logical consequence of P. Since $t_1\theta_1 \ldots \theta_n = t_2\theta_1 \ldots \theta_n$, it follows that $\forall(B_m\theta_1 \ldots \theta_n)$ is valid, hence, trivially, is a logical consequence of P. Hence $\forall((B_1 \wedge \ldots \wedge B_k)\theta_1 \ldots \theta_n)$ is a logical consequence of P.*

The result for relational goals naturally carries over to functional goals.

Corollary 1 (Soundness of functional SLV-resolution) *Let P be a relational-functional program and G_f a functional goal. Then every computed answer for $P \cup \{G_f\}$ is a correct answer for $P \cup \{G_f\}$.*

Proof
By lemmas 2 and 1 there is an equivalent relational goal with computed and correct answers for which the soundness result of theorem 1 holds.

Corollary 2 *The success set of a relational-functional program is contained in its least Herbrand crossbase model.*

Proof
Let the program be P and suppose $F \in X_P$ is in the success set of P. By proposition 3, the success set of P is the set of all $F \in X_P$ such that $P \cup \{\ \texttt{:-}\ F^{\otimes}\}$ has a relational refutation. By theorem 1, $F^{\otimes}$, hence F, is a logical consequence of P. Thus, F is true wrt all Herbrand crossbase models of P, hence is in P's least Herbrand crossbase model.

6 Least Herbrand Crossbase Models as Fixpoints

We now define T_P-like immediate-consequence operators on Herbrand crossbase interpretations. For this we employ *unnesting* of clause premises, a fixpoint-semantics, ground-formula analogue to flattening in SLV-resolution. Instead of introducing new variables, unnesting chooses any ground terms from the Herbrand universe, as "returned values", to link the subformulas generated from the original formula.

Definition 35 *A set of* unnested setters $unnestis_P(t\ \texttt{is}\ E)$ *of a ground setter* $t\ \texttt{is}\ E$ *for a program* P *is defined recursively as the non-deterministic mapping*

$unnestis_P(t\ \texttt{is}\ g(u_1, \ldots, u_m)) =$
$\quad \{t\ \texttt{is}\ g(u_1, \ldots, u_m)\}\ if\ \{u_1, \ldots, u_m\} \subseteq U_P$
$unnestis_P(t\ \texttt{is}\ g(E_1, \ldots, E_{i-1}, h(E_{i,1}, \ldots, E_{i,n_i}), E_{i+1}, \ldots, E_m)) =$
$\quad unnestis_P(u\ \texttt{is}\ h(E_{i,1}, \ldots, E_{i,n_i})) \cup unnestis_P(t\ \texttt{is}\ g(E_1, \ldots, E_{i-1}, u, E_{i+1}, \ldots, E_m))$
$\quad for\ some\ u \in U_P$

Definition 36 *A set of* unnested formulas $unnest_P(V)$ *of a ground relationship or setter* V *for a program* P *is defined as the non-deterministic mapping*

$unnest_P(r(u_1, \ldots, u_m)) =$
$\quad \{r(u_1, \ldots, u_m)\}\ if\ \{u_1, \ldots, u_m\} \subseteq U_P$
$unnest_P(r(E_1, \ldots, E_{i-1}, h(E_{i,1}, \ldots, E_{i,n_i}), E_{i+1}, \ldots, E_m)) =$
$\quad unnestis_P(u\ \texttt{is}\ h(E_{i,1}, \ldots, E_{i,n_i})) \cup unnest_P(r(E_1, \ldots, E_{i-1}, u, E_{i+1}, \ldots, E_m))$
$\quad for\ some\ u \in U_P$
$unnest_P(t\ \texttt{is}\ t) =$
$\quad \{\}\ if\ t \in U_P$
$unnest_P(t\ \texttt{is}\ g(E_1, \ldots, E_m)) =$
$\quad unnestis_P(t\ \texttt{is}\ g(E_1, \ldots, E_m))$

A first auxiliary immediate-consequence operator, TB_P, generates atoms from atoms and molecules.

Definition 37 *Let P be a relational-functional program. The mapping $TB_P : 2^{X_P} \to 2^{B_P}$ is defined as follows. Let $I \in 2^{X_P}$ be an Herbrand crossbase interpretation. Then:*

$$TB_P(I) = \{w \in B_P \mid \; w \text{ :- } V_1, \ldots, V_n \text{ is a ground instance of a clause in } P, \; unnest_P(V_k)^{\otimes} \subseteq I \text{ for } 1 \leq k \leq n\}$$

If each V_k has the Horn-premise form $r(u_1, \ldots, u_n)$ of an atom, $unnest_P(V_k)^{\otimes}$ just denotes the unit set $\{V_k\}$, hence TB_P becomes the T_P operator of M. H. van Emden and R. Kowalski.

Proposition 4 *Let P be a relational-functional program containing Horn clauses only and $I \in 2^{B_P}$ be an Herbrand interpretation. Then the mapping TB_P restricted to $2^{B_P} \subseteq 2^{X_P}$ specializes to the mapping $T_P : 2^{B_P} \to 2^{B_P}$ defined as:*

$$T_P(I) = \{w \in B_P \mid \; w \text{ :- } V_1, \ldots, V_n \text{ is a ground instance of a clause in } P, \; V_k \in I \text{ for } 1 \leq k \leq n\}$$

Note how the intuitive understanding of T_P is extended by TB_P: as $T_P(I)$ 'guesses' a ground clause of P and then checks whether its premise atoms are members of I, $TB_P(I)$ 'guesses' a ground clause of P, then 'guesses' an unnesting (zero/one atoms and one/zero or more setters) from each of its premises, and then checks whether the "$\otimes$"-corresponding atoms and molecules constitute subsets of I.

A second auxiliary immediate-consequence operator, TC_P, generates molecules from atoms and molecules.

Definition 38 *Let P be a relational-functional program. The mapping $TC_P : 2^{X_P} \to 2^{C_P}$ is defined as follows. Let $I \in 2^{X_P}$ be an Herbrand crossbase interpretation. Then:*

$$TC_P(I) = \{e \text{ :-\& } t \in C_P \mid \; e \text{ :- } V_1, \ldots, V_n \text{ \& } E \text{ is a ground instance of a clause in } P, \; unnest_P(V_k)^{\otimes} \subseteq I \text{ for } 1 \leq k \leq n, \; unnest_P(t \texttt{ is } E)^{\otimes} \subseteq I\}$$

Example 9 *The program P_2 (cf. example 8) with $U_{P_2} = \{a, b, c\}$ contains the footed clause $f(X)$:- $p(g(a), g(X))$ & $h(g(X))$. Suppose a TC_{P_2} application selects the ground instance $f(a)$:- $p(g(a), g(a))$ & $h(g(a))$, i.e. $V_1 = p(g(a), g(a))$ and $E = h(g(a))$. Then $unnest_{P_2}(V_1)$ can select $\{p(b, c),\; b \texttt{ is } g(a),\; c \texttt{ is } g(a)\}$, so that $unnest_{P_2}(V_1)^{\otimes} = \{p(b, c),\; g(a) \text{ :-\& } b,\; g(a) \text{ :-\& } c\}$. Further suppose TC_{P_2}'s set formation selects $t = b$ and $unnest_{P_2}(t \texttt{ is } E)$ selects $\{b \texttt{ is } h(c),\; c \texttt{ is } g(a)\}$, so that $unnest_{P_2}(t \texttt{ is } E)^{\otimes} = \{h(c) \text{ :-\& } b,\; g(a) \text{ :-\& } c\}$. Now, if some interpretation I has $\{p(b, c),\; g(a) \text{ :-\& } b,\; g(a) \text{ :-\& } c,\; h(c) \text{ :-\& } b\}$ as a subset, $TC_{P_2}(I)$ will contain the element $f(a)$:-& b.*

Since the sets produced by unnesting are always finite, the atoms and setters resulting from $unnest_P(V_k)$ and $unnest_P(t \texttt{ is } E)$ can be regarded as premises of a 'virtual' ground clause e :- $unnest_P(V_1)^{\epsilon}, \ldots, unnest_P(V_n)^{\epsilon}, unnest_P(t \texttt{ is } E)^{\epsilon}$ & t. ("$\{\ldots\}^{\epsilon}$" denotes the sequence of *elements* of "{...}".) The corresponding non-ground clause can be obtained by transforming the original program P via static flattening and denotative normalization [2]. Therefore, each application of TC_P can be regarded as a condensed form of the application of a less powerful operator indexed by the more lengthy transformed program (T_P's extension would be confined to clauses with atomic and flat-setter bodies and term foots).

Example 10 *A virtual ground clause of* $f(a)$:- $p(g(a), g(a))$ & $h(g(a))$ *from example 9 is* $f(a)$:- b is $g(a)$, c is $g(a)$, $p(b,c)$, c is $g(a)$, b is $h(c)$ & b. *Its non-ground abstraction* $f(X)$:- $Y1$ is $g(a)$, $Y2$ is $g(X)$, $p(Y1,Y2)$, $Y3$ is $g(X)$, $Y4$ is $h(Y3)$ & $Y4$ *is the flattened, denotative normalization of* $f(X)$:- $p(g(a), g(X))$ & $h(g(X))$, *the original non-ground clause.*

The main immediate-consequence operator, TX_P, just unites the two auxiliary ones.

Definition 39 *Let P be a relational-functional program. The mapping $TX_P : 2^{X_P} \rightarrow 2^{X_P}$ is defined as follows. Let $I \in 2^{X_P}$ be an Herbrand crossbase interpretation. Then:*

$$TX_P(I) = TB_P(I) \cup TC_P(I)$$

Example 11 *Let P_1 be the relational-functional program of example 5 and I the interpretation* $\{g(k[a],l[a])$:-& $k[a]$, $p(k[a])$, $q(l[a])\} \in 2^{X_{P_1}}$. *Since* $unnest_{P_1}(k[a] \texttt{ is } g(g(k[a], l[a]), l[a]))^{\otimes}$ *can select* $\{g(k[a], l[a])$:-& $k[a]\}$, *we obtain* $TX_{P_1}(I) = \{f(k[a])$:-& $k[a]$, $g(a,a)$:-& $k[u]$, $p(k[u])$, $q(l[u])\}$ *for* $u \in U_{P_1}$.

Clearly, TX_P is monotonic on the complete lattice 2^{X_P} under the partial order "$\subseteq$". Like T_P in [7], it can be shown to be continuous.

Proposition 5 *Let P be a relational-functional program. Then the mapping TX_P is continuous.*

Proof

Let S be a directed subset of 2^{X_P}, V_k be a ground relationship or setter, for $1 \leq k \leq n$, and t is E be a ground setter. Each $unnest_P(V_k)^{\otimes}$ being a finite set, we can first note that $\bigcup_{k=1}^{n} unnest_P(V_k)^{\otimes} \subseteq lub(S)$ iff $\bigcup_{k=1}^{n} unnest_P(V_k)^{\otimes} \subseteq I$ for some $I \in S$; furthermore, $unnest_P(t \texttt{ is } E)^{\otimes}$ being a finite set, $\bigcup_{k=1}^{n} unnest_P(V_k)^{\otimes} \cup unnest_P(t \texttt{ is } E)^{\otimes} \subseteq lub(S)$ iff $\bigcup_{k=1}^{n} unnest_P(V_k)^{\otimes} \cup unnest_P(t \texttt{ is } E)^{\otimes} \subseteq I$ for some $I \in S$. In order to show that TX_P is continuous we have to show $TX_P(lub(S)) = lub(TX_P(S))$ for each directed subset S. Since TX_P denotes the disjoint union of TB_P's and TC_P's values we show the equality of both subsets individually:

$w \in TB_P(lub(S))$
iff
w :- $V_1, \ldots, V_n$ *is a ground instance of a clause in* P *and* $\bigcup_{k=1}^{n} unnest_P(V_k)^{\otimes} \subseteq lub(S)$
iff
w :- $V_1, \ldots, V_n$ *is a ground instance of a clause in* P *and* $\bigcup_{k=1}^{n} unnest_P(V_k)^{\otimes} \subseteq I$ *for some* $I \in S$
iff
$w \in TB_P(I)$ *for some* $I \in S$
iff
$w \in lub(TB_P(S))$

e :-& $t \in TC_P(lub(S))$
iff
e :- $V_1, \ldots, V_n$ & E *is a ground instance of a clause in* P *and* $\bigcup_{k=1}^{n} unnest_P(V_k)^{\otimes} \cup$ $unnest_P(t$ **is** $E)^{\otimes} \subseteq lub(S)$
iff
e :- $V_1, \ldots, V_n$ & E *is a ground instance of a clause in* P *and* $\bigcup_{k=1}^{n} unnest_P(V_k)^{\otimes} \cup$ $unnest_P(t$ **is** $E)^{\otimes} \subseteq I$ *for some* $I \in S$
iff
e :-& $t \in TC_P(I)$ *for some* $I \in S$
iff
e :-& $t \in lub(TC_P(S))$

Herbrand crossbase models can be characterized in terms of TX_P.

Proposition 6 *Let* P *be a relational-functional program and* I *be an Herbrand crossbase interpretation of* P. *Then* I *is a crossbase model for* P *iff* $TX_P(I) \subseteq I$.

Proof
I *is a crossbase model for* P
iff
for each ground instance w :- $V_1, \ldots, V_n$ *or* e :- $V_1, \ldots, V_n$ & E *of each clause in* P *we have, respectively,* $\bigcup_{k=1}^{n} unnest_P(V_k)^{\otimes} \subseteq I$ *implies* $w \in I$ *or* $\bigcup_{k=1}^{n} unnest_P(V_k)^{\otimes} \cup$ $unnest_P(t$ **is** $E)^{\otimes} \subseteq I$ *implies* e :-& $t \in I$
iff
$TX_P(I) \subseteq I$

Using these propositions and general fixpoint results, we can extend the fixpoint characterization of the least Herbrand model of logic programs by M. H. van Emden and R. Kowalski to a characterization of the least Herbrand crossbase model of relational-functional programs (for the "↑"-notation see [7]).

Theorem 2 (Fixpoint characterization of the least Herbrand crossbase model) *Let* P *be a relational-functional program. Then* $M_P = lfp(TX_P) = TX_P \uparrow \omega$.

Proof

$$\begin{aligned} M_P &= glb\{I \mid I \text{ is an Herbrand crossbase model for } P\} \\ &= glb\{I \mid TX_P(I) \subseteq I\}, \text{ by proposition 6} \\ &= lfp(TX_P), \text{ by proposition 5.1 in [7]} \\ &= TX_P \uparrow \omega, \text{ by proposition 5.4 in [7] and proposition 5} \end{aligned}$$

Example 12 *The 8-element least Herbrand crossbase model of the program P_2 of example 8 (in section 4) can be computed bottom-up by the following TX_{P_2} iterations (details of the last step were shown in example 9):*

$TX_{P_2} \uparrow 0 =$
$\{\}$

$TX_{P_2} \uparrow 1 = TX_{P_2} \uparrow 0 \cup$
$\{g(a)$:-& $c,\ h(a)$:-& $b,\ h(b)$:-& $b,\ h(c)$:-& $b,$
$q(b)\}$

$TX_{P_2} \uparrow 2 = TX_{P_2} \uparrow 1 \cup$
$\{g(a)$:-& $b,$
$p(b,c)\}$

$M_{P_2} = lfp(TX_{P_2}) = TX_{P_2} \uparrow \omega = TX_{P_2} \uparrow 3 = TX_{P_2} \uparrow 2 \cup$
$\{f(a)$:-& $b\}$

This is equal to the success set of P_2 given in example 8.

7 Completeness of SLV-Resolution

Like for soundness, we will again use proposition 3 as well as lemmas 1 and 2; hence the following mgu and lifting lemmas will only be needed for relational goals. The symbol "$\stackrel{G}{=}$" will denote equality between substitutions after restriction of the rhs substitution to the variables of the goal G.

Lemma 3 (Mgu lemma) *Let P be a relational-functional program and G_r a relational goal. Suppose that $P \cup \{G_r\}$ has an unrestricted SLV-refutation. Then $P \cup \{G_r\}$ has an SLV-refutation of the same length such that, if $\theta_1, \ldots, \theta_n$ are the unifiers from the unrestricted SLV-refutation and $\theta'_1, \ldots, \theta'_n$ are the mgu's from the SLV-refutation, then there exists a substitution γ such that $\theta_1 \ldots \theta_n \stackrel{G_r}{=} \theta'_1 \ldots \theta'_n \gamma$.*

Proof
The induction proof is as for lemma 8.1 in [7] except that unifiers and mgu's need not derive from (body) resolution but can derive from the other rules of SLV-resolution (flattening in unrestricted SLV-refutations, like in SLV-refutations, produces identity substitutions).

Lemma 4 (Lifting lemma) *Let P be a relational-functional program, G_r a relational goal, and θ a substitution. Suppose there exists an SLV-refutation of $P \cup \{G_r\theta\}$. Then there exists an SLV-refutation of $P \cup \{G_r\}$ of the same length such that, if $\theta_1, \ldots, \theta_n$ are the mgu's from the SLV-refutation of $P \cup \{G_r\theta\}$ and $\theta'_1, \ldots, \theta'_n$ are the mgu's from the SLV-refutation of $P \cup \{G_r\}$, then there exists a substitution γ such that $\theta\theta_1 \ldots \theta_n \stackrel{G_r}{=} \theta'_1 \ldots \theta'_n\gamma$.*

Proof
The proof is as for lemma 8.2 in [7] with the qualification already noted for lemma 3, which is crucially applied here.

The converse of corrollary 2 extends the logic-programming completeness result of K. R. Apt and M. H. van Emden to relational-functional programming.

Theorem 3 *The success set of a relational-functional program is equal to its least Herbrand crossbase model.*

Proof
Let the program be P. By corrollary 2 it suffices to show that the least Herbrand crossbase model of P is contained in the success set of P. Let F denote the ground atom d or molecule f :-& t. By proposition 3 we need only consider the relational goals denoted by $F^{\otimes}$. Suppose F is in the least Herbrand crossbase model of P. By theorem 2, $F \in TX_P \uparrow n$ for some $n \in \omega$. We prove by induction on n that $F \in TX_P \uparrow n$ implies that $P \cup \{$:- $F^{\otimes}\}$ has a refutation (i.e., $d \in TX_P \uparrow n$ implies that $P \cup \{$:- $d\}$ has a refutation and f :-& $t \in TX_P \uparrow n$ implies that $P \cup \{$:- t `is` $f\}$ has a refutation). Hence F will be in the success set.
Suppose first that $n = 1$. Then $F \in TX_P \uparrow 1$ means that F is a ground instance of an atom or molecule from P. Clearly, $P \cup \{$:- $d\}$ and $P \cup \{$:- t `is` $f\}$ have a refutation (a body resolution and an `is`-rhs resolution followed by a term unification, respectively).
Now suppose that the result holds for $n-1$. We distinguish the two cases for F.
First, let $d \in TX_P \uparrow n$. By the definition of TX_P there exists a ground instance of a clause w :- $V_1, \ldots, V_m$ and an unnesting of its premises such that $d = w\theta$ and $\bigcup_{k=1}^{m} unnest_P(V_k\theta)^{\otimes} \subseteq TX_P \uparrow (n-1)$ for some unifier θ. By the induction hypothesis, for each formula A in the selected $unnest_P(V_k\theta)$, for $1 \le k \le m$, $P \cup \{$:- $A\}$ has a refutation. Hence, $P \cup \{$:- $V_k\theta\}$ has a refutation, mimicking unnesting by flattening. Because each $V_k\theta$ is ground and flattening only introduces new variables, these refutations can be combined into a refutation of $P \cup \{$:- $(V_1, \ldots, V_m)\theta\}$. Thus $P \cup \{$:- $d\}$ has an unrestricted refutation and we can apply the mgu lemma to obtain a refutation of $P \cup \{$:- $d\}$.
Second, let f :-& $t \in TX_P \uparrow n$. By the definition of TX_P there exists a ground instance of a clause e :- $V_1, \ldots, V_m$ & E and an unnesting of its premises such that $f = e\theta$ and $\bigcup_{k=1}^{m} unnest_P(V_k\theta)^{\otimes} \cup unnest_P(t$ `is` $E\theta)^{\otimes} \subseteq TX_P \uparrow (n-1)$ for some unifier θ. By the induction hypothesis, for each formula A in the selected $unnest_P(V_k\theta)$, for $1 \le k \le m$, and $unnest_P(t$ `is` $E\theta)$, $P \cup \{$:- $A\}$ has a refutation. Hence, $P \cup \{$:- $V_k\theta\}$ and $P \cup \{$:- t `is` $E\theta\}$ have a refutation, mimicking unnesting by flattening. Because each $V_k\theta$ and t `is` $E\theta$ are ground and flattening only introduces new variables, these refutations can be combined into a refutation of $P \cup \{$:- $(V_1, \ldots, V_m, t$ `is` $E)\theta\}$. Thus $P \cup \{$:- t `is` $f\}$

has an unrestricted refutation and we can apply the mgu lemma to obtain a refutation of $P \cup \{ \text{ :- } t \texttt{ is } f\}$.

For proving that every correct (relational or functional) answer is an instance of a computed (relational or functional) answer we first transfer lemma 8.5 from [7].

Lemma 5 *Let P be a relational-functional program and F a relationship or setter. Suppose that $\forall(F)$ is a logical consequence of P. Then there exists an SLV-refutation of $P \cup \{ \text{ :- } F\}$ with the identity substitution as the computed answer.*

Proof

Suppose F has variables $x_1, \ldots, x_n$, anywhere in the relationship or on both sides of the setter. Let $a_1, \ldots, a_n$ be distinct constants not appearing in P or F and let θ be the substitution $\{x_1/a_1, \ldots, x_n/a_n\}$. Then it is clear that $F\theta$ is a logical consequence of P. Also, $F\theta$ being ground, each formula A in some $unnest_P(F\theta)$ is a logical consequence of P. Since each A is ground, theorem 3 shows that $P \cup \{ \text{ :- } A\}$ has a refutation. Thus, $P \cup \{ \text{ :- } F\theta\}$ has a refutation, mimicking unnesting by flattening. Since flattening only introduces new variables and the a_i do not appear in P or F, by replacing a_i by x_i, for $1 \leq i \leq n$, in this refutation, we obtain a refutation of $P \cup \{ \text{ :- } F\}$ with the identity substitution as the computed answer.

Now, K. L. Clark's completeness result can be extended from logic to relational-functional programming. For relational goals we can adapt the formulation for definite goals in [7].

Theorem 4 (Completeness of relational SLV-resolution) *Let P be a relational-functional program and G_r a relational goal. For every correct answer θ for $P \cup \{G_r\}$ there exists a computed answer σ for $P \cup \{G_r\}$ and a substitution γ such that $\theta \stackrel{G_r}{=} \sigma\gamma$.*

Proof

Let the relational goal G_r be $\text{ :- } B_1, \ldots, B_k$. Since θ is correct, $\forall((B_1 \wedge \ldots \wedge B_k)\theta)$ is a logical consequence of P. By lemma 5 there exists a refutation of $P \cup \{ \text{ :- } B_i\theta\}$ such that the computed answer is the identity, for $1 \leq i \leq k$. We can combine these refutations into a refutation of $P \cup \{ \text{ :- } G_r\theta\}$ such that the computed answer is the identity.
Suppose the sequence of mgu's of the refutation of $P \cup \{ \text{ :- } G_r\theta\}$ is $\theta_1, \ldots, \theta_n$. Then $G_r\theta\theta_1 \ldots \theta_n = G_r\theta$. By the lifting lemma there exists a refutation of $P \cup \{ \text{ :- } G_r\}$ with mgu's $\theta'_1, \ldots, \theta'_n$ such that $\theta\theta_1 \ldots \theta_n \stackrel{G_r}{=} \theta'_1 \ldots \theta'_n\gamma'$, for some substitution γ'. Let σ be $\theta'_1 \ldots \theta'_n$ restricted to the variables in G_r. Then $\theta \stackrel{G_r}{=} \sigma\gamma$, where γ is an appropriate restriction of γ'.

Again, the result for relational goals naturally carries over to functional goals.

Corollary 3 (Completeness of functional SLV-resolution) *Let P be a relational-functional program and G_f a functional goal. For every correct answer (t, θ) for $P \cup \{G_f\}$ there exists a computed answer (s, σ) for $P \cup \{G_f\}$ and a substitution γ such that $\theta \stackrel{G_f}{=} \sigma\gamma$ and $t = s\gamma$.*

Proof

By lemmas 1 and 2 there is an equivalent relational goal with correct and computed answers for which the completeness result of theorem 4 holds.

References

[1] M. Bellia and G. Levi. The relation between logic and functional languages: A survey. *Journal of Logic Programming*, 3:217–236, 1986.

[2] Harold Boley. A relational/functional language and its compilation into the WAM. Technical Report SEKI SR-90-05, University of Kaiserslautern, Department of Computer Science, April 1990.

[3] Harold Boley. Extended Logic-plus-Functional Programming. In *Workshop on Extensions of Logic Programming, ELP '91, Stockholm1991*, LNAI. Springer, 1992.

[4] D. DeGroot and G. Lindstrom, editors. *Logic Programming: Functions, Relations, and Equations.* Prentice-Hall, 1986.

[5] Laurent Fribourg. SLOG: A logic programming language interpreter based on clausal superposition and rewriting. In *1985 Symposium on Logic Programming*, pages 172–184. IEEE Computer Society Press, 1985.

[6] E. Giovannetti, G. Levi, C. Moiso, and C. Palamidessi. Kernel-LEAF: A logic plus functional language. *Journal of Computer and System Sciences*, 42:139–185, 1991.

[7] John W. Lloyd. *Foundations of Logic Programming.* Springer-Verlag, Berlin, Heidelberg, New York, 1987.

[8] J.J. Moreno-Navarro and M. Rodriguez-Artalejo. Logic programming with functions and predicates: The language BABEL. *Journal of Logic Programming*, 12:191–223, 1992.

[9] M. J. O'Donnell. *Equational Logic as a Programming Language.* MIT Press, Cambridge, Mass., 1985.

[10] David H. D. Warren. Higher-order extensions to PROLOG: Are they needed? *Machine Intelligence*, 10:441–454, 1982.

Embedding Finite Sets in a Logic Programming Language

Agostino Dovier
Dipartimento di Informatica
Università di Pisa
C.so Italia 40, 56100 PISA
dovier@di.unipi.it

Eugenio G. Omodeo
Dip. di Informatica e Sistemistica
Università di Roma La Sapienza
Via Salaria 113, 00198 ROMA
omodeo@assi.ing.uniroma1.it

Enrico Pontelli
New Mexico State Univ.
Dept. of Computer Science
Las Cruces, NM 88003
epontell@nmsu.edu

Gianfranco Rossi
Dip. di Matematica
Università di Bologna
P.zza di Porta S.Donato 5,
40127 BOLOGNA
gianfr@dm.unibo.it

Abstract. A way of introducing simple (finite) set designations and operations as first-class objects of an (unrestricted) logic programming language is discussed from both the declarative and the operational semantics viewpoint. First, special set terms are added to definite Horn clause logic and an extended Herbrand Universe based on an axiomatic characterization of the kind of sets we are dealing with is defined accordingly. Moreover, distinguished predicates representing set membership and equality are added to the base language along with their negative counterparts ($\neq$ and $\notin$). A new unification algorithm which can cope with set terms is developed and proved to terminate. Usual SLD resolution is modified so as to incorporate the new unification algorithm and to properly manage the distinguished predicates for set operations (in particular, conjunctions of atoms containing $\neq$ and $\notin$ are dealt with as constraints, first reduced to a canonical form through a suitable canonization algorithm). Finally, the application of the resulting language to the definition of Restricted Universal Quantifiers is discussed.

1 Introduction

General agreement exists about the usefulness of sets as very high-level representations of complex data structures (cf. [2]) and of set abstractions in code specifications. In particular, sets and set abstractions can be conveniently used in rapid software *prototyping*, where efficiency is not a primary requirement while the availability of high level data and operation abstractions are key features of the prototype implementation language.

Only relatively few programming languages embody sets as primitive objects. Among them, the (non-executable) specification language Z [26], the procedural language SETL [5, 24] and the functional languages MIRANDA [25] and ME TOO [18]. A number of recent proposals have preferred, however, a more declarative programming framework. In particular, *logic programming* languages have been advocated by many as a suitable setting for *declarative programming* with sets. Among them, the proposals of the logic database languages LDL [3] and LPS [11]. Also the recent work by Legeard and Legros [13] introduces sets in a Prolog-like language dealing with set expressions as constraints, while [23] analyzes the problem of logic programming with sets in its generality (including infinite sets). A similar framework but stressing the notion of equational programming is also advocated in [9].

Actual Prolog systems already provide some facilities to support sets in the form of the built-in predicates *setof* and *bagof*. However, it is widely recognized that the definition of these facilities is quite unsatisfactory. In fact, no precise logical semantics can be attributed to them. Sets are simply represented *as lists* and therefore are dealt with as ordinary terms (e.g. by an implicit order among their elements). On the contrary, a logic language embodying sets ought to supply special *set former terms* along with a few basic operations on them as part of the language, and allow other more complex operations on sets (possibly including the *setof* operation), to become definable within the language itself, without having to further extend its semantics.

Aim of this paper is to define such an extended logic language, called {log} (read set-log). Unlike some of the above cited proposals, however, we do not restrict ourselves to any specific application domain. So our starting point is a *pure* logic programming language, that is Definite Horn clauses with no extra-logical constructs. Then simple *set constructs* are added to this language (namely, enumerated set terms, set membership and equality and their negative counterparts) and suitable *operational* and *declarative semantics* are defined for them. It is shown that the usual set operations, such as union, intersection, etc., can be defined in this extended language. Also Restricted Universal Quantifiers are shown to be definable within the language itself; so they can be added to it as a simple syntactic extension (dealt with by a suitable preprocessor).

The paper is organized as follows. Section 2 briefly describes a few extensions to ordinary logic programming language syntax that can support the introduction of set terms. Declarative semantics of the resulting language is presented in section 3 by defining an extended Herbrand Universe based on an axiomatic characterization of the kind of sets we are dealing with. The problem of unification of set terms is then addressed in section 4 and a new unification algorithm which can deal with set terms is described in detail. Section 5 presents the extended SLD procedure incorporating the new unification algorithm and the management of $\in$, $=$, $\notin$ and $\neq$, based on the so called constraint canonization algorithm. Section 6 shows how Restricted Universal Quantifiers can be defined in our language. Finally, a comparison with some other related proposals is carried out in section 7.

2 {log} Syntax

To begin with, we introduce in this section the *extensional* representation of *finite* sets. All that is presupposed is the availability of:

- an interpreted constant, *{}*, for the empty set $\emptyset$;
- a binary function symbol, *with* (used as an infix left associative operator), to be interpreted as follows: *s with t* stands for the set that results from adding *t* as a new element to the set *s*.

Apart from these two symbols, {log} contains the usual equipment of clausal Horn logic (cf. [14]) along with distinguished predicates for set membership and equality ($\in$ and $=$) and their negative counterparts ($\neq$ and $\notin$).

The extensional representation for sets referred to above is provided by a collection *G* of ground terms: this is the smallest collection such that

- the constant *{}* belongs to *G* ;
- *s with t*, *s*, *t* ground terms (not necessarily in *G*), belongs to *G* .

In view of the intended interpretation, any *s* in *G* will be called a ***set term***. A non-ground term *t* is called a set term if there exists an instantiation σ of the variables in *t* such that t^σ belongs to *G*; in particular a variable is a set term. Set terms of the form *t with* t_n *with* ... *with* t_1 wherein *t* is *not* a set term are intended to designate sets based on a ***kernel*** *t* other than *{}* (also called *colored sets*).

For the sake of simplicity we introduce special syntactic forms to designate set terms: $\{t_1,...,t_n|s\}$ stands for *s with* t_n *with* ... *with* t_1 and $\{t_1,...,t_n\}$ stands for *{} with* t_n *with* ... *with* t_1 where $n \geq 1$ and $s, t_1,...,t_n$ are terms. For example:

- `f(a,{5})`, i.e. `f(a,{} with 5)`, is a term, but not a set term;
- `{2,g(3),a}`, i.e. `{} with a with g(3) with 2`, is a ground set term;
- `{}`, `{1,X,Y,2}`, `{1,1,{2,{}},f(a,{b})}` and any term $\{t_1,...,t_n|R\}$ with a 'tail' variable R, are set terms
- `{a|f({b})}` is a colored set term based on the kernel `f({b})`.

For the rest of this paper, we will freely exploit the syntactic features available in Edinburgh Prolog in addition to the constructs discussed above. Three sample {log} clauses are:

```
- q(X) :- X ∈ {a,b,c,d} & p(X)
- singleton(X) :- X = {Y}.
- in_difference(X,Set1,Set2) :-
                    X ∈ Set1 &
                    X ∉ Set2.
```

Colored set terms (i.e. terms of the form $\{t_1,...,t_n|t\}$ wherein t is not a set term) do not designate sets of any conventional kind; one might therefore contend that such terms ought to be forbidden as they are unlikely to serve any serious purpose in programming. Nevertheless, we deem it convenient to always regard $\{t_1,...,t_n|t\}$ as a legal set term when $t_1,...,t_n$, t are legal, to make the language structure absolutely uniform and the inference mechanisms (e.g. unification) more straightforward.

3 {log} Declatative Semantics

To convey the meaning of our language, we are to formally characterize the legal interpretations of {log}. We begin by providing the *axioms* of a suitable first-order set theory with equality: the legal interpretations of {log} will be the models of these axioms (cf. [8]).

Next we will focus on a privileged interpretation domain formed by terms, U_H, resulting from suitable modifications to the classical Herbrand universe [14]; moreover, we will designate a fixed binary relation over U_H as the privileged interpretation of $\in$. (The predicate = will be interpreted as syntactic equality).

The interpretation of the predicate symbols of {log} other than $\in$ or = is left totally unspecified for the time being, as it must take into account a {log} program, viz. a set of application-specific clausal axioms enriching the initial axiom endowment we are presenting now.

3.1 Set axioms

Here are our basic axioms (X, Y, V, S and the X_is distinct variables ranging over the whole interpretation domain):

(Z) $V \notin \{\}$;

(W1) $V \neq Y \rightarrow (V \in X \textit{ with } Y \leftrightarrow V \in X)$;

(W2) $Y \in X \textit{ with } Y$;

(L) $Y \in X \rightarrow \exists z\,(Y \notin z \;\&\; X = z \textit{ with } Y)$;

(K_0) $(\forall z\; z \notin X) \rightarrow (X = ker(X))$;

(K_1) $V \notin ker(X)$;

(K_2) $ker(V \textit{ with } Y) = ker(V)$;

(E) $(ker(X) = ker(Y) \;\&\; \forall z\,(z \in X \leftrightarrow z \in Y)) \rightarrow X = Y$;

(R) $\exists z \forall w (w \in X \rightarrow (z \in X \& w \notin z))$;

(U) $f(X_1,...,X_n) \neq \{\} \& V \notin f(X_1,...,X_n)$, *where n is the arity of f and f/n* $\notin$ *{{}/0, ker/1, with/2}.*

Although rather conventional in the overall, and somewhat narrow in comparison to well-established set theories such as Zermelo-Fraenkel or von Neumann-Bernays-Gödel, our theory slightly deviates from the classical ones under two respects:

- Presence of ***urelements***. One refers by this word to member-less entities distinct from *{}*. It readily follows from (U) that a single function symbol, say *f/1*, can be used to generate infinitely many such entities, namely

  $f(\{\}), f(\{\{\}\}), f(\{\{\{\}\}\}), ...$.

- Each term *t* in the interpretation domain has an associated kernel, *ker(t)*, which can be an urelement or *{}*. Intuitively speaking, we think of *t* as resulting from repeated (possibly none) insertions of members into this initial kernel, insertions being achieved by the operation *with.* (Note that, *ker(f(a)) = f(a)*).[1]

Let us briefly comment upon the extensionality and regularity axioms, (E) and (R). The first of these states that in order to be equal *X* and *Y* must have the same kernel and the same members. It follows, in view of (W_1), (W_2) and (K_2) that *with* enjoys the following properties:

$(X \text{ with } Y_1) \text{ with } Y_2 = (X \text{ with } Y_2) \text{ with } Y_1,$ *(permutativity)*

$(X \text{ with } Y) \text{ with } Y = X \text{ with } Y.$ *(absorption)*

Another very useful consequence of (W_1), (W_2), (K_2) and (E) is that

$$Y \in X \leftrightarrow \exists z\, (X = z \text{ with } Y),$$

whereby one can express membership in terms of equality. By exploiting the element removal axiom (L) too, one obtains

$$(X \text{ with } Y = V \text{ with } S \;\&\; Y \neq S) \rightarrow \exists w\, (w \text{ with } S = X \;\&\; w \text{ with } Y = V),$$

which will prove crucial in our unification algorithm.

The regularity axiom (R) states that from each non-empty set *X* one can choose a member *z* which belongs to *X* and does not intersect *X*: this is a well-known expedient way to state that membership forms no cycles (and a little more).

It goes without saying that standard equality axioms (cf. [8]) are being postulated here. The Clark *freeness axioms* [21] are being adopted too:

$$f(X_1,...,X_n) \neq g(Y_1,...,Y_m);$$
$$f(X_1,...,X_n) = f(Y_1,...,Y_n) \rightarrow (X_1 = Y_1 \&...\& X_n = Y_n);$$
$$t[X] \neq X.$$

As usual *f/n* and *g/m* differ from one another in the first of these; we must further require that they differ from *ker/1* and from *with/2*. Moreover, in addition to requiring that *t[X]* be a term involving the variable *X* and distinct from it, we must require that *t[X] be not a set term.*

Technically, one can regard (U) as a novel freeness axiom, and (R) as an analogue about sets of the *occur axiom* $t[X] \neq X$. Actually, we must strengthen (R) for our purposes, by adding to it

(R') $t[X] \notin X \;\&\; ker(X) \neq t[X]$.

3.2 An adapted Herbrand universe

In order to define the *privileged interpretation domain* U_H one considers the ordinary Herbrand universe *H* (generated as usual by the collection *F* of functors, which is assumed

[1] These also are the main differences, so far, between our theory and the theory *T0* in [19].

to fulfil $\{\}/0$, $with/2 \in F$ and $ker/1 \notin F$), and takes the smallest equivalence relation $\equiv$ over H that fulfils the above permutativity and absorption properties (with $\equiv$ in place of $=$). Then, one takes a representative term from each one of the equivalence classes forming $H/\equiv$ (according to specific criteria to be hinted at below), and finally one puts $U_H = \{representative\ terms\}$ by definition.

Establishing an order < over H can help in filling up the details of this plan. For the sake of simplicity, it is reasonable to assume that a total ordering of F is given from the outset. By exploiting this ordering, < can be defined antilexicographically. This means – among others – that r *with* $t < s$ *with* u holds, recursively, when either $t < u$ or t coincides with u and $r < s$.

A ground term g is said to be *canonical* if either it is a constant or every one of its subterms is canonical and, moreover, $t < u$ holds for every subterm of the form s *with* t *with* u of g. U_H will be formed by all canonical terms. Let τ be the function that maps a ground term t to its canonical representative. If t has the form $f(t_1,...,t_n)$ with $f/n \neq with/2$, $\tau(t)$ will be $f(t_1',...,t_n')$ where $t_i' = \tau(t_i)$ for each i, $1 \leq i \leq n$. If t has the form k *with* t_1 *with* ...*with* t_n – where the main functor of k differs from $with/2$ – $\tau(t)$ is the term k' *with* t_{π_1}' *with*...*with* t_{π_m}' where $k', t_{\pi_1}',...,t_{\pi_m}'$ are the distinct canonical representatives of k, $t_1,...,t_n$ arranged so that $t_{\pi_1}' < ... < t_{\pi_m}'$. Of course the canonical representative of each term will be its value in the privileged interpretation.

To complete the picture of the privileged interpretation it suffices to add that for any $t, u \in U_H$:

- the kernel $k = ker(t)$ is obtained by decomposing t in the form k *with* t_1 *with* ... *with* t_n, $n \geq 0$, where the main functor of k differs from $with/2$;
- whether the relation $u \in t$ holds or not can be established by decomposing t in the same manner and by checking whether u occurs as one of the t_is.

The definition of the term canonization function τ described above can be extended so as to encompass atoms and clauses in the following way:

- for each ground atom $A = p(t_1,...,t_n)$, $\tau(A) = p(\tau(t_1),...,\tau(t_n))$;
- for each ground clause $C = A$:- B_1 &...& B_n, $\tau(C) = \tau(A)$:- $\tau(B_1)$ & ... & $\tau(B_n)$;
- for each set I of either ground atoms or ground clauses, $\tau(I) = \bigcup_{A \in I} \{\tau(A)\}$.

As anticipated at the beginning of the section, we are taking $U_H = \tau(H_P)$ as the interpretation domain of any given program P. Also, functors are so interpreted that each ground term t denotes $\tau(t)$. Then we will regard the collection $\tau(B_P)$ as the Herbrand base of P, where B_P is defined as usual (without atoms involving $=$ or $\in$, though, because these have a rigid meaning). A *(set) interpretation* I of P can be characterized simply as a subset of $\tau(B_P)$: it will be a *model* of P if it satisfies the whole $ground(P)$.

With the semantics thus restricted to set interpretations only, we can easily prove the usual model-theoretic and fixpoint semantics results. In particular, with

$$T_P(I) = \{a \mid a :\text{-}\ b_1 \ \&\ ...\ \&\ b_n \in \tau(ground(P))\ and, for\ each\ i \in \{1,...,n\},$$
$$either\ b_i \in \tau(I)\ or\ b_i\ is\ s\pi t\ where\ \pi \in \{=,\in,\neq,\notin\}\ and\ b_i\ is\ true\ w.r.t.\ the\ axioms\}$$

and

$$M_P = \bigcap_{M\ model\ of\ P} M$$

one will have

$$M_P = T_P \uparrow \omega.$$

3.3 Side remarks about set complementation

If we included in the {log} language a set complementation operator, $comp/1$, so that – among others –

- *comp({})* designates the whole interpretation domain, and
- *comp(comp(X) with Y)* designates *X* deprived of the element *Y*,

then co-finite sets ought to be taken into charge along with finite sets, which would significantly enrich the structure of any legitimate interpretation of {log}. We would then be forced to accept certain membership cycles – since $comp(\{\}) \in comp(\{\})$ –, and would have to modify the set axioms accordingly.

We refrain from this extension mainly because it would conflict with another very useful extension of {log}: the introduction of **intensional set formers** [6,7]. As a matter of fact, by adopting the two extensions together, one would run into paradoxical expressions like

$$\{ X \in comp(\{\}) : X \notin X \}.$$

Should the latter be regarded as an acceptable set expression, it would designate a set ξ fulfilling both $\xi \in \xi$ and $\xi \notin \xi$, as was first remarked by B. Russell in 1901.

4 Set Unification

The development of a procedural semantics for {log} requires that the unification algorithm is refined in order to deal with sets, and that the SLD procedure is modified in such a way as to include set unification and proper management of the equality and membership relations. We cope in what follows with the first of these two points, postponing the second one to the next section.

4.1 The set unification problem

As regards the unification problem we assume all the definitions (e.g., Herbrand system, substitution, solution, etc.) given in [15] and [16].

Standard unification is no more adequate to deal with set terms. A first reason is that the inherent lack of order inside a set causes the decay of the 'uniqueness' property of the most general unifier of standard unification. This is clear from the following example: consider the singleton Herbrand system $E = \{\{X,Y\} = \{1,2\}\}$; there are only two solutions, namely $\sigma_1 = \{X \leftarrow 1, Y \leftarrow 2\}$ and $\sigma_2 = \{X \leftarrow 2, Y \leftarrow 1\}$, neither of which is more general than the other. A second reason for the inadequacy of standard unification, is that duplicate elements in a set are not relevant as far as unification is concerned. Thus, for instance, the two set terms $\{1\}$ and $\{1,1\}$ should unify, although standard unification treats them as non-unifiable. Furthermore, the equation $X = \{1/X\}$, which does not admit any solution in the standard case (unless infinite terms are taken into account), has the solution $\sigma = \{X \leftarrow \{1/N\}\}$ in the extended framework we are considering.

What is needed is some form of ***generalized unification***, i.e. unification w.r.t. a theory *T* which describes the properties of a set of functional symbols (*with* and *{}* in our case) by means of a set of equations (axioms). In this connection, two terms *s* and *t* are said to be T-unifiable iff there exists a substitution σ such that $s^\sigma =_T t^\sigma$; such a σ is called a ***T-unifier***. The set of all T-unifiers of two terms *s* and *t* is denoted by $\cup\Sigma_T(s,t)$ (cf. for instance [22]). Of course, we are interested in the ***minimal set of unifiers*** $\mu\Sigma_T(s,t)$, that is, the set of substitutions satisfying:

(i) $\mu\Sigma_T(s,t) \subseteq \Sigma$;

(ii) $\forall \delta \in \Sigma\ (\exists \sigma \in \mu\Sigma_T(s,t)\ (\sigma \leq_T \delta))$;

(iii) $\forall \sigma,\delta \in \mu\Sigma_T(s,t)\ (\sigma \leq_T \delta \rightarrow \sigma = \delta)$

for each complete set of unifiers Σ of s and t (and in particular for $\Sigma = \cup\Sigma_T(s,t)$)[2].

The characterizing properties of our set constructor *with* are absorption and permutativity, as seen in section 3. Other properties for which a number of *extended unification* algorithms[3] have been developed in the past, such as associativity, commutativity, distributivity and their combinations, are unfortunately not satisfied by the *with* operator. In particular, ACI-unification cannot be directly applied in our case. In fact, the identity *(X with Y) with Z = X with (Y with Z)*, representing associativity, does not hold, for instance, under the substitution *{X←{} with c, Y←{} with b, Z←a}*, because the two sets *{a,{b},c}* and *{{a,b},c}* are distinct in our interpretation. Similarly, the idempotency property *X with X = X* does not hold under the substitution *{X←{} with a}* since *{{a},a} ≠ {a}*.

A viable approach could be to use a ***universal unification algorithm*** for a class of theories E (i.e. "an algorithm which takes as its input a pair of terms (s,t) and a theory E ∈ E and generates a complete set of unifiers for $<s=t>_E$" [22]), such as those based on narrowing or on some different rewriting technique (e.g. [17]). According to these approaches, the theory at hand should be represented as a canonical rewrite system. This is not the case of the theory we are interested in, since the permutativity rule for the *with* operator is non-terminating. By using suitable techniques (e.g. lazy evaluation) one can circumvent the ensuing problem of non-termination, but universal unification algorithms seem too inefficient for our purposes.

Therefore, we have developed a new unification algorithm that extends standard unification so as to embody the set axioms presented in section 3. For any given Herbrand system *E* involving set terms, the algorithm is able to compute through non-determinism each element of a complete set of unifiers of *E*.

4.2 Complexity

Before presenting our set-unification algorithm we notice that the problem of deciding whether two set terms are unifiable is *NP-complete*. The NP-hardness ensues from a reduction of 3-SAT to the problem at hand: Given the formula

$$\Phi = (l_1^{(1)} \vee l_2^{(1)} \vee l_3^{(1)}) \,\&\ldots\&\, (l_1^{(m)} \vee l_2^{(m)} \vee l_3^{(m)})$$

with

$$l_i^{(j)} = a_i^{(j)} \text{ or } l_i^{(j)} = \neg a_i^{(j)}, \text{ where}$$
$$a_i^{(j)} \in \{d_1,\ldots,d_k\},\ \forall i \in \{1,2,3\},\ \forall j \in \{1,\ldots,m\},\ k \leq 3*m,$$

find a truth-value assignment to the propositional variables $d_1,\ldots,d_k$ such that $\Phi \leftrightarrow true$.

We define the transformation function f as follows:

$$f(l) = \begin{cases} X_i & \text{if } l \equiv d_i \\ Y_i & \text{if } l \equiv \neg d_i \\ \{false, f(l_1), f(l_2), f(l_3)\} & \text{if } l \equiv l_1 \vee l_2 \vee l_3 \end{cases}$$

and translate Φ into the equation

$$\{\{X_1,Y_1\},\ldots,\{X_k,Y_k\}, f(l_1^{(1)} \vee l_2^{(1)} \vee l_3^{(1)}),\ldots f(l_1^{(1)} \vee l_2^{(1)} \vee l_3^{(1)})\} = \{\{false, true\}\},$$

which requires each of the sets $\{X_j,Y_j\}$ to become *{false, true}*, and at least one of $f(l_1^{(i)})$,

[2] Recall that: two substitutions δ, σ are **T-equal** (written $\delta =_T \sigma$) iff $X^\delta =_T X^\sigma$ for each variable X; a substitution δ is **more general than a substitution** σ (written $\delta \leq_T \sigma$) iff there exists a substitution μ such that $\delta \circ \mu =_T \sigma$ (for instance, $\delta = \{X \leftarrow \{f(X),b\}\}$ is more general than $\sigma = \{X \leftarrow \{b,f(a)\}\}$ in the theory we are considering here); two substitutions δ, σ are **T-equivalent** (written $\delta \equiv_T \sigma$) iff $\delta \leq_T \sigma$ and $\delta \geq_T \sigma$ (for instance, $\{X \leftarrow \{a\}\}, \{X \leftarrow \{a,a\}\}, \{X \leftarrow \{a,a,a\}\}$ are all equivalent substitutions in our theory). Note that, if the set $\mu\Sigma_T(s,t)$ exists, it is unique up to the equivalence $\equiv_T$ and therefore it is enough to compute just one $\mu\Sigma_T(s,t)$ as a representative of the equivalence class $[\mu\Sigma_T(s,t)]_{\equiv_T}$ (cf. [Sie86]).

[3] I.e. algorithms for special theories embodying the equality axioms of the theory itself.

$f(l_2^{(i)}), f(l_3^{(i)})$ to become *true* for every *i*. (To stay strictly inside the realm of pure sets, *false* could be replaced by *{}* and *true* by *{{}}* in this translation).

It is hence clear that an algorithm for unifying two sides of such an equation in polynomial time could also be exploited for solving 3-SAT in polynomial time.

The NP-completeness of the set unification problem ensues from the polynomial behaviour of standard unification. In fact, a set-set equation can be replaced by a set of equations between the elements of the two sets. This is a non-deterministic equivalent of the term decomposition action of standard unification algorithms (see, for instance, [16]).

4.3 Set unification algorithm

Let E be a Herbrand system, i.e. a set of equations $\{t_i = t_i', i = 1,...,n\}$, where the t_i's are terms (variable or not). A Herbrand system is said to be in *solved form* if all equations have the form $x_i = s_i$ $(i = 1,...,m)$, and every variable x_i occurs exactly once in E. Such a system has the obvious solution $\{x_1 \leftarrow s_1,...,x_n \leftarrow s_m\}$. Aim of the following algorithm is to bring any given system E to solved form or to report a failure if E has no solution.

UNIFICATION ALGORITHM

Let F be a set of functional symbols, V a denumerable set of variables and T be the set of first order terms over $F \cup V$. Let X, Y be generic variables (i.e. $X,Y \in V$), t, t_i, t_i' be terms in T, and r, s represent set terms.

function *unify*(E: Herbrand_system): Herbrand_system;
begin
 if E is in solved form
 then return E
 else select arbitrarily an equation e in E so that:
  case e **of**
  1) $X = X$: **return** *unify*$(E \setminus \{e\})$;
  2) $t = X, t \notin V$: **return** *unify*$((E \setminus \{e\}) \cup \{X = t\})$;
  3) $X = t$, t is not a set term and X occurs in t: fail;
  4) $X = t$ *with* t_n...*with* t_0 and X occurs in t $(t \notin V)$ or in t_0 or ... or in t_n: **fail;**
  5) $X = X$ *with* t_n...*with* t_0 and X does not occur in $t_0,...,t_n$:
  return *unify*$((E \setminus \{e\}) \cup \{X = N$ *with* t_n ... *with* $t_0\})$, N new variable;
  6) $X = t$, X does not occur in t, X occurs somewhere else in E:
  return *unify*$((E \setminus \{e\})\sigma \cup \{X = t\})$, where σ is the substitution $\{X \leftarrow t\}$;
  7) $f(t_1,...,t_n) = g(t_1',...,t_m')$, $f \neq g$ or $n \neq m$: **fail;**
  8) $f(t_1,...,t_n) = f(t_1',...,t_n')$, $f/n \neq$ *with*/2:
  return *unify*$((E \setminus \{e\}) \cup \{t_1 = t_1',...,t_n = t_n'\})$;
  9) $r = s$, where $r \equiv h$ *with* t_n *with*...*with* t_0 and $s \equiv k$ *with* t_m' *with*...*with* t_0',
   h, k terms with main functor $\neq$ *with*/2, using the notation $r\backslash t_i$ (resp., $s\backslash t_i$) to denote the term obtained from r (resp. s) by taking away its i-th element t_i:
  if h, k are not the same variable **then**
  9.1) choose one from among the following actions:
   a) **return** *unify*$((E \setminus \{e\}) \cup \{t_0 = t_0', r\backslash t_0 = s\backslash t_0'\})$
   b) **return** *unify*$((E \setminus \{e\}) \cup \{t_0 = t_0', r = s\backslash t_0'\})$
   c) **return** *unify*$((E \setminus \{e\}) \cup \{t_0 = t_0', r\backslash t_0 = s\})$
   d) **return** *unify*$((E \setminus \{e\}) \cup \{r\backslash t_0 = N$ *with* t_0', N *with* $t_0 = s\backslash t_0'\})$,
    N new variable;
  else $h, k \in V, h \equiv k \equiv X$
  9.2) select arbitrarily i from among $0,...,m$;

choose one from among the following actions:
a) **return** *unify*$((E \setminus \{e\}) \cup \{t_0 = t_i', r\backslash t_0 = s\backslash t_i'\})$
b) **return** *unify*$((E \setminus \{e\}) \cup \{t_0 = t_i', r = s\backslash t_i'\})$
c) **return** *unify*$((E \setminus \{e\}) \cup \{t_0 = t_i', r\backslash t_0 = s\})$
d) **return** *unify*$((E \setminus \{e\}) \cup \{X = N$ *with* $t_0,$
N with t_n *with...with* t_1 = *N with* t_m' *with...with* $t_0'\})$, *N* new
variable;
end.

The following theorems state the termination, correctness and completeness of *unify(E)* for any given system *E* of equations.

Theorem 4.1 (termination)
Let *E* be a Herbrand system. Then *unify(E)* terminates, provided a suitable strategy is adopted for selecting *e* across recursive levels.

Theorem 4.2 (soundness and completeness)
Given a system *E*, let $E_1,...,E_n$ be all the systems in solved form produced by the unification algorithm. Then $Soln(E) = Soln(E_1)' \cup ... \cup Soln(E_n)'$, where *Soln(X)* is the set of all the ground T-unifiers of *X* and $Soln(E_i)'$ is $Soln(E_i)$ restricted to the variables of *E*.

Let us briefly comment upon action 9 of the algorithm. Its aim is the reduction of set-set equations. In particular, cases (b), (c) and (d) take care of duplicates in the left-hand side term, duplicates in the right-hand side term and permutativity of the set constructor *with*, respectively.

As an example, let us consider the following system

{{a|X} = {b,a|Y}}.

The algorithm applies action 9.1 to it, requiring one of the following systems to be solved

a) *{a=b, X={a|Y}}*
b) *{a=b, {a|X}={a|Y}}*
c) *{a=b, X={b,a|Y}}*
d) *{X={b|N},{a|Y}={a|N}}.*

The first three clearly have no solution, whereas system (d) can be further transformed by applying again action 9.1 to its second equation, which leads to the following new systems:

a) *{X={b|N}, Y=N},*
from which, by variable substitution, we get *{X←{b|Y}}*;
b) *{X={b|N}, {a|Y}=N},*
from which, by variable substitution, we get *{X←{b,a|Y}}*;
c) *{X={b|N}, Y={a|N}},*
from which we get *{X←{b|N}, Y←{a|N}}*;
d) *{X={b|N}, Y={a|N'}, N={a|N'}}*
from which, by variable substitution, we get *{X←{b,a|N'}, Y←{a|N'}}.*

The substitutions we have got constitute the set of unifiers for the initial system we were looking for. Notice that this set is not *minimal* even though correct and complete. For instance, the fourth solution θ = *{X←{b,a|N'}, Y←{a|N'}}* can be obtained, apart from duplicates, from the second solution σ = *{X←{b,a|Y}}* by applying the substitution *{Y←{a|N'}}* to σ. In general, the set of substitutions computed by our unification algorithm can contain substitutions which are less general and/or equivalent (w.r.t. the given theory) to other substitutions in the set. However, the number of these "redundancies" is in any case finite and could be reduced by adding suitable checks to the algorithm so as to detect cases in which not all the alternatives of the algorithm are required.

Equations of the form X *with* t_n *with...with* $t_0 = X$ *with* t_m' *with...with* t_0', where the two sides are set terms with the same variable tail element, are dealt with as a special case by action 9.2. The problem here is how permutativity of the *with* operator can be guaranteed. In fact, it is easy to check that by applying action 9.1, and in particular case (d), to an equation of this form (e.g. $\{a|X\} = \{b|X\}$) the algorithm might go into an infinite loop. The solution we have adopted is to avoid action 9.1.d of the general case by requiring the algorithm non-deterministically considers each element of one of the two sets involved in the given set-set equation, thus trying all possible combinations.

Of course, this solution opens a great (though finite) number of alternatives, generating many redundant solutions. An alternative formulation of action 9.2 which is less uniform with the rest of the algorithm but more efficient as for the number of generated solutions is shown below.

9.2) X *with* t_m *with ... with* $t_0 = X$ *with* t_n' *with...with* t_0', X variable:
return *unify*$((E \setminus \{e\}) \cup T)$, where the set T is generated as follows:
choose $I = \{(i_1,j_1),\ldots,(i_p,j_p)\}$ from among the subsets of $\{0,\ldots,m\} \times \{0,\ldots,n\}$ such that either I or $\{(j,i) / (i,j) \in I\}$ is a single-valued map;
T is $\{t_i = t_j' \mid (i,j) \in I\} \cup \{X = N$ *with* r_1 *with ... with* $r_{m+n+2-p}\}$
where the r_ks are all terms t_i and t_j' such that $(\forall a \in \{0,\ldots,n\}\ (i,a) \notin I)$ and $(\forall b \in \{0,\ldots,m\}\ (b,j) \notin I)$ (the ordering of the r_ks is immaterial).

Finally, we want to remark that our unification algorithm is close in spirit to the algorithm proposed by Jayaraman and Plaisted in [9] but it manages to solve a larger number of cases. In particular the algorithm in [9] intentionally does not take into account duplicates in a set (e.g. the equation $\{a,a\} = \{a\}$ fails in that algorithm). Furthermore, as far as can be drawn from the presentation of the algorithm sketched in [9], that algorithm requires one of the terms in a set-set equation to be ground, and accordingly is not concerned at all with the situations dealt with by action 9.2 in our algorithm (e.g. $\{a|X\} = \{b|X\}$).

5 {log} Resolution Procedure

The resolution procedure developed for {log} is an extension of the usual SLD resolution procedure, where standard unification is replaced by the set unification algorithm presented above. In addition, some changes are required in order to properly manage equality and membership and their negative counterparts as predicates with a pre-assigned meaning.

The main idea behind the management of $\neq$ and $\notin$ is the use of a simple constraint logic programming scheme [10]. In our context, an *atomic constraint* is any disequation of the form $t_1 \neq t_2$ or $t_1 \notin t_2$; a *constraint* is a conjunction of atomic constraints. We proceed here to illustrate the basic resolution step of our constraint handling method, based on the so-called *disequation analyzer Can* (a non-deterministic algorithm complementary, in a sense, to unification).

The main purpose of *Can* is to transform a given constraint into an equivalent set of constraints in canonical form. A constraint is in *canonical form* if all of the atomic constraints in it (if any) have the form:

a) $X \neq t$ and X does not occur in t (X variable, t term), or

b) $t \notin X$ and X does not occur in t.

Given a constraint C, *Can* non-deterministically generates every element of an equivalent finite set $C_{Can} = \{\langle\Gamma_1,\theta_1\rangle,\ldots,\langle\Gamma_\delta,\theta_\delta\rangle\}$ where each Γ_i is a constraint in canonical form, and θ_i is a substitution which keeps track of the bindings for the auxiliary variables created by the canonization process. We will describe the canonization algorithm in detail in section 5.2.

5.1 Extended SLD Resolution Procedure

Let P be a {log} program and G be a goal :- C_1&...& C_n & B_1 &...& B_k (where the C_is, are atomic constraints and the B_js are {log} atoms). The goal G' is *derived* from G with substitution σ if the following conditions hold:

- if $k = 0$ then μ is the empty substitution ε and C' is $\emptyset$;
- if $k > 0$ then
  - B_i ($i \in \{1,...,k\}$) is the selected atom;
  - μ and C' are computed as follows:
    case B_i of
    a) $p(t_1,...,t_k)$, with p an ordinary predicate and there exists a clause $p(t_1',...,t_k')$:- C_1' &...& C_m' & B_1' &...& B_h' in P:
    μ is an mgu of the system $\{t_1 = t_1',...,t_k = t_k'\}$; C' is $\{C_1',...,C_m'\}$;
    b) $t = t'$: μ is an mgu of the system $\{t = t'\}$; C' is $\emptyset$;
    c) $t \in \{t_1,..,t_n|h\}$:
    μ is an mgu of one of the systems $\{t = t_1\},...,\{t = t_n\}$ or, alternatively, if h is a variable X not occurring in t, μ is the substitution $\{X \leftarrow \{t|N\}\}$, N new variable; C' is $\emptyset$;
- $<\{D_1,...D_d\},\theta>$ is one of the pairs generated by applying *Can* to $(\{C_1,...,C_n\} \cup C')^{\mu}$;
- G' is :- D_1 &...& D_d& $(B_0$ &...& B_{i-1} & B_1'&...& B_h' & B_{i+1} &...& $B_k)^{\sigma}$, where σ is $\mu \circ \theta$.

A *derivation* of $P \cup \{G\}$ is a (finite or infinite) sequence $G_0 = G, G_1, G_2,...$ of goals such that G_{i+1} is derived from G_i. A *refutation* of $P \cup \{G\}$ is a finite derivation of $P \cup \{G\}$ such that the last derived goal G_n only contains canonical atomic constraints.

Finally, a *computed answer* for a refutation $G, G_1,...,G_n$ of $P \cup \{G\}$ is a pair $<C,\sigma>$ where C is the constraint (in canonical form) occurring in G_n and σ is the substitution $\sigma_1 \circ \sigma_2 \circ ... \circ \sigma_n$ restricted to the variables of G where $\sigma_1, \sigma_2,...,\sigma_n$ are the substitutions generated at consecutive steps of the refutation.

It is interesting to notice that such a resolution algorithm involves four kinds of *non-deterministic* choice:

- which atom in the goal to select (don't care non-determinism);
- which clause in the program to select (don't know non-determinism);
- which mgu in the set of unifiers computed by the unification algorithm to select (don't know non-determinism)
- if the selected atom has the form $t \in \{t_1,...,t_n|X\}$, which one of the $n+1$ systems $\{t = t_1\},...,\{t = t_n\}$, $\{X = \{t|N\}\}$ to solve first (don't know non-determinism).

5.2 Constraint canonization algorithm

In this section we describe a non-deterministic algorithm which is able to compute, for any given constraint C, the corresponding set of constraints in canonical form C_{Can}. The algorithm starts with the pair $<C,\varepsilon>$ and generates, through non-determinism, each element of C_{Can}. Notice that a constraint is represented here as a set of atomic constraints; in particular, $\emptyset$ is a constraint in canonical form.

CONSTRAINT CANONIZATION ALGORITHM

Let t, t', t_i, t_i' be first order terms, X, Y be generic variables (i.e. $X, Y \in V$), and r, s be set terms.

function *Can*(<*C*: constraint, *σ*: substitution>): <constraint,substitution>;
begin
  if *C* is in canonical form
    then return <*C*,*σ*>
    else select arbitrarily an atomic constraint *c* **in** *C*;
    case *c* **of**
    1) $t \notin s$ *with* t': **return** $Can(<(C \setminus \{c\}) \cup \{t \neq t', t \notin s\}, \sigma>)$;
    2) $t \notin f(t_1,...,t_n), f \neq$ *with*: **return** $Can(<(C \setminus \{c\}), \sigma>)$;
    3) $t \notin X$, X variable, and X occurs in t: **return** $Can(<(C \setminus \{c\}), \sigma>)$;
    4) $f(t_1,...,t_n) \neq g(t_1',...,t_m'), f \neq g$: **return** $Can(<(C \setminus \{c\}), \sigma>)$;
    5) $f(t_0,...,t_n) \neq f(t_0',...,t_n'), f \neq$ *with*: choose i from among $0,...,n$;
       return $Can(<(C \setminus \{c\}) \cup \{t_i \neq t_i'\}, \sigma>)$;
    6) $f \neq f$ or $X \neq X$, X variable: **fail**;
    7) $t \neq X$ and t is not a variable: **return** $Can(<(C \setminus \{c\}) \cup \{X \neq t\}, \sigma>)$;
    8) $X \neq t$, t is not a set term and X occurs in t, or
       t is h *with* t_n...*with* t_1, h kernel or variable, and X occurs in t_1 or...or t_n:
       return $Can(<(C \setminus \{c\}), \sigma>)$;
    9) $X \neq X$ *with* t_n...*with* t_0: choose i from among $0,...,n$;
       return $Can(<(C \setminus \{c\}) \cup \{t_i \notin X\}, \sigma>)$;
    10) r *with* $t \neq s$ *with* t': choose one from among the following actions:
       a) δ is *member_solve*($Z \in r$ *with* t);
          return $Can(<(C \setminus \{c\}) \cup \{Z \notin s \text{ with } t'\})^{\delta}, \delta \circ \sigma>)$, Z new variable;
       b) δ is *member_solve*($Z \in s$ *with* t');
          return $Can(<(C \setminus \{c\}) \cup \{Z \notin r \text{ with } t\})^{\delta}, \delta \circ \sigma>)$, Z new variable;

where *member_solve* is a function which is able to solve set membership atoms (in the same way they are solved within the extended resolution procedure presented above)

function *member_solve*(*M*: membership atom): substitution;
begin
  case *M* **of**
  1) $Z \in s$ *with* t: choose one from among the following actions:
     a) **return** $\{Z \leftarrow t\}$;
     b) **return** *member_solve*($Z \in s$);
  2) $Z \in X$, X variable:
     return $\{X \leftarrow N \text{ with } Z\}$, N new variable;
  3) $Z \in f(t_1,...,t_n), f \neq$ *with*: **fail**
end.

Let us see how the {log} resolution procedure works on a simple example involving also a negative answer.

```
in_difference(X,Set1,Set2) :-
                     X ∈ Set1 &
                     X ∉ Set2.
```

Given the goal

```
:- in_difference(X,{1,2},{1,3})
```

the only clause of the program is selected as a possible resolvent of the goal. Solving the set membership goal in the body of the selected clause generates (see the definition of derived goal above) the two alternative substitutions $\{X \leftarrow 1\}$, $\{X \leftarrow 2\}$; then *Can* is applied non-deterministically to either the constraint $\{1 \notin \{1,3\}\}$ or $\{2 \notin \{1,3\}\}$. The first generates (action 1 of *Can*) the new constraint $\{1 \neq 1, 1 \notin \{3\}\}$ that clearly fails; the second generates the constraint $\{2 \neq 1, 2 \notin \{3\}\}$ from which, after few iterations of *Can*, we get the pair $<\emptyset,\varepsilon>$. So the final computed answer is

```
--> X = 2.
```

If the following goal is given instead

```
:- in_difference(X,Set1,{1,3})
```

solving the set membership atom in the body of the selected clause generates the following substitution $\{Set1 \leftarrow \{X/N\}\}$, whereas applying *Can* to the constraint $\{X \notin \{1,3\}\}$ generates the pair $<\{X \neq 1, X \neq 3\},\varepsilon>$. So the final computed answer is

```
--> Set1 = {X|N}, X ≠ 1, X ≠ 3.
```

The following theorems state the termination, correctness and completeness of the canonization algorithm for any given constraint C (formal proofs of these theorems and of those of the following section can be found in [7]).

Theorem 5.1 (termination)
Let C be a constraint; then $Can(C)$ always terminates.

Theorem 5.2 (soundness)
Let C be a constraint such that $C_{Can} = \{<C_1,\theta_1>,\ldots,<C_n,\theta_n>\}$. Then
1) if $n = 1$, $C_1 = C$, and θ_1 is empty, then C admits a solution;
2) if θ is a solution of C_i $(i \in \{1,\ldots,n\})$ then θ is a solution of C^{θ_i}.

Theorem 5.3 (completeness)
Let C be a constraint such that $C_{Can} = \{<C_1,\theta_1>,\ldots,<C_n,\theta_n>\}$. If θ is a solution of C then there exists an i among 1 and n and a solution σ of such C_i such that $\theta = \theta_i \circ \sigma$.

Actually, a specific ground substitution γ, such that $C\gamma$ is provable from the axioms can be exhibited in case 1 of theorem 5.2. In consequence of this fact, one has:

Theorem 5.4
The axiomatic set theory specified in Section 3.1 makes it possible to prove either C or $\neg C$ for any constraint C.

5.3 Soundness and completeness of the resolution procedure

Theorem 5.5 (soundness)
Let P be a {log} program and G be a goal. If G has a refutation in P with computed answer $<C,\theta>$ and σ is a solution for C then we have $P \models_{Set} G^{\theta \circ \sigma}$.

Lemma 5.1 (lifting lemma for {log})
Let P be a {log} program, G be a non empty conjunction of {log} atoms, C be a constraint, and σ be a substitution for the variables in (C,G). If :- $(C \,\&\, G)^{\sigma}$ does have a refutation in P with computed answer $<C',\theta'>$ then :- $(C \,\&\, G)$ has a refutation in P with computed answer $<C'',\theta''>$ such that

(i) θ'' is more general than $\sigma \circ \theta'$ and
(ii) for each α solution of C' there exists β such that $\beta \circ (\alpha|_{vars(C)})$ is a solution of C''.

Lemma 5.2
Let B be an atom of the form
(i) $t = s$ or (ii) $t \in s$.

If $\not\models_{Set} B^{\sigma}$ for some σ ground then there exists a refutation for $\{:\text{-}\ B^{\sigma}\}$ in any program P.

Lemma 5.3
Let $Succ(P) = \{\tau(a) \mid Pred(a) \notin \{=,\in,\neq,\notin\}$ *and there exists a refutation for* $P \cup \{:\text{-}\ a\}\}$.
Then $Succ(P) = M_P$, for each {log} program P.

Lemma 5.4
Let P be a {log} program, $G = (:\text{-}\ C\ \&\ L_1\ \&\ \ldots\ \&\ L_h)$ be a goal such that $P \cup \{\neg C \vee \neg L_1 \vee \ldots \vee \neg L_h\}$ is unsatisfiable in the set theory; then there is a refutation for G in P.

Theorem 5.6 (Completeness)
Let P be a {log} program, G be a goal and $P \models_{Set} (G^{\sigma})^{\forall}$; then G has a refutation in P.

6 Restricted Universal Quantifiers

Restricted Universal Quantifiers (*RUQs*) are formulas of the form $(\forall X \in s)\ F$, F formula, which stand for the quantified implication $\forall X\ ((X \in s) \rightarrow F)$. Usefulness of providing RUQs as part of the representation language has been demonstrated by several authors (e.g. [4,11]). In fact, RUQs allow basic set-theoretic operations (such as subset, union, intersection and so on) to be expressed in a clear and concise way. In what follows we will show how the language presented so far can be extended so as to encompass RUQs.

An *extended Horn clause* is a formula:

$$p(t_1,\ldots,t_n)\ :\text{-}\ B_1\ \&\ \ldots\ \&\ B_n$$

where each B_i can either be an atom or an RUQ formula of the form $(\forall X_1 \in t_1)\ldots(\forall X_n \in t_n)G$, G atom, satisfying the following properties:

- the variables $X_1,\ldots,X_n$ can occur only in G;
- if $i \neq j$ then $X_i \neq X_j$.

These two restrictions ensure that a B_i of the form $(\forall X_1 \in t_1)\ldots(\forall X_n \in t_n)G$ is logically equivalent to $\forall X_1\ldots\forall X_n(X_1 \in t_1\ \&\ldots\&\ X_n \in t_n \rightarrow G)$. (Note that the first restriction, motivated (cf. [20]) by our set finiteness requirement, is implicitly present in [11] since nesting of sets is not allowed there.)

For example, using RUQs, it is easy to define the following set-theoretic operations:

```
(A)   subset(S1,S2) :-
                  (∀X ∈ S1)(X ∈ S2)

(B)   disj(D,S1,S2) :-
                  (∀Z ∈ D)(Z ∉ S2 & Z ∈ S1)
```

where the second clause is intended to state that D is a subset of S1 \ S2.

One might proceed as in [11], by enhancing resolution so as to deal directly with RUQs. However, both for conceptual simplicity and for soundness concerns we prefer to transform extended Horn clauses into equivalent {log} clauses without RUQs (hints about a similar idea can be found in [12]). We have proved that such a transformation is always possible, and have developed an algorithm to perform it.

RUQs ELIMINATION ALGORITHM

Let $C = H\ :\text{-}\ B_1\ \&\ldots\&\ B_k\ \&\ B_{k+1}\ \&\ldots\&\ B_n$ be an extended Horn clause, where $B_1,\ldots,B_k$ $(k \leq n)$ are {log} formulas and $B_{k+1},\ldots,B_n$ are formulas containing RUQs.

1) Replace C by the set of clauses

$$I = \{H :\text{-}\ B_1 \,\&\ldots\&\, B_k \,\&\, D_1 \,\&\ldots\&\, D_{n-k},$$
$$D_1 :\text{-} B_{k+1},$$
$$\ldots,$$
$$D_{n-k} :\text{-}\ B_n\}$$

where each D_j is obtained by taking a new predicate symbol (different from all the others in the program) and applying it to all variables in B_{k+j} which are not quantified by an RUQ of B_{k+j}.

2) Replace each element of I of the form

$$p(t_1,\ldots,t_n) :\text{-}\ (\forall X_1 \in s_1)(\forall X_2 \in s_2)\ G$$

by the two clauses:

$$p(t_1,\ldots,t_n) :\text{-}\ (\forall X_1 \in s_1)\ r(Y_1,\ldots,Y_k)$$
$$r(Y_1,\ldots,Y_k) :\text{-}\ (\forall X_2 \in s_2)\ G,$$

where $Y_1,\ldots,Y_k$ are all variables (different from X_2) occurring in s_2 or free in G, and r is a new predicate symbol; repeat this step as long as possible.

3) Replace each extended Horn clauses of the form

$$p(t_1,\ldots,t_n) :\text{-}\ (\forall X \in \{t_1',\ldots,t_m' / h\})G.$$

by

$$p(t_1,\ldots,t_n) :\text{-}\ G^{\{X \leftarrow t_1'\}} \,\&\, \ldots \,\&\, G^{\{X \leftarrow t_m'\}}$$

if h is a term whose main functor differs from *with/2*, or by

$$p(t_1,\ldots,t_n) :\text{-}\ G^{\{X \leftarrow t_1'\}} \,\&\, \ldots \,\&\, G^{\{X \leftarrow t_m'\}} \,\&\, D$$
$$D :\text{-}\ (\forall X \in h)G$$

if h is a variable, where D is put together in the same way as in step 1).

4) Replace each simple extended Horn clause

$$p(t_1,\ldots,t_n) :\text{-}\ (\forall X \in Y)G[X,Z_1,\ldots,Z_m],$$

where Y is a variable and $X, Z_1,\ldots,Z_m$ $(m \geq 0)$ are all variables occurring in G, by the following three {log} clauses:

$$p(t_1,\ldots,t_n) :\text{-}\ r(Y,Z_1,\ldots,Z_m)$$
$$r(K,Z_1,\ldots,Z_m) :\text{-}\ K \neq \_\ with\ \_ \qquad \text{(i.e., } K \text{ is a set kernel)}$$
$$r(\{A \mid R\},Z_1,\ldots,Z_m) :\text{-}$$
$$(A \notin R) \,\&\, G^{\{X \leftarrow A\}} \,\&\, r(R,Z_1,\ldots,Z_k),$$

with r a new predicate symbol.

For example, the extended Horn clause (A) for the subset operation given at the beginning of the section gets transformed into the equivalent three {log} clauses (action 4 of the algorithm is applied):

```
subset(S1,S2)  :- r(S1,S2)

r(S1,_) :- S1 ≠ _ with _
r({A|R},S2) :-
          (A ∉ R) & (A ∈ S2) & r(R,S2).
```

Similarly, clause (B) for the predicate *disj/3* gets transformed into:

```
disj(D,S1,S2)  :- r(D,S1,S2)

r(K,S1,S2)  :- K ≠ _ with _
r({A|R},S1,S2):-
          (A ∈ S1) & (A ∉ S2) & (A ∉ R) &
          r(R,S1,S2).
```

Note that it is impossible to implement RUQs in a usable manner without resorting to ≠

and $\notin$. In particular, the constraint $A \notin R$ in the last step of the algorithm is needed to avoid that the program may loop forever trying to generate a set with infinite many occurrences of the same element (e.g. *{1,1,1,...}* instead of *{1}*).

In conclusion, RUQs are introduced in {log} only at a syntactic level, as a convenient notation, with no extension at the semantic level. The same approach can be adopted to introduce intensional set formers and the *setof* predicates by which such abstractions are implemented (see [6]). However, it turns out that in this case the language must be extended so as to provide either a built-in set collection mechanism (see [3]) or some form of negation in goals and clause bodies.

7 Related Work

In this paper we have addressed the problem of introducing sets in a logic programming language. The approach we have adopted is that of a ***deep integration*** between simple set designations and operations and the usual logic programming machinery. This has required primarily the development of a suitable semantical extension of Horn clause logic.

Among the proposals that have addressed this problem with a similar approach we briefly recall [3], [11] and [23].

The first paper defines LDL, a logic based language oriented to the manipulation of deductive databases. The main differences between LDL and {log} are:

- the procedural semantics: bottom-up in LDL, top-down (with set unification) in {log};
- in LDL the set manipulators (union, intersection etc.) are built-in predicates, while in {log} they are programmer-defined;
- the 'collector capability' is expressed in different ways: via set-grouping in LDL, using the *with* + negation combination in {log}.

It is interesting to note that the syntactic restrictions enforced in LDL are very similar to those necessary to introduce classical negation by failure in {log} (see [7]).

Kuper's proposal [11] basically consists in extending logic programming with RUQs (see section 6 above). Kuper shows the usefulness of this extension, but does not offer a full-blown semantics for the language.

Quite interesting is a comparison between our proposal and Sigal's work [23] which outlines, from a theoretical point of view, a complete logic language with sets, where set-theoretic operations are built-in. A model-theoretic semantics is developed for a subset of this language which bears some resemblance to {log}. Sigal's proposal copes with the rather intriguing task of manipulating infinite sets (even repeatedly nested one inside another). Although theoretically appealing, this approach leads to difficulties that are hard to surmount: whence the lack of a realistic procedural semantics for the proposed language.

8 Future Developments of {log}

The interpreted operator *ker*, which helped us in keeping the form of our set axioms simple (cf. section 3.1), has not been included among the symbols of {log}. Adding *ker* to the language would be useful, enabling one e.g. to define the *subset* predicate as

```
subset(S1,S2) :-
        ker(S1) = ker(S2) &
        (∀X ∈ S1)(X ∈ S2),
```

instead of in the less satisfactory way seen in section 6. Similarly one could define the element removal operation by the clause

```
less(A,X,B) :-
        ker(A) = ker(B) &
        (∀Y ∈ B)(Y ∈ A & Y ≠ X) &
        (∀Y ∈ A)(Y = X ∨ Y ∈ B).
```

This extension calls for a modification of the unification algorithm which ought to produce along with each substitution a conjunction of atomic constraints of the new form

$$ker(X) = t.$$

Our extended SLD resolution procedure ought to be modified too, to take into proper charge the new kind of constraints.

We have already announced a couple of times in this paper that {log} will be extended with intensional set formers. This extension poses problems of various kinds, one of the most obvious being that infinite sets can easily be described by means of intensional set formers, e.g.

```
natS({X : nat(X)})

nat(0)
nat(succ(X)) :- nat(X).
```

Suitable criteria could be adopted for rejecting expressions (such as `{X:nat(X)}` in the example) that denote (or might denote) infinite sets. Unfortunately such criteria must be, out of necessity, very conservative, and prone to refuse useful set formers together with dangerous ones. Alternatively infinite sets could be accepted as part of the language. In this case, however, a coherent attitude should be taken to deal with infinite sets at all levels: by having an explicit infinity axiom, by accordingly enriching the privileged interpretation, by enhancing the procedural semantics, etc. (cf. [23]).

We also envisage generalizations of {log} for the treatment of non-standard sets: for instance, non-well-founded sets (cf. [1]) among which membership can form cycles of all kinds.

Acknowledgments

This work originates from a project, named AXL, funded by ENI and ENIDATA. Partial support came from MURST 60%. We have enjoyed useful discussions with Alberto Policriti, in particular concerning the axiomatization in section 3 and the proof of termination of our unification algorithm.

References

1. P.Aczel. Non-well-founded sets. Vol.14, Lecture Notes, Center for the study of Language and Information, Stanford, 1988.
2. A.Aho, J.Hopcroft, J.Ullman. *The design and analysis of computer algorithms.* Addison-Wesley, 1975.
3. C.Beeri, S.Naqvi et al. Set and negation in a Logic Database Language (LDL1). *Proceedings 6th ACM SIGMOD Symposium,* 1987.
4. D.Cantone, A.Ferro, E.G.Omodeo. *Computable set Theory.* Oxford University Press, International Series of Monographs on Computer Science, 1989.
5. E.E.Doberkat, D.Fox. *Software Prototyping mit SETL.* B.G.Teubner Stuttgart, 1989.

6. A.Dovier, E.G.Omodeo, E.Pontelli, G.F.Rossi. {log}: A Logic Programming Language with Finite Sets, in *Logic Programming: Proceedings of the Eighth International Conference* (K.Furukawa, ed.), The MIT Press, 1991.
7. A.Dovier, E.G.Omodeo, E.Pontelli, G.F.Rossi. {log}: A Language for Programming in Logic with Finite Sets, Research Report, in preparation.
8. H.B.Enderton. *A mathematical introduction to logic*. Academic Press, 2nd printing, 1973.
9. B.Jayaraman, D.A.Plaisted. Programming with Equations, Subsets and Relations. *Proceedings of NACLP89*, Cleveland, 1989.
10. J.Jaffar, J.L.Lassez. From Unification to Constraints. *Proceedings Fifth Conference on Logic Programming*, Tokyo, 1987.
11. G.M.Kuper. Logic Programming with Sets. *Proceedings 6th ACM SIGMOD Symposium*, 1987.
12. G.M.Kuper. On the Expressive Power of Logic Programming with Sets. *Proceedings 7th ACM SIGMOD Symposium*, 1988.
13. B.Legeard, E.Legros. CLPS: A Set Constraints Logic Programming Language. Research Report, Laboratoire d'Automatique de Besançon, Institut de Productique, Besançon, France, Feb. 1991.
14. J.W.Lloyd. *Foundations of logic programming*. Springer Verlag, 2nd edition, 1987.
15. J.L.Lassez, M.J.Maher, K.Marriot. Unification revisited. *Lecture Notes in Computer Science*, Vol. 306, Springer Verlag, 1986.
16. A.Martelli, U.Montanari. An efficient unification algorithm. *ACM TOPLAS*, 4, April 1982.
17. A.Martelli, C.Moiso, G.F.Rossi. Lazy Unification Algorithms for Canonical Rewrite Systems, in *Resolution of Equations in Algebraic Structures*, vol II (H.Ait-Kaci and M.Nivat, eds), Academic Press, 1989.
18. M.Naftalin. An experiment in practical semantics. *ESOP 86 - Lecture Notes in Computer Science*, Vol. 213, Springer Verlag, 1986.
19. F.Parlamento, A.Policriti. Decision procedures for elementary sublanguages of set theory. IX. Unsolvability of the decision problem for a restricted subclass of Δ_0-formulas in set theory. *Communications of Pure and Applied Mathematics*, 41, 1988.
20. F.Parlamento, A.Policriti. Expressing infinity without foundation. *Journal of Symbolic Logic*, 56(3), 1991.
21. J.C.Shepherdson. Negation in Logic Programming. In *Foundations of deductive databases and Logic Programming* (J.Minker, ed). Morgan Kaufmann, Los Altos, CA, 1987.
22. J.H.Siekmann. Unification Theory. *Journal of Symbolic Computation*, 7, 1989.
23. R.Sigal. Desiderata for Logic Programming with sets. *Proceedings GULP89: Fourth National Conference on Logic Programming*, Bologna, 1989.
24. J.T.Schwartz, R.B.K.Dewar, E.Dubinsky, E.Schonberg. *Programming with sets, an introduction to SETL*. Springer-Verlag, 1986.
25. D.Turner. An overview of Miranda. *SIGPLAN Notices*, Vol.21, n.12, 1986.
26. *Z handbook*, Oxford University Computing Laboratory, Oxford 1986.

A Modal Framework for Structured Logic Programs

Laura Giordano and Alberto Martelli
Dipartimento di Informatica - Università di Torino
C.so Svizzera 185 - 10149 TORINO
E-mail: (laura, mrt)@di.unito.it

Abstract. Modal logic can be regarded as a unifying framework in which different logical languages with blocks and modules can be expressed. In particular, a modal characterization can be given to different languages which are obtained by extending Horn clause logic with implication goals D=>G (where G is a goal and D is a set of local clauses). Implication goals can be regarded as blocks of conventional programming languages and such an extension provides different kinds of block structured languages, according to the visibility rules chosen for the local clauses. The choices are mainly two: either lexical (static) visibility rules or dynamic visibility rules. The approach of this paper makes feasible the task of integrating the different kinds of blocks within a single language, the modal language. The main aim of this paper is to study the operational semantics of the language which integrates different kinds of blocks, to investigate how it can be used (and further extended) and to see how it compares to other logical languages proposed for dealing with blocks and modules.

1 Introduction

Many extensions of Horn clause logic have been proposed in order to add structuring constructs such as blocks and modules to logic programs. In particular, *local definitions* of clauses can be introduced by allowing implication goals to occur nested in goals and in clause bodies. Implication goals are implications of the form D=>G, where D is a set of clauses and G is a goal. The clauses in D are intended to be *local*, as they can be used only in a proof of G. This way, a goal G_i in a clause $G_1 \wedge ... \wedge G_n \rightarrow A$ can be not only an atom, but also an implication goal. Since implication goals introduce local clause definitions, we will call them ***blocks***, by analogy with conventional Algol-like programming languages.

Such an extension was introduced in N-Prolog [GaRe84] mainly to deal with hypothetical reasoning and the operational semantics of the extended language was proved to be sound and complete w.r.t. intuitionistic logic (by regarding both $\rightarrow$ and => as the intuitionistic implication). In [Mill86] a fixpoint semantics has been defined for a superset of this language (containing also the disjunction in goals). An analysis of these proposals shows that they use dynamic visibility rules for clauses, since, operationally, to prove a goal D => G in a program P they prove the goal G in the extended program P∪D (and thus P can use clauses in D and vice versa).

However, the same extended language with implication goals can be given a different operational semantics if different visibility rules for locally defined clauses are chosen. In particular, in [GMR88, GMR92, MoSh91] languages with *static scope rules* for clause definitions have been defined, in which, as in Algol-like languages, the rules for using clauses are determined by the *lexical* structure of the program (D can use clauses in P but not vice versa). Furthermore in [GMR92] a notion of closed block is defined (as opposed to open block) which mimics at the object level the metapredicate demo of Bowen and Kowalski [BoKo82], so that D => G can be read as demo(D,G).

In [GM91] it has been shown that these different languages with blocks can be given a modal characterization in the logic S4. The modal interpretation of the language with dynamic visibility rules is the obvious one, since such a language, as proved in [GaRe84], has an intuitionistic semantics, and intuitionistic logic can be interpreted within S4 modal logic. The modal characterization for the language with static blocks and closed blocks can be obtained by slightly modifying that one.

As a consequence, a modal extension of Horn clause logic can provide a *unifying framework* in which different kinds of blocks can be defined and integrated. The possibility of integrating the different kinds of blocks is provided by the similarity of their modal characterizations. In fact, the difference between the two languages, with static and dynamic visibility rules, does not reside in how the implication goal is defined, but in how clauses (both the local and the global ones) are defined. Thus, by allowing both of the two kinds of clause definitions, an integrated language can be defined.

In this paper, we define the operational semantics of this integrated language and investigate how it can be used. In particular we show that, by means of some syntactic sugar, also modules can be introduced. We will see how this extended language compares to other proposals for dealing with block and modules in logic programs.

In the following sections we recall the definition of the language in [Mill86] and those in [GMR92] with their operational semantics and we put forward their interpretation in the modal logic S4. For simplicity, in doing this, we will only consider the propositional case and we will ignore variables and quantifiers. The extension to the predicative case is analyzed in [GM92].

2 Block Languages with Different Visibility Rules

In this section we recall the syntax and the operational semantics of the propositional subset of the block languages in [Mill86] and in [GMR88] and we make a distinction among (open) blocks with dynamic or static visibility rules respectively and closed blocks, as proposed in [GMR92].

Let A be an atomic proposition and T a distinguished proposition (true). The syntax of the block language, which is the same for both static and dynamic blocks, is the following:

L:

$$G ::= T \mid A \mid G_1 \wedge G_2 \mid D \Rightarrow G$$
$$D ::= G \rightarrow A \mid D_1 \wedge D_2$$

In this definition G stands for a goal and D for a clause or a conjunction of clauses. A *program* is a set of clauses.

Contrary to [Mill86] we have introduced two different implications in goals and in clauses. In fact, though in the dynamic case both implications have the same semantics (they are both the intuitionistic implication) in the static case the two implications are different.

2.1 Open Blocks with Dynamic Scoping

We recall the operational semantics of the language defined in [Mill86]. Given a program P and a goal G, the meaning of G being ***operationally derivable*** from P, that is $P \vdash G$, is defined by induction on the structure of G as follows:

- $P \vdash T$;
- $P \vdash A$ *iff* there is a clause $G \rightarrow A \in P$ and $P \vdash G$;
- $P \vdash G_1 \wedge G_2$ *iff* $P \vdash G_1$ and $P \vdash G_2$;
- $P \vdash D \Rightarrow G$ *iff* $P \cup D \vdash G$.

(Note that, since P is a set, if D is a conjunction of clauses it has to be transformed into a set of clauses in the union $P \cup D$).

The scope rules of this block language are *dynamic* because the set of clauses that can be used to solve a goal G depends on the sequence of goals generated up to that point and can be determined only dynamically. In fact, an implication goal can simply be regarded as specifying a query in an *updated* program.

Example 2.1. The proof of the goal G=s in the program

P: $r \to q$

$(((q \to p) \wedge r) \Rightarrow p) \to s$

succeeds, since it amounts to prove

goal $((q \to p) \wedge r) \Rightarrow p)$ in P

goal p in $P' = P \cup \{ q \to p, r \}$

goal q in P'

goal r in P',

which succeeds. The proof of q uses the clause r defined in the inner block, which is visible at that point since the block has been added to the program P. If, on the contrary, the goal q is called directly from the outer environment its proof fails.

2.2 Open Blocks with Static Scoping

Given the above language L with implication goals, static scope rules for local definitions of clauses can be obtained by modifying the previously given operational semantics (as done in [GMR88, GMR92]).We want the rules for using a clause to be determined only by the static nesting of blocks in the program text. In this way, to solve a goal coming from the body of a clause declared in a block we want to use only the clauses declared in that block or in externally nested blocks. With this choice, we fail in proving the goal a=>b from the program $P=\{a \to c, c \to b\}$, since the atom a introduced to prove b is local to the goal and cannot be used to solve the subgoal a coming from the body of clause $a \to c$. For this reason, when static scoping rules are chosen, implication goals cannot be used to model the updating of the set of clauses nor to perform hypothetical reasoning. However, static blocks allow more efficient implementations of the language by means of compilation techniques (see [GMR88] for further motivations).

Let us define the operational semantics for the language with static scoping. In this case it is necessary to consider the derivability of a goal G from a list of programs $D_1|...|D_n$, i.e. a ***list*** of sets of clauses. The list allows us to record the ordering between blocks given by their ***lexical nesting*** in the program text. The higher is the index i of D_i in $D_1|...|D_n$, the deeper is the nesting of D_i in the program. We can now define the derivability of a goal G from a list of programs $D_1|...|D_n$ by induction on the structure of G as follows:

- $D_1|...|D_n \vdash T$;
- $D_1|...|D_n \vdash A$ *iff*, for some i, $1 \le i \le n$, there is a clause $G \to A \in D_i$ and $D_1|...|D_i \vdash G$;
- $D_1|...|D_n \vdash G_1 \wedge G_2$ *iff* $D_1|...|D_n \vdash G_1$ and $D_1|...|D_n \vdash G_2$;
- $D_1|...|D_n \vdash D \Rightarrow G$ *iff* $D_1|...|D_n|D \vdash G$.

Notice that when a clause $G \rightarrow A$ in D_i is used to refute an atomic goal A, then the clauses in $D_{i+1}|...|D_n$ cannot be used any more to prove G, since the clauses of inner blocks are not visible from external ones (and thus from G). To prove a goal D=>G, the set of local declarations D is added to the list of programs as the tail element, so that the clauses in D can be used only to refute goals coming from D itself or from G.

It is easy to see that, with this operational semantics, given the program P and the goal G of Example 2.1, G is not provable in P. The following is an example of successful derivation.

Example 2.2.

The proof of the goal G=s in the program

P: q

$(((r \wedge q \rightarrow p) \wedge r) \Rightarrow p) \rightarrow s$

succeeds, since the local clauses $(r \wedge q \rightarrow p) \wedge r$ introduced by proving the implication goal $((r \wedge q \rightarrow p) \wedge r) \Rightarrow p$ are used only locally to the block.

2.3 Closed Blocks

From the language of open static blocks defined in section 2.2 it is easy to define a language with closed blocks, by modifying the operational semantics of implication goals. The idea is to see an implication goal D=>G as specifying a change of context: to prove the goal D=> G from the program P, prove G from the program D (the set of local clauses). For this reason the goal D=>G can be regarded as mimicking the metapredicate demo(D,G) defined by Bowen and Kowalski [BoKo82].

The derivability of a closed goal G from a program P is defined by induction on the structure of G as follows (we do not require a list of programs in this case):

- $P \vdash T$;
- $P \vdash A$ *iff* there is a formula $G \rightarrow A \in P$ and $P \vdash G$;
- $P \vdash G_1 \wedge G_2$ *iff* $P \vdash G_1$ and $P \vdash G_2$;
- $P \vdash D \Rightarrow G$ *iff* $D \vdash G$.

3 Modal Interpretations

In this section we give the S4 modal interpretation of the languages with blocks defined in the previous section. Since the formal details of the modal interpretation have been already presented in [GM91], we try to give here just some intuitive motivations to explain why it works.

As regards the language with **dynamic blocks**, in [GaRe84] it is proved that the above operational semantics is sound and complete w.r.t. intuitionistic logic (also in the first order case) when the two implications => and → are regarded as the same implication, the intuitionistic one. Therefore, such a language has the semantics of intuitionistic logic and the well known mapping from the language of intuitionistic propositional logic to the language of propositional S4 modal logic can be applied to it. We recall this mapping (denoting it by *) on the propositional formulas of the language L.

$p^* = \Box p$ (p is an atom)

$(A \wedge B)^* = A^* \wedge B^*$

$(A \Rightarrow B)^* = \Box (A^* \supset B^*)$

$(A \rightarrow B)^* = \Box (A^* \supset B^*)$

where $\supset$ is the material implication and $\Box$ is the universal modal operator. Of course, the two different implications are translated in the same way, since both of them stand for the intuitionistic implication.

By applying this mapping, the language L can be translated into the following language L_1 in S4 modal logic:

L_1:

$G ::= T \mid \Box A \mid G_1 \wedge G_2 \mid \Box (D \supset G)$

$D ::= \Box (G \supset \Box A) \mid D_1 \wedge D_2.$

The correspondence between the language L with dynamic blocks and its modal interpretation L_1 can be stated as follows: for all programs P and goals G

$$P \vdash G \text{ iff } \models_{S4} P^* \supset G^*,$$

according to the definition of operational derivability given in section 2.1.

Let us give an intuitive reading of this modal language. By the semantics of S4 modal logic, an implication goal $\Box$ (D $\supset$ G) is true in an interpretation M at a world w if in every world w' reachable from w in which D is true G is also true. We can see the modal operator $\Box$ as specifying a change of world from the current world to a new reachable world. This makes clear how an implication goal $\Box$ $(D \supset G)$ can be regarded as specifying the proof of the goal G in a new world obtained by adding D.

Besides, when moving to a new world, the clauses present in the initial program continue to hold. In fact, in the language L_1, a program contains clauses of the form

$$\Box (G \supset \Box A)$$

and (by the transitivity of the accessibility relation in the logic S4) if a clause $\Box(G \supset \Box A)$ is true in an interpretation M at a world w, then it is true in that interpretation at any world w' reachable from w.

Thus, if we go from the world w to the world w' by updating the database, in w' the clause of the program $\Box$ $(G \supset \Box A)$ will still be available. This models the fact that, operationally, in the case of dynamic scoping rules, the clauses in the global program are always available for further inferences when new clauses are introduced by an update. In particular, the clauses added by an implication goal (and coming from a certain block) can always be used to prove subgoals coming from the body of a clause defined in an external block. In other words, when a clause $\Box$ $(G \supset \Box A)$ is entered in the database (by an update) then the possibility of proving its body G is affected by the successive updates.

As an example, consider the program $P=\{a \rightarrow b\}$ and the goal G= a=>b. G is operationally provable in the program P. In fact, when a is added to the program then b is derivable. In the modal interpretation the program and the goal become respectively

$$P^* = \{ \Box (\Box a \supset \Box b) \} \quad \text{and} \quad G^* = \Box (\Box a \supset \Box b);$$

therefore it is quite obvious that $\models_{S4} P^* \supset G^*$.

The S4 modal interpretation for the language with **open static blocks** can be obtained by slightly modifying the one for dynamic blocks in the following way:

L_2:

$$G ::= T \mid \Box A \mid G_1 \wedge G_2 \mid \Box (D \supset G)$$
$$D ::= G \supset \Box A \mid D_1 \wedge D_2.$$

The difference w.r.t. to the language L_1 (for dynamic blocks) is that, in this case, the two implications (in goals and in clauses) are translated in two different ways:

$$(A => B)^* = \Box (A^* \supset B^*)$$
$$(A \rightarrow B)^* = A^* \supset B^*.$$

That is, the modal operator $\Box$ is not put in front of the implications in clause definitions.

Notice that the only difference between the languages L_1 and L_2 is that, in the static case, no modal operator occurs in front of a clause, while the implication goal is interpreted in both cases in the same way. By considering the possible world semantics for S4 modal logic, the difference between the languages L_1 and L_2 becomes quite intuitive. We said that the modal operator specifies a change of world and an implication goal $\Box\ (D \supset G)$ is true in an interpretation M at a world w if G is true when we move to any new (reachable) world w' in which D holds. Since in the language L_2 the clauses of a program have the form $G \supset \Box\ A$, then it is not true that if a clause is true in an interpretation M at the world w, then it is also true at any world w' reachable from w, for clauses have no modal operator in front of them.

Thus, if we go from the world w to the world w' by updating the database, in w' the clause $G \supset \Box\ A$ may not be available. In fact, in the case of static scoping, if the clause $G \supset \Box\ A$ occurs in the program, then proving G cannot be affected by successive updates of the program by implication goals: the clauses introduced by the successive updates cannot be used to prove G. Only the atomic consequences of the clauses in the global program remain available in all the reachable worlds and, therefore, clauses in the program can be used to prove the body of a clause in a block, but not vice versa.

Therefore, the language L_2 is a very static language in which, given a program, the updates occurring in the goal or in the program itself can't have much influence on what is derivable form the initial program. A block allows new atoms to be derived by introducing new clauses (procedure), but it does not affect the initial program.

In [GMR88, GMR92] a fixpoint and a model-theoretic semantics have been defined for the language L with static blocks w.r.t. which the above operational semantics is sound and complete. The peculiarity of the model-theoretic semantics is that, in this case, the two implications are given a different semantics: roughly speaking, => is the intuitionistic implication while $\rightarrow$ is the classical one. This model-theoretic semantics, which is a Kripke semantics, has been used in [GM91] to prove the *correctness* of the above interpretation of the language with open static blocks within S4 modal logic, i.e. to prove that, for all programs P and goals G,

$$P \vdash G \quad \text{iff} \quad \models_{S4} P^* \supset G^*,$$

according to the definition of operational derivability given in section 2.2.

As an example, consider again the program $P=\{ a \rightarrow b\}$ and the goal G= a=>b. If static visibility rules are adopted, G is not operationally provable in the program P. In fact, to prove a=>b, a is added to the program, but it cannot be used to prove the goal a coming from the body of the clause $a \rightarrow b$ in the global program since it is not visible. In the modal interpretation the program and the goal are

$$P^* = \{ \Box\, a \supset \Box\, b \} \text{ and } G^* = \Box\, (\Box\, a \supset \Box\, b),$$

and it is not true that $\models_{S4} P^* \supset G^*$.

Also the language of **closed blocks** can be interpreted within S4-modal logic as follows:

L_3:

$$G ::= T \mid A \mid G_1 \wedge G_2 \mid \Box (D \supset G)$$
$$D ::= G \supset A \mid D_1 \wedge D_2.$$

The difference w.r.t. the language L_2 is that in this case there is no modal operator in front of the atomic formulas. As for the language L_2, there is no modal operator in front of the clause definitions. Therefore, the only occurrence of the modal operator is the one in front of the implication in goals.

For this reason, intuitively, the modal operator has the effect of closing a context: there is nothing which has a box in front of it and can pass through the modal context. So, when we have to prove a goal $\Box(D \supset G)$ at a world w, we have to move to a new reachable world w' where D holds. But, maybe nothing which holds at w holds also at w', so G has to be proved in a completely new context where only D holds.

4 An Integrated Language

In this section we want to integrate the languages L_1 and L_2 presented before in a single modal language which subsumes the previous ones by allowing different kinds of blocks in the same program. Since the two languages are subsets of propositional S4, then their combination will have the same model-theoretic semantics (the Kripke semantics of S4 modal logic). What has to be defined is an operational semantics for the integrated language.

Since the languages L_1 (dynamic open blocks) and L_2 (static open blocks) only differ as regards clause definitions, it is straightforward to think of combining them by allowing both *static* clause definitions (i.e. definitions of the form $G \supset \Box A$) and *dynamic* clause definitions (of the form $\Box (G \supset \Box A)$) in the same language. This makes feasible to distinguish among the static and the dynamic parts of a program, thus allowing a partial use of compilation techniques when static blocks are employed.

The syntax of the integrated language can be defined as follows:

L_4:

$$G ::= T \mid \Box A \mid G_1 \wedge G_2 \mid \Box (D \supset G)$$
$$D ::= \Box (G \supset \Box A) \mid G \supset \Box A \mid D_1 \wedge D_2.$$

To define its operational semantics, since *static* clause definitions are allowed, it is necessary to consider the derivability of a goal G from a list of programs $D_1|...|D_n$, as in the case of open static blocks. The derivability of a closed goal G from a list of programs $D_1|...|D_n$ can be defined by induction on the structure of G as follows:

- $D_1|...|D_n \vdash T$;
- $D_1|...|D_n \vdash \Box A$ *iff*, for some i, $1 \le i \le n$,
  there is a clause $\Box (G \supset \Box A) \in D_i$ and $D_1|...|D_n \vdash G$
  or
  there is a clause $G \supset \Box A \in D_i$ and $D_1|...|D_i \vdash G$;
- $D_1|...|D_n \vdash G_1 \wedge G_2$ *iff* $D_1|...|D_n \vdash G_1$ and $D_1|...|D_n \vdash G_2$;
- $D_1|...|D_n \vdash \Box (D \supset G)$ *iff* $D_1|...|D_n|D \vdash G$.

The operational semantics of the implication goal $\Box (D \supset G)$ is the same as for open static blocks (the set of local declarations D is added to the list of programs as the tail element), but a different use of the list of programs is done each time a new clause is selected, according to its kind. Notice that when a *static clause* $G \supset \Box A$ is selected from D_i to refute an atomic goal A, then the clauses in $D_{i+1}|...|D_n$ cannot be used any more to prove G, since the clauses of inner blocks are not visible from external ones (and thus from G). On the contrary, when a *dynamic clause* $\Box (G \supset \Box A)$ is selected in D_i to prove A, then all the programs $D_1,...,D_n$ in the list can be used to prove G (i.e. the clauses in the different blocks are regarded as being undistinguishable).

When writing a program, a static clause can be used when its body can be considered as completely defined in the enclosing blocks, and we do not want any successive update to affect it. On the contrary, if we want the body of a clause to be proved dynamically also using clauses introduced by updates, then a dynamic clause is needed.

To allow closed blocks in the language L_4, it is not correct to integrate it with the language of closed blocks L_3. In this case, in fact, the presence of clauses of the form $G \supset A$ would not produce closed blocks any more, since this feature in the language L_3 is due to the modal operator only occurring in front of implication goals. However, to recover this possibility, it suffices to introduce in the language a new modal operator. Let $\boxtimes$ be another universal modal operator (we have moved to a multimodal logic) for which the axioms of S4 modal logic hold. Consider an extended language with the following syntax:

L_5:

$$G ::= T \mid \Box A \mid G_1 \wedge G_2 \mid \Box(D \supset G) \mid \boxtimes(D \supset G)$$
$$D ::= \Box(G \supset \Box A) \mid G \supset \Box A \mid D_1 \wedge D_2.$$

Since the modal operator $\boxtimes$ only occurs in front of implication goals, its effect consists in closing a context, i.e. to allow closed blocks. In fact, to deal with such *closed implications* the following new rule has to be added to the operational semantics for the language L_4:

- $D_1|...|D_n \vdash \boxtimes(D \supset G)$ *iff* $D \vdash G$.

When a closed implication $\boxtimes(D \supset G)$ has to be proved, the current context (list of programs) is removed and G is proved in the local set of clauses D.

The language defined above is probably too complex to be used in practice. However the purpose of this paper is to explore the potential uses of the modal constructs in building structured logic programs and to single out the most useful constructs, which will be provided by a high level language to be subsequently defined.

5 Using Blocks to Modularize the Program

In [GM91] it has been shown that modal logics are also well suited for supporting the notion of module by making use of multimodal logics. In this section we will follow another approach to define modules: we will define them by introducing some syntactic sugar on the block language. The reason for introducing modules is that they are a better ground to compare this proposal with the others in the literature, whose main concern are modules, rather then blocks.

In the following we will consider several kinds of modules and ways to combine them. All of them will be based on the idea that a module m can be defined as consisting of the set of clauses D, by the definition (syntactic sugar)

m is-mod D,

where m is a name and the language of the clauses in D is the modal language L_5 or one subset of it.

Once the name of the module has been associated with a set of clauses in this way, then the module name can be used in implication goals. We can write

$$\Box(m \supset G)$$

to say that the goal G has to be proved in the module m. The operational semantics of this language with modules is the same as for the block language, once each occurrence of a module name has been replaced with the corresponding set of clauses. Of course, this preprocessing can be performed only if the modules are not recursively defined. The different kinds of clauses that a module contains cause how the module interacts with other modules. We will now consider some different possibilities.

In a very simplistic view, we can assume that a module is a closed environment which *exports* every proposition defined inside it and *imports* a proposition from other modules by explicitly referring to those modules. We can define a module system in which the modules $m_1,..,m_k$ behave like this by allowing each module to contain only clauses in the language L_3 (except for the fact that in each implication goal a module name and not a set of local clauses has to occur). In fact, in this way, each module will be closed (since the modal operator can only occur in implication goals) and a module m_i will be able to import a predicate A from m_j explicitly by the implication goal $\Box\ (m_j \supset A)$. More generally, a module m_i can ask for the proof of a goal G in another module m_j by the implication goal $\Box\ (m_j \supset G)$. Every proposition defined in a module is exported, in the sense that it can be queried from other modules. This is the very simple kind of modules defined in [GMR90].

A more complex kind of open modules have been defined in [MoPo89]. Apart from the presence of module names, that they call *units*, their operational semantics is quite similar to the one for static open blocks. A difference is that they employ *predicate overriding*, that is, the most recent definition of a predicate in a sequence overrides the previous ones. To model this kind of modules in our language (apart from predicate overriding) is straightforward: it suffices to allow each module to contain only clauses of the language L_2, i.e. clauses of the form $G \supset \Box\ A$, where G can contain also implication goals of the form $\Box\,(m_j \supset G)$ corresponding to the "context extension formulas" m>>G in [MoPo89]. In this way, modules are not closed any more and can be composed. It has to be noticed however that the language in [MoPo89] also allows the definition of mutually recursive units, while we don't.

In this paper we have not tackled the problem of modelling predicate overriding. This might be done, however, in a modal framework by making use of a multimodal logic, as suggested in [FaHe92].

An example of module composition is the following (adapted from [MoPo89]):

authors **is-mod** { $\Box$ wrote(Person, Something) $\supset$ $\Box$ author(Person)}

books is-mod { T ⊃ □ wrote(plato, republic).
T ⊃ □ wrote(homer, iliad).
□ (authors ⊃ □ author(Person)) ⊃ □ writer(Person)},

where the goal □ (books ⊃ □ writer(plato)) has the following derivation:

	⊢ □ (books ⊃ □ writer(plato))
books	⊢ □ writer(plato)
books	⊢ □ (authors ⊃ □ author(plato))
books | authors	⊢ □ author(plato)
books | authors	⊢ □ wrote(plato, Something)
books	⊢ T

Here, according to the static visibility rules, the inner module authors implicitly imports all the facts that are provable in module books, but not vice versa.

Note that modules can also be composed by nesting them in the initial goal. For instance, given a module sort defining a predicate quicksort

sort **is-mod** { ...
... □ greater_than(X,Y) .... ⊃ □ quicksort(......).
.....}

and two different modules defining a predicate greater_than

integers **is-mod** {...
.... ⊃ □ greater_than(X,Y).
....}

char **is-mod** {...
.... ⊃ □ greater_than(X,Y).
....}

the two goals
□(integers ⊃ □(sort ⊃ □quicksort(...))) and
□(char ⊃ □(sort ⊃ □quicksort(...)))
will compute quicksort in two different environments.

In the same way, it is possible to define a module system in which the composition of modules consists of the union of the modules. This happens if the clauses contained in the modules are all dynamics, i.e. of the form □ (G ⊃ □ A). In this case, given the query □ (m_i ⊃ □ (m_j ⊃ G)), the goal G is proved in the union of the modules m_i and m_j. These, of course, correspond to the modules defined in [Mill89] obtained by adding some syntactic sugar to the language with dynamic blocks.

However, if the block language on which the modules are built is the language L_5, it is also possible to have in the same program different modules, each one of a different kind (closed modules, modules with static or with dynamic clauses), and even to have a module containing both static and dynamic clauses. This gives a big flexibility, since it allows to make use of the dynamic features only when needed, while leaving the other part of the program static.

The presence of static or dynamic clause definitions in a module specifies what of the clause is *exported* to the other modules. Thus, if a module m contains a dynamic clause of the form □ (G ⊃ □ A) such a clause is intended to be exported to other modules. Of course, since modules are composed by means of implication goals as

$$\Box\,(m_1 \supset \Box\,(m_2 \supset \Box\,(m_3 \supset G))),$$

the direction of the export is determined by the nesting of implication goals: the module m_1 exports toward all the more deeply nested modules (m_2 and m_3), while m_2 only exports to m_3 (and not to m_1). So, each dynamic clause defined in m is visible to the more nested modules or, in other words, can be affected by successive updates.

On the contrary, a clause of the form G ⊃ □ A in the module m is not exported by m. Only its consequent A is exported to the internal modules. The possibility of proving G is not affected by successive updates. Consider, for instance, the following example.

Example 5.1.
If we have the two modules

m_4 **is-mod** { □ d ⊃ □ a
□ (□ b ⊃ □ d) }

m_5 **is-mod** {T ⊃ □ b }

then the goal □ (m_4 ⊃ □ (m_5 ⊃ □ d)) succeeds from the program consisting of the two modules (since the body □ b of the second clause of m_4 can be proved in the module m_5), while the goal □ (m_4 ⊃ □ (m_5 ⊃ □ a)) fails, since the first clause in m_4 is static and the proof of its body □ d cannot make use of clauses defined in more internal modules as m_5. Notice that not only $\Box$ d has to be resolved with a clause in m_4, but all the proof of $\Box$ d has to be done in m_4.

A different framework for structuring logic programs has been defined in [BLM90]. There a distinction is made between *conservative and evolving policies* and between *statically and dynamically configured systems.* The distinction between *conservative and evolving policies* roughly corresponds to our distinction between static and dynamic visibility rules.

A *statically configured system* is defined as a system where hierarchies among units (i.e. modules) are specified when units are defined. In these systems the context in which a unit is used does not depend on the dynamic sequence of goals, but is always fixed. To define statically configured units, in [BLM90], the definition

$$\text{unit}(m_1, \text{static}([m_2,m_3,m_4])$$

is introduced, whose meaning is that whenever the unit m_1 is used, it is used in the context of the modules m_2,m_3,m_4.

In our language, statically configured modules can be allowed by regarding the above static unit definition as syntactic sugar. Its meaning is that each occurrence of the implication goal $\Box\ (m_1 \supset G)$ in the program has to be replaced with the implication goal

$$\boxtimes\ (m_4 \supset \Box\ (m_3 \supset \Box\ (m_2 \supset \Box\ (m_1 \supset G)))).$$

In this way, the context in which m_1 is used is always the closed context containing m_2,m_3 and m_4. A preprocessing step is needed to make the replacement above and, in general, more steps are needed if more then one unit is defined as statically configured.

If a module is not defined as statically configured, i.e. it is *dynamically configured*, it can be used in different contexts, if it occurs in different implication goals in the program.

We said that the proposal in [BLM90] makes a distinction between conservative and evolving policies, which roughly corresponds to our distinction between static and dynamic visibility. More precisely, while we regard clauses as being either static or dynamic, in [BLM90] such a behavior is referred to the goals in the body of a clause.

As regards atomic goals, it is possible to put the symbol # in front of the atoms. #A means that A is a *lazy atom* and, operationally, it has to be solved dynamically from the current list of modules. This gives the *evolving policy.* Intuitively, a clause of the form

$$\#B \wedge \#C \supset A$$

corresponds, in our modal approach, to the dynamic clause

$$\Box(\Box B \wedge \Box C \supset \Box A).$$

On the other hand if # is not used in front of an atom *(eager atom)*, it means that the atom coming from a module has to be solved statically only using clauses defined in that module or in externally nested modules. This gives the *conservative policy*. A clause of the form

$$B \wedge C \supset A$$

corresponds, in our modal approach, to the static clause

$$\Box B \wedge \Box C \supset \Box A.$$

As atomic goals, also implication goals can have a static or dynamic behavior. In fact, the language in [BLM90] contains two kinds of implication goals:

$$m >> G \quad \text{and} \quad m >>> G.$$

In terms of our modal language, the first one can be regarded as an implication goal occurring in a static clause, while the second one as an implication goal occurring in a dynamic clause.

In [BLM90] it is argued that the combination of the different policies and the different kind of configuration of modules allows to deal with the best-known proposals for structuring logic programs. In particular, the choice of statically configuration evolving systems is recognized as the proper one to deal with inheritance based systems. Indeed, statically configured modules can be used to represent the static dependencies among modules in a hierarchy. We rephrase in our language an example presented in [BLM90] and taken from [McCa88].

Example 5.2.

Let us consider three modules, named respectively *animal, bird* and *tweety*. Since what is true for animals is also true for birds, the *bird* module inherits from the *animal* module. Moreover, the module *tweety* inherits from *bird* and thus from *animal*. Let assume that there are no modules more general than *animal*. To model this situation, the following static unit declarations have to be introduced:

unit(animal, static([])).
unit(bird, static([animal])).
unit(tweety, static([bird])).

The modules *animal, bird* and *tweety* are defined as follows:

animal **is-mod**
{ $T \supset \Box$mode(walk).
$\Box(\Box$ no_of_legs(2) $\supset \Box$ mode(run)).
$\Box(\Box$ no_of_legs(4) $\supset \Box$ mode(gallop)). }

bird **is-mod**

{ $T \supset \Box$no_of_legs(2).

$T \supset \Box$covering(feather). }

tweety **is-mod**

{ $T \supset \Box$owner(fred). }

Because of the static configuration, when a goal $\Box(\Box$tweety $\supset \Box$mode(run)) is called, it is replaced, by preprocessing, by the goal

$$\boxtimes(\Box\text{animal} \supset \Box(\Box\text{bird} \supset \Box(\Box\text{tweety} \supset \Box\text{mode(run)})))$$

So, the goal $\Box$mode(run) is proved in the list of modules animal | bird | tweety. Since the clause for $\Box$mode(run) in the module *animal* is dynamic the subgoal $\Box$no_of _legs(2) can be proved in the nested module *bird* and, therefore, the call succeeds. In this way we get the same behavior as in the corresponding example of [BLM90] where lazy atoms #no_of _legs(2) and #no_of _legs(4) are used.

Though there is a correspondence between the conservative and evolving policies in [BLM90] and the notion of static and dynamic visibility rules we have introduced, this correspondence is not perfect. In fact, if we come back to the example 5.1, we can write the two modules m_4 and m_5 in the language in [BLM90] as follows:

unit(m_4):

$d \supset a$.

$\#b \supset d$.

unit(m_5):

b.

As in example 5.1, the goal m_4>> (m_5 >> d) succeeds from the program, but, also the goal m_4>> (m_5 >> a) succeeds, while it doesn't in the modal language. In fact, in this case, though the atom d in the body of the clause $d \supset a$ is eager (it is not preceded by #) and therefore has to be resolved with a clause in m_4 (in this case there are no externally nested modules), the subgoals generated by it can be solved dynamically. Indeed, the proof of the eager goal d can make use of the atom b defined in the nested module m_5.

This kind of behavior, which allows a static goal to depend on dynamic subgoals, is reflected in a rather complex operational semantics [BLM90], which makes use of two lists of modules instead of a single one as the operational semantics we have defined above.

As another difference wrt. our proposal, the language in [BLM90] allows all kind of atoms (both lazy and eager ones) and implication goals to occur in the same clause body. For instance, it is legal to write the following clause:

$$B \wedge \#C \supset A$$

where B is an eager atom and #C a lazy atom. Such a clause cannot be represented in our modal language, since it only allows static clauses (whose body only contain eager atoms or implication goals of the form m >> G) or dynamic clauses (whose body only contains lazy atoms or implication goals of the form m >>> G) to be defined. In order to represent clauses like this, however, it suffices to make use of two clauses instead of a single one, as follows:

$$\Box(\Box D \wedge \Box C \supset \Box A)$$

$$\Box B \supset \Box D$$

where D is a dummy proposition. In this way the subgoal $\Box$C is proved dynamically, while $\Box$B is proved statically.

6 Conclusions

In this paper we have shown how modal logic can provide a unifying framework for expressing implication goals (blocks) with different visibility rules for clauses, so that different kinds of blocks can be integrated into a single modal language. The language has been extended, by some syntactic sugar, so as to allow module definitions as well. We have proved the flexibility of the language through several examples, by showing how to obtain behaviours similar to those proposed in the literature on structured logic programming, in particular by Miller, Monteiro and Porto, Brogi, Lamma and Mello. This language can be considered as a base language upon which to design other languages providing suitable constructs for building blocks and modules at a higher level.

Possible extensions of the language concern the introduction of multimodal operators of the kind [m], which allow to deal semantically with modules by considering m as a module name [GM91]. Further study will also be devoted to devising efficient implementation techniques, in particular by making use of the techniques developed for theorem proving in modal logic.

Acknowledgement

This work has been partially supported by C.N.R. - Progetto Finalizzato "Sistemi Informatici e Calcolo Parallelo" under grant n. 90.00668.PF69.

References

[BoKo82] Bowen K.A., Kowalski R.A.: "Amalgamating Language and Metalanguage in Logic Programming", in *Logic Programming* (Clark and Tarnlund, eds.), Academic Press, 1982, 153-172.

[BLM90] Brogi A., Lamma E., Mello P.: "A General Framework for Structuring Logic Programs", Technical Report *Progetto Finalizzato Sistemi Informatici e Calcolo Parallelo*, 1990.

[FaHe92] Fariñas del Cerro L., Herzig A., Metaprogramming through Intensional Deduction: some examples, in: *Proc. META92*, Stockholm, 1992.

[GaRe84] Gabbay D.M., Reyle N.: "N_Prolog: An Extension of Prolog with Hypothetical Implications.I.", *Journal of Logic Programming*, no.4 1984, 319-355.

[GM91] Giordano L., Martelli A.: "A Modal Reconstruction of blocks and modules in logic programming", in *Proc. 1991 Int. Logic Programming Symposium*, San Diego, October 1991, 239-253.

[GM92] Giordano L., Martelli A.: "Structuring Logic Programs: A Modal Approach", submitted for publication.

[GMR88] Giordano L., Martelli A., Rossi G.F., "Local Definitions with static Scope Rules in Logic Programming", in *Proc. Int. Conf. on Fifth Generation Computer Systems*, Tokyo, 1988, 389-396.

[GMR90] Giordano L., Martelli A., Rossi G.F.: "Extending Horn Clause Logic with Module Costructs", Research Report 04-90-RR, Dipartimento di Matematica e Informatica, Universita' di Udine, 1990.

[GMR92] Giordano L., Martelli A., Rossi G.F.: "Extending Horn Clause Logic with Implication Goals", *Theoretical Computer Science*, 95 (1992) 43-74.

[McCa88] Mc Cabe F.G.: "Logic and Objects: Language, Applications and Implementation", *Doctorate Thesis*, University of London, 1988.

[Mill86] Miller D.A.: "A Theory of Modules for Logic Programming", *IEEE Symp. on Logic Programming*, Sept.1986, 106-114.

[Mill89] Miller D.A.: "A Logica Analysis of Modules in Logic Programming", in *Journal of Logic Programming*, n.6, 1989, pp.79-108.

[MoPo89] Monteiro L., Porto A.: "Contextual Logic Programming", in *Proc. Sixth Int. Conf. of Logic Programming*, Lisbon, 1989, 284-299.

[MoSh91] Moscowitz Y., Shapiro E.: "Lexical Logic Programs", *Proc. 8th Int. Conf. on Logic Programming*, Paris, 1991, 349-363.

Metalogic for State Oriented Programming

Antonio Brogi and Franco Turini

Dipartimento di Informatica, Corso Italia 40, 56125 Pisa, Italy

Abstract. Object-oriented programming and blackboard systems have proven to be two of the most successful approaches to the construction of complex software systems. Both of them rely upon the ability of maintaining either a distributed or a centralised state. On the other hand, logic programming has proven to be one of the most sophisticated and semantically well defined paradigms for declarative programming. We show how logic programming and state management can be reconciled, and how object-oriented and blackboard based systems can stand on this ground. The main instrument of the construction is a suitable form of metalogic, which takes into account a collection of logic programs and an operator for their dynamic composition.

1 Introduction

The origins of logic programming date back to the early 70's when a procedural interpretation for a subset of predicate logic was formulated [13]. The definition of the semantics of predicate logic as a programming language [26] and the realisation of an interpreter for the PROLOG language set the foundations for the theory and the practice of programming with logic. The possibility of using logic as a programming language has attracted several researchers in the last twenty years and it has generated a lively area of research. Logic programming is today one of the most active areas of computer science, as shown by the number of international journals and conferences dedicated to the topic. Logic programming is continuing to grow in different important areas of computer science, such as programming, databases and artificial intelligence. The procedural interpretation of logic was originally defined in terms of the clausal form of logic, and in particular by considering Horn clauses [13]. An extensive description of the possible uses of logic as a programming language and of its applications to problem solving is reported, for instance, in [14].

During the development of logic programming, the formalism of Horn clauses has been extended in several ways to improve its knowledge representation and problem solving capabilities. Horn programs, in fact, are not suited for a number of actual uses, such as building large systems in a modular way, and for various artificial intelligence applications, such as nonmonotonic reasoning and object-oriented programming. Several proposals radically extend logic programming by introducing additions to the language both on a syntactic and on a semantic ground. Many of these extensions are equipped with semantics departing from the standard semantics of logic programming. As a consequence, different proposals are difficult to compare, and are often incompatible each other.

We apply here a general methodology, based on metalogic, for the definition of extensions of logic programming. We show that several extensions can be defined from inside logic programming by exploiting the metaprogramming features of the language. In previous work [6], we have shown that the expressive power of metalogic suffices to reconstruct a number of knowledge representation techniques and inference methods, such as forms of hypothetical reasoning, hierarchical reasoning and object-orientation of programs. The main advantages of the methodology is the definition of a uniform framework, from both the syntax and the semantics point of view, for

- Rapid prototyping of needed extensions,
- Evaluating different extensions, and
- Comparing alternative proposals.

A further advantage is that metalogical definitions show that several extensions can be expressed from inside the standard logic programming framework in a simple way.

It is a widespread opinion that logic programming should be extended with features for the realisation of typical artificial intelligence architectures, such as object-oriented and blackboard systems (see for instance [4] and [18]). All of these architectures require in one way or another the ability of handling some notion of *state* to cope with the dynamic evolution of knowledge bases. In object-oriented programming, a state is associated with an object to determine its current configuration. In blackboard systems, a notion of state is employed as a communication medium among separate (possibly concurrent) agents.

Here, we describe a two-step process for creating an object-oriented framework and a blackboard-oriented framework starting from the basic kernel of logic programming. We first establish a basic conservative extension, which can provide the firm ground for any other object-oriented flavoured and blackboard-oriented flavoured extensions.

This basic extension consists of

- Moving from a single logic program to a collection of logic programs (theories), and
- Providing a composition operator (union) over theories.

The operational meaning of this extension is captured by axiomatising the provability relation of the new framework via metalogical axioms. More important than that, the new framework can be given more abstract semantics (denotational and model-theoretic) which properly and conservatively extend the semantic kernel of logic programming. On this ground, we will build typical object-oriented and blackboard-oriented features by axiomatising two abstract models via metalevel axioms.

The advantages of the abstract model for the object-oriented framework are many:

- On one side, it provides a logical understanding of object-oriented features, much in the same sense a denotational model provides a functional understanding of an imperative language. Typical object-oriented mechanisms,

such as inheritance and message passing can be understood in terms of deduction processes.
- On another side, it exemplifies a proper extension of typical object-oriented formalisms by allowing the logical definition of methods, internal states, hierarchical links and message passing.
- Finally, it is an executable prototype of the system.

Similar advantages can be claimed for the blackboard-oriented model.

Both abstract models need to embody a notion of state. A state is viewed as a logic program (theory) consisting of unit clauses only. Updates on a state, such as insertions and deletions of items, are defined through metalevel transformations of a theory. The metalevel definition of state and state updates is then employed for the rational reconstruction of object-oriented and blackboard systems.

Logic programming can be naturally object-oriented by viewing both objects and the associated states as theories. An object with a certain state is represented through a metalevel composition of the corresponding theories. A multi-object setting is then studied where separate objects may cooperate each other through message passing.

Blackboard systems [9, 21], instead, are based on a model of computation where separate agents communicate through a shared medium (the blackboard). Such a communication model relates to production systems and to some programming languages, such as SHARED PROLOG [4], LINDA [10] and the concurrent constraint paradigm [22]. Logic programming can be blackboard-oriented by viewing both the agents and the blackboard as theories. Updates on the shared blackboard are defined through metalevel transformations of the theory which represents the blackboard.

The plan of the paper follows. Some preliminaries on logic programming and on the use of metalogic are introduced in the next Subsection. The basic multi-theory framework is presented in Section 2. The representation of a state as a theory, and the updates of a state are discussed in Section 3. The object-orientation and the blackboard-orientation of logic programming are presented in Section 4 and 5, respectively. Finally, some conclusions are drawn in Section 6.

Background

We use standard notations of Apt [1] and Lloyd [16]. Object level programs (or theories) are finite sets of definite clauses. In the definitions, we refer to generic theories by using capital letters such as P, Q (possibly indexed). The minimal Herbrand model of a theory P is denoted by M_P.

The *immediate consequence operator* T_P maps Herbrand interpretations to Herbrand interpretations, and it is defined as follows [1]:

$$T_P(I) = \{ A \mid A \leftarrow B_1, \ldots, B_n \in ground(P) \text{ and } \{B_1, \ldots, B_n\} \subseteq I \}.$$

The powers of the T_P operator are defined as follows:

$$\begin{aligned} T_P \uparrow 0 &= \emptyset \\ T_P \uparrow (n+1) &= T_P(T_P \uparrow n) \\ T_P \uparrow \omega &= \bigcup_{n<\omega} T_P \uparrow n \end{aligned}$$

A well known result by van Emden and Kowalski [26] states that the T_P operator is monotonic and continuous, and that the minimal Herbrand model of a definite logic program can be obtained as the least fixpoint of the T_P.

This work heavily relies on the notion of metalogic [2]. In metalogic, object level expressions are represented by metalevel terms, while object level provability is defined by metalevel axioms. The simplest application of metalogic is the so called *vanilla* metainterpreter [23], which is a three-clause program describing the SLD derivation procedure of logic programming. The predicate $demo(P, X)$ states that the formula X is provable in the theory P. The standard provability relation of logic programming may be defined by the following metalevel axioms.

Definition 1. The vanilla metainterpreter is defined as follows.

(v1) $demo(P, true) \leftarrow$

(v2) $demo(P, (X, Y)) \leftarrow$
$\quad demo(P, X),$
$\quad demo(P, Y)$

(v3) $demo(P, X) \leftarrow$
$\quad demo(P, X \leftarrow Y),$
$\quad demo(P, Y)$

For the sake of homogeneity, the predicate *demo* is employed for representing both the axioms of a theory and the formulae which are provable in the theory. More precisely, object level theories are referred to by means of constant names and they are represented by unit clauses of the *demo* predicate. For instance, a theory consisting of the clauses

$a \leftarrow$
$b \leftarrow c$

can be named $p1$ and it can be represented as follows.

$demo(p1, a \leftarrow true) \leftarrow$
$demo(p1, b \leftarrow c) \leftarrow$

2 The Basic Framework

We extend the basic framework of logic programming by considering a collection of logic programs (we have used and we will use the word theories with identical meaning) and a union composition operator defined over them. Some of the results of this Section have already been reported in [5, 17]. The union operator (denoted by $\cup$) allows one to compose theories into a single theory according to the following definition.

Definition 2. Given two theories P and Q, $P \cup Q$ is a theory valued expression which denotes the theory obtained by putting the clauses of theories P and Q together.

We provide three definitions of the semantics of the above composition operator:

- An operational semantics based on metalogic,
- A denotational semantics based on the immediate consequence operator, and
- A model-theoretic semantics.

The three definitions extend the basic semantic definitions of the logic programming kernel in a conservative and proper way. We start with the operational semantics.

Definition 3. The operational semantics of the operator $\cup$ is given by the following two clauses to be added to the vanilla metainterpreter:

(v4) $demo(P \cup Q, X \leftarrow Y) \leftarrow demo(P, X \leftarrow Y)$

(v5) $demo(P \cup Q, X \leftarrow Y) \leftarrow demo(Q, X \leftarrow Y)$

The denotational semantics can now be given by defining how the immediate consequence operator of the union of two theories relates to the immediate consequence operators of the two argument theories.

Definition 4. Given two theories P and Q, for any Herband interpretation I:

$$T_{P \cup Q}(I) = T_P(I) \cup T_Q(I)$$

where we have overloaded the symbol $\cup$ by letting it mean union between theories in the left hand side and set-union (between sets of ground atoms) in the right hand side.

It is worth observing that the above definition captures the step by step interaction of the two argument theories when they are composed via $\cup$. In fact the following property holds.

Proposition 5. *Given theories P and Q*

$$T_P \uparrow \omega \cup T_Q \uparrow \omega \subseteq T_{P \cup Q} \uparrow \omega$$

As the above proposition already suggests, the model-theoretic semantics of $\cup$ cannot be simply given as "the minimal Herbrand model of $P \cup Q$ is the union of the minimal Herbrand models of P and Q". This is true only for special cases, such as if P and Q are disjoint with respect to predicate names - a not so interesting case. The following definition captures the more general case.

Definition 6. Given two theories P and Q

$$M_{P\cup Q} = \bigcap \{M \mid M \models P \wedge M \models Q\}$$
$$= min\ \{M \mid M \models P \wedge M \models Q\}$$

We are now in a position of proving the equivalence of the semantic definitions given above. We first prove the equivalence between the denotational and the model theoretic semantics and, then, we prove the equivalence between the denotational and the operational semantics.

Theorem 7. *Given two theories P and Q*

$$T_{P\cup Q} \uparrow \omega = M_{P\cup Q}$$

Proof
By mutual inclusion.

i) $T_{P\cup Q} \uparrow \omega \subseteq M_{P\cup Q}$
In fact, $M_{P\cup Q}$ is a model of both P and Q by definition, hence $T_P(M_{P\cup Q}) \subseteq M_{P\cup Q}$ and $T_Q(M_{P\cup Q}) \subseteq M_{P\cup Q}$.
As a consequence, $T_{P\cup Q}(M_{P\cup Q}) = T_P(M_{P\cup Q}) \cup T_Q(M_{P\cup Q}) \subseteq M_{P\cup Q}$, that is $M_{P\cup Q}$ is a Herbrand model of $P \cup Q$ and hence it contains the minimal Herbrand model, i.e. $T_{P\cup Q} \uparrow \omega$.
ii) $M_{P\cup Q} \subseteq T_{P\cup Q} \uparrow \omega$, since $T_{P\cup Q} \uparrow \omega$ is a model of both P and Q.

Theorem 8. *Given two theories P and Q and an object level atom A, let $\mathcal{M}$ be the logic program containing axioms v1-v5, and the metalevel representation of P and Q. Then*

$$A \in T_{P\cup Q} \uparrow \omega \Leftrightarrow \mathcal{M} \vdash demo(P \cup Q, A)$$

Proof
We show first

(1) $A \in T_{P\cup Q}(I) \Longleftrightarrow \exists G : \mathcal{M} \vdash demo(P \cup Q, A \leftarrow G) \wedge G \subseteq I$

$A \in T_{P\cup Q}(I)$
$\Longleftrightarrow$ $\{$definition of $T_{P\cup Q}\}$
$A \in T_P(I) \cup T_Q(I)$
$\Longleftrightarrow$ $\{$definition of $T_P\}$
$(\exists G_1 : A \leftarrow G_1 \in ground(P) \wedge G_1 \subseteq I) \vee$
$(\exists G_2 : A \leftarrow G_2 \in ground(Q) \wedge G_2 \subseteq I)$
$\Longleftrightarrow$ $\{$definition of metalevel representation$\}$
$(\exists G_1 : demo(P, A \leftarrow G_1) \in ground(\mathcal{M}) \wedge G_1 \subseteq I) \vee$
$(\exists G_2 : demo(Q, A \leftarrow G_2 \in ground(\mathcal{M}) \wedge G_2 \subseteq I)$
$\Longleftrightarrow$ $\{$completeness of SLD$\}$
$(\exists G_1 : \mathcal{M} \vdash demo(P, A \leftarrow G_1) \wedge G_1 \subseteq I) \vee$

$$
\begin{array}{ll}
 & (\exists G_2 : \mathcal{M} \vdash demo(Q, A \leftarrow G_2) \wedge G_2 \subseteq I) \\
\Longleftrightarrow & \quad \{(\text{v4}),(\text{v5})\} \\
 & (\exists G_1 : \mathcal{M} \vdash demo(P \cup Q, A \leftarrow G_1) \wedge G_1 \subseteq I) \vee \\
 & (\exists G_2 : \mathcal{M} \vdash demo(P \cup Q, A \leftarrow G_2) \wedge G_2 \subseteq I) \\
\Longleftrightarrow & \quad \{\vee \text{ idempotence}\} \\
 & (\exists G : \mathcal{M} \vdash demo(P \cup Q, A \leftarrow G) \wedge G \subseteq I)
\end{array}
$$

We define now a program $\mathcal{D}$ as follows:

$$
\begin{array}{lll}
\mathcal{D} & = & \{demo(P \cup Q, A) \leftarrow demo(P \cup Q, B_1), \ldots, demo(P \cup Q, B_n) \\
 & & \mid \mathcal{M} \vdash demo(P \cup Q, A \leftarrow B_1, \ldots, B_n)\}
\end{array}
$$

and we prove that

(2) $T_{\mathcal{D}} \uparrow \omega = T_{\mathcal{M}} \uparrow \omega$

by proving that $T_{\mathcal{D}'} \uparrow \omega = T_{\mathcal{M}'} \uparrow \omega$, where $\mathcal{D}' = ground(\mathcal{D})$ and $\mathcal{M}' = ground(\mathcal{M})$. To prove (2) we show that $\mathcal{D}'$ can be obtained from $\mathcal{M}'$ via unfolding.

In fact, each clause $demo(P \cup Q, A) \leftarrow demo(P \cup Q, B_1), \ldots, demo(P \cup Q, B_n)$ of $\mathcal{D}'$ can be obtained as follows starting from an instance of clause $(v3)$ of $\mathcal{M}'$.

$$
\begin{array}{ll}
 & demo(P \cup Q, A) \leftarrow demo(P \cup Q, A \leftarrow B_1, \ldots, B_n), demo(P \cup Q, B_1, \ldots, B_n) \\
\mapsto & \quad \{\text{unfold}, \mathcal{M}' \vdash demo(P \cup Q, A \leftarrow B_1, \ldots, B_n)\ \} \\
 & demo(P \cup Q, A) \leftarrow demo(P \cup Q, B_1, \ldots, B_n) \\
\mapsto & \quad \{\text{unfold } (v2)\} \\
 & demo(P \cup Q, A) \leftarrow demo(P \cup Q, B_1), demo(P \cup Q, B_2, \ldots, B_n) \\
 & \quad \vdots \\
\mapsto & \quad \{\text{unfold } (v2)\} \\
 & demo(P \cup Q, A) \leftarrow demo(P \cup Q, B_1), \ldots, demo(P \cup Q, B_n)
\end{array}
$$

We now show that:

(3) $A \in T_{P \cup Q}(I) \Longleftrightarrow demo(P \cup Q, A) \in T_{\mathcal{D}'}(I')$

where $I' = \{demo(P \cup Q, A) \mid A \in I\}$. We calculate:

$$
\begin{array}{ll}
 & A \in T_{P \cup Q}(I) \\
\Longleftrightarrow & \quad \{\text{ by } (1)\ \} \\
 & \mathcal{M}' \vdash demo(P \cup Q, A \leftarrow B_1, \ldots, B_n)\ \wedge\ B_i \in I \\
\Longleftrightarrow & \quad \{\text{ definition of } I'\ \} \\
 & \mathcal{M}' \vdash demo(P \cup Q, A \leftarrow B_1, \ldots, B_n)\ \wedge\ demo(P \cup Q, B_i) \in I' \\
\Longleftrightarrow & \quad \{\text{ definition of } \mathcal{D}'\ \} \\
 & demo(P \cup Q, A) \in T_{\mathcal{D}'}(I')
\end{array}
$$

We are now in the position of concluding the proof as follows

$$
\begin{array}{ll}
& A \in T_{P \cup Q} \uparrow \omega \\
\Longleftrightarrow & \quad \{ \text{ by (3) } \} \\
& demo(P \cup Q, A) \in T_{\mathcal{D}} \uparrow \omega \\
\Longleftrightarrow & \quad \{ \text{ by (2) } \} \\
& demo(P \cup Q, A) \in T_{\mathcal{M}} \uparrow \omega \\
\Longleftrightarrow & \quad \{ \text{ by completeness of SLD } \} \\
& \mathcal{M} \vdash demo(P \cup Q, A)
\end{array}
$$

The operator of union over theories has the typical properties of set-union operators, as it stated by the following proposition.

Proposition 9. *Given the theories P,Q,R, we have*

- Idempotence $P \cup P = P$
- Commutativity $P \cup Q = Q \cup P$
- Associativity $P \cup (Q \cup R) = (P \cup Q) \cup R$

where the equality sign denotes semantic equivalence.

The proof of the above properties have been given in [17] with respect to the denotational semantics.

3 Updating a Knowledge Base

Pure logic programs are not suited for representing the dynamic evolution of knowledge. A definite logic program is a finite set of Horn clauses which does not change during a computation.

The introduction of the extra-logical primitives "assert" and "retract" in the PROLOG programming language [23] was the first attempt to address the problem of representing the dynamic evolution of logic programs. The operation of updating a knowledge source can be naturally viewed as a transformation of a given knowledge base into a new knowledge base, which incorporates the effects of the update. If knowledge bases are represented as logic programs, updates may be naturally interpreted as metalevel operators over object level programs. According to this interpretation, metalevel approaches have been proposed in [2, 3, 11] to provide assert and retract operations with a logical meaning .

We consider a knowledge base Kb consisting of unit clauses only. (Equivalently, Kb can be viewed as a set of atomic formulae.) Unit clauses can be used to represent the state of an object in a straightforward way, for example by representing an attribute-value pair (a, v) via the unit clause $a(v) \leftarrow$. Basic updates on a knowledge base are the insertion and the deletion of formulae. In addition to them, we consider a special kind of update ($known(X)$) which checks whether a certain formula X holds in the knowledge base, without actually modifying the knowledge base. The predicate $update(Kb, U, Newkb)$ states that knowledge base Kb evolves into $Newkb$ due to the update U. The following axioms formally define the three kinds of updates.

(u1) $update(Kb, insert(X), \{X \leftarrow\} \cup Kb) \leftarrow$

(u2) $update(\{X \leftarrow\} \cup Kb, delete(X), Kb) \leftarrow$

(u3) $update(Kb, known(X), Kb) \leftarrow demo(Kb, X)$

In axioms (u1-3), a knowledge base is represented by the composition by union of its clauses. The axioms rely on the basic properties (idempotence, associativity and commutativity) of the theory-composition operator union. The dynamic construction of theories and their subsequent use require the addition of the following axiom to the vanilla metainterpreter:

$$demo(\{X \leftarrow Y\}, X \leftarrow Y) \leftarrow$$

This axiom extends the representation of object level theories by means of constant names by supporting the reference to unnamed theories. For instance, a theory consisting of the clause

$$a \leftarrow b$$

can be represented by

$$demo(\{a \leftarrow b\}, a \leftarrow b) \leftarrow$$

Notice that both the use of metalogic and the use of the union operator, have a well defined meaning in the basic framework presented in Section 2.

The deletion of a clause from a knowledge base presents two order of problems. The first one may be posed by the presence of a mixture of ground and non-ground clauses in the knowledge base. The second one concerns multiple occurrences of the same unit clause. The problem of retracting non-ground formulae has been addressed in [5] by using constructive negation techniques and will not be considered here. The problem of multiple occurrences of the same unit clause can be suitably addressed by substituting axiom (u2) with the following axioms.

(d1) $update(\{\}, delete(X), \{\}) \leftarrow$

(d2) $update(\{X \leftarrow\} \cup Kb, delete(X), Newkb) \leftarrow$
$\quad update(Kb, delete(X), Newkb)$

(d3) $update(\{Y \leftarrow\} \cup Kb, delete(X), \{Y \leftarrow\} \cup Newkb) \leftarrow$
$\quad X \neq Y,$
$\quad update(Kb, delete(X), Newkb)$

Intuitively, axioms (d1-3) correspond to viewing the state Kb as a set rather than as a multi-set of unit clauses. In axiom (d3), moreover, $X \neq Y$ stands for "X is not unifiable with Y".

4 Object-Orientation of Logic Programming

In object-oriented programming, each object has a state which determines its current configuration, and separate objects may cooperate each other by exchanging messages. Metaprogramming in a multi-theory setting parallels some typical aspects of object-oriented programming. As pointed out in [6], a natural object-orientation of a multi-theory setting is to view each theory as an object. We have shown in the previous Section how update operations can be suitably expressed in terms of metalogic, where a state is viewed as a theory consisting of unit clauses. We present now a rational reconstruction of some typical features of the object-oriented paradigm. We consider the notions of object with state, the mechanism of message passing and the definition of inheritance relations among objects.

4.1 Objects with State

We first consider the case of a single object O with an associated state S, which may be updated by O during the computation. The object O is represented by a logic theory, possibly including *insert* and *delete* commands, while the state S is represented by a theory of unit clauses. The combination of the object with its state is represented through a metalevel composition $O+S$ of the corresponding object level theories.

Roughly, rather than querying a single theory O, we are interested in considering a pair $O+S$ where O is an object and S is the current state of O. The main novelty is that the computation performed by theory O does depend on its state S.

We use a three-argument predicate $demo(O+S, X, News)$ which states that the formula X is provable in the theory O starting with state S and terminating with a (possibly updated) state $News$.

(o1) $demo(O+S, true, S) \leftarrow$

(o2) $demo(O+S, X, News) \leftarrow$
$\quad demo(O, X \leftarrow Y),$
$\quad demo(O+S, Y, News)$

(o3) $demo(O+S, (X, Y), News) \leftarrow$
$\quad demo(O+S, X, S'),$
$\quad demo(O+S', Y, News)$

(o4) $demo(O+S, X, News) \leftarrow update(S, X, News)$

Axioms (o1-3) correspond to axioms (v1-3) of the vanilla metainterpreter suitably extended to deal with the notion of state. Axiom (o4) deals with the case of an update operation executed by the theory O. Furthermore, notice that axiom (o3) implies a sequentiality in the execution of subgoals. The sequentiality is necessary to take into account the sequentiality of side-effects on the state. It is worth observing that axioms (o1-4) properly extend (v1-3). Actually, for all the theories which do not contain update operations, the two sets of axioms are equivalent. More precisely, for any theory O and any formula X which can be proved in O without using axiom (o4) we have that if $demo(O + S, X, News)$ is provable then $S = News$. As a consequence, for any pure logic program we have that: $demo(O + S, X, S)$ is provable if and only if $demo(O, X)$ is provable. Notice that the converse is not always true. If a formula X can be proved in $O + S$ without modifying S, this does not necessarily imply that $demo(O, X)$ can be proved with (v1-3). For example, consider the provability of a w.r.t. the theory

$$a \leftarrow insert(b), delete(b)$$

The axioms (o1-4), along with the axioms for updating a knowledge base, provide a semantic account for the behaviour of an object with state. Notice that the functor + does not play the role of a full-fledged theory constructor. It rather plays the role of an abstract syntax operator which allows the meta-axioms to distinguish between different sets of clauses. The only operator which is actually used for constructing theories dynamically and which deserves a specific semantic treatment is the union operator, which is used inside *update* to construct new theories. This observation will carry over to the theory functors which will be introduced in the next Sections.

4.2 Communicating Objects

We now turn our attention to the case of multi-object environments, where several objects — each with its local state — may communicate.

In our setting, the configuration of a multi-object system may be suitably represented by a set of pairs (*theory* + *state*) of the form

$$(O_1 + S_1)\&(O_2 + S_2)\& \dots \&(O_n + S_n)$$

A computation is started by a query of the form $O_i : X$. The intended meaning of $O_i : X$ is "prove the formula X in theory O_i". We obviously expect O_i to modify its state during the derivation of X.

Objects can exchange messages, for instance an object O_i might send a message Msg to another object O_j:

O_i

$$\dots$$
$$\dots \leftarrow send(O_j, Msg)$$
$$\dots$$

Such a message passing primitive can be naturally interpreted by a metalevel call of the form $demo(Oj, Msg)$ where unification provides a bi-directional communication mechanism. In other words, a metalevel call of the form $demo(O_j, G)$

invoked by some theory O_i can be interpreted as a message sent from O_i to O_j, whose answer will consist of the answer substitution (possibly) computed by Oj.

The predicate $demo(C, X, Newc)$ states that the formula X can be proved in the configuration of objects C terminating in the configuration $Newc$.

(mo1) $demo(C, O : true, C) \leftarrow$

(mo2) $demo(C, O : X, Newc) \leftarrow$
$demo(O, X \leftarrow Y)$,
$demo(C, O : Y, Newc)$

(mo3) $demo(C, O : (X, Y), Newc) \leftarrow$
$demo(C, O : X, C')$,
$demo(C', O : Y, Newc)$

(mo4) $demo(C, O : X, Newc) \leftarrow$
$C = (O + S)\&C'$,
$update(S, X, News)$,
$Newc = (O + News)\&C'$

(mo5) $demo(C, O : send(O', X), Newc) \leftarrow demo(C, O' : X, Newc)$

It is worth observing that axioms (mo1-5) properly extend (o1-4). Actually, when the configuration of objects consists of a single object (with state), the two sets of axioms are equivalent. (See the considerations at the end of the previous Subsection.)

4.3 Inheritance

We now consider the possibility of defining inheritance relations among objects. Following the interpretation of objects as theories, inheritance relations among objects can be interpreted as hierarchical links among theories.

In [5] some hierarchical operators between logic theories have been defined. The first link, called *isa*, between a theory P and a theory Q intensionally defines a new theory which contains all the predicate definitions of P and inherits the definitions of predicates occurring in Q only. Notice that the definitions in Q of predicates defined in both theories are replaced by the corresponding definitions in P. A metalevel definition of *isa* can now be given as follows:

(i1) $demo(P\ isa\ Q, X \leftarrow Y) \leftarrow$
$demo(P, X \leftarrow Y)$

(i2) $demo(P\ isa\ Q, X \leftarrow Y) \leftarrow$
$undefined(X, P)$
$demo(Q, X \leftarrow Y)$

The predicate $undefined(X, P)$ checks whether the predicate symbol of X does not belong to the set predicate symbols of theory P.

An example of a knowledge base management system based on multiple theories is the one developed within the EPSILON project [7]. In EPSILON, each theory contains a chunk of knowledge and is associated to a specific inference engine. There are mechanisms for defining inheritance relations among theories and there are two possible types of inheritance: *open* and *closed*. With the so called *isa* link, for instance, a theory P inherits from Q clauses to be evaluated in the environment of P. If the inheritance is *closed* (P *closedisa* Q), only the clauses defining predicates which are not defined in P are inherited, while if the inheritance is *open* (P *openisa* Q) all the clauses of Q are inherited by P. It is worth observing that these two inheritance links of the EPSILON system can be mapped onto some of the previously described operators. More precisely, the *openisa* link is nothing but the *union* operator, while the *closedisa* corresponds to the *isa* operator.

(i3) $demo(P\ openisa\ Q, X) \leftarrow demo(P \cup Q, X)$

(i4) $demo(P\ openisa\ Q, X) \leftarrow demo(P\ isa\ Q, X)$

Another inheritance link defined in EPSILON is the *consultance* link. A theory P, which is linked to another theory Q via a *consultance* link, sends queries to the metainterpreter of Q. If the link is *closed* (P *closedconsult* Q) a query is sent only for those predicates which are not defined in P, if it is *open* (P *openconsult* Q) for each predicate. The difference between *openconsult* and *openisa* only concerns implementation matters, that is which is the actual inference engine which proves the goal. As far as their logical definition is concerned, the two links are semantically equivalent.

(i5) $demo(P\ openconsult\ Q, X) \leftarrow demo(P \cup Q, X)$

(i6) $demo(P\ closedconsult\ Q, X) \leftarrow$
$demo(P, X \leftarrow Y)$,
$demo(P\ closedconsult\ Q, Y)$

(i7) $demo(P\ closedconsult\ Q, X) \leftarrow$
$undefined(X, P)$,
$demo(Q, Y)$

So far, we have defined some hierarchical operators between logic theories and we have shown how to use them explicitly in the queries (e.g. $demo(P\ isa\ Q, G)$). In most object-oriented systems, however, when trying to prove a certain property of an object, there is no need of specifying in the query all the structure of the hierarchy including the object. The inheritance mechanisms are automatically triggered during the computation in order to exploit the hierarchy. Such a behaviour can be obtained within a metalogical framework by representing links between objects with meta-axioms with the form:

$link(P, Q) \leftarrow$

and suitably extending definition of *demo* with the following clauses:

$$demo(P, X) \leftarrow \\ \quad link(P, Q), \\ \quad demo(P \; link \; Q, X)$$

If we consider, for example, the definition of the *isa* operator, it is immediate to see that also nested hierarchies (e.g P *isa* (Q *isa* R)) can be dynamically captured this way.

5 Blackboard-Orientation of Logic Programming

The blackboard architecture and paradigm have been used for many different purposes. Historically, the blackboard model was introduced as the main feature of the HEARSAY-2 speech understanding system. Later on, HASP (a system for ocean surveillance) contributed to define a more precise model of a blackboard system [21]. The blackboard model of problem solving consists of partitioning the knowledge about a particular problem into distinct subsets, in order to keep domain knowledge separated from control knowledge and to organise communications via a central data structure, named blackboard.

A blackboard architecture basically contains three kinds of components: a number of knowledge sources (KSs), a blackboard and a control module. A knowledge source is a program reading and writing data onto the blackboard. Communication and interaction among different KSs are allowed via the blackboard only. Each KS is responsible for knowing the conditions under which it may contribute to a solution (preconditions for activation). The blackboard data structure is a global database maintaining the state of the currently elaborated solution. The control module monitors the changes on the blackboard and decides which action to execute next, that is which knowledge source has to be activated, and on which goal. The blackboard model is well suited for expressing the cooperation of both parallel and concurrent agents: in particular, the control module can select several theories to be activated in parallel. A control mechanism is then needed in order to organise and rule concurrent accesses to the shared memory.

LINDA is a linguistic framework based on an abstract shared memory (Tuple Space) which is used as a general model for specifying inter-process communication [10]. The *generative communication* of LINDA relies on three primitives:

- *in(Tuple)*: reads and consumes a message,
- *read(Tuple)*: reads a message without consuming it, and
- *out(Tuple)*: produces a message.

These primitives refer to a communication medium called the Tuple Space, that is a set of persistent messages produced by a set of parallel programs. Linda's primitives may be virtually embedded in all programming languages, though they have been mainly proposed for imperative languages, like FORTRAN and C. An example of integration of Linda's primitives with logic programming is reported in [19].

The communication model of Linda relates to other programming languages, such as SHARED PROLOG [4] and the concurrent constraint paradigm [22]. In the concurrent constraint paradigm, for instance, computations emerge from the interaction of concurrently executing agents that communicate by placing, checking and instantiating constraints on shared variables. It is worth observing that both the *concurrent constraint paradigm* and LINDA share the same idea of letting several parallel agents synchronise via a centralised medium, respectively a store of constraints and a set of tuples. In this perspective, LINDA's primitives may be seen as a means for specifying simple constraints, concerning the addition/deletion (under pattern matching) of tuples to/from the tuple space, while in the *concurrent constraint paradigm* arbitrary constraints can be used to rule the synchronisation of parallel agents.

We now define a scenario where several separate logic programs cooperate by updating and querying a shared knowledge base (the blackboard). Having in mind software reusability as a primary requirement of program construction, we consider a set of standard, possibly existing, logic programs. A logic program can be executed sequentially and does not hold the ability of communicating with other programs. Each program has therefore to be extended with means for communicating with a shared knowledge base (the state). Each program can be extended with a set of *communication patterns* specifying the modes of interaction with the state. In SHARED PROLOG [4], for instance, each pattern has the form:

$$program(P, pattern(Precondition, Goal, Postcondition))$$

Precondition is a condition which must hold in order to start a local computation (*Goal*) in P. *Postcondition* is a condition to be evaluated at the end of the possibly successful computation of *Goal* in P. The conditions are updates and queries to be evaluated on the shared state. In their most general form, both *Precondition* and *Postcondition* consist of a (possibly empty) set of:

- Insertions of axioms in the state,
- Deletions of axioms from the state, and
- Queries to the state.

Given a state S, a program P can be executed if there is a pattern

$$program(P, pattern(Pre, G, Post))$$

and *Pre* can be successfully evaluated on S. As we have shown in Section 3, updates (such as *Pre* and *Post*) can be described in an elegant way with a metaprogram. The evaluation of the sequence (*Pre*, *Goal*, *Post*) can be therefore simply expressed by means of the metainterpreter defined in Subsection 4.1 with a goal of the form:

$demo(P + S, (Pre, Goal, Post), News)$

We now define how to combine a set of separate logic programs, suitably extended with communication patterns, to perform computations. Given a set of programs, $P_1, \ldots, P_n$ say, their composition with respect to a state S is denoted by the term:

$S :: P_1; \ldots; P_n$

The metainterpreter describing the behaviour of a set of programs w.r.t. a state is the following:

$$\begin{aligned} & demo(S :: P_1; \ldots; P_n) \leftarrow \\ & \quad program(P_i, pattern(Pre, G, Post)), \\ & \quad demo(P_i + S, (Pre, Goal, Post), News), \\ & \quad demo(News :: P_1; \ldots; P_n) \end{aligned}$$

At each step, one program (P_i) is selected along with one of its communication patterns. If the *Precondition* of P_i is satisfied w.r.t. the current state S, the program performs its sequential computation (*Goal*) and then its *Postactivation* is evaluated. Finally, the top-level metainterpreter restarts with the updated state.

6 Conclusions

Abstraction is the key to successful programming and language abstraction, that is the ability of designing your own language and using it for your own problem, is the most powerful form. The LISP and logic programming tradition has proven that metaprogramming is the key to successful language abstraction. The work reported in [25] and in [12] are examples, taken from the LISP culture, of ways of enriching the structure of the basic language processor in order to facilitate the construction of language abstractions via metaprogramming.

In this paper we have embarked into a similar enterprise in the realm of logic programming. We have strengthened the basic programming facilities by allowing the programmer to refer to a multi-theory setting and to exploit a composition operator. The framework has been given a firm semantic account.

Given this basic language, we have been able to build two language abstractions, an object-oriented language and a blackboard-oriented language, which share the feature of state manipulation. The definitions of the two languages consist of only a few axioms written in the metalogic extended with the union operator. The axioms are so straightforward that they can be considered a formal semantics for the abstract languages, that is you can reason about the properties of object-oriented or blackboard-oriented languages by using the axioms.

From a practical viewpoint, the axioms can be considered an easy and understandable, but slow, executor of the languages (see for instance [8]). Several proposals [15, 24] have been put forward to lower the burden of metainterpretation on the execution speed. Partial evaluation can solve most of the problems but it falls short when a dynamic modification of the program is required, as in our case.

We are currently running an experiment in which the basic Warren Abstract Machine [27] is extended to handle a multi-theory environment and operators over theories. Actually we are extending the WAM to take into account all the operators described in [5]. Although we do not have yet a fully working system, able to support a thorough experimentation, the preliminary results seem to be encouraging.

Acknowledgements

This work has been partially supported by Esprit Project 3012 COMPULOG and by "Progetto Finalizzato Sistemi Informatici e Calcolo Parallelo" under grant no. 92.01564.PF69.

References

1. K.R. Apt. Logic programming. In J.van Leeuwen, editor, *Handbook of Theoretical Computer Science*, pages 493-574. Elsevier, 1990. Vol. B.
2. K.A. Bowen and R.A. Kowalski. Amalgamating Language and Metalanguage in Logic Programming. In K.L. Clark and S.A. Tarnlund, editors, *Logic Programming*, pages 153–173. Academic Press, 1982.
3. K.A. Bowen and T. Weinberg. A Meta-Level Extension of Prolog. In J. Cohen and J. Conery, editors, *Proceedings of IEEE Symposium on Logic Programming*, pages 48–53. IEEE Computer Society Press, 1985.
4. A. Brogi and P. Ciancarini. The Concurrent Language Shared Prolog. *ACM Transactions on Programming Languages and Systems*, 1(1):99–123, 1991.
5. A. Brogi, P. Mancarella, D. Pedreschi, and F. Turini. Composition Operators for Logic Theories. In J.W. Lloyd, editor, *Computational Logic, Symposium Proceedings*, pages 117–134. Springer-Verlag, Brussels, November 1990.
6. A. Brogi and F. Turini. Metalogic for Knowledge Representation. In J.A. Allen, R. Fikes, and E. Sandewall, editors, *Principles of Knowledge Representation and Reasoning: Proceedings of the Second International Conference*, pages 100–106, Cambridge, CA, 1991. Morgan Kaufmann.
7. P. Coscia, P. Franceschi, G. Levi, G. Sardu, and L. Torre. Metalevel definition and compilation of inference engines in the Epsilon logic programming environment. In R.A. Kowalski and K.A. Bowen, editors, *Proc. Fifth International Conference on Logic Programming*, pages 359–373. The MIT Press.
8. E.Denti, E.Lamma, P.Mello, A.Natali and A.Omicini. Techniques for Implementing Contexts in Logic Programming. 1992. In these Proceedings.
9. R. Engelmore and T. Morgan. *Blackboard Systems*. Addison-Wesley, 1988.
10. D. Gelernter. Generative Communication in Linda. *ACM Transactions on Programming Languages and Systems*, 7(1):80–112, 1985.
11. P.M. Hill and J.W. Lloyd. Meta-Programming for Dynamic Knowledge Bases. Technical Report CS-88-18, Department of Computer Science, University of Bristol, 1988.
12. G. Kiczales, J. de Rivieres and D.G. Bobrow *The Art of the Metaobject Protocol* MIT Press, 1991.

13. R.A. Kowalski. Predicate logic as a programming language. In *IFIP 74*, pages 569–574, 1974.
14. R.A. Kowalski. *Logic for problem solving.* North-Holland, 1979.
15. G.Levi and G.Sardu. Partial Evaluation in a "Multiple Worlds" Logic Language. *New Generation Computing,* 6(2,3):227-248, 1988.
16. J.W. Lloyd. *Foundations of logic programming.* Springer-Verlag, second edition, 1987.
17. P.Mancarella and D.Pedreschi. An Algebra of Logic Programs In *Fifth International Conference, Symposium of Logic Programming* pages 1006-1023 (1988).
18. F.G. McCabe. *Logic and Objects.* PhD thesis, University of London, November 1988.
19. P.Mello and A,Natali. Extending Prolog with Modularity, Concurrency and Metarules. *New Generation Computing,* 10(4), August 1992.
20. L. Monteiro and A.Porto. A Transformational View of Inheritance in Logic Programming. In D.H.D. Warren and P. Szeredi, editors, *Proc. Seventh International Conference on Logic Programming,* pages 481–494. The MIT Press.
21. H.P. Nii. Blackboard Systems: the blackboard model of problem solving and the evolution of blackboard architectures. *AI Magazine,* pages 38–106, Summer 1986.
22. V.A. Saraswat and M. Rinard. Concurrent Constraint Programming. In *Proceedings seventeenth POPL.* ACM, 1990.
23. L. Sterling and E. Shapiro. *The Art of Prolog.* The MIT Press, 1986.
24. A.Takeuchi and K.Furukawa. Partial evaluation of Prolog programs and its application to metaprogramming. In H.J. Kugler, editor, *Information Processing 86,* pages 415-420. North-Holland, 1986.
25. F.Turini. Magma2: a Language Oriented Towards Abstractions of Control. *ACM Transactions on Programming Languages and Systems* 6(4):468-486, 1985.
26. M.H. van Emden and R.A. Kowalski. The semantics of predicate logic as a programming language. *Journal of the ACM,* 23(4):733–742, 1976.
27. D.H.D. Warren. An Abstract Prolog Instruction Set. SRI Technical Note 309, SRI International, 1983.

On the Semantics of Inheritance in Logic Programming: Compositionality and Full Abstraction

Michele Bugliesi

Dipartimento di Matematica Pura ed Applicata
University of Padova
Via Belzoni 7, 35131 Padova ITALY
e-mail: michele@blues.unipd.it

Abstract. We give an account of various semantics for hierarchical logic programs and discuss their properties in terms of compositionality and full abstraction when inheritance is assumed as the underlying composition mechanism. The analysis is carried out along the guidelines of [7] and leads us to conclude that a logical semantics is inherently inadequate to fully capture the computational aspects of program composition by inheritance.

1 Introduction

The interest in modular logic programmming has motivated the work of a growing research community in the last few years. Originated by Miller's seminal paper on the subject ([13]), modularity has been studied from two main perspectives. It has been seen as an object-level mechanism and defined in terms of various extensions of Horn-clause logic to accommodate new constructs: implication goals ([13]), context extension ([15]) and messages ([3] and [6]) among others. Alternatively, and for our present concerns more interestingly, it has been conceived as a (meta-level) composition mechanism defined over programs in terms of the standard operations of union, intersection and deletion of clauses (see [1] and [4] for examples). At this level, modularity simply amounts to viewing programs as subprograms, or fragments, to be composed to form larger programs. In spite of its intuitive flavour, this simple idea has a number of fairly interesting consequences.

Considering a program as part of an enclosing context changes radically our standard intuition about its computational behaviour. Two fragments, that are computationally equivalent if considered as stand-alone programs, are likely to exhibit a completely different behaviour when viewed as part of a context. Consider for instance the two (equivalent) programs $P = \{\}$ and $Q = \{p \text{ :- } q\}$ and contrast them with the (non-equivalent) programs obtained by taking the union of P and Q with the program $R = \{q\}$. In general terms, we may say that program composition changes, refining it, our notion of computational equivalence: two programs are considered to be equivalent if they can be interchanged in any context without affecting the visible results of the computation ([12]). More precisely:

> two programs P and Q are observationally congruent ($P \equiv_{obs} Q$) iff for every context $C[\cdot]$, $C[P]$ and $C[Q]$ exhibit the same observational behaviour.

Associated with this computational characterisation, there is a corresponding issue related to our mathematical notion of semantics and its adequacy to the computational framework. As suggested in [7] and [12], the adequacy of a semantic characterisation for a computational system can be formally established in terms of the two fundamental notions of ***compositionality*** and ***full abstraction***. Compositionality ensures that two semantically equivalent programs are also observationally equivalent; full abstraction guarantees that any distinction made at the semantic level has also an observational counterpart. Formally:

> a semantics is said to be compositional if semantic equality implies observational congruence. It is fully abstract if semantic equality coincides with $\equiv_{obs}$.

1.1 Outline

Every given composition mechanism (coupled with a notion of observable) induces an associated observational equivalence relation. In this paper we focus on program composition via inheritance, the goal being to study the corresponding computational equivalence and possibly to define an adequate abstract semantics. We consider a definition of inheritance which encompasses the standard Object-Oriented notions of overriding and late binding and analyse the relationship between various logical semantics for logic programs (their associated equivalences) and the computational equivalence induced by the hierarchical composition via inheritance.

The analysis is carried out along the guidelines of [9]. We first consider the choice of the invariant $[\![P]\!] = T_P$ and give a formal proof of its compositionality as well as a counter-example to its full abstractness. We then consider more abstract invariants (coarser equivalences) to achieve fully abstract semantics while retaining compositionality. The study of the various choices highlights (some of) the distinguishing properties of inheritance and their impact on the computational framework. The conclusion we are lead to is that the computational aspects of inheritance do not have a natural logical counterpart: observational and semantic equivalence do not coincide under any logical choice of the semantic invariant.

In the next section we introduce the notation and the terminology which is used in the sequel. In section 3 we consider a compositional semantics for inheritance. In section 4 we discuss the choice of other invariants and study the properties of their associated equivalences. We then conclude in 5 with some final observations.

2 Preliminaries

2.1 Inheritance

We begin by informally introducing the interpretation of inheritance we use throughout. Given two programs, P and Q, we use the notation $P \lhd Q$ to stand for the composition of P and Q into a hierarchy where Q is P's immediate ancestor. We also assume an overriding semantics for $\lhd$ whereby if both P and Q contain a definition for same predicate, then the definition in P overrides the one found in Q. The intended interpretation of the $\lhd$-composition is best illustrated by showing how the evaluation of the goal is accomplished in a $\lhd$-composite program.

Example 1. Consider the composition $P \lhd Q$ where P inherits from Q the predicate $q/1$ and overrides Q's definition of $p/1$.

$$P = \{p(2)\} \qquad Q = \left\{\begin{array}{l} p(1) \\ q(x)\text{:-}p(x) \end{array}\right\}$$

We want to look at the evaluation of the goal $q(x)$ in $P \lhd Q$. Since the predicate symbol $q/1$ is not defined in P, it is inherited from Q and then evaluating $q(x)$ reduces to evaluating $p(x)$. Now the result of the computation depends on the binding for $p/1$ in Q. We have two possible choices: we can either bind it to Q's local definition, or consider $P \lhd Q$ as a modified version of Q where $p/1$ is bound to the definition provided in P. The two choices correspond to two different definitions of inheritance which are qualified respectively as *static* (with *early* binding) and *dynamic* (with *late* binding) in [17]. □

In the sequel of the paper we will adhere to the definition which is currently standard in Object-Oriented programming and assume dynamic inheritance as the underlying mechanism. Under this assumption, for the programs of the previous example, the call $p(x)$ is bound to the definition provided by P and this, in turn, yields the binding $\{x/2\}$ as the answer substitution for the goal $q(x)$.

This operational behaviour can be formally defined in several ways. In [2] and [15] it is formalized in terms of ad-hoc inference rules that specify the underlying selection strategy for the clauses of the component programs.

An equivalent characterisation can be given in terms of a syntactic composition operator over programs. Let *Pred(A)* denote the predicate symbol of any given atom A and let $\delta(P)$ be the set predicate symbols *defined* by P (a predicate p is defined by a program P, if P contains a clause whose head's predicate symbol is p).

Definition 1. Let P and Q be two programs. $P \prec Q$ denotes the program obtained as the union of the clauses of P with the clauses of Q which do not define any of the predicates in $\delta(P)$.

$$P \prec Q = P \cup \{A\text{:-}G \in Q : Pred(A) \notin \delta(P)\}$$ □

A formal proof of the equivalence (in terms of answer substitutions) between the syntactic $\prec$-composition and the $\lhd$-composition can be found in [5] (see also [14]). For an intuitive argument, consider the two programs of example 1. According to the previous definition, $P \prec Q$ is the program

$$\left\{ \begin{array}{l} p(2) \\ q(x) \text{ :- } p(x) \end{array} \right\}$$

which exhibits, under SLD resolution, the same behaviour as the composition $Q \lhd P$ described above.

2.2 Observational Equivalence

To determine the equivalence induced by the operator $\prec$, we need a notion of observable. In the classical approach, the computational behaviour of a program is defined in terms of its success set (the set of atomic consequences in the program's Herbrand base). However, as suggested in [7], we can get a more accurate characterisation by taking as observables the set of all the atomic consequences of the program (without restricting to the program's Herbrand base). Other (more refined) definitions of observables are also possible, (see for instance [11]) but the specific choice will make no difference for the results which follow. Let then:

$$Ob(P) \;=\; \{A \mid P \models A \text{ and } A \text{ is an atom}\}$$

Following [7], we will also use the following terminology. Let $\mathcal{P}$ denote the class of our programs and Com be a class of composition operators.

An equivalence relation $\equiv$ over $\mathcal{P}$ *preserves Ob* if

$$P \equiv Q \;\Rightarrow\; Ob(P) = Ob(Q)$$

An equivalence $\equiv$ is a *congruence* for Com if for every $f \in Com$

$$P_i \equiv Q_i \;\Rightarrow\; f(P_1, \ldots, P_n) \equiv f(Q_1, \ldots, Q_n)$$

Taking Ob as above and $Com = \{\prec\}$, we can define the *equivalence induced by* $(Ob, \prec)$ as follows:

$$P \equiv_{Ob,\prec} Q \iff \text{for all } R \left\{ \begin{array}{l} Ob(R \prec P) = Ob(R \prec Q) \\ Ob(P \prec R) = Ob(Q \prec R) \end{array} \right.$$

Correspondingly, we can restate in terms of Ob and $\prec$ the properties of compositionality and full abstraction for any given semantic function (or invariant) $[\![\;]\!]$. Let $\equiv_{[\![\;]\!]}$ be the equivalence induced by $[\![\;]\!]$:

$$P \equiv_{[\![\;]\!]} Q \iff [\![P]\!] = [\![Q]\!]$$

We say that $[\![\;]\!]$ is $(Ob, \prec)$-compositional if $\equiv_{[\![\;]\!]}$-equivalence implies observational equivalence (i.e. $\equiv_{[\![\;]\!]}$ preserves Ob and is a congruence for $\prec$). $[\![\;]\!]$ is fully abstract if $\equiv_{[\![\;]\!]}$ coincides with $\equiv_{Ob,\prec}$.

Given two equivalences $\equiv_1$ and $\equiv_2$, we will henceforth say that $\equiv_1$ is *finer* or *stronger* than $\equiv_2$ (dually $\equiv_2$ *weaker*, or *coarser* than $\equiv_1$) whenever $\equiv_1$ implies $\equiv_2$.

3 Compositionality for $(Ob, \prec)$

As noted in [10], compositionality for a syntactic operator defined in terms of union of clauses can only be achieved by resorting to a *function-level* semantics. The classical model-theoretic approach to the semantics of logic programming fails in fact to provide an adequate characterisation when programs are viewed as part of enclosing contexts. The idea of having functions over Herbrand sets as the semantic objects used to interpret our programs has motivated several proposals in the recent literature. See for instance the semantics based on the closure operator of [8] and the definition based on the immediate-consequence operator T_P of [10] and [16]. Various function-level invariants have also been considered in [9] and compared on the account of the relative strength of the induced equivalence relations.

The purpose of this and of the following sections is to study the adequacy of all these invariants within the framework of the hierarchical type of program composition provided by $\prec$. We start off the analysis by discussing the choice of the invariant $[\![P]\!] = T_P$ proposed in [6] as the basis for a model-theoretic semantics for inheritance. Other invariants addressed in [9] will be studied in the sequel of the paper.

We first introduce a new operator (from [6]) which provides the formal device for declaratively modeling the overriding semantics of $\prec$. We denote with $\mathcal{B}$ the Herbrand base of a program and with $\mathcal{P}(\mathcal{B})$ the power-set of $\mathcal{B}$.

Definition 2. Let π be an arbitrary set of predicate symbols and let S_1 and S_2 be two sets in $\mathcal{P}(\mathcal{B})$. Then the function $\diamond_\pi : \mathcal{P}(\mathcal{B}) \times \mathcal{P}(\mathcal{B}) \mapsto \mathcal{P}(\mathcal{B})$ is defined as follows: $S_1 \diamond_\pi S_2 = S_1 \cup \{t \in S_2 \mid pred(t) \notin \pi\}$ □

Let now Φ denote the set of continuous mappings from $\mathcal{P}(\mathcal{B})$ to $\mathcal{P}(\mathcal{B})$. Φ is a complete lattice under the order relation $\leq$ obtained from $\subseteq$ in the standard way (given $T_1, T_2 \in \Phi$, $T_1 \leq T_2 \iff \forall I \in \mathcal{P}(\mathcal{B})\ T_1(I) \subseteq T_2(I)$).

The definition of $\diamond$ can be directly lifted at the function level. With an abuse of notation, we will use the same symbol to denote the two different operators defined on $\mathcal{P}(\mathcal{B})$ and Φ.

Definition 3. Let T_1, T_2 be two functions in Φ and π be a set of predicate symbols. The composition $T_1 \diamond_\pi T_2$ is defined as follows:

$$T_1 \diamond_\pi T_2 \;=\; \lambda I \,.\, T_1(I) \diamond_\pi T_2(I)$$ □

Notice that for any π, $\diamond_\pi$ is continuous on $(\mathcal{P}(\mathcal{B}), \subseteq)$, and consequently on $(\Phi, \leq)$. Hence, $T_1 \diamond_\pi T_2$ is also continuous and $\diamond$ is well defined on Φ. The following result characterizes $\diamond$ as the semantic counterpart of the syntactic operator $\prec$.

Theorem 4. *[6] For any two programs P and Q,* $T_{(P \prec Q)} \;=\; T_P \diamond_{\delta(P)} T_Q$. □

In view of this result, the semantics of $P \prec Q$ is defined in [6] as the least fixpoint of the continuous transformation $T_P \diamond_{\delta(P)} T_Q$. The invariant $[\![P]\!] = T_P$ enjoys however other interesting properties. Theorem 4 can in fact be used as the basis for proving the $(Ob, \prec)$-compositionality of the invariant itself.

The proof of the next theorem uses the result from [9] that for two programs P and Q, $T_P = T_Q$ iff P and Q are are subsumption equivalent. For this reason, in the sequel the invariant $[\![P]\!] = T_P$ will be denoted by $[\![\,]\!]_s$ and the associated equivalence by $\equiv_s$.

Theorem 5. $[\![\,]\!]_s$ *is* $(Ob, \prec)$*-compositional.*

Proof. That $\equiv_s$ preserves Ob is obvious since subsumption equivalence implies logical equivalence and this in turn implies sameness of (atomic) logical consequences. To show that $\equiv_s$ is a congruence for $\prec$, consider the programs $P \equiv_s P'$ and $Q \equiv_s Q'$. The proof that $P \prec Q \equiv_s P' \prec Q'$ follows by simply applying the result of theorem 4,

$$[\![P \prec Q]\!]_s \;=\; [\![P]\!]_s \Diamond_{\delta(P)} [\![Q]\!]_s \;=\; [\![P']\!]_s \Diamond_{\delta(P')} [\![Q']\!]_s \;=\; [\![P' \prec Q']\!]_s$$

and noting that $\delta(P) = \delta(P')$ is a consequence of the fact that P and P' are subsumption equivalent. □

3.1 Full Abstraction

A reasonable objection to the choice of the invariant $[\![\,]\!]_s$ is that it does not provide a very useful tool for reasoning about programs. The induced equivalence – subsumption equivalence – is in fact too fine grained to fully capture the computational properties of the $\prec$-composition. As a matter of fact, it is immediate to show that $\equiv_s$ is not a fully abstract congruence for $(Ob, \prec)$.

Example 2. Consider the two following programs defining the set of natural numbers:

$$P = \left\{ \begin{array}{l} n(0) \\ n(s(x)) \text{ :- } n(x) \end{array} \right\} \qquad Q = \left\{ \begin{array}{l} n(0) \\ n(s(0)) \\ n(s(s(x))) \text{ :- } n(s(x)) \end{array} \right\}$$

P and Q are not subsumption equivalent (take $I = \oslash$ to see that there exists I such that $T_P(I) \neq T_Q(I)$). Yet, they are equivalent under $\equiv_{Ob,\prec}$. In fact, given any program R we can easily show that

$$Ob(R \prec P) = Ob(R \prec Q) \quad \& \quad Ob(P \prec R) = Ob(Q \prec R)$$

To verify the first equality, observe that R either defines $n/1$ or it doesn't. If it does, then $R \prec P = R \prec Q = R$. Otherwise the $\prec$-composition of P and Q reduces to taking the union of the two programs and, since $n/1$ can only appear as a goal in R, $Ob(R \cup P) = Ob(R \cup Q)$. Hence $Ob(R \prec P) = Ob(R \prec Q)$.

A similar argument applies to the second equality. □

It follows from this example that subsumption equivalence is strictly finer, or stronger, than observational equivalence. More abstract invariants (coarses equivalences) are therefore needed to achieve a fully abstract semantics for $(Ob, \prec)$. The next section is dedicated to the analysis of various possible choices.

4 More Abstract Semantics

As already mentioned, the set of candidate invariants at our disposal is limited by the fact that we are imposing $(Ob, \prec)$-compositionality as a key requirement. This dispenses us from considering any conventional model-theoretic semantics which would not be compositional, being $\prec$ defined in terms of union of clauses. We now proceed by considering the equivalences proposed in [9] moving from $\equiv_s$ in the direction of growing abstraction. *Weak subsumption equivalence* provides the next choice.

4.1 Weak Subsumption Equivalence

It is shown in [9] that weak subsumption equivalence ($\equiv_{ws}$) is the equivalence induced by the invariant $[\![P]\!]_{ws} = T_P + Id$. It is easy to see that $[\![\,]\!]_{ws}$ in itself is not $(Ob, \prec)$-compositional. Take a program P and construct a program P' by taking the union of P with a tautological clause of the form $\{p'(x) \colon\!\!- p'(x)\}$ with $p' \notin \delta(P)$. Clearly, $[\![P]\!]_{ws} = [\![P']\!]_{ws}$ and thus $P \equiv_{ws} P'$, but the two programs are not necessarily observationally equivalent.

Example 3. Let P be the program $\{p(a)\}$ let P' be defined as $P \cup \{p'(x) \colon\!\!- p'(x)\}$. Then consider the two composite programs $P \prec R$ and $P' \prec R$ with $R = \{p'(b)\}$.

$$P \prec R \;=\; \left\{ \begin{matrix} p(a) \\ p'(b) \end{matrix} \right\} \qquad\qquad P' \prec R \;=\; \left\{ \begin{matrix} p(a) \\ p'(x) \colon\!\!- p'(x) \end{matrix} \right\}$$

Clearly $P \prec R \models p'(b)$ and $P' \prec R \not\models p'(b)$. □

Notice that the inequivalence of P and P' above is simply a consequence of the fact that the two programs define two different sets of predicate symbols. This is in fact a key property of the computational equivalence entailed by Ob and $\prec$.

Proposition 6. *For any two programs P and Q, $P \equiv_{Ob,\prec} Q \;\Rightarrow\; \delta(P) = \delta(Q)$.*

Proof. By contradiction, immediate from example 3. □

The consequence, at the semantic level, is that no invariant can be compositional if it identifies two programs which define different sets of predicate symbols. Two such programs can be in fact always distinguished at the computational level. Hence, neither $[\![\,]\!]_{ws}$ nor any invariant more abstract than $[\![\,]\!]_{ws}$ are $(Ob, \prec)$-compositional.

Compositionality for these invariants can be recovered by enriching the notion of semantic equivalence $\equiv_{[\,]}$ to capture the computational aspects of $\prec$ more accurately. The following definition suits our purposes:

Definition 7. For any invariant $[\![\,]\!]$, let $\equiv^{\delta}_{[\,]}$ denote the following equivalence relation:

$$P \equiv^{\delta}_{[\,]} Q \iff \delta(P) = \delta(Q) \text{ and } [\![P]\!] = [\![Q]\!] \qquad \square$$

Obviously, for any choice of invariant $[\![\,]\!]$, $\equiv^{\delta}_{[\![\,]\!]}$ is finer than the corresponding equivalence $\equiv_{[\![\,]\!]}$ (the two equivalences coincide for $[\![\,]\!] = [\![\,]\!]_s$).

In view of the above definition, $[\![\,]\!]_{ws}$ does induce a congruence for $\prec$. The proof of the next result is a straightforward consequence of theorem 5.

Proposition 8. *$\equiv^{\delta}_{ws}$ is $(Ob, \prec)$-compositional.* □

Now, being $\equiv^{\delta}_{ws}$ coarser than $\equiv^{\delta}_{s}$, it follows that $\equiv^{\delta}_{ws}$ is (strictly) coarser than subsumption equivalence. However, it is still too fine grained to provide a fully abstract congruence for $(Ob, \prec)$. Example 2 gives an immediate counter-example: the two programs are observationally indistinguishable, they defined the same predicates $(n/1)$ but they are not weakly subsumption equivalent.

4.2 Logical Equivalence

The next (and final) invariant we consider is the closure operator $[\![P]\!]_l = (T_P + Id)^{\omega}$ of [8]. Two observations motivate the choice of $[\![\,]\!]_l$ as a reasonable candidate for a compositional and fully abstract semantics for inheritance. Firstly $[\![\,]\!]_l$ is strictly (and by far) weaker than all the invariants we have studied so far. Secondly, and more importantly, the equivalence relation induced by $[\![\,]\!]_l$ ($\equiv_l$) is proved in [9] to coincide with logical equivalence and logical equivalence, in turn, provides a fully abstract congruence for program composition by union ([7]).

Notice that $\equiv_l$ in itself also is not compositional for it has the same problems as $\equiv_{ws}$. Consider then the new equivalence $\equiv^{\delta}_l$ obtained from $[\![\,]\!]_l$ according to definition 7. Again, it is easy to see that also $\equiv^{\delta}_l$ is not $(Ob, \prec)$-compositional.

Example 4. Let P and P' be the two following programs:

$$P = \left\{ \begin{array}{l} p(a)\!:\!-q(b) \\ q(b) \end{array} \right\} \qquad\qquad P' = \left\{ \begin{array}{l} p(a) \\ q(b) \end{array} \right\}$$

P and P' are obviously logically equivalent (they have the same models), and $\delta(P) = \delta(P')$. Hence, $P \equiv^{\delta}_l P'$. Now, by taking $R = \{q(a).\}$, we have:

$$R \prec P = \left\{ \begin{array}{l} p(a)\!:\!-q(b) \\ q(a) \end{array} \right\} \qquad\qquad R \prec Q = \left\{ \begin{array}{l} p(a) \\ q(a) \end{array} \right\}$$

and these two program are no longer logically equivalent. Thus $R \prec P \not\equiv^{\delta}_l R \prec P'$ and consequently $\equiv_l$ is not a congruence for $\prec$. □

We are already in a position to draw some conclusions. We have shown that $[\![\,]\!]_{ws}$ induces the compositional and not fully abstract equivalence $\equiv^{\delta}_{ws}$. We have then shown that $\equiv^{\delta}_l$, which is coarser than $\equiv^{\delta}_{ws}$, is not compositional. Hence, what we could by now assume is that the $(Ob, \prec)$-compositional and fully abstract invariant is bound to fall somewhere in between $[\![\,]\!]_{ws}$ and $[\![\,]\!]_l$. The next example shows that this cannot be the case.

Example 5. Consider the programs $P = \{p(a)\text{:-}p(b)\}$ and $P' = \{p(b)\text{:-}p(a)\}$. P and P' are clearly not logically equivalent. Thus they are distinguished by $\equiv_l^\delta$ and by any equivalence stronger than $\equiv_l^\delta$. Yet the two programs are indistinguishable with respect to $\equiv_{Ob,\prec}$. □

As a consequence, we have that $\equiv_l^\delta$ is actually neither finer nor coarser than $\equiv_{Ob,\prec}$ (the two relations are simply unrelated). Hence, no equivalence finer than $\equiv_l^\delta$ can possibly coincide with $\equiv_{Ob,\prec}$ or, equivalently, every invariant in between $[\![\,]\!]_{ws}$ and $[\![\,]\!]_l$ is bound to be either non-compositional or non fully abstract.

5 Discussion

The following picture gives a schetch of the invariants we have considered so far and displays the relationships between the associated equivalence relations. Needless to say, the set of alternatives we have considered is by no means exaus-

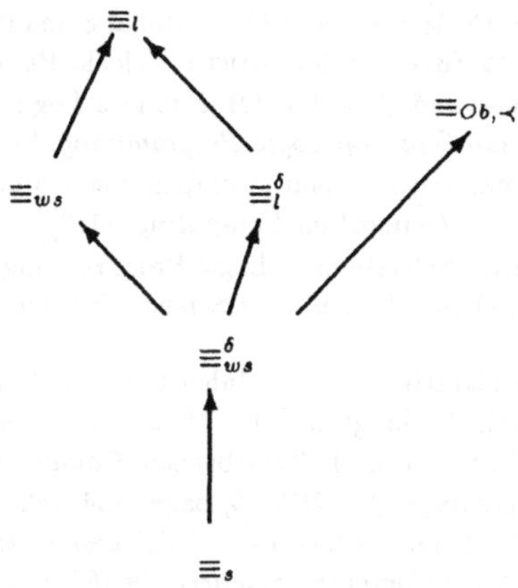

Fig. 1. Relationships between Equivalences: abstraction grows from bottom to top

tive. Thus the above picture does not imply that we couldn't define a compositional and fully abstract semantics using alternative semantic characterisations. As a matter of fact such characterization exists for any choice of Ob and Com ([7]): define $[\![P]\!]$ to be P's equivalence class under Ob and Com. However, the picture does suggest that any *logical* semantics does not satisfy these two properties.

As a matter of fact, the problem addressed in the last example points out the inherent non-logical flavour of the $\prec$-composition. The only *logical* semantics that would identify the two programs of example 5 as equivalent is the classical minimal Herbrand model semantics (another possible solution would be to consider the completed programs but the notion of completion in the context of program composition does not seem that reasonable). Yet, the choice of minimal models as invariants would then fall short of capturing the compositional properties of the union of clauses which is used to define the $\prec$-composition. Then, the implied conclusion is that the two operations of union and deletion, which are both necessary to achieve a syntactic characterisation of composition via inheritance, are inherently incompatible at the (logical) semantic level.

Acknowledgements This work was partially supported by the Italian C.N.R. under "Progetto Finalizzato Sistemi Informatici e Calcolo Parallelo" grant n. 89.00026.69.

References

1. A. Bossi, M. Gabbrielli, G. Levi, and M. Meo. Contributions to the Semantics of Open Logic Programs. In *Proceeding of FGCS'92*, 1992.
2. A. Brogi, E. Lamma, and P. Mello. Structuring Logic Programs: A Unifying Framework and its Declarative and Operational Semantics. Technical Report 4/1, Progetto Finalizzato Sistemi Informatici e Calcolo Parallelo, 1990.
3. A. Brogi, E. Lamma, and P. Mello. Objects in a Logic Programming Framework. In *Proc. 2nd Russian Conf. on Logic Programming*, Leningrad, 1991.
4. A. Brogi, E. Lamma, and P. Mello. Compositional Model-theoretic Semantics for Logic Programs. *New Generation Computing*, 11(2), 1992.
5. M. Bugliesi. Inheritance Systems in Logic Programming: Semantics and Implementation. Ms Thesis, Dept. of Computer Science, Purdue University, West-Lafayette IN, USA.
6. M. Bugliesi. A Declarative View of Inheritance in Logic Programming. In *Proceedings JICSLP'92*, Washington D.C., 1992. MIT press.
7. H. Gaifman and E. Shapiro. Fully Abstract Compositional Semantics for Logic Programs. In *Proceedings of POPL'89*, pages 134–142. ACM, 1989.
8. J. L. Lassez and M. Maher. Closures and Fairness in the Semantics of Logic Programming. *Theoretical Computer Sciences*, 29:167–184, 1984.
9. M. Maher. Equivalences of Logic Programs. In J. Minker, editor, *Foundations of Deductive Databases and Logic Programming*. M. Kaufmann, 1988.
10. P. Mancarella and D. Pedreschi. An Algebra of Logic Programs. In *Proc. 5th Int. Conf. on. Logic Programming*, Seattle, 1988. ALP.
11. M. Martelli, M. Falaschi, G. Levi, and C. Palamedessi. A new Declarative Semantics for Logic Languages. In *Proceedings JICSLP'88*, Seattle, 1988. MIT press.
12. A. Meyer. Semantical paradigms: Notes for and Invited Lectures. In *Proceedings of 3rd Annual Sym. on Logic in Computer Science*. IEEE, 1988.
13. D. Miller. A Logical Analysis of Modules in Logic Programming. *Journal of Logic Programming*, 6(2):79–108, 1989.
14. L. Monteiro and A. Porto. Syntactic and Semantic Inheritance in Logic Programming. PHOENIX Workshop and Seminar on Declarative Programming (to appear).
15. L. Monteiro and A. Porto. Contextual Logic Programming. In *Proc. 6th Int. Conf. on. Logic Programming*, Lisbon, 1989. ALP.

16. R. A. O'Keef. Towards an Algebra for Constructing Logic Programs. In *Proc. Symposium on Logic Programming.* IEEE, 1985.
17. U. Reddy. Objects as Closures: Abstarct Semantics of Object Oriented Languages. In *Proc. Lisp and Functional Programming,* pages 289–297. ACM, 1988.

The AbstrAct Scheme for Concurrent Programming

António Porto and Paulo Rosado

Departamento de Informática
Universidade Nova de Lisboa
2825 Monte da Caparica
Portugal

Abstract

We present a new model for concurrent programming, which we call AbstrAct. A system is specified through collections of rules defining all possible state transformations that may occur. The activity of a system is driven by goals (actions) organized in parallel and sequence in a structure called the agenda. Actions in the agenda communicate and synchronize by atomically consulting and updating a global shared space, the blackboard, which may, in general, be regarded as a logic program. An action rule corresponds to an atomic step in the execution of an action in the agenda, that replaces it by a structure of subactions while changing the blackboard; the rule specifies conditions on the current and new blackboard.

We give operational semantics to AbstrAct through a variant of Fair Transition Systems, and ilustrate the expressiveness and programming style of AbstrAct derived languages through small examples.

1 Introduction

With the current plethora of proposed concurrent languages and notations (see [5, 24, 25, 10, 6, 12, 2, 15, 18] for representative examples), there is always some disbelief in the relevance of some new proposal, and usually one cannot help uttering the usual – "Oh, no, yet another...".

We have decided to face these odds by presenting not just one language but a programming scheme illustrated by a particular language instance. Actually our presentation is in two steps, first the propositional version and then the first-order version of the scheme, accompanied in both cases by a language instance. With this work we aim at providing an expressive notation for designing (re)active systems[2] and contribute to a better understanding of what should be the high level concepts behind a general purpose concurrent language.

* Work carried out with partial support from ESPRIT project BRA 3020 "Integration", JNICT project PMCT/C/TIT/844.90 "Pérola", and INIC.

[2] We consider as *reactive* the systems whose purpose goes beyond the *transformation* of an input in an output according to some function denoted by the program [14].

The paper is organized as follows. In section 2, the main concepts are informally presented by stepwise development of a solution to a simplified variant of the Dining Philosophers problem. We start the formal presentation of the basic concepts in section 3 by restricting ourselves to the propositional fragment of AbstrAct. All aspects informally introduced in the preceding section are formalized and operational semantics are given by associating each AbstrAct system to a variant of a Fair Transition System, following Pnueli [19]. The following section, 4, illustrates a particular instantiation of the propositional scheme, the language AbstrActα. In section 5 we move on to first-order, again by presenting first the extensions of the previous formalization that account for the use of terms, and then, in section 6 a language instance, AbstrActβ. In subsection 6.1 we try to show the expressiveness and the programming style introduced by the language AbstrActβ through examples. In section 8 we make some comparisons with related work, and we end with section 9 of Conclusions where, basically, we justify our design decisions.

2 Basic Notions

An AbstrAct system is defined by an *initial state* plus a collection of *action rules* which denote the state transitions that may occur in any particular computation. Operational semantics of such a system will be examined in the light of the state-transition model. An action rule is an expression of the form

$$a \rightarrow K : C \qquad (1)$$

and has the following declarative reading: an *action a* to be executed *reduces* to the actions K, an expression possibly involving parallel and sequential composition of actions, if *it is possible* to change the state of the system so that the *conditions C* hold for the pair of current and new state. Notions of *action*, *reduction*, *task expression* and *conditions* on pairs of states will be formalized in sections below. For now, we will try to give intuitions about their meaning through examples.

Let's consider a problem which is a simplification of the Dining Philosophers. Instead of five philosophers eating spaghetti with forks, we will consider two philosophers improperly eating spaghetti with a fork and a spoon which are shared between them. We will call this exercise "The Two Philosophers".

Let's consider, for example, the action rule that defines the action *eat* in the context of this problem

$$eat \rightarrow eating : getfork,\ getspoon. \qquad (2)$$

This rule states that the action *eat* reduces to actually *eating* if it is possible to execute, in the current state, the actions of picking the fork and the spoon from the table. Let's consider that, in a certain state of the computation, there

The reason why we have enclosed the prefix *re* in brackets is grounded in our belief that a lot of these systems are more *active* than *reactive*, in the sense that they have some inner purpose that drives their actions.

is evidence that the action *eat* is to be executed. At this state the system may transit to another state, according to the above rule, if *both* actions *getfork* and *getspoon* are performed in that transition. These actions are seen as *conditions on the pair of states* which correspond to the transition. It so happens that *getfork* and *getspoon* may only take place if some conditions hold in the current state, namely, that both the fork and the spoon are currently on the table. The resulting state reflects not only the effects of the execution of *getfork* and *getspoon* (the fork and the spoon are no longer on the table) but also the fact that the action *eating* replaces *eat* as an action that has to be executed, driving future transitions of the system.

It is not difficult to see that from an initial state where both the spoon and the fork are on the table and where all removals of the cutlery from the table are modeled by the above rule, there is no feasible computation of this system that results in a deadlock situation [3], according to the above mentioned operational semantics. This is equivalent to state that in rule 2 the actions *getfork* and *getspoon* are to be executed as an *atomic* step.

General rules with the above structure may have particular instances. A rule of the form

$$a \rightarrow \mu : C \tag{3}$$

states that action a reduces to the *void action*, μ, if the corresponding state change satisfies the conditions C. Actually this means that *a completely executes* in the transition satisfying C. This particular instance of an action rule may also be represented in the short form $a : C$. The action *getfork* can be defined by the rule

$$getfork : \leftarrow fork, \rightarrow(\neg\ fork) \tag{4}$$

which states that the complete execution of the action of getting the fork is performed in a transition that goes from a state where the *precondition fork* holds to a new state where the *postcondition* $\neg$*fork* holds. Operationally this amounts to say that the state has to be *updated* so that, in this particular example, the fork no longer remains on the table ($\neg$*fork* is true in the resulting state).

At this point, it is convenient to clarify what we mean by the "state of the system". We consider the state as being defined by a *set of logical formulæ*. In this example, it simply represents the relations between the fork, the spoon and the table (we will postpone discussing the other component of the state which holds the actions that have to be executed.) Pre- and postconditions are also formulæ. To test if a precondition holds is to *deduce* it from the current set of logic formulæ. To *update* the state is to change this set of formulæ so that the postconditions can be deduced from it. We call this set of formulæ the *blackboard*, reflecting its role as that of a passive entity holding information, being queried and changed concurrently by actions.

In this example, when a philosopher wants to eat, actions *getfork* and *getspoon* have to be executed in a single transition. The execution of these actions

[3] A deadlock would correspond to a philosopher holding the fork and the other holding the spoon, and both waiting for the other piece of cutlery to be available on the table.

actually corresponds to deducing the conjunction of the corresponding preconditions from the current blackboard and updating it so that the conjunction of the postconditions can be deduced from the result. The action of getting both the fork and the spoon from the table involves deducing from the blackboard the formulæ

$$\{fork, spoon\}$$

and from the next blackboard deducing the formulæ

$$\{\neg fork, \neg spoon\}.$$

Let's now look at how to represent a philosopher. Each philosopher is mapped to an action *live* whose execution corresponds to its life. The definition of what is the life of a philosopher is expressed by the following action rule

$$live \rightarrow eat\,.\,think\,.\,live \tag{5}$$

which states that to *live* is to *eat*, to *think* and to keep on living, and all these in sequence. This rule is a short form for rule 1 where C is defined to be μ, the action that executes in any state and never changes it. Operationally, if there is an action *live* to execute, a transition governed by the above rule may occur, no matter what the current blackboard is. The blackboard is not changed by this transition but the action *live* reduces to the sequence of actions (***eat* . *think* . *live***).

Actions which have to be executed are organized in a structure called the *agenda* through parallel (|) and sequential (.) connectives, arbitrarily nested. Together with an initial blackboard and action rules, the initial agenda is part of the system specification. The initial agenda, for the Two Philosophers system, can be defined by the expression

$$live \mid live$$

representing two philosophers with similar lives, living in parallel. The agenda defines a partial order of actions, which results from the existence of explicit sequential connectives. An action a in the agenda that reduces through a general rule 1 is replaced by the structure of actions K. When K is μ (rule 3), what is meant is that a completely executes and actions which were in sequence with a in the agenda become eligible for execution. Consider the following rules which define the action of *eating*,

$$eating \rightarrow putfork \mid putspoon \tag{6}$$

and the action rules for *putfork* and *putspoon*

$$putfork : \rightarrow fork,$$
$$putspoon : \rightarrow spoon.$$

Rule 6 states that *eating* amounts to releasing the fork and the spoon. The acts of releasing the cutlery are the last actions that have to be done in order to terminate the act of eating. We've just skipped all actions that involve putting spaghetti in the mouth, swallowing, etc. since they are not relevant. However, if we had abstracted all these actions in terms of the action *chompchomp*, *eating* could have been defined in the following way

$$\textit{eating} \rightarrow \textit{chompchomp}\,.\,(\textit{putfork}\,|\,\textit{putspoon}).$$

Now consider the initial state where the agenda is (*live* | *live*) and the cutlery is on the table. The reduction of *live* in the agenda via action rule 5 results in the agenda

$$\textit{live}\,|\,(\textit{eat}\,.\,\textit{think}\,.\,\textit{live}).$$

In this situation there are only two actions that may execute, *live* and *eat*. Action *think* will only become *executable* after *eat* completely executes. The *complete execution* of an executable action in the agenda involves either the reduction of the action to μ, or the recursive process of reducing it to an expression of actions and then completely execute all actions in it. Let's carry on with this computation just to ilustrate what we mean. Reducing *eat* to *eating* (via rule 2) would make the agenda become

$$\textit{live}\,|\,(\textit{eating}\,.\,\textit{think}\,.\,\textit{live})$$

and further execution of *eating* via rule 6 would bring up the agenda

$$\textit{live}\,|\,((\textit{putfork}\,|\,\textit{putspoon})\,.\,\textit{think}\,.\,\textit{live}).$$

Only after the complete execution of both *putfork* and *putspoon* (they must both reduce to μ) with a resulting agenda

$$\textit{live}\,|\,(\textit{think}\,.\,\textit{live}),$$

does *think* become an executable action.

3 Propositional AbstrAct

The next four sections should be seen as a stepwise presentation of our first attempt at defining a precise, real AbstrAct programming language, AbstrActβ.

This first section will be devoted to the formal definition of the propositional fragment of AbstrAct. By restricting ourselves to the propositional case we abstract from all the subtleties brought about by manipulation of data in computations, and concentrate on the fundamental ideas. The same motivation of first abstracting away from details made us choose to start by presenting in this section a programming language scheme rather than a concrete language. The presentation of the propositional language AbstrActα will be done in the following section, by filling in definitions left open in the scheme. The following two sections follow the same pattern, but now for the first-order case, culminating with the definition of the language AbstrActβ.

3.1 Syntax

The vocabulary

The vocabulary consists of a set $\mathcal{P}$ of ***propositions***, a set $\mathcal{A}$ of ***actions***, the *condition* connectives (,), ($\leftarrow$) and ($\rightarrow$), and the ***task*** connectives (μ), (|) and (.).

Task expressions

In every state of the computation a system will have a component, the ***agenda***, which is an expression of actions. These actions can be regarded in two ways: as a "still to be done" part of an ongoing "long range" action, or as ***tasks*** or duties the system is committed to execute in the future. For example, in the context of the computation described in section 2, the action ***putfork*** in the agenda

$$live \mid ((putfork \mid putspoon) \,.\, think \,.\, live)$$

plays the role of a task the system has to accomplish. It also denotes part of the ongoing action of *eat* which will only terminate when the actions ***putfork*** and *putspoon* terminate. The agenda is accordingly called a ***task expression.***

Definition 1. The set of *task expressions* is defined as the least set $\mathcal{K}$ satisfying the following:

(*void*) $\mu \in \mathcal{K}$,
(*action*) $\mathcal{A} \subseteq \mathcal{K}$,
(*parallel*) $(T_1 \mid T_2) \in \mathcal{K}$ if $T_1, T_2 \in \mathcal{K} - \{\mu\}$,
(*sequence*) $(T_1 \,.\, T_2) \in \mathcal{K}$ if $T_1, T_2 \in \mathcal{K} - \{\mu\}$.

Condition expressions

Condition expressions occur solely in the rightmost part of action rules. The strangest thing about the definition of condition expressions is that they may include actions. Actions in this context have to be accomplished in a single transition, and the fact that they may or may not do so ***conditions*** the reduction of some action via that particular action rule. Actions in this context correspond to conditions on *pairs of consecutive states* of the computation (a similar definition is given for the term *action* in [16]) considering a state-transition operational model.

A condition expression can also be an annotated proposition, which is seen as conditioning only one of the two states in a transition, i.e. it can be seen as either a *precondition* or a *postcondition.*

Definition 2. The set of *condition expressions* is defined as the least set $\mathcal{C}$ satisfying the following:

(*void*) $\mu \in \mathcal{C}$,
(*action*) $\mathcal{A} \subseteq \mathcal{C}$,
(*precondition*) $\{\leftarrow p \mid p \in \mathcal{P}\} \subseteq \mathcal{C}$,
(*postcondition*) $\{\rightarrow p \mid p \in \mathcal{P}\} \subseteq \mathcal{C}$,
(*conjunction*) $(C_1, C_2) \in \mathcal{C}$ if $C_1, C_2 \in \mathcal{C} - \{\mu\}$.

Action rules

Definition 3. The set of *action rules* is the set of triples

$$\mathcal{R} = \{a \to K : C \mid a \in \mathcal{A}, K \in \mathcal{K}, C \in \mathcal{C}\}.$$

The action a in the rule is said to be the rule *head*, and such a rule is seen as part of the *definition* of action a.

Rules of the form $a : C$ and $a \to K$ are short form notation for $a \to \mu : C$ and $a \to K : \mu$, respectively,.

3.2 Operational semantics

To the propositions $\mathcal{P}$ we must associate a set $\mathcal{F}$ of formulæ to be used in the blackboard. $\mathcal{P}$ and $\mathcal{F}$ are part of the same underlying logical language, so the notion of logical consequence is defined among them, but the exact relation is not fixed.

AbstrAct systems

An AbstrAct *system* is a triple $S = \langle R, A_0, D_0 \rangle$ where $R \subseteq \mathcal{R}$ is a set of action rules, $A_0 \in \mathcal{K}$ is the initial *agenda*, and $D_0 \subseteq \mathcal{F}$ constitutes the initial *blackboard*.

Now, in order to define the operational semantics of a system, we define its mapping to a variant of a *Fair Transition System* (TS) as defined in [19].

Transition systems

The TS associated with the system $S = \langle R, A_0, D_0 \rangle$ is the tuple $\mathbf{S} = \langle \Sigma, \mathcal{T}, \Theta, \mathcal{J} \rangle$ where:

Σ (the set of states) is the set of all pairs $\langle A, D \rangle$ such that $A \in \mathcal{K}$ and $D \subseteq \mathcal{F}$. They are called respectively the agenda and the blackboard.

$\mathcal{T}$ (the set of transitions) is the set

$$\{\tau_r \mid r \in R\}$$

where τ_r is the *transition* associated with a rule r, this being a function $\tau_r : \Sigma \to \wp(\Sigma)$ from states into sets of states. For each $r = (a \to K : C) \in R$ we have

$$\begin{aligned} \langle A', D' \rangle \in \tau_r(\langle A, D \rangle) \text{ iff } & A \overset{a \to K}{\longrightarrow} A', && (1) \\ & C \rightsquigarrow \langle P, P' \rangle, && (2) \\ & D \vdash P, && (3) \\ & D \overset{P'}{\mapsto} D'. && (4) \end{aligned}$$

Each transition involves 1) reducing an action to a task in the agenda, 2) obtaining pre- and postconditions satisfying a condition expression, 3) testing if the preconditions are entailed by the current blackboard, and 4) updating the current blackboard to make the postconditions hold.

Θ (the set of initial states) is the singleton $\{(A_0, D_0)\}$.

$\mathcal{J}$ (the justice set) is the set of sets of transitions

$$\begin{aligned}\mathcal{J} = &\{\{\tau_r\} \mid r \in R\}\\ &\cup\\ &\{\{\tau_r \mid r = (a \to K : C) \in R\} \mid a \in \mathcal{A}\}.\end{aligned}$$

Each set in the first component contains the transition corresponding to a single rule, thus guaranteeing that no rule is forever enabled without being used. In the second component, each set contains all possible transitions for a single task, thus guaranteeing that no task remains forever enabled in the agenda without being reduced.

Agenda reduction

An *action reduction* $a \to K$ pairs an action $a \in \mathcal{A}$ and a task expression $K \in \mathcal{K}$. The *agenda reduction* $A \xrightarrow{a \to K} A'$ via an action reduction is defined as the least relation satisfying the following rules:

Action reduction

$$\frac{}{a \xrightarrow{a \to K} K}$$

Parallel reduction

$$\frac{}{(a \mid A) \xrightarrow{a \to \mu} A} \qquad \frac{A \xrightarrow{a \to K} A'}{(A \mid B) \xrightarrow{a \to K} (A' \mid B)} \; \{A' \neq \mu\}$$

$$\frac{}{(A \mid a) \xrightarrow{a \to \mu} A} \qquad \frac{B \xrightarrow{a \to K} B'}{(A \mid B) \xrightarrow{a \to K} (A \mid B')} \; \{B' \neq \mu\}$$

Sequential reduction

$$\frac{}{(a \,.\, B) \xrightarrow{a \to \mu} B} \qquad \frac{A \xrightarrow{a \to K} A'}{(A \,.\, B) \xrightarrow{a \to K} (A' \,.\, B)} \; \{A' \neq \mu\}$$

Condition unfolding

$C \leadsto \langle P, P' \rangle$ is a relation between a condition expression C and a pair of *preconditions* P and *postconditions* P', which is inductively defined as the least relation satisfying the following rules:

Void

$$\frac{}{\mu \leadsto \langle \emptyset, \emptyset \rangle}$$

Precondition

$$\frac{}{\leftarrow P \leadsto \langle \{P\}, \emptyset \rangle}$$

Postcondition

$$\frac{}{\rightarrow P \rightsquigarrow \langle \emptyset, \{P\} \rangle}$$

Conjunction

$$\frac{A \rightsquigarrow \langle P_A, P'_A \rangle \qquad B \rightsquigarrow \langle P_B, P'_B \rangle}{(A, B) \rightsquigarrow \langle P_A \cup P_B, P'_A \cup P'_B \rangle}$$

Rule

$$\frac{C \rightsquigarrow \langle P, P' \rangle}{a \rightsquigarrow \langle P, P' \rangle} \ \{(a : C) \in R\}$$

Notice the dual use of a rule of the form $a \rightarrow \mu : C$. In the context of an agenda reduction, it represents a complete execution of an *action* a via a transition corresponding to condition C. In the context of a condition unfolding, it states that an abstract *condition* a on a pair of consecutive states is implied by condition C.

Entailment

The *entailment* relation $D \vdash P$ between sets of formulæ and sets of propositions must be sound and complete for the logical language of $\mathcal{F}$ and $\mathcal{P}$ in the following sense:

$$D \vdash P \qquad \text{iff} \qquad \forall p \in P \ \ D \models p$$

Update

The *update* relation is any that satisfies

$$D \overset{P}{\mapsto} D' \Rightarrow D' \vdash P$$

In fact it would be desirable to state a stronger condition about the *minimal change* of D, but this is hard to characterize in a sufficiently general manner. It may be specified for particular instances of the scheme, as indeed is the case with the language in the next section.

Computations

The operational semantics of a system S can be defined as the set of computations of the TS $\mathbf{S}$ associated with S.

A *computation* σ of a TS $\mathbf{S} = \langle \Sigma, \mathcal{T}, \Theta, \mathcal{J} \rangle$ is a finite or infinite sequence of states $s_i \in \Sigma$ and transitions $\tau_i \in \mathcal{T}$

$$\sigma : \ s_0 \xrightarrow{\tau_0} s_1 \xrightarrow{\tau_1} s_2 \xrightarrow{\tau_2} \cdots$$

satisfying the requirements of *initiality* ($s_0 \in \Theta$), *consecution* ($\forall i \ s_{i+1} \in \tau_i(s_i)$), *termination*

$$\sigma : \ s_0 \rightarrow \cdots \rightarrow s_k \ (\sigma \text{ is finite}) \Rightarrow \forall \tau \in \mathcal{T} \ \tau(s_k) = \emptyset,$$

and *justice*, this being the requirement that for any $T \in \mathcal{J}$, if σ is an infinite sequence $\cdots s_i \xrightarrow{\tau_i} \cdots$ such that some transition in T is always enabled after some point k of the computation ($\forall i \geq k\ \exists \tau \in T\ .\ \tau(s_i) \neq \emptyset$) then some transition in T occurs after that point ($\exists i \geq k\ \tau_i \in T$.)

A *terminal* state s_k is one such that $\forall \tau \in T\ \tau(s_k) = \emptyset$. We define a ***deadlocked*** computation as a finite computation

$$s_0 \longrightarrow \cdots \longrightarrow s_k$$

where s_k is terminal and $s_k = \langle A, D \rangle, A \neq \mu$.

Nondeterminism

The definition of the justice set $\mathcal{J}$ reflects the existence of two types of nondeterminism in the model: the selection of the executable action to execute and the selection of the action rule which will be used in the reduction of the action. The model exhibits a weak fair behaviour in the two situations.

The model also exibhits nondeterminism in the selection of the pair of pre- and postconditions in the relation $C \rightsquigarrow \langle P, P' \rangle$ and of the updated blackboard D' in the relation $D \overset{P}{\mapsto} D'$. We haven't specified any fairness conditions for these situations. While practical programming languages may live with nondeterminism in the conditions, the indefinition of what is the update may be problematic. In the languages AbstrActα and AbstrActβ that we define below we adopt a conservative position and restrict the blackboard so that updates become deterministic.

4 The Language AbstrActα

We will now propose a language, AbstrActα, based on the above model. This language will be a straigthforward instantiation of several notions left undefined, namely the characterization of propositions and actions, of the logical formulæ built from propositions, and of the entailment and update relations.

Propositions and actions

Propositions are built out of a set of propositional symbols $\mathcal{P}_0$ and connectives for negation and conjunction. $\mathcal{P}$ is the least set satisfying

(*positive*)	$\mathcal{P}_0 \subset \mathcal{P}$,
(*negative*)	$\{\neg p \mid p \in \mathcal{P}_0\} \subset \mathcal{P}$,
(*conjunction*)	$(P_1, P_2) \in \mathcal{P}$ if $P_1, P_2 \in \mathcal{P}$.

Elements of both $\mathcal{P}_0$ and the set $\mathcal{A}$ of actions are constants built out of lowercase letters.

The blackboard

The set of formulæ $\mathcal{F}$ appearing in a blackboard coincides with the set of propositional constants $\mathcal{P}_0$.

Programs

An AbstrActα program is an expression

$$\frac{\frac{A}{D}}{R}$$

where A is a task expression which constitutes the initial agenda, D is a collection of propositional constants separated by commas which stands for the initial blackboard, and R is a set of action rules (rules just follow one another, with no extra syntax). Such a program has equivalent semantics to the AbstrAct system $\langle R, A, D\rangle$.

Entailment and update

To each proposition P we associate a positive part $P^+ \subseteq \mathcal{P}_0$ and a negative part $P^- \subseteq \mathcal{P}_0$, defined as follows:

$$\begin{aligned} (A,B)^+ &= A^+ \cup B^+, & (A,B)^- &= A^- \cup B^-, \\ (\neg A)^+ &= \emptyset, & (\neg A)^- &= \{A\}, \\ A^+ &= \{A\} \text{ if } A \in \mathcal{P}_0. & A^- &= \emptyset \text{ if } A \in \mathcal{P}_0. \end{aligned}$$

The entailment relation between blackboards and sets of propositions is defined as

$$D \vdash P \text{ iff } P^+ \subseteq D,\ P^- \cap D = \emptyset.$$

This definition reflects a *closed world assumption*. Propositions which are not stated in D are considered to be false.

The update relation between blackboards through a proposition is defined as follows:

$$D \overset{P}{\mapsto} D' \text{ iff } D' = D \cup P^+ - P^-,\ P^+ \cap P^- = \emptyset.$$

4.1 An example: The Two Philosophers

The program in Figure 1 is a solution for "The Two Philosophers" problem presented in section 2. Since we already went through it we will restrict ourselves to some short comments.

The Two Philosophers is a trivial problem of two processes (the philosophers) sharing a resource (the cutlery) which must be accessed in mutual exclusion. In spite of the simplification, solving this exercise involves accounting for the possibility of deadlock in a situation when a philosopher holds the fork and the other holds the spoon.

Conflicting situations of the philosophers trying to grab the same object are trivially avoided since the act of grabbing the cutlery is an atomic operation: either it is fully accomplished or not at all, being in this case delayed until better oportunity. Notice the constrast between the definitions of this act (of getting the cutlery) and the act of cutlery release which corresponds to executing ***putfork*** and ***putspoon*** in parallel with no constraints whatsoever.

So the presented solution is trivially deadlock free. It is not, however, starvation free. It is possible that one of the philosophers, after putting down the cutlery, always picks it up again before the other one does. This is no violation of the justice requirement, since the transition rule for the other philosopher is

$$live \mid live$$

$$\frac{\frac{}{fork,\ spoon}}{}$$

$$live \rightarrow eat\,.\,think\,.\,live$$

$$eat \rightarrow eating : getfork,\ getspoon$$

$$eating \rightarrow putfork \mid putspoon$$

$$\begin{array}{l} getfork : \leftarrow fork,\ \rightarrow(\neg\ fork) \\ getspoon : \leftarrow spoon,\ \rightarrow(\neg\ spoon) \\ putfork : \rightarrow fork \\ putspoon : \rightarrow spoon \end{array}$$

Fig. 1. The Two Philosophers.

never enabled for an infinite amount of time, although it is enabled infinitely often for a finite amount of time. This is the well-known distinction between *weak* fairness (the one we impose) and *strong* fairness.

5 First-Order AbstrAct

When stepping to a first-order language we introduce variables, constants and function symbols, with which terms are constructed. These are used as arguments of predicate symbols to form the atoms, which correspond to the propositional constants in a propositional language. In our setting, an analogous enrichment of the language is done for actions, which become the application of action symbols to terms. Terms then become informational glue between the two worlds of actions and propositions, i.e. the agenda and the blackboard. However, some care must be taken because variables simply cannot play a "logical" role inside actions. There are two ways one can look at the role of a variable inside an action:

1. as specifying (part of) a generic action which can be specialized,
2. as specifying a result of the action accomplishment.

In the first case instantiation must precede execution, for it makes no sense to specialize a task while it is being carried out or after; by doing so one might be ruling out an already taken execution path, whose effects upon the system cannot simply be undone. In the second case an instantiation done during execution must only be used (through other actions it is specializing) after the complete execution of the action. This guarantees that no other action is further specialized after it has started. We will therefore consider tasks to have two distinct types of arguments, which we call *input* and *output* arguments.

In the propositional model, an action rule denotes a possible reduction of an action. In this extension it denotes a possible reduction for a family of actions, the ones whose input is an instance of the input of the action in the rule head. So several actions, with the same action symbol but different inputs, may reduce via the same action rule. Each rule head action is parameterized by the input of the executing action, and this parameterization extends to the whole rule. Therefore, condition expressions in the rule may have variables that are instantiated by this parameterization.

First-order AbstrAct extends propositional AbstrAct but does not change the basic principle of attaining synchronization between parallel actions solely by atomic deduction and update of the blackboard. So, variables in task expressions act as channels for information flow but *never* as a synchronization mechanism (as opposed to CLP languages [24]). We will make simple syntactic restrictions on the definition of action rules and initial agenda that will enforce this constraint.

5.1 Syntax

Vocabulary

The vocabulary is extended to include a set of *variables*, a set of *constants*, a set of *function symbols* and a set of *predicate symbols*, with which we construct *terms*, *atoms* and *literals* as usual.

We denote by $\|E\|$ the set of variables occuring in an expression E.

Actions

An *action* is written in the form

$$a(i_1, \ldots, i_n)[o_1, \ldots, o_m]$$

where a is an $n \times m$-ary action symbol and $i_1, \ldots, i_n$ and $o_1, \ldots, o_m$ are terms (respectively the *input* and *output arguments.*) In the sequel we will sometimes write $\bar{t}$ to stand for $t_1, \ldots, t_n$.

Task expressions

Task expressions are defined as for the propositional case. However, we now have to define *well-formed task expressions*, to account for the required constraint between input and output in actions.

Definition 4. The *output set* of a task expression K, denoted by $\|K\|^o$, is inductively defined as follows:

$$\begin{aligned}
\|\mu\|^o &= \emptyset, \\
\|a(\bar{\imath})[\bar{o}]\|^o &= \|\bar{o}\|, \\
\|K\,.\,K'\|^o &= \|K\|^o \cup \|K'\|^o, \\
\|K \mid K'\|^o &= \|K\|^o \cup \|K'\|^o.
\end{aligned}$$

Definition 5. The *input set* of a task expression K, denoted by $\|K\|^i$, is inductively defined as follows:

$\|\mu\|^i = \emptyset,$
$\|a(\bar{\imath})[\bar{o}]\|^i = \|\bar{\imath}\|,$
$\|K\,.\,K'\|^i = \|K\|^i \cup \|K'\|^i - \|K\|^o,$
$\|K \mid K'\|^i = \|K\|^i \cup \|K'\|^i.$

Definition 6. The set $\mathcal{W}$ of *well-formed* task expressions is defined inductively as the least set satisfying the following:

$$\mu \in \mathcal{W},$$

$$a(\bar{\imath})[\bar{o}] \in \mathcal{W} \quad \text{iff} \quad a(\bar{\imath})[\bar{o}] \in \mathcal{A}, \; \|\bar{\imath}\| \cap \|\bar{o}\| = \emptyset, \; \bar{o} \text{ are distinct variables},$$

$$(K\,.\,K') \in \mathcal{W} \quad \text{iff} \quad \|K\| \cap \|K'\|^o = \emptyset, \; K, K' \in \mathcal{W},$$

$$(K \mid K') \in \mathcal{W} \quad \text{iff} \quad \|K\|^o \cap \|K'\|^o = \emptyset, \; \|(K \mid K')\|^i \cap \|(K \mid K')\|^o = \emptyset, \; K, K' \in \mathcal{W}.$$

This ensures that any output variable of a task will only occur as an input variable of another task that is scheduled to start after complete execution of the first.

Definition 7. An action rule $a \rightarrow K : C \in \mathcal{R}$ is *well formed* if $K \in \mathcal{W}$ and $\|K\|^o \cap (\|a\|^i \cup \|C\|) = \emptyset$.

Basically this restriction prevents output variables of K to be instantiated in the transition corresponding to the rule. Since K is to be executed *after* this transition its output variables must remain free.

5.2 Operational Semantics

An AbstrAct system is now defined as the triple $S = \langle R, A_0, D_0 \rangle$ where every action rule $r \in R$ ($R \subseteq \mathcal{R}$) is well formed and A_0, the initial agenda, is a well formed task expression. D_0 is again a subset of the set $\mathcal{F}$ of logic formulæ.

The operational semantics are defined as for the propositional case, again as the set of computations of the Transition System associated to the corresponding AbstrAct system. The difference is in the definition of the transition τ_r associated to a rule r, where we now have to consider variable substitutions.

For any $r = (a \rightarrow K : C) \in R$ we now have

$$\langle A', D' \rangle \in \tau_r(\langle A, D \rangle) \quad \text{iff} \quad A \overset{a\theta - K\theta}{\longrightarrow} A', \; C\theta \rightsquigarrow \langle P, P' \rangle, \; D \vdash P, \; D \overset{P'}{\mapsto} D'.$$

where θ is a variable substitution.

The substitution θ appearing above represents a solution to two problems: 1) make the input part of the rule head a identical to that of an action in the agenda (see section below on the definition of the Agenda reduction relation); 2) instantiate the conditions so that they can reduce, eventually using action rules of the system, to pre- and postconditions such that the preconditions hold in the current state (see section below on Condition Reduction).

Agenda reduction

The agenda reduction relation $A \overset{a \rightarrow K}{\longrightarrow} A'$ has also to be modified. The idea is that a (a rule head with a substitution applied) will have exactly the same name and input arguments as the action a' to be replaced by K in A, and the substitution that makes the output variables of a' (all output arguments are variables) identical to the output arguments of a has to be applied to the rest of the agenda to produce the new agenda A'. The formal definition is as follows.

$$A \overset{a \rightarrow K}{\longrightarrow} A' \Leftrightarrow \exists \sigma \; A \overset{a \rightarrow K}{\longrightarrow} A' \, [\sigma]$$

The auxiliary relation has an extra argument consisting of an ***output substitution*** σ. It is defined as the least relation satisfying the following rules:

Action reduction

$$\frac{}{a \overset{a' \rightarrow K}{\longrightarrow} K \, [\sigma]} \quad \left\{ \begin{array}{l} a = n(\overline{\imath})[\overline{o}], \; \overline{o'} = \overline{o}\sigma \\ a' = n(\overline{\imath})[\overline{o'}], \; dom(\sigma) = \|\overline{o}\| \end{array} \right\}$$

Parallel reduction

$$\frac{a \overset{a' \rightarrow \mu}{\longrightarrow} \mu \, [\sigma]}{(a \,|\, A) \overset{a' \rightarrow \mu}{\longrightarrow} A[\sigma]}, \qquad \frac{a \overset{a' \rightarrow \mu}{\longrightarrow} \mu \, [\sigma]}{(A \,|\, a) \overset{a' \rightarrow \mu}{\longrightarrow} A[\sigma]},$$

$$\frac{A \overset{a \rightarrow K}{\longrightarrow} A' \, [\sigma]}{(A \,|\, B) \overset{a \rightarrow K}{\longrightarrow} (A' \,|\, B) \, [\sigma]} \quad \left\{ \begin{array}{l} A' \neq \mu \\ (A' \,|\, B) \in \mathcal{W} \end{array} \right\},$$

$$\frac{B \overset{a \rightarrow K}{\longrightarrow} B' \, [\sigma]}{(A \,|\, B) \overset{a \rightarrow K}{\longrightarrow} (A \,|\, B') \, [\sigma]} \quad \left\{ \begin{array}{l} B' \neq \mu \\ (A \,|\, B') \in \mathcal{W} \end{array} \right\}.$$

Sequential reduction

$$\frac{a \overset{a' \rightarrow \mu}{\longrightarrow} \mu \, [\sigma]}{(a \,.\, B) \overset{a' \rightarrow \mu}{\longrightarrow} B\sigma \, [\sigma]} \quad \{ B\sigma \in \mathcal{W} \},$$

$$\frac{A \overset{a \rightarrow K}{\longrightarrow} A' \, [\sigma]}{(A \,.\, B) \overset{a \rightarrow K}{\longrightarrow} (A' \,.\, B\sigma) \, [\sigma]} \quad \left\{ \begin{array}{l} A' \neq \mu \\ (A' \,.\, B\sigma) \in \mathcal{W} \end{array} \right\}.$$

Notice that the output substitution is only applied to tasks in sequence in the agenda. By the well-formedness condition, an output variable of an action is not shared (either as input or as output) by actions in parallel with it.

Condition reduction

The condition reduction relation has also to be modified, to account for variable bindings necessary to match rule heads to actions. The only rule that needs to be modified is the *Rule reduction* rule.

$$\frac{C\gamma \leadsto \langle P, P' \rangle}{a\gamma \leadsto \langle P, P' \rangle} \; \{(a : C) \in R\}$$

where γ is a variable substitution.

Substitutions

These definitions are "synthetic" because they do not hint at how to compute the substitution θ. Operationally a substitution for making the input part of the rule identical to that of an action in the agenda is constructed first, and applied to the rest of the rule. Then the conditions C are reduced to pre- and postconditions using action rules, a process that produces a substitution corresponding to *unifications* of actions with rule heads. More precisely this corresponds to computing an answer substitution for the problem of deriving the preconditions from the current blackboard, much as in the execution of a goal for a logic program [17]. The composition of all these substitutions is θ. The other substitution remaining to be made is the one for the output variables of the reduced action in the agenda, which is implicit in the definition of $A \xrightarrow{a \to K} A'$.

The requirement of well-formedness for action rules and agendas in practice assures that the synchronization model does not change with the introduction of variables, by restricting a variable to have at most one producer (one write operation) and several consumers that will issue read operations only *after* it has been written.

The nonexistence of conflicts in the access to variables in the agenda is implied by the above constraints. Also, variables retain the single assignment property of logic variables. Take a transition corresponding to the reduction of an action a in the agenda via an action rule $a' \to K : C$. Write operations are done on the output of a either 1) by propagating the substitution resulting from the matching of the inputs of a and a' (the rule head a' may share variables between the output and input – note that the rule head does not need to be a well formed action), 2) from the evaluation of C (output variables of a' may be shared with variables of C) or 3) from the ensuing execution of subactions K (output variables of a' may occur as output variables of K). The restriction $\|K\|^o \cap (\|a\|^i \cup \|C\|) = \emptyset$ on well formed action rules guarantees that there is at most a write operation on the variable, either issued in this transition (cases 1) or 2)) or postponed to a subsequent transition (case 3)). Notice that the input of a is not further instantiated.

As a last remark, our definition allows more substitutions θ than needed. We could have used *most general* substitutions, but the definitions would become a bit more cumbersome.

6 The Language AbstrActβ

The language AbstrActβ is the first-order equivalent of AbstrActα.

All constant, function, predicate and action symbols are strings of lowercase letters, while variables are strings of letters the first of which is uppercase. Terms are variables, constants or expressions $f(t_1, \ldots, t_n)$ where p stands for a predicate symbol and $t_1, \ldots, t_n$ for terms. Remember that the basic propositions (corresponding to propositional constants in AbstrActα) are the *atoms*, i.e. expressions of the form $p(t_1, \ldots, t_n)$ where p stands for a predicate symbol and $t_1, \ldots, t_n$ for terms. When the predicate symbol p has arity zero we just write p for the corresponding atom.

The rest of the syntax has already been introduced. Programs are written as for AbstrActα.

The set of formulæ $\mathcal{F}$ appearing in a blackboard is the set of *ground* atoms, i.e. those with no occurrences of variables.

The entailment and update are the same as for AbstrActα.

6.1 Programming examples

Readers/Writers

The readers/writers exercise in its simplest version is a problem of assuring that typical operations of reading and updating components of a data structure shared by several concurrent processes are accomplished in a coherent way. The result of executing several of these operations concurrently must be equivalent to that of executing them in some serial order, which basically means that each operation execution has to be seen as an atomic step.

The solution is trivial in AbstrActβ since the concept of atomic action is primitive in the language. Processes are mapped to tasks in parallel in the agenda which issue read and write operations via the actions $read[T]$ and $write(T)$. The data structure is represented by some collection of facts in the blackboard, and if we represent the operations on these facts as being defined in terms of abstract atomic actions $consult[T]$ and $update(T)$, the definitions of read and write are trivially defined by the transition rules

$$read[T] : consult[T]$$
$$write(T) : update(T).$$

A more elaborated version of the problem requires that the data structure be updated as soon as possible, assigning to the write operations a higher priority than to the read operations.

Figure 2 presents a solution. [4] The blackboard is augmented with a relation

[4] Some patterns of pre- and postconditions in condition expressions are so common in AbstrActβ programs that we've decided to use a compact notation for them. A "sweet" AbstrActβ program allows that

$\leftarrow A, \rightarrow(\neg A)$ may be written $A\rightarrow$ and

$\leftarrow A[t], \rightarrow(\neg A[t]), \rightarrow A[r]$ may be written $A[t \rightarrow r]$

where A is an atom.

$$read[T] \rightarrow reading[T] : \leftarrow writers(0)$$
$$reading[T] : consult[T]$$

$$write(T) \rightarrow writing(T) : writers(W \rightarrow s(W))$$
$$writing(T) : update(T),\ writers(s(W) \rightarrow W)$$

Fig. 2. Action rules for *read*[T] and *write*(T) in the readers/writers problem. Writers have priority over readers on the assumption of stronger fairness conditions.

writers/1 representing the number (in successor notation) of writers currently writing. Every *write* reduces to *writing* while incrementing the number of active writers, this being decremented upon termination of the *writing*. The reduction of *read* to *reading* is conditioned by there being no active writers, so any read operation is delayed until all *writing* operations terminate.

This solution does not guarantee the priority of writers over readers, the fairness conditions of the execution model not being strong enough. The desired behaviour will be obtained on the assumption that executable actions in the agenda which may reduce by some action rule will do so as soon as possible.

The Dining Philosophers

Here is a solution to the original problem of the Dining Philosophers.

This solution is equivalent to the one for the Two Philosophers. The aditional complication derived from the fact that each philosopher may conflict with two different philosophers to get its forks is not apparent at the language level. The only relevant idea is that getting both forks is an atomic action. It is perhaps worth commenting upon the sligthly different way the *eat* action is defined. The atomic grabbing of the cutlery has been abstracted in the action *getforks*, and *eating* has been separated from the cutlery release which is abstracted in *putforks*. Since *getforks* is an atomic operation, by its rule definition, it can be used as a task on its own rather than as a precondition for reducing *eat*. We could have written the rule

$$eat(L, R) \rightarrow eating\,.\,putforks(L, R) : getforks(L, R)$$

but the form in figure 3 (operationally equivalent as *getforks* is itself atomic) avoids the redundant atomicity requirement and gives a more symmetrical structure to *eat*.

A queue

The definitions of the AbstrActβ language result in a programming style where complex data structures accessed in parallel are distributed through multiple facts in the blackboard. This increases concurrency since a prospective implementation enforcing atomicity of actions would *lock* only the relevant facts accessed in that particular action. The possibility of abstracting actions on

$$live(1,2) \mid live(2,3) \mid live(3,4) \mid$$
$$live(4,5) \mid live(5,1)$$

$$ontable(1),\ ontable(2),\ ontable(3),$$
$$ontable(4),\ ontable(5)$$

$$live(L,R) \rightarrow eat(L,R)\,.\,think\,.\,live(L,R)$$

$$eat(L,R) \rightarrow getforks(L,R)\,.\,eating\,.\,putforks(L,R)$$

$$getforks(L,R) : getfork(L),\ getfork(R)$$
$$putforks(L,R) \rightarrow putfork(L) \mid putfork(R)$$

$$getfork(F) : ontable(F)\rightarrow$$
$$putfork(F) : \rightarrow ontable(F)$$

$$eating \rightarrow \mu$$
$$think \rightarrow \mu$$

Fig. 3. The Dining Philosophers.

several facts in the blackboard hides the implementation details of these data structures.

The example we present here is that of a queue of elements accessed by two operations *get* and *put* represented by atomic actions. The data structure is distributed in three relations *head*, *tail* and *elem*. The *head* and *tail* relations denote pointers to, respectively, the first element of the queue and the next element to be inserted in the queue. The relation $elem(Z,X)$ states that the element pointed to by Z is X.

$$put(X) : tail(Z \rightarrow s(Z)), \rightarrow elem(Z,X)$$

$$get[X] : head(Z \rightarrow s(Z)),\ elem(Z,X)\rightarrow$$

Fig. 4. Action rules representing the *put* and *get* operations of a *fifo* queue.

The execution of a *put* action is done in an atomic operation where the tail is incremented and a new element is added. Execution of a *get* atomically increments the head and removes the first element from the queue. The *empty* condition is implicitly tested when deducing the existence of an element at the head of the queue. If the queue is empty, corresponding to a blackboard

$$\{head(Z), tail(Z)\}$$

for some ground term Z, no definitions exist for predicate ***elem***, and any ***get*** will be delayed until some element is inserted by a *put* operation. The first argument Z of the $elem(Z, X)$ relation has a twofold purpose: it acts as a unique identifier of X and implicitly defines the order of the element in the queue. Operations to increment and decrement Z are trivially defined since Z is a natural number represented in sucessor notation.

7 Implementation

No serious attempt has yet been made at an efficient low-level implementation of an AbstrAct language. There is, however, a prototype implementation of a language which is an extension of AbstrActβ. It relies on a translation to Prolog and uses its internal database to simulate the blackboard (you can see it's not efficient.) The language is described in [22], where a sketch of the implementation can be found, along with a description of bugs and missing features.

8 Related Work

AbstrAct shares with several proposals (UNITY [12], Concurrent Logic Programming Languages (CLPL) [24], Shared Prolog [6], Linear Objects [2]) and even with OPS5 [7] the declarative style of programming through ***assertions*** of what are the possible state transformations of the system. The explicit definition of entities driving the activity of the system (goals or tasks) is absent from UNITY, OPS5 and Linear Objects, and only weakly present in Shared Prolog. The concept of a global shared state used in the communication and synchronization of activities (processes, actions, objects or goals) are characteristic of models present in Linda (the Tuple Space), Shared Prolog (the blackboard) and Linear Objects (the forum). The Linda model does not give the possibility of directly expressing user defined atomic operations to access multiple components of the shared state (this is added to the Linda model in Shared Prolog). AbstrAct differs from all these in offering general deductive capabilities over the shared state, through user-defined abstractions. Explicit sequentiality is absent from all referred proposals (in the Linda case this is not relevant), with the exception of some members of the CLPL family.

Concurrent Logic Programming Languages

Concurrent Logic Programming Languages [24] share with AbstrAct the goal-oriented characteristic and declarative style of the programs. However, the CLPLs computation state is composed solely by the current instantiated resolvant and a transition corresponds to the reduction of an atom in the resolvant via a clause of the program. The resolvant can be seen as both the AbstrAct agenda and blackboard, where the former is represented by the processes in the resolvant and the latter by the current instantiated terms of the whole resolvant. Evaluation of the expressive power in representing shared data structures through logic programs or by terms is difficult and both approaches have merits and disadvantages. A discussion on the expressive power of Linda languages and the CLP family in [11] may shed some light on the compromises and features of representing data by terms shared between goals or by assertions on a global shared space (tuples or relations).

The main difference to AbstrAct lies in the model of communication / synchronization. Processes in the resolvant communicate and synchronize by instantiating and waiting for instantiation of shared "logical" variables, while parallel actions in the agenda communicate and synchronize by atomically consulting and updating a shared blackboard.

The choice of not incorporating sequentialization in the most famous representants of the CLPL family results in a model with fewer concepts to handle but forcing the use of shared variables with the sole purpose of monitoring and controling the flow of execution. Detection of termination of an abstract action involving multiple transitions is an example of a problem whose solution is trivial when recurring to an explicit sequential operator. The solution for an equivalent problem in CLPLs (the detection of the termination of a tree of processes) requires that all involved predicates have an extra pair of control variables in their definition (the switch) which "close" when the corresponding process terminates (short circuit technique [23]).

Linear Objects

Linear Objects (LO) is a logic programming language where computations are seen as proofs of sequents. LO has its roots on Linear Logic and it inherits from that logic the concept of formulæ as resources which may be consumed after having being used in the proof [2, 13]. The state of an LO computation is a two level structure of atoms (the resolvant), enough to give an idea of context which the authors associate to objects. Transitions are modeled by methods (clauses which may have multiple atoms in their heads). Methods state what atoms are deleted from and added to the resolvant in each transition.

In LO there is no explicit representation of the goals of the system, and everything from objects to operations, distributed data structures and messages is represented by atoms (or terms in them). A latter enhancement of the language proposes a form of interobject communication/synchronization (the forum communication) which, operationally, relies on a shared context between objects where atoms are added ("telled") and deleted [3, 4]. This shared context is comparable with the blackboard of AbstrAct. A notorious difference between both approaches is that in LO the deletion of an atom previously added to the shared context has a local effect, whereas telling an atom is like broadcasting it to every other object of the system. In AbstrAct every change to the blackboard (stating a proposition or negating it) is global.

Linda

In what concerns the definition of complex data structures the style of programming introduced by AbstrActβ has many similarities with the one introduced by Linda based languages [1]. In both approaches there is a state shared by concurrent processes or actions where one may represent distributed data structures. This is the *Tuple Space* of Linda whose equivalent counterpart here is the blackboard. Tuples can be roughly mapped to facts, and data structures are distributed through tuples in a similar way to our distribution of them through relations. The major difference at this level is that the Tuple Space is a multiset whereas the blackboardis a set, and the corresponding updates are in terms of additions/deletions versus statements of truth (which may already hold for the current state.) The implementation of a queue in C-Linda [10] is a good example to stress the similarities of both approaches. The queue is partially represented in the tuple space by two tuples

$$\langle \text{"}head\text{"}, N\rangle$$
$$\langle \text{"}tail\text{"}, M\rangle$$

which correspond to relations *head/1* and *tail/1* in the example in section 6.1. Elements of the queue are represented by tuples $\langle \text{"}elem\text{"}, N, E\rangle$, corresponding to the relation *elem/2*. The *get* operation is defined by the instructions

$$in(\text{"}head\text{"}, N);$$
$$in(\text{"}elem\text{"}, N, E);$$
$$out(\text{"}head\text{"}, N+1);$$

which have a counterpart in the action rule that defines *get* as an atomic composed action, but notice that for exclusive access the instruction *in("head", N)* acts as a *p* operation on a semaphore of initial value 1. Other conflicting *get* operations block in the first instruction, as long as the winner *get* operation does not terminate and inserts again the tuple $\langle \text{"}head\text{"}, N\rangle$ in the tuple space.

Further comparisons must be done in the light of the expressiveness/efficiency tradeoff. We provide a high level notion of atomic action, whereas in the Linda model notions of atomicity have to be explicitily programmed; atomicity is guaranteed only at the level of the system primitives which are provided to access the tuple space: *in*, *out* and *read*. From this point of vue Linda languages can be seen to lie at a lower level than AbstrAct languages. AbstrAct combines deductions and updates in arbitrarily complex atomic actions, which (at the expenses of a higher degree of complexity in the implementation) increases the expressive power of the derived languages. The difference in expressiveness is highlighted when comparing the respective deadlock-free solutions for the Dining Philosophers problem. The C-Linda solution [9] requires the existence of a doorman that forbids the entrance in the room to more than four philosophers. AbstrActβ does not have to worry about this because atomicity of actions is ensured by an implementation which deals with the arising deadlock situations. What is gained in expressiveness is lost in efficiency. While some Linda based languages have efficient implementations on distributed architectures, an equivalent AbstrActβ implementation is of comparable complexity to that of implementations of Distributed Transactions Systems.

Shared Prolog

Shared Prolog [6] uses the Linda communication model along with sets of activation rules indexed by processes which are launched in parallel. The activation part of a rule uses unification rather than pattern matching for accessing tuples with *in* and *read* operations and is executed as an atomic operation. The rule also contains a Prolog goal and a set of *out* operations.

Being based on the Linda model, the set/multiset distinction already alluded to above is again valid when comparing Shared Prolog with AbstrAct.

Atomic operations in Shared Prolog are composed solely out of *in* and *read* operations, excluding both the use of *out* operations and user-defined abstractions. In contrast, in AbstrAct arbitrary actions can be composed for atomic execution (see the Dining Philosophers example.) The only place to use abstractions in Shared Prolog is in a Prolog goal which does not access the state, its only connection being data passed in arguments.

In contrast to AbstrAct, Shared Prolog behaves much as OPS5 in having action rules which are not goal-directed, their activation depending on the evaluation of a pattern on the current state. In such languages the programmer has to explicitly encode goal-directedness in the form of 'goal' tokens in the state.

There is no general parallel or sequential composition of actions in Shared Prolog. There is only an initial parallel configuration, but from then on each process proceeds through a sequence of activations of rules in its assigned theory (in each step one of the executable rules is nondeterministically chosen to fire.) We find the ability of composing actions in parallel and sequence essential for the abstract description of tasks, as we do in AbstrAct.

UNITY

The pragmatics of AbstrAct differ from UNITY [12] in that we are primarily interested in constructing high-level languages that enhance expressiveness at the expense of dealing with a bigger set of concepts, while UNITY appears as a programming notation, part of a theory of programming. The pragmatics of UNITY involve the formal derivation of programs from the properties of the systems and the formal proofs that systems represented by programs have certain properties. It is not surprising that the resulting notation is so frugal in the number of concepts it deals with.

The initial and assign sections of a UNITY program are comparable with, respectively, the initial state and the set of transition rules of an AbstrAct specification (the other sections are not relevant for this comparison). A (guarded) multiple assign statement is comparable with a transition rule, the guard having an equivalent in the preconditions of the conditional action and the multiple assignment reflecting the existence of several changes to the state accomplished atomically (postconditions). The agenda and all the definitions in the rules concerning reductions of actions in subactions has no equivalent in UNITY since there are no goals driving the activity of the system. Also, the abstraction on the definition of atomic actions in AbstrAct has no equivalent in UNITY. We encapsulate both conditions (guards) and updates (assignments) in actions.

The if-then-else construct of UNITY has no parallel in AbstrAct. Each condition driving a different change of state has to go in a different rule as a condition expression. This fact is sometimes annoying and may redund in some inefficiency, since we may have situations where complex preconditions and their negation are evaluated at the same time. A solution for an equivalent problem in the context of the CLPLs languages consisted in defining an *otherwise* guard. An interesting discussion on the negative (or positive) influence of *otherwise* on the modularity of rules (clauses in CLP languages) can be found in [24].

The termination detection of AbstrAct programs is a direct consequence of its goal oriented semantics. A computation terminates when the agenda is empty, in opposition to UNITY where termination is equivalent to reaching a state fixed-point.

9 Conclusions

AbstrAct is the result of the development of some basic ideas proposed in [20] and followed in [21]. The primordial motivation for AbstrAct is the belief that the success of concurrent languages with roots in Logic Programming does not lie in its claimed logical nature but rather in certain orthogonal features of logic programming which these above mentioned proposals inherited (like the rule based style of programming, the representation of all data as terms, the notion of reduction of a goal in subgoals, etc.). All these aspects are addressed in AbstrAct, but in our case action rules represent only atomic state transformations and have no dubious logical connotation.

Why rule based programming?

Changes of the state are represented through *assertions*, basically stating that if some preconditions are true in the current state then the state may be updated resulting in a new state. Considering an underlying state-transition model each of these assertions represents the possible transitions of such a system. This approach is regarded as having the advantages of incrementality and declarativity.

Why logic programs?

Representing the blackboard by a logic program avoids the need to define an ad-hoc collection of operators to evaluate the conditions on the blackboard that trigger a corresponding transition. We represent conditions by logic formulæ and rely on the notion of deduction of a formula from a logic program to evaluate conditions. Changes of state are expressed in an equivalent way. We express them through postconditions, which are logic formulæ that have to be true in the resulting state.

Why goal-orientedness?

We believe that many systems which are said to be reactive are actually perceived by most people to be more active than reactive, by which we mean that we tend to identify in such systems some purpose that drives their actions. This amounts to saying that we model such systems as having a goal directed behaviour, and we argue that this goal directedness should be directly expressible in the programming language. In fact, with rule based languages that do not provide goal orientedness, programmers tend to encode that notion in ways which are not transparent (see for example the programming style of Linear Objects and OPS5). Besides some increase in expressiveness, goal orientedness increases the efficiency of programs, since the choice of the rule to govern the transition does not rely solely on the evaluation of the preconditions (or guards) of the rules which would mean considering all rules of the program. The rules that may be used are those that *define* goals to be solved, so indexing mechanisms can be used.

Why explicit sequentiality?

The inclusion of an explicit connective to express sequentiality is justified by the fact that the absence of explicit control structures enforces sequenced sub-computations to be expressed through unattractive manipulation of boolean flags (as referred in [8] and [7]), a characteristic of, for example, OPS5 systems. It is our belief that a lot of computational phenomena are naturally perceived by the programmer as being necessarily sequential, which justifies the possibility of having a way of directly representing this notion in the programs.

Why user-defined atomicity?

Synchronization between concurrent ongoing actions is achieved solely by enforcing subactions of these actions to be accomplished in single steps of execution. This feature frees the programmer from having to explicitly program synchronization policies with low level mechanisms, such as semaphores, therefore allowing elegant solutions, expressed using abstractions from the problem domain, for typical situations when defining concurrent systems.

The way atomic actions are defined in AbstrAct results from a compromise between expressiveness, simplicity and the prospective efficiency of implementations. A possible extension of the definition of atomic actions could encompass long range actions which take arbitrarily many reductions to accomplish. This is conceptually a different type of atomicity, and is a topic for future research.

Why "AbstrAct"?

The name "AbstrAct" honors two fundamental notions: the concept of *action* which is central to this proposal since what we are basically doing is providing notations to define systems that *(re)act*, and the concept of ***abstraction*** as we provide for actions to be defined in terms of abstractions of other actions.

References

1. S. Ahuja, N. Carriero, D. Gelertner. *Linda and Friends*. IEEE Computer. August 1986.
2. JM. Andreoli, R. Pareschi. *LO and Behold! Concurrent Structured Processes*. Proc. of the OOPSLA'90. ACM Press. 1990.
3. JM. Andreoli, R. Pareschi. *Communication as Fair Distribution of Knowledge*. Proc. of the OOPSLA'91. ACM Press. 1991.

4. JM. Andreoli, R. Pareschi. *Dynamic Programming as Multiagent Programming.* Presented in the Workshop on Object Based Concurrent Programming (at ECOOP). 1991.
5. H. Bal, J. Steiner, A. Tanenbaum *Programming Languages for Distributed Computing Systems.* ACM Computing Surveys, Vol. 21, N. 3, September 1989.
6. A. Brogi, P. Ciancarini. *The Concurrent Language, Shared Prolog.* ACM TOPLAS, V. 13, N. 1, January 1991.
7. L. Brownston, R. Farrell, E. Kant, N. Martin. *Programming Expert Systems in OPS5: an Introduction to Rule-Based Progamming.* Addison-Wesley, Reading, Mass., 1985.
8. R. Back, R. Kurki-Suonio. *Distributed Cooperation with Action Systems.* ACM Trans. on Programming Languages and Systems, Vol. 10, N 4, 1988.
9. N. Carriero, D. Gelernter. *"Linda in Context".* Communications of the ACM, Vol. 32, N. 4, April 1989.
10. N. Carriero, D. Gelertner. *How to Write Parallel Programs: A Guide to the Perplexed.* ACM Computing Surveys, Vol. 21, N 3. September 1989.
11. *Comments on "Linda in Context".* Technical Correspondence, Communications of the ACM, Vol. 32, N. 10, October 1989.
12. K. Chandy, J. Misra. *Parallel Program Design.* Addison-Wesley, Reading, Massachusetts, 1988.
13. J.Y. Girard. *Linear Logic.* Theoretical Computer Science, 50 (1). 1987.
14. D. Harel, A. Pnueli. *On the development of Reactive Systems.* Logics and Models of Concurrent Systems, Ed. K. Apt, Springer Verlag, 1985.
15. C. Hoare. *Communicating Sequential Processes.* Communications of the ACM, Vol. 21, N. 8, August 1978.
16. L. Lamport. *A Temporal Logic of Actions.* Technical Report 57. SRC, 1990.
17. J. Lloyd. *Foundations of Logic Programming (second, extended edition).* Symbolic Computation Series. Sringer-Verlag. 1987.
18. R. Milner. *Communication and Concurrency.* Prentice-Hall, 1989.
19. A. Pnueli. *Application of Temporal Logic to the Specification and Verification of Reactive Systems: A Survey of Current Trends.* In Lecture Notes in Computer Science. Eds. J. de Bakker, W. de Roever, G. Rozenberg. Springer-Verlag. 1986.
20. A. Porto. *Logical Action Systems.* Proc. of the Logic Programming Workshop, Albufeira. UNL Portugal, 1983.
21. A. Porto, P. Rosado. *Deductions for Actions RT55/91-DI/UNL.* Technical Report. Dep. of Computer Science. Universidade Nova de Lisboa. Portugal. April 1991.
22. P. Rosado. *The AbstrAct Language.* Technical Report UNL-DI RT-16/92, Departamento de Informática, Universidade Nova de Lisboa, 1992.
23. V. Saraswat, D. Weinbaum, K.Kahn, E. Shapiro. *Detecting Stable Properties of Networks In Concurrent Logic Programming Languages.* Proc. of the ACM Conf. on principles of Distributed Computing, ACM Press. 1988.
24. E. Shapiro. *The Family of Concurrent Logic Programming Languages.* ACM Computing Surveys, Vol. 21, N. 3, September 1989.
25. *Object-Oriented Concurrent Programming.* Eds. A. Yonezawa, M. Tokoro, The MIT Press, 1987.

The π-calculus as a theory in linear logic: Preliminary results

Dale Miller

Computer Science Department
University of Pennsylvania
Philadelphia, PA 19104-6389 USA
dale@cis.upenn.edu

Abstract. The agent expressions of the π-calculus can be translated into a theory of linear logic in such a way that the reflective and transitive closure of π-calculus (unlabeled) reduction is identified with "entailed-by". Under this translation, parallel composition is mapped to the multiplicative disjunct ("par") and restriction is mapped to universal quantification. Prefixing, non-deterministic choice (+), replication (!), and the match guard are all represented using non-logical constants, which are specified using a simple form of axiom, called here a *process clause*. These process clauses resemble Horn clauses except that they may have multiple conclusions; that is, their heads may be the par of atomic formulas. Such multiple conclusion clauses are used to axiomatize communications among agents. Given this translation, it is nature to ask to what extent proof theory can be used to understand the meta-theory of the π-calculus. We present some preliminary results along this line for π_0, the "propositional" fragment of the π-calculus, which lacks restriction and value passing (π_0 is a subset of CCS). Using ideas from proof-theory, we introduce *co-agents* and show that they can specify some testing equivalences for π_0. If negation-as-failure-to-prove is permitted as a co-agent combinator, then testing equivalence based on co-agents yields observational equivalence for π_0. This latter result follows from observing that co-agents directly represent formulas in the Hennessy-Milner modal logic.

1 Introduction

In this paper we address the question "Can we view a given process calculus as a logic?" This is different (although certainly related) to the question "Can logic be used to characterize a given process calculus?" Such a question would view logic as an auxiliary language to that of the process calculus: for example, the Hennessy-Milner logic has such a relationship to CCS. Our approach here will be to use logic more immediately by trying to match combinators of the given process calculus directly to logical connectives and, if a combinator fails to match, trying to axiomatized it directly and uniformly in logic.

For our purposes here, we shall consider a formal system to be a logic if it has a sequent calculus presentation that admits a cut-elimination theorem. Of course, this definition of logic is not formal unless formal definitions of sequent calculi and cut-elimination are provided. We shall not attempt formal definitions of these two terms here: we simply make use of a couple examples of sequent calculus systems. A constant of the formal system will be considered *logical* if it has left and right introduction rules. A *non-logical* constant is any other constant whose meaning is specified by axioms or theories: such constants do not, in general, participate in a cut-elimination theorem.

There seems to be two broad ways in which connections between concurrency and proof theory can be and are being developed: one uses proof reduction and the other proof search.

The functional programming approach. Functional programs can be viewed as natural deduction proofs and computation on them as the process of proof normalization. Using familiar correspondences between natural deduction proofs and normalization with sequent calculus and cut-elimination in intuitionistic logic [Pot77, Fel91], functional programs can be seen as sequent proofs and computation as cut-elimination. Traditionally, the sequents used are of the form $\Delta \longrightarrow G$, where Δ is a set of propositions (generally typing judgments) and G is a single proposition. Such sequents are called ***single-conclusion*** sequents.

Following ideas of Girard presented in [Gir87], Abramsky [Abr90, Abr91] has extended this interpretation of computation to multiple-conclusion sequents, that is, sequents of the form $\Delta \longrightarrow \Gamma$, where Δ and Γ are both sets (actually, multisets) of propositions. In this setting, cut-elimination specifies concurrent programming. In particular, Abramsky presents a method for "realizing" the computational content of multiple-conclusion proofs in linear logic that yields concurrent programs in CCS, CSP, and the π-calculus. In these realized programs, cut-elimination in proofs is modeled by communication.

The logic programming approach. In the logic programming setting, programs are theories (collections of formulas) describing the meaning of non-logical constants and computation is identified with the search for cut-free sequent proofs. Here, the sequent $\Sigma; \Delta \longrightarrow G$ is used to represent the state of an idealized logic programming interpreter in which the current set of non-logical constants is Σ, the current logic program (theory) about those constants is the set of formulas Δ and the formula to be established, called the query or goal, is G.

A logic and proof system will be consider a logic programming language if a simple kind of ***goal-directed*** search is complete. This kind of definition of logic programming was first given in [MNPS91] for single-conclusion sequents, where the technical notion of ***uniform proof*** provides an analysis of goal-directed search. A uniform proof is a cut-free, single-conclusion sequent proof where every sequent whose right-hand side is non-atomic is the conclusion of a right-introduction rule. In an interpreter attempting to find a uniform proof, the structure of the right-hand side (the goal) can be reflected directly into the proof being constructed. The given logic and proof system is called an ***abstract logic programming language*** if a sequent has a proof if and only if it has a uniform proof. First-order and higher-order variants of Horn clauses and the more expressive hereditary

Harrop formulas can be used as the basis of abstract logic programming languages [MNPS91].

In abstract logic programming languages, the search semantics of a logical connective in the goal is independent from its context (the program): contexts are only considered to help in proving atomic formulas. For example, if our logical system is intuitionistic logic, an attempt to prove the sequent $\Sigma; \Delta \longrightarrow G_1 \vee G_2$ could be replaced by a proof of either $\Sigma; \Delta \longrightarrow G_1$ or $\Sigma; \Delta \longrightarrow G_2$, no matter what formulas are contained in Δ. This is not a complete strategy for full intuitionistic logic: while there is a proof of the sequent $\Sigma; p \vee q \longrightarrow q \vee p$, its last inference rule is not $\vee$-R, that is, there are no proofs of $\Sigma; p \vee q \longrightarrow q$ or of $\Sigma; p \vee q \longrightarrow p$. When the syntax of programs are restricted adequately, completeness of uniform proofs can be established. The resulting restriction then determines a logic programming language. Within this setting, cut-elimination plays the meta-theoretic role of guarantor of canonical models for logic programs (see, for example, [Mil92, HM92]).

Unfortunately, the definition of uniform proofs given here is restricted to only single-conclusion sequent proofs systems. Extending this notion of goal-directed search to multiple conclusion sequents runs into the following simple problem: if the right-hand side of a sequent contains two or more non-atomic formulas, how should the logical connectives at the head of those formulas be introduced? There seems to be two choices. One approach simply requires that one of the possible introductions be done. This has the disadvantage that there might be an interdependency between right-introduction rules in that one may need to appear lower is a proof than another. In this case, logical connectives in the goal would not reflect directly and simply into the structure of the proof. A second approach requires that all right-hand rules should be done simultaneously. Although it is difficult to deal with simultaneous rule application in the sequent calculus, we can employ permutations of inference rules within the sequent calculus [Kle52]. That is, we can require that if two or more right-introduction rules can be use to derive a given sequent, then all possible orders of applying those right-introduction rules can be obtained from any other order simply by permuting right-introduction inferences. Using this second approach, we shall say that a cut-free sequent proof Ξ is *uniform* if for every subproof Ψ of Ξ and for every non-atomic formula occurrence B in the right-hand side of the endsequent of Ψ, there is a proof Ψ' that is equal to Ψ up to permutation of inference rules and is such that the last inference rule in Ψ' introduces the top-level logical connective occurring in B. It is easy to see that this definition of uniform proof generalizes the one given above for single-conclusion sequents.

As we shall see , the π-calculus can be viewed as a multiple-conclusion logic programming language in the sense that certain sequents are provable if and only if they have multiple-conclusion uniform proofs.

Our analytic tools are taken from the sequent calculus, especially the refinement of that subject found in linear logic [Gir87], and from logic programming, particularly the topics of goal-directed provability and negation-as-failure. We shall investigate to what extent the framework of introduction rules, λ-

abstraction in terms and in proofs (also know as eigen-variables), and the central notion of cut-elimination helps in analyzing a process calculus. This work is preliminary: we shall only look at the π-calculus [MPW89a, MPW89b, Mil91, MPW91] as a particular example of a process calculus. This calculus is, of course, rich and presents several interesting challenges.

2 Translating π-calculus expressions into logic

Besides assuming some familiarity with sequent calculus, we shall also assume that the reader is familiar with the π-calculus as given in either [Mil90] or [MPW89a]. The principle mechanism of the π-calculus is the synchronization of two agents and the sending of a name from one agent to another. Synchronization is familiar from CCS; value passing is new to the π-calculus. The expression $\bar{x}z.P$ describes an agent that is willing to transmit the value z on the wire x (x and z are names). The expression $x(y).Q$ denotes an agent that is willing to receive a value on wire x and formally bind that value to y. The bound variable y in this expression is scoped over Q. The central computational step of the π-calculus is the reduction of the parallel composition $\bar{x}z.P \mid x(y).Q$ to the expression $P \mid Q[z/y]$. The agents P and $Q[z/y]$ are now able to continue their interactions with their environment independently.

The π-calculus differs from CCS also in that it has a notion of scope restriction: in the agent expression $(x)P$, x is bound and invisible to the outside. The scoped value x, however, can be communicated outside its scope, providing a phenomenon known as "scope extrusion." For example, $(z)(\bar{x}z.P \mid Q) \mid x(y).R$ is structurally equivalent to $(z)(\bar{x}z.P \mid Q \mid x(y).R)$, provided that z is not free in $x(y).R$. This scope restriction is always easy to accommodate since we shall assume that α-conversion is available for changing the name of bound variables. This expression can now be reduced to $(z)(P \mid Q \mid R[z/y])$, where the scope of the restriction (z) is larger since it contains the agent $R[z/y]$ in which z may be free. This mechanism of generating new names (using α-conversion) and sending them outside their scope is an important part of the computational power of the π-calculus.

The silent transition τ is not discussed at all in this paper: although the techniques described below should be able to address τ, the appropriate methods for this have not yet been investigated.

Below we describe three translations of π-calculus agent expressions into logical expressions. The first two are simple duals of each other; the third is a simplification of the first.

The disjunctive translation. The first translation requires the logical constants $\oplus$ (additive disjunction), $⅋$ (par, multiplicative disjunction), ? (the exponential "why not"), $\forall$, and $\bot$ (the identity for $⅋$). Given its dependence on the additive and multiplicative disjunctions of linear logic, this translation is called the disjunctive translation. The following three simply typed, non-logical constants are also required (assuming that the type of logical expressions is o and that of names is i):

$$\mathtt{send} : i \to i \to o \to o, \quad \mathtt{get} : i \to (i \to o) \to o, \quad \mathtt{match} : i \to i \to o \to o.$$

As should be clear from these types, we shall freely make use of higher-order types and λ-calculus to smooth the treatment of bound variables and variable scoping. All those details will be pressed into a simple meta-level that contains the simply typed λ-calculus and quantification at higher-order types.

The disjunctive translation is given by the following induction on the structure of agent expressions.

$$\langle\!\langle P + Q \rangle\!\rangle = \langle\!\langle P \rangle\!\rangle \oplus \langle\!\langle Q \rangle\!\rangle \qquad \langle\!\langle P \mid Q \rangle\!\rangle = \langle\!\langle P \rangle\!\rangle \parr \langle\!\langle Q \rangle\!\rangle$$
$$\langle\!\langle (x)P \rangle\!\rangle = \forall x \langle\!\langle P \rangle\!\rangle \qquad \langle\!\langle !\, P \rangle\!\rangle = ?\langle\!\langle P \rangle\!\rangle \qquad \langle\!\langle nil \rangle\!\rangle = \bot$$
$$\langle\!\langle \bar{x}y.P \rangle\!\rangle = \mathtt{send}\ x\ y\ \langle\!\langle P \rangle\!\rangle \qquad \langle\!\langle x(y).P \rangle\!\rangle = \mathtt{get}\ x\ \lambda y \langle\!\langle P \rangle\!\rangle$$
$$\langle\!\langle [x = y]P \rangle\!\rangle = \mathtt{match}\ x\ y\ \langle\!\langle P \rangle\!\rangle$$

To describe the meaning of the three non-logical constants, we have the following axioms.

$$\forall_i x \forall_i y \forall_o S \forall_{i \to o} R\ [Ry \parr S \multimap \mathtt{get}\ x\ R \parr \mathtt{send}\ x\ y\ S]$$
$$\forall_i x \forall_{i \to o} P\ [P \multimap \mathtt{match}\ x\ x\ P]$$

Notice that these axioms are higher-order in the sense that they allow quantification over predicate symbols. Such quantification is intended here to be purely syntactic: the type $i \to o$ denotes the set of closed, simply typed λ-terms of type $i \to o$ and not some abstract domain of functions. A similar treatment of higher-order type quantification for Horn clauses can be found in [NM90].

The conjunctive translation. It is trivial to dualize the disjunctive translation completely. That is, it is possible to map the "logical" combinators into the dual logical connectives.

$$\langle\!\langle P + Q \rangle\!\rangle = \langle\!\langle P \rangle\!\rangle \,\&\, \langle\!\langle Q \rangle\!\rangle \qquad \langle\!\langle P \mid Q \rangle\!\rangle = \langle\!\langle P \rangle\!\rangle \otimes \langle\!\langle Q \rangle\!\rangle$$
$$\langle\!\langle (x)P \rangle\!\rangle = \exists x \langle\!\langle P \rangle\!\rangle \qquad \langle\!\langle !\, P \rangle\!\rangle = !\langle\!\langle P \rangle\!\rangle \qquad \langle\!\langle nil \rangle\!\rangle = 1$$

In this case, the non-logical axioms would be axiomatized with the formulas

$$\forall_i x \forall_i y \forall_o S \forall_{i \to o} R\ [\mathtt{get}\ x\ R \otimes \mathtt{send}\ x\ y\ S \multimap Ry \otimes S]$$
$$\forall_i x \forall_o P\ [\mathtt{match}\ x\ x\ P \multimap P]$$

This translation is called *conjunctive* because it uses the multiplicative and additive conjunctions.

The formal analysis below is completely dualizable, so there appears to be no formal reason to pick one translation over the other. This seems to be the case because process calculus is fundamentally about reduction, while logic has made a commitment to both reduction (implies/implied-by) and to truth values. Truth values do not naturally map into processes. The disjunctive translation maps reduction to implied-by; the conjunctive translation to implies.

The following two extra-logical motivations can be offered for choosing the disjunctive translation over the conjunctive translation.

Goal reduction in logic programming and agent reduction in the π-calculus. In logic programming based on single-conclusion sequents, a uniform proof that results from the successful search for a proof of a sequent $\Sigma; \Delta \longrightarrow G$ records the goal reductions applied to G in the right-hand side of the proof's sequent when read from the bottom of the proof. If the disjunctive translation is used, a similar observation can be applied to the π-calculus: agent reduction is recorded in the right-hand sides of the sequents when read from the bottom. Andreoli and Pareschi [AP91] have made a similar choice in the representation of agent reduction using a kind of multiple-conclusion Horn clause. The conjunctive translation estranges this parallel since reductions would take place on the left-hand side.

Scope extrusion as a multiple-conclusion phenomenon. A natural notion of scoping occurs in logic programming based on single-conclusion sequents. For example, the search for a uniform proof of the sequent $\Sigma; \Delta \longrightarrow D \supset G$ reduces to the search for a uniform proof of the sequent $\Sigma; \Delta, D \longrightarrow G$. If Δ is considered to be the current program held by a logic programming interpreter, then D can be seen as a program unit that is added to the current program during a computation. A notion of modular programming for logic programming was developed in [Mil89] based on this simple observation. To enforce that this notion of modular programming obeys the correct notion of scoping, single conclusion sequent calculus is required. Consider, for example, searching for a uniform proof of the sequent $\Sigma; \Delta \longrightarrow G_1 \vee (D \supset G_2)$ using the usual intuitionistic introduction rules for $\vee$-R and $\supset$-R [Gen69]. This search would lead to the search for proofs of either the sequent $\Sigma; \Delta \longrightarrow G_1$ or $\Sigma; \Delta, D \longrightarrow G_2$. In particular, the formula D is only available to help prove the formula G_2: its scope does not include G_1. This formula is, however, classically equivalent to $(D \supset G_1) \vee G_2$ and $D \supset (G_1 \vee G_2)$. Thus the scope of D can move in ways not supported in intuitionistic logic. In particular, $p \vee (p \supset q)$ is not provable intuitionistically but it is classically. Gentzen's characterization of the differences between intuitionistic and classical logics as arising from differences in using single and multiple conclusion sequents provides an elegant analysis of scope extrusion. Consider the following sequent proof.

$$\cfrac{\cfrac{\overline{p \longrightarrow p, q}}{\longrightarrow p, p \supset q}}{\longrightarrow p \vee (p \supset q)}$$

The occurrence of p in the left of the initial sequent has as its scope all the formulas on the right: in the intuitionistic case, there can only be one such formula on the right and, hence, scope cannot be liberalized in this way.

If the disjunctive translation is used, scope extrusion in the π-calculus can be accounted for in an analogous fashion. In this case, however, scope extrusion arises between the interaction of the $\forall$-R rule and multiple conclusions. For a simple example, consider the sequent $\Sigma; p \longrightarrow (\forall x_i.q) \vee (\exists y_i.p)$, where we assume that Σ has no constant whose type contains i. This sequent is provable only if we admit multiple conclusion sequents in its proof. Below is a proof of this sequent.

$$\dfrac{\dfrac{\dfrac{\overline{\Sigma, x : i; p \longrightarrow q, p}}{\Sigma, x : i; p \longrightarrow q, \exists y_i.p}}{\Sigma; p \longrightarrow \forall x_i.q, \exists y_i.p}}{\Sigma; p \longrightarrow (\forall x_i.q) \vee (\exists y_i.p)}$$

Here, it is an eigen-variable that has its scope liberated. As we shall see, scope extrusion in the π-calculus will be explained by this use of eigen-variables. In the conjunctive translation, similar proofs are possible but the correspondence to scope extrusion in logic programming would disappear and the distinctions between single-conclusion and multiple-conclusion sequents would not then be relevant.

Structural equivalence. Before describing our final translation (a variant of the disjunctive translation), we present a simple method for determining structural equivalence between two agents. By $\Sigma; P \vdash Q$ we mean that the formula Q is provable from the formula P given the signature of constants Σ: a formal definition for this three-place predicate is given shortly. The notation $\Sigma; P \dashv\vdash Q$ simply means that $\Sigma; P \vdash Q$ and $\Sigma; Q \vdash P$. We shall extend the domain of $\vdash$ and $\dashv\vdash$ by allowing P and Q to be agent expressions: in this case, one of the above two translations is used to coerce an agent into a formula. Notice that the extension of $\Sigma; P \dashv\vdash Q$ is independent of which translation is used and if Σ is held fixed, the resulting binary relation is an equivalence. Also, since no axioms about communication or matching are used, only the logical identities are used to determine this equivalence. As a result, this equivalence to a good candidate for structural equivalence. Figure 1 provides some examples of $\Sigma; P \dashv\vdash Q$ and $\Sigma; P \vdash Q$ (for which we assume the use of the disjunctive translation described above).

A final translation. A much more serious aspect of the translation given above is the choice of which combinators should be genuine logical constants and which are axiomatized, non-logical constants. It seems an advantage to make as few of the combinators into logical connectives as possible as long as the remaining combinators can be described uniformly in terms of the logical ones. One reason for this advantage is that reduction steps map rather naturally into right introduction rules of the sequent calculus (this will be clear from the proof of Proposition 5), while the left introduction rules do not generally yield plausible reduction steps. For example, if $+$ is mapped to the logical constant $\oplus$ and if we wish reduction to be identified with entailed-by, then we are forced to admit the reduction rule: if P reduces to Q_1 and to Q_2, then P reduces to $Q_1 + Q_2$: a dubious "reduction" rule. Fortunately, it is possible to axiomatize the reduction nature of $+$ and ! by using the clauses

$$\forall_o P \forall_o Q\, [P \multimap P + Q] \qquad \forall_o P \forall_o Q\, [Q \multimap P + Q]$$
$$\forall_o P\, [\bot \multimap !P] \qquad \forall_o P\, [!P \parr !P \multimap !P] \qquad \forall_o P\, [P \multimap !P]$$

P	Q	$\Sigma; P \vdash Q$	$\Sigma; Q \vdash P$	$\Sigma; P \dashv\vdash Q$
$P \mid P$	P	no	no	no
$P + P$	P	yes	yes	yes
$(x)P$	$P[y/x]^{\S}$	yes	no	no
$(x)P^{\dagger}$	P	yes‡	yes	yes‡
$P \mid !P$	$!P$	yes	no	no
$!P$	$!P \mid !P$	yes	yes	yes
$!P$	nil	no	yes	no
$P_1 \mid (P_2 \mid P_3)$	$(P_1 \mid P_2) \mid P_3$	yes	yes	yes
$P_1 + (P_2 + P_3)$	$(P_1 + P_2) + P_3$	yes	yes	yes
$P \mid nil$	P	yes	yes	yes
$P \mid Q$	$Q \mid P$	yes	yes	yes
$P + Q$	$Q + P$	yes	yes	yes
$(x)(y)P$	$(y)(x)P$	yes	yes	yes
$(x)(P \mid Q)^{\dagger}$	$P \mid (x)Q$	yes	yes	yes
$(x)(P + Q)^{\dagger}$	$P + (x)Q$	no	yes	no
$(P_1 \mid P_2) + (P_1 \mid P_3)$	$P_1 \mid (P_2 + P_3)$	yes	no	no
$(P_1 + P_2) \mid (P_1 + P_3)$	$P_1 + (P_2 \mid P_3)$	no	no	no
$!P \mid !Q$	$!(P + Q)$	yes	yes	yes

(†) x is not free in P. (‡) Σ is not empty. (§) $y \in \Sigma$.

Fig. 1. Some logical implications and equivalences assuming the disjunctive translation and assuming that + and ! are mapped to logical constants.

These clauses encode right introduction rules without forcing us to accept the corresponding left introduction rules.

Instead of translating π-calculus expressions into the syntax of linear logic, we shall simply use the syntax of the π-calculus. We shall not make any distinction now between agents and formulas over the logical constants $\mid : o \to o \to o$, $(-) : (i \to o) \to o$, $nil : o$ and the non-logical constants $! : o \to o$, $+ : o \to o \to o$, plus the constructors for prefixing and matching, written $x(y).P$, $\bar{x}y.P$, and $[x = y]P$ of types $i \to (i \to o) \to o$, $i \to i \to o \to o$, and $i \to i \to o \to o$, respectively. We shall also assume that there is a denumerably infinite set of constants of type i.

Let Δ and Γ be finite, multisets of formulas. Let Σ be a *signature*, that is, a (possibly empty) set of typed constants. A term t is a Σ*-term* if t is closed and all constants in t are members of Σ. A sequent is a triple $\Sigma; \Delta \longrightarrow \Gamma$ where $\Delta \cup \Gamma$ contains formulas all of whose non-logical constants are from the set Σ. The notation $\Sigma; \Delta \vdash \Gamma$ means that the sequent $\Sigma; \Delta \longrightarrow \Gamma$ has a proof in linear logic (inference rules for the fragment of linear logic needed here are in Figures 2 and 3). The rule $(-)R$ has the proviso that $y \notin \Sigma$, and the rule $(-)L$ has the proviso that t is a Σ-term. Notice that the only inference rule with more than one premise is the left introduction rules for multiplicative disjunction. The structural rules of contraction and weakening are not present. The notation $\Sigma; \Delta \dashv\vdash \Gamma$ means $\Sigma; \Delta \vdash \Gamma$ and $\Sigma; \Gamma \vdash \Delta$. Again, the relation $\dashv\vdash$ will be used as structural equivalence. Since we have reduced the number of logical connectives, this equivalence is now weaker than is described in Figure 1. For example, $P+Q$ is no longer $\dashv\vdash$ related to $Q+P$.

The cut-elimination theorem for linear logic [Gir87] shows that the inference rules in Figure 3 are admissible with respect to the basic set of rules. Given the cut-elimination theorem, provability in this proof system is obviously decidable. Note that we have not given any status to the non-logical constants and their axioms in this proof system. We do this in the next section.

$$\frac{}{\Sigma; P \longrightarrow P}\ \text{initial} \qquad \frac{}{\Sigma; nil \longrightarrow}\ nil\text{-}L \qquad \frac{\Sigma; \Delta \longrightarrow \Gamma}{\Sigma; \Delta \longrightarrow nil, \Gamma}\ nil\text{-}R$$

$$\frac{\Sigma; P, \Delta_1 \longrightarrow \Gamma_1 \quad \Sigma; Q, \Delta_2 \longrightarrow \Gamma_2}{\Sigma; P \mid Q, \Delta_1, \Delta_2 \longrightarrow \Gamma_1, \Gamma_2}\ \mid L \qquad \frac{\Sigma; \Delta \longrightarrow P, Q, \Gamma}{\Sigma; \Delta \longrightarrow P \mid Q, \Gamma}\ \mid R$$

$$\frac{\Sigma; P[t/x], \Delta \longrightarrow \Gamma}{\Sigma; (x)P, \Delta \longrightarrow \Gamma}\ (-)L \qquad \frac{\Sigma \cup \{y\}; \Delta \longrightarrow P[y/x], \Gamma}{\Sigma; \Delta \longrightarrow (x)P, \Gamma}\ (-)R$$

Fig. 2. Basic inference rules

$$\frac{\Sigma; \Delta_1 \longrightarrow P, \Gamma_1 \quad \Sigma; P, \Delta_2 \longrightarrow \Gamma_2}{\Sigma; \Delta_1, \Delta_2 \longrightarrow \Gamma_1, \Gamma_2} \qquad \frac{t \text{ a } \Sigma\text{-term} \quad \Sigma \cup \{x\}; \Delta \longrightarrow \Gamma}{\Sigma; [t/x]\Delta \longrightarrow [t/x]\Gamma}$$

Fig. 3. Two forms of the cut-rule

3 Process clauses and process theories

We now step back from the particular example of the π-calculus to consider some general considerations of the logical framework we have picked.

A *process clause* is a closed formula of the form

$$\forall \bar{x}\, [P \multimap Q_1 \mid \cdots \mid Q_m]$$

where $m \geq 1$, P is an agent expression, $Q_1, \ldots, Q_m$ are atomic (formulas with non-logical constants as their head symbols), and all free variables in P (called the *body* of the clause) are free in $Q_1 \mid \cdots \mid Q_m$ (called the *head* of the clause). The quantified variables $\bar{x}$ may be of type i and o, as well as higher-order types, for example, $i \rightarrow o$. If $m = 1$, such a clauses is also called a *single-conclusion* clause; otherwise, it is called a *multiple-conclusion* clause. An instance of a process clause using Σ-terms (for a given Σ) is called a Σ-instance of that clause.

The propositional structure of process clauses is similar to the clauses studied by Andreoli and Pareschi [AP91] where & and $\top$ (erasure) are also permitted in the body of clauses: their formalism, however, permits neither universal quantification in the body of clauses nor quantification of higher-type variables.

A *process theory* is a finite, possibly empty, set H of process clauses. An H-*proof* is a proof built using the rules in Figure 2 and one inference of the form

$$\frac{\Sigma;\Delta \longrightarrow \Gamma, P}{\Sigma;\Delta \longrightarrow \Gamma, Q_1,\ldots,Q_m}$$

for every clause $\forall\bar{x}\,[P \multimap Q_1 \mid \cdots \mid Q_m]$ in H. When an H-clause is written as an inference rule in this way, that inference rule is called an H-inference rule. Let Σ be a signature that contains all the non-logical constants contained in clauses of H. We write $\Sigma;\Delta \vdash_H \Gamma$ to mean that the sequent $\Sigma;\Delta \longrightarrow \Gamma$ has an H-proof. The structure of H-proofs are particularly simple, as we shall now see.

The *site* of an instance of an inference rule is a multiset of occurrence of formulas in the concluding sequent defined using the following cases: if the inference rule is the initial rule proving the sequent $\Sigma; P \longrightarrow P$, then the site is the multiset containing both occurrences of P; the site for an introduction rule is the singleton multiset containing the formula occurrence containing the introduced logical constant; and the site for an H-inference rule based on the clause $\forall\bar{x}\,[P \multimap Q_1 \mid \cdots \mid Q_m]$ is the multiset containing the occurrences of the instances of the formulas $Q_1,\ldots,Q_m$. Two inference rules *permute* if whenever instances of these two rules have a common sequent as a conclusion and the sites of these two inference rule instances are disjoint, then those inference rules can be composed in either order to yield identical premises to their composition. When doing a bottom-up search for proofs, the order in which permuting inference rules are applied is not important. For example, the following two proof fragments demonstrate that $(-)R$ and $|R$ permute over each other.

$$\frac{\dfrac{\Sigma, y:i;\Delta \longrightarrow P, Q, [y/x]R, \Gamma}{\Sigma;\Delta \longrightarrow P, Q, (x)R, \Gamma}}{\Sigma;\Delta \longrightarrow P \mid Q, (x)R, \Gamma} \qquad \frac{\dfrac{\Sigma, y:i;\Delta \longrightarrow P, Q, [y/x]R, \Gamma}{\Sigma, y:i;\Delta \longrightarrow P \mid Q, [y/x]R, \Gamma}}{\Sigma;\Delta \longrightarrow P \mid Q, (x)R, \Gamma}$$

We assume here that $y \notin \Sigma$.

Proposition 1 *All pairs of right rules (nil-R, |R, and (−)R) and H-inference rules permute over each other.*

Proof. This proposition follows from simply checking all cases. The case where a $(-)R$ inference rule is below an H-inference rule requires the assumption about process clauses that all free variables in the body of clauses are also free in their head. □

Consider the process theory that contains the single process clause

$$\forall P \forall Q \forall x [P \mid Q \multimap x.P \mid \bar{x}.Q].$$

Here, prefixing is represented by two non-logical constants, both of type $i \rightarrow o \rightarrow o$. The order of the two H-rules in the proof fragment

$$\frac{\dfrac{\Sigma; P \mid Q \mid R \longrightarrow P, Q, R}{\Sigma; P \mid Q \mid R \longrightarrow b.P, Q, \bar{b}.R}}{\Sigma; P \mid Q \mid R \longrightarrow a.b.P, \bar{a}.Q, \bar{b}.R}$$

cannot be switched: the site of the lower rule contains a subformula that is in the site of the upper rule. Notice also that a sequent with right-hand side $a.P, \bar{a}.Q, \bar{a}.R$ can be the result of an H-inference rule in two ways: the choice of one of these precludes the other choice.

Proposition 2 *If $\Sigma; \Delta \longrightarrow \Gamma$ has an H-proof, it has an H-proof Ξ such that Ξ has an occurrence of a sequent $\Sigma'; \Delta \longrightarrow \Gamma'$ where all inference rules above this sequent occurrence are left introduction rules and instances of the initial inference rule and all inference rules below this sequent occurrence are right introduction rules or H-inference rules.*

The sequent $\Sigma'; \Delta \longrightarrow \Gamma'$ is called the *crossover sequent* for the proof Ξ.

Proof. Let Ψ be an H-proof of $\Sigma; \Delta \longrightarrow \Gamma$. If there is no pair of inference rules such that the lower one is a left introduction rule and the upper one is a right introduction rule or an H-inference rule, then Ψ has the structure described for the Ξ in the proof. Otherwise, assume that such a pair of inference rules exists. It is then possible to permute the order of these two rules and still have a proof of the same endsequent. The fact that a |-L below a (−)-R rule can be permuted requires observing the general fact that if $\Sigma; \Delta \longrightarrow \Gamma$ has an H-proof then $\Sigma'; \Delta \longrightarrow \Gamma$ has an H-proof whenever Σ' is a signature that contains Σ. A simple inductive argument then shows that by doing enough permutations, all such pairs of inference rules can be removed. □

Corollary 1. *If $\Sigma; \Delta \longrightarrow \Gamma$ has an H-proof then Δ must be a singleton multiset.*

Proof. Assume not and let $\Sigma; \Delta \longrightarrow \Gamma$ be a sequent in which Δ contains more than one member and which has an H-proof Ξ of minimal height. Clearly, $\Sigma; \Delta \longrightarrow \Gamma$ is not an initial sequent. But it is simple to check that no matter what its last inference rule is, Ξ must contain a proper subproof of a sequent containing more than one formula on its left. This contradicts the choice of Ξ. □

Proposition 3 *The two cut rules of Figure 3 are admissible in H-proofs.*

Proof. Let Ξ_1 be an H-proof for $\Sigma; Q \longrightarrow P, \Gamma_1$ and let Ξ_2 be an H-proof for $\Sigma; P \longrightarrow \Gamma_2$. We must show that there is an H-proof for $\Sigma; Q \longrightarrow \Gamma_1, \Gamma_2$. First, we can assume that the last inference rule in Ξ_2 is a left introduction rule or the initial sequent rule since cut permutes up through all the right introduction rules and H-inference rules for proofs of this premise. Similarly, we can assume that the last inference rule in Ξ_1 is either a right introduction rule or an H-inference rule in which the occurrence of P is in the site. Now, if P has a top-level logical constant, then Ξ_1 ends in a right introduction of that constant and Ξ_2 ends in a left introduction of that constant. The usual movement of cut upwards in a proof will work in this case. Finally, if P is atomic, then Γ_2 is the multiset that consists of just P, so we can simply use Ξ_1 as the proof of $\Sigma; Q \longrightarrow \Gamma_1, \Gamma_2$.

The proof that the other cut rule involving substitution is admissible is simpler and more direct. □

The following proposition demonstrates that process theories can be viewed as multiple conclusion logic programming languages.

Proposition 4 ***The sequent has an H-proof if and only if it has a uniform H-proof.***

Proof. Assume that Ξ is a cut-free, atomically closed sequent proof. An ***atomically closed*** proof is a proof in which all initial sequents contain only atomic formulas: it is easy to show that a sequent has a proof if and only if it has an atomically closed proof. Using the definition of uniform proofs for multiple conclusion sequents given in the introduction, we now show that Ξ is, in fact, a uniform proof. Let Ψ be a subproof of Ξ that proves the sequent $\Sigma; \Delta \longrightarrow \Gamma$ and let B be a non-atomic formula occurrence in Γ. Since the sites of H-rules contain only atoms and since initial sequent rules involve only atoms, the top-level logical connective of B must be introduced somewhere is Ψ. Given that all left rules can be permuted upward through a proof and that all right-rules and H-inference rules also permute over each other, a series of permutations can carry the proof Ψ into a proof Ψ' in which the last inference rule introduces the top-level logical connective of B. Thus, Ξ is a uniform proof. □

Process calculi are generally described using a notion of reduction. We will focus on unlabeled reduction, such as is found in [Mil90]; an example of labeled reductions is used in Section 5. Figures 4, 5, and 6 present a proof system for a formulation of reduction determined by a process theory H. The following proposition shows the close relation between $\vdash_H$ and such reduction.

$$\frac{}{\Sigma; S \Longrightarrow R}\ \mathrm{H}$$

Fig. 4. Theory reduction rules: provided that $R \multimap S$ is a Σ-instance of a clause in H.

$$\frac{\Sigma \cup \{x\}; P \Longrightarrow P'}{\Sigma; (x)P \Longrightarrow P'}\ \mathrm{INS} \qquad \frac{t \text{ is a } \Sigma\text{-term} \quad \Sigma; Q \Longrightarrow P[t/x]}{\Sigma; Q \Longrightarrow (x)P}\ \mathrm{GEN}$$

$$\frac{\Sigma; P \Longrightarrow P'}{\Sigma; P \mid Q \Longrightarrow P' \mid Q}\ \mathrm{PAR}$$

Fig. 5. Descent reduction rules: In INS, x is not free in P'.

$$\frac{\Sigma; P \dashv\vdash Q}{\Sigma; P \Longrightarrow Q}\ \mathrm{REF} \qquad \frac{\Sigma; P \Longrightarrow Q \quad \Sigma; Q \Longrightarrow R}{\Sigma; P \Longrightarrow R}\ \mathrm{TRANS}$$

Fig. 6. Structural reduction rules.

Proposition 5 *Let H be a process theory and let reduction be defined with respect to it. Then $\Sigma; Q \Longrightarrow P$ has a proof if and only if $\Sigma; P \vdash_H Q$.*

Proof. First, assume that $\Sigma; Q \Longrightarrow P$ has a reduction proof. Proceed by induction on the structure of that proof. If the proof is of height 1, then it is an instance of either a theory reduction rule or the REF rule. In each case, it follows immediately that $\Sigma; P \vdash_H Q$.

To handle the remaining structural rule, assume that the proof ends in an instance of the TRANS rule. By induction, $\Sigma; R \vdash_H Q$ and $\Sigma; Q \vdash P$, and thus $\Sigma; R \vdash_H P$ by cut.

Assume that the last inference rule was a descent reduction rule. If that rule is INS, then induction guarantees that $\Sigma \cup \{x\}; P' \longrightarrow P$ has a proof. Adding the $(-)R$ rules yields a proof for $\Sigma; P' \longrightarrow (x)P$. Similarly, if that rule is GEN then induction provides a proof of $\Sigma; P[t/x] \longrightarrow Q$ where t is a Σ-term. Adding the $(-)L$ rule yields a proof of $\Sigma; (x)P \longrightarrow Q$. If that rule is PAR, then induction provides a proof of $\Sigma; P' \longrightarrow P$. Using the initial sequent $\Sigma; Q \longrightarrow Q$ and the $|L$ and $|R$ rules yields a proof of $\Sigma; P' \mid Q \longrightarrow P \mid Q$.

Now consider the converse of this proposition. That is, assume that $\Sigma; P \longrightarrow Q_1, \ldots, Q_n$ has an H-proof. We prove by induction on the structure of a (cut-free) H-proof that $\Sigma; Q_1 \mid \cdots \mid Q_n \Longrightarrow P$ has a reduction proof. (If $n = 0$ then $Q_1 \mid \cdots \mid Q_n$ is simply *nil*.)

Case initial: If the proof is an instance of the initial rule, then $n = 1$ and Q_1 is P. The reduction proof is simply an instance of the REF rule.

Case nil-R: The final sequent is $\Sigma; P \longrightarrow nil, Q_1, \ldots, Q_n$ and induction provides a proof of $\Sigma; Q_1 \mid \cdots \mid Q_n \Longrightarrow P$. Noticing that $\Sigma; nil \mid R \dashv\vdash R$ for any R, use the REF and TRANS rules to provide a reduction proof for $\Sigma; nil \mid Q_1 \mid \cdots \mid Q_n \Longrightarrow P$.

Case $|R$: The final sequent is $\Sigma; P \longrightarrow P \mid Q, Q_1, \ldots, Q_n$ and induction provides a proof of $\Sigma; (P \mid Q) \mid Q_1 \mid \cdots \mid Q_n \Longrightarrow P$. If this is not the desired reduction sequent already, simply use REF and TRANS to associate the $|$'s differently.

Case $(-)R$: The final sequent is $\Sigma; P \longrightarrow (x)Q, Q_1, \ldots, Q_n$ and induction provides a proof of $\Sigma \cup \{y\}; Q[y/x] \mid Q_1 \mid \cdots \mid Q_n \Longrightarrow P$. Adding the INS proof rule yields a proof of $\Sigma; (y)(Q[y/x] \mid Q_1 \mid \cdots \mid Q_n) \Longrightarrow P$. Since $\Sigma; (y)(Q[y/x] \mid Q_1 \mid \cdots \mid Q_n) \dashv\vdash (x)Q \mid Q_1 \mid \cdots \mid Q_n$, a use of REF and TRANS yields a proof of $\Sigma; (x)Q \mid Q_1 \mid \cdots \mid Q_n \Longrightarrow P$.

Case H-inference rule: The final sequent is $\Sigma; P \longrightarrow Q_1, \ldots, Q_i, \ldots, Q_n$ and $R \multimap Q_1 \mid \cdots \mid Q_i$ is a Σ-instance of a rule in H. Thus, induction provides a proof of $\Sigma; R \mid Q_{i+1} \mid \cdots \mid Q_n \Longrightarrow P$. But by the H-rule (Figure 4), we have $\Sigma; Q_1 \mid \cdots \mid Q_i \Longrightarrow R$. By $n - i$ applications of PAR, we have $\Sigma; Q_1 \mid \cdots \mid Q_n \Longrightarrow R \mid Q_{i+1} \mid \cdots \mid Q_n$. A use of TRANS and we are finished.

Case nil-L: The final sequent is $\Sigma; nil \longrightarrow$. But $\Sigma; nil \Longrightarrow nil$ follows from REF.

Case $|L$: The final sequent is $\Sigma; P_1 | P_2 \longrightarrow Q_1, \ldots, Q_n$ and induction provides proofs of $\Sigma; Q_1 \mid \cdots \mid Q_i \Longrightarrow P_1$ and $\Sigma; Q_{i+1} \mid \cdots \mid Q_n \Longrightarrow P_2$, so $i = 1, \ldots, n$. (Of course, it is permitted to permute the Q's prior to splitting them.) Using

$n-i$ applications of PAR provides a reduction proof of $\Sigma; Q_1 \mid \cdots \mid Q_n \Longrightarrow P_1 \mid Q_{i+1} \mid \cdots \mid Q_n$. One application of PAR yields $\Sigma; P_1 \mid Q_{i+1} \mid \cdots \mid Q_n \Longrightarrow P_1 \mid P_2$. Thus, one use of TRANS provides a reduction proof of $\Sigma; Q_1 \mid \cdots \mid Q_n \Longrightarrow P_1 \mid P_2$.

Case $(-)L$: The final sequent is $\Sigma; (x)P \longrightarrow Q_1, \ldots, Q_n$ and induction provides a proof of $\Sigma; Q_1 \mid \cdots \mid Q_n \Longrightarrow P[t/x]$ for t a Σ-term. The GEN rule immediately yields $\Sigma; Q_1 \mid \cdots \mid Q_n \Longrightarrow (x)P$. □

4 Reduction in the π-calculus

We should like to identify reduction in the π-calculus with the reduction relation defined in the previous section using the signature

$$\Sigma_\pi = \{\mathtt{send} : i \to i \to o \to o,\ \mathtt{get} : i \to (i \to o) \to o,\ \mathtt{match} : i \to i \to o \to o,\ ! : o \to o,\ + : o \to o \to o\}$$

and the following theory, which we shall call the π-theory.

$$\forall_i x \forall_i y \forall_o S \forall_{i \to o} R\, [Ry \parr S \multimap \mathtt{get}\ x\ R \parr \mathtt{send}\ x\ y\ S]$$
$$\forall_i x \forall_{i \to o} P\, [P \multimap \mathtt{match}\ x\ x\ P]$$
$$\forall_o P \forall_o Q\, [P \multimap P + Q] \qquad \forall_o P \forall_o Q\, [Q \multimap P + Q]$$
$$\forall_o P\, [\bot \multimap !P] \qquad \forall_o P\, [!P \parr !P \multimap !P] \qquad \forall_o P\, [P \multimap !P]$$

A π-proof is an H-proof, where H is the set of axioms displayed above. We write $\Sigma; \Delta \vdash_\pi \Gamma$ if the sequent $\Sigma_\pi \cup \Sigma; \Delta \longrightarrow \Gamma$ has a π-proof. Notice that since Σ_π contains no constructors for type i, the signature Σ can be restricted to being composed only of tokens of type i. Thus, t is a Σ-term if and only if $t \in \Sigma$: the only values used during computations (search for proofs) are names and not general terms.

Notice that it is very easy to accommodate definition of agents using process clauses: the definition $C(\bar{x}) = P$, where the free variables of P are contained in the list $\bar{x}$, can be translated to the process clauses $\forall \bar{x}[P \multimap C(\bar{x})]$. Such clauses can be added to the base π-theory.

Since the notion of reduction is central to the definition of a process calculus, we must be very careful in making any claim to having captured the π-calculus as it is described in, say, [MPW89a, MPW89b]. There seems to be at least the following significant differences with the description given in those reports.

1. Signatures are made explicit and reductions depend on them.
2. The $+$ and $!$ combinators are treated only via computation rules: there are no rules for explicitly descending through them. Thus several reduction steps defined here may be needed to account for a single reduction step of the π-calculus.
3. The GEN and INS rules do not correspond to any rules of [MPW89a, MPW89b]. As a reduction rule, GEN does seem odd since it does not seem to be making anything simpler. Its main purpose seems to be that it allows the result of a reduction to discharge its dependence on any part of the surrounding signature. Notice that a version of the reduction rule for restriction

in the π-calculus can be proved here: if $\Sigma \cup \{x\}; P \Longrightarrow Q$ can be proved then by one instance each of GEN and INS, we have a proof of $\Sigma; (x)P \Longrightarrow (x)Q$.

Given our plan to use proof theory to organize the syntax of process calculi, these differences seem forced. Probably only additional results will tell us if what is defined here is significantly different from the π-calculus of [MPW89a]. Of course, the process calculi defined here may be of their own interest.

5 An analysis of the propositional fragment

Because the π-calculus communicates values of type i only, we shall think of the π-calculus as a first-order theory. In this section we analysis the "propositional" fragment of the π-calculus. In particular, we shall only be interested in synchronization and not with value passing, binding, or restriction, or with match. Thus, agent expressions in the propositional calculus are defined via the grammar

$$P ::= nil \quad | \quad P_1 \,|\, P_2 \quad | \quad P_1 + P_2 \quad | \quad !P \quad | \quad a.P \quad | \quad \bar{a}.P,$$

where, a ranges over some fixed, finite set of names Σ_0. We refer to this propositional theory as the π_0-calculus. It is determined by the signature

$$\Sigma_{\pi_0} = \{\mathbf{send} : i \rightarrow o \rightarrow o,\ \mathbf{get} : i \rightarrow o \rightarrow o,\ ! : o \rightarrow o,\ + : o \rightarrow o \rightarrow o\}$$

and the following set of process clauses.

$$\forall_i x \forall_o S \forall_o R\, [R \parr S \multimap \mathbf{get}\ x\ R \parr \mathbf{send}\ x\ S]$$
$$\forall_o P \forall_o Q\, [P \multimap P + Q] \qquad \forall_o P \forall_o Q\, [Q \multimap P + Q]$$
$$\forall_o P\, [\bot \multimap !P] \qquad \forall_o P\, [!P \parr !P \multimap !P] \qquad \forall_o P\, [P \multimap !P]$$

We shall, of course, identify $\mathbf{get}\ a\ P$ and $\mathbf{send}\ a\ P$ with $a.P$ and $\bar{a}.P$, respectively, and identify $\bar{\bar{a}}$ with a. A π_0-proof is an H-proof, where H is the set of axioms displayed above. We write $\Delta \vdash_{\pi_0} \Gamma$ if the sequent $\Sigma_{\pi_0} \cup \Sigma_0; \Delta \longrightarrow \Gamma$ has a π_0-proof. Since agents of the π_0-calculus do not contain universal quantification, all occurrences of signatures in any π_0-proof are equal and, therefore, we shall choose not to display signatures. The π_0-calculus is essentially a subset of CCS.

Given this proof-theoretic setting, a natural way to attribute meaning $[\![P]\!]$ to an agent P is via the definition

$$[\![P]\!] = \{W \mid\ \vdash_{\pi_0} P \,|\, W, \text{ where } W \text{ is an agent}\}.$$

The goal would then be to say that two agents, P and Q, are equivalent, in some sense, if $[\![P]\!] = [\![Q]\!]$. Unfortunately, using this definition, all agents are equivalent since $[\![P]\!]$ is always empty: there is no notion of a "true" agent. The only notion we have so far is that of one agent reducing to (implied-by) another.

Since we are inside a logic containing many more logical constants than we are using so far, it is possible to extend the notion of agents to *co-agents*, one of which will be "truth." Given some notion of co-agents, we shall define the meaning of agents using

$$[\![P]\!] = \{W \mid \vdash_{\pi_0} P \mid W, \text{ where } W \text{ is a co-agent}\}.$$

Thus, co-agents will be used to probe the behavior of agents. It is important to make the following observation: no matter what we choose for co-agents, if $[\![P]\!] \subseteq [\![Q]\!]$ then $[\![P+Q]\!] = [\![Q]\!]$. Thus, if $[\![P]\!] \subseteq [\![Q]\!]$ is ever strictly true, we have not captured deadlock within our theory of equivalence.

$$\frac{}{\Sigma;\Delta \longrightarrow \top, \Gamma}\ \top\text{-R} \qquad \frac{\Sigma;\Delta \longrightarrow \Gamma, W_1 \quad \Sigma;\Delta \longrightarrow \Gamma, W_2}{\Sigma;\Delta \longrightarrow \Gamma, W_1 \,\&\, W_2}\ \&\text{-R}$$

Fig. 7. Proof rules for the two co-agent connectives $\top$ and &.

In analyzing the π_0-calculus, we shall first introduce two co-agents, identified as the two (linear) logical connectives $\top$ (erasure) and & (additive conjunction) for which their right introduction rules are given in Figure 7. Assume for now that we define a co-agent to be any expression that contains at least one occurrence of either $\top$ or &. We can make the following observations regarding occurrences of $\top$ in $[\![P]\!]$.

- It is always the case that $\top \in [\![P]\!]$.
- The agent P has an a-transition if and only if $\bar{a}.\top \in [\![P]\!]$.
- The agent P has an a-transition followed by a b-transition if and only if $\bar{a}.\bar{b}.\top \in [\![P]\!]$.

Thus, P has a trace $a_1, \ldots, a_n$ if and only if $\bar{a}_1.\cdots.\bar{a}_n.\top \in [\![P]\!]$. If $\top$ were the only co-agent, then the equivalence described by $[\![P]\!] = [\![Q]\!]$ would be that of trace equivalence.

By allowing & as a co-agent expression, we can make more distinctions between the behaviors of agents. For example, let P be $a.b.nil + a.(c.nil + d.nil)$ and let Q be $a.(b.nil + c.nil) + a.d.nil$. While these have the same traces, the co-agent $\bar{a}.(\bar{c}.\top \,\&\, \bar{d}.\top)$ is a member of $[\![P]\!]$ but not of $[\![Q]\!]$. Notice, however, that since $[\![a.b.nil]\!] \subseteq [\![a.(b.nil + c.nil)]\!]$, it follows that $[\![a.(b.nil + c.nil)]\!] = [\![a.b.nil + a.(b.nil + c.nil)]\!]$.

Clearly, co-agents are acting as testers. The logical constant $\top$ behaves very much as the w tester in [Hen88]. The logical constant & specifies two tests that a process must satisfy simultaneous: in a sense, the process must be copied and the two copies must be able to satisfy two separate tests. Thus co-agents treat agents extensionally, that is, as black boxes whose internal structure is not examined directly. Consider what would happen if $\otimes$ (the multiplicative conjunction) were permitted to also be a co-agent connective. The co-agent $W_1 \otimes W_2$ would require that the agent being tested be divided into two pieces, one of which must pass

W_1 and the other W_2. While such a tensor tester may have its uses, we do not consider it any further here.

It will be important for a subsequent result (regarding bisimilarity) that we allow possibly infinite conjunctions. Let I be a denumerable set (possibly empty). The right introduction rule for $\&_{i\in I}$ is given by the inference figure

$$\frac{\longrightarrow \Gamma, W_{i_1} \cdots \longrightarrow \Gamma, W_{i_j} \cdots}{\longrightarrow \Gamma, \&_{i\in I} W_i},$$

where $I = \{i_1, \ldots, i_j, \ldots\}$. If the index set is empty, then $\&_{i\in I}$ is the same as $\top$ and if the index set has two element, then $\&_{i\in I}$ is the same as $\&$. The term *co-agent* now refers to any agent expression containing at least one occurrence of $\&_{i\in I}$, where I is not a singleton.

The following proposition shows that if co-agents are only used to define testing equivalence, they only need to be built up out of prefixing and the co-agent combinator $\&_{i\in I}$.

Proposition 6 *Define $[\![\Gamma]\!]_1$ to be the set of all multisets of agents and co-agents Δ such that $\vdash_{\pi_0} \Gamma, \Delta$. Define $[\![\Gamma]\!]_2$ to be the set of co-agents W built exclusively from occurrences of the indexed & and prefixing so that $\vdash_{\pi_0} \Gamma, W$. For multisets of agents Γ and Ψ, $[\![\Gamma]\!]_1 = [\![\Psi]\!]_1$ if and only if $[\![\Gamma]\!]_2 = [\![\Psi]\!]_2$.*

Proof. The proof that $[\![\Gamma]\!]_1 = [\![\Psi]\!]_1$ implies $[\![\Gamma]\!]_2 = [\![\Psi]\!]_2$ is immediate. Thus, assume that $[\![\Gamma]\!]_2 = [\![\Psi]\!]_2$ and that Δ is a multiset of agents and co-agents such that $\vdash_{\pi_0} \Gamma, \Delta$. Consider the proof system given Figure 8. A π_0-proof of $\longrightarrow \Gamma, \Delta$ can then be extended to a proof in Figure 8 of $\longrightarrow \Gamma \boxed{R} \Delta$, for some R built exclusively from occurrences of the indexed & and prefixing. Thus, $R \in [\![\Gamma]\!]_2$ and $R \in [\![\Psi]\!]_2$. Now given a π_0-proof of $\longrightarrow \Psi, R$ and the proof of $\longrightarrow \Gamma \boxed{R} \Delta$, it is an easy to construct a proof of $\longrightarrow \Psi \boxed{R} \Delta$. Thus, $\vdash_{\pi_0} \Psi, \Delta$ and $\Delta \in [\![\Psi]\!]_1$. The converse inclusion is similar. □

The following proposition describes the fact that in the bottom-up search for proofs involving co-agents, the top-level logical structure of co-agents can be addressed first. We shall strive to preserve this property when we add one more connective to the structure of co-agents.

Proposition 7 *If $\longrightarrow \Gamma, W$ has a proof, where Γ is a multiset of agents and W is a co-agent built exclusively from occurrences of the indexed & and prefixing, then this sequent has a proof Ξ such that for every occurrence of a sequent in Ξ, if the co-agent expression in that sequent is a top-level $\&_{i\in I}$ then that sequent occurrence is the conclusion of a $\&_{i\in I}$-R introduction rule.*

Proof. This can be proved by a observing that if there is an inference rule in a proof of $\longrightarrow \Gamma, W$ immediately below an instance of a $\&_{i\in I}$-R introduction rule, then the $\&_{i\in I}$-R introduction rule can be permuted lower. □

$$\frac{\longrightarrow \Gamma \boxed{R} \Delta}{\longrightarrow nil, \Gamma \boxed{R} \Delta} \qquad \frac{\longrightarrow P, Q, \Gamma \boxed{R} \Delta}{\longrightarrow P \mid Q, \Gamma \boxed{R} \Delta} \qquad \frac{\longrightarrow \Gamma, Q \boxed{R} \Delta}{\longrightarrow \Gamma, P \boxed{R} \Delta}\dagger$$

$$\frac{\longrightarrow \Gamma \boxed{R} \Delta}{\longrightarrow \Gamma \boxed{R} nil, \Delta} \qquad \frac{\longrightarrow \Gamma \boxed{R} P, Q, \Delta}{\longrightarrow \Gamma \boxed{R} P \mid Q, \Delta} \qquad \frac{\longrightarrow \Gamma \boxed{R} Q, \Delta}{\longrightarrow \Gamma \boxed{R} P, \Delta}\dagger$$

$$\frac{\longrightarrow P, Q, \Gamma \boxed{R} \Delta}{\longrightarrow a.P, \bar{a}.Q, \Gamma \boxed{R} \Delta} \qquad \frac{\longrightarrow P, \Gamma \boxed{R} Q, \Delta}{\longrightarrow a.P, \Gamma \boxed{\bar{a}.R} \bar{a}.Q, \Delta} \qquad \frac{\longrightarrow \Gamma \boxed{R} P, Q, \Delta}{\longrightarrow \Gamma \boxed{R} a.P, \bar{a}.Q, \Delta}$$

$$\frac{\text{for all } i \in I \quad \longrightarrow \Gamma \boxed{R_i} W_i, \Delta}{\longrightarrow \Gamma \boxed{\&_{i \in I} R_i} \&_{i \in I} W_i, \Delta}$$

Fig. 8. A proof system used for "interpolating" between agents and co-agents. The † proviso: $Q \multimap P$ is a instance of a single conclusion π_0-axiom.

So far co-agents are extracting only positive information. The equivalence of processes, $[P] = [Q]$, does not come close to the notion of bisimulation since it is not possible to test for what a process cannot do. For this, it appears necessary to leave the usual logical connectives and their introduction rules and develop a notion of negation as "failing to pass a test" or of "negation-as-failure," as it is often called in the logic programming literature.

A notion of negation-as-failure cannot be achieved by simply adding introduction rules. Instead we shall use a hierarchy of proof systems $\{S_n \mid n = 0, 1, 2, \ldots\}$ such that S_n can handle a nesting of at most n occurrences of negation and where non-provable sequents in the S_n proof system yield initial sequents (axioms) for negation in the S_{n+1} proof system (S_0 is identified with the π_0 proof system). Even given this hierarchy of proof systems, negation can still cause us one serious problem. Notice that the sequent $\longrightarrow a.nil, \bar{b}.\top$ has no π_0-proof. Thus, in the S_1 proof system, we shall accept the sequent $\longrightarrow a.nil, \neg\bar{b}.\top$ as initial. If we do not add any further restrictions, there will also be an S_1 proof of $\longrightarrow a.nil + b.nil, \neg\bar{b}.\top$. This conclusion is not acceptable since there is a S_0-proof (and, hence, S_1 proof) of $\longrightarrow a.nil + b.nil, \bar{b}.\top$. Thus, it would be possible for an agent $(a.nil + b.nil)$ to pass a test $(\bar{b}.\top)$ and its complement. A suitable solution to this problem is to insist that proofs in S_n introduce $\neg$ as early as possible; that is, require that any S_{n+1} proof of a sequent $\longrightarrow \Gamma, \neg W$ be, in fact, an initial sequent of S_{n+1}. Notice that this condition is essentially equivalent to the one which can be verified for $\&_{i \in I}$ (Proposition 7). With negation, however, this condition cannot be inferred so we must enforce it.

Given this motivation, we can now make the following definitions. Let C_n for $n \geq 0$ be sets of expressions defined by the following recursion on the structure of formulas.

- If I is a denumerable (possibly empty) set and for all $i \in I$, $W_i \in C_n$ then $\&_{i\in I} W_i \in C_n$.
- If $P \in C_n$ then $a.P \in C_n$ and $\bar{a}.P \in C_n$.
- If $P \in C_n$ then $\neg P \in C_{n+1}$.

We now introduce, for each $n \geq 0$, a proof system S_n. Sequents in S_n-proofs will be of the form $\longrightarrow \Gamma, W$ where Γ is a multiset of agents and $W \in C_n$. For each $n \geq 0$, S_n contains the right introduction rules for *nil*, $|$, and $\&_{i\in I}$ as well as the inference rules for all the π_0-theory axioms. In particular, the only initial sequents in S_0 are given by the $\&_{i\in I}$-R rule when I is empty. The systems S_{n+1} have as additional initial sequents $\longrightarrow \Gamma, \neg W$, where the sequent $\longrightarrow \Gamma, W$ does not have an S_n-proof. Such initial sequents are called ***negative initial sequents.*** An S_n-proof is a tree structure arrangement of such initial sequents and inferences with the following proviso: if the sequent $\longrightarrow \Gamma, \neg W$ has an occurrence in the tree, then that occurrence is an initial sequent. For $n \geq 0$, we write $\vdash^n \Gamma, W$ to mean that there is an S_n-proof of $\longrightarrow \Gamma, W$. Notice that $\vdash_{\pi_0} \Gamma, W$ if and only if $\vdash^0 \Gamma, W$. Let $C_\omega = \bigcup_{n\geq 0} C_n$.

Notice that it is easy to extend Proposition 7 to S_n for $n \geq 0$. That is, S_n-proofs can be assumed to be such that whenever a sequent occurrence has an occurrence of a $\&_{i\in I}$ co-agent, that sequent occurrence is the conclusion of the $\&_{i\in I}$ introduction rule.

Proposition 8 *Let $W \in C_n$, let $m \geq n$, and let Γ be a multiset of agent expressions. Then $\vdash^m \Gamma, W$ if and only if $\vdash^{m+1} \Gamma, W$.*

Proof. By induction on m. If $m = 0$ then $n = 0$. Since W has no occurrences of negations, the result is immediate. Assume that $m > 0$. Let Ξ be an S_m-proof of $\longrightarrow \Gamma, W$. If Ξ has no negative initial sequents, then Ξ is both an S_0 and S_{m+1}-proof. Thus, assume that Ξ contains the initial sequent $\longrightarrow \Delta, \neg W'$. Since $\neg W'$ is a subformula of W, $W' \in C_{n-1}$. Also, there is no S_{m-1}-proof of $\longrightarrow \Delta, W'$. By the inductive hypothesis, there is no S_m-proof of $\longrightarrow \Delta, W'$ so S_{m+1} contains the initial sequent $\longrightarrow \Delta, \neg W'$. Since every initial sequent of Ξ is initial in S_{m+1}, Ξ is an S_{m+1} proof of $\longrightarrow \Gamma, W$. Conversely, let Ξ be an S_{m+1}-proof of $\longrightarrow \Gamma, W$. Again, let $\longrightarrow \Delta, \neg W'$ be a negative initial sequent in Ξ. Thus, $W' \in C_{n-1}$ and there is no S_m-proof of $\longrightarrow \Delta, W'$. By the inductive hypothesis, there is no S_{m-1} proof of $\longrightarrow \Delta, W'$ so $\longrightarrow \Delta, W'$ is an initial sequent in S_m. Thus, Ξ is also an S_m proof. □

Let Γ be a multiset of agent expressions and let $W \in C_\omega$. We write $\vdash^\omega \Gamma, W$ if there is some $n \geq 0$ such that $\vdash^n \Gamma, R$. Notice that if $W \in C_n$ for some $n \geq 0$, Proposition 8 implies that $\vdash^\omega \Gamma, W$ if and only if $\vdash^n \Gamma, W$.

Proposition 9 *Let Γ be a multiset of agent expressions and let $W \in C_\omega$.*

(i) Either $\vdash^\omega \Gamma, W$ or $\vdash^\omega \Gamma, \neg W$.
(ii) It is not the case that $\vdash^\omega \Gamma, W$ and $\vdash^\omega \Gamma, \neg W$.
(iii) $\not\vdash^\omega \Gamma, W$ if and only if $\vdash^\omega \Gamma, \neg W$.

(iv) $\vdash^\omega \Gamma, W$ *if and only if* $\vdash^\omega \Gamma, \neg\neg W$.

Proof. To prove *(i)*, let n be such that $W \in C_n$. Then $\longrightarrow \Gamma, W$ is either provable or not provable in S_n. In the first case, $\vdash^\omega \Gamma, W$. In the second case, $\vdash^{n+1} \Gamma, \neg W$ and therefore $\vdash^\omega \Gamma, \neg W$.

To prove *(ii)*, let n be such that $W \in C_n$ and assume that $\vdash^\omega \Gamma, W$ and $\vdash^\omega \Gamma, \neg W$. By Proposition 8, $\vdash^n \Gamma, W$ and $\vdash^{n+1} \Gamma, \neg W$. Given the restriction on proofs involving negations in proofs, $\longrightarrow \Gamma, \neg W$ is an initial sequent of S_{n+1} and thus there is no S_n-proof of $\longrightarrow \Gamma, W$, which is a contradiction.

To prove *(iii)*, let n be such that $W \in C_n$. Thus by Proposition 8 $\not\vdash^\omega \Gamma, W$ if and only if $\not\vdash^n \Gamma, W$. But this is equivalent to $\vdash^{n+1} \Gamma, \neg W$. By Proposition 8 again, this is equivalent to $\vdash^\omega \Gamma, \neg W$.

To prove *(iv)*, notice that by *(iii)*, $\vdash^\omega \Gamma, W$ is equivalent to $\not\vdash^\omega \Gamma, \neg W$, which (by *(iii)* again) is equivalent to $\vdash^\omega \Gamma, \neg\neg W$. □

For Γ a multiset of agent expressions, define $[\![\Gamma]\!] = \{W \in C_\omega \mid \vdash^\omega \Gamma, W\}$.

Proposition 10 *Let P and Q be two agent expressions. Then $[\![P]\!] \subseteq [\![Q]\!]$ if and only if $[\![P]\!] = [\![Q]\!]$.*

Proof. Assume that $[\![P]\!] \subseteq [\![Q]\!]$ and that $[\![P]\!] \neq [\![Q]\!]$. Thus, there is a $W \in C_\omega$ such that $\vdash^\omega Q, W$ but $\not\vdash^\omega P, W$. By Proposition 9 *(iii)*, $\vdash^\omega P, \neg W$. But this implies that $\neg W \in [\![P]\!]$ and $\neg W \in [\![Q]\!]$ which contradicts Proposition 9 *(ii)*. □

Before connecting the equivalence given by $[\![P]\!] = [\![Q]\!]$ to known equivalences, we need to define the notion of labeled transition. Let a be an action (that is, a constant of type i). The three place relation $P \overset{a}{\Longrightarrow} P'$ is defined to hold if $P' \mid 1 \vdash_{\pi_0} P \mid \bar{a}.1$. Here, the constant 1 is some anonymous symbol for which no inference rule or axiom is provided. (It is possible to identify 1 with the constant of the same name used in linear logic [Gir87] since the inference rules given for 1 there cannot be used in any cut-free π_0-proof of the sequent $P' \mid 1 \longrightarrow P \mid \bar{a}.1$.) Given this definition, it follows that if $P \overset{a}{\Longrightarrow} P'$ and Q is an agent expression then $P \mid \bar{a}.Q \Longrightarrow P' \mid Q$ (simply replace 1 with Q).

If Γ is a multiset of formulas then $|\Gamma$ denotes the parallel composition (using $|$) of all the formulas Γ in some fixed but arbitrary order.

Proposition 11 *Let Γ be a multiset of agents, let a be an action, and let $W \in C_\omega$. Then $\vdash^\omega \Gamma, \bar{a}.W$ if and only if there is a multiset of agents Ψ such that $|\Gamma \overset{a}{\Longrightarrow} |\Psi$ and $\vdash^\omega \Psi, W$.*

Proof. First assume that $\vdash^\omega \Gamma, \bar{a}.W$. A proof of $\longrightarrow \Gamma, \bar{a}.W$ must contain a subproof where the last inference rule is

$$\frac{\longrightarrow \Gamma', R, W}{\longrightarrow \Gamma', a.R, \bar{a}.W},$$

for some multiset of agents Γ' and some agent R. Set Ψ equal to the multiset $\Gamma' \cup \{R\}$. Now the sequent $(|\Psi) \mid 1 \longrightarrow \Gamma', R, 1$ clearly has a π_0-proof (involving only |L rules and initial sequents). If we now add to this sequent all the right rules that were applied to build the proof of $\longrightarrow \Gamma, a.W$ from $\longrightarrow \Gamma', R, W$, we can construct a proof of $(|\Psi) \mid 1 \longrightarrow \Gamma, \bar{a}.1$ and of $(|\Psi) \mid 1 \longrightarrow (|\Gamma) \mid \bar{a}.1$. Thus, $|\Gamma \stackrel{a}{\Longrightarrow} |\Psi$.

For the converse, assume that Ψ is such that $|\Gamma \stackrel{a}{\Longrightarrow} |\Psi$ and $\vdash^\omega \Psi, W$. The crossover sequent of the proof of $(|\Psi) \mid 1 \longrightarrow \Gamma, \bar{a}.1$ must be $(|\Psi) \mid 1 \longrightarrow \Gamma', 1$ for some multiset of agents Γ' (see Proposition 2). Since $(|\Psi)$ and $(|\Gamma')$ are equal agent expressions up to associativity and commutativity of $|$, $\vdash^\omega \Gamma', W$. Now applying to the sequent $\longrightarrow \Gamma', W$ all those right rules that were used to prove $(|\Psi) \mid 1 \longrightarrow (|\Gamma) \mid \bar{a}.1$ from $(|\Psi) \mid 1 \longrightarrow \Gamma', 1$ yields a proof of $\longrightarrow \Gamma, \bar{a}.W$. □

We can now show that co-agents act the same as formulas of the Hennessy-Milner modal logic. ***Assertion formulas*** are formulas containing the indexed conjunction $\bigwedge_{i \in I}$ (for a denumerable index set I), the possibility modal $\langle a \rangle$ (for a an action), and the negation $\neg$. The logical constant ***true*** is defined to be $\bigwedge_{i \in I} A_i$ for the empty index set I. The satisfaction of an assertion A by a process expression P, written as $P \models A$, is defined by the following induction on the structure of assertions.

- $P \models \bigwedge_{i \in I} A_i$ if $P \models A_i$ for every $i \in I$.
- $P \models \langle a \rangle A$ if there is an agent P' such that $P \stackrel{a}{\Longrightarrow} P'$ and $P' \models A$.
- $P \models \neg A$ if it is not the case that $P \models A$.

Define the following bijection of C_ω into assertion formulas: $(\&_{i \in I} W_i)^\circ = \bigwedge_{i \in I} W_i^\circ$, $(a.W)^\circ = \langle \bar{a} \rangle W^\circ$, and $(\neg W)^\circ = \neg W^\circ$.

Proposition 12 *Let $W \in C_\omega$ and let P be an agent expression. Then $\vdash^\omega P, W$ if and only if $P \models W^\circ$.*

Proof. This proof is by induction on the structure of co-agents in C_ω. The cases for $\&_{i \in I}$ and $\neg$ are immediate. Let W be $a.W'$. If $P \models \langle \bar{a} \rangle (W')^\circ$ then there is a P' such that $P \stackrel{\bar{a}}{\Longrightarrow} P'$ and $P' \models (W')^\circ$. By the inductive hypothesis, $\vdash^\omega P', W'$ and by Proposition 11, $\vdash^\omega P, W$. Conversely, if $\vdash^\omega P, a.W'$ then, by Proposition 11, there is a P' such that $P \stackrel{\bar{a}}{\Longrightarrow} P'$ and $\vdash^\omega P', W$. By the inductive hypothesis, $P' \models W^\circ$ and by the definition of $\models$, $P \models \langle \bar{a} \rangle (W')^\circ$. □

The following proposition is now immediate.

Proposition 13 *Let P and Q be agents. Then $[\![P]\!] = [\![Q]\!]$ if and only if for every assertion A, $P \models A$ if and only if $Q \models A$.*

Since the Hennessy-Milner logic characterizes observational equivalence, P and Q are observational equivalence if and only if $[\![P]\!] = [\![Q]\!]$. It is possible to show this result directly without making use of the Hennessy-Milner logic but the proof would be essentially identical to the proof using this modal logic.

This derivation of the Hennessy-Milner logic via co-agents is rather satisfactory for at least two reasons. First, it is possible to understand agents and assertion formulas as part of the same logical system, here a theory in a fragment of linear logic. Second, the intensional prefixing operator gives rise to the intensional modal operator: the latter does not need to be added separately. Representing prefixing as two non-logical constants of higher-order type might be considered one of the more controversial aspects of this representation. The fact that this choice also explains the modal operator provides us with more confidence in this choice.

In fact, the parsimony of our presentation of co-agents can be improved even further: negation $\neg$ is the only co-agent combinator that is necessary. For example, the expression $\neg nil$ can be used for $\top$ ($\neg P$ for any agent P will also do) and the expression $\neg(\neg W_1 + \neg W_2)$ can be used for $W_1 \& W_2$. Thus, if we admit indexed sums $\sum_{i \in I}$ into π_0, the only co-agent combinator we need to introduce is the negation-as-failure-to-prove operator.

Of course, there is a great deal of work left to be done in getting a full picture of the relationship between multiple-conclusion sequent calculus and process calculi. For example, Abramsky's work on bisimulation as testing equivalence [Abr87] should be related to the material just presented. A very good test of our approach would be to see if the modal logics recently described for the π-calculus in [MPW91] can be motivated using the notion of co-agents.

6 Conclusions

In this paper we have attempted to show one way that proof theory can be used to represent and organize the details of the π-calculus. This approach seems successful on more than one level: not only can the reflective and transitive closure of reduction be identified with entailed-by but also proof-theoretic notions of semantics provide a natural link to well studied semantics for concurrency. The derivation of the Hennessy-Milner modal logic via the notion of co-agents speaks strongly for the directness of this approach.

Acknowledgements. The anonymous reviewers of an earlier draft of this paper have suggested several improvements to presentation of this paper. The author has been funded in part by ONR N00014-88-K-0633, NSF CCR-91-02753, and DARPA N00014-85-K-0018.

References

[Abr87] Samson Abramsky. Observation equivalence as a testing equivalence. *Theoretical Computer Science*, 53:225–241, 1987.

[Abr90] Samson Abramsky. Computational interpretations of linear logic. Technical Report Research Report DOC 90/20, Imperial College, October 1990.

[Abr91] Samson Abramsky. Proofs as processes. Copy of transparencies, 1991.

[AP91] J.M. Andreoli and R. Pareschi. Linear objects: Logical processes with built-in inheritance. *New Generation Computing*, 9:3-4, 1991. (Special issue of papers selected from ICLP'90).

[Fel91] Amy Felty. A logic program for transforming sequent proofs to natural deduction proofs. In Peter Schroeder-Heister, editor, *Extensions of Logic Programming: International Workshop, Tübingen FRG, December 1989*, volume 475 of *Lecture Notes in Artificial Intelligence*. Springer-Verlag, 1991.

[Gen69] Gerhard Gentzen. Investigations into logical deductions, 1935. In M. E. Szabo, editor, *The Collected Papers of Gerhard Gentzen*, pages 68–131. North-Holland Publishing Co., Amsterdam, 1969.

[Gir87] Jean-Yves Girard. Linear logic. *Theoretical Computer Science*, 50:1–102, 1987.

[Hen88] Matthew Hennessy. *Algebraic Theory of Processes*. MIT Press, 1988.

[HM92] Joshua Hodas and Dale Miller. Logic programming in a fragment of intuitionistic linear logic. *Journal of Information and Computation*, 1992. Invited to a special issue of papers from the 1991 LICS conference.

[Kle52] Stephen Cole Kleene. Permutabilities of inferences in gentzen's calculi LK and LJ. *Memoirs of the American Mathematical Society*, 10, 1952.

[Mil89] Dale Miller. A logical analysis of modules in logic programming. *Journal of Logic Programming*, 6:79 – 108, 1989.

[Mil90] Robin Milner. Functions as processes. Research Report 1154, INRIA, 1990.

[Mil91] Robin Milner. The polyadic π-calculus: A tutorial. LFCS Report Series ECS-LFCS-91-180, University of Edinburgh, October 1991.

[Mil92] Dale Miller. Abstract syntax and logic programming. In *Logic Programming: Proceedings of the First and Second Russian Conferences on Logic Programming*, number 592 in Lecture Notes in Artificial Intelligence, pages 322–337. Springer-Verlag, 1992. Also available as technical report MS-CIS-91-72, UPenn.

[MNPS91] Dale Miller, Gopalan Nadathur, Frank Pfenning, and Andre Scedrov. Uniform proofs as a foundation for logic programming. *Annals of Pure and Applied Logic*, 51:125–157, 1991.

[MPW89a] Robin Milner, Joachim Parrow, and David Walker. A calculus of mobile processes, Part I. LFCS Report Series ECS-LFCS-89-85, University of Edinburgh, June 1989.

[MPW89b] Robin Milner, Joachim Parrow, and David Walker. A calculus of mobile processes, Part II. LFCS Report Series ECS-LFCS-89-86, University of Edinburgh, June 1989.

[MPW91] Robin Milner, Joachim Parrow, and David Walker. Modal logics for mobile processes. LFCS Report Series ECS-LFCS-91-136, University of Edinburgh, April 1991.

[NM90] Gopalan Nadathur and Dale Miller. Higher-order Horn clauses. *Journal of the ACM*, 37(4):777 – 814, October 1990.

[Pot77] Garrel Pottinger. Normalization as a homomorphic image of cut-elimination. *Annals of Mathematical Logic*, 12(3):223–357, 1977.

Natural Deduction Proof Theory for Logic Programming

Seppo Keronen

Wilhelm-Schickard-Institut, Universität Tübingen, Sand 13
D-7400 Tübingen, Germany
seppo@logik.informatik.uni-tuebingen.de

Abstract. The SLD resolution proof theory for the Prolog family of logic programming languages is well known. The extended syntactic forms of these languages, however, distance them from the Horn language required by SLD resolution. We propose a direct proof theoretic account for logic programming. The derivations built by the inference engine are not refutations, but direct proofs of the query from the program formulae as premisses. Derivations correspond to a deductively complete subclass of natural deduction proofs called atomic normal form (ANF) proofs. The new proof theory suggests efficient implementations for more expressive logic programming languages. Also, ANF proofs are readily understood as formal counterparts of informal (but rigorous) arguments constructed by humans. Powerful explanation, debugging and control facilities can be based on this correspondence.

1 Introduction

The SLD resolution proof theory for Horn languages [1] [9] and its extension to SLDNF resolution [2] [11] is well known. In this paper, we initiate a similar development for a proof theory based on natural deduction [6] [15] [18], rather than resolution refutation. The ANF proof theory, presented here, represents the first stage of the development.

Natural deduction offers several outstanding advantages as a base for logic programming:

- Proofs are readily understood as formal counterparts of informal (but rigorous) arguments constructed by humans. Powerful explanation, debugging and control facilities can be provided, based on simply inspecting the state of a proof construction computation.
- Strictly classical reasoning is inappropriate for many deductive problems faced by mechanical reasoners. Alternative logics are commonly formulated as natural deduction systems. For example, deductive systems for intuitionistic logic, and logics that can supply coherent answers in the presense of contradictory knowledge, are available.

Compared to resolution refutation, little is known about the efficient implementation of natural deduction based systems. The ANF proof theory is designed to address this shortcoming. The special advantages of ANF are:

- The impressive implementation technology of logic programming systems is directly applicable to the task of constructing ANF proofs. The fundamental computational unit of the new theory is the unification of two atomic formulae [16]. The data structures built by current logic programming implementations represent ANF proofs.
- The extended syntactic forms of the Prolog family of logic programming languages distance them from SLD resolution. The transformation of expressive program clauses into the simpler language [12] destroys their procedural reading. In contrast ANF provides a direct proof theoretic account for these languages.
- There is a simple correspondence between the expressive power of a language and the natural deduction machinery required for its implementation. For each logical operator admitted by either the assertion or goal syntax, there is a corresponding rule of inference to be incorporated in the inference engine. Efficient implementations for more expressive languages are suggested, based on this correspondence.

As motivation and gentle introduction to the new proof theory, we run through a very simple propositional example in both the resolution refutation and ANF regimes. The example deductive problem is:

$$\{a \wedge b\} \ ?\!- \ a \vee c$$

That is, deduce the formula $a \vee c$ given the singleton set of axioms $\{a \wedge b\}$.

The resolution scheme requires that we translate axioms into clausal form. The translation for the example problem is shown in (1).

assertion:	$a \wedge b$
set of clauses:	$\{a, b\}$

(1)

We make a corresponding move, take the axiomatic assertion (2) and apply the and-elimination rule of inference yielding the two proof fragments (3) and (4).

$$\frac{}{a \wedge b} \qquad\qquad \cfrac{\overline{a \wedge b}}{a} \qquad\qquad \cfrac{\overline{a \wedge b}}{b}$$

(2) (3) (4)

The query formula $a \vee c$ is rewritten for consumption by the resolution strategy as shown in (5).

We also break down the query into two components, take the goal (6) and apply the or-introduction rule yielding the two proof fragments (7) and (8).

query: $a \vee c$
negated assertion: $\sim(a \vee c)$
set of clauses: $\{\sim a, \sim c\}$

(5)

$$\begin{array}{c} a \vee c \\ \hline \end{array} \qquad \begin{array}{c} a \\ \hline a \vee c \\ \hline \end{array} \qquad \begin{array}{c} c \\ \hline a \vee c \\ \hline \end{array}$$

(6) (7) (8)

For resolution the problem of deducing $a \vee c$ from $\{a \wedge b\}$ is rerepresented as the problem: Derive the null clause, using the resolution rule of inference, from the union of the two sets of clauses of (1) and (5). Only the one derivation, displayed in (9), is possible.

Our representation for the same problem is: Is it possible to construct a natural deduction proof by "pasting" together some of the proof fragments (3), (4), (7) and (8). Only the one proof, displayed in (10), is possible.

(9)

$$\begin{array}{c} \hline a \wedge b \\ \hline a \\ \hline a \vee c \\ \hline \end{array}$$

(10)

The natural deduction proof is readily understood as an argument for the query from the axioms. In this case the argument consists of just two steps:

- Since $a \wedge b$ holds then a alone must hold.
- Since a holds then $a \vee c$ must also hold.

The clarity of natural deduction proofs makes the task of explaining the conclusions reached by the inference engine easier. Given the Prolog backward chaining search strategy, intermediate states of computation correspond to conditional proofs for the query formula. Debugging based on the inspection of intermediate computation states therefore also benefits. In [8] the prospect of a control language based on the introspection of computation states is examined.

The rest of the paper presents an outline of the ANF proof theory as it relates to logic programming. Following the necessary preliminaries, natural deduction is briefly introduced in section 3. The formal deductive system for ANF proofs in classical logic is presented in section 4. The subsystem for the Prolog language and associated computational concerns are then covered in section 5. Finally, in section 6, we discuss briefly the relationship of the new theory to other work in computational logic and the prospects for further development.

2 Preliminaries

The deductive systems to be described are intended for the familiar language of first order predicate calculus formulae. We follow the usual practice for natural deduction formulations and enrich the language slightly. The symbol # (read contradiction) is admitted as a well formed atomic formula. Also we distinguish syntactically between occurrences of bound (quantified) variables (denoted by $\ldots, x, y, z$) and free variables or parameters (denoted by $\ldots, X, Y, Z$).

The symbols A, B and C will stand for atomic formulae — E, F, G and H will stand for formulae with various syntactic restrictions — Δ for a set of formulae — Π and Σ for proofs (bipartite graphs with formula and inference rule nodes). Substitutions (of terms for parameters) are denoted by conjunctions of equality assertions in solved form [10]. To denote a substitution instance of a formula F using substitution Θ we write $F\Theta$. Analogously, the substitution Θ applied to a proof Π is denoted by $\Pi\Theta$. Any of the above symbols may be decorated by various subscripts and superscripts.

3 Natural Deduction

The natural deduction rules of inference for classical logic are displayed in figure 1. We first look at the role these rules play in the formal definition of proof, and then take a closer look at the rules themselves.

The natural deduction rules of inference provide the clauses for a formal, inductive definition of the notion of *proof*:

base An ocurrence of a formula standing alone is a proof supporting the given formula as conclusion, and depending on just that same formula as premiss. Such a trivial argument, for formula F, is represented by the deducibility assertion

$$\{F\} \vdash F$$

step The rules of inference provide the clauses of the inductive definition. Given proofs matching each of the premisses of the rule, a proof for the instantiated conclusion may be constructed. The new proof may discharge some of the premisses of its component proofs as assumptions. Such a complex argument with conclusion G and depending on the set of premisses $\{F_1, F_2, \ldots, F_n\}$ is summarized by the deducibility assertion

$$\{F_1, F_2, \ldots, F_n\} \vdash G$$

In accordance with the above definition, proofs generated by single conclusion rules of inference are trees. The root of the tree is the *conclusion*, the leaves of the tree are either *premisses* or *assumptions* of the proof.

introduction rules / **elimination rules**

$$ {\scriptstyle \wedge I}\ \frac{\dfrac{\Pi_1}{G} \quad \dfrac{\Pi_2}{H}}{G \wedge H} \qquad\qquad {\scriptstyle \wedge E}\ \frac{\dfrac{\Pi}{E \wedge F}}{E} \qquad {\scriptstyle \wedge E}\ \frac{\dfrac{\Pi}{E \wedge F}}{F} $$

$$ {\scriptstyle \vee I}\ \frac{\dfrac{\Pi}{G}}{G \vee H} \qquad {\scriptstyle \vee I}\ \frac{\dfrac{\Pi}{H}}{G \vee H} \qquad\qquad {\scriptstyle \vee E}\ \frac{\dfrac{\Pi}{E \vee F} \quad \dfrac{\begin{matrix}[E]\\ \Pi_1\end{matrix}}{G} \quad \dfrac{\begin{matrix}[F]\\ \Pi_2\end{matrix}}{G}}{G} $$

$$ {\scriptstyle \Rightarrow I}\ \frac{\dfrac{\begin{matrix}[F]\\ \Pi\end{matrix}}{G}}{F \Rightarrow G} \qquad\qquad {\scriptstyle \Rightarrow E}\ \frac{\dfrac{\Pi}{G \Rightarrow F} \quad \dfrac{\Pi_1}{G}}{F} $$

$$ {\scriptstyle \forall I}\ \frac{\dfrac{\Pi}{G(X)}}{\forall x G(x)} \qquad\qquad {\scriptstyle \forall E}\ \frac{\dfrac{\Pi}{\forall x F(x)}}{F(t)} $$

$$ {\scriptstyle \exists I}\ \frac{\dfrac{\Pi}{G(t)}}{\exists x G(x)} \qquad\qquad {\scriptstyle \exists E}\ \frac{\dfrac{\Pi}{\exists x F(x)} \quad \dfrac{\begin{matrix}[F(X)]\\ \Pi_1\end{matrix}}{G}}{G} $$

$$ {\scriptstyle \sim I}\ \frac{\dfrac{\begin{matrix}[G]\\ \Pi\end{matrix}}{\#}}{\sim G} \qquad\qquad {\scriptstyle \sim E}\ \frac{\dfrac{\Pi}{\sim F} \quad \dfrac{\Pi_1}{F}}{\#} $$

absurdity / **excluded middle**

$$ {\scriptstyle \#}\ \frac{\dfrac{\Pi}{\#}}{G} \qquad\qquad {\scriptstyle \mathrm{AXIOM}}\ \frac{}{F \vee \sim F} $$

x – variable
X – parameter
t – term
$\#$ – contradiction
E, F, G, H – formula
Π, Π_1, Π_2 – proof

Fig. 1. deductive system for classical logic

Some notation for proofs:

$$\frac{\Pi}{G} \qquad \begin{matrix}(F)\\ \Pi\end{matrix} \qquad \begin{matrix}[F]\\ \Pi\end{matrix} \qquad \begin{matrix}\frac{\Sigma}{(F)}\\ \Pi\end{matrix}$$

(11) (12) (13) (14)

(11) Proof Π has conclusion G.
(12) Formula F occurs as a premiss in proof Π.
(13) Formula F may occur as an assumption in proof Π.
(14) A proof Σ with conclusion F, has been "grafted" onto Π at each occurrence of F as premiss.

Natural deduction rules of inference can be recognized as formal counterparts of methods used in common reasoning practice. For instance, putting the rules on the top row of figure 1 into words:

And introduction ($\wedge$I): The conjunction $G \wedge H$ follows given both a proof Π_1 for the formula G and a proof Π_2 for the formula H.
And elimination ($\wedge$E): Given a proof Π of the conjunction $E \wedge F$ the formula E follows. Also, from the same premiss the formula F follows.

We adopt a slightly more verbose notation for inference rules than is common. For example, instead of the conventional notation (15) for the implication elimination (modus ponens) rule, we write (16).

$$\frac{G \Rightarrow F \quad G}{F} \qquad\qquad \frac{\dfrac{\Pi_1}{G \Rightarrow F} \quad \dfrac{\Pi_2}{G}}{F}{\scriptstyle \Rightarrow E}$$

(15) (16)

The fomula F is the *conclusion* of the rule, $G \Rightarrow F$ and G are *premiss formulae*, and Π_1, Π_2 are *premiss proofs*. This rule is read as the inductive clause:

Given a proof $\dfrac{\Pi_1}{G \Rightarrow F}$ and a proof $\dfrac{\Pi_2}{G}$ then $\dfrac{\dfrac{\Pi_1}{G \Rightarrow F} \quad \dfrac{\Pi_2}{G}}{F}{\scriptstyle \Rightarrow E}$ is a proof.

The rules of inference appearing in figure 1 are partitioned into four subsets:

Introduction Rules: The generic introduction rule, with premiss proofs $\Pi_1 \ldots \Pi_n$ and conclusion formula G, is expressed in the pattern:

$$\frac{\Pi_1 \ldots \Pi_n}{G}\,{-_I}$$

For each logical operator, $\Pi_1 \ldots \Pi_n$ express the conditions under which a formula G, with that operator dominant, may be introduced as conclusion. The premiss formulae are subformulae of the conclusion.

Elimination Rules: The elimination rule with major premiss Π, minor premisses $\Pi_1 \ldots \Pi_n$ and conclusion F is expressed in the pattern:

$$\frac{\dfrac{\Pi}{E} \quad \Pi_1 \ldots \Pi_n}{F}\,{-_E}$$

For each logical operator, given formula E has that operator dominant, $\Pi_1 \ldots \Pi_n$ and F assert nothing more than would be required to establish E by the corresponding introduction rule. All minor premiss formulae and the conclusion are subformulae of the major premiss formula.

Together the introduction and elimination rules define a subsystem of classical logic called *minimal logic*.

Absurdity Rule: This rule expresses the principle that given a proof of contradiction, any formula whatsoever follows. The rule is often referred to as *ex falso quodlibet*. The addition of the absurdity rule to minimal logic yields *intuitionistic logic*.

Current logic programming languages are not expressive enough to yield contradictions. Many theorem proving systems that are, however, do not implement this rule in its full generality.

Excluded Middle: This rule expresses the principle that for any formula whatsoever either it or its negation holds. The addition of this principle to the intuitionistic system yields *classical logic*.

Natural deduction proofs are constructed not only by application of the above rules of inference — It is common practice to "graft" one proof (lemma) that establishes a desired conclusion, on top of a proof requiring that conclusion as premiss. This principle, called CUT [6], is expressed by the inductive clause:

Given proofs $\dfrac{\Pi_1}{F}$ and $\begin{array}{c}(G)\\ \Pi_2\end{array}$ and that $(F\Theta = G\Theta)$ then $\left(\begin{array}{c}\Pi_1\\ \hline F\\ \hline\hline (G)\\ \Pi_2\end{array}\right)\Theta$ ${=}\text{CUT}$

is a proof.

A double inference stroke is used here to emphasize the structural character of the CUT rule.

4 Atomic Normal Form

The rules of inference for ANF proof in classical logic are displayed in figure 2. An ANF proof is a natural deduction proof satisfying both a ***normal form constraint*** and an ***atomicity constraint***, as described below.

The inductive definition of proof, given in the preceding section, is too weak to capture the notion that a proof should arrive at its conclusion as directly as possible. A *normal form* proof [15] is a natural deduction proof that satisfies the following additional constraint:

Normal Form Constraint: Every major premiss formula of an elimination rule instance, occurring in the proof, is not the conclusion of an introduction rule instance.

This constraint simply recognises the so called ***inversion principle*** relating the introduction and elimination rules for each of the logical operators. The inversion principle implies that no deductive gain is to be had by using a formula, constructed by an introduction rule, as the major premiss for an elimination rule.

The above constraint confers two important properties for a normal form proof Π_N:

Subformula Property: Every formula occurrence in Π_N is a subformula of one of the premisses of Π_N or of the conclusion of Π_N.

Minimal Formula Property: Every branch of a Π_N consists of two segments. Tracing a branch from the leaf premiss or assumption, a sequence of elimination rule instances only is followed by a sequence of introduction rule instances only. The two segments are separated by a ***minimal formula*** occurrence [15].

The above two properties form the basis for partitioning a proof into proof fragments. A proof fragment is a subgraph of a normal form proof, delineated by minimal formula occurrences. We recognise two kinds of proof fragmrnts. An ***introduction fragment*** represents the inferential contribution of a particular ***goal*** formula to the overall proof. An ***elimination proof fragment*** represents the inferential contribution of a particular ***assertion formula***. For any normal form proof:

Goal Formula: Just the following are goal formula occurrences:

- The query
- Any premiss formula of an introduction rule
- Any minor premiss formula of an elimination rule

Assertion Formula: Just the following are assertion formula occurrences:

- An axiom
- An assumption
- The conclusion formula of an elimination rule

introduction rules

$$\begin{array}{c}\dfrac{G \quad H}{(G\wedge H)}{\scriptstyle \wedge I}\\ \Pi_I\end{array}$$

$$\begin{array}{c}\dfrac{G}{(G\vee H)}{\scriptstyle \vee I}\\ \Pi_I\end{array} \qquad \begin{array}{c}\dfrac{H}{(G\vee H)}{\scriptstyle \vee I}\\ \Pi_I\end{array}$$

$$\begin{array}{c}[F]\\ \dfrac{G}{(F\Rightarrow G)}{\scriptstyle \Rightarrow I}\\ \Pi_I\end{array}$$

$$\begin{array}{c}\dfrac{G(X)}{(\forall x G(x))}{\scriptstyle \forall I}\\ \Pi_I\end{array}$$

$$\begin{array}{c}\dfrac{G(t)}{(\exists x G(x))}{\scriptstyle \exists I}\\ \Pi_I\end{array}$$

$$\begin{array}{c}[G]\\ \dfrac{\#}{(\sim G)}{\scriptstyle \sim I}\\ \Pi_I\end{array}$$

$$\begin{array}{c}\dfrac{\#}{(G)}{\scriptstyle \#}\\ \Pi_I\end{array}$$

elimination rules

$$\dfrac{\dfrac{\Pi_E}{E\wedge F}}{E}{\scriptstyle \wedge E} \qquad \dfrac{\dfrac{\Pi_E}{E\wedge F}}{F}{\scriptstyle \wedge E}$$

$$\dfrac{\dfrac{\Pi_E}{E\vee F}}{E \qquad F}{\scriptstyle \vee E}$$

$$\dfrac{\dfrac{\Pi_E}{G\Rightarrow F} \quad \dfrac{\Pi_I}{G}}{F}{\scriptstyle \Rightarrow E}$$

$$\dfrac{\dfrac{\Pi_E}{\forall x F(x)}}{F(t)}{\scriptstyle \forall E}$$

$$\dfrac{\dfrac{\Pi_E}{\exists x F(x)}}{F(X)}{\scriptstyle \exists E}$$

$$\dfrac{\dfrac{\Pi_E}{\sim F} \quad \dfrac{\Pi_I}{F}}{\#}{\scriptstyle \sim E}$$

$$\dfrac{}{F \vee \sim F}{\scriptstyle \text{AXIOM}}$$

cut rule

$$\left(\begin{array}{c}\dfrac{\dfrac{\Pi_E}{A}{\scriptstyle E}}{(B)}{\scriptstyle =\text{CUT}}\\ \dfrac{}{\Pi_A}{\scriptstyle I}\end{array}\right)\Theta \qquad \text{where: } A\Theta = B\Theta$$

x – variable
X – parameter
t – term
$\#$ – contradiction
Θ – substitution

A, B – atomic formula
E, F, G, H – formula
Π_I – introduction proof
Π_E – elimination proof
Π_A – atomic normal form proof

Fig. 2. atomic normal form proof

Introduction Proof Fragment (Π_I): A Π_I is characterized by the inductive definition:

base A goal formula standing alone is a Π_I.

step The inference rules shown on the left of figure 2 form the clauses of the definition. (The assumptions "thrown up" by the application of ⇒I and ~I rules generate elimination proof fragments.)

The introduction rules are framed to work "backwards", reducing a goal into simpler subgoals and assumptions.

Elimination Proof Fragment (Π_E): A Π_E is characterized by the inductive definition:

base An assertion formula standing alone is a Π_E.

step The inference rules shown on the right of figure 2 form the clauses of the definition. Notice that introduction proof fragments may occur as parts of an elimination fragment.

Just like the inductive definition of proof in the preceding section, the elimination rules here work "forwards", reducing an asserted formula into simpler assertions and subgoals.

Notice that the subformula property of the inference rules limits the number of rule instances constituting a proof fragment to the number of logical operator occurrences in the axiom, assumption or query formula from which the fragment is derived.

An *atomic normal form (ANF) proof* is a normal form proof that satisfies the additional constraint:

Atomicity Constraint: Every minimal formula occurrence in the proof is an atom (positive literal).

An ANF proof is constructed from instances of introduction and elimination proof fragments "pasted" together using the CUT rule of inference as "glue".

Atomic Normal Form Proof: An ANF proof (Π_A) is determined by the inductive definition:

base: A Π_I is a Π_A.

step: Given a Π_A with atomic premiss B, a Π_E with conclusion A, and that $A\Theta = \mathbf{B}\Theta$ (A and B unify) then we can compose $\Pi_A\Theta$ and $\Pi_E\Theta$ (substitution instances of the Π_A and Π_E). This step is symbolised as the CUT rule of inference at the bottom of figure 2.

Reflecting the above definition, the construction of an ANF proof proceeds in two distinct phases, **extend** and **compose**. There are a number of perspectives on what happens during the two phases and why this division into two phases is desirable:

- The inferential resources implicit in the logic program and the query are made explicit as a set of proof fragments (inferential extensions of the axioms and query) by **extend**. The task of **compose** is to build a proof by joining together instances of these fragments.

- In the **extend** phase, the introduction and elimination rules for the logical operators are removed by combining rules, resulting in a reduced number of more powerful inference rules. During **compose** reasoning is carried out using these derived rules of inference.
- Current theorem prover technology has largely developed on the assumption that the fundamental operation of an inference engine is the unification of two atomic formulae. **Extend** partially evaluates the problem to be presented to **compose**, which is such an inference engine.

The above description of ANF proof was framed for the full first order classical calculus. In the next section we will examine a simple subsystem, sufficient for the pure Edinburgh Prolog [3] language.

5 Prolog

There is a simple correspondence between the expressive power of the language in which a deductive problem is stated and the rules of inference that occur in any normal form proof that is a solution for that problem. The relationshiop is this:

- Only introduction rules for connectives that appear as the primary connective of a goal formula occur in a proof.
  and
- Only elimination rules for connectives that appear as the primary connective of an assertion formula occur in the proof.

The notion of a *Prolog*[1] *proof* is pinned down by the deductive system of figure 3. Prolog is a sublanguage of the full first order language, augmented with the negation as failure (NAF) rule of inference. The following deductive machinery is represented in figure 3:

Introduction Rules: The introduction rules for $\wedge$, $\vee$ and $\exists$ reflect the goal syntax of embedded conjunctions and disjunctions with existential quantifiers bracketing queries.

Elimination Rules: The elimination rules for the operators $\Rightarrow$ and $\forall$ reflect the fact that only implications with atomic conclusions and bracketed by universal quantifiers may be asserted. The antecedents of these implications are of course goals.

CUT: The CUT rule with atomic premiss and conclusion is implemented by the familiar unification operation of Robinson [16].

NAF: The goal syntax of Prolog permits negated goals but not negated assertions. In this situation a negation based on contradiction would be meaningless. Instead, the absence of a proof for a formula (negation as failure [2]) is taken as sufficient evidence for the negation of that formula to follow.

[1] The pure Edinburgh dialect of [3]

A deductive problem Δ ?– G is represented by the inference engine as follows:

$$\frac{\quad}{F}\ \text{AXIOM} \qquad\qquad \frac{G}{\quad}\ \text{QUERY}$$

(17) (18)

(17) Each axiom formula F, member of Δ, is represented by an occurrence of the AXIOM rule. The AXIOM rule has a single conclusion but no premisses.
(18) The query formula G is represented by an occurrence of the QUERY rule. The QUERY rule has a single premiss, but no conclusion.

The **extend** phase of the computation maps axiom and query rule occurrences into their inferential extensions by exhaustive application of the inductive definitions of introduction and elimination proof fragments respectively. For the Edinburgh Prolog language very axiom rule occurrence (17) is mapped into an AND/OR tree of the form (19), and the single query rule occurrence into the form (20). The AND branchings arise from inference rules with multiple premisses — The OR branchings from multiple inference rule applications.

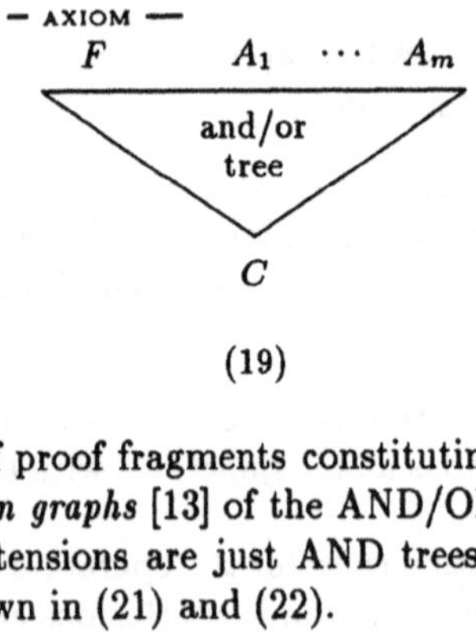

(19)

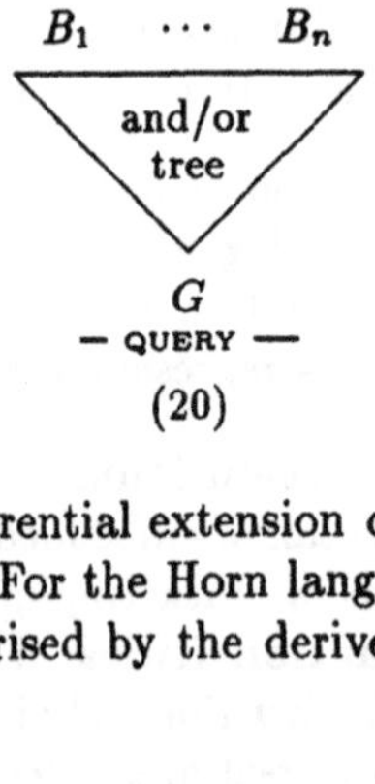

(20)

The set of proof fragments constituting an inferential extension correspond to the *solution graphs* [13] of the AND/OR graph. For the Horn language these inferential extensions are just AND trees, summarised by the derived rules of inference shown in (21) and (22).

$$\frac{A_1 \quad \cdots \quad A_m}{C} \qquad\qquad \frac{B_1 \quad \cdots \quad B_n}{\quad}$$

(21) (22)

For Prolog the mapping between the formulae of the deductive problem and their inferential extensions is still simple enough to make an explicit **extend** phase unnecessary. Disjunctive goals give rise to OR branches in the inferential

introduction rules   elimination rules

$$\frac{G \quad H}{(G \wedge H)} {\scriptstyle -\wedge I} \atop \Pi_I$$

$$\frac{\Pi_E \quad \Pi_I}{F} \atop \frac{G \Rightarrow F \quad G}{F} {\scriptstyle -\Rightarrow E}$$

$$\frac{G(t)}{(\exists x G(x))} {\scriptstyle -\exists I} \atop \Pi_I$$

$$\frac{\Pi_E}{\forall x F(x)} \atop \frac{\forall x F(x)}{F(t)} {\scriptstyle -\forall E}$$

$$\frac{G}{(G \vee H)} {\scriptstyle -\vee I} \atop \Pi_I \qquad \frac{H}{(G \vee H)} {\scriptstyle -\vee I} \atop \Pi_I$$

structural rules

$$\frac{\Pi_F}{G} \atop {\scriptstyle =NAF} \frac{}{(\neg G)} {\scriptstyle -I} \atop \Pi_I$$

$$\left({\scriptstyle =CUT} \frac{\Pi_E}{A} {\scriptstyle -E} \atop \frac{(B)}{\Pi_P} {\scriptstyle -I} \right) \Theta$$

where:
$A\Theta = B\Theta$

x – variable
X – parameter
t – term
$\#$ – contradiction
Θ – substitution

A, B – atomic formula
E, F, G, H – formula
Π_I – introduction proof
Π_E – elimination proof
Π_F – failure proof
Π_P – Prolog proof

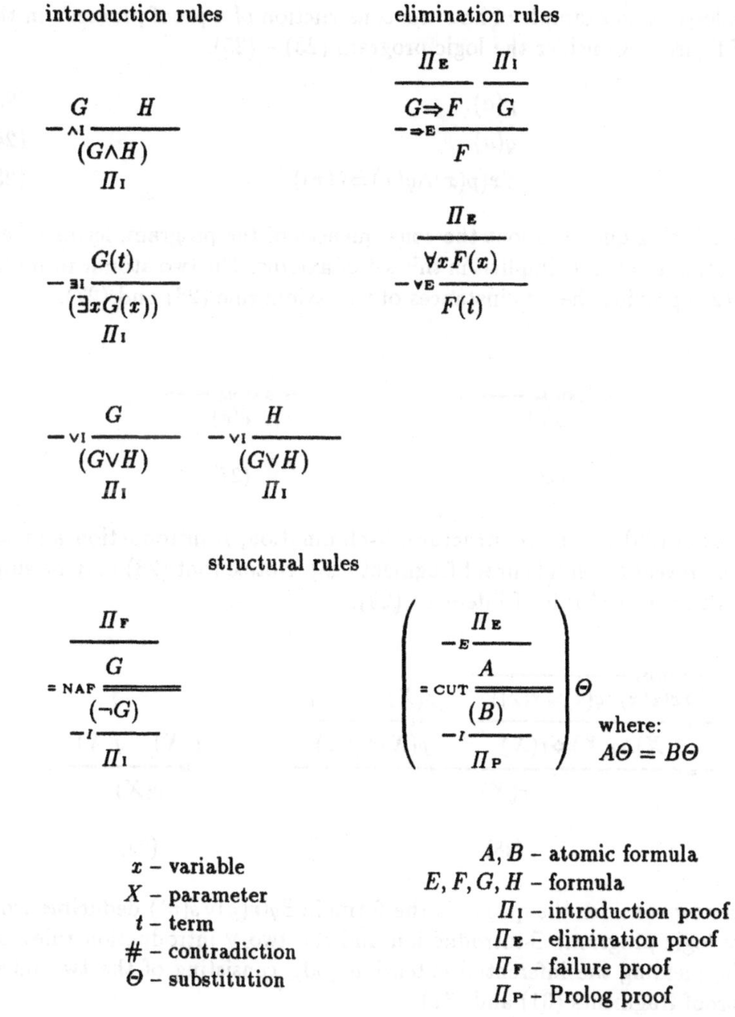

Fig. 3. Prolog proof

extensions of Prolog clauses and queries. These AND/OR trees can be found in Prolog implementations as the data structures representing goals. In this sense the new proof theory reflects implementation issues more faithfully than does the SLD resolution theory.

The **compose** phase is confronted with the problem of constructing an ANF proof given the set of proof fragments (derived rules of inference) produced by **extend**. The procedural semantics of Prolog correspond directly to a depth first, left to right application of our inductive definition of ANF proof.

Let us look at an example of how the construction of a proof proceeds in the system of figure 3. Consider the logic program (23) – (25).

$$p(a). \tag{23}$$

$$q(a). \tag{24}$$

$$\forall x(p(x)\wedge q(x)\Rightarrow r(x)). \tag{25}$$

Before inviting queries about the consequences of the program, let us reveal the elimination fragments implicit in this set of axioms. The two atomic formulae (23) and (24) provide the two instances of the axiom rule (26) and (27).

$${\scriptstyle\text{AXIOM}}\frac{}{p(a)} \qquad\qquad {\scriptstyle\text{AXIOM}}\frac{}{q(a)}$$

(26) (27)

The axiom (25) has more structure: $\forall$-elimination, $\wedge$-introduction and $\Rightarrow$-elimination, reveal the single proof fragment (28). Notice that (28) may be summarised as the derived rule of inference (29).

$${\scriptstyle\Rightarrow\text{E}}\frac{{\scriptstyle\forall\text{E}}\dfrac{{\scriptstyle\text{AXIOM}}\dfrac{}{\forall x(p(x)\wedge q(x)\Rightarrow r(x))}}{p(X)\wedge q(X)\Rightarrow r(X)} \quad {\scriptstyle\wedge\text{I}}\dfrac{p(X)\quad q(X)}{p(X)\wedge q(X)}}{r(X)} \qquad\qquad {\scriptstyle 28}\frac{p(X)\quad q(X)}{r(X)}$$

(28) (29)

Let us now consider the query: Is the formula $\exists y(r(y)\vee s(y))$ deducible from the above logic program? $\exists$-introduction and the two $\vee$-introduction rules are applicable, yielding the inferential extension (30), consisting of the two introduction proof fragments (31) and (32).

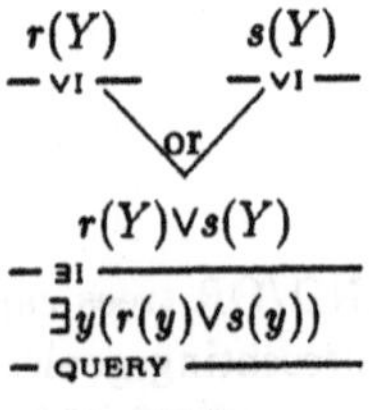

$${\scriptstyle\text{QUERY}}\frac{{\scriptstyle\exists\text{I}}\dfrac{{\scriptstyle\vee\text{I}}\dfrac{r(Y)}{r(Y)\vee s(Y)}}{\exists y(r(y)\vee s(y))}}{} \qquad\qquad {\scriptstyle\text{QUERY}}\frac{{\scriptstyle\exists\text{I}}\dfrac{{\scriptstyle\vee\text{I}}\dfrac{s(Y)}{r(Y)\vee s(Y)}}{\exists y(r(y)\vee s(y))}}{}$$

(30) (31) (32)

We now have in hand the set of proof fragments, (26), (27), (28), (31) and (32), from instances of which a proof is to be constructed, using instances of the CUT rule as glue. Only the one proof (33) is achievable. The equality assertions (substitutions) associated with instances of CUT are generated by a unification algorithm. The well-formedness of the result proof demands the consistency of the entire set of equality assertions (within a simple syntactic equality theory). This constraint is maintained by the composition of substitutions operation of [19], built into the unifier and representation mechanisms of implementations.

$$\dfrac{\dfrac{\dfrac{\dfrac{\dfrac{}{\forall x(p(x)\wedge q(x)\Rightarrow r(x))}\,\text{AXIOM}}{p(X_1)\wedge q(X_1)\Rightarrow r(X_1)}\,\forall\text{E} \qquad \dfrac{\dfrac{\dfrac{}{p(a)}\,\text{AXIOM}}{p(X_1)}\,\text{CUT}\; X_1=a \qquad \dfrac{\dfrac{}{q(a)}\,\text{AXIOM}}{q(X_1)}\,\text{CUT}\; X_1=a}{p(X_1)\wedge q(X_1)}\,\wedge\text{I}}{\dfrac{r(X_1)}{r(Y_1)}\,\text{CUT}\; Y_1=X_1}\,\Rightarrow\text{E}}{\dfrac{r(Y_1)\vee s(Y_1)}{\exists y(r(y)\vee s(y))}\,\exists\text{I}}\,\vee\text{I}$$

$$\text{— QUERY —}$$

(33)

The computational scaffolding may be removed from (33) by applying substitutions and hiding the CUTs. The result is the *cut free proof* (34).

$$\dfrac{\dfrac{\dfrac{\dfrac{}{\forall x(p(x)\wedge q(x)\Rightarrow r(x))}\,\text{AXIOM}}{p(a)\wedge q(a)\Rightarrow r(a)}\,\forall\text{E} \qquad \dfrac{\dfrac{}{p(a)}\,\text{AXIOM} \qquad \dfrac{}{q(a)}\,\text{AXIOM}}{p(a)\wedge q(a)}\,\wedge\text{I}}{r(a)}\,\Rightarrow\text{E}}{\dfrac{r(a)\vee s(a)}{\exists y(r(y)\vee s(y))}\,\exists\text{I}}\,\vee\text{I}$$

$$\text{— QUERY —}$$

(34)

Another variant of (33) is in terms of derived rules of inference, as shown in (35). Finally, the cut free version of this is shown in (36).

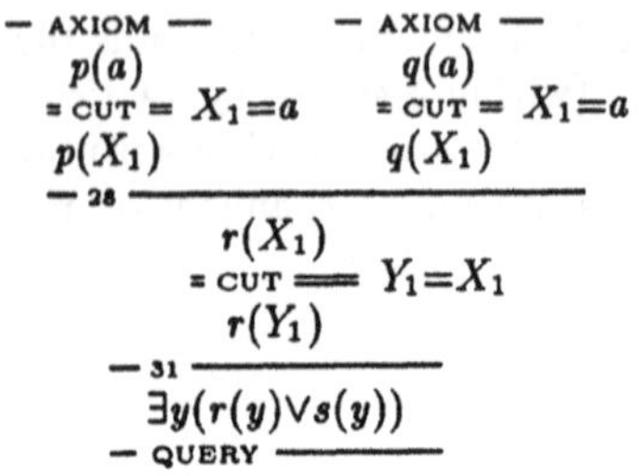

$$
\dfrac{\dfrac{\dfrac{\dfrac{}{p(a)}\,\text{AXIOM}}{p(X_1)}\,{=}\text{CUT}{=}\;X_1{=}a \qquad \dfrac{\dfrac{}{q(a)}\,\text{AXIOM}}{q(X_1)}\,{=}\text{CUT}{=}\;X_1{=}a}{\dfrac{r(X_1)}{r(Y_1)}\,{=}\text{CUT}{=}\;Y_1{=}X_1}\,28}{\exists y(r(y)\vee s(y))}\,31 \quad \text{QUERY}
$$

(35)

$$
\dfrac{\dfrac{\dfrac{}{p(a)}\,\text{AXIOM} \qquad \dfrac{}{q(a)}\,\text{AXIOM}}{r(a)}\,28}{\exists y(r(y)\vee s(y))}\,31 \quad \text{QUERY}
$$

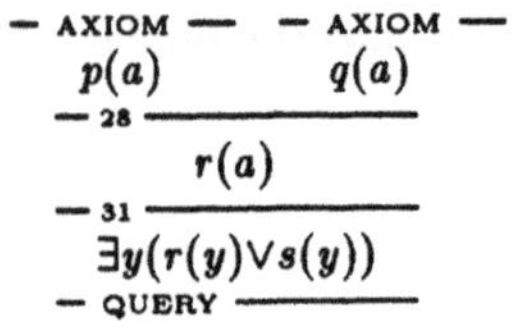

(36)

6 Conclusion

The formal properties and some of the practical consequences of the ANF scheme for subsystems of classical logic are investigated in [8]:

- The deductive completeness of ANF systems is established.
- The prospect of more expressive logic programming languages, achieved by incorporating the "missing" rules of inference is examined.
- The advantages of the natural deduction based approach for explanation, debugging and program analysis are demonstrated.
- A meta-language to control inference, based on the introspection of intermediate computation states, is proposed.

References

1. Krzysztof R. Apt and M. H. van Emden. *Contributions to the Theory of Logic Programming.* JACM, 29(3) 841–862 1982.
2. Keith L. Clark. 'Negation as Failure'. in H. Gallaire and J. Minker (eds). *Logic and Databases.* Plenum Press, 1978.
3. W. F. Clocksin and C. S. Mellish. *Programming in Prolog.* Springer-Verlag, 1981.
4. Haskell B. Curry. *Foundations of Mathematical Logic.* Dover Publications, 1977.
5. D. M. Gabbay and U. Reyle. *N-Prolog: An Extension of Prolog with Hypothetical Implications.* Journal of Logic Programming 1984:4:319-355
6. Gerhard Gentzen. *Untersuchungen über das logische Schliessen.* Mathematische Zeitschrift 39 176-210, 405-431, 1935. English translation in M. E. Szabo (ed). *The Collected Papers of Gerhard Gentzen.* North Holland, 1969.
7. Seif Haridi. *Logic Programming Based on a Natural Deduction System.* Technical Report TRITA-CS-8104, Department of Telecommunication Systems - Computer Systems, The Royal Institute of Technology, Stockholm, Sweden.
8. Seppo Keronen. *Computational Natural Deduction.* PhD Thesis, Department of Computer Science, Australian National University, Canberra, 1991.
9. Robert A. Kowalski and D. Kuehner. *Linear Resolution with Selection Function.* Artificial Intelligence 2 227–260, 1971.

10. J-L. Lassez, M. J. Maher and K. Marriott. 'Unification Revisited'. in J. Minker (ed.) *Deductive Databases and Logic Programming.* Morgan Kaufmann, 1988.
11. John W. Lloyd. *Foundations of Logic Programming.* Springer-Verlag, 1984
12. John W. Lloyd and Rodney W. Topor. *Making Prolog More Expressive.* Journal of Logic Programming 3 225-240, 1984.
13. Nils J. Nilsson. *Principles of Artificial Intelligence.* Tioga, 1980.
14. Lawrence C. Paulson. *Logic and Computation (Interactive Proof with Cambridge LCF).* Cambridge University Press, 1987.
15. Dag Prawitz. *Natural Deduction (A Proof-Theoretical Study).* Almqvist & Wiksell, 1965.
16. J. A. Robinson. *A Machine-Oriented Logic Based On the Resolution Principle.* JACM, 12(1) 23–41, 1965.
17. D. J. Shoesmith and T. J. Smiley. *Multiple-conclusion Logic.* Cambridge University Press, 1978.
18. Neil W. Tennant. *Natural Logic.* Edinburgh University Press, 1978.
19. J. van Vaalen. *An extension of unification to substitutions with an application to automatic theorem proving.* in IJCAI-4.

A Typed Foundation for Directional Logic Programming

Uday S. Reddy

Department of Computer Science
University of Illinois at Urbana-Champaign
Urbana, IL 61801
Net: reddy@cs.uiuc.edu

Abstract. A long standing problem in logic programming is how to impose ***directionality*** on programs in a safe fashion. The benefits of directionality include freedom from explicit sequential control, the ability to reason about algorithmic properties of programs (such as termination, complexity and deadlock-freedom) and controlling concurrency. By using Girard's linear logic, we are able to devise a type system that combines types and modes into a unified framework, and enables one to express directionality declaratively. The rich power of the type system allows outputs to be embedded in inputs and *vice versa*. Type checking guarantees that values have unique producers, but multiple consumers are still possible. From a theoretical point of view, this work provides a "logic programming interpretation" of (the proofs of) linear logic, adding to the concurrency and functional programming interpretations that are already known. It also brings logic programming into the broader world of typed languages and types-as-propositions paradigm, enriching it with static scoping and higher-order features.

Keywords Directionality, modes, types, concurrent logic programming, linear logic, Curry-Howard isomorphism, sequent calculus, logic variables.

1 Introduction

Logic programming was heralded with the slogan [29]:

Algorithm = Logic + Control

While the "logic" part of the algorithm, formalized by declarative semantics, has been well-studied (see, *e.g.*, [35]), procedural semantics—the semantics of control—has not progressed far. Since the theory offers only certain unreachable mechanisms for complete strategies [33], practical logic programming languages have resorted to low-level operational mechanisms that are not entirely satisfactory. The sequential control of Prolog [9] and the read-only variables of Concurrent Prolog [49] are examples of such mechanisms. At the same time, the desire for higher-level *declarative* mechanisms for specifying control has been certainly present, as seen in the mode declarations of Parlog [21] and MU-Prolog [41].

We believe that a formal approach to procedural semantics is necessary so that one can reason about algorithmic properties of programs such as termination, complexity and deadlock freedom *etc.* To address such questions one needs to specify not only the "logic" of an algorithm but also how the logic is to be used, *i.e.*, what kind of parameters we intend to supply to a predicate.

We propose the concept of a *procedure* as the foundation for algorithmically sound logic programming. A procedure is like a predicate, but has a specific input-output directionality. It is not necessary for an entire argument of a predicate to be an input or output. Outputs can be embedded in input arguments and inputs can be embedded in output arguments. Thus, the interesting applications of logic variables such as partially instantiated data structures and back communication in concurrent programs are still possible. What is required is a certain well-formedness condition: If a value is given as an input to a procedure, there must be another procedure (in fact, precisely one procedure) which produces the value as an output. We call logic programming via such procedures *directional logic programming.*[1] Conventional logic programs can then be thought of as short hand notations which stand for multiple directional logic programs.

Historically, this work was begun in [42, 43] where a "simple theory of directionality" was outlined. The qualifier "simple" signifies the fact that entire arguments of predicates are treated as inputs or outputs. (Undoubtedly, such a simple theory is not adequate to handle all logic programs of interest). Ideas similar to this proposal were used in Parlog [8, 21] and MU-Prolog [41] for controlling evaluation order, and by Deville [13] for reasoning about algorithmic properties of logic programs. However, the subset of programs treated by the simple modes is too weak, and all these applications found need for extensions which, unfortunately, lacked the conviction of the simple modes. The author had been of the opinion that "combining modes with types" would provide a way to obtain a richer theory of directionality. But, this project had never been carried to its conclusion. With Girard's invention of *linear logic* [17], all the technical tools necessary for the synthesis of types and modes were suddenly found to be in place. This paper reports on the application of linear logic to the problem of directionality.

Linear logic was formulated by Girard as a constructive logic that is "larger" than intuitionistic logic. In particular, it incorporates features of classical logic such as the law of negation $\neg\neg A = A$ and a version of the excluded middle: $A \vee \neg A$. This feat is accomplished by controlling the use of *structural rules*, weakening and contraction, which would otherwise allow a hypothesis to be used an arbitrary number of times (as in classical or intuitionistic logic). In fact, Girard notes that intuitionistic logic itself owes its constructive nature to restrictions on the structural rules. By making these restrictions uniform, we obtain a constructive logic that is able to go beyond the intuitionistic one.

[1] The concept of procedures is, in fact, present in most concurrent logic programming languages including Concurrent Prolog [49], Parlog [21], Janus [45] and other concurrent constraint languages [46]. Our notion of directional logic programming includes them and provides a *theory* for their well-formedness.

The proofs in a constructive logic are recipes for computation, *i.e.*, they are programs. For instance, functional programs are textual representations of the proofs of intuitionistic logic. (See [2, 10, 20, 37, 52]). The proofs of linear logic must similarly have a computational interpretation as programs. What kind of programs? It seems that the symmetries of linear logic permit a wide spectrum of interpretations. Girard himself formulated a concurrent computation framework called proof nets [17, 19]. Lafont [31] uses similar structures called "interaction nets". However, the abstract nature of this framework does not readily lend itself to use as a programming language. Abramsky [2] was the first to propose a concrete computational interpretation as a concurrent programming language in the framework of the "chemical abstract machine" [5]. Filinski [14] and Reddy [44] proposed functional programming interpretations in terms of continuations and "acceptors" respectively. It seems that the asymmetry between inputs and outputs present in functional programming does not fit well with linear logic. The present work forms yet another interpretation of the proofs of linear logic: as directional logic programs. Not only do logic programs avoid the asymmetry of functional programs, but many of their features, such as Horn clause notation, find a ready correspondence with linear logic concepts.

Curry-Howard isomorphism In interpreting this work, one must separate in one's mind two distinct ways of relating programming languages and logic. In the *declarative programming* tradition, one has the correspondence:

$$\begin{aligned} \text{programs} &\longleftrightarrow \text{propositions} \\ \text{computations} &\longleftrightarrow \text{proofs} \end{aligned}$$

This is sometimes called "proofs as computations" correspondence. There is a large body of work in using this correspondence to interpret linear logic for declarative programming (including logic programming [3, 24, 26, 30] and concurrent systems [4, 6, 15, 22, 36]). On the other hand, as outlined in the previous paragraph, a deeper correspondence exists with *constructive* logics:

$$\begin{aligned} \text{types} &\longleftrightarrow \text{propositions} \\ \text{programs} &\longleftrightarrow \text{proofs} \\ \text{computation} &\longleftrightarrow \text{proof normalization} \end{aligned}$$

This correspondence is often called "propositions as types" correspondence or Curry-Howard isomorphism (following the work of [11, 27]). Here, programs are treated as purely recipes for computation and their potential declarative reading remains in the background. To emphasize this aspect—and to prevent confusion between the two correspondences—we will avoid the terminology of "predicate" and "goal formula" and use "procedure" and "command" in their place. The role of propositions in the programming context is played not by programs but by their types. To see why this is so, think of the type of a program as a weak form of specification. If p is a constructive proof of a proposition A, then the recipe for computation involved in p satisfies the specification corresponding to A. In fact, types need not really be weak specifications. By enriching types to include equality propositions and dependent type constructors, one obtains a rich type system that can express arbitrary specifications [10, 37, 52]. We will say no more about this important topic. The reader may refer to the above references and [20] for further discussion of the Curry-Howard correspondence.

Directionality It is well-known that the selection of literals for resolution in logic programming crucially determines the search space. (See [43, 50] for a discussion). Take, for example, the list reversal program:

```
reverse(nil, nil).
reverse(a.x, y) ← reverse(x,z), append(z, a.nil, y).
```

and the goal **reverse**(L**, x)** where L is a specific list. Using left-to-right literal selection, the evaluation of the goal terminates in $O(n)$ time with one solution. But, using right-to-left literal selection, the same goal takes $O(n^2)$ time for the first solution and fails to terminate upon backtracking. These effects are roughly reversed for the goal reverse(x, L). Therefore, logic programs are well-behaved for only certain sets of goals. We want to be able to specify the acceptable sets of goals and use such specifications for literal selection.

Suppose we specify input-output modes such as

```
mode reverse(in, out).
mode append(in, in, out).
```

Using a "strong" interpretation of modes as in [43], the acceptable goals are those which have ground terms in the input argument positions and variables in the output positions. Thus, **reverse**(L**, x)** is acceptable, but **reverse(x,** L**)** is not. A concurrent evaluation strategy can be devised where goals are suspended until the arguments in input positions have sufficient information for evaluation. The undesirable effects mentioned in the previous paragraph are thus eliminated.

However, specifying acceptable goals is not enough. We must also ensure that only acceptable goals are produced during evaluation. This involves checking that every variable in a clause appears in a single output position and cyclic waits do not arise. The "theory of directionality" of [43] and the "directionality check" of [21] are automatic methods of ensuring this.

The limitation of simple modes is that entire arguments are considered input or output. We cannot embed outputs in inputs and *vice versa*. For instance, we cannot use **reverse** to reverse a list of unbound variables. As argued by Shapiro [48] embedding outputs in inputs is crucial for concurrent applications. Parlog weakens its mode system to allow such embedding, but does not provide a way to check whether it is used consistently.

A little thought reveals that a solution for this problem lies in considering types. The type

```
reverse : Pred (List(t), List(t))
```

is polymorphic in the element type t [23, 32, 40], *i.e.*, **reverse** works uniformly for all types of list elements. If we combine mode information with types, this polymorphism is enough to indicate that ground terms, unbound variables and all other kinds of mixtures are acceptable as list elements for **reverse**. In the linear-logic based type system proposed here, every type t has a dual type $t^\perp$ whose meaning is to switch the input-output notion of t. We can then specify the (directional) type of **reverse** as

```
reverse : proc (List(t), List(t)⊥)
```

This states that the first argument is an *input* of type List(t) and the second argument is an *output* of type List(t). If we instantiate t to, say, int, we obtain the effect that a list of integers is reversed. On the other hand, if we instantiate it to $\texttt{int}^\perp$, we have the effect that a list of place holders for integers (such as unbound variables) is reversed.

Overview The rest of this paper is organized as follows. We first give a brief overview of linear logic in Section 2 and mention its meaning in terms of propositions as well types. In Section 3, we informally motivate the concepts of directional logic programming. A concrete logic programming language is presented in Section 4 together with its type rules and procedural semantics. We also give several examples to illustrate its use and the constraints of the type system. Its theoretical properties are mentioned in Section 5. Finally, in Section 6, we consider various extensions such as adding functions, nondeterminism *etc.*

2 Overview of Linear Logic

The syntax of propositions (or types) in linear logic is as follows. Let β range over atomic propositions (atomic type terms) and $A, B, \ldots$ over propositions. Then,[2]

$$\begin{array}{rll} A ::= & \beta \mid A^\perp & \\ & \mid A \otimes B \mid A \,||\, B \mid 1 \mid \bot & \text{- multiplicatives} \\ & \mid A \,\&\, B \mid A \oplus B \mid \top \mid 0 & \text{- additives} \\ & \mid\, !A \mid ?A & \text{- exponentials} \end{array}$$

That is a lot of connectives for a propositional fragment of a logic! We will describe the meaning of these connectives (from a type-theoretic point of view) in the remainder of the paper. For now, we note that each classical connective has two versions in linear logic—a multiplicative one and an additive one. On each of these rows, the listed connectives correspond to $\wedge$, $\vee$, true and false of classical logic. The operator $(\ )^\perp$ corresponds to negation. The operators ! and ? are new. They indicate permission to carry out the structural rules of *weakening* (representing $A \Rightarrow$ true and false $\Rightarrow A$) and *contraction* ($A \Rightarrow A \wedge A$ and $A \vee A \Rightarrow A$) on the propositions.

[2] The type constructor "||" is written as an upside down & in Girard's original notation. Our change of notation is due to typographical reasons.

The most important feature of linear logic is that negation is involutive (just as in classical logic), *i.e.*, $A^{\perp\perp} = A$.[3] Moreover, all other connectives satisfy the following De Morgan laws:

$$
\begin{array}{rcl@{\qquad}rcl}
(A \otimes B)^{\perp} &=& A^{\perp} \mathbin{||} B^{\perp} & (A \mathbin{||} B)^{\perp} &=& A^{\perp} \otimes B^{\perp} \\
1^{\perp} &=& \perp & \perp^{\perp} &=& 1 \\
(A \,\&\, B)^{\perp} &=& A^{\perp} \oplus B^{\perp} & (A \oplus B)^{\perp} &=& A^{\perp} \,\&\, B^{\perp} \\
\top^{\perp} &=& 0 & 0^{\perp} &=& \top \\
(!A)^{\perp} &=& ?A^{\perp} & (?A)^{\perp} &=& !A^{\perp}
\end{array}
$$

This means that many of the expressible propositions are equal to each other. We obtain unique representations (negation normal forms) if we restrict negation to atomic propositions. Implication is defined in the classical fashion: $A \multimap B = A^{\perp} \mathbin{||} B$. So, $A^{\perp}$ can also be thought of as $A \multimap \perp$.

We are interested in the use of linear logic as a "constructive" logic, *i.e.*, in modelling programs as proofs of linear logic propositions. A linear logic proof from a collection of hypotheses Γ must use each of the hypotheses precisely once. This is called the *linearity* property. Now, consider, what is a proof of $A^{\perp}$? It should be a "proof method" that transforms proofs of A into contradictions. We can think of such a method as a "pure consumer" of proofs of A. How about a proof of $A^{\perp\perp}$? A method for transforming proofs of $A^{\perp}$ into contradictions must implicitly produce a proof of A and use it for contradicting $A^{\perp}$. So, it is effectively a proof of A. What we have just given is an informal argument that proofs of $A^{\perp\perp}$ and A are isomorphic. The requirement of linearity is crucial to this. Without it, we cannot be sure if the proof method for $A^{\perp\perp}$ is just ignoring $A^{\perp}$ or using it multiple times. In the first case, it would have produced no proof of A at all, and, in the second, it would have produced multiple proofs of A. Thus, by imposing the restriction of linearity, we obtain the all-important negation law: $A^{\perp\perp} = A$.

Let us switch gears and think of propositions as types and proofs as computations. If a computation of type A produces a value of type A, then a computation of type $A^{\perp}$ *consumes* values of type A. So, a computations of type $A^{\perp\perp}$ consumes consumers of A-typed values. As argued above, it effectively produces an A-typed value. So, the negation operator $(\ )^{\perp}$ means ***inverting the input-output notion*** of a type. An input of type A is an output of type $A^{\perp}$ and an output of type A is an input of type $A^{\perp}$. Thus, input-output modes are incorporated into types.

The best way to study linear logic proofs is by a sequent calculus [16, 18, 20, 51]. A derivation of a sequent $\Gamma \vdash \Delta$ represents a proof of (the disjunction of) the conclusions Δ from (the conjunction of) the hypotheses Γ. In a logic with involutive negation, it is not strictly necessary to treat hypotheses and conclusions separately. The sequent $\Gamma \vdash \Delta$ is equivalent to a right-sided sequent $\vdash \Gamma^{\perp}, \Delta$. This is the format used in [2, 17]. However, we will find it convenient to work with symmetric sequents. In Figure 1, we give a sequent calculus presentation of linear logic which uses symmetric sequents, but still does most of its work on the right hand side alone. For the most part, the logical intuitions

[3] We adopt the convention that $(\ )^{\perp}$ binds closely. So $A^{\perp\perp}$ is to be parsed as $(A^{\perp})^{\perp}$.

$$\text{Exchange} \quad \frac{\Gamma, A, B, \Gamma' \vdash \Delta}{\Gamma, B, A, \Gamma' \vdash \Delta} \quad \frac{\Gamma \vdash \Delta, A, B, \Delta'}{\Gamma \vdash \Delta, B, A, \Delta'}$$

$$\text{Id} \quad \frac{}{A \vdash A} \qquad \text{Cut}_R \quad \frac{\Gamma \vdash A, \Delta \quad \Gamma' \vdash A^{\perp}, \Delta'}{\Gamma, \Gamma' \vdash \Delta, \Delta'}$$

$$(\,)^{\perp}\mathcal{R} \quad \frac{\Gamma, A \vdash \Delta}{\Gamma \vdash A^{\perp}, \Delta} \qquad (\,)^{\perp}\mathcal{L} \quad \frac{\Gamma \vdash A, \Delta}{\Gamma, A^{\perp} \vdash \Delta}$$

$$\otimes\mathcal{R} \quad \frac{\Gamma \vdash A, \Delta \quad \Gamma' \vdash B, \Delta'}{\Gamma, \Gamma' \vdash A \otimes B, \Delta, \Delta'} \qquad \parallel \mathcal{R} \quad \frac{\Gamma \vdash A, B, \Delta}{\Gamma \vdash A \parallel B, \Delta}$$

$$\mathbf{1}\,\mathcal{R} \quad \frac{}{\vdash \mathbf{1}} \qquad \perp \mathcal{R} \quad \frac{\Gamma \vdash \Delta}{\Gamma \vdash \perp, \Delta}$$

$$\oplus\mathcal{R} \quad \frac{\Gamma \vdash A, \Delta}{\Gamma \vdash A \oplus B, \Delta} \quad \frac{\Gamma \vdash B, \Delta}{\Gamma \vdash A \oplus B, \Delta} \qquad \&\,\mathcal{R} \quad \frac{\Gamma \vdash A, \Delta \quad \Gamma \vdash B, \Delta}{\Gamma \vdash A \,\&\, B, \Delta}$$

$$\text{no rule for } \mathbf{0}\ \mathcal{R} \qquad \top\mathcal{R} \quad \frac{}{\Gamma \vdash \top, \Delta}$$

$$!\mathcal{R} \quad \frac{!\Gamma \vdash A, ?\Delta}{!\Gamma \vdash !A, ?\Delta} \qquad ?\mathcal{R} \quad \frac{\Gamma \vdash A, \Delta}{\Gamma \vdash ?A, \Delta}$$

$$?\mathcal{W} \quad \frac{\Gamma \vdash \Delta}{\Gamma \vdash ?A, \Delta} \qquad ?\mathcal{C} \quad \frac{\Gamma \vdash ?A, ?A, \Delta}{\Gamma \vdash ?A, \Delta}$$

Fig. 1. Sequent calculus for linear logic

given earlier should explain the rules. The annotations $\mathcal{L}$, $\mathcal{R}$, $\mathcal{W}$ and $\mathcal{C}$ stand for left-introduction, right-introduction, weakening and contraction respectively. In $!\mathcal{R}$, the notation $!\Gamma$ $(?\Delta)$ means a sequence all of whose formulas are of the form $!X$ $(?Y)$. The reason for this requirement is explained in Section 6.1. See [34, 47] for informal introductions to linear logic and [2, 17] for fuller treatments.

3 Towards Directional Logic Programming

In this section, we informally motivate the concepts of directional logic programming. Our starting point is Typed Prolog [32]. A predicate definition in Typed Prolog is of the form:

$$\begin{array}{l} P : \mathit{pred}\ (A_1 \times \ldots \times A_k) \\ P(\bar{t}_1) \leftarrow \phi_1 \\ \quad \vdots \\ P(\bar{t}_n) \leftarrow \phi_n \end{array}$$

For our purpose, it will be better to work with iff-completions of the Horn clauses as defined in [7]:

$$P(\bar{x}) \iff (\exists \bar{y}_1, \bar{z}_1 .\, \bar{x} = \bar{t}_1, \phi_1);\ \ldots;\ (\exists \bar{y}_n, \bar{z}_n .\, \bar{x} = \bar{t}_n, \phi_n)$$

($\bar{y}_i$ are the variables of $\bar{t}_i$ and $\bar{z}_i$ are the variables of ϕ_i which do not occur in $\bar{t}_i$). We will also use a similar iff-completion for type definitions. If

$$f_1 : A_1 \to \beta \quad \ldots \quad f_n : A_n \to \beta$$

are *all* the function symbols with the atomic type β as their range type, then we assume a (possibly recursive) definition of β as

$$type\ \beta = f_1\ A_1 + \cdots + f_n\ A_n$$

Here, "+" is the *disjoint union* (or *sum*) type constructor and the symbols f_i are taken to be the "constructor tags" used for injection of the summands into β.

SLD-resolution with respect to the original Horn clause program can now be viewed as a certain reduction semantics with respect to the iff-completion. Treat each predicate definition as a *rewrite rule*. In addition, add the following reductions:

$$\begin{array}{rcll}
x = t, \phi[x] & \longrightarrow & x = t, \phi[t] & \text{if } x \notin V(t) \quad (1)\\
x = x & \longrightarrow & & (2)\\
x = t & \longrightarrow & \mathit{false} & \text{if } x \in V(t) \text{ and } t \neq x \quad (3)\\
(t_1, \ldots, t_k) = (u_1, \ldots, u_k) & \longrightarrow & t_1 = u_1, \ldots, t_k = u_k & (4)\\
f\,t = f\,u & \longrightarrow & t = u & (5)\\
f\,t = g\,u & \longrightarrow & \mathit{false} & \text{if } f \neq g \quad (6)\\
\mathit{false}, \phi & \longrightarrow & \mathit{false} & (7)\\
\exists x.\, \phi & \longrightarrow & \phi & \text{if } x \notin V(\phi) \quad (8)\\
\exists x.\, x = t, \phi & \longrightarrow & \phi & \text{if } x \notin V(\phi) \quad (9)\\
\mathit{false}; \phi & \longrightarrow & \phi & (10)\\
(\phi_1; \phi_2), \phi' & \longrightarrow & (\phi_1, \phi'); (\phi_2, \phi') & (11)
\end{array}$$

In reduction (1), $\phi[x]$ denotes a formula with one or more occurrences of x. Reductions (1-6) handle unification, (7) handles failure, (8-9) handle "garbage collection" and (10-11) handle backtracking. The reduction system is Church-Rosser. (In traditional theory [35], this result is stated as the independence of the answer substitutions on the selection function). Now, the reduction of a goal of the form $P(\bar{t})$, if it converges, yields a possibly infinite normal form:

$$\exists \bar{y}_1.\, \bar{x} = \bar{u}_1;\ \exists \bar{y}_2.\, \bar{x} = \bar{u}_2;\ \ldots$$

which denotes the answer substitutions obtained by SLD-resolution. (Handling the divergent case requires some more work; but that would lead us too far astray). For example, given the Typed Prolog program:

```
nil : List α
"." : α × List α → List α
append : pred (List α × List α × List α)
append(nil, ys, ys) ←
append(x.xs, ys, x.zs) ← append(xs,ys,zs)
```

we have the iff-completion:

```
type List α = nil + α.(List α)
append : pred (List α × List α × List α)
append(xs, ys, zs) ⟺
    (∃ ys'. xs = nil, ys = ys', zs = ys');
    (∃ x,xs',ys',zs'. xs = x.xs', ys = ys', zs = x.zs',
       append(xs', ys', zs'))
```

The goal **append(1.nil, 2.nil, ans)** reduces to the normal form

```
ans = 1.2.nil
```

From now on, we refer to this as *relational* logic programming in order to distinguish it from *directional* logic programming.

Procedural notions Predicate calls in logic programs involve various procedural notions. In using a predicate as a *condition*, we typically give it ground arguments and use both the true and false cases of the result. In using it as a *test*, we use only the true case of the result; the false case is considered a "failure". Such use as tests is found, for example, in generate-and-test programs. Finally, in using a predicate as a *procedure*, we give it both ground and nonground arguments, expecting some or all of the variables in the arguments to get bound at the end of the procedure. A further distinction can be made based on *determinacy*. Deterministic procedures are always expected to succeed and yield a single answer substitution upon success. A failure of a deterministic procedure is tantamount to an "error", *e.g.*, accessing the top of an empty stack. A nondeterministic procedure may yield multiple answer substitutions upon backtracking or fail indicating that there are no further answers. The above description paints a rich and varied picture of procedural notions used in logic programming. The challenge is to formulate a procedural semantics that supports such notions.

Our proposal is mainly directed at the use of predicates as procedures, even though conditions and tests are supported by indirect means. Even among procedures, we concentrate mainly on deterministic procedures. Our understanding of nondeterministic procedures is still preliminary.

Inputs and outputs In using a predicate as a procedure, we need to distinguish between inputs and outputs. While in the declarative reading of a predicate, all its arguments are formally treated as inputs, in the procedural reading, some quantities among the arguments are actually "place holders" for outputs, *e.g.*, **ans** in the call **append(1.nil, 2.nil, ans)**. One way to handle these distinctions is to annotate arguments as input or output. But, linear logic suggests a much more comprehensive treatment. For every type A, it provides a dual type $A^{\perp}$ which switches the input-output notion of A. That is, an input of type $A^{\perp}$ is really an output of type A and an output of type $A^{\perp}$ is really an input of type A. It is reasonable to think of $A^{\perp}$ as the type of place holders for A-typed values. Such place holders, when given to procedures, must necessarily be filled in with values. This is a property guaranteed by the type system. So, giving an argument of type $A^\perp$ has the effect of demanding an A-typed value as an output.

Using these notions, we can define an append procedure with the type:

$$\texttt{append : proc (List } \alpha \otimes \texttt{List } \alpha \otimes \texttt{(List } \alpha)^\perp\texttt{)}$$

This constrains the append procedure so that its first two arguments are always list inputs and the third argument is always a list output. Other versions of append procedures can be similarly defined with different input-output directionality. A single predicate of relational logic programming can thus correspond to many procedures in directional logic programming. All of them share the *same* declarative semantics, but have different procedural semantics.

The advantage of combining input-output modes with types is that directionality specification is not limited to procedure arguments. It can also apply to data structures or parts of data structures. For instance, the type $List\,\alpha \otimes (List\,\alpha)^\perp$ is the type of pairs which have lists as their first components and place holders for lists as their second components. Such a type is useful in formulating difference lists, for example.

Every type constructor of Typed Prolog splits into two versions in directional logic programming: one that plays the standard input-output role and the other that plays the dual role. This is summarized in the following table:

Typed Prolog	Standard direction	Dual direction
Unit	1	$\perp$
$\times$	$\otimes$	$\|\|$
$+$	$\oplus$	$\&$

This means that a single type of Typed Prolog can have many directional versions. For example, the directional incarnations of $A \times B$ include $A \otimes B$, $A^\perp \otimes B$, $A \otimes B^\perp$, $A^\perp \otimes B^\perp$ and four other types which use $||$ in place of $\otimes$. And, even more combinations if we look inside A and B!

The "terms" of Typed Prolog split into two kinds of constructs in directional logic programming: *patterns*, when used in their input role (*e.g.*, left hand sides of clauses), and *terms*, when used in their output role (*e.g.*, as arguments of procedures). The unification operation "=" becomes a (bi-) directional unification operation "$\Leftrightarrow$". Whereas in $t_1 = t_2$, t_1 and t_2 are of the same type A, in $t_1 \Leftrightarrow t_2$, t_1 and t_2 are of dual types: A and $A^\perp$ respectively. So, t_1 is a producer of A's and t_2 is a consumer of A's and the unification $t_1 \Leftrightarrow t_2$ makes them communicate.

In the next section, we present a concrete programming language based on these ideas.

4 The Core Language

The language we present is quite large. Notice that there are 10 type constructors and, for each of them, there must be a way to produce a value of the type and a way to consume a value of the type (with some exceptions). That gives something like 20 type rules! The symmetries of linear logic mean that only half of them are essential. The other half are just variants. However, defining the language by only half the rules sacrifices convenience and understandability. We use a compromise where the "official" definition of the language (Fig. 1, 2) chooses economy but our explanation of it chooses convenience. In this section, we present the core language which involves the type constructors $\otimes$, $\mathbf{1}$ and $\oplus$ (together with their duals $||$, $\perp$ and $\&$). We omit $\top$ and $\mathbf{0}$ because they seem to play no role in a programming language, and relegate exponentials to a cursory treatment in Section 6.

A *computation* in a directional logic program, in general, accepts some number of *inputs* (say, of types $A_1, \ldots, A_n$) and some number of *outputs* (say, of types $B_1, \ldots, B_m$). Such a computation can be viewed as a network of the following form:[4]

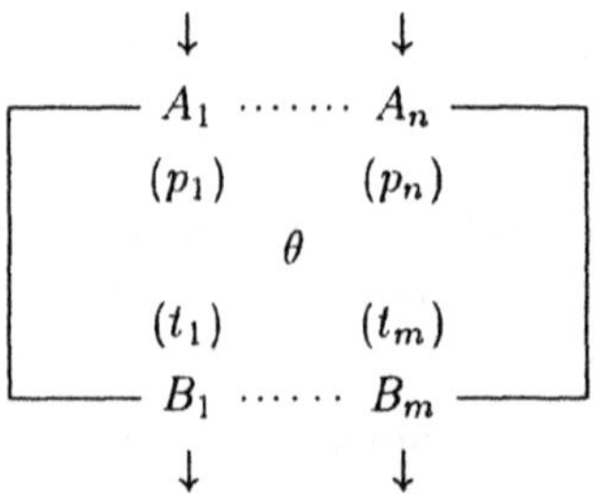

In the concrete syntax, the inputs are represented by what are called *patterns* $(p_1, \ldots, p_n)$, outputs by *terms* $(t_1, \ldots, t_m)$ and the internal connections of the network by a *command* (θ).[5] We also represent the same computation as a sequent:

$$p_1 : A_1, \ldots, p_n : A_n \vdash \{\theta\}\ t_1 : B_1, \ldots, t_m : B_m$$

We use the symbols Γ and Δ to denote collections of typings on the left and right hand sides of $\vdash$. So, for example, $\Gamma \vdash \{\theta\}\Delta$ is a schematic sequent.

The directional versions of predicates are called *procedures*. Their definitions are of the form:

$$\begin{array}{l} P : proc\ A \\ P\,p \;=\; \theta \end{array}$$

Note that only patterns occur on the left hand side of a definition and the procedure body only contains a command. So, a procedure is a computation of

[4] In [17], these computations are called "proof nets".

[5] Note that, in traditional logic programming, input-output distinctions are ignored. So, patterns and terms merge into a single class, *viz.*, terms. Commands map to their non-directional versions, formulas.

the form:

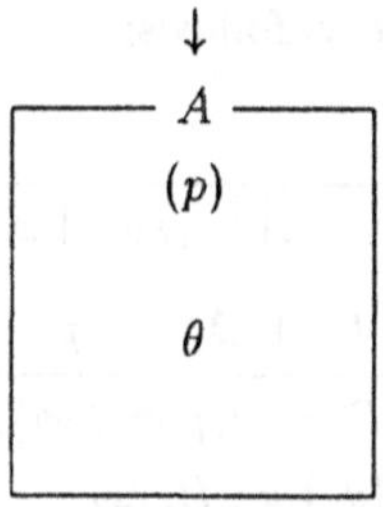

It does not produce a *direct* output though it may produce outputs indirectly by assigning values to its output arguments.

The context-free syntax of patterns, terms and commands is as follows. Assume the syntactic classes

$$x \in Variable$$
$$P \in Procedure$$

The set of variables is partitioned into two isomorphic subsets:

$$Variable = Variable^{+} \uplus Variable^{-}$$
$$(\,)^{\perp} : Variable^{+} \cong Variable^{-} : (\,)^{\perp}$$

If x is a variable in one of the subsets, then its image in the other subset is denoted $x^{\perp}$. This is similar to the naming convention used in CCS [39]. The abstract syntax is given by

$$\begin{aligned} p, q &\in Pattern \\ t, u &\in Term \\ \theta, \phi &\in Command \end{aligned}$$

$$\begin{aligned} p &::= x \mid () \mid (p_1, p_2) \mid [\,] \mid [p_1, p_2] \\ &\quad \mid case(inl\; p_1 \Rightarrow \theta_1 \mid inr\; p_2 \Rightarrow \theta_2) \mid \langle p_1, \_\rangle \mid \langle \_, p_2\rangle \\ t &::= x \mid () \mid (t_1, t_2) \mid [\,] \mid [t_1, t_2] \\ &\quad \mid inl\; t \mid inr\; t \mid \langle \{\theta_1\}t_1,\ \{\theta_2\}t_2\rangle \\ \theta &::= succ \mid p \Leftarrow t \mid t_1 \Leftrightarrow t_2 \mid \theta_1, \theta_2 \mid \nu x.\theta \mid P\, t \\ &\quad \mid error \mid fail \mid \theta_1 ; \theta_2 \end{aligned}$$

The meaning of these constructs is explained in the remainder of the section together with their type rules.

4.1 Traditional data structures

We start with the constructs that the reader can easily relate to: term formation rules for traditional data structures. $A \otimes B$ is the type of pairs, $\mathbf{1}$ is the unit type (consisting of the empty tuple) and $A \oplus B$ is the sum type (consisting of variants). The type rules are as follows:

$$\frac{}{x : A \vdash \{succ\}\ x : A}\ \mathsf{Id}$$

$$\frac{\Gamma \vdash \{\theta\}\ t : A, \Delta \quad \Gamma', p : A \vdash \{\phi\} \Delta'}{\Gamma, \Gamma' \vdash \{\theta, p \Leftarrow t, \phi\} \Delta, \Delta'}\ \mathsf{Cut}$$

$$\frac{\Gamma_1 \vdash \{\theta_1\}\ t : A, \Delta_1 \quad \Gamma_2 \vdash \{\theta_2\}\ u : B, \Delta_2}{\Gamma_1, \Gamma_2 \vdash \{\theta_1, \theta_2\}\ (t, u) : A \otimes B, \Delta_1, \Delta_2}\ \otimes\mathcal{R} \qquad \frac{\Gamma, p : A, q : B \vdash \{\theta\} \Delta}{\Gamma, (p, q) : A \otimes B \vdash \{\theta\} \Delta}\ \otimes\mathcal{L}$$

$$\frac{}{\vdash \{succ\}\ () : \mathbf{1}}\ \mathbf{1}\mathcal{R} \qquad \frac{\Gamma \vdash \{\theta\}\ \Delta}{\Gamma, () : \mathbf{1} \vdash \{\theta\} \Delta}\ \mathbf{1}\mathcal{L}$$

$$\frac{\Gamma \vdash \{\theta\}\ t : A, \Delta}{\Gamma \vdash \{\theta\}\ inl\, t : A \oplus B, \Delta}\ \oplus\mathcal{R}_1 \qquad \frac{\Gamma \vdash \{\theta\}\ u : B, \Delta}{\Gamma \vdash \{\theta\}\ inr\, u : A \oplus B, \Delta}\ \oplus\mathcal{R}_2$$

$$\frac{\Gamma, p : A \vdash \{\theta\}\ \Delta \quad \Gamma, q : B \vdash \{\phi\}\ \Delta}{\Gamma, case(inl\ p \Rightarrow \theta \mid inr\ q \Rightarrow \phi) : A \oplus B \vdash \{succ\}\ \Delta}\ \oplus\mathcal{L}$$

The rules are mostly self-explanatory, but some minor comments are in order. In the rule Id, *succ* (short for "succeed") is to be thought of as the empty command which always succeeds (similar to *true* in Prolog). We often omit writing $\{succ\}$ in a sequent. In the rule Cut, the command $p \Leftarrow t$ means a pattern match and "," denotes symmetric composition. The computation constructed by the Cut rule is of the following form:

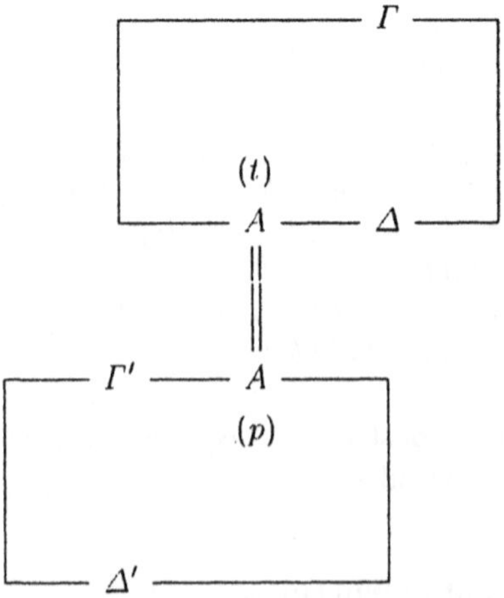

The A-typed output of the first computation is plugged into the A-typed input of the second computation. Similarly, the computations formed by $\otimes\mathcal{R}$ and $\otimes\mathcal{L}$

are

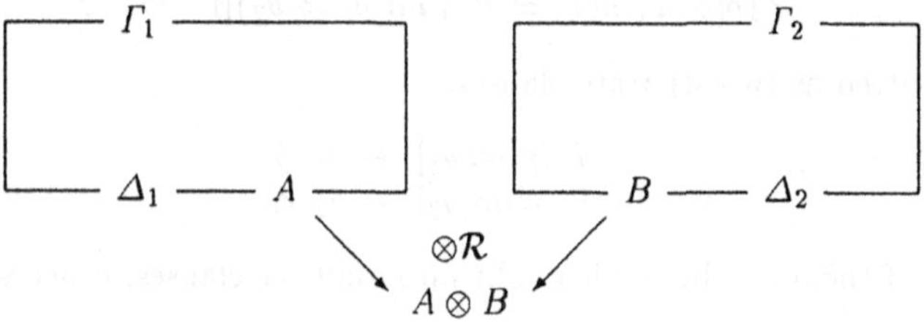

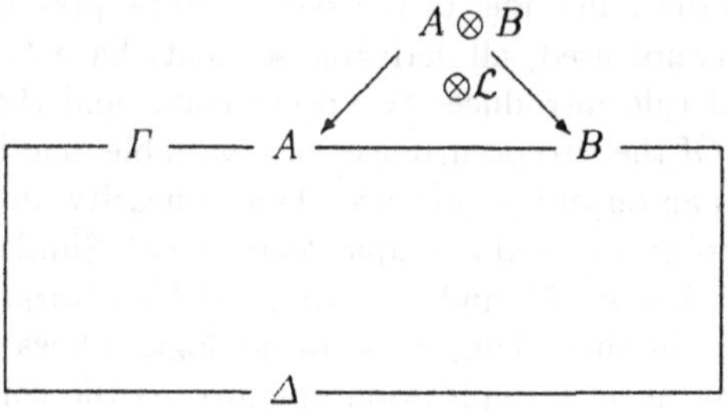

Note that a pair is produced by producing its components from two *separate* computations. In contrast, the consumption of a pair involves consuming both its components in the *same* computation. This difference in how pairs are produced and consumed is crucial.

In the $\oplus\mathcal{R}$ rules, *inl* and *inr* are constructors to indicate which summand the value is in. A pattern of the form $case(inl\, p \Rightarrow \theta \mid inr\, q \Rightarrow \phi)$ constructed in the rule $\oplus\mathcal{L}$, can only be matched with *inl* t or *inr* u. One of the cases is selected, as appropriate, and the other case is discarded. It may be surprising that the *case* pattern introduced in this rule has to be so complex. The pattern cannot be something as simple as $case(inl\, p|inr\, q)$ because the commands that need to be performed in each case have to be *suspended* until one of the cases is selected. Hence, the need to associate commands with the cases. Another special feature of $\oplus\mathcal{L}$ is that the contexts Γ and Δ in the two premises must be identical. If we need to join premises with different pattern/term constructions, new variables can be introduced (using Cut) so that the patterns/terms of the premises match up. For example, the derivation

$$\cfrac{\cfrac{\cfrac{}{x : X \vdash x : X}\,\mathsf{Id} \qquad p' : X, p : A \vdash \{\theta\}\, t : Y}{x : X, p : A \vdash \{p' \Leftarrow x, \theta\}\, t : Y}\,\mathsf{Cut} \qquad \cfrac{}{y : Y \vdash y : Y}\,\mathsf{Id}}{x : X, p : A \vdash \{p' \Leftarrow x, \theta, y \Leftarrow t\}\, y : Y}\,\mathsf{Cut}$$

replaces p' and t with fresh variables x and y.

In practice, this notation for case-patterns would be too cumbersome. We use Horn-clause syntax as "syntactic sugar" for writing the cases separately.

The rule is that a predicate definition

$$P\,(p[case(inl\; q_1 \Rightarrow \theta_1 \mid inr\; q_2 \Rightarrow \theta_2)]) \quad = \quad \phi$$

can be written as two separate clauses:

$$\begin{array}{l} P\,(p[inl\; q_1]) \leftarrow \theta_1, \phi \\ P\,(p[inr\; q_2]) \leftarrow \theta_2, \phi \end{array}$$

and each of them can be further split into multiple clauses, if necessary.

Linearity We must now state an important property of the type system (which also extends to the remainder of the system to be presented later). Note that, as long as $\oplus\mathcal{L}$ is not used, all derivable sequents have *two* occurrences of each variable. The Id rule introduces two occurrences and the other rules preserve this property.[6] Of the two occurrences of a variable, one is an input occurrence and the other is an output occurrence. Thus, linearity means that each variable has a unique "producer" and a unique "consumer". Similar restrictions are used in Doc [25] and Janus [45], and the "directed logic variables" of Kleinman *et. al.* [28]. Also, as in these languages, linear logic allows duplication operators (Section 6.1). By using a duplication operator as the consumer of a value, we obtain the effect that two copies of the value are generated. Thus, linearity is not a restriction in *practice*.

The property of linearity, suitably generalized, holds for the use of $\oplus\mathcal{L}$ rule as well. The basic difference is that, for the pattern $case(inl\; p \Rightarrow \theta \mid inr\; q \Rightarrow \phi)$ a free occurrence of x in θ as well as ϕ counts as a single occurrence.

Any variable that is both produced and consumed within a command is really a "local" variable and it is treated as such in the theory. In practice, it would be clearer to use an explicit restriction operator to indicate such binding. Let $V^+(\theta)$ and $V^-(\theta)$ denote the set of variables that have free (unrestricted) occurrences in θ as terms and patterns respectively. Then, we can introduce restriction by:

$$\frac{\Gamma \vdash \{\theta\}\Delta}{\Gamma \vdash \{\nu x.\theta\}\Delta}\ \text{Restrict} \qquad \text{if } x \in V^+(\theta) \cap V^-(\theta)$$

Reduction semantics To formalize the meaning of the above constructs, we first impose a few equivalences:

$$\theta_1, \theta_2 = \theta_2, \theta_1 \tag{12}$$

$$\theta_1, (\theta_2, \theta_3) = (\theta_1, \theta_2), \theta_3 \tag{13}$$

$$succ, \theta = \theta \tag{14}$$

The equations state that the order of the occurrence of commands in a composite command are immaterial and that *succ* is the empty command. Note that these

[6] Whenever two sequents are joined using a type rule, their respective variables must be renamed apart from each other, unless the rule requires otherwise. An example of the latter is $\oplus\mathcal{L}$ where Γ and Δ in the two premises must be identical.

are essentially the equations of the linear CHAM [2, 5]. The semantics of the constructs is defined by the following reduction rules:

$$x \Leftarrow t, \theta[x]^T \longrightarrow \theta[t] \tag{15}$$

$$p \Leftarrow x, \theta[x]^P \longrightarrow \theta[p] \tag{16}$$

$$() \Leftarrow () \longrightarrow succ \tag{17}$$

$$(p_1, p_2) \Leftarrow (t_1, t_2) \longrightarrow p_1 \Leftarrow t_1,\ p_2 \Leftarrow t_2 \tag{18}$$

$$case(inl\, p \Rightarrow \theta_1 \mid inr\, q \Rightarrow \theta_2) \Leftarrow inl\, t \longrightarrow p \Leftarrow t,\ \theta_1 \tag{19}$$

$$case(inl\, p \Rightarrow \theta_1 \mid inr\, q \Rightarrow \theta_2) \Leftarrow inr\, u \longrightarrow q \Leftarrow u,\ \theta_2 \tag{20}$$

$\theta[x]^T$ and $\theta[x]^P$ denote commands that contain at least one occurrence of x as a term and pattern respectively. Note that linearity means that there is exactly one such occurrence (modulo the proviso for *case* patterns). The semantics of procedure call is given by

$$P\, t \quad \longrightarrow \quad p \Leftarrow t, \theta \tag{21}$$

whenever P is defined by $P\, p = \theta$.

Note that the reductions (15–16) are the directional versions of the reduction (1) of unification, (17–18) capture (4) and (19–20) capture (5). The reductions (2,3,6) of unification do not arise in directional logic programming. This is significant. It means that directional logic programs do not "fail" in the conventional sense. On the other hand, there is need for two forms of failure mechanisms. The first is a way to escape from an erroneous case. For this purpose, we use an *error* command:

$$\frac{}{\Gamma \vdash \{error\}\ \Delta}\ \mathsf{ERROR}$$

with the equivalence:

$$error, \theta \quad = \quad error \tag{22}$$

We often abbreviate $case(inl\, p \Rightarrow error \mid inr\, q \Rightarrow \theta)$ to $case(inr\, q \Rightarrow \theta)$ (and, similarly for *error* in the *inr* case). The second mechanism is an explicit failure command for terminating backtracking. (See Sections 4.3 and 6.2).

We also use an equivalence similar to (16) on Horn clause notation for syntactically simplifying clauses:

$$P\,(p[x]^P) \leftarrow (q \Leftarrow x, \theta) \quad = \quad P\,(p[q]) \leftarrow \theta \tag{23}$$

(Note that this equivalence is of no significance for evaluation because it is commands—not clauses—that are are evaluated).

4.2 Negation

The negation operator $(\ )^\perp$ switches the input-output notion of a type. An output of type $A^\perp$ is really an input of type A. Similarly, an input of type $A^\perp$ is really an output of type A. Since inputs and outputs are represented in the concrete syntax by patterns and terms respectively, we need a way to convert patterns to terms and *vice versa*. For this purpose, we will define two syntactic functions

$$(\ )^+ : \mathit{Pattern} \to \mathit{Term}$$
$$(\ )^- : \mathit{Term} \to \mathit{Pattern}$$

as inverses of each other. We refer to them as ***dualizing maps***. Using these maps, the type rules for negation are expressed as follows:

$$\frac{\Gamma, p : A \vdash \{\theta\}\ \Delta}{\Gamma \vdash \{\theta\}\ p^+ : A^\perp, \Delta}\ ()^\perp\mathcal{R} \qquad \frac{\Gamma \vdash \{\theta\}\ t : A, \Delta}{\Gamma, t^- : A^\perp \vdash \{\theta\}\ \Delta}\ ()^\perp\mathcal{L}$$

In the $(\ )^\perp\mathcal{R}$ rule, an input p of type A is viewed as an output p^+ of type $A^\perp$. (Similarly, in $(\ )^\perp\mathcal{L}$, an output t of type A is viewed as an input t^- of type $A^\perp$). This is merely a change of view point:

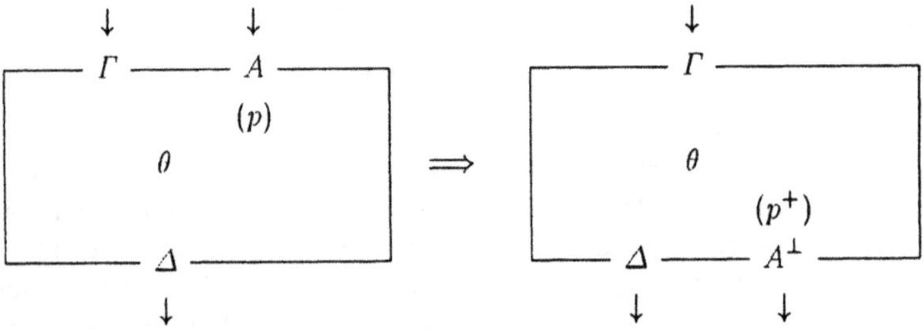

The computation net remains the same in this transformation. Only the labels (and concrete syntax) change using the dualizing maps.

Negation and identity The syntax for dualizing variable symbols is the expected:

$$x^+ \ = \ x^\perp \qquad x^- \ = \ x^\perp \tag{24}$$

By combining negation rules with Id, we obtain two interesting variants as derived rules:

$$\frac{}{\vdash \{succ\}\ x^\perp : A^\perp, x : A}\ \mathsf{Id}_R \qquad \frac{}{x : A, x^\perp : A^\perp \vdash \{succ\}}\ \mathsf{Id}_L$$

Since these rules are the key to understanding linear logic and directional logic programming, we will spend some time in explaining them.

The original Id rule denotes a computation of the following form:

This represents a "communication link" that accepts an A-typed value at its input-end and communicates it to its output-end. In traditional syntax, the input occurrences are always used in variable binding positions and the output occurrences in term positions. Directional logic programming requires us to take a symmetric view of this phenomenon. In particular, it is admissible to have both the input and output occurrences of a variable link to be in term positions or both to be in binding positions.

The computation of Id_R can be pictured as

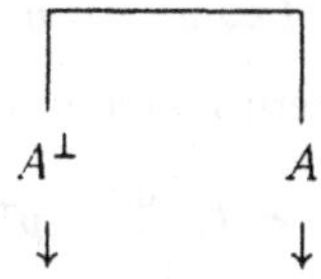

This says that an $A^\perp$-typed value and an A-typed value are simultaneously produced at two ends of the communication link. But, producing an $A^\perp$-typed value means the same as *receiving* an A-typed value. Thus, the link can be thought of as propagating an A-typed value from its $A^\perp$-end to its A-end. At the same time, whatever has been said about A-typed values can be said about $A^\perp$-typed values in the opposite direction. So, the link can *also* be thought of as propagating an $A^\perp$-typed value from right to left. Which of the two propagations "actually happens" depends on various considerations including irrelevant run-time factors. So, it is best to think of the two propagations, A-typed values from left to right and $A^\perp$-typed values from right to left, as being *equivalent*.

The computation denoted by Id_L is just another view of the communication link:

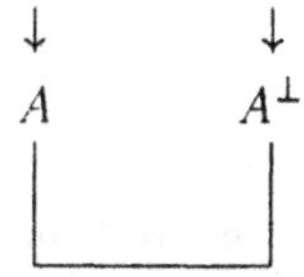

Here, either an A-typed value is communicated from left to right or, equivalently, an $A^\perp$-typed value from right to left.

Negation and cut Combining the Cut rule with negation rules gives the following interesting derivation:

$$\dfrac{\dfrac{\Gamma, p : A \vdash \{\theta\}\ \Delta}{\Gamma \vdash \{\theta\}\ p^+ : A^\perp, \Delta}\,()^\perp\mathcal{R} \qquad \dfrac{\Gamma' \vdash \{\phi\}\, t : A, \Delta'}{\Gamma', t^- : A^\perp \vdash \{\phi\}\Delta'}\,()^\perp\mathcal{L}}{\Gamma, \Gamma' \vdash \{\theta, t^- \Leftarrow p^+, \phi\}\Delta, \Delta'}\,\mathsf{Cut}$$

Since we maintain that the negation rules do not alter the underlying computation, the effect of this ought to be the same as cutting the original premises. In other words, $t^- \Leftarrow p^+$ must be equivalent to $p \Leftarrow t$. The dualizing functions make $\Leftarrow$ a "symmetric" operation.

However, the syntax of $\Leftarrow$ is badly asymmetric. The left hand side is required to be a pattern and the right hand side a term. To fix this problem, we take the following version of the cut rule as more basic:

$$\frac{\Gamma \vdash \{\theta\}\, t : A, \Delta \quad \Gamma' \vdash \{\phi\}\, u : A^{\perp}, \Delta'}{\Gamma, \Gamma' \vdash \{\theta, t \Leftrightarrow u, \phi\}\, \Delta, \Delta'}\ \mathsf{Cut}_R$$

The notation $t \Leftrightarrow u$ has the advantage that both the operands are terms. We impose the equivalence

$$t \Leftrightarrow u \quad = \quad u \Leftrightarrow t \tag{25}$$

and define the traditional pattern match in terms of "$\Leftrightarrow$":

$$p \Leftarrow t \quad \stackrel{\text{def}}{=} \quad p^{+} \Leftrightarrow t$$

Thus, $t \Leftrightarrow u$ is equivalent to $t^{-} \Leftarrow u$ as well as $u^{-} \Leftarrow t$.

The command $t \Leftrightarrow u$ can be thought of as a *directional unification* operation. The term t produces an A-typed value and the term u produces an $A^{\perp}$-typed value, *i.e.*, u is prepared to *accept* an A-typed value. The execution of $t \Leftrightarrow u$ instantiates the variables of t and u such that the value produced by t is the same as the value accepted by u and *vice versa*. It is important to note that "$\Leftrightarrow$" denotes *bidirectional* communication. For instance, if $A = int \otimes int^{\perp}$, t produces the first component of the pair and consumes the second component whereas u does exactly the opposite. Such bidirectional communication, which gives logic programming its expressive power, is preserved in directional logic programming.

Example 1. The identity procedure can be defined as

```
id : proc (α ⊗ α⊥)
id (x, x⊥) = succ
```

For all types α, the identity procedure transfers the first argument of type α to the second argument as an output. However, since α can also be a negative type, the same procedure can also transfer the second argument to the first argument.

The identity procedure can also be defined, somewhat frivolously, as

```
id (x, y) = (x ⇔ y)
```

To type check this definition, we need to derive the sequent $x : \alpha, y : \alpha^{\perp} \vdash \{x \Leftrightarrow y\}$. This may be split into two sequents using Cut_R:

$$x : \alpha \vdash \{succ\}\, x : \alpha$$
$$y : \alpha^{\perp} \vdash \{succ\}\, y : \alpha^{\perp}$$

each of which is an instance of Id. □

Example 2. Assume a polymorphic type definition of lists as follows:

```
List α = nil 1 ⊕ cons (α ⊗ List α)
```

The constructors `nil` and `cons` replace the formal constructors *inl* and *inr*.

A conventional procedure for appending lists may be defined as follows:

```
append : proc (List α ⊗ List α ⊗ (List α)⊥)
append(xs, ys, zs) =
    case(nil() ⇒ zs ⇔ ys
       | cons(x,xs') ⇒ ν zs'. append(xs',ys,zs'⊥),
                                zs ⇔ cons(x,zs'))
    ⇐ xs
```

Using Horn clause notation, the same definition can also be written as

```
append(nil(), ys, zs) ← zs ⇔ ys
append(cons(x,xs'), ys, zs) ←
    ν zs'. append(xs',ys,zs'⊥), zs ⇔ cons(x,zs')
```

Two comments are in order. First, we are unable to use pattern matching syntax for the third parameter of *append*. This is remedied in Section 4.3. Secondly, the *append* procedure, as defined above, can only be used to append lists. It cannot be used "backwards" to split a list into two parts. This restriction is directly stated in types. The first two arguments are list inputs and the third argument is a list output. Operationally, the pattern match **case(...)** ⇐ **xs** cannot be executed until xs is instantiated to a *nil* or a *cons* term. Thus, directionality is built into the procedure. □

It may be seem that we have lost some of the convenience of logic programming by not being able to run procedures like *append* backwards. But, note that sequential control, such as that of Prolog, also loses the ability to run procedures backwards in any practical sense. We noted this for the *reverse* predicate in Section 1. In fact, it appears that most Prolog programs are written with a specific input-output directionality in mind. Our objective is to formalize these directionality notions and, then, to replace the low-level operational mechanisms of control used in conventional logic languages with high-level declarative mechanisms.

4.3 Dual data structures

This section is essentially an exercise in syntax. All the computations were already introduced in Section 4.1 while, in Section 4.2, we introduced "change of view point". We must now introduce enough syntax to execute the change of view point. This involves defining new type constructors that are dual to the traditional ones, and pattern and term forms for these type constructors.

The dual type constructors are defined by the following equations:

$$(A \otimes B)^\perp = A^\perp \parallel B^\perp$$
$$\mathbf{1}^\perp = \perp$$
$$(A \oplus B)^\perp = A^\perp \,\&\, B^\perp$$

The new type constructors are dual to the old ones in that, forming an output of an old type is similar to forming an input of its dual type and forming an input of an old type is similar to forming an output of its dual type. With this understanding, we propose the following syntax for new pattern/term forms:[7]

$$\begin{aligned} (p,q)^+ &= [p^+, q^+] & (t,u)^- &= [t^-, u^-] \\ ()^+ &= [\,] & ()^- &= [\,] \\ case(inl\ p \Rightarrow \theta \mid inr\ q \Rightarrow \phi)^+ &= \langle\{\theta\}p^+, \{\phi\}q^+\rangle & (inl\ t)^- &= \langle t^-, \_\rangle \\ & & (inr\ u)^- &= \langle \_, u^-\rangle \end{aligned} \tag{26}$$

The type rules for the new constructs are obtained as derived rules by combining the type rules of Section 4.1 with negation rules:

$$\frac{\Gamma \vdash \{\theta\}\, t : A, u : B, \Delta}{\Gamma \vdash \{\theta\}\, [t,u] : A \,\|\, B, \Delta} \,\|\mathcal{R} \qquad \frac{\Gamma_1, p : A \vdash \{\theta_1\}\, \Delta_1 \quad \Gamma_2, q : B \vdash \{\theta_2\}\, \Delta_2}{\Gamma_1, \Gamma_2, [p,q] : A \,\|\, B \vdash \{\theta_1, \theta_2\}\, \Delta_1, \Delta_2} \,\|\mathcal{L}$$

$$\frac{\Gamma \vdash \{\theta\}\, \Delta}{\Gamma \vdash \{\theta\}\, [\,] : \bot, \Delta} \,\bot\mathcal{R} \qquad \frac{}{[\,] : \bot \vdash \{succ\}} \,\bot\mathcal{L}$$

$$\frac{\Gamma \vdash \{\theta\}\, t : A, \Delta \quad \Gamma \vdash \{\phi\}\, u : B, \Delta}{\Gamma \vdash \{succ\}\, \langle\{\theta\}t, \{\phi\}u\rangle : A \,\&\, B,\ \Delta} \,\&\mathcal{R}$$

$$\frac{\Gamma, p : A \vdash \{\theta\}\, \Delta}{\Gamma, \langle p, \_\rangle : A \,\&\, B \vdash \{\theta\}\,, \Delta} \,\&\mathcal{L}_1 \qquad \frac{\Gamma, q : B \vdash \{\theta\}\, \Delta}{\Gamma, \langle \_, q\rangle : A \,\&\, B \vdash \{\theta\}\, \Delta} \,\&\mathcal{L}_2$$

We briefly explain each of these constructions:

- The type constructor "$\|$" (read as "par" — short for *parallelization*) is dual to $\otimes$. Recall that a $\otimes$-pair is produced by producing its components independently and consumed by consuming its components in the same computation. Dually, a $\|$-pair is produced by producing both its components from the same computation and consumed by consuming its components in separate computations. We call pairs $[t, u]$ of type $A \,\|\, B$ "connected pairs" because the two components are connected via a computation. They are extremely useful for building data structures whose components are dependent on each other. (See Examples 4 and 5).
- The type $\bot$ is useful for constructing a dummy input, just as **1** is useful for constructing a dummy output. Note that $\bot\mathcal{L}$ is the only rule, other than Id_L, that builds an empty command from scratch. (See Example 6).
- $A \,\&\, B$ is the type of pairs whose computation is delayed until one of its components is selected. Hence, we call them *lazy pairs*. Note that precisely one component of a lazy pair may be used; the other component is discarded.

When a type is defined, we can introduce *selector* symbols for lazy pairs:

$$\texttt{type}\ A = s_1\ B_1 \,\&\, \ldots \,\&\, s_n\ B_n$$

Given such a definition, the pattern $\langle \_, \ldots, p_i, \ldots, \_\rangle$ can be written as $s_i\ p_i$ and the term $\langle\{\theta_1\}t_1, \ldots, \{\theta_n\}t_n\rangle$ can be written as $\langle s_1 \Rightarrow \{\theta_1\}t_1, \ldots, s_n \Rightarrow \{\theta_n\}t_n\rangle$.

If the list type is defined by

[7] Unfortunately, our notation for duals of tuples ("[...]") conflicts with the Prolog notation for lists. Note that we never use "[...]" for lists in this paper.

```
List α = nil 1 ⊕ cons (α ⊗ List α)
```

its dual type gets the definition

```
(List α)⊥ = nil ⊥ & cons (α⊥ || (List α)⊥)
```

This definition says that an acceptor for lists is a lazy pair of two acceptors. In the *nil* case, we use the first component which is an acceptor of ()'s. The second component, used in the *cons* case, is a connected pair of an element acceptor and another list acceptor. Thus, an acceptor of lists does not have to be simply a "place holder". It can have interesting structure. To illustrate how this structure gets used, we look at the reduction semantics.

Reduction semantics First we complete the definition of dualizing maps:

$$
\begin{array}{rlrl}
[p,q]^+ &= (p^+,q^+) & [t,u]^- &= (t^-,u^-) \\
[\,]^+ &= () & [\,]^- &= () \\
\langle p,\_\rangle^+ &= inl\, p^+ & \langle\{\theta\}t,\{\phi\}u\rangle^- &= case(inl\, t^- \Rightarrow \theta \mid inr\, u^- \Rightarrow \phi) \\
\langle \_,q\rangle^+ &= inr\, q^+ & &
\end{array}
\tag{27}
$$

The reduction semantics for the full language is shown in Figure 2. Recall that

Equivalences

$$
\begin{aligned}
\theta_1,\theta_2 &= \theta_2,\theta_1 \\
\theta_1,(\theta_2,\theta_3) &= (\theta_1,\theta_2),\theta_3 \\
succ,\theta &= \theta \\
t \Leftrightarrow u &= u \Leftrightarrow t
\end{aligned}
$$

Reductions

$$
\begin{array}{rl}
x \Leftrightarrow t, \theta[x^\perp] &\longrightarrow \theta[t] \\
[\,] \Leftrightarrow () &\longrightarrow succ \\
[t_1,t_2] \Leftrightarrow (u_1,u_2) &\longrightarrow t_1 \Leftrightarrow u_1, t_2 \Leftrightarrow u_2 \\
\langle\{\theta_1\}t_1,\{\theta_2\}t_2\rangle \Leftrightarrow inl\, u &\longrightarrow t_1 \Leftrightarrow u, \theta_1 \\
\langle\{\theta_1\}t_1,\{\theta_2\}t_2\rangle \Leftrightarrow inr\, u &\longrightarrow t_2 \Leftrightarrow u, \theta_2 \\
P\, t &\longrightarrow p^+ \Leftrightarrow t, \theta \quad \text{where } P\,p = \theta \text{ is in program}
\end{array}
$$

Fig. 2. Reduction semantics of the core language

we take the unification operation "⇔" to be basic and define "⇐" in terms of "⇔". Thus, commands in Fig. 2 do not have any patterns in them. Using the definition of dualizing maps, (24), (26), (27), the earlier reductions (15–20) are seen as syntactic variants of the official reduction rules in the figure. In addition, the following reductions are also obtained as syntactic variants:

$$[p_1,p_2] \Leftarrow [t_1,t_2] \longrightarrow p_1 \Leftarrow t_1, p_2 \Leftarrow t_2 \tag{28}$$

$$[\,] \Leftarrow [\,] \longrightarrow succ \tag{29}$$
$$\langle p, \_\rangle \Leftarrow \langle\{\theta\}t, \{\phi\}u\rangle \longrightarrow p \Leftarrow t, \theta \tag{30}$$
$$\langle \_, q\rangle \Leftarrow \langle\{\theta\}t, \{\phi\}u\rangle \longrightarrow q \Leftarrow u, \phi \tag{31}$$

Example 3. We return to the *append* program of Example 2 and rewrite it using the new constructs:

```
append : proc (List α ⊗ List α ⊗ (List α)⊥)
append(nil(), ys, ys⊥) ← succ
append(cons(x,xs'), ys, cons[x⊥,zs'⊥]) ←
    append(xs', ys, zs'⊥)
```

The third parameter of *append* is an acceptor of lists. The definition of $(List\,\alpha)^\perp$ shows that such acceptors have an interesting structure. This structure is used in writing the pattern for the third parameter in the second clause. Type checking the clauses involves deriving the following sequents:

$$() : \mathbf{1},\ ys : L,\ ys^\perp : L^\perp \ \vdash\ \{succ\}$$
$$(x, xs') : \alpha \odot L,\ ys : L,\ cons[x^\perp, zs'^\perp] : L^\perp \ \vdash\ \{append(xs', ys, zs'^\perp)\}$$

where L stands for $List\ \alpha$. We leave them for the reader to verify.

To see how the pattern of the third parameter works, suppose *append* is invoked with a variable $zs^\perp$ as the third argument. This involves the following pattern match:

$$cons[x^\perp, zs'^\perp] \Leftarrow zs^\perp$$

If its dual zs is passed to another procedure, it must eventually execute a case analysis on zs of the following form:

$$case(nil() \Rightarrow \theta_1 \mid cons(a, as) \Rightarrow \theta_2) \Leftarrow zs$$

This is equivalent to the unification

$$zs \Leftrightarrow \langle nil \Rightarrow \{\theta_1\}[\,],\ cons \Rightarrow \{\theta_2\}[a^\perp, as^\perp]\rangle$$

So, the acceptor-pair on the right may get substituted for $zs^\perp$ in the first pattern match. This gives

$$cons[x^\perp, zs'^\perp] \Leftarrow \langle nil \Rightarrow \{\theta_1\}[\,],\ cons \Rightarrow \{\theta_2\}[a^\perp, as^\perp]\rangle$$

which reduces to $x^\perp \Leftarrow a^\perp,\ zs'^\perp \Leftarrow as^\perp,\ \theta_2$.

On the other hand, the first pattern match is equivalent to the unification

$$zs^\perp \Leftrightarrow cons(x, zs')$$

So, $cons(x, zs')$ may be substituted for zs in the second pattern match. Thus, whether values are passed in one direction or acceptors in the opposite direction, the same results are obtained. □

Example 4. The type of difference lists can be defined in a directional logic program as

```
type DList α = List α || (List α)⊥
```

We will refer to the two components as the "head" and the "tail" respectively. The head of a difference list is a list and its tail is an acceptor of lists. The two components are *connected*: the list accepted in the tail is used in the head.

Dually, an acceptor of difference lists is of the type:

```
type (DList α)⊥ = (List α)⊥ ⊗ (List α)
```

It accepts the head of the difference list and gives a list for its tail.

Procedures for creation and concatenation of difference lists may be defined as follows:

```
new : proc (DList α)⊥
concat : proc (DList α ⊗ DList α ⊗ (DList α)⊥)

new (x, x⊥) = succ
concat([x,y⊥], [y,z⊥], (x⊥,z)) = succ
```

Note that the only parameter of *new* and the third parameter of *concat* are output parameters.

Type checking the definition of *concat* illuminates how ⊗ and || interact in derivations. Let L stand for *List* α. Then, we need to derive

$$[x, y^\perp] : L \parallel L^\perp,\ [y, z^\perp] : L \parallel L^\perp,\ (x^\perp, z) : L^\perp \otimes L \ \vdash\ \{succ\}$$

First, use $\otimes\mathcal{L}$ to decompose the pair $(x^\perp, z)$ into separate hypotheses $x^\perp : L^\perp$ and $z : L$. Next, use $\parallel\mathcal{L}$ to decompose $[x, y^\perp]$ giving the sequents:

$$x : L, x^\perp : L^\perp \vdash \{succ\}$$
$$y^\perp : L^\perp, [y, z^\perp] : L \parallel L^\perp, z : L \vdash \{succ\}$$

The first sequent follows by Id_L. The second sequent may be derived by further decomposing $[y, z^\perp]$ and using Id_L twice.

Here are some more operations on difference lists. (The reader is encouraged to work through the type derivations for these clauses).

```
addl : proc (α ⊗ DList α ⊗ (DList α)⊥)
addr : proc (DList α ⊗ α ⊗ (DList α)⊥)
out : proc (DList α ⊗ (List α)⊥)

addl (i, [h,t⊥], (cons[i⊥,h⊥], t)) = succ
addr ([h, cons[i⊥,t⊥]], i, (h⊥,t)) = succ
out ([h, nil[]], h⊥) = succ
```

Interestingly, it does not seem possible to define a procedure to delete the first element of a difference list in the same fashion as above. The problem is that the first element itself is dependent on the tail input of the difference list. So, it cannot be separated away from the tail input. □

Example 5. We illustrate how to achieve back communication required in concurrent message passing programs. The following is a "stack manager" process that maintains an internal stack and services messages for pushing and popping values.

```
type Msgs α = done ⊥ ⊕ push(α ⊗ Msgs α) ⊕ pop(α⊥ || Msgs α)
stack : proc (Msgs α)
stackloop : proc (Msgs α ⊗ List α)

stack ms = stackloop(ms, nil())
stackloop(done dummy, st) ← dump(st, dummy)
stackloop(push(x, ms'), st) ← stackloop(ms', cons(x,st))
stackloop(pop[x⊥, ms'], nil()) ← error
stackloop(pop[x⊥, ms'], cons(x,st')) ← stackloop(ms', st')
```

Note that a **push** message comes with an α, but a **pop** message comes with an acceptor for α's. The stack process sends back an α to the originator of the message via this acceptor. (See the last clause).

Traditionally, in concurrent logic languages, messages are structured as a stream (list) with components of the form *push v* and *pop x*. Expressing it in our type system would yield the following type:

```
type Msgs' α = List (push α ⊕ pop α⊥)
```

This type subtly differs from our *Msgs* type: the *pop*-acceptor is combined with the remaining stream using $\otimes$ rather than $\|$. This would mean that the last clause would not type check (because $x^\perp$ and ms' are consumed separately). More importantly, it does not allow the user process to use the popped value in future messages. Our *Msgs* type corrects these problems and provides the right structure for bidirectional communication.

In the first clause of **stackloop**, we would ideally like to have an empty clause body. But, that would mean that **st** is not used, violating linearity. (Such a clause body would not type check). We use here a procedure **dump** which magically discards the stack. See Example 6 for its definition. □

Type checking in directional logic programming guarantees certain desirable properties for concurrent programming. For example, a *Msgs* stream can be consumed by one and only one stack process, and, unless there is an error, the stream is consumed completely and all the acceptors in it are satisfied. In general, there is a single process that has "write access" to a variable and this process is guaranteed to write the variable (unless there is an error or nontermination). In other words, no race conditions or deadlocks arise. The "directionality checks" of Parlog [21] are meant to guarantee similar properties. However, these checks are possible only for "strong" modes, not for "weak" modes. Strong modes would rule out back communication as in the above example. In contrast, our proposal allows the so-called weak modes and, at the same time, guarantees safety and liveness properties.

This guarantee is obtained, in large part, by distinguishing between the two kinds of pairs: *independent* pairs belonging to $\otimes$-types and *connected* pairs belonging to $\|$-types. The components of independent pairs are separately constructed; so, it is all right to use both the components in the same computation. On the other hand, the components of connected pairs are dependent on each other. Were we to assume that the components are independent and subsequently link them, we are likely to create cycles. For example, if we disregard the connectedness of the pair $[x^\perp, x]$ and treat is as being of type $A^\perp \otimes A$ then we can create the cyclic computation:

$$x^\perp \Leftrightarrow x$$

This command waits forever for the value of x in an effort to produce a value for x! Thus, the distinction between $\otimes$ and $\|$ is crucial.

However, there is a sense in which the distinction between $\otimes$ and $\|$ is overstated. While cycles result if we assume that $\|$-pairs are disconnected, nothing really goes wrong if we use disconnected components to form a $\|$-pair. In this case, $A \parallel B$ is the type of *possibly* connected pairs. Since the use of such pairs still assumes that the components may be connected, this is a safe loss of information. The easiest way to add such loss of information is via the so-called MIX rule [12, 17]:

$$\frac{\Gamma \vdash \{\theta\}\ \Delta \quad \Gamma' \vdash \{\theta'\}\ \Delta'}{\Gamma, \Gamma' \vdash \{\theta; \theta'\}\ \Delta, \Delta'}\ \mathsf{MIX}$$

The command $\theta; \theta'$ denotes the formal "joining together" of the separate computations θ and θ'. There can be no interactions between them. We will see, in Section 6.2, that the ";" operator allows backtracking-nondeterminism. This motivates the nullary version of the MIX rule:

$$\frac{}{\vdash \{\mathit{fail}\}}\ \mathsf{FAIL}$$

The following equivalences hold for ";" and *fail*:

$$\theta_1; \theta_2 = \theta_2; \theta_1 \tag{32}$$

$$\theta_1; (\theta_2; \theta_3) = (\theta_1; \theta_2); \theta_3 \tag{33}$$

$$\mathit{fail}; \theta = \theta \tag{34}$$

See Section 6.2 for applications of these constructs.

5 Properties of Directional Logic Programs

In this section, we briefly mention the important theoretical properties of the type system presented here.

First, we establish the *linearity* property. This is done in a somewhat roundabout fashion. We define functions $V(\cdot)$ which give the free variables of terms, patterns and commands as *multisets* of variables. The definition is "conditional".

Then we show, by induction on type derivations, that the condition is satisfied and, at the same time, the derivable sequents are linear and acyclic. The free variables of a term are defined by:

$$V(x) = \{x\}$$

$$\begin{array}{rlrl} V(()) &= \emptyset & V([]) &= \emptyset \\ V((t,u)) &= V(t) \cup V(u) & V([t,u]) &= V(t) \Delta V(u) \\ V(inl\, t) &= V(t) & V(\langle\{\theta\}t, \{\phi\}u\rangle) &= V(\theta) \Delta V(t) \\ V(inr\, t) &= V(t) & &= V(\phi) \Delta V(u) \end{array}$$

where $V_1 \Delta V_2 = (V_1 \setminus V_2^{\perp}) \cup (V_2 \setminus V_1^{\perp})$. The definition involves a condition for the case of lazy pairs. Free variables of patterns are defined by dualization: $V(p) = V(p^{+})$. For commands, we have the definition:

$$\begin{array}{rll} V(succ) &= \emptyset & \\ V(t_1 \Leftrightarrow t_2) &= V(t_1) \cup V(t_2) & \\ V(\theta_1, \theta_2) &= V(\theta_1) \Delta V(\theta_2) & \\ V(\nu x.\theta) &= V(\theta) & \text{if } x, x^{\perp} \notin V(\theta) \\ V(P\, t) &= V(t) & \end{array}$$

Theorem 1. *Suppose*

$$p_1 : A_1, \ldots, p_n : A_n \vdash \{\theta\}t_1 : B_1, \ldots, t_m : B_m$$

is a derivable sequent. Then, for all p_i $(i = 1, n)$, θ, t_j $(j = 1, m)$,

- $V(\cdot)$ *is well-defined.*
- linearity: $V(\cdot)$ *is a set,* i.e., *has at most one occurrence of a variable x.*
- acyclicity: $V(\cdot)$ *does not have both x and $x^{\perp}$ for any variable x.*
- $V(\theta) \Delta V([t_1, \ldots, t_m]) = V((p_1, \ldots, p_n))^{\perp}$.

We have that evaluation preserves types (called "semantic soundness" in [40]).

Theorem 2 (subject reduction). *If $\Gamma \vdash \{\theta\}$ is a derivable sequent and $\theta \longrightarrow^{*} \theta'$ by the reduction system, then $\Gamma \vdash \{\theta'\}$ is derivable.*

Note that this means, in particular, that the evaluation maintains linearity and acyclicity.

The confluence or Church-Rosser property follows by a proof similar to Abramsky's [2]:

Theorem 3 (confluence). *If $\theta \longrightarrow^{*} \theta_1$ and $\theta \longrightarrow^{*} \theta_2$, then there exists a command ϕ such that $\theta_1 \longrightarrow^{*} \phi$ and $\theta_2 \longrightarrow^{*} \phi$.*

This means that the results of evaluation are independent of the evaluation order. In conventional terminology, the results are independent of the "selection function".

We now show the correspondence between directional logic programs and relational logic programs. The correspondence is defined by a series of translations

$(\cdot)^\circ$ from the directional type system to Typed Prolog. For types, we have the translation:

$$(A^\perp)^\circ = A^\circ$$
$$1^\circ = \perp^\circ = \mathit{Unit}$$
$$(A \otimes B)^\circ = (A \,||\, B)^\circ = A^\circ \times B^\circ$$
$$(A \oplus B)^\circ = (A \,\&\, B)^\circ = A^\circ + B^\circ$$

The translation of a directional term t is a pair (t', ϕ) which we write as $(t' \mathsf{where} \phi)$, and, when ϕ is empty, abbreviate to t'. In the following equations, assume $t^\circ = (t' \text{ where } \phi_1)$ and $u^\circ = (u' \text{ where } \phi_2)$.

Terms :

$$x^\circ = (x^\perp)^\circ = x$$
$$()^\circ = [\,]^\circ = ()$$
$$(t, u)^\circ = [t, u]^\circ = (t', u') \text{ where } \phi_1, \phi_2$$
$$(\mathit{inl}\ t)^\circ = \mathit{inl}\ t' \text{ where } \phi_1$$
$$(\mathit{inr}\ t)^\circ = \mathit{inr}\ t' \text{ where } \phi_1$$
$$\langle \{\theta_1\} t, \{\theta_2\} u \rangle^\circ = x \text{ where } (x = \mathit{inl}\ t', \phi_1, \theta_1^\circ;\ x = \mathit{inr}\ u', \phi_2, \theta_2^\circ)$$

Patterns :

$$p^\circ = (p^+)^\circ$$

Commands:

$$\mathit{succ}^\circ = \text{the empty formula}$$
$$(t \Leftrightarrow u)^\circ = t' = u', \phi_1, \phi_2$$
$$(\theta_1, \theta_2)^\circ = \theta_1^\circ, \theta_2^\circ$$
$$(\nu x.\, \theta)^\circ = \exists x.\, \theta^\circ$$
$$(P\, t)^\circ = P\, t',\ \phi_1$$

Finally, to translate procedure definitions

$$P : \mathit{proc}\ A$$
$$P\, p = \theta$$

we assume that p is a pattern made of distinct variables and tupling constructs "(...)" and "[...]". (If it is not originally in that form, it can be easily converted to that form using the equivalence (23) backwards). The translation of the procedure definition is

$$P : \mathit{pred}\ A^\circ$$
$$P\, p^\circ = \theta^\circ$$

It is rather obvious that:

Lemma 4. *The translation of a well-typed directional program is a well-typed Typed Prolog program.*

Next, we show that the translation preserves semantics. Let $\longrightarrow_T$ denote the Typed Prolog reduction relation defined by (1–11) and $\longrightarrow_D$ denote the reduction relation of directional programs defined in Fig. 2. Then, we have:

Theorem 5. *Let $\mathcal{P}$ be a directional logic program and $\Gamma \vdash \{\theta\}$ a well-typed command with respect to $\mathcal{P}$. (So, "$\Gamma^\circ \vdash \theta^\circ$ Formula" is a well-typed goal with respect to $\mathcal{P}^\circ$). Then, whenever $\theta \longrightarrow_D^* \theta'$, $\theta^\circ \longrightarrow_T^* \theta'^\circ$.*

The converse does not hold. There are fewer reductions in directional setting than in the relational setting. Essentially, a consumer of a variable can "fire" in Typed Prolog even without the variable being bound, whereas in the directional program it is made to wait. Thus, the best we can aim for is the following result. Call a type *lazy* if it has an unnegated & constructor. A command $\Gamma \vdash \{\theta\}$ is said to be lazy if $V(\Gamma)$, which is the same as $V(\theta)^{\perp}$, contains a variable of a lazy type.

Theorem 6. *Let $\mathcal{P}$ be a directional logic program and $\Gamma \vdash \{\theta\}$ a non-lazy command with respect to $\mathcal{P}$. (We have that "$\Gamma^{\circ} \vdash \theta^{\circ}$ Formula" is a well-typed goal with respect to $\mathcal{P}^{\circ}$). Whenever $\theta^{\circ} \longrightarrow_T^* \phi$ and the reduction of θ° is convergent, there exist θ', ϕ' such that $\theta \longrightarrow_D^* \theta'$, $\theta'^{\circ} = \phi'$ and $\phi \longrightarrow_T^* \phi'$.*

Since Typed Prolog can fire the consumer of a variable even without the variable being bound, to simulate the reduction in the directional setting, we have to first evaluate the producer of the variable. If $\phi \longrightarrow_T^* \phi'$ represents the evaluation of the producer, then we can represent the combination $\theta^{\circ} \longrightarrow_T^* \phi \longrightarrow_T^* \phi'$ in the directional reduction system.

We should point out, however, that there are reduction rules, called *commutative* reductions, which achieve the effect of firing consumers. See [20, 17]. In our setting, commutative reductions are expressed as:

$$
\begin{array}{rcl}
u[\langle\{\theta_1\}t_1, \{\theta_2\}t_2\rangle] & \longrightarrow & \langle\{\theta_1\}u[t_1], \{\theta_2\}u[t_2]\rangle \\
\langle\{\theta_1\}t_1, \{\theta_2\}t_2\rangle \Leftrightarrow u,\ \phi & \longrightarrow & \langle\{\theta_1, \phi\}t_1, \{\theta_2, \phi\}t_2\rangle \Leftrightarrow u
\end{array}
$$

These rules transport computations into lazy pairs (equivalently, case branches) so that they can proceed even without a choice being made. Note, in particular, the similarity between the second reduction and the backtracking rule (11). Thus, directional logic programming *can* be made to perform all the reductions available in the relational setting. But, it is not our program to do so.

6 Extensions

In this section, we briefly review various extensions and pragmatic concerns.

6.1 Repetition

The language considered so far is completely linear (except for procedures). Each value has a single producer and a single consumer. However, we do need to use some values multiple times. This is tricky business. As noted in [25, 28], allowing multiple consumers implicitly allows multiple producers as well because the consumed value may have an embedded acceptor. But, multiple producers lead to inconsistencies.

Linear logic includes a safe treatment of multiply usable values. However, the constructs involved in this treatment are extremely rich and powerful. In particular, they go beyond Horn clause logic. It is not yet clear what is the best way to incorporate these features into directional logic programming. For the sake of completeness, we briefly indicate the features provided by linear logic and point to the issues they raise.

The type "$!A$" (read "of course" A) denotes computations that may be discarded or duplicated (in addition to being used linearly). If such computations use other computations, it is easy to see that the latter must in turn be discardable/duplicatable. For, in discarding/duplicating the final computation, we are also discarding/duplicating its subcomputations. This explains the intricacies involved in the $!\mathcal{R}$ rule below:

$$!\mathcal{R} \quad \frac{p_1 : !B_1, \ldots, p_k : !B_k \vdash \{\theta\}\, t : A}{x_1 : !B_1, \ldots, x_k : !B_k \vdash \{succ\}\, (![p_1 \Leftarrow x_1, \ldots, p_k \Leftarrow x_k]\{\theta\}t) : !A}$$

$$!\mathcal{L} \quad \frac{\Gamma, p : A \vdash \{\theta\}\, \Delta}{\Gamma, !p : !A \vdash \{\theta\}\, \Delta}$$

$$!\mathcal{W} \quad \frac{\Gamma \vdash \{\theta\}\, \Delta}{\Gamma, \_ : !A \vdash \{\theta\}\, \Delta} \qquad !\mathcal{C} \quad \frac{\Gamma, p_1 : !A, p_2 : !A \vdash \{\theta\}\, \Delta}{\Gamma, p_1 @ p_2 : !A \vdash \{\theta\}\, \Delta}$$

The $!\mathcal{R}$ rule "promotes" a linear computation to a discardable/duplicatable computation. The term constructed by such promotion encapsulates the entire computation, including the command θ, and introduces fresh variables for the interface $x_1, \ldots, x_k$. (The reason for this complexity becomes clear once we look at the reduction semantics below). The rule $!\mathcal{L}$ allows an $!A$-typed value to be used once (linearly), $!\mathcal{W}$ allows it to be discarded and $!\mathcal{C}$ allows it to be duplicated. The reduction semantics of these constructs is as follows:

$$!q \Leftarrow (![p_1 \Leftarrow t_1, \ldots]\{\theta\}u) \longrightarrow p_1 \Leftarrow t_1, \ldots, \theta, q \Leftarrow u \tag{35}$$

$$\_ \Leftarrow (![p_1 \Leftarrow t_1, \ldots]\{\theta\}u) \longrightarrow \_ \Leftarrow t_1, \ldots \tag{36}$$

$$\begin{aligned} q_1 @ q_2 \Leftarrow (![p_1 \Leftarrow t_1, \ldots]\{\theta\}u) \longrightarrow\ & y_1 @ z_1 \Leftarrow t_1, \ldots, \\ & q_1 \Leftarrow (![p_1 \Leftarrow y_1, \ldots]\{\theta\}u), \\ & q_2 \Leftarrow (![p_1 \Leftarrow z_1, \ldots]\{\theta\}u) \end{aligned} \tag{37}$$

Note that, in reductions (36) and (37), the demands to discard and duplicate a promoted computation are propagated to its inputs. The complexity of the promotion construction is due, in part, to the need for such propagation.

Linear logic's promotion construct takes us beyond Horn clause logic programming. Since entire computations can be discarded (reduction 36), lazy evaluation is required in computing with ! types. Similarly, reduction (37) requires entire computations to be explicitly copied. The effect of copying can be achieved by sharing in some instances, but not always. For example, consider $x_1 @ x_2 \Leftarrow d$ where d is a difference list. Since d has an internal local variable, it cannot be simply shared from x_1 and x_2. Instead, separate copies of d must be bound to the two variables. It seems that copying can be avoided by restricting the use of "!" to "positive" types, *i.e.*, types built from primitive types, $\otimes$, $\mathbf{1}$ and $\oplus$. Similarly, the lazy evaluation may be avoided by requiring θ to be empty in the promotion rule. All of this needs further investigation.

Example 6. To be able to "dump" the stack of Example 5, we must require that all its elements are discardable. Then, we can define *dump* as:

```
dump : proc (List !α ⊗ ⊥)
dump(nil(), []) ← succ
dump(cons(__, st), dummy) ← dump(st, dummy)
```

One may wonder if we could discard the stack directly, instead of discarding its elements individually. It is possible to do so by using a type of "nonlinear" lists:

```
type NList α = nil 1 ⊕ cons (!α ⊗ !(NList α))
```

Then, *stackloop* can be redefined as follows:

```
stackloop : proc (Msgs !α ⊗ !(NList α))
stackloop(nil[], nst) ←
    __ ⇐ nst
stackloop(push(x, ms'), nst) ←
    stackloop(ms', ![x' ⇐ x, nst' ⇐ nst] cons(x', nst'))
stackloop(pop[x⊥, ms'], !st) ←
    case st of
       nil() ⇒ error
     | cons(y, nst') ⇒ x⊥ ⇐ y, stackloop(ms', nst')
```

□

6.2 Nondeterminism

Just as we introduced dual type constructors for data structures in Section 4.3, we can introduce a dual constructor for "!". This is written as "?" and pronounced "why not". The type $?A$ denotes computations whose acceptors can be multiply used. Thus, $?A$-typed computations are nondeterministic: they denote multiple A-typed values. The constructions for ?-types are obtained by extending the dualizaton maps:

$$\begin{aligned}(![p_1 \Leftarrow t_1, \ldots]\{\theta\}u)^- &= (?[p_1 \Leftarrow t_1, \ldots]\{\theta\}u^-)\\ (!p)^+ &= ?p^+\\ \_^+ &= noval\\ (p_1 @ p_2)^+ &= p_1^+ \ or \ p_2^+\end{aligned}$$

For example, we can define a procedure for producing all the members of a list as a nondeterministic value as follows:

```
members : proc ((?α)⊥ ⊗ List α)
members(x⊥, nil()) ←
    x⊥ ⇔ noval, fail
members(x⊥, cons(y,ys)) ←
    x⊥ ⇔ (?y) or x', (succ; members(x'⊥, ys))
```

Note that the goal `member(x⊥, cons(1,cons(2,nil())))` reduces to the following command:

```
x⊥ ⇔ ?1 or x1, (succ;
                x1⊥ ⇔ ?2 or x2, (succ;
                                 x2⊥ ⇔ noval, fail))
```

which is nothing but a representation of the backtracking behaviour.

6.3 Higher-order features

If we add unrestricted "of course" types, the language becomes higher-order. The type *proc* A, denoting procedures that accept A-typed arguments, is essentially equivalent to the type $!A^{\perp}$. Consider the notations $\varepsilon p : A.\,\theta$ for procedure abstraction and $t_1\, t_2$ for procedure application. These can be defined as

$$\varepsilon p : A.\,\theta \stackrel{\text{def}}{=} ![\bar{x} \Leftarrow \bar{x}]\{\theta\}p^{+}$$
$$t_1\, t_2 \stackrel{\text{def}}{=} !P \Leftarrow t_1, P \Leftrightarrow t_2$$

Therefore, procedure abstraction can be made a legitimate term and treated as a first-class value. Note that adding higher-order features to directional logic programming does not involve higher-order "unification" as in Lambda Prolog [38]. We have procedure application, but not equality testing of procedures.

6.4 Conditions and functions

We have deliberately avoided introducing functions into the language to keep it simple and "logic programming-like". However, it is clear that at least one kind of function is necessary, *viz.*, condition. In our procedural view of logic programs, the unification operator can only be used to bind variables. It cannot be used to test for the equality of two values. (See [25] for a similar sentiment). In fact, since the language is higher-order, a universal equality test is not possible. So, we need at least a type `Bool` and a function `=` : $\alpha \otimes \alpha \multimap$ `Bool` where α is restricted to testable types. One quickly sees the need for defining new conditions. So, why not introduce a general function abstraction construct:

$$\multimap\mathcal{R}\quad \frac{\Gamma, p : A \vdash \{\theta\}\, t : B}{\Gamma \vdash \{\theta\}\ \lambda p{:}\, A.\, t : A \multimap B} \qquad \text{if } V(\Gamma) \cap V(p) = \emptyset$$

In fact, using the definition $A \multimap B = A^{\perp} \parallel B$, $\lambda p{:}\, A.\, t$ is equivalent to $[p^{+}, t]$. Function application $f\,t$ is equivalent to $\{f \Leftrightarrow (t, x^{\perp})\}\, x$. One can follow the ideas of [44] to make the language of terms as rich as the language of commands.

6.5 Sequencing

The language described here is inherently concurrent. So, it is not translatable to Prolog. There are two possible approaches. Notice that the only place where dependencies crop up in the operational semantics is in the reduction rules for the additive type constructors. One can perform static analysis on programs to determine if all such dependencies are in the forward direction. A sequential evaluation would then be complete.

A second possibility is the following: There exists a translation from the language presented here into the functional language of [44]. (Both the languages are computational interpretations of the same logic). This gives a sequential implementation of some sort. It would still not be translatable into sequential Prolog because the translation into the functional language uses suspensions (lazy evaluation) to simulate concurrency.

7 Related Work

7.1 Distributed logic programming

A significant class of concurrent logic programming languages evolved from Hirata's proposal to make logic variables linear and directed [25, 28, 45]. The motivation behind these restrictions is the same as that of directional logic programming. Many of the technical details also bear a close similarity. For example, Janus appears to be an untyped (*i.e.*, dynamically typed) version of the language presented in Sections 4.1 and 4.2. Patterns and terms correspond to "ask" and "tell" terms respectively. Even our $x^\perp$ notation appears in Janus as the related "!" constructor: permission to tell a constraint on a variable. However, an important difference between $x^\perp$ and $!x$ must be noted. Whereas $x^\perp$ notation is merely a syntactic annotation (nothing would change even if we chose to write $x^\perp$ as merely x), the $!x$ annotation is an integral part of the operational semantics of Janus. Essentially, some of the type checking is done at run-time. Moreover, since the dual data structures of Section 4.3 are not present in Janus, cyclic deadlocks are possible. From our point of view, all the concerns we raise about relational logic programming are present for distributed logic programming with an even greater force. How does one specify the behaviour of a program? The type system presented here makes a contribution in this regard.

7.2 Computational interpretation of linear logic

Our work draws considerable inspiration from Abramsky's computational interpretation of linear logic [2]. The reduction semantics in Fig. 2 is essentially a notational variant of the linear chemical abstract machine defined there. (For example, Abramsky writes our $t_1 \Leftrightarrow t_2$ as $t_1 \perp t_2$). The main difference is that we use symmetric sequents in place of his right sided sequents. This leads to a more accessible notation and gives a direct correspondence with the notation of logic programming.

In separate work, carried out independently from ours, Abramsky, Jagadeesan and Panangaden showed that the proofs of linear logic can be interpreted in a cc language. (See [1]). In addition, Lafont [30] seems to foresee many of our ideas.

8 Conclusion

We have given a typed foundation for logic programs with input-output directionality. Our type system combines (what were previously called) types and modes and provides a framework for writing safe logic programs with good algorithmic properties. In addition, this work forms a concrete computational interpretation of Girard's linear logic based on the Curry-Howard correspondence.

The proposed type system extends "simple" modes with facilities for embedding outputs in input arguments and *vice versa*. It provides a theoretical basis for previous extensions of the same nature made in languages like Parlog and MU-Prolog. It also gives a safe type system for distributed logic programming languages.

On the theoretical front, it brings logic programming into the mainstream of typed languages by interpreting logic programs as proofs of a constructive logic. In this respect, it is closely related to the chemical abstract machine and continuation-based interpretations of linear logic. Working out the precise connections with these other interpretations should enrich our understanding of logic programs as well as the other paradigms.

Acknowledgements I am indebted to Dick Kieburtz and Boris Agapiev for introducing me to the fascinating world of linear logic. The work of Abramsky [2] formed the impetus for this work and many of his ideas form an integral part of this type system. Discussions with Peter O'Hearn, Radha Jagadeesan, Sam Kamin, Dale Miller and Phil Wadler helped clarify many issues I failed to notice. In particular, Phil Wadler persuaded me to use the $x^{\perp}$ notation for dual occurrences of variables which seem to clarify the presentation greatly.

References

1. S. Abramsky. Computational interpretation of linear logic. Tutorial Notes, International Logic Programming Symposium, San Diego, 1991.
2. S. Abramsky. Computational interpretations of linear logic. Research Report DOC 90/20, Imperial College, London, Oct 1990. (available by FTP from theory.doc.ic.ac.uk; to appear in *J. Logic and Computation*).
3. J.-M. Andreoli and R. Pareschi. Logic programming with linear logic. In P. Schroeder-Heister, editor, *Extensions of Logic Programming,* (Lect. Notes in Artificial Intelligence). Springer-Verlag, Berlin, 1991. (LNAI).
4. A. Asperti, G. L. Ferrari, and R. Gorrieri. Implicative formulae in the "proofs as computations" analogy. In *Seventeenth Ann. ACM Symp. on Princ. of Program. Lang.*, pages 59–71. ACM, 1990.

5. G. Berry and G. Boudol. The chemical abstract machine. In *Seventeenth Ann. ACM Symp. on Princ. of Program. Lang.*, pages 81–94. ACM, 1990.
6. C. Brown and D. Gurr. A categorical linear framework for petri nets. In *Fifth Ann. Symp. on Logic in Comp. Science*, pages 208–218. IEEE, June 1990.
7. K. L. Clark. Negation as failure. In H. Gallaire and J. Minker, editors, *Logic and Data Bases*, pages 293–322. Plenum Press, New York, 1978.
8. K. L. Clark and S. Gregory. Parlog: A parallel logic programming language. Research Report DOC 83/5, Imperial College of Science and Technology, London, May 1983.
9. A. Colmerauer, H. Kanouri, R. Pasero, and P. Roussel. Un systeme de communication homme-machine en francais. Research report, Groupe Intelligence Artificielle, Universite Aix-Marseille II, 1973.
10. R. L. Constable, *et. al. Implementing Mathematics with the Nuprl Proof Development System.* Prentice-Hall, New York, 1986.
11. H. B. Curry and R. Feys. *Combinatory Logic.* North-Holland, Amsterdam, 1958.
12. V. Danos and L. Regnier. The structure of multiplicatives. *Archive for Mathematical Logic*, 28:181–203, 1989.
13. Y. Deville. *Logic Programming: Systematic Program Development.* Addison-Wesley, Wokingham, 1990.
14. A. Filinski. Linear continuations. In *ACM Symp. on Princ. of Program. Lang.*, pages 27–38. ACM, Jan 1992.
15. V. Gehlot and C. Gunter. Normal process representatives. In *Symp. on Logic in Comp. Science*, pages 200–207. IEEE, June 1990.
16. G. Gentzen. *The Collected Papers of Gerhard Gentzen, edited by M. E. Szabo.* North-Holland, Amsterdam, 1969.
17. J.-Y. Girard. Linear logic. *Theoretical Comp. Science*, 50:1–102, 1987.
18. J.-Y. Girard. *Proof Theory and Logical Complexity*, volume 1. Bibliopolis, Napoli, 1987.
19. J.-Y. Girard. Towards a geometry of interaction. In J. W. Gray and A. Scedrov, editors, *Categories in Computer Science and Logic*, pages 69–108, Boulder, Colorado, June 1987. American Mathematical Society. (Contemporary Mathematics, Vol. 92).
20. J-Y. Girard, Y. Lafont, and P. Taylor. *Proofs and Types.* Cambridge Univ. Press, Cambridge, 1989.
21. S. Gregory. *Parallel Logic Programming in PARLOG: The Language and its Implementation.* Addison-Wesley, Reading, Mass., 1987.
22. C. Gunter and V. Gehlot. Nets as tensor theories. Technical Report MS-CIS-89-68, University of Pennsylvania, Oct 1989.
23. M. Hanus. Horn clause programs with polymorphic types: Semantics and resolution. *Theoretical Comp. Science*, 89:63–106, 1991.
24. J. Harland and D. Pym. The uniform proof-theoretic foundation of linear logic programming. Technical Report ECS-LFCS-90-124, University of Edinburgh, Nov 1990.
25. M. Hirata. Programming language Doc and its self-description, or $x = x$ considered harmful. In *Third Conference of Japan Society of Software Science and Technology*, pages 69–72, 1986.
26. J. Hodas and D. Miller. Logic programming in a fragment of intuitionistic linear logic. In *Sixth Ann. Symp. on Logic in Comp. Science.* IEEE, 1991.

27. W. A. Howard. The formulae-as-types notion of construction. In J. R. Hindley and J. P. Seldin, editors, *To H. B. Curry: Essays on Combinatory Logic, Lambda Calculus and Formalism*, pages 479–490. Academic Press, New York, 1980.
28. A. Kleinman, Y. Moscowitz, A. Pnueli, and E. Shapiro. Communication with directed logic variables. In *Eighteenth Ann. ACM Symp. on Princ. of Program. Lang.*, pages 221–232. ACM, 1991.
29. R.A. Kowalski. Algorithm = logic + control. *Communications of the ACM*, 22:424–431, 1979.
30. Y. Lafont. Linear logic programming. In P. Dybjer, editor, *Porc. Workshop on Programming Logic*, pages 209–220. Univ. of Goteborg and Chalmers Univ. Technology, Goteborg, Sweden, Oct 1987.
31. Y. Lafont. Interaction nets. In *Seventeenth Ann. ACM Symp. on Princ. of Program. Lang.*, pages 95–108. ACM, Jan 1990.
32. T.K. Lakshman and U. S. Reddy. Typed Prolog: A Semantic Reconstruction of the Mycroft-O'Keefe Type System. In V. Saraswat and K. Ueda, editors, *Logic Programming: Proceedings of the 1991 International Symposium*, pages 202 - 217. MIT Press, Cambridge, Mass., 1991.
33. J.-L. Lassez and M. J. Maher. Closures and fairness in the semantics of programming logic. *Theoretical Computer Science*, pages 167–184, May 1984.
34. P. Lincoln. Linear logic. *SIGACT Notices*, 23(2):29–37, 1992.
35. J. W. Lloyd. *Foundations of Logic Programming.* Springer-Verlag, Berlin, second edition, 1987.
36. N. Marti-Oliet and J. Meseguer. From Petri nets to linear logic. *Math. Structures in Comp. Science*, 1:69–101, 1991.
37. P. Martin-Löf. Constructive mathematics and computer programming. In L. J. Cohen, J. Los, H. Pfeiffer, and K.-P. Podewski, editors, *Proc. Sixth Intern. Congress for Logic, Methodology and Philosophy of Science*, pages 153–175. North-Holland, 1982.
38. D. A. Miller and G. Nadathur. Higher-order logic programming. In *Intern. Conf. on Logic Programming*, 1986.
39. R. Milner. *A calculus for communicating systems.* (LNCS). Springer-Verlag, 1979.
40. A. Mycroft and R. A. O'Keefe. A polymorphic type system for Prolog. In *Logic Programming workshop*, pages 107–122, Universidade Nova de Lisboa, 1983.
41. L. Naish. Automating control of logic programs. *J. Logic Programming*, 2(3):167–183, 1985.
42. U. S. Reddy. Transformation of logic programs into functional programs. In *Intern. Symp. on Logic Programming*, pages 187–197. IEEE, 1984.
43. U. S. Reddy. On the relationship between logic and functional languages. In D. DeGroot and G. Lindstrom, editors, *Logic Programming: Functions, Relations and Equations*, pages 3-36. Prentice-Hall, 1986.
44. U. S. Reddy. Acceptors as values: Functional programming in classical linear logic. Preprint, Univ. Illinois at Urbana-Champaign, Dec 1991.
45. V. A. Saraswat, K. Kahn, and J. Levy. Janus: A step towards distributed constraint programming. In S. Debray and M. Hermenegildo, editors, *North American Conf. on Logic Programming*, pages 431–446. MIT Press, Cambridge, 1990.
46. V. A. Saraswat and M. Rinard. Concurrent constraint programming. In *Seventeenth Ann. ACM Symp. on Princ. of Program. Lang.*, pages 232–245. ACM, 1990.
47. A. Scedrov. A brief guide to linar logic. *Bulletin of the European Assoc. for Theoretical Computer Science*, 41:154–165, June 1990.

48. E. Shapiro. The family of concurrent logic programming languages. *ACM Computing Surveys*, 21(3):412–510, 1989.
49. E. Y. Shapiro. A subset of concurrent prolog and its interpreter. Technical Report TR-003, ICOT- Institute of New Generation Computer Technology, January 1983.
50. L. Sterling and E. Shapiro. *The Art of Prolog.* MIT Press, Cambridge, Mass., 1986.
51. G. Takeuti. *Proof Theory*, volume 81. North-Holland, Amsterdam, 1987. Second edition.
52. S. Thompson. *Type Theory and Functional Programming.* Addison-Wesley, Wokingham, England, 1991.

An Architecture for Prolog Extensions

Micha Meier
Joachim Schimpf

European Computer Industry Research Centre,
Arabellastr. 17, 8000 Munich 81, Germany
michaecrc.de, joachim@ecrc.de

Abstract. We address the task of an efficient implementation of Prolog extensions. Prolog is a very good language for prototyping and almost any extension can be quickly written in Prolog using a Prolog interpreter and tested on small examples. It is harder to find out if the results scale up to large, real life problems, though. A Prolog interpreter, even if partially evaluated with respect to a given problem, quickly hits the space and time limitations and so more elaborate approaches to the implementation are necessary. In this article we describe an architecture of a Prolog system that gives the user enough support to quickly prototype new extensions and at the same time to implement them efficiently and incrementally. This architecture has been used to build the **SEPIA** and **ECL^{i}PS^e** systems.

1 Introduction

Prolog is a very good language for prototyping and for implementation of various new extensions of logic programming. Its declarative semantics, ability to handle program as data and interactive processing give the user enough flexibility to quickly test new ideas. If, however, the researchers want to test the applicability of the extension to large, real-life problems, more elaborate approaches to the implementation have to be taken. Some of them require more work and are more efficient, others have other advantages and disadvantages. We can compare them for instance with the following criteria:

- how easy it is to implement the extension, how much of the normal Prolog functionality has to be duplicated
- the execution speed
- the space usage
- how easily can two or more extensions be combined together.

The most obvious methods to implement extensions are then the following:

1. **Interpreters** can be very quickly written in Prolog, they are simple and easy to understand, often it is even possible to combine several extensions just by combining their interpreters or by slightly modifying them. However, the additional interpretation layer causes a significant overhead and often it is even not possible to use the built-in unification algorithm and thus the whole

unification has to be re-implemented in Prolog. Furthermore, the space usage of interpreters is quite high, because all information has to be represented explicitly, it cannot be 'compiled away'. Determinacy detection in interpreted programs is often difficult or impossible and this causes another increase in space usage. The last but not least drawback of this approach is that the whole input program might have to be executed with the interpreter, even if only a small fraction of it requires extended functionalities and the rest is plain Prolog which could be otherwise compiled and executed directly.

2. **Translation by specialising an interpreter**. By partially evaluating a Prolog interpreter with respect to a given program we obtain a translation of the extended program into Prolog. Since this process can be completely automated, it is a very convenient way to obtain a faster implementation without further implementation cost. All advantages of a metainterpreter are kept. This approach may also be more efficient because the additional interpretation layer may be partly removed. The space usage and determinacy detection is better than for a plain interpreter.

   This scheme is however usually limited to small and pure programs. In the presence of real-life problems it is often difficult to obtain a significant improvement by the partial evaluation (at least this is what we can say from our experience). Significant extensions also depend largely on dynamic parameters, e.g. data, and cannot be statically transformed into straightforward Prolog programs. For instance, extensions that change the default control rule must explicitly store and process the resolvent if the control depends on dynamic parameters (which it usually does).

3. **Compilation to Prolog**. In this case the extended program is translated into plain Prolog by means of a specialised translator or compiler. Writing an extension compiler is not always an easy task and since its complexity often does not match its efficiency, it is much easier to develop a specialised metainterpreter.

   Combining two extensions in this way may pose some nontrivial problems.

4. **New system from scratch**. This is obviously the most efficient and also the most difficult possibility. Even when one utilizes publicly available Prolog libraries, e.g. the parser, compiler and some built-in predicates, one has to write a huge amount of low level code that has nothing to do with the extension, just to implement a plain Prolog system.

   Currently it makes much more sense to modify an available Prolog system like SICStus or SB-Prolog.

5. **Modifying an existing system** also yields a very efficient implementation, however its cost is still quite high:
   - To modify its functionality, one has first to understand the implementation of the whole system.
   - When modifying the abstract machine, it might be quite difficult to change the compiler to cope with it efficiently. Particularly, we do not consider WAM modifications as a good idea for implementing new extensions. The WAM was an important step in the history of Prolog,

but future compilers will have to be based on global analysis and use information for which the WAM is too coarse grained. Taking this into account, extensions through WAM modifications are very complex tasks which lead nowhere.

- When a new release of the host Prolog system becomes available, the changes for the extension have to be carefully repeated in the new sources, and sometimes the new release may be incompatible with it. The extensions are likely not to gain anything from advanced techniques like global analysis and partial evaluation.
- As parts of the extension have to be implemented in the low level implementation language and parts in Prolog, it is far too easy to miss the right balance and to put too much emphasis on the low level programming, trying to make the implementation more efficient. The parts programmed at low level cannot be easily modified or extended and their effect may be outweighed by implementation costs and increased complexity of the system.
- Combining two extensions is extremely difficult and it is usually not even worth trying.

It can be seen that none of these approaches offers the right balance between simplicity and efficiency. It is obvious that efficient implementations have to be *integrated* into the Prolog machine at a low level. However, to make such an integration easy, the Prolog system itself must be built with precisely this goal in mind. Our idea is to define 'sockets' in the Prolog kernel which allow the extensions to be plugged in efficiently. Extended programs are then compiled and run just like the normal ones except that, when some extended feature is required, the control is given through the 'socket' to the extension code, which does the appropriate processing. In this way, the implementation has the simplicity of a metainterpreter and (almost) the efficiency of a modified native Prolog system.

2 What 'Sockets' Are Necessary for an Extension?

It is quite difficult to think of a scheme that would suit every possible Prolog extension. We have tried to cover all areas researched at our institute, ECRC, and our has been shown to be applicable even for other areas, but it is likely that still more sockets could be useful. The processing of a Prolog program can be generally divided into areas like

- reading in the program and storing it in memory,
- control,
- data processing, unification,
- execution of built-in predicates, ...

Every Prolog extension will have to modify at least one of these areas, most extensions will modify several of them. In the following sections we will discuss how the corresponding 'sockets' can be defined to allow efficient and straightforward processing.

2.1 Compilation and Program Storage

First of all, there should be no sockets in the code generator. An optimizing compiler has to have all the knowledge about the compiled code and if at some point an undefined action could be taken, or unknown instructions generated, the possibility for code improvement would be severely restricted. We believe that we can avoid changes in the compiler by preprocessing the source and by exploiting the event mechanism (see below).

Some extensions use special syntax to denote their objects or their special constructs. Although it is possible to use Prolog operators and compound terms to represent extension objects, this might not always be efficient enough. This problem is solved by introducing *input macros* as a 'socket' in the parser, whose presence in the input triggers an event or simply calling of a specified transformation predicate. In this way, some functors can be reserved to represent special objects and these objects are created by the transformation procedure.

2.2 Built-In Predicates

Every Prolog system contains a number of built-in predicates. Some of them are implemented in Prolog itself, others in the implementation language. When an extension is being connected to Prolog, often it is necessary to modify the behaviour of some of the built-in predicates so that it reflects the extension functionality. Although it is possible to do this by modifying the source code of the predicates, this approach is tedious and error-prone, and usually requires identical or similar changes for many of the predicates. For example, performing arithmetic with the successor function only (i.e. 2 is s(s(0))) would require the modification of all predicates that evaluate arithmetic expressions and inclusion of code that translates between the number and successor representation of the integers. The same would apply if e.g. rational numbers were included in the language.

This problem can be solved in a much more coherent way by including *event handling* in the Prolog engine. Whenever the built-in predicate encounters a situation which is not strictly regular, e.g. a compound term when a number is expected, it raises an event. Depending on the event type, an appropriate event handler is invoked, which will solve the problem, if there is any, and then return to the normal execution. This is equivalent to replacing every built-in predicate with another one that first makes a series of checks to find out whether there are some irregularities present, and if so, a corresponding handler predicate is directly called.

As soon as an event handling scheme is available, it can be used for various other purposes, e.g. to customize the system, to keep control even if things go wrong, etc. The event handling scheme is described in detail in [8].

2.3 Control

Coroutining The usual left-to-right Prolog selection rule has often to be modified in Prolog extensions. A simple, context-free approach is to specify syntactical conditions which a literal must satisfy in order to be selected. The selection rule proceeds as usual, except that literals which fail to satisfy the selection condition are suspended until the condition is satisfied. This is the so-called *coroutining*, introduced for the first time in Prolog-II [4].

Prolog systems that provide coroutining have often only simple facilities based on Prolog-II's **freeze/2** to suspend a predicate call [3]. For advanced extensions like constraint propagation a more sophisticated design is necessary:

- The user must be able to specify several delaying conditions for one goal, which implies that the goal might be woken by more than one variable. Although this feature can be simulated by **freeze/2**, it has to be provided by the system for efficiency.
- **freeze/2** or declarations as in NU-Prolog [11] are not flexible enough to directly specify complex control strategies. The **delay clauses** introduced in **SEPIA** represent a completely declarative approach to coroutining control – they are meta clauses with a syntax like normal Prolog clauses, e.g.

delay p(X, 1) if var(X).

The delay clauses allow the specification of even quite complicated control very naturally. For example, the logical conjunction **and(In1, In2, Out)** with its usual definition has to be delayed if both *In1* and *In2* are un-instantiated (otherwise the result is 0 or equal to the other input), and different (otherwise the output is equal to the inputs) and *Out* is not 1 (otherwise both inputs must be 1). Such a condition is naturally expressed with a delay clause as

delay and(Op1, Op2, Res) if var(Op1), var(Op2),
Op1 \== Op2, Res \== 1.

Several delay clauses may be specified for a predicate to allow disjunctive conditions. When executing a delay clause, its head uses pattern matching instead of unification, and no variables in the call may be bound by it.

Another advantage of delay clauses is that they are extensible - although only built-in test predicates are allowed in the body of a delay clause, the user can also add external predicates (written in C) for specialised control. This option has been preferred to completely general subgoals in delay clauses, because the latter would cause problems in the semantics and in the implementation and we have had no extensions that actually required it.

Manipulation of the Resolvent For more advanced extensions it is necessary to introduce some context in which a literal can or has to be selected. A general principle that allows processing of the resolvent and selection of the next literal is difficult to implement. Such a mechanism is also very likely to degrade the performance of ordinary Prolog programs and bring them close to metainterpretation. However, a flexible and efficient mechanism can be built on top of coroutining. It is only necessary to allow access to suspended literals, so that the list of all suspended goals can be processed, from which a suspended literal may possibly be selected. Thus e.g. the predicate **suspended_goals(Var,**

GoalList) returns the list of all goals suspended due to the specified variable, and **suspended_goals/1** returns all suspended goals.

Occur Check and Other Search Rules Prolog's lack of the *occur check* and use of *depth-first* search is, for some extensions, a serious problem, because the underlying solver is then neither sound nor complete. Fixing this in an existing system may cause significant overheads as unification with the occur check must be completely coded in Prolog. Therefore, an architecture for Prolog extensions must contain the occur check and alternatives to depth-first search as an option. Using compiler technology, it is possible to have an optional occur check and an optional (e.g. depth-first iterative deepening) search, by specifying different compiler modes so that the compiler either generates the additional instructions (to perform the occur check or to test the execution depth), or not. In this way, we can keep both efficiency and extensibility.

In **SEPIA** we have used this approach to implement depth-bounded search and depth-first iterative deepening search. Predicates compiled in this mode fail if the execution depth exceeds the limit, and a corresponding top-level predicate controls how the limit is set.

Connection to External Systems Some extensions may need a connection to an external system, usually a non-logical one. The inclusion of such a system into the backtracking scheme of Prolog may pose some problems and new requirements. Our architecture supports external systems with the following features:

- Prolog and C are mutually callable (this is more or less standard in current systems); C functions can also backtrack and suspend.
- Most of the external data can be directly used in Prolog; the number and string formats are compatible and structured data can be mapped on Prolog arrays.
- We provide hooks to notify the external system of
  - failure
  - cut
  - garbage collection of data related to the external system.

The necessity of failure and cut notifications may not be obvious; a typical example of their use is a tight connection of a relational database to Prolog. When a database query starts, it is necessary to open the relation, allocate buffers etc. Since the answer is passed into Prolog by backtracking over all tuples, the relation has to stay open until either all answers have been exhausted and the query fails, or if the execution commits to one tuple with a cut. Using the hook, the database is notified about the cut or failure and it can close the relation and/or remove the write locks on it immediately.

As long as external systems use data in the Prolog format, all garbage can be collected automatically. If this is not possible, the hooks in the garbage collector can be used to define the format of data that can appear on the Prolog heap and all pointers to it.

2.4 Unification

Unification is the core of Prolog and thus many extensions require a modification of the basic unification algorithm, either to include new cases (new data types or an extended notion of unify-ability), or to disallow some existing ones (e.g. unification of non-matching types). When extending unification, it is absolutely crucial to keep the speed of the ordinary, non-extended unification.

Extended unification is therefore provided by a generic data type, called a **metaterm**. A metaterm can be seen as a normal free variable X which has some Prolog term as its associated attribute:

Whenever a metaterm is unified with another one or with a non-variable, an event is raised, and the appropriate event handler takes care of the processing. In **SEPIA** it is the event 10 for the former and 11 for the latter. When a normal free variable is unified with a metaterm, it is directly bound without raising an event, because it carries no internal information that could influence the unification. In this way, Prolog is extended at a conceptually high level, while keeping the efficiency of a compiled WAM, because normal execution is not at all influenced or slowed down. The operations supported for metaterms are the following:

- Creation, i.e. coupling a variable with an attribute using the predicate **meta_term(Var, Attr)**.
- Accessing the attribute, using the same predicate.
- Test if a term is a metaterm using **meta(Term)**.
- Deletion – the attribute is removed and the variable is bound to some term with the **meta_bind(Meta, Term)** predicate, which strips off the attribute from **Meta** and binds it to **Term**.

The metaterms do not represent a separate meta-level of the program – it is rather a data type that supports the amalgamation of the meta and object level. The attribute of the metaterm may be any term, and free variables in it are subject to normal unification.

Metaterms represent a data type with interesting properties which can be used not only for a plain extended unification, but also for a number of other purposes. A metaterm can be seen and processed in several different ways:

- a variable with an attribute
- a variable whose value is known only partially
- a generic data type
- user-definable extension of unification
- a reference data type.

As the last item shows, metaterms can be also used to implement extra-logical and impure features. This, in general, can be an advantage, if the impure features are only used to efficiently implement pure logical mechanisms (like implementing Prolog using C). However, care must be taken not to destroy declarative semantics of the programs.

Metaterms can be used for an efficient and straightforward implementation of various extensions. Below, we list a few of them, although there are certainly many more.

Static Attribute Sometimes we need to associate some simple and fixed information with a variable, for instance

- the source name of the variable,
- marking quantified variables,
- marking void variables,
- marking selected variables.

Example 1. This example shows how metaterms can be used to trace successive instantiations of a term:

```
trace_subst(Var) :-
    meta_term(Var, _).        % add a dummy attribute

meta_unify(M, T) :-
    printf("variable %w bound to %w\n", [M, T]),
    % call vars_to_meta recursively for all subterms of T
    apply_to_subterms(vars_to_meta, T),
    meta_bind(M, T).          % do the actual binding

vars_to_meta(X) :-
    meta(X) -> true ; var(X) -> meta_term(X, _) ; true.

% set meta_unify/2 to be called whenever a metaterm is bound
:- set_error_handler(10, meta_unify/2).
:- set_error_handler(11, meta_unify/2).
```

The predicate **trace_subst(Var)** marks the variable with a dummy attribute and whenever such variable is bound, a message is displayed and all variables occurring in the bound term are in turn marked:

```
% An example code:
p(f(X, Y, Z)) :- q(X), r(Y, Z).
```

```
q(g(a, U)) :- s(U).

r(Y, Y) :- Y = [a|T], s(T).

s([]).

% The execution trace:
[sepia]: trace_subst(A), p(A).
variable A bound to f(X, Y, Z)
variable X bound to g(a, U)
variable U bound to []
variable Y bound to Z
variable Z bound to [a|T]
variable T bound to []

A = f(g(a, []), [a], [a])
yes.
```

Dynamic Attribute A more advanced technique is to give the metaterm an attribute which changes during the execution. This attribute can represent e.g.

- a list of goals that have to be executed when the variable becomes instantiated - "classical coroutining"
- a goal to be executed to obtain or update the value of the variable
- a ψ-term [1]
- implementation of order-sorted logic.

Example 2. This example generates a lazy list of 1's. The tail of the list is initialised with a metaterm, whose attribute stores the goal **ones/1**. As soon as the list tail is unified, the handler procedure **tail_handler/2** drops the attribute, unifies the list tail and calls the goal **ones/1** which produces a new list element.

```
% Generate a lazy list of ones.
ones([1|X]) :- meta_term(X, ones(X)).

% The handler for metaterm unification
tail_handler(M, T) :-
    meta_term(M, Goal),
    meta_bind(M, T),        % bind the metaterm to T
    call(Goal).             % and execute the goal

:- set_error_handler(10, tail_handler/2).
:- set_error_handler(11, tail_handler/2).

% Example of use:
add_list([X|L], [Y|M], [S|R]) :-
        S is X + Y,
        add_list(L, M, R).
add_list([], _, []) :- !.
```

```
add_list(_, [], []).
```

```
[sepia]: ones(Ones), add_list([1, 2, 3], Ones, Result).

Ones = [1, 1, 1|M]
Result = [2, 3, 4]      More? (;)
yes.
```

Generic Data Types Metaterms can represent a typed variable with run-time type testing. The attribute can store the type name, type value, a list of possible type values or a goal that checks the type when the variable is unified.

Example 3. Here is an example of a simple type hierarchy which uses built-in type testing predicates.

```
:- op(1150, fx, type), op(700, xfx, :).
type Name = (Type; Rest) :-
    type(Name = Type),
    type(Name = Rest).
type Name = Type :-
    atom(Type),
    assert(type(X, Name) :- type(X, Type)),
    assert(subt(Type, Name)).

Var:Type :-
    meta_term(Var1, Type),
    Var = Var1.

type_type_unify(M1, M2) :-
    meta_term(M1, T1),
    meta_term(M2, T2),
    (subtype(T1, T2) -> meta_bind(M2, M1) ;
    subtype(T2, T1) -> meta_bind(M1, M2)).

type_term_unify(M, Term) :-
    meta_term(M, Type),
    type(Term, Type),
    meta_bind(M, Term).

:- set_error_handler(10, type_type_unify/2).
:- set_error_handler(11, type_term_unify/2).

subtype(T, T).
subtype(T1, T2) :-
    subt(T1, T),
    subtype(T, T2).

% built-in types
type(I, integer) :- integer(I).
```

```
type(F, float) :- real(F).
type(A, atom) :- atom(A).
type(S, string) :- string(S).
type(C, compound) :- compound(C).

% Now define a simple type hierarchy
:- type term = (var; nonvar).
:- type nonvar = (atomic; compound).
:- type atomic = (number; atom; string).
:- type number = (integer; float).

% An example of its use
[eclipse 2]: X:atom, Y:number, X=Y.

no (more) solution.
[eclipse 3]: X:atomic, Y:number, X=Y, X=1.

Y = 1
X = 1      More? (;)
yes.
```

Object-Oriented Programming If the metaterm is used to represent an object, the metaterm variable represents a reference to the object and the attribute stores the state of the object. If the object changes its state and if it is certain that no references to the old state exist, the state can be modified just by exchanging the attribute of the metaterm.

Constraint Propagation The attribute of the metaterm stores all constraints imposed on the variable. In combination with the goal suspension (either built-in or also implemented using metaterms), we obtain a powerful tool to implement various kinds of CLP languages, without having to modify the low level code of the Prolog machine. The constraint solver(s) are quite naturally invoked by the event handlers of metaterm unification.

We have been able to implement a package for arithmetic constraints over finite domains of integers and another for (non)equality over arbitrary terms. The whole code is written in Prolog and uses a simple list representation of the domains, but its performance is quite good, it is only 4 – 10 times slower than the CHIP compiler [5], which is a dedicated CLP system using a bit field representation for domains, and low-level C coding for all constraints processing.

Below are several examples of the definition of simple constraints. The first defines only variables over finite integer domains and their unification.

Example 4. Defining variables, whose value is from a specified integer finite domain:

```
% Constrain a variable to be from the specified integer interval.
:- coroutine.
:- op(300, xfx, [in, #, <., <..]).
```

```
:- import initial/2 from sepia_kernel.

X in [L,H] :-
    (number(X) ->         % only test the bounds
        L =< X, X =< H
    ;
    meta(X) ->            % already constrained
        New in [L, H],
        X = New
    ;                     % constrain the variable
        make_list(L, H, D),   % make a list of integers
        meta_term(X, D)
    ).

make_list(H, H, [H]) :- !.
make_list(L, H, [L|R]) :-
    H > L,
    L1 is L + 1,
    make_list(L1, H, R).

meta_unify(T1, T2) :-
    meta_term(T1, D1) ->
        (meta_term(T2, D2) ->   % both constrained
            intersection(D1, D2, D),
            new_attribute(T1, D1, D),
            meta_bind(T2, T1)
        ;
            memberchk(T2, D1),  % one instantiated
            meta_bind(T1, T2))
    ;
    meta_term(T2, D2) ->
        memberchk(T1, D2),
        meta_bind(T2, T1)
    ;
        T1 = T2.                % both instantiated

:- set_error_handler(10, meta_unify/2).
:- set_error_handler(11, meta_unify/2).

% Common handling of constants and constrained vars
attribute(A, DA) :-
    meta(A) -> meta_term(A, DA) ; DA = [A].

% Give the variable a new attribute
new_attribute(_, OldD, OldD) :- !.      % no change
new_attribute(Var, _, [Val]) :-         % instantiate it
    !,
    meta_bind(Var, Val).
new_attribute(Var, _, [V|R]) :-         % new domain most be non-empty
    meta_term(New, [V|R]),
```

```
    meta_bind(Var, New).                    % modify the attribute

domain_range([Min|R], Min, Max) :-
    last_element(Min, R, Max).

last_element(Max, [], Max) :- !.
last_element(_, [E|R], Max) :-
    last_element(E, R, Max).

% Print the variable together with its attribute.
portray(Stream, Var) :-
    meta(Var),
    meta_term(Var, Domain),
    printf(Stream, "<%w%Pw>", [Var, Domain]).

% Example:
[eclipse 2]: X in [1,10], Y in [5,15], X=Y.

X = New<[5, 6, 7, 8, 9, 10]>
Y = New<[5, 6, 7, 8, 9, 10]>
yes.
[eclipse 3]: X in [1, 6], X in [6, 8].

X = 6
yes.
```

The next example adds to the functionality of the previous one the inequality constraint over integers. The inequality must be delayed until one argument is ground as no pruning can be done before this, but then it is completely solved (*forward checking* in the terms of [6]). Note that the control could be extended to delay also in the case when one argument is a plain free variable.

Example 5. Inequality over integer finite domains.

```
% Delay #/2 until one argument is a non-variable or
% both are equal.
delay A # B if var(A), var(B), A \== B.
A # B :-
    nonvar(A) -> delete_value(A, B) ;
    nonvar(B) -> delete_value(B, A).

delete_value(N, Var) :-
    attribute(Var, D),
    delete(N, D, ND) -> new_attribute(Var, D, ND) ; true.

% Example of use:
[eclipse 4]: X in [1,5], Y in [3,7], X # Y, X = 4.

Y = New<[3, 5, 6, 7]>
X = 4
```

```
yes.
[eclipse 5]: X#Y, X=Y.

no (more) solution.
```

The last example shows a more advanced constraint type – inequality < /2 of two integer domain variables. This constraint prunes those elements from the domains of the two variables which are incompatible with the constraint, but then, unless it is trivially satisfied or falsified, it has to wait to be woken as soon as one of the domains is updated, but not necessarily reduced to a single element (this is termed *partial lookahead* in [6]). Note that, without sophisticated control primitives, defining such a predicate would be quite difficult.

Example 6. The < /2 relation for two domain variables.

```
A < B :-
        A <. B.

A <. B :-
        attribute(A, DA),
        attribute(B, DB),
        domain_range(DA, MinA, MaxA),
        domain_range(DB, MinB, MaxB),
        (MinB > MaxA ->
            true                          % solved
        ;
            remove_greatereq(DA, MaxB, NewDA),
            new_attribute(A, DA, NewDA),
            attribute(B, DB1),
            remove_smallereq(DB1, MinA, NewDB),
            new_attribute(B, DB, NewDB),
            (MinB > MinA,
             MaxB > MaxA ->
                A <.. B                           % nothing done
            ;
                A <. B                    % repeat
            )
        ).

% initial/2 succeeds if (A, B) contains more than one variable,
% but it lets the goal continue as soon as A or B is updated,
% e.g. by modifying their attribute.
delay A <.. B if initial(1, (A, B)).
A <.. B :-
        A <. B.

remove_smallereq([X|Rest], Min, L) :-
    X =< Min,
    !,
    remove_smallereq(Rest, Min, L).
```

```
remove_smallereq(L, _, L).

remove_greatereq([X|Rest], Max, [X|L]) :-
    Max > X,
    !,
    remove_greatereq(Rest, Max, L).
remove_greatereq(_, _, []).

% Example:
[eclipse 6]: X in [1, 5], Y in [2, 10],
        Y < X, printf("X = %Pw, Y = %Pw\n", [X, Y]),
        X # 5, printf("X = %Pw, Y = %Pw\n", [X, Y]),
        Y # 2.
X = <New[3, 4, 5]>, Y = <New[2, 3, 4]>
X = <New[3, 4]>, Y = <New[2, 3]>

X = 4
Y = 3
yes.
```

True Metaterms A term which contains metaterms can be seen as a potential representation of many other terms (instances) and, depending on the context where it is used, it is interpreted as the appropriate one. This means that the term represents an amalgamation of the object level with a meta level and this amalgamation is quite an efficient one.

A typical example of this metaterm interpretation is the representation of the object program in a meta program. Object variables cannot be represented by free variables because this would cause conflicts with the meta variables. Usually this is solved by representing the object variables by ground terms (e.g. using **numbervars/3**), so that they can be easily recognised at the meta level. In this way, however, an object goal must be either fully interpreted by the meta program, or the goal has to be first reflected to the object level, i.e. the grounded variables transformed again to free ones, and then the goal can be directly executed. Moreover, to obtain the answer substitution, an explicit list of all variables and their ground representations must be created.

When metaterms are available, they can be used to represent object variables, or even any terms, and, the term containing them is interpreted differently depending on the level at which it is being processed.

In the following example a goal is executed directly. However, none of its variables is being bound – a list of substitutions is returned instead. This is achieved by replacing every variable by a metaterm whose attribute is a free variable, and performing all unification on this attribute. When the goal succeeds, the substitution list is simply created from all the attributes.

Example 7. Execution without variable binding.

```
% Call a goal and return a list of substitutions.
call_subst(Goal, SubstList) :-
```

```
    % collect the vars from Goal replaced by metaterms into Vars
    sumnodes(vars, Goal, Vars, []),
    call(Goal),
    var_subst(Vars, SubstList).

% This procedure is applied recursively to every argument of Goal
vars(X) -->
    {meta(X)} -> [] ;    % already meta, ignore
    {var(X)} -> {meta_term(X, _)},
                 [X] ;   % add the attribute and put into the list
    [].

% The unification handler. When a metaterm is unified,
%  we unify its attribute instead.
meta_unify(M, Term) :-
    meta_term(M, Term).

:- set_error_handler(10, meta_unify/2).
:- set_error_handler(11, meta_unify/2).

% Build the list of substitutions.
var_subst([], []).
var_subst([Var|Rest], SubstList) :-
    meta_term(Var, Term),
    (var(Term), not meta(Term) ->
        SubstNew = SubstList
    ;
        SubstList = [Var/Term|SubstNew]
    ),
    var_subst(Rest, SubstNew).

% Examples:
[eclipse 4]: call_subst(f(D, A, g(B)) = f(a, B, C), List).

D = D
A = A
B = B
C = C
List = [D / a, A / B, C / g(B)]
yes.
[eclipse 5]: call_subst(append(A, B, [1, 2]), List).

List = [A / [], B / [1, 2]]
A = A
B = B     More? (;)

List = [A / [1], B / [2]]
A = A
B = B     More? (;)
```

```
List = [A / [1, 2], B / []]
A = A
B = B
yes.
```

In fact, there are so many completely different uses for the attributed variables, that it is hard to give an exhaustive list of areas where they can be applied. Attributes or similar concepts have already been proposed in [10, 3, 7], but in **SEPIA** and **ECL^{i}PS^e** the metaterms are a primitive which is fully accessible to the user, independent of coroutining and fully supported by the system, which includes also the garbage collection and event handling.

2.5 Other Data Types

The metaterms are suitable for representing data that has a Prolog format and/or requires some particular control. Some extensions, however, may require data in a strictly non-Prolog format. An example can be numbers in double precision or IEEE format - which need several words of consecutive memory space. Most Prolog systems use tagged architecture where every word denotes a Prolog term and is tagged by a special combination of bits. Thus, to introduce a data type which occupies several consecutive words without tags, it would be necessary to define a new data type with a new tag, which would denote that the next *n* words in memory represent some particular object. Every time such a data type is introduced, the whole system kernel has to be updated to take it into account, e.g. the compiler (for **assert/1**), the emulator (for unification), the garbage collector and built-in predicates.

To overcome this problem, we have defined in **SEPIA** the data type **string**, which represents a sequence of consecutive bytes in the memory. Although the system uses this data type only to represent sequences of ASCII characters, it in fact represents a buffer located on the heap (global stack) which can be used for any purpose. Its advantage is that it is already recognised by the whole system and only the output predicates give it a particular interpretation. So an extension writer can easily use it for various purposes.

Some built-in predicates raise an event if they encounter strings, in particular all arithmetic predicates. In this way it is straightforward to write packages that provide new number formats, e.g. infinite precision integers or rationals.

2.6 Modules

Modules are necessary for managing source programs as well as for providing a way to encapsulate run-time data into various compound objects. The former requires a static module system with a fixed structure (which can be easier compiled), but the latter needs a module system where new modules and their interfaces can be created, modified and erased at run time. The **SEPIA** module system matches the latter objective – it is predicate-based and it is fully dynamic, so that new items can be created and modified at any time. This mechanism can then be used to implement e.g. contexts.

3 Conclusion and Future Work

The architecture presented here has two main goals: simplicity and efficiency of extensions. We believe that the extensions must be written in a high level language so that they can be easily modified and further extended. It has often been our experience that the benefits from hard-coding a feature in C were short-lived, and the disadvantages of rigidity, complexity and decreased maintainability soon took over.

The lesson is that, while the system is being prototyped, even if it is a commercial prototype, as much as possible must be written in Prolog, and general solutions should be preferred to specialised ones. Only in the last step, when 'freezing' the system to a product, identified system bottlenecks can be hard-coded in C. As there is no such thing as 'a stable system' because all software is evolving, the high-level prototype can be further used for modifications and extensions of the product. All this may seem obvious, but a quick look at conference papers and common practice teaches us otherwise.

The architecture presented in this article describes the **SEPIA** system [9]. Recently, the **SEPIA** system has been merged with the MegaLog system [2] into **ECL^{i}PS^e** . **ECL^{i}PS^e** is fully compatible with **SEPIA** and keeps its extensibility, but it also has the MegaLog knowledge base, which makes its area of application wider and constitutes another type of support for extension writers.

Our experiences with the system are mostly positive. It was in fact quite surprising that it has taken some time to realize how extensible the system is and how its features should be correctly used. Sometimes we have written system parts in C and have later discovered that the available sockets already provided this functionality almost for free; with time we have learned to appreciate it. In our opinion, the fact that the **SEPIA** sources are not publicly distributed is not a drawback, because it imposes a discipline on extension writers to exploit the available functionality, rather than to modify the sources on every occasion. The benefits are obvious – apart from the ones mentioned at the beginning: an extension written completely in Prolog is more flexible and is compiled faster (the **SEPIA** compiler compiles about 2000 lines/sec.) than by recompiling sources or loading C code.

Since **ECL^{i}PS^e** is being used as the basis for most LP work at ECRC, we have received many suggestions and requests for further extensions. Some of the work planned for the near future includes:

- generalisation of the coroutining mechanism. Often users want to wake suspended goals in some particular order, usually the simple built-in predicates first, but sometimes a much more complex scheme is required. Another requirement is to give every woken goal a precedence and not to wake any goals with lower precedence while goals with higher precedences are executing.
  To accommodate such schemes, we have decided to shift much of the coroutining implementation to the Prolog level and leave the task of suspending and waking almost completely to the user. The machine will only raise an event when suspending a goal and when a suspending variable is bound.

Although this change will almost certainly decrease the performance of some programs, users will be able to experiment with a much larger class of control strategies very easily. Successful strategies could then be coded again at a lower level (if necessary) to increase the performance again.

- Distributed coroutining. Coroutining can be quite naturally combined with interrupt processing. If an interrupt is processed synchronously, it can interact with the main execution and e.g. bind some variables and wake some goals. This will make it possible to extend coroutining to a distributed system where some goals are woken and executed on different machines and on success they bind the variables in the main process.
- Guard-like control. Although many applications require that suspending be performed at the procedure level, some applications or some predicates would benefit from a clause-level processing, i.e. suspending if the head unification or guard execution instantiates a variable.
- Since **ECL^{i}PS^e** will be used for various extensions in the CLP area, alternative number formats will be provided using the mechanism described above.

References

1. Hassan Aït-Kaci and Roger Nasr. LOGIN: A logic programming language with built-in inheritance. *Journal of Logic Programming*, 3(3):185–215, 1986.
2. J. Bocca. MegaLog - A Platform for Developing Knowledge Base Management Systems. In *Proc. Second Int. Symposium on Database Systems for Advanced Applications (DASFAA '91), Tokyo*, April 1991.
3. Mats Carlsson. Freeze, indexing and other implementation issues in the WAM. In *Proceedings of the 4th ICLP*, pages 40–58, Melbourne, May 1987.
4. Alain Colmerauer. Prolog II manuel de reference et modele theorique. Technical Report ERA CNRS 363, Groupe Intelligence Artificielle, Faculte des Sciences de Luminy, March 1982.
5. M. Dincbas, P. Van Hentenryck, H. Simonis, A. Aggoun, T. Graf, and F. Berthier. The constraint logic programming language CHIP. In *International Conference on FGCS 1988*, Tokyo, November 1988.
6. Pascal Van Hentenryck. *Constraint Satisfaction in Logic Programming.* MIT Press, 1989.
7. Serge Le Huitouze. A new data structure for implementing extensions to prolog. In *PLILP*, pages 136–150, 1990.
8. Micha Meier. Event handling in Prolog. In *Proceedings of the North American Conference on Logic Programming*, Cleveland, October 1989.
9. Micha Meier, Abderrahmane Aggoun, David Chan, Pierre Dufresne, Reinhard Enders, Dominique Henry de Villeneuve, Alexander Herold, Philip Kay, Bruno Perez, Emmanuel van Rossum, and Joachim Schimpf. SEPIA - an extendible Prolog system. In *Proceedings of the 11th World Computer Congress IFIP'89*, San Francisco, August 1989.
10. Ulrich Neumerkel. Extensible unification by metastructures. In *Proceedings of META'90*, 1990.

11. James A. Thom and Justin Zobel. Nu-Prolog reference manual version 1.1. Technical Report 86/10, Department of Computer Science, University of Melbourne, 1986. Revised May 1987.

Techniques for Implementing Contexts in Logic Programming

Enrico Denti, Evelina Lamma, Paola Mello, Antonio Natali, Andrea Omicini

DEIS, Università di Bologna
Viale Risorgimento, 2
40136 Bologna - Italy
{enrico, evelina, paola, natali, andrea}@deis33.cineca.it

Abstract. In this paper we discuss different techniques for implementing an extension of logic programming for knowledge structuring. The extension we consider, in particular, is based on Contextual Logic Programming. Three different implementation approaches are considered first: meta-interpretation, translation into Prolog code and compilation on an extended Warren Abstract Machine. These approaches are compared from the point of view of both methodology and efficiency. In the last part of the paper we consider a more effective implementation, developed on an industrial Prolog enhanced with the module construct.

1 Introduction

Horn Clause Logic as a programming language considers a logic program as an unstructured set of axioms which can be interpreted, in turn, as procedure definitions.

The intensive use of logic programming languages, and Prolog in particular, implies in some frequent and significant cases the need for structuring concepts - and thus the introduction of linguistic extensions - into the basic logic programming paradigm to enhance its expressive power.

Most recent Prolog implementations (e.g., SICStus Prolog [SICS91]) try to address the need for structuring concepts by providing *modules* as software components for programming-in-the-large. The Prolog name space for procedures is partitioned into separate modules, and explicit import/export rules are introduced in order to modify the visibility of predicate names.

This mechanism, however, is unsatisfactory when looking for higher dynamicity in program structuring and composition. For instance, both software engineering and artificial intelligence frequently demand for applications and knowledge bases to be structured into different theories that can be statically or dynamically combined, in order to represent blocks, nested modules, objects, inheritance relationships, viewpoints and perform hypothetical reasoning ([Bow85, Mil86, BLM90]).

A number of proposals exists to address theses issues (see, for example, [Mil86, GMR88, MP89, MNR89, McC88]), ranging from the conventional notion of scope-rule and block-based programming to the integration of logic and object-oriented programming. In these proposals, Horn Clause Logic is usually extended by adding mechanisms for the definition and manipulation of local clauses. The basic mechanism is still to partition clauses into separate components (called modules, units, objects), and allowing implication goals of the form D⊃G in clause bodies, where D is a set of clauses local to the goal G (i.e. they can be used only to prove G). The intuitive meaning of such an implication is that G is proved in a set of clauses which results from extending or replacing the current set of clauses with the set of clauses in D. For that reason, hereafter, we will refer to the above implication as the *extension goal* (also called embedded implication or implication goal in the literature). After successful completion of G, the clauses introduced in D become inaccessible when solving subsequent goals.

Thus, the set of clauses which can be used (i.e., that are visible) in the proof of a goal is now determined by both the modular structure of the program and the extension goals encountered.

Once such linguistic extensions have been defined, the problem is how to implement them. Two main approaches can be considered.

The first is a *Prolog-based approach*, which adds a (Prolog) layer between the user and the underlying Prolog machine (fig. 1.1), while the machine itself remains untouched. For this reason, this approach does not require the development of complex, specialised execution models and environments. Such an approach is exploited by two well known techniques for implementing logic language extensions:

- Meta-programming and, in particular, meta-interpretation.
  In this case, an extended meta-interpreter ([SaS86]) is defined, which reproduces at meta-level the Prolog interpretation cycle, enhanced with the new linguistic extensions. This approach, frequently adopted in the logic programming community, is elegant and easy to follow, and allows us to quickly build a first prototype supporting the extension introduced. The main problem is that, due to the added interpretation level, this approach is too inefficient to be adopted for real applications.
- Translation into standard Prolog.
  This implementation technique is based on a "naive" translation of extended logic programs into standard Prolog ones and does not require any modification to the execution model of Prolog that is based on the Warren Abstract Machine (WAM [War83]). This approach is less natural and easy to follow than meta-interpretation, but it is more efficient.

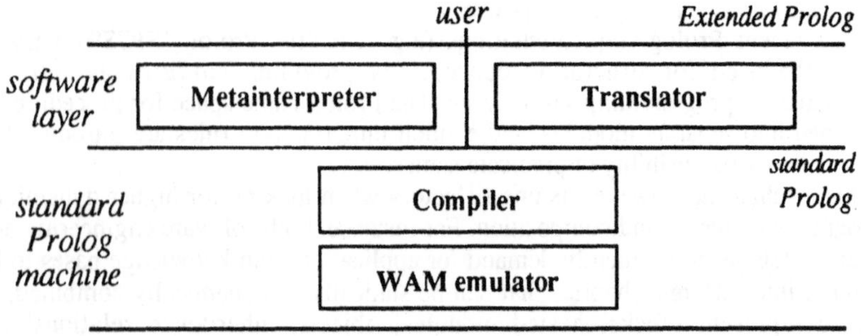

Figure 1.1 A scheme for the Prolog-based approach

The second is the *virtual-machine-based approach*, which consists of enhancing the Prolog machine so to enable it to directly support the new language features. Its most natural exploitation is the *WAM-based approach*:

- In this case, the extended languages is compiled on an enhanced Prolog abstract machine. The standard Prolog abstract machine (WAM) is extended with a minimal set of new instructions and new data structures to directly support the extensions introduced (see [Bac87, LMN89]). This technique is the most efficient but also the most complex in practice, since it implies the building of an "ad hoc" environment for the new language with a new compiler and a new emulator for the extended abstract machine.

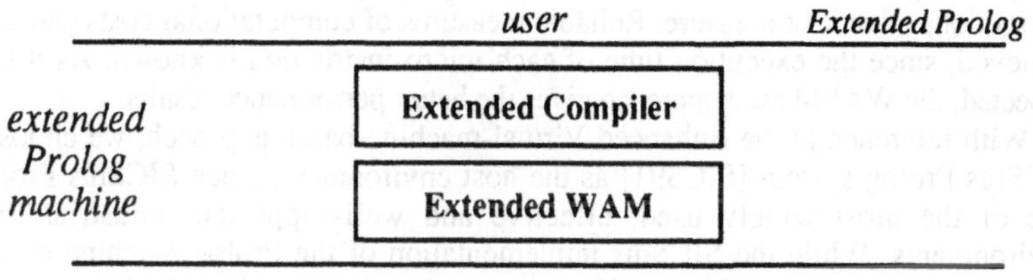

Figure 1.2 A scheme for the WAM-based approach

If we consider a real implementation, extended logic programs should rely on a fully developed (industrial) programming environment, including an optimising compiler, an efficient run-time support and all the classic programming tools like debuggers, graphical interface, etc. The implementation can take advantage from additional features embedded into the virtual machine of the chosen system, which is not necessarily a standard WAM. We call this approach *enhanced virtual-machine-based*.

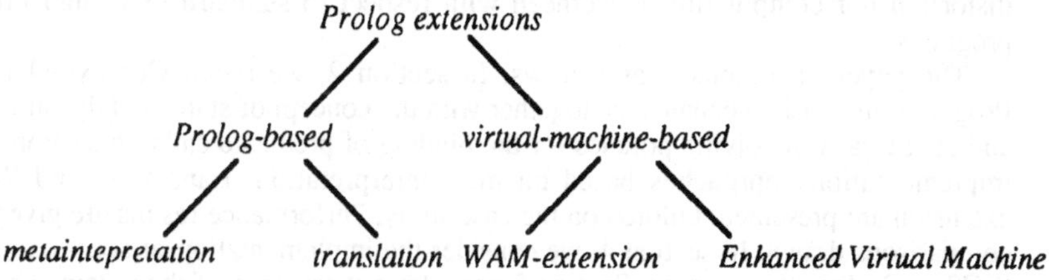

Figure 1.3. A taxonomy of implementation techniques

The aim of the paper is to discuss different techniques for implementing *contexts* ([MP89]) following the approaches outlined so far (see the taxonomy of figure 1.3). Contexts are a useful extension of logic programming for the introduction of structuring mechanisms. In *contextual logic programming* ([MP89, MNR89, BLM90a]) a logic program can be structured into separate modules, called *units*, that can be statically or dynamically combined into structures called contexts through the static definition of hierarchies of theories or by introducing extension goals in clause bodies.

We discuss the implementation of contexts by considering the approaches mentioned above, and compare them from the point of view of both methodology and performance. In fact, each of these approaches implies a different trade-off between simplicity and flexibility (at the first stage of the development) and efficiency (when real applications are built).

Prolog-based and WAM extension approach have been compared, from the efficiency point of view, on the basis of a common emulation environment grounded on a dedicated VLSI micro-coded architecture [CLM90]. In order to achieve comparable performance results, an emulator of the VLSI Prolog coprocessor described in [CLM90] has been used. Two versions of such emulator have been employed, the first supporting standard Prolog (i.e. implementing the standard WAM), the second supporting the extended WAM for Contextual Logic Programming (S-WAM) described in [LMN89, LMN]. Since both machines share the same set of micro-coded instructions, this set has been used as common ground, and the number of micro-coded instructions as unit of measure. Reliable measures of computational costs can also be achieved, since the execution time of each micro-instruction is known. As it can be expected, the WAM-based approach gives the better performance results.

With reference to the Enhanced Virtual-machine-based approach, we choose the SICStus Prolog system [SICS91] as the host environment, since SICStus Prolog is one of the most widely used, effective and well-supported industrial Prolog environments. While the SICStus implementation of the Prolog machine emulator (henceforth called the SICS-WAM) has been strongly shaped on the Warren model, the fundamental difference of SICS-WAM is the structure of the abstract machine code. This code relies on a program representation which is a complex data structure rather than on a plain sequence of WAM instructions. The increased complexity of the code structure aims to support some non-standard features, such as a flat module system and the incremental loading of clauses and dynamic predicates.

The implementation of contexts on the SICStus Prolog virtual machine has been grounded on this code representation and takes advantage from the module system. The resulting implementation (see [DNO92]) does introduce neither semantic distortion nor computational overhead with respect to standard (SICStus) Prolog programs.

The paper is organised as follows. In section 2, we recall Contextual Logic Programming basic mechanisms, together with the concept of static and dynamic unit and conservative/evolving policies for the binding of predicate calls. In section 3 the implementation approaches based on meta-interpretation, translation and WAM extension are presented, tailored on the case study. Performance results are given and comparisons drawn. In section 4, we consider the implementation of contexts on the SICStus Prolog environment. Section 5 provides a discussion of the obtained results together with some hints on optimisations.

2 Contextual Logic Programming

The Contextual Logic Programming paradigm (CLP for short in the following) was introduced first in [MP89]. The key idea in Contextual Logic Programming is that a logic program can be conceived as a collection of independent components called *units*. A unit is simply identified by the set of clauses it defines and by a unique, atomic name used to denote it. Units can be (possibly dynamically) composed into *contexts* and contexts, in turn, provide the set of definitions for the evaluation of goals. Contexts can be represented as ordered lists of unit names of the form $[u_N, ..., u_i, ..., u_1]$, and roughly denote the union of the sets of clauses of the composing units.

Contexts are dynamically built by using a suitable extension operator, here denoted by >>. In particular, the execution of the extension goal u_{N+1}>>G (where u_{N+1} is a unit name and G a goal formula) with respect to the context

C = `[uN,...,ui,...,u1]` causes the proof of G to be executed in a new context `C1 = [uN+1, uN,...,ui,...,u1]`, obtained by pushing u_{N+1} on top of C. In other words, a context represents the ordered, dynamic nesting of extension operators. At each instant of the computation, the *current context* (i.e., the current list of units built through a sequence of context extension operations) determines the set of predicate definitions to which predicate calls are to be bound.

Example 2.1
Let us consider the following CLP program:

```
unit(u1):          unit(u2):          unit(u3):
a:- b.             b.                 c:- a.
```

The extension `u1>>u2>>u3>>c` is successfully executed. In particular, `c` is proved in the context `[u3,u2,u1]`, which virtually corresponds to the set of clauses:

```
c:- a.
b.
a:- b.
```

□

Example 2.2
As a further example, let us consider the following program P composed of two units:

```
unit(list):
member(X,[Y|_]):- eq>>equal(X,Y).
member(X,[_|Z]):- member(X,Z).

permutation([],[]).
permutation([X|Y],Z):- del(X,Z,W),
                       permutation(Y,W).
del(X,[X|Z],Z).
del(X,[Y|Z],[Y|W]):- del(X,Z,W).

unit(eq):
equal(X,X).
equal([X|Y],[Z|W]):- permutation([X|Y],[Z|W]).
```

The first one (`list`) defines the predicates `member/2`, `permutation/2` and `del/3`; the second one (`eq`) defines the predicate `equal/2` which implements an equality relation in the case of lists by using the `permutation/2` predicate.

Notice the different ways in which a predicate that is not locally defined is called. For instance, the unit `list` calls the predicate `equal/2` by explicitly naming the unit `eq` where it is defined, while the "external" call of the predicate `permutation/2` in the unit `eq` does not specify any unit name.

The definition of predicate `permutation/2` to be used by the predicate `equal/2` can be dynamically specified. In fact, it depends on the current context which evolves during the computation. Thus, the definition of predicate `permutation/2` can change at run-time without modifying the code for `equal/2`. For instance, if the top-level goal is

```
:- list>>member([a,b],[e,d,[f,g],h,[b,a]]),
```

when `permutation/2` is called in `eq` the current context is `[eq,list]`, so that the definition of `permutation/2` present in `list` will be used. Notice that, if the current context is changed, a different definition will be used, thus giving to the unit `eq` a high degree of reusability.

□

In basic CLP [MP89] clauses at a given level in the context can see clauses at a lower level but not vice versa. Informally, given a context `C=[uN,...,ui,...,u1]`, predicate calls of the unit u_i in `C` are bound with respect to the definitions contained in the sub-context `[ui,...,u1]`. In the following, we refer to this binding policy as *conservative policy*. In practice, if a conservative policy is adopted, new extensions nested within the extension involving u_i cannot give any contribution to the proof of goals of u_i.

The need for a conservative policy is related to the aim of building "static" systems (such as block-based systems or nested modules), where the binding of procedure calls of a program component U can be performed as soon as U is used. The procedure calls are bound with respect to the definitions of U and its enclosing components (i.e., units which precede U in the current context).

Nevertheless, more dynamic policies of binding can be introduced in CLP, in the style of [Mil86]. In this case, no restriction on clause visibility within the context is imposed, and the context is really treated as a set of predicate definitions. Informally, given a context `C=[uN,...,ui,...,u1]`, all the predicate definitions present in `C` are taken into account for solving goals of the unit u_i independently of its position in `C`. In the following, we refer to this case as *evolving policy*.

Evolving systems follow dynamic scope rules, and are suitable to model hypothetical reasoning through viewpoints and knowledge updating (see for instance [War84]).

Example 2.3
Let us consider the program P of example 2.2, and a new unit `del` where a different definition for the `del/3` predicate is given. If we call the goal

```
:- list>>del>>member([a,b],[e,d,[f,g],h,[b,a]])
```

and adopt an evolving policy, the definition of `del/3` used in `list` will be the new one defined in the unit `del`. If a conservative policy is adopted, the definition of `del/3` in unit `list` will be used, and we will get the same behaviour of example 2.2 independently of the unit `del` that is part of the current context. □

Up to now we have considered the composition of (*dynamic*) units into context obtained through context extension operations. However, in some cases it could be useful to define a more static way of composing units, e.g. statically fixing the nesting of components within the program. *Static* units have been introduced in CLP (see [MNR89, BLM90a]) by associating them a fixed context. In this way, a "lexical closure" is set at unit definition time so that the behaviour of each static unit does not depend on the evolution of the computational environment.

When a static unit is defined, one specifies the context visible from it as a parameter of the unit definition (see example 2.4). Whenever a context extension involving a static unit `u` takes place, the context (statically) associated with `u` is enforced as current context.

Example 2.4
Let us consider the following program P:

```
unit(u1,closed([u2])):
p:- q.
unit(u2,closed([])):
q.
```

P is composed of two static units, `u1` and `u2`. `u2` refers to an empty context, while `u1` refers to the context `[u2]`. The goal `:- u1>>G` enforces the proof of `G` in the context `[u1,u2]` whatever the current context was. □

The context associated with a static unit u is actually the transitive closure of the relation determined by the "closed" declaration.

Blocks, modules and inheritance-based systems can be easily implemented as statically configured hierarchies of units, whereas dynamic configurations provide a natural support for artificial intelligence techniques such as viewpoints and hypothetical reasoning (see [BLM90a] for a deeper discussion).

In the following two sections we consider the implementation of Contextual Logic Programming by following the approaches outlines in the introduction.

We limit ourselves to the case of the evolving policy for the binding of predicate calls to predicate definitions, and the dynamic configuration of units. Comparisons are therefore performed by considering the most dynamic case (that is, late binding for all predicate calls). This is justified by the following issues:

- It is the most frequent in the case of artificial intelligence applications, where Prolog is widely used.
- In the dynamic case, it is less evident the advantage, in terms of efficiency, of compilation techniques such as WAM-extension with respect to (meta-)interpretation, thus performance results are more significant.

3 The Prolog-Based and WAM-Extension Approach

In this section we consider the implementation of Contextual Logic Programming by following the approaches based on meta-interpretation, translation into Prolog code and WAM extensions.

Implementing extensions of logic programming based on extension goals conceptually entails "asserting" and "retracting" program clauses. Since extension goals are usually nested during a computation, several layers of these operations have to be performed during execution. However, the assertion and retraction of program clauses follows a stacking discipline, and may as such be implemented using or simulating a run-time stack.

This can be accomplished by maintaining a list representation for the run-time program, which is useful from the perspective of understanding the addition and deletion of program clauses.

Such a list records data structures at different abstraction levels depending on the implementation approach we are considering. Moreover, the list is maintained at different implementation levels in the underlying machinery. In the case of meta-interpretation and translation, for instance, we can record the list of the units composing the current context, and explicitly maintain this list as an argument of the meta-interpreter or as an extra-argument of the translated program. In both cases, this allows one to deal with contexts as first-class objects, being contexts mapped onto a logical variable which can be directly inspected and manipulated, but introduces overhead.

In the case of WAM extensions, we can hold both reference to the units composing the context and bindings for the predicate calls occurring in each unit in a (new) WAM data area. This is the case of the implementation described in [LMN89] for dynamic conservative systems. Obviously this approach is more efficient than the previous one, but contexts are data structures no more directly accessible.

An intermediate approach can be followed, that allows to handle contexts as first class objects maintaining at the same time a good degree of efficiency. This approach is possible when the underlying machine is enhanced with new features. For instance, if reflection mechanisms and reification are provided, the lists representing contexts can be explicitly maintained by the underlying machine, and bound to a meta-variable (reification) when needed. This approach is followed in [LMN91], and could be also easily adopted for implementing contexts in systems like Sepia [Mei89] where meta-terms are provided. A similar approach is followed in [DNO92] which relies on the SICStus Prolog virtual machine where contexts are mapped into SICStus modules. We will describe this last implementation in section 4.

3.1 The Meta-interpretation Approach

Meta-programming is a technique which treats other programs as data. Meta-programs analyse, transform, and simulate other programs [BK82].

In particular, writing meta-interpreters is a common technique to add functionalities to the basic Prolog machine (see [SaS86, StS86]). In general, meta-interpreters use direct access to the program internal representation through the built-in predicate `clause/2` whose arguments are the clause head and body, and reproduce the interpretation cycle at Prolog level. Since we consider programs which have been partitioned into units, we suppose that the representation of program clauses is given by means of a `rule/3` predicate, where the first argument represents the unit name to which the clause belongs, and the second and third arguments represent the clause head and body respectively. The program of example 2.2 is therefore represented as shown in figure 3.1.

```
rule(list,  member(X,[Y|_]),eq>>equal(X,Y)).
rule(list,  member(X,[_|Z]),member(X,Z)).

rule(list,  permutation([],[]),true).
rule(list,  permutation([X|Y],W),
            (del(X,W,Z),permutation(Y,Z))).

rule(list,  del(X,[X|Z],Z),true).
rule(list,  del(X,[Y|W],[Y|Z]),del(X,W,Z)).

rule(eq,    equal(X,X),true).
rule(eq,    equal([X|Y],[W|Z]),
            permutation([X|Y],[W|Z])).
```

Figure 3.1: Program representation

As concerns the meta-interpreter code (see figure 3.2), subgoal selection and reduction is described by the clauses C1, C2 and C4. Clause C4 implements the binding mechanism, non-deterministically selecting a unit `U` of context `Ctx`; a subgoal `G` is proved by finding in `U` some clause whose head unifies with `G`, and subsequently solving the clause body. Moreover, through `member/2`, it explores on backtracking all units of Ctx in which a definition for G can be found, thus implementing *predicate extension.*

Notice that the meta-interpreter has an additional argument with respect to the "vanilla" meta-interpreter [StS86]. This arguments represents the current context, that is the run-time program representation. This is, in turn, the list of unit names encountered so far and involved in an extension goal.

Clause C3 is responsible for supporting the new operator ">>", and handles the dynamic extension of the current context. In order to solve a goal of the kind U>>G, the meta-interpreter simply adds a unit name U on the top of the current context Ctx and then solves G, recursively.

Notice that the binding of predicate calls requires a search to be performed along the context (by means of predicate member/2) in order to identify a unit U where to look for an applicable clause definition.

```
solve(_,true):- !.                                    %C1
solve(Ctx,(G1,G2)):-!,  solve(Ctx,G1),
                        solve(Ctx,G2).                %C2
solve(Ctx,U>>G):- !,    solve([U|Ctx],G).             %C3
solve(Ctx,G):-          member(U,Ctx),                %C4
                        rule(U,G,Body),
                        solve(Ctx,Body).
member(X,[X|_]).                                      %C5
member(X,[_|Z]):-       member(X,Z).                  %C6
```

Figure 3.2: Meta-interpreter code

3.2 The Translation Approach

Besides meta-interpretation, another common approach for supporting linguistic extensions is to translate the extended code into Prolog one. This is usually obtained by adding extra-arguments to Prolog clauses. The resulting code can be therefore executed on a standard Prolog machine.

In the case of Contextual Logic Programming, we maintain a new data structure (i.e., a Prolog list) for holding the context. The major overhead of this solution is due to the fact that, in the most general case, we perform a greater number of unifications, since we add extra-arguments to each predicate definition and predicate call.

In figure 3.3 the translated code for the program of example 2.2 is reported.

```
member([list|_],Ctx,X,[Y|_]):-
        equal([eq|Ctx],[eq|Ctx],X,Y).                 %C1
member([list|_],Ctx,X,[_|Z]):-
        member(Ctx,Ctx,X,Z).                          %C2
permutation([list|_],Ctx,[],[]).                      %C3
permutation([list|_],Ctx,[X|Y],Z):-
        del(Ctx,Ctx,X,Z,W),                           %C4
        permutation(Ctx,Ctx,Y,W).
del([list|_],Ctx,X,[X|Z],Z).                          %C5
del([list|_],Ctx,X,[Y|Z],[Y|W]):-                     %C6
        del(Ctx,Ctx,X,Z,W).
```

```
equal([eq|_],Ctx,X,X).                                      %C7
equal([eq|_],Ctx,[X|Y],[Z|W]):-                             %C8
          permutation(Ctx,Ctx,[X|Y],[Z|W]).
member([_|T],Ctx,X,Y):- member(T,Ctx,X,Y).                  %C9
permutation([_|T],Ctx,X,Y):-
          permutation(T,Ctx,X,Y).                           %C10
del([_|T],Ctx,X,Y,Z):- del(T,Ctx,X,Y,Z).                    %C11
equal([_|T],Ctx,X,Y):- equal(T,Ctx,X,Y).                    %C12
```

Figure 3.3: The translated code

We add two arguments to each clause head and subgoal. The second argument represents the global set of clauses which constitute the current context (*global context*), while the first one represents the subcontext (*partial context*) we are considering for finding some clause to apply. Moreover, additional clauses (C9-C12) are added for each predicate definition, in order to consider the overall set of definitions in the context (thus supporting predicate extension).

3.3 The WAM-based Approach

The third approach supports extensions to the Prolog language by directly extending the basic abstract machine defined by D.H.D. Warren. The resulting abstract machine (called S-WAM) is only sketched here. It is better described in [LMN89, LMN].

The basic difference of this approach with respect to the meta-interpretation and the automatic translation one is that in S-WAM contexts are not explicitly represented as extra-arguments in program clauses, but are held in an internal data structure (called the *context stack*) following a stacking discipline. Thus, the run-time program representation is directly handled by the underlying machinery.

In particular, in S-WAM the context stack maintains data structures (called *instance environments*) associated with units and corresponding to unit "closures". For a unit U, such closures virtually consist of bindings $<p_i, c_i>$, where p_i is a predicate name and c_i a pointer to the code of a clause for p_i visible from U. Actually, c_i can be determined at compile time for static units whatever the binding policy is (see [LMN] for the conservative case, and [Bug92] where the implementation is based on virtual predicate tables in the style of object-oriented languages), at context-extension time for dynamic units and predicate calls following the conservative policy, and at predicate call time only for dynamic units and predicate calls following the evolving policy (see [LMN] for details).

Moreover, each instance environment refers to the previous one, thus originating an environment chain to be considered when binding predicates at run-time.

The context stack grows whenever an extension of the kind U>>G occurs, and shrinks when G is deterministically solved or definitely fails. An instance environment associated with U is allocated on the context stack whenever U is involved in a context extension (allocate_ctx U S-WAM instruction), and logically deallocated when G is solved (deallocate_ctx S-WAM instruction). Physical deallocation is performed whenever G is deterministically solved, or on backtracking.

New registers refer to the context stack, and new instructions are also added to the WAM instruction set in order to expand and shrink this data area. The structure of both WAM choice-points and environments have been expanded to consistently handle new registers, and suitably follow the stacking discipline for the run-time program representation.

In figure 3.4 the overall S-WAM registers, data structures, and instructions are depicted.

NEW INSTRUCTIONS:

```
allocate_ctx          allocate_last_ctx
allocate_l_ctx        allocate_l_last_ctx
deallocate_ctx        deallocate_last_ctx
call_lazy             execute_lazy
call_eager            execute_eager
trust_extends
```

NEW MEMORY AREAS:

unit descriptor area — context-stack area

NEW STRUCTURES:

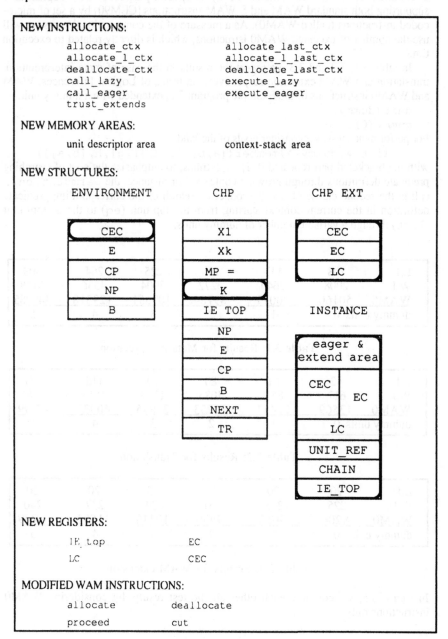

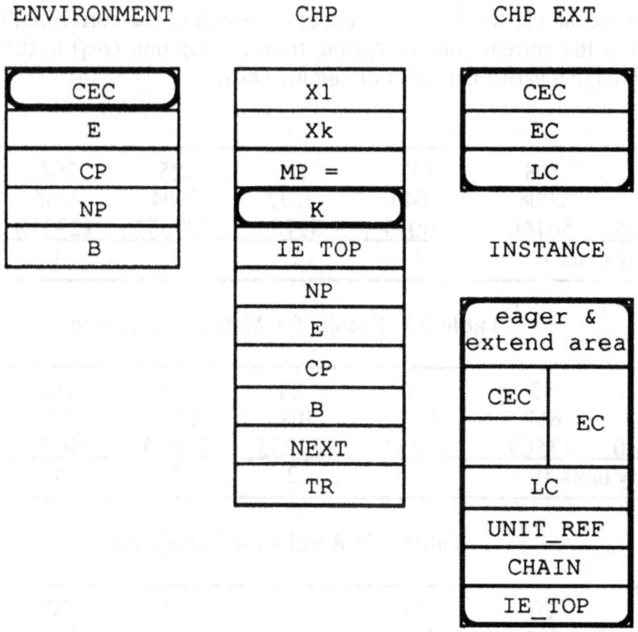

NEW REGISTERS:

```
IE_top      EC
LC          CEC
```

MODIFIED WAM INSTRUCTIONS:

```
allocate    deallocate
proceed     cut
```

Figure 3.4: S-WAM at a glance

3.4 Comparisons and Performance Results

The three implementation techniques discussed so far can be compared on the basis of a common environment, constituted by a special-purpose VLSI coprocessor supporting both standard WAM and S-WAM instructions [CLM90] by a set of micro-coded instructions (called WAM0). As a measure of the computational costs we will use the number of executed WAM0 istructions, which is directly related to execution time.

In table 3.1, 3.2 and 3.3 we report the results in the case of meta-interpretation, translation and WAM extension respectively, in terms of Logical Inferences, WAM and WAM0 instructions of the Example program 2.2, extended with a dummy unit:

```
unit(dummy).
dummy(0).
```

For performance tests we consider goals of the kind:

```
:- list>>{dummy>>}member([a,b],[e,d,[f,g],h,[b,a]]).
```

with the bracketed part repeated 0, 1, ..., 5 times, to emphasise the cost of searching predicate definitions through growing contexts. For instance, the `permutation/3` call in the second clause of `eq/2` produces a search of the corresponding predicate definition in the current context starting from the top unit (`eq`) to the bottom unit (`list`) through a variable number of dummy units.

L.I.	108	147	186	225	264	303
W.I.	2008	2640	3272	3904	4536	5168
WAM0	50160	70017	89784	109551	129318	149085
dummy units	0	1	2	3	4	5

Table 3.1: Results for Meta-interpretation

L.I.	42	61	80	99	118	137
W.I.	617	851	1085	1319	1553	1787
WAM0	13569	20411	27253	34095	40937	47779
dummy units	0	1	2	3	4	5

Table 3.2: Results for Translation

L.I.	20	20	20	20	20	20
W.I.	225	228	231	234	237	240
WAM0	8206	9053	9900	10746	11593	12439
dummy units	0	1	2	3	4	5

Table 3.3: Results for WAM extension

In figure 3.5, we compare each other all the test results by considering WAM0 instructions only.

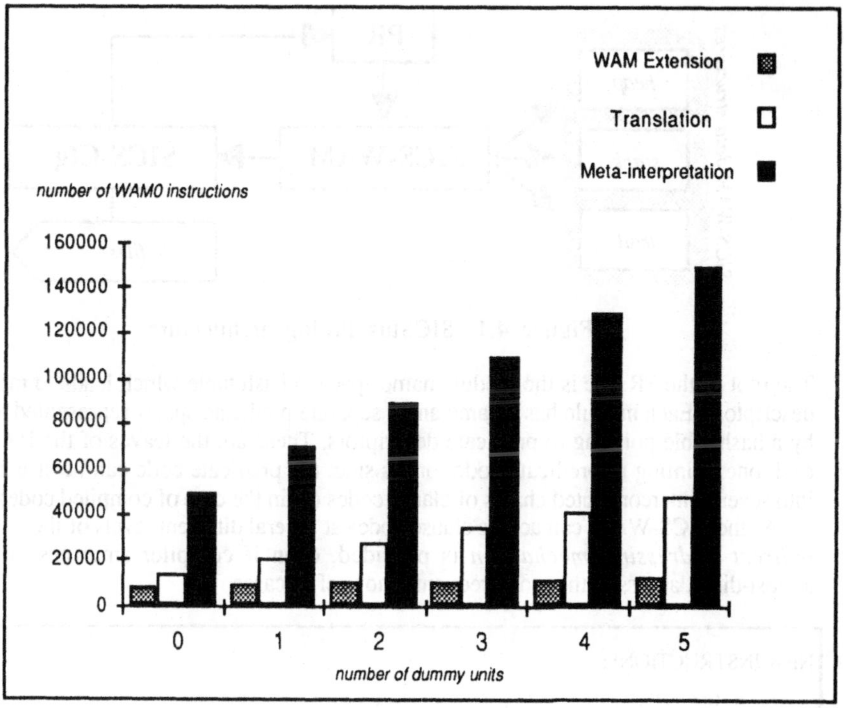

Figure 3.5: Performance comparisons

As expected the WAM-extension solution is the most efficient. It shows only a slight increment of the number of executed WAM0 istructions (about 10% with respect to the 0-dummy test) for each dummy unit added. This is mainly due to the fact that here units and contexts, in particular, are part of the low-level machine and directly manipulated by WAM instructions, while in the case of translation and meta-interpretation they are handled as Prolog data structures (i.e., list of unit names) accessed through unification at each predicate call.

Moreover, the results would be even better for the conservative policy of binding (see [LMN]), since in the S-WAM bindings for predicate calls are recorded in the instance environment, while they have to be newly determined at each call in the case of both meta-interpretation and translation into Prolog code.

4 The Enhanced Virtual Machine Approach

In [DNO92] contexts are implemented on the basis of the SICStus Prolog system (hereinafter we call this implementation CSM - Contexts as SICStus Modules).

Actually, the SICStus Prolog machine emulator (SICS-WAM) relies on a program representation which is structured as a tree, rather than a plain sequence of WAM instructions: then, figure 4.1 depicts the program representation as a separate block (PR), controlled by a subsystem here called SICStus configurator (SICS-Cfg).

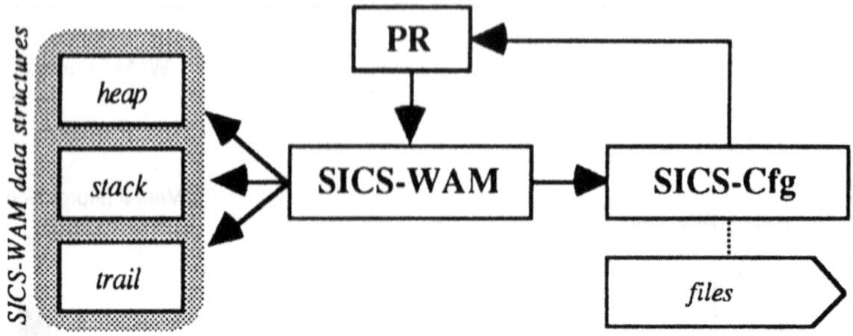

Figure 4.1 SICStus Prolog architecture

The root of the PR tree is the module name space, a hash table which leads to module descriptors. Each module has a name and a separate predicate space, represented again by a hash table pointing to predicate descriptors. These are the leaves of the PR tree, each one pointing to predicate code; on its side, the predicate code can be structured into several interconnected chains of clause codes (as in the case of compiled code).

As the SICS-WAM can access clause codes at several different levels of the tree, an *indirect addressing mechanism* is provided, even if compiler smartness forces almost-direct access in the most frequent (and useful) cases.

NEW INSTRUCTIONS:

(none)

NEW MEMORY AREAS:

CSM Knowledge Base Area

NEW STRUCTURES:

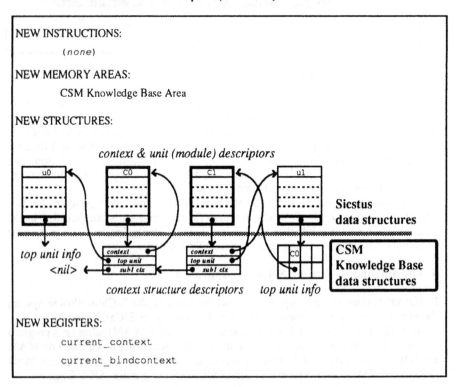

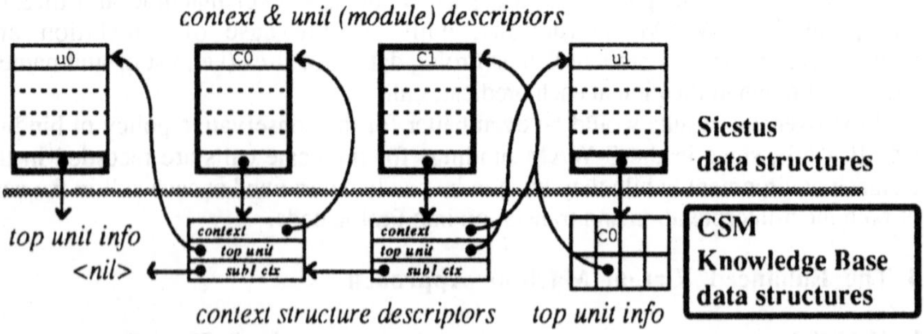

NEW REGISTERS:

`current_context`

`current_bindcontext`

Figure 4.2 CSM extensions at a glance

CSM implementation takes advantage from the SICStus Prolog system, by modifying the PR part only, with no change to the SICS-WAM. Both units and contexts are mapped into SICStus modules. This allows us to reuse module names and separate predicate spaces, together with the SICStus indirect addressing scheme for predicate binding.

CSM adds few structures to SICStus ones. Nothing is added to SICS-WAM; two extra-WAM registers hold the current contexts as module pointers, while the *CSM knowledge base* keeps track of contexts as (top-unit, first-subcontext) pairs (*context structure descriptor*, fig 4.2). For better dynamic performance, this information is duplicated: every unit u in the knowledge base points to a table (*top-unit info*, fig 4.2) where all contexts whose top-unit is u are recorded; so, each context can be retrieved via a hash function through its first-subcontext identifier (in figure 4.2, context `C1 = [u1,u0]` can be retrieved by accessing its top unit `u1` table using as a key its first-subcontext `C0 = [u0]` identifier).

CSM computation evolves as a normal Prolog computation (no new registers to hold, no new data structures to fill) until a suitable CSM operator or an *undefined predicate* exception is caught. In these cases, a non-local call is performed, using the proper context (*current context* for evolutive policy, *current bindcontext* for conservative policy) as binding environment. When the call has been bound and the correspondent CSM state changes have been done, computation proceeds as a normal SICStus Prolog one, till the next CSM event.

Thus, no overhead is introduced with respect to both SICStus Prolog and local CSM computations.

4.1 Discussion and Comparisons

The main distinguishing feature of the CSM approach is that contexts are persistent data structures. Then, context creation (which consists essentially of a memory area allocation, a first-subcontext table copy and a bunch of hash accesses to insert top-unit predicate references) represents the main CSM computational cost.

On the other hand, this has several consequences:

- contexts can be referred to by logic variables. Explicit context creation and handling (for instance, by-name context switch or context structure checking, etc.) can be easily performed, and a number of utility predicates can also be provided with no great effort (see [DNO92]);
- each context creation needs to be performed only once: when a context has to be used again during a computation (for instance, after backtracking), it can be simply restored from the CSM knowledge base (*smart context creation*);
- CSM can build at run-time those structures that static languages usually configure at compile-time; thus, contexts can be used to represent static software components (hierarchies, for instance) which can be dynamically specialized with no dramatic loss of computational efficiency.

Thus, pure performance comparisons make little sense when applied to the whole CSM system with respect to Prolog-based approaches which do not support CSM features. Moreover, the WAM-based approach should be extended and possibly redesigned in order to accomplish CSM new features. So, when considering CSM with respect to other approaches, we must take into account that we are comparing a fully developed programming environment with basic kernels.

Anyway, it can be interesting to give some figures as well, in order to provide a raw view of the overall CSM system performance, and to check whether CSM well behaves when facing "real" programs.

In particular, our performance tests have been thought in order to show that the cost of CSM contextual binding is not sensibly affected by the size of units and contexts.

For this purpose, we used a variant of the example used in Section 3 and run it in both real-contextual and Prolog-based (meta-interpreted and translated) versions, by repeatedly increasing the example size. In more detail, we run tests with

1. an increasing number of clauses in a unit, and
2. an increasing number of units in the binding context.

Since a rigorous unit of measure like the number of executable instructions is not available, we take the average execution time of several executions of some tests. Figures are normalized, by taking as 1 the least value for the metainterpreted solution.

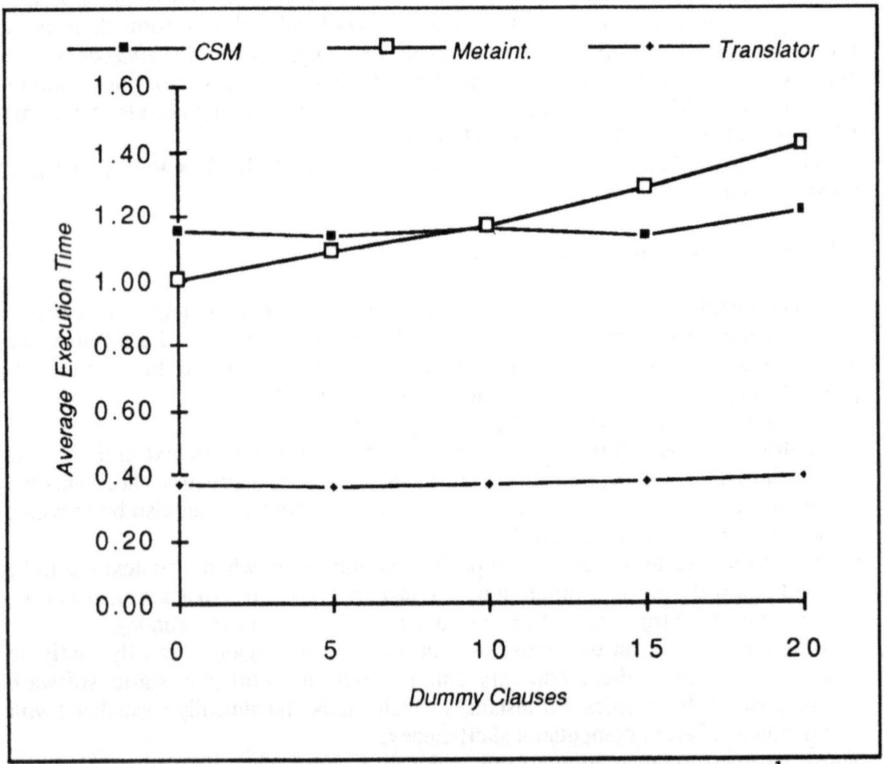

Figure 4.3. Results for an increasing number of dummy clauses.[1]

[1] Lazy binding is performed in the context `[eq, dummy, list]`, where unit `dummy` has a dummy clause number varying from 0 to 20.

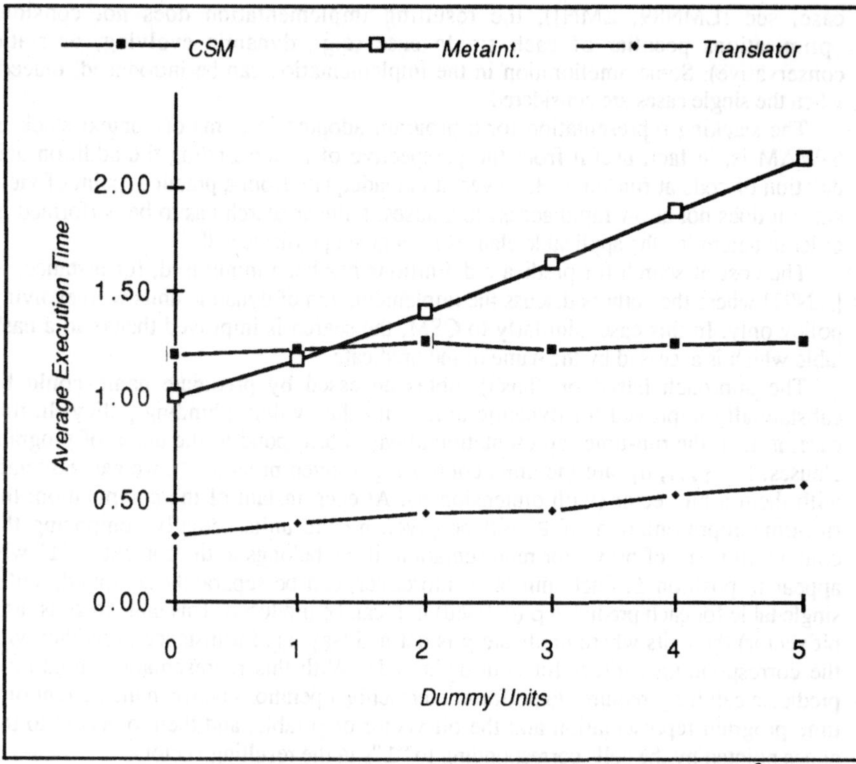

Figure 4.4. Results for an increasing number of dummy units.[2]

It could be surprising to see that absolute figures of CSM performance are so high: but, even forgetting differences between features, we must consider that tests were performed on a non-optimized version of CSM, where some critical points are still written as Prolog extensions to SICStus and where no static optimization is made.

Tests basically confirm the above assumptions: that is, when facing a normally-sized "real" program, CSM already has a substantial gain on the other approaches since it is not sensibly affected by the size of the program.

5 Final Remarks

In this paper we have compared different techniques for implementing contexts in logic programming. As expected, figures show that the virtual-machine based approach (both in the case of S-WAM and CSM) gives better results than the Prolog-based one.

It is worth noting that both S-WAM and CSM support conservative and evolving binding policy, and static and dynamic units. In the case of S-WAM, even if some optimisation have already been introduced (in particular for the dynamic conservative

---

[2] Every dummy unit has five dummy clauses, and lazy binding is performed in a context having the form `[eq, dummy, ..., dummy, list]`, with the number of dummy unit varying from 0 to 5.

case, see [LMN89, LMN]), the resulting implementation does not consider optimisations peculiar of each single case (e.g., dynamic evolving, or static conservative). Some amelioration in the implementation can be introduced, indeed, when the single cases are considered.

The stacking representation for a program adopted in terms of context stack in S-WAM is, in fact, useful from the perspective of understanding the addition and deletion of code at run-time. However, it is inadequate from a practical point of view since it does not allow rapid access to clauses: a linear search has to be performed in order to determine the applicable clauses for a given predicate call.

The cost of search for predicate definitions has been minimised, for instance, in [JaN91] where the authors discuss the implementation of dynamic units with evolving policy only. In this case, similarly to CSM, the search is improved thanks to a hash table which is accessed by the name of the predicate.

The approach based on (hash) tables accessed by predicate name could be substantially improved for dynamic units with the evolving binding policy. In this case, in fact, the run-time representation always correspond to the union of program clauses. If $u_1, \ldots, u_n$ are the units composing a given program P, we can associate with them a bit vector (with dimension n). At each instant of the computation, the run-time representation of P will be given by the units actually composing the context. In terms of bit vector representation, if u_i belongs to the context, a "1" will appear in position i. Each unit of P, moreover, can be separately compiled, and a single table for each predicate p (defined) in P can be produced. This table records (as a bit vector) the units where predicate p is defined (say u_i, for instance), together with the corresponding address for p in u_i's code. With this representation, binding a predicate call for p requires to perform intersection operations between the current run-time program representation and the bit vector of p table, and then to access to the codes pointed by the cells corresponding to "1"s in the resulting vector.

Finally, for static units only, one can take advantage from virtual predicate tables in the style of the implementation of object-oriented language virtual methods. In [Bug92], the author discusses the implementation of static units through the static creation of such tables for each (sub-)hierarchy of the program. In these tables, each predicate corresponds to a fixed offset, and the table reports the address of the procedure code in the proper unit of the hierarchy.

It is worth noticing that performance comparisons between the Prolog-based and the virtual-machine based approaches might be subject to change if partial evaluation techniques [LS87] are applied. We may expect that after the application of partial evaluation the overhead of the Prolog-based approach would be reduced.

In the future, we intend both to consider all these optimisations, and to verify the results on most significant examples.

Acknowledgements

We would like to thank Michele Bugliesi, for the useful discussions we had with him, and Pierluigi Civera, Gianluca Piccinini, and Maurizio Zamboni, who worked with us on the implementation of the emulation environment. We also thank DS Logics for sponsoring the CSM implementation. This work has been partially supported by the C.N.R. "Progetto Finalizzato Sistemi Informatici e Calcolo Parallelo", under grant nº 9201606.PF69.

References:

[Bac87] H. Bacha: Meta-level Programming: A Compiled Approach. In: J-L. Lassez (ed.): Proceedings 4th International Conference on Logic Programming, The MIT Press, Cambridge (USA), 1987.

[BK82] K. Bowen, R.A. Kowalski: Amalgamating language and meta-language in logic programming. In: K.L. Clark and S-A. Tarnlund (eds.): Logic Programming, Academic Press, London (UK), pp. 153-172, 1982.

[Bug92] M. Bugliesi: Virtual Predicate Tables for Implementing Inheritance in Logic Programming. Technical Report, University of Padova, 1992.

[BLM90] A. Brogi, E. Lamma, P Mello: Inheritance and Hypothetical Reasoning in Logic Programming. In: L. Carlucci Aiello (ed.): Proceedings of 9th European Conference on Artificial Intelligence ECAI-90, Pitman Publishing, London (UK), 1990.

[BLM90a] A. Brogi, E. Lamma, P Mello: A General Framework for Structuring Logic Programs. C.N.R. Technical Report "Progetto Finalizzato Sistemi Informatici e Calcolo Parallelo", N. 4/1, May 1990.

[Bow85] K. Bowen: Meta-level Programming and Knowledge Representation. New Generation Computing, Vol. 3, no. 4, OHMSHA LDT. and Springer-Verlag, Tokyo (J), pp. 359-383, 1985.

[CLM90] P.L. Civera, E. Lamma, P. Mello, A. Natali, G. Piccinini, G., M. Zamboni: Implementing Structured Logic Programs on a Dedicated VLSI Coprocessor. In: Proceedings Workshop on VLSI for Artificial Intelligence and Neural Networks, Oxford University, September 1990.

[DNO92] E. Denti, A. Natali, A. Omicini: Contexts as First-class Objects in SICStus Prolog. In: S. Costantini (ed.): Proceedings 7th Italian Conference on Logic Programming, Tremezzo, Italy, June 1992.

[GMR88] L. Giordano, A. Martelli, G.F. Rossi: Local Definitions with Static Scope Rules in Logic Languages. In: Proceedings International Conference on Fifth Generation Computer Systems FGCS84, ICOT, Tokyo (J), 1988.

[JaN91] B. Jayaraman, G. Nadathur: Implementation Techniques for Scoping Constructs in Logic Programming. In: K. Furukawa (d.): Proceedings of the 8th International Conference on Logic Programming, Paris (F), The MIT Press, Cambridge (USA), pp. 871-886, 1991.

[LMN89] E. Lamma, P. Mello, A. Natali: The Design of an Abstract Machine for Efficient Implementation of Contexts in Logic Programming. In: G. Levi and M. Martelli (eds.): Proceedings 6th International Conference and Symposium on Logic Programming, The MIT Press, Cambridge (USA), 1989.

[LMN91] E. Lamma, P. Mello, A. Natali: Reflection mechanisms to combine Prolog databases. Software, Practice and Experience, Vol. 21, No. 6, pp. 603-624, John Wiley & Sons, Chichester (UK), 1991.

[LMN] E. Lamma, P. Mello, A. Natali: An Extended Warren Abstract Machine for the Execution of Structured Logic Programs. Journal of Logic Programming, North-Holland, Forthcoming.

[LS87] J.W. Lloyd, J.C. Shepherdson: Partial Evaluation in Logic Programming. Journal of Logic Programming, Vol. 13, N0. 3&4, pp. 217-242, North-Holland, 1991

[Mei89] M. Meier et alii: SEPIA - An Extendible Prolog System. Proceedings of the 11th World Compuetr Congress IFIP'89, San Francisco (USA), August 1989.

[McC88] F.G. McCabe: Logic and Objects: Language, application and implementation. PhD Thesis, Imperial College, London (UK), November 1988.

[Mil86] D. Miller: A Theory of Modules for logic Programming. In: Proceedings 1986 International Symposium on Logic Programming, 106-114; 1986.

[MNR89] P. Mello, A. Natali, C. Ruggieri: Logic Programming in a Software Engineering Perspective. In: E.L. Lusk and R.A. Overbeek (eds.): Proceedings of the North American Conference on Logic Programming NACLP89, The MIT Press, Cambridge (USA), 1989.

[MP89] L. Monteiro, A. Porto: Contextual Logic Programming, In: G. Levi and M. Martelli (eds.): Proceedings 6th International Conference and Symposium on Logic Programming, The MIT Press, Cambridge (USA), 1989.

[SaS86] S. Safra, E. Shapiro: Meta-interpreters for Real. In: H.G. Kugler (ed.): Information Processing 86, pp. 271-278, Elsevier Science Publisher, 1986.

[SICS91] Swedish Institute of Computer Science: SICStus Prolog User's Manual. Kista, Sweden, 1991.

[StS86] L. Sterling, E. Shapiro: The Art of Prolog. The MIT Press, 1986.

[War83] D.H.D. Warren: An Abstract Prolog Instruction Set. SRI Technical Note 309, SRI International, October 1983.

[War84] D.S. Warren: Database Updates in Prolog. In: Proceedings International Conference on Fifth Generation Computer Systems 1984, Tokyo (J), 1984.

Implementing a Notion of Modules in the Logic Programming Language λProlog

Keehang Kwon, Gopalan Nadathur and Debra Sue Wilson

Department of Computer Science, Duke University, NC 27707

Abstract. Issues concerning the implementation of a notion of modules in the higher-order logic programming language λProlog are examined. A program in this language is a composite of type declarations and procedure definitions. The module construct that is considered permits large collections of such declarations and definitions to be decomposed into smaller units. Mechanisms are provided for controlling the interaction of these units and for restricting the visibility of names used within any unit. The typical interaction between modules has both a static and a dynamic nature. The parsing of expressions in a module might require declarations in a module that it interacts with, and this information must be available during compilation. Procedure definitions within a module might utilize procedures presented in other modules and support must be provided for making the appropriate invocation during execution. Our concern here is largely with the dynamic aspects of module interaction. We describe a method for compiling each module into an independent fragment of code. Static interactions prevent the compilation of interacting modules from being completely decoupled. However, using the idea of an interface definition presented here, a fair degree of independence can be achieved even at this level. The dynamic semantics of the module construct involve enhancing existing program contexts with the procedures defined in particular modules. A method is presented for achieving this effect through a linking process applied to the compiled code generated for each module. A direct implementation of the dynamic semantics leads to considerable redundancy in search. We present a way in which this redundancy can be controlled, prove the correctness of our approach and describe run-time structures for incorporating this idea into the overall implementation.

1 Introduction

This paper' concerns the implementation of a notion of modules in the logic programming language λProlog. Logic programming has traditionally lacked devices for structuring the space of names and procedure definitions: within this paradigm, programs are generally viewed as monolithic collections of procedure definitions, with the names of constants and data constructors being implicitly defined and visible everywhere in the program. Although the absence of such facilities is not seriously felt in the development of small programs, structuring mechanisms become essential for programming-in-the-large. This fact has spurred investigations into mechanisms for constructing programs in a modular fashion (*e.g.*, see [11, 14, 19, 20]) and has also resulted in structuring devices being included in some implementations of a Prolog-like language on an *ad hoc* basis. Most proposals put forth have, at the lowest level, been based on the use of the logic of Horn clauses. This logic does not directly support the realization of structuring devices, and consequently these have had to be built in at an extra-logical level. The logic of hereditary Harrop formulas, a recently discovered extension to Horn clause logic [13], is interesting in this respect because it contains logical primitives for controlling the visibility of names and the availability of predicate definitions. The language λProlog is based on this extended logic and thus provides logical support for several interesting scoping constructs [10, 11]. The notion of modules whose implementation we describe in this paper is in fact based on these new mechanisms.

The language λProlog is in reality a typed language. One manifestation of this fact is that programs in this language consist of two components: a set of type declarations and a set of procedure definitions. The module concept that we consider is relevant to a structuring of programs with respect to both components. In a simplistic sense, a module corresponds to a named collection of type declarations and procedure definitions. This view of modules reveals that the use of this structuring notion has both static and dynamic effects. The typical use that might be expected of any module is that of making it contents available in some fashion within a program context such as another module. The main impact of making the declarations in a module visible must clearly be a static one: to take one example, the type associated with some constant by the module in question may be needed for parsing expressions in the new context. The effect with regard to predicate definitions is, on the other hand, largely dynamic. Thus, procedure definitions in the new context might contain invocations to procedures defined in the "imported" module. The important question to be resolved, then, is that of how a reference to code is to be resolved in a situation where the available code is changing dynamically.

From the perspective of implementing the module notion, the main concern is really with the dynamic aspects. In particular, our interest is largely in a method for compiling the definitions appearing in modules and in the run-time structures needed for implementing the prescribed semantics for this construct. We examine these questions in detail in this paper and suggest solutions to them. Now, λProlog has several new features in comparison with a language such as Prolog and a complete treatment of compilation requires methods to be presented for handling these features as well. We have studied the implementation issues arising out the other extensions in recent work and have detailed solutions to them [7, 16, 17]. We outline the nature of these solutions here but do not present them in detail. In a broad sense, our solutions to the other problems can be embedded in a machine like the Warren Abstract Machine (WAM) [21]. We start with this machine and describe further enhancements to it that serve to implement the dynamic aspects of the module notion. There are several interesting characteristics to the scheme we ultimately suggest for this purpose, and these include the following:

(i) A notion of separate compilation for modules is supported. As we explained above, there is a potential for static interaction between modules that makes completely independent compilation impossible. However, this situation is no different from that in any other programming language. We propose the idea of an interface definition to overcome this problem. Relative to such definitions, we show that the separate compilation goal can actually be achieved.

(ii) A notion of linking is described and implemented. The dynamic use of modules effectively reduces to solving goals of the form M ==> G where M is a module name. The expected action is to enhance an existing program context with the definitions in M before solving G. The symbol ==> can, in a certain sense be viewed as a primitive for linking the compiled code generated for a module into a program context. Using ideas from [8] and [16] we show how this primitive can be implemented.

(iii) A method for controlling redundancy in search is described. The dynamic semantics presented for modules in [11] can lead to the definitions in a module being added several times to a program context, leading to considerable redundancy in solving goals. We present a sense in which this redundancy can be eliminated, prove the correctness of our approach and show how this idea can be incorporated into the overall implementation. The general idea in avoiding redundancy has been used in earlier implementations of λProlog [2, 9]. However, ours is, to our knowledge, the first proof of its correctness and the embedding of the idea within our compilation model is interesting in its own right.

The remainder of this paper is structured as follows. We describe the language of λProlog without the module feature in the next section, focussing eventually on the general structure of an implementation for this "core". In Section 3, we present the module notion that is the subject of this paper and outline the main issues in its implementation. In Section 4, we present our first implementation scheme. This scheme permits separate compilation and contains the run-time devices needed for linking. However, it has the drawback that it is may add several copies of a module to a program context leading to the mentioned redundancy in search. We discuss this issue in detail in Section 5 and show a way in which redundancy can be controlled. In Section 6 we use this idea in describing mechanisms that can be incorporated into the basic scheme of Section 4 to ensure that only one copy of a module is available in a program context at any time. Section 7 concludes the paper.

2 The Core Language

We describe in this section the part of the λProlog language that can be thought of as its core. Our presentation will be at two levels: we shall describe the logical underpinnings of the language and also attempt to describe it at the level of a usable programming language. Both aspects are required in later sections. The exposition at a logical level are needed to understand the semantics of the modules notion and to justify optimizations in its implementation. The presentation of the programming language is necessary to understand the value of modules as a pragmatic structuring construct.

1.1 Syntax

The logical language that underlies λProlog is ultimately derived from Church's simple theory of types [1]. This language is ***typed*** in the sense that every well-formed expression in it has a type associated with it. The language of types that is actually used permits a form of polymorphism. The type expressions are obtained from a set of ***sorts***, a set of ***type variables*** and a set of ***type constructors***, each of which is specified with a unique arity. The rules for constructing types are the following: (i) each sort and type variable is a type, (ii) if c is an n-ary type constructor and $t_1, \ldots, t_n$ are types, then $(c\ t_1\ \ldots\ t_n)$ is a type, and (iii) if α and β are types then so is $\alpha \rightarrow \beta$. Types formed by using (iii) are called ***function*** types. In writing function types, parentheses can be omitted by assuming that $\rightarrow$ is right associative. Type variables have a largely abbreviatory status in the language: they can appear in the types associated with expressions, but at a conceptual level such expressions can be used in a computation only after all the type variables appearing in them have been instantiated by closed types. A type is closed if it contains no type variables. However, these variables permit a succinct presentation of predicate definitions and, as we mention later, their instantiations at run-time can often be delayed. Thus, type variables provide a sense of polymorphism in λProlog.

At the level of concrete syntax, type variables are denoted by names that begin with an uppercase letter. The set of sorts initially contains only o, the boolean type, and int, the type of integers, and no type constructors are assumed. The user can define type constructors by using declarations of the form

kind c $\quad$ *type* $\rightarrow \ldots \rightarrow$ *type*.

The arity of the constructor c that is thus declared is one less than the number of occurrences of *type* in the declaration. Noting that a sort might be viewed as a nullary type constructor, a declaration of the above kind may also be used to add new sorts. As specific examples, the declarations

kind i $\quad$ *type*.
kind *list* $\quad$ *type* $\rightarrow$ *type*.

add i to the set of sorts and define *list* as a unary constructor. The latter will be used below as a means for constructing types corresponding to lists of objects of a homogeneous type .

The ***terms*** of the language are constructed from given sets of constant and variable symbols, each of which is assumed to be specified with a type. The constants are categorized as the ***logical*** and the ***nonlogical*** ones. The logical constants consist of the following:

true	of type o, denoting the true proposition,
$\wedge$	of type $o \rightarrow o \rightarrow o$, representing conjunction,
$\vee$	of type $o \rightarrow o \rightarrow o$, representing disjunction,
$\supset$	of type $o \rightarrow o \rightarrow o$, representing implication,
sigma	of type $(A \rightarrow o) \rightarrow o$, representing existential quantification,
pi	of type $(A \rightarrow o) \rightarrow o$, representing universal quantification.

The symbols *sigma* and *pi* have a polymorphic type associated with them. These symbols really correspond to a family of constants, each indexed by a choice of ground instantiation for τ and a similar interpretation is intended for other polymorphic symbols.

In the machine presentation of nonlogical constants and variables, conventions similar to those in Prolog are used: both variables and constants are represented by tokens formed out of sequences of alphanumeric characters or sequences of "sign" characters, and those tokens that begin with uppercase letters correspond to variables. The underlying logic requires a type to be associated with each of these tokens. Symbols that consist solely of numeric characters are assumed to have the type *int*. For other symbols, an association is achieved by declarations of the form

type *constant* *type-expression*.

Such a declaration identifies the type of *constant* with the corresponding type expression. As examples, the declarations

type *nil* (*list* A).
type :: $A \rightarrow$ (*list* A) $\rightarrow$ (*list* A).

define the constants *nil* and :: that function as constructors for homogeneous lists. Types of constants and variables may also be indicated by writing them in juxtaposition and separated by a colon. Thus the notation X : *int* corresponds to a variable X of type *int*.

The terms in our logical language are obtained from the constant and variable symbols by using the mechanisms of function abstraction and application. In particular (i) each constant and variable of type τ is a term of type τ, (ii) if x is a variable of type τ and t is a term of type τ', then $\lambda x t$ is a term of type $\tau \rightarrow \tau'$, and (iii) if t_1 is a term of type $(\tau_2 \rightarrow \tau_1)$ and t_2 is a term of type τ_2, then $(t_1\ t_2)$ is a term of type τ_1. A term obtained by virtue of (ii) is referred to as an ***abstraction*** whose bound variable is x and whose scope is t. Similarly a term obtained by (iii) is called the application of t_1 to t_2.

Several conventions are adopted towards enhancing readability. Parentheses are often omitted by assuming that application is left associative and that abstraction is right associative. The logical constants $\wedge$, $\vee$ and $\supset$ are written as right associative infix operators. It is often useful to extend this treatment to nonlogical constants, and a device is included in λProlog for declaring specific constants to be prefix, infix or postfix operators. For instance, the declaration

infix 150 *xfy* ::.

achieves the same effect that the declaration $op(150, xfy, ::)$ achieves in Prolog: it defines :: to be a right associative infix operator of precedence 150.

An important notion is that of a ***positive*** term which is a term in which the symbol $\supset$ does not appear. We define an ***atomic formula*** or ***atom*** to be a term of type o that has the structure $(P\ t_1\ \ldots\ t_n)$ where P, the ***head*** of the atom, is either a nonlogical constant or a variable and $t_1, \ldots, t_n$, the ***arguments*** of the atom, are positive terms. Such a formula is referred to as a ***rigid*** atom if its head is a nonlogical constant, and as a ***flexible*** atom otherwise. Using the symbol A to denote arbitrary atoms and A_r to denote rigid atoms, the classes of G-, D- and E-formulas are identified as follows:

$$G ::= \mathit{true} \mid A \mid (G_1 \wedge G_2) \mid (G_1 \vee G_2) \mid \mathit{sigma}\ (\lambda x G) \mid \mathit{pi}\ (\lambda x G) \mid (E \supset G)$$

$$D ::= A_r \mid G \supset A_r \mid \mathit{pi}\ (\lambda x D) \mid (D_1 \wedge D_2)$$

$$E ::= D \mid \mathit{sigma}\ (\lambda x E)$$

A curious aspect of these syntax rules is the use of the symbols *pi* and *sigma*. These symbols represent universal and existential quantification respectively. The quantifiers that are used in conventional presentations of logic play a dual role: in the expression $\forall x P$, the quantifier has the function of binding the variable x over the expression P in addition to that of making a predication of the result. In the logical language considered here, these roles are separated between the abstraction operation and appropriately chosen constants. Thus the expression $\forall x P$ is represented here by $(\mathit{pi}\ (\lambda x P))$. The former expression may be thought of as an abbreviation for the latter, and we use this convention at a metalinguistic level below. A similar observation applies to the symbol *sigma* and existential quantification.

The G- and D-formulas determine the ***programs*** and ***queries*** of λProlog. A program consists of a list of closed D-formulas each element of which is referred to as a ***program clause***, and a query or goal is an closed G-formula[1]. In writing the program clauses in a program in λProlog, the universal quantifiers appearing at the front are left implicit. A similar observation applies to the existential quantifiers at the beginning of a query. There are some other conventions used in the machine presentation of programs. Abstraction is depicted by \, written as an infix operator. Thus, the expression $\lambda X(X :: \mathit{nil})$ is represented by $X\backslash(X :: \mathit{nil})$. The symbols $\wedge$ and $\vee$ are denoted by , and ; as in Prolog. Implications appearing at the top-level in program clauses are written backwards with :- being used in place of $\supset$, and the symbol $\supset$ in goal formulas is written as =>. Finally, a program is depicted by writing a sequence of program clauses, each clause being terminated by a period. An example of the use of these conventions is provided by the following clauses defining the familiar ***append*** predicate, assuming the types for ***nil*** and :: that were presented earlier.

[1] This definition is more general than the one usually employed in that existential quantification is permitted over D formulas appearing to the left of implications in goals. This feature does not add anything new at a logical level, but is pragmatically useful as we see later. This extended definition is also used in [4].

(append nil L L).
(append H :: L1 L2 H :: L3) :- *(append L1 L2 L3)*.

Notice that not all the needed type information has been presented in these clauses: the types of the variables and of *append* have been omitted. These types could be provided by using the devices explained earlier. However, type declarations can be avoided in several situations since the desired types can be reconstructed [15]. For example, the type of *append* in the above program can be determined to be $(list\ A) \rightarrow (list\ A) \rightarrow (list\ A) \rightarrow o$. The type reconstruction algorithm that is used is sensitive to the set of clauses contained in the program. For example, if the program above included the clause

(append (1 :: *nil*) (2 :: *nil*) (1 :: 2 :: *nil*)).

as well, then the type determined for *append* would be $(list\ int) \rightarrow (list\ int) \rightarrow (list\ int) \rightarrow o$ instead.

The example above shows the similarity of λProlog syntax to that of Prolog. The main difference is a curried notation, which is convenient given the higher-order nature of the language. There are similarities in the semantics as well as we discuss below.

1.1 Answering Queries from Programs

We present an operational semantics for λProlog by providing rules for solving a query in the context of a given program. The rules depend on the top-level logical symbol in the query and have the effect of producing a new query and a new program. Thus, the operational semantics induces a notion of computational state given by a program and a query. We employ structures of the form $\mathcal{P} \longrightarrow G$ where $\mathcal{P}$ is a listing of closed program clauses and G is a closed G-formula to represent such a state. We refer to these structures as *sequents*, and the idea of solving a query from a set of closed program clauses corresponds to that of constructing a derivation for an appropriate sequent.

Several auxiliary notions are needed in presenting the rules for constructing derivations. One of these is the notion of equality assumed in our language. Two terms are considered equal if they can be made identical using the rules of λ-conversion. We assume a familiarity on the part of the reader with a presentation of these rules such as that found in [5]. We need a substitution operation on formulas. Formally, we think of a substitution as a finite set of pairs of the form $\langle x, t\rangle$ where x is a variable and t is a term whose type is identical to that of x; the substitution is said to be closed if the second component of each pair in it is closed. Given a substitution $\{\langle x_i, t_i\rangle | 1 \leq i \leq n\}$, we write $F[t_1/x_1, \ldots, t_n/x_n]$ to denote the application of this substitution to F. Such an application must be done carefully to avoid the usual capture problems. The needed qualifications can be captured succinctly by using the λ-conversion rules: $F[t_1/x_1, \ldots, t_n/x_n]$ is equal to the term $((\lambda x_1 \ldots \lambda x_n F)\ t_1\ \ldots\ t_n)$. We also need to talk about *type instances* of terms. These are obtained by making substitutions for type variables that appear in the term. Finally, we are particularly interested in terms that do not have any type variables in them and we call such terms *type variable free*.

The various notions described above are used in defining the idea of an instance of a program clause.

Definition 1. An instance of a closed program clause D is given as follows:

(i) If D is of the form A_r or $G \supset A_r$, then any type variable free type instance of D is an instance of D.
(ii) If D is of the form $D_1 \wedge D_2$ then an instance of D_1 or of D_2 is an instance of D.
(iii) If D is of the form $\forall x D_1$, then an instance of $D_1[t/x]$ for any closed positive term t of the same type as x is an instance of D.

The restriction to (closed) positive terms forces an instance of a program clause to itself be a program clause. In fact, instances of program clauses have a very simple structure: they are all of the form A_r or $G \supset A_r$.

In describing the derivation rules, and thus the operational semantics of our language, we restrict our attention to type variable free queries. We present a more general notion of computation later based on this restricted definition of derivation.

Definition 2. Let G be a type variable free query and let $\mathcal{P}$ be a program. Then a derivation is constructed for $\mathcal{P} \longrightarrow G$ by using one of the following rules:

SUCCESS By noting the G is equal to an instance of a program clause in $\mathcal{P}$.

BACKCHAIN By picking an instance of a program clause in $\mathcal{P}$ of the form $G_1 \supset G$ and constructing a derivation for $\mathcal{P} \longrightarrow G_1$.

AND If G is equal to $G_1 \wedge G_2$, by constructing derivations for the sequents $\mathcal{P} \longrightarrow G_1$ and $\mathcal{P} \longrightarrow G_2$.

OR If G is equal to $G_1 \vee G_2$, by constructing a derivation for either $\mathcal{P} \longrightarrow G_1$ or $\mathcal{P} \longrightarrow G_2$.

INSTANCE If G is equal to $\exists x G_1$, by constructing a derivation for the sequent $\mathcal{P} \longrightarrow G_1[t/x]$, where t is a closed positive term of the same type as x.

GENERIC If G is equal to $\forall x G_1$, by constructing a derivation for the sequent $\mathcal{P} \longrightarrow G_1[c/x]$, where c is a nonlogical constant of the same type as x that does not appear in $\forall x G$ or in the formulas in $\mathcal{P}$.

AUGMENT If G is equal to $(\exists x_1 \ldots \exists x_n D) \supset G$, by constructing a derivation for $D[c_1/x_1, \ldots, c_n/x_n], \mathcal{P} \longrightarrow G$, where, for $1 \leq i \leq n$, c_i is a nonlogical constant of the same type as x_i that does not appear in $(\exists x_1 \ldots \exists x_n D) \supset G$ or in the formulas in $\mathcal{P}$.

To understand the operational semantics induced by these rules, let us assume a program given by the following clauses

```
(rev L1 L2) :-
        (((rev_aux nil L2),
        (pi (X\(pi (L1\(pi (L2\
                ((rev_aux X :: L1 L2) :- (rev_aux L1 X :: L2)))))))))
                => (rev_aux L1 nil)).
```

and consider solving the query (*rev* 1 :: 2 :: *nil* 2 :: 1 :: *nil*). The first rule that must be used in a derivation is BACKCHAIN. Using it reduces the problem to that of solving the query

```
((rev_aux nil 2 :: 1 :: nil),
(pi (X\(pi (L1\(pi (L2\
        ((rev_aux X :: L1 L2) :- (rev_aux L1 X :: L2)))))))))
=> (rev_aux 1 :: 2 :: nil nil)
```

from the same program. The AUGMENT rule is now applicable and using it essentially causes the program to be enhanced with the clauses

```
(rev_aux nil 2 :: 1 :: nil).
(rev_aux X :: L1 L2) :- (rev_aux L1 X :: L2).
```

prior to solving the query (*rev_aux* 1 :: 2 :: *nil nil*). Using the BACKCHAIN rule twice in conjunction with the last clause produces the goal (*rev_aux nil* 2 :: 1 :: *nil*). The derivation attempt now succeeds because the goal is an instance of program clause.

The above example indicates the programming interpretation given to logical formulas and symbols by the operational semantics. Program clauses of the form $\forall x_1 \ldots \forall x_n A_r$ and $\forall x_1 \ldots \forall x_n(G \supset A_r)$ function in a sense as procedure definitions: the head of A_r represents the name of the procedure and, in the latter case, the body of the clause, G, corresponds to the body of the procedure. From an operational perspective, every program clause is equivalent to a conjunction of clauses in this special form, and a program is equivalent to a list of such clauses. Thus both correspond to a collection of procedure definitions. Goals correspond to search requests with the logical symbols appearing in them functioning as primitives for specifying the search structure. Thus, in searching for a derivation, $\wedge$ gives rise to an AND branch, $\vee$ to an OR branch and *sigma* to an OR branch parameterized by a substitution. These symbols are used in a similar fashion in Prolog. The symbols $\supset$ and *pi*, on the other hand, do not appear in Prolog goals. The treatment of these symbols is interesting from a programming viewpoint. The first symbol has the effect of augmenting an existing program for a limited part of the computation. Thus, this symbol corresponds to a primitive for giving program clauses a scope. The symbol *pi* similarly corresponds to a primitive for giving names a scope; processing this symbol requires a new name to be introduced for a portion of the search. A closer look at the operational semantics reveals a similarity between the interpretation of *pi* and the treatment given to existential quantifiers in E-formulas through the AUGMENT rule. This is not very surprising since the formulas $\forall x(D(x) \supset G)$ and $(\exists x D(x)) \supset G$ are equivalent in most logical contexts, assuming x does not appear free in G. From a pragmatic perspective, then, the existential quantifier in E-formulas enables a name to be made local to a set of procedure definitions, *i.e.*, it provides a means for information hiding.

A computation in λProlog corresponds to constructing a derivation for a query from a given program. We are generally interested in extracting a value from a computation. In the present context, this can be made clear as follows.

Definition 3. Let $\mathcal{P}$ be a collection of program clauses and let G be a type variable free query of the form $\exists x_1 \ldots \exists x_n G_1$; the variables $x_1, \ldots, x_n$ are assumed to be implicitly quantified here. An answer to G in the context of $\mathcal{P}$ is a closed substitution $\{\langle x_i, t_i \rangle | 1 \leq i \leq n\}$ such that $\mathcal{P} \longrightarrow G_1[t_1/x_1, \ldots, t_n/x_n]$ has a derivation.

In general our queries may have type variables in them. The answers to such a query are given by the answers to each of its type variable free type instances.

Our ultimate interest is in a procedure for carrying out computations of the kind described above and for extracting results from these. The rules for constructing derivations provide a structure for such a procedure but additional mechanisms are needed. One problem involves instantiations for type variables. There is usually insufficient information for choosing instantiations for these at the points indicated. This problem can be overcome by allowing type variables into the computation and by using unification to incrementally determine their instantiations. A similar problem arises with existential quantifiers in queries. For example, solving a query of the form $\exists x G$ requires a closed term t to be produced that makes $G[t/x]$ solvable. The usual mechanism employed in these cases is to replace x with a *logic* variable, *i.e.*, a place-holder, and to let an appropriate instantiation be determined by unification. However, this mechanism must be used with care in the present situation. First, the unification procedure that is used must incorporate our enriched notion of equality, *i.e.*, higher-order unification [6] must be used. Second, the treatment of universal quantifiers requires unification to respect certain constraints. For example, consider the query $\exists x \forall y p(x, y)$, where p is a predicate constant. Using the mechanisms outlined, this query will be transformed into $p(X, c)$, where c is a new constant and X is a logic variable. Notice, however, that X must not be instantiated with a term that contains c in it. A solution to this problem is to add a numeric tag to every constant and variable and to use these tags in constraining the unification process [3, 18].

A suitable abstract interpreter can be developed for λProlog based on the above ideas[2]. In actually implementing this interpreter, two additional questions arise. First, there is some nondeterminism involved: in solving an atomic goal, a choice has to be made between program clauses and in solving $G_1 \vee G_2$ a decision has to be made between solving G_1 and G_2. The usual device employed here is to use a depth-first search with backtracking. The second question concerns the implementation of implications in queries. To understand the various problems

[2] Actually, the proper treatment of type variables in a computation is still an open issue. However, a discussion of this matter is orthogonal to our present purposes.

that arise here, let us consider a query of the form $(D \supset G_1) \wedge G_2$. This query results in the query $D \supset G_1$ which must be solved by adding (the clauses in) D to the program, solving the clauses in G_1 and then removing D. The addition of code follows a stack based discipline and can be implemented as such. However, if a compilation model is used, some effort is involved in spelling out a scheme for achieving the addition and deletion of code. Moreover the "program clauses" that are added might now contain logic variables in them. Thus, consider solving the goal $\exists L(\textit{rev}\ 1 :: 2 :: \textit{nil}\ L)$ using the clause for *rev* presented earlier in this section. The program would at a certain stage have to be augmented with the clause $(\textit{rev\_aux}\ \textit{nil}\ L)$ where L is now a logic variable. In general, we need now to think of procedures as blocks of code *and* bindings for some variables. Continuing now with the solution of the query $(D \supset G_1) \wedge G_2$, the goal G_2 will be attempted after the first conjunct is solved. A failure in solving this goal might require an alternative solution to G_1 to be generated. Notice, however, that an attempt to find such a solution must be made in a context where the program once again contains D. An implementation of our language must support the needed context switching ability.

Implementation techniques have been devised for solving the various problems mentioned above [7, 16, 17], resulting in an abstract machine and a compilation scheme for the core language described in this section. We do not discuss this explicitly here, and will rely on the reader's intuition and indulgence when alluding to these ideas later in the paper. However, the discussion of modules will require a closer acquaintance with the scheme used for implementing implications in queries, and we then supply some further details.

Before concluding this section, it is interesting to note the connection between our notion of computation and deduction in a logical context. The following proposition describes this connection.

Proposition 4. *Let $\mathcal{P}$ be a program and let $\mathcal{P}'$ be the collection of all the type variable free type instances of formulas in $\mathcal{P}$. Further, let G be a type variable free query. Then there is a derivation for $\mathcal{P} \longrightarrow G$ if and only if G follows from $\mathcal{P}'$ in intuitionistic logic.*

Only the *only if* part of this proposition is non-trivial. For the most part, this follows from the existence of uniform proofs for sequents of the kind we are interested in; see, *e.g.*, [13] and [18] for details. One additional point to note is the treatment of existential quantifiers in E-formulas. However, this causes no problem because the introduction of existential quantifiers in assumptions can always be made the last step in intuitionistic proofs.

3 Modules

The language described thus far only permits programs that are a monolithic collection of kind, type, and operator declarations together with a set of procedure definitions. Modules provide a means for structuring the space of declarations and also for tailoring the definitions of procedures depending on the context.

The ultimate purpose of this feature is to allow programs to be built up from logical segments which are in some sense separate.

At the very lowest level, the module feature allows a name to be associated with a collection of declarations and program clauses. An example of the use of this construct is provided by the following sequence of declarations that in effect attaches the name *lists* with the list constructors and some basic list-handling predicates:

```
module      lists.
infix 150   ::       xfy.
kind  list  type → type.
type  nil   (list A).
type  ::    A → (list A) → (list A).

(append nil L L).
(append (H :: L1) L2 (H :: L3)) :- (append L1 L2 L3).

(member H (H :: L)).
(member X (H :: L)) :- (member X L).

(length 0 nil).
(length N (H :: L) :- ((length N1 L), N is N1 + 1).
```

One way to think of this module declaration is as a declaration of a list "data type". This data type can be made available in specific contexts by using the name *lists* in a manner that we describe presently. This discussion will bring out the intended purpose of the modules feature. However, there is one use that can already be noted. Looking at the *lists* module above, we see that the types of the predicates defined in it have not been provided. These types can be reconstructed, but, as we noted in Section 2, the types "inferred" depend on the set of available program clauses. The module boundary provides a notion of scope that is relevant to this reconstruction process: looked at differently, the types of all the symbols appearing in the clauses in a module are completely determined once the module is parsed.

The meaning of the module feature is brought out by considering its use in programming. In the presence of modules, we enhance our goals to include a new kind of expression called a *module implication*. These are expressions of the form *M* ==> *G*, where *M* is a module name. Goals of the new sort have the intuitive effect of adding *M* to the program before solving *G*. In making this precise, however, the effect of *M* on two different components have to be made clear: on the type, kind and operator declarations and on the procedure definitions.

The effect on the space of declarations that we assume here is simple. All the associations present in *M* become available on adding *M* to the context. This is really a *static* effect in that it provides a context in which to parse the goal *G* in a larger goal *M* ==> *G*. As a concrete example, consider the goal

```
lists ==> (append 1 :: 2 :: nil  3 :: nil L).
```

In parsing this query, there is a need to determine the types of *append* and of ::. The semantics attributed to the modules feature requires the types associated with these tokens in the module *lists* to be assumed for this purpose. This appears to be the most natural course, given that we expect the definition of *append* provided in *lists* to be useful in solving this query.

From the perspective of procedure definitions, we assume the semantics for modules that is presented in [11]. Within this framework, the dynamic aspects of the module feature are explained by a translation into the core language. Thus, a module is thought of as the conjunction of the program clauses appearing in it. For instance, the *lists* module corresponds to the conjunction of the clauses for *append*, *member* and *length*. Under this interpretation, a module corresponds to a *D*-formula as described in the last section. Now if module *M* corresponds to the formula *D*, the query *M* ==> *G* is thought of as the goal *D* => *G*. The run-time treatment of module implication is then determined by the AUGMENT rule presented in the last section. In particular, solving the goal *M* ==> *G* calls for solving the goal *G* after adding the predicate definitions in the module *M* to the existing program.

The analogy between a module and a data type raises the question of whether some aspects of an implementation might be hidden. Our language permits constant names to be made local to a module, thus allowing for the hiding of a data structure. To achieve this effect, a declaration of the form

local ***constant*,...,*constant*.**

can be placed within a module. The names of the constants listed then become unavailable outside the module. For example, adding the declaration

local ::.

to the *lists* module has the effect of hiding the list constructor ::.

The static effect of the local construct is easy to understand: only some names are available when the module is added to a context. From a dynamic perspective, another issue arises. Can constants defined to be local eventually become visible outside through computed answers? The expectation is that they should not become so visible. This effect can be achieved by thinking of local constants really as variables quantified existentially over the scope of the conjunction of program clauses in the module. As an example, consider the following module

module **store.**
local **emp, stk.**
kind **store type → type.**
type **emp (store A).**
type **stk A → (store A) → (store A).**
initialize emp.
(enter X S (stk X S)).
(remove X (stk X S) S).

This module implements a *store* data type with initializing, adding and removing operations. At a level of detail, the store is implemented as a stack. However, the intention of the local declarations is to hide the actual representation of the store. Now, from the perspective of dynamic effects, the module corresponds to the formula

$$\exists Emp \exists Stk($$
(*initialize Emp*) ,
(*pi* (*X*\(*pi* (*S*\(*enter X S* (*Stk X S*)))))),
(*pi* (*X*\(*pi* (*S*\(*remove X* (*Stk X S*) *S*)))))).

This formula has the structure of an E-formula and in fact every module corresponds in the sense explained to an E-formula. Referring to this formula as *EStore*, let us consider solving a goal of the form $\exists X$(*Store* ==> $G(X)$). The semantics of this goal requires solving the goal $\exists X$(*EStore* => $G(X)$). Under the usual treatment of existential quantifiers, this results in the goal (*EStore* => $G(X)$) where X is now a logic variable. Using the AUGMENT rule, this goal is solved by instantiating the existential quantifiers at the front of *EStore*, adding the resulting D-formula to the program and then solving $G(X)$. The important point to note now is that any substitution that is considered for X must not have the constants supplied for *Emp* and *Stk* appearing in it. Thus the semantics attributed to modules and local declarations achieves the intended dynamic effect.

While module implication is useful for making modules available at the top-level, modules may themselves need to interact. For instance, a module that contains sorting predicates might need the declarations and procedure definitions in the *lists* module and a module that implements graph-search might similarly need the *store* and *lists* modules. The needed interaction is obtained in λProlog by placing an *import* declaration in the module which needs other modules. The format of such a declaration is the following:

import $M1, \ldots, Mk$.

In a declaration of this sort, $M1, \ldots, Mk$ must be names of other modules that are referred to as the *imported* modules. A declaration of this sort has, once again, a static and a dynamic effect on the module in which it is placed, *i.e.*, the *importing* module. The static effect is to make all the declarations in the imported modules, save those hidden by local declarations, available in the importing module. These declarations can be used in parsing the importing module and also become part of the declarations provided by that module. The intended dynamic effect, on the other hand, is to make the procedure definitions in the imported modules available for solving the goals in the bodies of program clauses that appear in the importing module. This effect can actually be explained by using module implication [11]. Let us assume that the clause P :- G appears in a module that imports the modules $M1, \ldots, Mk$. The dynamic semantics involves interpreting this clause as the following one instead:

P :- ($M1$ ==> $\cdots$ (Mk ==> G)).

Observe that using this clause involves solving the goal ($M1$ ==> ⋯ (Mk ==> G)) that ultimately causes the program to be enhanced with the clauses in $M1, \ldots, Mk$ before solving G.

```
module graph_search.
import lists, store.

(g_search Soln) :-
        ((init_open Open), (expand_graph Open nil Soln)).

(init_open Open) :-
        ((start_state State), (initialize Op), (enter State Op Open)).

(expand_graph Open Closed Soln) :-
        (remove State Open ROp),
        (((final_state State), (soln State Soln));
        ((expand_node State NStates),
        (add_states NStates ROp (State :: Closed) NOp),
        (expand_graph NOp (State :: Closed) Soln))).

(add_states nil Open Closed Open).
(add_states (St :: RSts) Open Closed NOpen) :-
        ((member St Closed), (add_states RSts Open Closed NOpen)).
(add_states (St :: RSts) Open Closed NOpen) :-
        ((enter St Open NOp), (add_states RSts NOp Closed NOpen)).
```

Fig. 1. A Module Implementing Graph Search

The definition of the module *graph_search* presented in Figure 1 illustrates the usefulness of the module interaction facility provided by *import*. The definitions of the predicates *start_state*, *final_state*, *soln* and *expand_node* have not been presented here, but we anticipate the reader can supply these. The important aspect to note is the use that is made of the declarations and procedure definitions in the modules *lists* and *store*. For example, the type

$$(list\ A) \rightarrow (store\ A) \rightarrow (list\ A) \rightarrow (store\ A) \rightarrow o$$

will be reconstructed for *add_states*. This type uses type constructors defined in in the modules *lists* and *store*. Similarly, the procedure *member* defined in *lists* and the procedures *initialize*, *enter* and *remove* defined in *store* are used in the program clauses in the module *graph_search*. A particularly interesting aspect is the interaction between the modules *graph_search* and *store*. Notice that the "constants" *emp* and *stk* used in *store* are not visible in *graph_search* and

cannot be used explicitly in the procedures appearing there. Thus, importing *store* provides an abstract notion of a store without opening up the actual implementation. For example, the current stack-based realization of the store can be replaced by a queue-based one without any need to change the *graph_search* module so long as the operations *initialize*, *enter* and *remove* are still supported. This change will have an effect on the behavior of *g_search* though, changing it to a procedure that conducts breadth-first search as opposed to the current depth-first search.

The pragmatic utility of the module feature and of the scoping ability provided by the new logical symbols in our language is an important issue to consider and detailed discussions of this aspect appear in [10] and [11]. Our interest in this paper is largely on implementation issues, especially those arising out of the module notion. From this perspective, it is necessary to understand carefully the dynamic interactions that can arise between modules through the use of the *import* statement. We therefore present an example that illustrates some of these interactions. Figure 2 contains a collection of interacting modules and Figure 3 exhibits the process of solving the query (*m*1 ==> (*p X*)) given these definitions. In presenting this solution attempt, we use a linear format based on the notion of derivation presented in Section 2 but augmented with the use of logic variables. Further, we use lines of the following form

$$M1, \ldots, Mn \text{ ?- } G(X)$$

where $G(X)$ is an atomic goal and $M1, \ldots, Mn$ are module names. Such a line indicates that $G(X)$ is to be solved from a program given by the collection of clauses in $M1, \ldots, Mn$. We refer to this list of modules as a program context. Now, the attempt to solve this goal proceeds by trying to match the goal with the head of some clause. If this attempt is successful, the line is annotated by a binding for the logic variables, *e.g.*, by an expression such as X <- a. In the case that the match results in additional goals, the following lines pertain to the solution of these goals. If no match is possible or if the match results directly in a success, the line is further annotated with the word *FAIL* or *SUCC*. In the former case, the succeeding lines indicate the solution attempt after backtracking and in the latter case they indicate an attempt to solve the remaining goals.

*module m*1.	*module m*2.	*module m*3.
*import m*2.	*import m*3.	*type r i* → *o*.
(*p X*) :- (*q X*), (*t X*).	(*p b*).	(*r a*).
(*t b*).	(*q X*) :- (*s X*).	(*r b*).
(*s X*) :- (*r X*).		

Fig. 2. A Set of Interacting Modules

$$
\begin{array}{rll}
m1\ ?\text{-}\ (p X) & & \\
m2, m1\ ?\text{-}\ (q\ X) & & \\
m3, m2, m1\ ?\text{-}\ (s\ X) & & \\
m2, m3, m2, m1\ ?\text{-}\ (r\ X) & X \text{<-}\ a & SUCC \\
m2, m1\ ?\text{-}\ (t\ a) & FAIL & \\
m2, m3, m2, m1\ ?\text{-}\ (r\ X) & X \text{<-}\ b & SUCC \\
m2, m1\ ?\text{-}\ (t\ b) & SUCC &
\end{array}
$$

Fig. 3. Solving ($m1$ ==> (p X)) Given the Modules in Figure 2

Let us consider now the attempt to solve the mentioned goal, ($m2$ ==> ((p X)). The initial program context is empty, but dealing with the module implication causes $m1$ to be added to it. The goal to be solved now is (p X). There is only one clause available for p and this is interpreted as if it were

$$(p\ X)\ \text{:-}\ (m2 \text{ ==> } ((q\ X), (t\ X)))$$

since $m1$ imports $m2$. Module $m2$ is therefore added to the program context and the goal to be solved reduces to (q X), (t X). Although not relevant to the solution of the present goal, notice that module $m2$ also contains a clause for p. The new program context thus contains an enhanced definition for this predicate and an implementation must be capable of combining code from different sources to produce the desired effect. Tracing through the solution attempt a few more steps, we see that the use of the second clause in module $m1$ results in an attempt to solve (r X). There are two clauses for this predicate in the relevant program context and these are used in order. Note that this interaction could not have been predicted from the static structure of $m1$ alone: there is no compile-time indication that code in module $m3$ might be used in solving goals appearing in the bodies of clauses in $m1$. A compilation scheme must therefore be sensitive to the fact that the definition of procedures used within modules are determined dynamically. Continuing with the solution attempt, (r X) is solved successfully with X being bound to the constant a. The task now becomes one of solving the goal (t a). Notice that the program context for this goal includes only $m1$ and $m2$, *i.e.*, an implementation must support this kind of context switching. When this goal fails, backtracking now requires an alternative solution to (r X) to be found. However, this solution attempt must take place in a resurrected context, as indicated in the figure. Once again, an implementation of the module feature must be capable of supporting this kind of reinstatement of earlier contexts.

We consider in the next section the various implementation issues pertaining to the dynamic behavior of modules that are raised by the above example. We note that a desirable feature of an implementation scheme is that it should permit a separate compilation of each module; this is in some sense indicative of the ability of this feature to split up a program into logically separate parts. The scheme that we present for implementing the dynamic behavior exhibits this facet — separate segments of compiled code are produced for each module and these are linked together dynamically to produce a desired program context. However, the idea of separate compilation is somewhat more problematic at the level of static interaction. The main issue is that the parsing of an importing module requires the various type, kind and operator declarations in the imported modules, implying a dependence in compilation. This kind of behavior is, however, not unique to our context. The usual solution to this problem is to introduce the idea of an interface between modules. Specialized to our context, this involves assigning a set of declarations to a module name. This assignment may act in a prescriptive fashion on the actual set of declarations appearing in the module in the sense that they may be required to conform to the "interface" requirements. With regard to importation, on the other hand, the interface declarations could control what is visible. One consequence of this view is that the association of types with constants might be hidden. Such an occlusion must be accompanied with a hiding of the constant itself and thus affects the dynamic behavior. However, this behavior can be modelled by the use of implicit local declarations[3]. A proper use of this idea will require predicate definitions also to be hidden. This ability is not supported within the current language: the ability to quantify existentially over predicate names requires an extension of the syntax of D-formulas. The extension in syntax can be easily accomplished as indicated in [4] and [10]. Although we do not treat this matter explicitly here, the desired extension does not cause any semantical problems and, as indicated in [16], can also be accommodated within our implementation scheme.

While the use of an interface as a method for prescribing interactions in this manner has several interesting aspects, a more conservative view of it is also possible. The interface declarations may be viewed simply as a distillate of the compilation of the module in question. Regardless of which view is taken, we assume here that, when a module is being compiled, all the type, kind and operator declarations obtainable from the imported modules are known. The scheme that we present in the next section then generates the code for capturing the dynamic behavior of a module by using only these interfaces and parsing the module in question. In this sense, our scheme is capable of supporting the idea of separate compilation.

4 Implementing the Dynamic Semantics of Modules

The crucial issue that must be dealt with in an implementation of the dynamic aspects of modules is the treatment of module implication. In particular, we are interested in the compilation of goals of the form M ==> G. Within a model that supports separate compilation, the production of code from the predicate definitions appearing in M must be performed independently of this goal. The compiled effect of this goal must then be to enhance the program context by

[3] A related proposal is contained in [12]. However, the suggestion there is to determine the local declarations dynamically, depending on the goal to be solved. This appears not to help with the "static" problem discussed here and also makes it difficult to generate code for a module independent of its use.

adding the code in M to it. Under this view, the symbol ==> becomes a primitive for linking code. The crucial issues within an implementation thus become those of what structures are needed for realizing this linking function and of what must be produced as a result of the compilation of a module to facilitate the linking process at run-time.

We have developed a scheme elsewhere [16] for implementing goals that contain implications. The dynamic semantics of module implication coupled with some features of the mentioned scheme make it an apt one to adapt to the present context. The essence of our scheme is to view a program as a composite of compiled code and a layered access function to this code. The execution of an implication goal causes a new layer to be added to an existing access function. Thus, consider an implication goal of the form $(C_1, \ldots, C_n) \Rightarrow G$ where, for $i \leq i \leq n$, C_i is a closed program clause of the form $\forall x_1 \ldots \forall x_n A_r$ or $\forall x_1 \ldots \forall x_n (G \supset A_r)$[4]. Each C_i corresponds to a partial definition of a procedure that must be added to the front of the program while an attempt is made to solve G. These clauses can be treated as an independent program segment and compiled in a manner similar to that employed in the WAM. Let us suppose that the clauses define the predicates $p_1, \ldots, p_r$. The compilation process then results in a segment of code with r entry points, each indexed with the name of a predicate. In our context, compilation must also produce a procedure that we call *find_code* that performs the following function: given a predicate name, this procedure returns the appropriate entry point in the code segment if the name is one of $p_1, \ldots, p_r$ and an indication of failure otherwise. This function can be implemented in several different ways such as through the use of a hash-function, but the details will not concern us here. Returning now to the implication goal, its execution results in a new access function that behaves as follows. Given a predicate name, *find_code* is invoked with it. If this function succeeds, then the code location that it produces is the desired result. Otherwise the code location is determined by using the access function in existence earlier.

The process of enhancing a context described above is incomplete in one respect: the new clauses provided for $p_1, \ldots, p_r$ may in fact be adding to earlier existing definitions for these predicates. To deal with this situation, the compilation process must produce code for each of these predicates that does not fail eventually, but instead looks for code for the relevant predicate using the access function existing earlier. Rather than carrying out this task each time it is needed, using an idea from [8], it can be done once at the time the new program context is set up. The idea used is the following. A vector of size r can be asso-

---

[4] In the general case, every implication goal can be transformed into one of the form

$$Q_1 X_1 \ldots Q_m X_m ((C_1(X_1, \ldots, X_m), \ldots, C_n(X_1, \ldots, X_m)) \Rightarrow G(X_1, \ldots, X_m))$$

where Q_i is $\exists$ or $\forall$ and $C_i(x_1, \ldots, x_m)$ is a program clause of the sort indicated but which may depend on the variables $x_1, \ldots, x_m$. Existential quantifiers may arise in considerations of module implication only if the module notion is enriched to allow for parameterization. Universal quantifiers do arise indirectly through *local* declarations whose treatment is considered later in this section.

ciated with the implication goal, with the ith entry in this vector corresponding to the predicate p_i. Now, the compilation of the body of the implication goal creates a procedure called *link_code* whose purpose is to fill in this vector when the implication goal is executed. This procedure essentially uses the name of each of the predicates and the earlier existing access function to compute an entry point to available code or, in case the predicate is previously undefined, to return the address of a failing procedure. To complement the creation of this table, the last instruction in the code generated for each of the predicates p_i must actually result in a transfer to the location indicated by the appropriate table entry.

In the framework of a WAM-like implementation, the layered access function described above can be realized by using what are called ***implication point records***. These records are allocated on the local stack and correspond essentially to layers in the access function. The components of such a record, based on the discussions thus far, are the following:

(i) the address of the *find_code* procedure corresponding to the antecedent of the implication goal,
(ii) a positive integer r indicating the number of predicates defined by the program clauses in the antecedent,
(iii) a pointer to an enclosing implication point record, and thereby to the previous layer in the access function, and
(iv) a vector of size r that indicates the next clause to try for each of the predicates defined in the antecedent of the implication goal.

The program context existing at a particular stage is indicated by a pointer to a relevant implication point record which is contained in a register called `I`. Now a goal such as $(C_1, \ldots, C_n)$ => G is compiled into code of the form

push_impl_point t
{ Compiled code for G }
pop_impl_point

In this code, t is the address of a statically created table for the antecedent of the goal that indicates the address of its *find_code* and *link_code* procedures and the number of predicates defined. The *push_impl_point* instruction causes a new implication point record to be allocated. The first three components of this record are set in a straightforward manner using the table indicated and the contents of the `I` register. Filling in the last component involves running *link_code* using the access function provided by the `I` register. The final action of the instruction is to set the `I` register to point to the newly created implication point record. The effect of the *pop_impl_point* instruction is to reset the program context. This is achieved simply by setting the `I` register to the address of the enclosing implication point record, a value stored in the record the `I` register currently points to.

There are a few points about the scheme described that are worth mentioning. First, under this scheme the compilation of an atomic goal does not yield an instruction to transfer control to a particular code address. Rather, the instruction produced must use an existing access function (indicated by the I register) and an index generated from the name of the predicate to locate the relevant code. Notice that this behavior is to be anticipated, given the dynamic nature of procedure definitions. The second observation pertains to the resurrection of a context upon backtracking. Under our scheme, the program context is reduced to the contents of a single register. By saving these contents in a WAM-like choice point record and by retaining implication point records embedded within choice points, the necessary context switching can be easily achieved.

We turn finally to the implementation of module implication. Let us consider first the treatment of a module implication of the form M ==> G where M is a module with no local declarations and no import statements. From the perspective of dynamic semantics, M can be reduced to a conjunction of closed D-formulas of the form $\forall x_1 \ldots \forall x_n A_r$ or $\forall x_1 \ldots \forall x_n (G \supset A_r)$, *i.e.*, of the form just considered. Thus the scheme outlined above can be applied almost without change to the treatment of this kind of module implication. Under this scheme, the compilation of the module M must produce code that implements the relevant *find_code* and *link_code* procedures in addition to the compiled code for the various predicates defined. The linking operation corresponding to ==> effectively amounts to setting up an implication point record. The main task involved in this regard is that of executing the *link_code* function which in a sense links the predicate definitions in the module to those already existing in the program.

The handling of local declarations does not pose any major complications. The treatment of a goal of the form E => G that is indicated by the operational semantics essentially requires the existential quantifiers at the front of E to be replaced by new constants and the resulting D-formula to be added to the existing program. Implementing this idea results in the local constants in E being conceived of as constants but with a numeric tag that prevents them from appearing in terms substituted for logic variables in G. At a level of detail, these constants can be identified with cells in an implication point record and the *push_impl_point* instruction has the additional task of allocating these cells and of tagging them with the appropriate numeric value.

The only remaining issue is the treatment of import declarations. Let us assume that a module M imports the modules $M1$,$M2$ and $M3$. From the perspective of dynamic semantics, this importation has an effect largely on the clauses appearing in M. Let P :- G be one of these clauses. Based on the semantics of importing, this clause is to be interpreted as the clause

$$P \text{ :- } (M1 \text{ ==> } (M2 \text{ ==> } (M3 \text{ ==> } G))).$$

This translation actually indicates a straightforward method for implementing the effect of importation: the body of the clause can be compiled into the code generated for G nested within a sequence of *push_impl_point* and *pop_impl_point* instructions. Noting that module M may contain several clauses, an improvement is possible in this basic scheme. We identify with a module two additional functions that we call *load_imports* and *unload_imports*. In the case of module M, executing the first of these corresponds conceptually to executing the sequence

> *push_impl_point* $M1$
> *push_impl_point* $M2$
> *push_impl_point* $M3$

and, similarly, executing the second corresponds to executing a sequence of three *pop_impl_point* instructions. The address of these two functions is included in the implication point record created when a module is added to the program context. From the perspective of compilation, the code that is generated for the clause considered now takes the following shape:

> {Code for unifying the head of the clause }
> *push_import_point* M
>   {Compiled code for goal G}
> *pop_import_point* M

The *push_import_point* instruction in this sequence has the effect of invoking the *load_imports* function corresponding to module M and the *pop_import_point* instruction similarly invokes the *unload_imports* function.

The scheme described above assumes that the address of the compiled code and the various functions associated with a module can be indexed by the name of the module. This information is organized into entries in a global table with each entry having the following components:

(i) r, the number of predicates defined in the module,
(ii) the starting address for the compiled code segment for the predicates defined in the module; *find_code* will return offsets from this address,
(iii) the address of the *find_code* routine for the module,
(iv) the address of the *link_code* routine for the module,
(v) the address of the *load_imports* routine for the module, and
(vi) the address of the *unload_imports* routine for the module.

In reality not every module is loaded into memory at the beginning of a program and hence not every module has an entry in the global table. If a module that does not already reside in memory is needed, then a loading process brings the various segments of code in and creates an appropriate entry in the global table for the module. It should be clear by this point that the codes and information needed for each module can be obtained by a compile-time analysis of that module and the necessary interface definitions.

5 Controlling Redundancy in Search

The semantics presented for module implication and for the *import* statement could result in the same module being added several times to a program context. This has a potential drawback: it may result in redundancy in the search for a solution to a goal and the same solution may also be produced several times. To understanding this possibility, let us consider the following definition of a module called *sets* which imports the module *lists* presented in Section 3.

> *module sets.*
> *import lists.*
> *type subset* (*list A*) → (*list A*) → *o.*
> *subset nil L.*
> (*subset X* :: *L*1 *L*2) :- ((*member X L*2), (*subset L*1 *L*2)).

Assume now that an attempt is made to solve the goal

> ***sets*** ==> ***subset*** 1 :: 2 :: 4 :: ***nil*** 1 :: 2 :: 3 :: ***nil***.

Using the linear format described in Section 3, part of the effort in solving this goal is represented by the following sequence:

```
                        sets ?- (subset 1 :: 2 :: 4 :: nil 1 :: 2 :: 3 :: nil)
                  lists, sets ?- (member 1 1 :: 2 :: 3 :: nil)   SUCC
                  lists, sets ?- (subset 2 :: 4 :: nil 1 :: 2 :: 3 :: nil)
           lists, lists, sets ?- (member 2 1 :: 2 :: 3 :: nil)
           lists, lists, sets ?- (member 2 2 :: 3 :: nil)   SUCC
           lists, lists, sets ?- (subset 4 :: nil 1 :: 2 :: 3 :: nil)
    lists, lists, lists, sets ?- (member 4 1 :: 2 :: 3 :: nil)
```

It is easily seen that the attempt to solve the last goal in this sequence in the indicated program context will fail. Notice however, that a considerable amount of redundant search will be performed before this decision is reached: there are three copies of the module *lists* in the program context and the clauses for *member* in each of these will be used in turn in the solution attempt. A similar redundancy is manifest in the answers that are computed under the semantics provided. For instance, the query

> ***sets*** ==> ***subset*** *S* 1 :: 2 :: ***nil***

will result in the substitution 1 :: 2 :: *nil* for *S* being generated twice through the use of the clauses in two different copies of the module *lists*.

The extra copies of the module *lists*, while leading to redundancy in search, do not result in an ability to derive new goals or to find additional answers. Adding these copies also results in a runtime overhead: given the implementation scheme of the previous section, the addition of each copy results in the creation of an implication point record, thereby consuming both space and time. A pragmatic question to ask, therefore, is whether the number of copies of any module in a program context can be restricted to just one. In answering this question there is an important principle to adhere to. It is desirable that the *logical semantics* of our language not be altered. In particular, we still want to be able to understand our language by using the derivation rules presented in Section 2 and to understand the dynamic semantics of modules through the devices discussed in Section 3. This principle is important because, as argued in [12], several interesting tools for analyzing the behavior of programs depend on this kind of a logical understanding of programming language constructs. In light of this principle, the question raised can be changed to one of the following sort: is it possible to preserve the important *observable* aspects of the given semantics while perhaps changing the details of the operational semantics so as to produce a preferred computational behavior. An affirmative answer to this question permits us to have the best of both worlds. The original semantics can be used for analyzing the interesting aspects of the behavior of programs while an actual implementation can be based on a modified set of derivation rules.

In the context being considered, the important aspects of program behavior are the set of queries that can be solved and the answers that can be found to any given query. Both aspects are completely determined by the set of sequents that have derivations. Thus, based on the above discussion, we might contemplate changing the underlying derivation rules for our language so as to reduce the *number* of derivations for any sequent while preserving the set of sequents that have derivations. With this in mind, we observe that the main source of redundancy in the example considered above is the *AUGMENT* rule. Assume that we want to solve a goal of the form $D \Rightarrow G$. The *AUGMENT* rule requires D to be added to the program context before attempting to solve G. Notice, however, that if D is already available in the program context, this addition is not likely to make a derivation of G possible where it earlier was not. A more interesting case is when the implication goal is of the form $(\exists x_1 \ldots \exists x_n D) \Rightarrow G$. In this case the AUGMENT rule requires the addition of $D[c_1/x_1, \ldots, c_n/x_n]$ (for a suitable choice of c_is) to the program prior to the attempt to solve G. However, if the program already contains a clause of the form $D[c'_1/x_1, \ldots, c'_n/x_n]$, the addition is again redundant from the perspective of being able to solve G.

In the rest of the section we prove the observations contained in the previous paragraph. Towards this end, we define an alternative to the AUGMENT rule.

Definition 5. Let G be a type variable free query and let $\mathcal{P}$ be a program. Then the AUGMENT′ rule is applicable if G is of the form $(\exists x_1 \ldots \exists x_n D) \Rightarrow G'$ and can be used to construct a derivation for $\mathcal{P} \longrightarrow G$ as follows:

(i) If a formula of the form $D[c'_1/x_1, \ldots, c'_n/x_n]$ does not appear in $\mathcal{P}$, then by constructing a derivation for $D[c_1/x_1, \ldots, c_n/x_n], \mathcal{P} \longrightarrow G'$ where, for $1 \leq i \leq n$, c_i is a nonlogical constant of the same type as x_i not appearing in the formulas in $\mathcal{P}, G$.

(ii) If a formula of the form $D[c'_1/x_1, \ldots, c'_n/x_n]$ appears in $\mathcal{P}$, then by constructing a derivation for $\mathcal{P} \longrightarrow G'$.

Let us refer to the derivation rules presented earlier as $DS1$ and let $DS2$ be obtained from $DS1$ by replacing AUGMENT with AUGMENT′. We say that a sequent has a derivation in $DS1$ ($DS2$) if a derivation can be constructed for it by using the rules in $DS1$ (respectively, $DS2$). We now make the following observation about derivations in $DS2$.

Lemma 6. *Let G be a type variable free query, let D be a program clause whose free variables are included in $x_1, \ldots, x_n$ and let $\mathcal{P}_1$ and $\mathcal{P}_2$ be programs that between them contain a formula of the form $D[c'_1/x_1, \ldots, c'_n/x_n]$ where, for $1 \leq i \leq n$, c'_i is a nonlogical constant of the same type as x_i. Further, for $1 \leq i \leq n$, let c_i be a nonlogical constant of the same type as c'_i that do not appear in D. Finally, let $\mathcal{P}'_1$, $\mathcal{P}'_2$ and G' be obtained from $\mathcal{P}_1$, $\mathcal{P}_2$ and G, respectively, by replacing, for $1 \leq i \leq n$, c_i with c'_i. Now, if $\mathcal{P}_1, D[c_1/x_1, \ldots, c_n/x_n], \mathcal{P}_2 \longrightarrow G$ has a derivation of length l in DS2, then there must also be a derivation in DS2 for $\mathcal{P}'_1, \mathcal{P}'_2 \longrightarrow G'$ that is of length l or less.*

Proof. We prove the lemma by an induction on the length of the derivation in DS2 of the first sequent. If this derivation is of length 1, it must have been obtained by using the SUCCESS rule. Now, if G is equal to an instance of $D[c_1/x_1, \ldots, c_n/x_n]$, then G' must be equal to an instance of $D[c'_1/x_1, \ldots, c'_n/x_n]$. Further, if G is an instance of a clause in $\mathcal{P}_1$ or in $\mathcal{P}_2$ it must be the case that G' is an instance of a clause in $\mathcal{P}'_1$ or in $\mathcal{P}'_2$. From these observations it follows that the SUCCESS rule is applicable to $\mathcal{P}'_1, \mathcal{P}'_2 \longrightarrow G'$ as well and so this sequent also must have a derivation of length 1.

Suppose now that the derivation of $\mathcal{P}_1, D[c_1/x_1, \ldots, c_n/x_n], \mathcal{P}_2 \longrightarrow G$ is of length $(l+1)$. We assume that the requirements of the lemma are satisfied by all sequents that have derivations of length l or less and show this must also be the case for the sequent being considered. The argument proceeds by examining the possible cases for the first rule used in the derivation in question.

Let us assume that this rule is an *AND*. In this case G must be of the form $G_1 \land G_2$ and there must be derivations of length l or less for the sequents $\mathcal{P}_1, D[c_1/x_1, \ldots, c_n/x_n], \mathcal{P}_2 \longrightarrow G_1$ and $\mathcal{P}_1, D[c_1/x_1, \ldots, c_n/x_n], \mathcal{P}_2 \longrightarrow G_2$. By hypothesis, there are derivations of length l or less for $\mathcal{P}'_1, \mathcal{P}'_2 \longrightarrow G_1$ and $\mathcal{P}'_1, \mathcal{P}'_2 \longrightarrow G_2$. Using these derivations together with an *AND* rule, we obtain one of length $l+1$ or less for $\mathcal{P}'_1, \mathcal{P}'_2 \longrightarrow G'_1 \land G'_2$. Now, G' must be equal to the formula $G'_1 \land G'_2$. Thus the desired conclusion is obtained in this case.

Arguments similar to that for *AND* can be supplied for the cases when OR or INSTANCE is the first rule used. In the case that GENERIC is used, G must be of the form $\forall y G_1$ and there must be a derivation of length l for

$$\mathcal{P}_1, D[c_1/x_1, \ldots, c_n/x_n], \mathcal{P}_2 \longrightarrow G_1[a/y]$$

for some nonlogical constant a of the same type as y that does not appear in G, $D[c_1/x_1, \ldots, c_n/x_n]$ or in the formulas in $\mathcal{P}_1$ and $\mathcal{P}_2$. We can almost use an argument similar to that employed for AND. The only problem is that a might be identical to some c'_i for $1 \leq i \leq n$. However, the following fact is easily seen: a derivation of length l for a sequent Ξ can be transformed into one of identical length for a sequent obtained from Ξ by replacing all occurrences of a nonlogical constant b with some other (nonlogical) constant of the same type. Using this together with the "newness" condition on a, we may assume that a is distinct from all the c'_is. The argument in this case can then be completed without trouble.

In the case that the first rule employed is BACKCHAIN, a combination of the observations used for SUCCESS and AND must be employed. In particular, let G_1' be the result of replacing, for $1 \leq i \leq n$, all occurrences of c_i by c_i' in G_1. Now, if $G_1 \supset G$ is an instance of $D[c_1/x_1, \ldots, c_n/x_n]$, then $G_1' \supset G'$ must be an instance of $D[c_1'/x_1, \ldots, c_n'/x_n]$. Further, if $G_1 \supset G$ is an instance of a program clause in $\mathcal{P}$, then $G_1' \supset G'$ must also be an instance of the same clause. Finally, using the hypothesis, if $\mathcal{P}_1, D[c_1/x_1, \ldots, c_n/x_n], \mathcal{P}_2 \longrightarrow G_1$ has a derivation of length l, then $\mathcal{P}_1', \mathcal{P}_2' \longrightarrow G_1'$ has a derivation of length l or less. Using these various facts, it is easily seen that if the first rule used in the derivation for $\mathcal{P}_1, D[c_1/x_1, \ldots, c_n/x_n], \mathcal{P}_2 \longrightarrow G$ is BACKCHAIN, then a derivation can be provided for $\mathcal{P}_1', \mathcal{P}_2' \longrightarrow G'$ in which the last rule is once again a BACKCHAIN and, further, this derivation will satisfy the length requirements.

Suppose now that the first rule used is AUGMENT′ and that case (i) of this rule is the applicable one. Then G must be of the form $(\exists y_1 \ldots \exists y_m D_1) \supset G_1$ and further, no formula of the form $D_1[a_1'/y_1, \ldots, a_m'/y_m]$ must appear in $\mathcal{P}_1, D[c_1/x_1, \ldots, c_n/x_n], \mathcal{P}_2$. By assumption, there is a derivation of length l for

$$D_1[a_1/y_1, \ldots, a_m/y_m], \mathcal{P}_1, D[c_1/x_1, \ldots, c_n/x_n], \mathcal{P}_2 \longrightarrow G_1$$

where, for $1 \leq i \leq m$, a_i is a constant of appropriate type and meeting the needed requirements of newness. By an argument similar to that used in the case of BACKCHAIN, we can assume that the a_js are distinct from the c_is and the c_i's. Then, using the induction hypothesis, there must be a derivation of length l or less for

$$D_1'[a_1/y_1, \ldots, a_m/y_m], \mathcal{P}_1', \mathcal{P}_2' \longrightarrow G_1'$$

where D_1' and G_1' are obtained from D_1 and G_1 by the replacement, for $1 \leq i \leq n$, of c_i by c_i'. Now, if a formula of the form $D_1[a_1'/y_1, \ldots, a_m'/y_m]$ did not appear in $\mathcal{P}_1$ or $\mathcal{P}_2$, then one of the form $D_1'[a_1'/y_1, \ldots, a_m'/y_m]$ cannot appear in $\mathcal{P}_1'$ or $\mathcal{P}_2'$. Thus, the derivation of the indicated sequent can be used together with an AUGMENT′ rule to obtain one for $\mathcal{P}_1', \mathcal{P}_2' \longrightarrow (\exists y_1 \ldots \exists y_m D_1') \supset G_1'$; a newness condition has to be satisfied by $a_1, \ldots, a_m$ for the AUGMENT rule to be used, but this can be seen to be the case, using particularly the assumption of distinctness from the c_i's. The derivation of the last sequent is obviously of length $(l+1)$ or less. Observing that $(\exists y_1 \ldots \exists y_m D_1') \supset G_1'$ is the same formula as G', the lemma is seen to hold in this case.

The only situation remaining to be considered is that when the first rule corresponds to case (ii) of AUGMENT′. The argument in this case is similar to that employed for case (i) of the same rule. The details are left to the reader.

Using the above lemma we now show the equivalence of $DS1$ and $DS2$ from the perspective of derivability of sequents of the kind we are interested in.

Theorem 7. *Let $\mathcal{P}$ be a program and let G be a type variable free query. There is a derivation for $\mathcal{P} \longrightarrow G$ in $DS1$ if and only if there is a derivation for the same sequent in $DS2$.*

Proof. Consider first the forward direction of the theorem. The only reason why the derivation in $DS1$ might not already be one in $DS2$ is because the AUGMENT rule that is used is in some cases not an instance of the AUGMENT′ rule. Consider the last occurrence of such a rule in the derivation. In this case, a derivation is constructed for a sequent of the form $\mathcal{P}' \longrightarrow (\exists x_1 \ldots \exists x_n D') \supset G'$ from one for the sequent $D'[c_1/x_1, \ldots, c_n/x_n], \mathcal{P}' \longrightarrow G'$, where the c_is are appropriately chosen constants. Given that we are considering the last occurrence of an errant rule, the derivation for the latter sequent must be one in $DS2$ as well. Since the application of the AUGMENT rule being considered does not conform to the requirements of the AUGMENT′ rule, it must be the case that, for some choice of constants $c'_1, \ldots, c'_n$, $D'[c'_1/x_1, \ldots, c'_n/x_n]$ appears in $\mathcal{P}'$. But then, using Lemma 6 and the fact that the constants $c_1, \ldots, c_n$ must not appear in G' or in the formulas in $\mathcal{P}'$, we see that $\mathcal{P}' \longrightarrow G'$ has a derivation in $DS2$. Using this derivation together with case (i) of the AUGMENT′ rule, we obtain a derivation in $DS2$ for the original sequent, *i.e.*, for $\mathcal{P}' \longrightarrow (\exists x_1 \ldots \exists x_n D') \supset G'$. We repeat this form of argument to ultimately transform the derivation in $DS1$ for $\mathcal{P} \longrightarrow G$ into one in $DS2$.

To show the theorem in the reverse direction, we observe the following fact: for any program $\mathcal{P}'$, type variable free query G' and program clause D', if $\mathcal{P}' \longrightarrow G'$ has a derivation in $DS1$, then $D', \mathcal{P}' \longrightarrow G'$ also has a derivation in $DS1$. Now, a derivation in $DS2$ may not be a derivation in $DS1$ only because case (i) of AUGMENT′ was used in some places. However, this can be corrected by using the observation just made. In particular, we consider the last occurrence of an errant rule in the derivation and convert it into an occurrence of the AUGMENT rule by using the above fact. A repeated use of this transformation yields the theorem.

An easy consequence of the above theorem is the following:

Corollary 8. *Let $\mathcal{P}$ be a program and let G be a query. The set of answers to G in the context of $\mathcal{P}$ is independent of whether rules in $DS1$ or in $DS2$ are used in constructing derivations.*

We have thus shown that, from the perspective of solving queries and computing answers, it is immaterial whether the rules in $DS1$ or those in $DS2$ are used to construct derivations. By virtue of Proposition 4, we can in fact use the notion of intuitionistic derivability for the purpose of analyzing programs in our language while using the rules in $DS2$ to carry out computations. At a pragmatic level, there is a definite benefit to using the AUGMENT′ rule instead of the AUGMENT rule in solving queries, since considerable redundancy in search can be eliminated by this choice. We use this observation to yield a more viable implementation of module implication and of the *import* statement in the next section. We note that another approach to controlling the redundancy arising out of the module semantics is suggested in [12]. However, this approach is less general than the one considered here in that it applies only to *import* statements and not to module implications. Moreover, the correctness of the approach is only conjectured in [12]. The observations in this section can be used in a straightforward fashion to verify this conjecture.

6 An Improved Implementation of Modules

We now consider an implementation of our language that uses the AUGMENT′ rule instead of the AUGMENT rule whenever possible. Under the new rule, solving an goal of the form $(\exists x_1 \ldots \exists x_n D) \supset G$ requires checking if there is already a clause of the form $D[c_1/x_1, \ldots, c_n/x_n]$ in the program. Clearly an efficient procedure for performing this test is a key factor in using the changed rule in an actual implementation. It is difficult to achieve this goal in general. One problematic case is when the goal $(\exists x_1 \ldots \exists x_n D) \supset G$ arises as part of a larger goal and D contains variables that are bound only in this larger context. Instantiations for these variables may be determined in the course of execution, thus making it difficult to perform the desired test by a simple runtime operation. In fact, the device of delaying instantiations might even make it impossible to determine the outcome of the test at the time the implication goal is to be solved because "clauses" in the program might contain logic variables. An example of this kind was seen in Section 2. The attempt to solve the goal $\exists L(rev\ 1 :: 2 :: nil\ L)$ resulted there in the clause $(rev\_aux\ nil\ L)$ being added to the program. The precise shape of this clause clearly depends on the instantiation chosen for L. A test of the sort needed by AUGMENT′ cannot be performed with regard to this clause prior to this shape being determined.

The above discussion demonstrates that the optimization embodied in the AUGMENT′ rule can be feasibly implemented only relative to a restricted class of program clauses, namely, clauses that do not contain logic variables. Of particular interest from this perspective is a statically identifiable closed E-formula that has the potential for appearing repeatedly in the antecedent of implication goals. Given such a formula E, a mark can be associated with it that records whether or not the current goal is dynamically embedded within the invocation of an implication goal of the form E => G. If it is so embedded and if the current goal is itself of the form E => G', then, in accordance with the AUGMENT′ rule, the computation can proceed directly to solving G' without affecting additions to the program.

The dynamic semantics of module implication provides a particular case of the kind of formula discussed above, namely the (closed) E-formula identified with a module. Thus, assume that we are trying to solve the goal M ==> G. If we know that the module M has already appeared in the antecedent of a module implication goal within which the current one is dynamically embedded, then no enhancements to the program need be made. The implementation scheme presented in 4 provides a setting for incorporating this test in an efficient manner. The essential idea is that we include an extra field called *added* in the record in the global table corresponding to each module. This field determines whether or not the clauses in a particular module have been added to the program in the path leading up to the current point in computation. When the goal M ==> G is to be solved, the *added* field for *M*'s entry in the global table is checked. If this indicates that the clauses in *M* has not previously been added, then the addition is performed and the status of the field is changed. Otherwise the computation proceeds directly to solving *G*.

While the idea described above is simple, some details have to be paid attention to in its actual implementation. One issue is the action to be taken on the completion of a module implication goal. At a conceptual level, the successful solution of the goal *M* ==> *G* must be accompanied by a removal of the code for *M*; this is accomplished in our earlier scheme by the instruction *pop_impl_point*. However, given the current approach, an actual removal must complement only an actual addition. To facilitate a determination of the right action to be taken, the *added* field is implemented as a counter rather than as a boolean. This field is initialized to 0. Each time a module is conceptually added to the program context, its *added* value is incremented. A conceptual removal similarly causes this value to be decremented. An actual removal is performed only when the counter value reaches 0.

The second issue that must be considered is the effect of backtracking. As we have noted, this operation might require a return to a different program context. An important characteristic of a program context now is the status of the *added* fields, and backtracking must set these back to values that existed at an earlier computation point. To permit an accomplishment of this resetting action, changes made to this field must be trailed. A naive implementation would trail the old value every time a change needs to be made, *i.e.*, every time a module is added or removed. A considerable improvement on this can be obtained by trailing a value only if there is a possibility to return to a state in which it is operative. Thus consider a goal of the form

m ==> (*G*1, (*m* ==> *G*2))

When the *added* field for *m* is incremented for the second time, there is a need to trail the old value only if unexplored alternatives exist in the attempt to solve *G*1. There is a simple way to determine this within a WAM-like implementation. Let us suppose we record the address of the most recent choice point at the time of processing the outermost (module) implication in the global table entry corresponding to *m*. Now, when the embedded implication is processed, we compare the address of the current most recent choice point with the recorded value. There is a backtracking point in the solution of *G*1 only if the first is greater than the second. Similarly, consider the decrement that is made to the *added* field when a goal of the form *m* ==> *G* is completed. The old value needs to be trailed only if choice points exist within the solution for *G*. A test identical to that described above suffices to determine whether this is the case.

In order to implement the above idea, one more field must be added to the entries in the global table for modules, *i.e.*, one that records the most recent choice point prior to the latest change to the *added* field. This field is called *mrcp* and is initialized to the bottom of the stack. Notice that this field needs to be updated each time *added* has to be trailed, and this change must also be trailed. Accordingly, each cell in the trail introduced for managing the *added*

```
pushimpl(m)
begin
    if m.added = 0
    then create an implication point record for m;
    if m.mrcp < B
    then
    begin
        trail ⟨m, m.mrcp, m.added⟩;
        m.mrcp := B;
    end;
    m.added := m.added + 1
end;

popimpl(m)
begin
    if m.mrcp < B
    then
    begin
        trail ⟨m, m.mrcp, m.added⟩;
        m.mrcp := B;
    end;
    m.added := m.added − 1;
    if m.added = 0 then
        Set I to most recent implication point
        in record pointed to by I
end
```

Fig. 4. Adding and Removing Modules from Program Contexts

values contains three items: the name of a module, the old value of *added*, and the old contents of the *mrcp* field. Pointers to this trail must be maintained in choice points and the trail must be unwound in the usual fashion upon backtracking. Module implication is compiled as before, although the interpretation of *push_impl_point m* and *pop_impl_point m* changes. In particular, these can be understood as though they are invocations to the procedures *pushimpl*(m) and *popimpl*(m) that are presented in pseudo-code fashion in Figure 4. In this code we write *m.mrcp* and *m.added* to denote, respectively, the *mrcp* and *added* fields in the global table entry corresponding to the module m. We also recall that the B register in the WAM setting indicates the most recent choice point.

There is an auxiliary benefit to two fields that has been added under the present scheme to the records in the global table. As mentioned in Section 4, our implementation permits modules to be loaded on demand, and hence does not require all modules to be available in main memory during a computation. A question that arises is whether modules can also be unloaded to reclaim code space. This unloading must be done carefully because a module not currently included in the program context might still be required because of the possibility of backtracking. A quick check of whether a module can be unloaded is obtained by examining the two new fields in the global table entry for a module. If the *mrcp* field points to the bottom of the stack and *added* is 0, then the module is not needed and can be unloaded.

The implementation of the dynamic effects of *import* can, in principle, be left unchanged. However, a significant efficiency improvement can be obtained by noting the following: once a clause from a module *m* has been used by virtue of the BACKCHAIN rule, there is no further need to check if the modules imported by *m* have been added to the program context. To utilize this idea, we include two more fields in each implication point record:

(i) A field called *backchained* that records the number of times a clause from the module to which the implication point record corresponds has been backchained upon.
(ii) A field called *mrcp* that records the most recent choice point prior to the last change to *backchained*.

When the implication point record is created, the *backchained* field is initialized to 0 and the *mrcp* field is set to point to the bottom of the stack. Whenever a clause from a module corresponding to the implication point record is backchained upon, a conceptual addition of the imported modules must be performed. An actual addition must be contemplated within the present scheme only if the *backchained* field is 0. In any case, this field is incremented before the "body" of the clause is invoked. The increment to *backchained* is complemented by a decrement when the clause body has been successfully solved. Finally, an actual removal of the imported modules from the program context must be contemplated only when *backchained* becomes 0 again. For the purpose of backtracking, it may be necessary to trail an old value of *backchained* each time this field is updated. The *mrcp* field is useful for this purpose. Essentially, we compare this field with the address of the current most recent choice point, obtained in the WAM context from the B register. If the latter is greater than the *mrcp* field, then the old value of *backchained* must be trailed. This action must also be accompanied by a trailing of the existing *mrcp* value and the update of this field to the address of the current most recent choice point.

The rationale for the various actions described for handling imports is analogous to that in the case of module implication, and should be clear from the preceding discussions. At a level of detail, another trail is needed for maintaining the old values of the *backchained* and *mrcp* fields. The cells in this trail correspond once again to triples: the address of the relevant implication point record and the *backchained* and *mrcp* values. Pointers to this trail must also be maintained in choice points and backtracking must cause the trail to be unwound. The compilation of clauses in modules is performed as before: the code produced for the body of a clause in module *m* must be embedded within the instructions *push_import_point m* and *pop_import_point m*. These instructions can be understood as though they are invocations to the procedures *pushimport*(*m*) and

```
pushimport(m)
begin
    if CI.backchained = 0
    then call load_imports for m
    if CI.mrcp < B
    then
    begin
        trail ⟨CI,CI.mrcp,CI.backchained⟩;
        CI.mrcp := B;
    end;
    CI.backchained := CI.backchained + 1
end;

popimport(m)
begin
    if CI.mrcp < B
    then
    begin
        trail ⟨CI,CI.mrcp,CI.backchained⟩;
        CI.mrcp := B;
    end;
    CI.backchained := CI.backchained − 1;
    if CI.backchained = 0 then
        invoke unload_imports for m
end
```

Fig. 5. Adding Imported Modules to a Program Context

popimport(m) that are presented, in pseudo-code fashion, in Figure 5. Use is made in these procedures of a register called CI that points within our implementation to the implication point record from which the clause currently being considered is obtained. Further, we write CI.*mrcp* and CI.backchained to denote the *mrcp* and *backchained* fields in the implication point record that *CI* points to.

It is important to note that once a clause from a module has been backchained upon, the two instructions *push_import_point* and *pop_import_point* incur very little overhead with respect to clauses in that module. In particular, at most two tests, a trailing and two updates are necessary for each instruction. This is much less work than the creation of implication point records that was necessary under a direct implementation of the operational semantics. Further, this overhead appears to be acceptable even if these instructions are executed repeatedly.

We consider an example to illustrate the manner in which redundancy is controlled within the changed implementation. Let us assume that the modules $m0$, $m1$ and $m2$ are defined as below.

module m0.	***module m1.***	***module m2.***
import m1, m2.	***import m2.***	***kind i type.***
type p i → o.	***type q i → o.***	***type a i.***
$(p\ X)$:- $(q\ X), (t\ X)$.	$(q\ X)$:- $(r\ X)$.	***type b i.***
$(r\ X)$:- $(s\ X)$.		$(r\ a)$.
		$(s\ b)$.
		$(t\ b)$.

The attempt to solve the goal *m0* ==> (*p X*) is presented below. We augment the linear format of Section 3 as follows in this presentation: Each module in the program context is presented by a pair consisting of its name and the value of the *backchained* field in the implication point record created for it. At the end of each line, a list of pairs is presented that indicates module names and the values of the *added* field in the global table entry for each of them.

$(m0,0)$?- $(p\ X)$		$[(m0,1),(m1,0),(m2,0)]$
$(m2,0),(m1,0),(m0,1)$?- $(q\ X)$		$[(m0,1),(m1,1),(m2,1)]$
$(m2,0),(m1,1),(m0,1)$?- $(r\ X)$	X <- a *SUCC*	$[(m0,1),(m1,1),(m2,2)]$
$(m2,0),(m1,0),(m0,1)$?- $(t\ a)$	*FAIL*	$[(m0,1),(m1,1),(m2,1)]$
$(m2,0),(m1,1),(m0,1)$?- $(r\ X)$		$[(m0,1),(m1,1),(m2,2)]$
$(m2,0),(m1,1),(m0,2)$?- $(s\ X)$	X <- b *SUCC*	$[(m0,1),(m1,1),(m2,2)]$
$(m2,0),(m1,0),(m0,1)$?- $(t\ b)$	*SUCC*	$[(m0,1),(m1,1),(m2,1)]$

An interesting point to note in this computation is that the clause (*r a*) in module *m2* is used only once in solving the subgoal (*r X*) even though there are conceptually two copies of *m2* in the program context when the subgoal is invoked. Similarly, an attempt to find another solution to the query will fail, even though the same solution can be found five more times under a naive interpretation of the given semantics.

7 Conclusion

We have examined a notion of modules for the logic programming language λProlog in this paper. The notion considered provides a means for structuring the two components that determine programs in this language: the type, kind and operator declarations and the procedure definitions. Using a module typically involves making its contents available in some other context. As explained in some detail, this operation has static and dynamic effects within λProlog. Our focus here has been on the implementation of the dynamic aspects of modules. At a level of detail, we have proposed an implementation method that is based on a WAM-like machine and that has several interesting features:

(i) It supports the idea of compiling modules separately. In particular, the compilation of a module produces WAM-like code based on only the program clauses appearing in the module.

(ii) Interpreting a logical operation as a primitive for linking a module into a given program context, it uses a compilation process to generate linking code and includes run-time structures for accomplishing the linking function.

(iii) Based on a theoretical analysis of this notion, it includes mechanisms for reducing redundancy inherent in the given dynamic semantics of the module feature. The redundancy check is based on a two-level test that in the usual situation can be carried out with very little overhead.

There are several significant enrichments to a Prolog-like language that are embodied in λProlog in addition to the module feature. A complete implementation of this language must include mechanisms for dealing with all these features. As mentioned already, a detailed consideration has been given to the features other than the module notion elsewhere, resulting in an abstract machine for the core language described in Section 2. An actual implementation of this machine is currently being undertaken. The mentioned machine is entirely compatible with the ideas for handling modules that are presented in this paper and we plan to include these ideas within our implementation effort in the near future.

8 Acknowledgements

Work on this paper has been supported by NSF Grant CCR-89-05825.

References

1. Alonzo Church. A formulation of the simple theory of types. *Journal of Symbolic Logic*, 5:56–68, 1940.
2. Conal Elliott and Frank Pfenning. eLP, a Common Lisp Implementation of λProlog. Implemented as part of the CMU ERGO project, May 1989.
3. Conal Elliott and Frank Pfenning. A semi-functional implementation of a higher-order logic programming language. In Peter Lee, editor, *Topics in Advanced Language Implementation*, pages 289–325. MIT Press, 1991.
4. Elsa L. Gunter. Extensions to logic programming motivated by the construction of a generic theorem prover. In Peter Schroeder-Heister, editor, *Extensions of Logic Programming: International Workshop, Tübingen FRG, December 1989*, pages 223–244. Springer-Verlag, 1991. Volume 475 of *Lecture Notes in Artificial Intelligence*.
5. J. Roger Hindley and Jonathan P. Seldin. *Introduction to Combinatory Logic and Lambda Calculus*. Cambridge University Press, 1986.
6. Gérard Huet. A unification algorithm for typed λ-calculus. *Theoretical Computer Science*, 1:27–57, 1975.
7. Keehang Kwon, Gopalan Nadathur, and Debra Sue Wilson. Implementing polymorphic typing in a logic programming language. Submitted, August 1992.
8. Evelina Lamma, Paola Mello, and Antonio Natali. The design of an abstract machine for efficient implementation of contexts in logic programming. In *Sixth International Logic Programming Conference*, pages 303–317, Lisbon, Portugal, June 1989. MIT Press.

9. Dale Miller and Gopalan Nadathur. λProlog version 2.7. Distributed in C-Prolog and Quintus Prolog source code, August 1988.
10. Dale Miller. Lexical scoping as universal quantification. In *Sixth International Logic Programming Conference*, pages 268–283, Lisbon, Portugal, June 1989. MIT Press.
11. Dale Miller. A logical analysis of modules in logic programming. *Journal of Logic Programming*, 6:79 – 108, 1989.
12. Dale Miller. A proposal for modules in λProlog. In *Workshop on the λProlog Programming Language*, Philadelphia, July 1992.
13. Dale Miller, Gopalan Nadathur, Frank Pfenning, and Andre Scedrov. Uniform proofs as a foundation for logic programming. *Annals of Pure and Applied Logic*, 51:125–157, 1991.
14. Luís Monteiro and António Porto. Contextual logic programming. In *Sixth International Logic Programming Conference*, pages 284–299, Lisbon, Portugal, June 1989. MIT Press.
15. Gopalan Nadathur and Frank Pfenning. The type system of a higher-order logic programming language. In Frank Pfenning, editor, *Types in Logic Programming*, pages 245–283. MIT Press, 1992.
16. Gopalan Nadathur, Bharat Jayaraman, and Keehang Kwon. Scoping constructs in logic programming: Implementation problems and their solution. Submitted, May 1992.
17. Gopalan Nadathur, Bharat Jayaraman, and Debra Sue Wilson. Implementation considerations for higher-order features. Submitted, November 1992.
18. Gopalan Nadathur. A proof procedure for the logic of hereditary Harrop formulas. To appear in the *Journal of Automated Reasoning*.
19. Richard O'Keefe. Towards an algebra for constructing logic programs. In *1985 Symposium on Logic Programming*, pages 152–160, Boston, 1985.
20. D.T. Sannella and L.A. Wallen. A calculus for the construction of modular Prolog programs. *Journal of Logic Programming*, 12:147 – 178, January 1992.
21. D.H.D. Warren. An abstract Prolog instruction set. Technical report, SRI International, October 1983. Technical Note 309.

Implementational Issues in GCLA: A-Sufficiency and the Definiens Operation

Martin Aronsson

Swedish Institute of Computer Science
Box 1263, S - 164 28 Kista, Sweden
email: martin@sics.se

Abstract. We present algorithms for computing $\mathcal{A}$-sufficient substitutions and constraint sets together with the definiens operation. These operations are primitive operations in the language GCLA. The paper first defines those primitives, which together form a dual rule to SLD resolution, and then describes the different algorithms and some of their properties together with examples. One of the algorithms shows how a definition can be compiled into a representation holding all possible $\mathcal{A}$-sufficient substitutions/constraint sets together with their corresponding definiens. This representation makes the computation in runtime of a definiens and an $\mathcal{A}$-sufficient substitution/constraint set having the same complexity as the operation `clause/2` in Prolog. The paper also describes the generalisation from unification (sets of equalities) to constraint sets and satisfiability of systems of equalities and inequalities.

1. Introduction

GCLA is a programming system developed at SICS for some years [Aro90, Aro92a, Kre92, HS-H90, HS-H91]. It is best regarded as a logic programming language, although it does not have the same theoretical foundation as most other logic programming languages. While traditional logic programming languages are based on logic, GCLA is based on the more general concept of inductive definitions, called *Partial Inductive Definitions* [Hal91].

One of the basic ideas in GCLA is that the program, called the *definition*, forms a partial inductive definition, and to that definition a consequence relation is associated, denoted by $\vdash_{\mathcal{D}}$, where $\mathcal{D}$ denotes a particular definition. A GCLA goal consists of a *sequent*, $\Gamma \vdash_{\mathcal{D}} C$, where Γ is called the *antecedent* and C the *consequent*. Assuming something is the same as adding that element to the antecedent. It is here that GCLA differs from most other logic programming languages, since that is not the same as adding something to the definition.

An atom in the antecedent can be replaced by its defining conditions, which is called its *definiens*. The corresponding inference rule is called the *definiton-left* inference rule ($\mathcal{D}\vdash$), and it is this operation that gives GCLA most of its power compared to ordinary horn clause logic programming systems (e.g. Prolog). The operation described in [HS-H91] is complex and laborious to perform, and it is divided into two suboperations; the ***definiens operation*** and the calculation of ***A-sufficient*** substitutions. It is in the latter one much of the execution time is spent, and therefore it is of great interest to develop better algorithms for this operation.

Section 2 gives the background and the necessary definitions. Section 3 of the paper presents three algorithms; the 'original' one presented in [HS-H91], and two others of which one compiles the definition into a new representation that is used to compute a definiens and an $\mathcal{A}$-sufficient substitution. We also present some test values and comparisons of various data, such as execution time, number of mgu's calculated, number of mgu's needed etc.

By replacing unification of terms with systems of (syntactic) equalities and inequalities, an interesting and more expressive language is defined. Unification guards in the head of the clauses are introduced, and the algorithms are generalised to handle the new satisfiability conditions. The constraint solving system can be further generalised, although the paper does not present any material on that. Section 4 presents the changes and additional terminology relative to section 2 as well as the generalised algorithms.

Section 5 contains a brief discussion to related work, and section 6 contains a brief discussion and some references to future work.

The GCLA system is implemented on top of Sicstus Prolog, and thus the presentation is influenced by some Prolog operations, notably the use of *cannot prove*, '\+', at some places, and we assume that the reader is familiar with Prolog's general operational behaviour.

2. Background and Definitions

Although in GCLAII [Kre92, Aro92a] the programmer is free to write any inference rule he wants, we will stick to the original rules presented in [HS-H90, HS-H91]. The definiens operation and the computation of $\mathcal{A}$-sufficient substitutions are primitive operations of GCLAII, with which the user can utilize in his own inference rules, and thus these primitives must have an efficient implementation.

2.1 Background

A GCLA goal is a sequent on the form $\Gamma \vdash_{\mathcal{D}} C$, where the consequence relation $\vdash_{\mathcal{D}}$ is defined by a particular definition $\mathcal{D}$, together with some rules for handling non-atomic conditions (we will often omit the $\mathcal{D}$-subscript in $\vdash_{\mathcal{D}}$ when it is clear what the definition is). Rules handling non-atomic conditions are those rules that do not use the definition, for example arrow right, which adds an element to the antecedent. Those rules do not use the definition, and therefore we will not further discuss the implementation of the structural rules in this paper (see [Aro92b]), but look at algorithms and representational ideas for definitions, in particular together with the definiens operation and $\mathcal{A}$-sufficient substitutions.

Before going into detail, we define the syntax of a GCLA definition. Since we talk about inductive definitions, we have no predicates or functions, just terms and conditions.

A *constant* is a *term*, and so is a *variable*. Constants begin with a lowercase letter, while variables begin with an uppercase letter, or '_'. The single symbol '_' denotes an anonymous variable. If $A_1, ..., A_n$ are terms and f is a functor (term constructor) of arity n, then $f(A_1, ..., A_n)$ is a *term*. All terms are *conditions*, and if C_1 and C_2 are conditions, then so are $(C_1 \rightarrow C_2)$, (C_1, C_2), $(C_1; C_2)$. `true` and `false` are conditions, and if X is a variable and C a condition, then `(pi X\ C)` is a *condition*, where X occurs bound in the condition C.

An *atom* is a term which is not a variable. If A is an atom, C a condition, then `A <= C` is a *clause*. We will refer to A as the *head* of the clause and C as the *body* of the clause. Often we will use H to denote a head and B to denote a body of a clause.

An ordered set of clauses forms a *definition* $\mathcal{D}$.

It is obvious that the universe of constants and atoms are infinite, as well as the number of variables, but that each term is finite.

An example definition is

```
p(X,1) <= q(X).
p(X,Y) <= r(X,Y).

q(2).
```

There are two GCLA inference rules that use the definition; $\vdash\mathcal{D}$ and $\mathcal{D}\vdash$. The inference rule $\vdash\mathcal{D}$ has the definition

$$\frac{\Gamma\sigma \vdash B\sigma}{\Gamma \vdash A}\vdash\mathcal{D}$$

if $(H \Leftarrow B) \in \mathcal{D}$ and $\sigma = mgu(H, A)$.

This rule corresponds to SLD resolution. Thus we can use the same representation technique as in Prolog's clause, which gives good performance.

The $\mathcal{D}\vdash$ rule is the dual to the $\vdash\mathcal{D}$ rule. While the $\vdash\mathcal{D}$ rule operates on one clause at a time, the $\mathcal{D}\vdash$ rule considers all clauses in a definition. The operation that collects all bodies of the clauses considered is called the *definiens operation* and is denoted by $\mathcal{D}(A)$, where A is an atom, and is explained in section 2.2.2 The rule $\mathcal{D}\vdash$ is defined as

$$\frac{\{\Gamma_1\sigma, B, \Gamma_2\sigma \vdash C\sigma \mid B \in \mathcal{D}(A\sigma)\}}{\Gamma_1, A, \Gamma_2 \vdash C}\ \mathcal{D}\vdash$$

if σ is an A-sufficient substitution (explained in section 2.2.1) with respect to $\mathcal{D}$.

Note that there is one instance of this rule for every σ, and if there are no members in $\mathcal{D}(A\sigma)$ there are no premises to the $\mathcal{D}\vdash$ rule, which means that it holds unconditionally. In this way, the negation of a condition C, '*not* (C)', is accomplished by posing the query $C \vdash$ `false`, and if C is not defined in $\mathcal{D}$ the query holds unconditionally.

This rule is much more interesting from an implementational point of view, since it is a "new" rule, i.e. it has little or no correspondence with some other operation in some other language. We will concentrate on the new operations, i.e. on the definiens operation and the generation of A-sufficient substitutions.

2.2 Definitions

We will now give the definitions of the definiens operation and A-sufficient substitutions.

2.2.1 Notations

We will denote substitutions with the letters θ, σ and τ, possible with subscripts. The empty substitution will be denoted by ε. A set of items will be denoted by {...}, a conjunctive vector will be denoted by $(e_1, \ldots, e_n)$, and a disjunctive sum will be denoted by $(e_1; \ldots; e_n)$. The concatenation of an element e to a vector L is denoted by (e, L), and the concatenation of an element e to a sum L is denoted by $(e; L)$. The empty set/vector/sum is denoted by Ø. Application of a substitution σ to a term T (sequent, set etc) will be denoted as $T\sigma$.

2.2.2 The Definiens Operation

The definiens operation is defined formally as: The definiens $\mathcal{D}(A)$ of an atom A, is the set of all instances $B\tau$ of all bodies B such that the instances of their corresponding heads $H\tau$ are equal to A, i.e.

$$\mathcal{D}(A) = \{B\tau \mid A = H\tau \text{ and } H \Leftarrow B \in \mathcal{D}\}$$

2.2.3 A-Sufficient Substitutions

Given an atom A, a substitution σ is called *A-sufficient* if for $A\sigma$ the condition $\mathcal{D}(A\sigma\tau) = (\mathcal{D}(A\sigma))\tau$ is fulfilled, for all τ. The reason for this condition is to ensure that $\mathcal{D}\vdash$ is closed under substitution, i.e. that derivability of $\Gamma \vdash C$ implies that $\Gamma\sigma \vdash C\sigma$, for any substitution σ.

The definiens operation and the calculation of an A-sufficient substitution is closely connected, as we shall see later. It is the case that given a definition and an A-sufficient substitution, the definiens is completely determined. The computation of these two can be combined into one operation, which we will call $suff_{\mathcal{D}}$.

2.2.4 Variable-Check

A definition clause $H \Leftarrow B$ is said to fulfil the *no-extra-variable condition* if every free variable occuring in B also occurs in H. Suppose now that T is fixed. Then we say that σ passes the *variable-check* if all program clauses $H \Leftarrow B$ for which $H\tau = T\sigma$ holds for some τ, fulfil the no-extra-variable condition. Intuitively, the variable-check for σ means that every clause from which $T\sigma$ can be obtained by substitution, fulfils the no-extra-variable condition.

The variable check must be fulfilled to be sure that the algorithms presented here produce A-sufficient substitutions. Once explicit quantifiers are introduced into the language, as in [Eri92], the variable check could be replaced by explicit quantifiers. In the rest of this paper we will assume that the σ considered passes the variable check.

3. Algorithms Without Constraints

We will present three algorithms. The first one is the original one described in [HS-H91]. Algorithm 2 is a refined version of the first, while the third one generates a new representation of a definition $\mathcal{D}$ to hold the set of all possible A-sufficient substitutions together with their corresponding definiens. One can regard the third algorithm as a pre-computation, or partial evaluation, of the possible A-sufficient substitutions for every possible term.

We will represent an empty definiens with the symbol `false`, and when $\mathcal{D}(A)$ contains more than one element, it will be written as a sum $(B_1 ; \ldots ; B_n)$, which is close to how it is represented in the GCLA system. For further details on how sums and other constructs are handled the reader should consult [Kre92].

3.1 Algorithm 1

The first algorithm was presented in [HS-H91], and could be very inefficient. The complexity is $O(n!)$, where n is the number of heads of clauses considered, and '!' is the factorial operation. The number of answers produced by this algorithm (before making the answer a set, where all redundancies are removed) is in the worst case equal to the factorial of the number of the clauses considered.

3.1.1 Definition

Let the clauses be ordered in some way. The heads of the definition $\mathcal{D}$ that should be considered are those that are unifiable with the atom A considered:

$$\{H \mid (H \Leftarrow B) \in \mathcal{D} \text{ and } mgu(A, H) \text{ exists}\}$$

Call this set $\mathcal{L}$. Let k denote the cardinality of $\mathcal{L}$. Now consider all the permutations $H_1, \ldots, H_k$ of $\mathcal{L}$ and define the following algorithm for generating an A-sufficient substitution:

Let

$$mgu'(H, H') = \begin{cases} mgu(H, H') & \text{if it exists} \\ \varepsilon & \text{otherwise} \end{cases}$$

Then define

$$\sigma_0 = \varepsilon$$
$$\sigma_{m+1} = \sigma_m mgu'(A\sigma_m, H_{m+1})$$
$$\sigma = \sigma_k$$

The factorial complexity comes from the permutation of the set $\mathcal{L}$, where all permutations are considered. The algorithm depends on the permutation and is deterministic once the permutation is fixed.

It is easy to see how the algorithm can be extended to also compute the definiens operation. Just associate for every head H_i where there exists an mgu the corresponding body to H_i, and collect them in a sum in parallel with σ_i, which we call $\mathcal{B}$. Thus, define the operation $suff_{\mathcal{D}}$ to return both an A-sufficient substitution σ and the sum $\mathcal{B}$:

$$suff_{\mathcal{D}}(A) = \langle \sigma, \mathcal{B} \rangle$$

and the corresponding algorithm is

$$\langle \sigma_0, \mathcal{B}_0 \rangle = \langle \varepsilon, \varnothing \rangle$$
$$\langle \sigma_{m+1}, \mathcal{B}_{m+1} \rangle = \begin{cases} \langle \sigma_m\tau, (B_{m+1}\tau \,;\, \mathcal{B}) \rangle & \text{if } \tau = mgu'(A\sigma_m, H_{m+1}) \\ \langle \sigma_m, \mathcal{B} \rangle & \text{otherwise} \end{cases}$$
$$\langle \sigma, \mathcal{B} \rangle = \langle \sigma_k, reverse(\mathcal{B}_k) \rangle$$

where B_{m+1} is the body of clause m+1, and *reverse* reverses its argument. The reverse operation is performed in order to get the bodies in the order the considered permutation is.

Note that there could be several sums returned by the algorithm corresponding to one substitution, but if we regard the sums as sets, they will be equal (see the example below).

3.1.2 Example

1) Consider the definition

```
p(1) <= b1.
p(X) <= b2(X).
```

where b_1 and b_2 stand for arbitrary bodies. To the term p(Z) the algorithm returns two equal substitutions, {Z / 1}; $suff_{\mathcal{D}}$(p(Z)) = ⟨{Z/1}, (b_1 ; b_2(1))⟩ and $suff_{\mathcal{D}}$(p(Z)) = ⟨{Z/1}, (b_2(1) ; b_1)⟩. Note that the second position of the pair is swapped in the two solutions, but that the p(Z)-sufficient substitution is the same.

These two solutions stems from the fact that all permutations of the heads are considered. Those two solutions would be regarded as the same, if we regard the second position of the pair as a set.

3.1.3 Soundness

That the algorithm above produces an A-sufficient substitution σ is proved in [HS-H91], provided that the variable-check for σ is fulfilled. That it is not complete is shown by the following example: Consider the program

```
p(1) <= b1.
```

and let $A = p(X)$. Then $\sigma = \{X/3\}$ is an A-sufficient substitution, since $\mathcal{D}(p(3)) = \emptyset$ and $\mathcal{D}(p(X)\sigma\tau) = \mathcal{D}(p(X)\sigma)\tau$, for all τ, but $\{X/3\}$ cannot be generated by the algorithm.

3.2 Algorithm 2

Algorithm 2 is a refinement of algorithm 1. The refinement lies in how the generation of the permutations is performed. Instead of considering all permutations of the heads of the set $\mathcal{L}$, just some are considered. If the clauses are numbered from top to bottom, it is easy to see that if a clause's head at position *i* is unifiable with a clause's head at position *j*, it does not matter if we first take *i* and then *j*, or if we first take *j* and then *i*. This means that an ordering condition can be imposed on the permutation algorithm: do not consider permutations which result in an ordered set of heads (bodies) whose clause numbers are not in ascending order. This makes this algorithm having a complexity of $\mathcal{O}(2^{n+1})$.

A version of this algorithm is also described in [Kre92], but without step 3) below.

3.2.1 Definition

The heads that should be considered are those that are unifiable with the atom A considered:

$$\{H \mid (H \Leftarrow B) \in \mathcal{D} \text{ and } mgu(H,A) \text{ exists}\}$$

Call this set $\mathcal{L}$. Let k denote the cardinality of $\mathcal{L}$, and consider some ordering $H_1, \ldots, H_k$ of $\mathcal{L}$. Define a set $\mathcal{S}$, which collects the heads that should not contribute to the A-sufficient substitution. Define a set $\mathcal{B}$ which collects those bodies that are part of the definiens. Define the following algorithm for calculating $suff_{\mathcal{D}}$:

0) $\langle \sigma_0, \mathcal{S}_0, \mathcal{B}_0 \rangle = \langle \varepsilon, \emptyset, \emptyset \rangle$

1) $\langle \sigma_{m+1}, \mathcal{S}_{m+1}, \mathcal{B}_{m+1} \rangle = \langle \sigma_m\tau, \mathcal{S}_m, (B_{m+1} ; \mathcal{B}_m) \rangle$ if $\tau = mgu(A\sigma_m, H_{m+1})$
2) $\langle \sigma_{m+1}, \mathcal{S}_{m+1}, \mathcal{B}_{m+1} \rangle = \langle \sigma_m, \{H_{m+1}, \mathcal{S}_m\}, \mathcal{B}_m \rangle$ if $\tau = mgu(A\sigma_m, H_{m+1})$
3) $\langle \sigma_{m+1}, \mathcal{S}_{m+1}, \mathcal{B}_{m+1} \rangle = \langle \sigma_m, \mathcal{S}_m, \mathcal{B}_m \rangle$ if $\neg\exists\tau(\tau = mgu(A\sigma_m, H_{m+1}))$

4) $\langle \sigma, \mathcal{B} \rangle = \langle \sigma_k, \mathcal{B}_k \rangle$ provided that $\forall H \in \mathcal{S}_k : (\neg\exists\tau(\tau = mgu(A\sigma_k, H)))$

Instead of considering all permutations of L as in the first algorithm, this algorithm is centred around the fact that either a head H_i contributes to the A-sufficient substitution, or not. This is reflected in the three clauses 1), 2) and 3), together with the provided-check in 4). Instead of always adding H_i to S when there does not exist a unifier of H_i and A, clause 3) is introduced to keep the set S as small as possible. There is a nondeterministic choice between 1) and 2), whenever there exist an mgu of A and H_i. If the mgu τ is added to σ_m, then the head H_i is not collected in the set S. If τ is not added to σ_m, then H_i is added to S, and when all k elements of L have been considered, the heads in S are checked that they are not unifiable with $A\sigma_k$. This last check checks that the elements cannot contribute to σ, which was assumed in clause 2) at some step $j < k$.

By always trying clause 1) first, we get a natural order of the solutions. To get all possible pairs of A-sufficient substitutions and defining conditions $\mathcal{B}$, a complete search is performed.

3.2.3 Examples

1) Consider again the first example of the previous section,

```
p(1) <= b1.
p(X) <= b2(X).
```

We get one answer substitution {Z/1} to the term p(Z), since the only permutation that will be considered is the permutation: first $\sigma_1 = \mathit{mgu}$(p(Z), p(1)), then $\sigma_2 = \mathit{mgu}$(p(Z)σ_1, p(X)). The permutation $\tau_1 = \mathit{mgu}$(p(Z), p(X)), $\tau_2 = \mathit{mgu}$(p(Z)τ_1, p(1)) will not be considered. Thus $\mathit{suff}_{\mathcal{D}}$(p(Z)) = ⟨{Z/1}, ($b_1$; b_2(1))⟩, to be compared with the result in algorithm 1.

2) Consider the definition

```
p(1) <= b1.
p(2) <= b2.
```

We get two answers substitutions {Z/1} and {Z/2} to the term p(Z), since the substitution depends on which of the clauses 1) or 2) in the algorithm that is chosen first. $\mathit{suff}_{\mathcal{D}}$(p(Z)) = ⟨{Z/1}, b_1⟩ or $\mathit{suff}_{\mathcal{D}}$(p(Z)) = ⟨{Z/2}, b_2⟩, and the definiens $\mathcal{D}$(p(Z)) equals {b_1} or {b_2}. To see a trace of the algorithm working, see the appendix.

3.2.2 Soundness

That the substitutions that this algorithm computes are also computed by the first algorithm is easy to see. There are just some permutations that are cut off. That all substitutions that are computed by the first algorithm also are computed by this algorithm is not as clear. We just give an informal comment, where the details are left.

For every two terms T_1 and T_2 that are unifiable, there are two possibilities considered by the first algorithm: $\tau = \mathit{mgu}(T_1, T_2)$ and $\sigma = \mathit{mgu}(T_2, T_1)$. τ and σ

will be considered equal since $T_1\tau = T_1\sigma$ and $T_2\tau = T_2\sigma$ (modulo variable renaming). Therefore, it suffices to consider just one case of the two possibilities. By ordering the heads, we can impose that just one of the two possibilities are considered, which is done implicitly by the accumulating set $\mathcal{S}$ combined with the redundancy check performed in the last clause of the algorithm.

3.3 Algorithm 3

Algorithm 1 and 2 was performed at runtime, i.e. given an atom A, they calculate an A-sufficient substitution. It is possible to calculate all possible A-sufficient substitution for all possible A's given the definition in beforehand. It can be seen as a compilation of the definition, from the definition itself to a new representation of the definition, which is a table of the possible A-sufficient substitutions and their corresponding definiens. It can also be seen as partially evaluating algorithm 2 with respect to a particular definition $\mathcal{D}$.

The algorithm that uses the calculated representation has complexity $O(2^n)$, but as shown in section 3.4, the actual numbers of mgu's computed in runtime is less than the other two algorithms.

3.3.1 Definition

Compared to algorithm 2, the first pass of algorithm 3 delays the fourth clause of algorithm 2 until runtime. A variable is given as input instead of an atom A, and all possible A-sufficient substitutions are generated combined with their delayed redundancy-checks.

We will use '\+' as cannot-prove, i.e. negation by failure. It will only be used together with unifiability, i.e. '=', and is used to express "not unifiable with", so $\backslash+(T_1 = T_2)$ is equal to $\neg\exists\tau(\tau{=}mgu(T_1,T_2))$. If T_2 does not share variables with any other term considered, which is the case when T_2 is a head of some clause in the definition, $\backslash+(T_1 = T_2)$ is the same as $\neg\exists y_1, ..., y_n(T_1 = T_2)$ where $y_1, ..., y_n$ are the variables in T_2, i.e. T_1 should not be an instance of T_2. $\mathcal{S}$ is defined to be a comma-separated vector instead of a set, as it was in algorithm 2. This is to reflect that the check of the elements in $\mathcal{S}$ is postponed until runtime.

Start with partially evaluate algorithm 2 with respect to a given definition $\mathcal{D}$. The heads that should be considered are all heads of the definition $\mathcal{D}$. Call this set $\mathcal{L}$. Let k denote the cardinality of $\mathcal{L}$. Now consider the ordered list $H_1, ..., H_k$ of $\mathcal{L}$ and define the following algorithm for generating all possible A-sufficient substitutions

0) $\langle\sigma_0, \mathcal{S}_0, \mathcal{B}_0\rangle = \langle\varepsilon, \emptyset, \emptyset\rangle$

1) $\langle\sigma_{m+1}, \mathcal{S}_{m+1}, \mathcal{B}_{m+1}\rangle = \langle\sigma_m\tau, \mathcal{S}_m, (B\tau;\ \mathcal{B}_m)\rangle$ if $\tau{=}mgu(A\sigma_m, H_{m+1})$
2) $\langle\sigma_{m+1}, \mathcal{S}_{m+1}, \mathcal{B}_{m+1}\rangle = \langle\sigma_m, (\backslash+(A = H_{m+1}), \mathcal{S}_m), \mathcal{B}_m\rangle$ if $\tau{=}mgu(A\sigma_m, H_{m+1})$
3) $\langle\sigma_{m+1}, \mathcal{S}_{m+1}, \mathcal{B}_{m+1}\rangle = \langle\sigma_m, \mathcal{S}_m, \mathcal{B}_m\rangle$ if $\neg\exists\tau(\tau{=}mgu(A\sigma_m, H_{m+1}))$

4) $\langle\sigma, \mathcal{R}, \mathcal{B}\rangle = \langle\sigma_k, \mathcal{S}_k\sigma_k, \mathcal{B}_k\rangle$

Number all the possible triples $\langle \sigma, \mathcal{R}, \mathcal{B} \rangle$ from 1 to n and let

$$\mathcal{A} = \{D(A\sigma_i, \mathcal{B}_i\sigma_i) \Leftarrow \mathcal{R}_i \mid 1 \leq i \leq n\}$$

where $\mathcal{B}_i$ is the definiens of $A\sigma_i$, and the relation D holds the possible instances of A together with its corresponding $\mathcal{B}$'s. Thus D is a representation of $suff_{\mathcal{D}}(A)$, where $\mathcal{R}$ contains the restrictions on when this particular $suff_{\mathcal{D}}$ is applicable. $\mathcal{A}$ as a whole contains all possible A-sufficient substitutions together with their definiens for all possible A's.

3.3.2 Simplifications

$\mathcal{A}$ is perhaps not the least set of clauses that represents the set of defining conditions, there could be clauses whose bodies, $\mathcal{R}$, can never be fulfilled. Such clauses are clauses where there exists a term \+ (A = H) in $\mathcal{R}$, where A is an instance of H. Since A and H will always be unifiable, \+ (A = H) will always fail, and such clauses can be removed safely. Furthermore, there could be redundant terms in $\mathcal{R}$. The terms \+ (A = H) in $\mathcal{R}$ where there does not exist a unifier of A and H will always fail, and therefore \+ (A = H) will always succeed, and such terms can therefore be removed safely.

3.3.3 Example

1) Consider again the definition

```
p(1) <= b1.
p(X) <= b2(X).
```

The new representation is

```
D(p(1), (b1 ; b2)).
D(p(X), b2) <= \+(p(X) = p(1)).
```

3.3.4 Soundness

Compared to algorithm 2 the possible A-sufficient substitutions have been computed in advance. The heads that were unifiable with A in algorithm 2 are represented in the new $A\sigma_i$ term in the new representation, and those heads that should not be unifiable with the term A are represented in the body $\mathcal{R}_i\sigma_i$ of the new representation. Thus there is a one-to-one correspondence between the new representation and the answers that are computed by algorithm 2.

3.4 Comparison of the Algorithms

Below is a table showing the number of mgu's calculated at runtime for computing all possible A-sufficient substitutions in the three different algorithms. n is the number of clauses considered.

n	Algorithm 1	Algorithm 2 Best case	Algorithm 2 Worst case	Algorithm 3 Best case	Algorithm 3 Worst case
1	1	2	2	2	2
2	4	6	6	3	4
3	18	13	14	4	8
4	96	23	30	5	16
5	600	36	62	6	32
n	n*n!	n(3n-1)/2+1	$2^{n+1}-2$	n+1	2^n

Best case is when no head is unifiable with any other head, in which case there is as many possible A-sufficient substitutions as there are clauses, plus one for the case when no head was unifiable with A.

Worst case is when all heads are unifiable with each other, but differ from each other at some place, which gives 2^n possible A-sufficient substitutions, depending on A. For example, the definition

```
p(1,Y,Z) <= b1.
p(X,2,Z) <= b2.
p(X,Y,3) <= b3.
```

is such a case for n = 3. One can note that the third algorithm computes exactly those.

Note that more mgu's are calculated in algorithm 2 than in algorithm 1 when n is less than 3, but when n equals 2 algorithm 1 often computes two equal substitutions and thus gives the GCLA system less efficient overall behaviour.

4. Algorithms Incorporating Guards and Constraints

In section 3 we dealt with A-sufficient substitutions without constraints. Since clauses in GCLA can have a guard putting constraints on variables, the algorithms must cope with those too. Thus, we are now going to generalise the algorithms to deal with *constraint sets* instead of substitutions. We will look upon a constraint set as a specification of a possible substitution, which means that a set of constraints should always have at least one solution, i.e. it should represent at least one grounding substitution. We will only deal with one type of constraints, 'not unifiable with' or more precisely 'not instance of', which is denoted by the relation '\='. However, one can think of other kinds of constraints that can be added, such as type conditions (for example X must be a number), ordering conditions (for example X must be greater than some Y given an order relation) etc. But when adding a new type of constraint, satisfiability in the new constraint system must be decidable.

4.1 Guards and Constraints

We will use the same terminology as described in section 2, with the following additional definitions and changes.

4.1.1 Unification Constraints and Guards

The constraint `X \= Template` is a restriction on `X` such that `X` should not be an instance of `Template`. We define `X \= T` as $\forall y_1, ..., y_n$ $(X \neq T)$, where $y_1, ..., y_n$ are the variables in *T*. *X* may be any term. For example

1) `(X \= s(Y))`σ, where σ = {`X/s(Z)`}, is not satisfiable, since we are looking for an `X` such that `X` is not an instance of `s(Y)`, for all `Y`, but `X` is `s(Z)`, and `s(Z)` is an instance of `s(Y)`, for all values of `Z`.
2) `(X \= s(Y))`σ, where σ = {`X/0`}, is satisfiable, since `0` $\neq$ `s(Y)`, for all `Y`.
3) `(X \= s(0))`σ where σ = {`X/s(Y)`} is satisfiable provided that `Y` is constrained to `(Y \= 0)`.
4) `(X \= s(Y))`σ where σ = {`X = s(0)`} is not satisfiable, since we are looking for an `X` such that `X` is not an instance of `s(Y)`, for all `Y`, and `s(0)` is an instance of `s(Y)`.
5) `(X \= f(1,2))`σ where σ = {`X = f(Y,Z)`} is satisfiable provided that at least one of `Y` and `Z` are constrained to `(Y \= 1)` and `(Z \= 2)` respectively, i.e. `((Y \= 1)` $\vee$ `(Z \= 2))`.

If $g_1, ..., g_n$ are constraints, then $\{g_1, ..., g_n\}$ is a *guard*. We will use the letter *G* to denote a guard.

If `A` is an atom, *C* is a condition, and *G* is a guard, then `A#G <= C` is a *guarded clause*. We will as before use *H* to denote the head of a clause and `B` to denote the body of a clause. We will call a guarded clause just a clause.

A set of equalities and inequalities will be called a *constraint set*, and will be denoted by θ, ζ, σ, τ or γ, possible with subscripts or superscripts. These corresponds to substitutions in section 2 and 3.

4.1.2 The Definiens Operation and A-sufficient Constraint Sets

We need a new operation, $\bullet$, for combining constraint sets, corresponding to combining substitutions.

Define $\bullet$ as:

$$\begin{cases} \bot \bullet \mathcal{B} & = \bot \\ \mathcal{A} \bullet \bot & = \bot \\ \bot \bullet \bot & = \bot \\ \mathcal{A} \bullet \mathcal{B} & = \begin{cases} \mathcal{A} \cup \mathcal{B} & \text{if } \mathcal{A} \cup \mathcal{B} \text{ is satisfiable} \\ \bot & \text{otherwise} \end{cases} \end{cases}$$

where $\bot$ is the unsatisfiable symbol. That $\bullet$ is associative is easy to show. We can note that when two substitutions σ and τ are combined, if σ and τ substitutes a variable `X` with t_1 and t_2 respectively, the combined substitution $\sigma\tau$ defines `X` to be substituted with t_1. In the constraint set analogue $\sigma \bullet \tau$, $\sigma \bullet \tau$ is defined to be $\bot$.

Furthermore, define $not(A = H, G)$ as

$$not(A = H, G) = \begin{cases} \{A \setminus= H\} & \text{or} \\ \{A = H, X_i = T_i\} & \text{where } X_i \setminus= T_i \in G \end{cases}$$

not is the complement to $\{A = H\} \cup G$, i.e. the negation of $A=H \;\&\; g_1 \;\&\; ... \;\&\; g_n$, where $g_i \in G$, which is $(A \setminus= H \vee A = H \;\&\; (g_1 \vee ... \vee g_n))$. To see this, consider the following informal discussion with the guard $\{X \setminus= T\}$.

$\{A = H, X \setminus= T\}$ represents at least one of all grounding substitutions σ such that $\{A = H, X \setminus= T\}\sigma$ holds. Let the function *subst* of a constraint set have the following definition:

$$subst\ (\mathcal{M}) = \{\sigma \mid \mathcal{M}\sigma \text{ holds and } \mathcal{M}\sigma \text{ is ground}\}$$

i.e. $subst\ (\mathcal{M})$ is the set of all possible grounding substitutions such that $\mathcal{M}\sigma$ holds.

Then $subst(\{A = H, X \setminus= T\}) = \{\sigma \mid A\sigma = H\sigma, X\sigma \setminus= T\sigma\}$. The complement $comp(subst(\{A = H, X \setminus= T\}))$ is then $\{\tau \mid \tau \notin subst(\{A = H, X \setminus= T\})\}$ = $\{\tau \mid \tau \in subst(\{A \setminus= H\}) \cup subst(\{X = T\})\} = \{\tau \mid A\tau \setminus= H\tau\} \cup \{\tau \mid X\tau = T\tau\}$, and, without loss of generality, we get $\{\tau \mid A\tau \setminus= H\tau\} \cup \{\tau \mid A\tau = H\tau, X\tau = T\tau\}$, which is represented as $not(A = H, \{X \setminus= T\})$.

We define the definiens operation for constraint sets as:

$$\mathcal{D}(A, \theta) = \{\langle B, \{A = H\} \cup G \rangle \mid H \# G <= B \in \mathcal{D} \text{ and } \{H = A\} \bullet G \bullet \theta \neq \bot\}$$

or in words

> $\mathcal{D}(A, \theta)$ is the set of all pairs of bodies B and sets $\{A = H\} \cup G$ such that $\theta \cup \{A = H\} \cup G$ is satisfiable, where θ is a (satisfiable) constraint set. If θ is unsatisfiable, $\mathcal{D}(A, \theta)$ is undefined.

We will need a set consisting of only the bodies B of a definiens $\mathcal{D}(A, \theta)$. Define $\mathcal{D}^b(A, \theta)$ as

$$\mathcal{D}^b(A, \theta) = \{B \mid \langle B, \sigma \rangle \in \mathcal{D}(A, \theta)\}$$

where σ is a constraint set.

In the proof we assume that the bodies of the clauses do not introduce new, free variables (i.e. that variables in the body also occurs in the head of a clause), in which case the proofs below do not hold, i.e. we assume that the no-extra-variable condition is fulfilled. We also assume that variables in clauses can be freely renamed.

We have to prove that the new definiens operation $\mathcal{D}$ is closed under $\bullet$, i.e. the corresponding condition to $\mathcal{D}(A\sigma)\tau = \mathcal{D}(A\sigma\tau)$ in the substitution case.

$$\mathcal{D}^b(A, \theta) = \mathcal{D}^b(A, \theta \bullet \tau), \text{ for all } \tau \text{ such that } \theta \bullet \tau \neq \bot$$

and for the calculated A-sufficient constraint set σ;

(*) $\mathcal{D}^b(A, \theta\bullet\sigma) = \mathcal{D}^b(A, \theta\bullet\sigma\bullet\tau)$, for all τ such that $\theta\bullet\sigma\bullet\tau \neq \perp$.

We will show that (*) can be replaced by another condition, namely that the calculated constraint set σ is total, where total is defined as:

> A constraint set σ is *total* if for every clause $H\#G <= B$, either $\{A = H\} \cup G \cup \sigma$ is satisfiable or $not(A{=}H, G) \cup \sigma$ is satisfiable.

Proposition: If σ is total, then the condition (*) is fulfilled.

Proof: $\mathcal{D}^b(A, \theta\bullet\sigma) = \{B \mid H\#G <= B \in \mathcal{D}$ and $\{H = A\}\bullet G\bullet\theta\bullet\sigma \neq \perp\}$, and since σ is total (hypothesis), either $\{A = H\} \cup G$ is in σ or $not(A = H, G)$ is in σ, for all heads H and guards G such that $H\#G <= B \in \mathcal{D}$. This means that the only sets $\{A = H\} \cup G$ for which $\{H = A\}\bullet G\bullet\theta\bullet\sigma \neq \perp$ holds are those terms where $\{A = H\}\bullet G \subseteq \sigma$. Since $\theta\bullet\sigma\bullet\tau \neq \perp$ holds (see (*)), we can conclude that $\{H = A\}\bullet G\bullet\tau \neq \perp$, for all sets $\{H = A\} \cup G \subseteq \sigma$. Therefore $\{H = A\}\bullet G\bullet\theta\bullet\sigma\bullet\tau \neq \perp$ for all sets $\{H = A\}\bullet G\bullet\theta\bullet\sigma \neq \perp$, and therefore $\mathcal{D}^b(A, \theta\bullet\sigma) \subseteq \mathcal{D}^b(A, \theta\bullet\sigma\bullet\tau)$.

That the cardinality of $\mathcal{D}(A, \theta\bullet\sigma\bullet\tau)$, denoted by $\#(\mathcal{D}(A, \theta\bullet\sigma\bullet\tau))$, is not greater than $\#(\mathcal{D}(A, \theta\bullet\sigma))$ is easy to show. Since σ is total, it holds that for all H, G, B such that $H\#G <= B \in \mathcal{D}$, if $\sigma\bullet\{H = A)\bullet G = \perp$, then $\sigma\bullet\{H = A)\bullet G\bullet\tau = \perp$ (intuitively, τ cannot make $\mathcal{D}(A, \theta\bullet\sigma)$ larger). Thus $\#(\mathcal{D}(A, \theta\bullet\sigma\bullet\tau)) \leq \#(\mathcal{D}(A, \theta\bullet\sigma))$. Together with $\mathcal{D}^b(A, \theta\bullet\sigma) \subseteq \mathcal{D}^b(A, \theta\bullet\sigma\bullet\tau)$ we have $\mathcal{D}^b(A, \theta\bullet\sigma) = \mathcal{D}^b(A, \theta\bullet\sigma\bullet\tau)$.

Q.E.D.

We have defined and proved the condition (*) for a constraint system where the only condition on the algorithm is that it produces a total constraint set σ, i.e. that it considers all clauses of a definition $\mathcal{D}$.

With the new definitions of the definiens operation and A-sufficient constraint sets, the two inference rules $\vdash\mathcal{D}$ and $\mathcal{D}\vdash$ are changed. Instead of applying the substitutions on the conditions directly, we have an accumulating set of constraints, that must be satisfiable in each step:

$$\frac{\Gamma \vdash B \qquad\qquad \{H = A\} \cup G \cup \gamma}{\Gamma \vdash A \qquad\qquad \gamma} \vdash\mathcal{D}$$

if $(H\#G <= B) \in \mathcal{D}$, and $\{H = A\} \cup G \cup \gamma$ is satisfiable.

and

$$\frac{\{\Gamma_1, B, \Gamma_2 \vdash C \qquad\qquad \zeta \cup \sigma \cup \gamma \mid \langle B, \zeta\rangle \in \mathcal{D}(A, \sigma \cup \gamma)\}}{\Gamma_1, A, \Gamma_2 \vdash C \qquad\qquad \gamma} \mathcal{D}\vdash$$

if σ is an A-sufficient constraint set with respect to $\mathcal{D}$, $\mathcal{D}(A, \sigma \cup \gamma)$ is the definiens operation and $\sigma \cup \gamma$ is satisfiable.

4.1.3 Satisfiability

The equality theory we will use has syntactic equality, $T_1 = T_2$, and syntactic inequality, $T_1 \backslash= T_2$, or more precise, T_1 is not an instance of T_2. To see that satisfiability of a set of equalities and inequalities is computable and terminating, consider the algorithm below, based on Herbrands algorithm [LMM88] for computing an unifier of a set of equalities. For other algorithms see [Wal87] and [Smi91]. Especially [Smi91], where the notion of U-constraints (universally quantified disequalities) is described, is very close to the satisfiability discussed here, although he considers inequalities where arbitrary arguments of terms can be universally declared variables (see section 5).

> Non-deterministically choose an equation from the equation set to which a numbered step applies. The action taken by the algorithm is determined by the form of the equation:
>
> 1) $f(t_1, \ldots, t_n) = f(s_1, \ldots, s_n)$
> replace by the equations $t_1 = s_1, \ldots, t_n = s_n$.
>
> 2) $f(t_1, \ldots, t_n) = g(s_1, \ldots, s_m)$ where $f \not\equiv g$
> halt with failure
>
> 3) $x = x$ delete the equation
>
> 4) $t = x$ where t is not a variable
> replace by the equation $x = t$
>
> 5) $x = t$ where $t \not\equiv x$ and x has another occurrence in the set of equations
> if x appears in t then halt with failure
> otherwise replace x by t in every other term of the set.
>
> The algorithm terminates when no step can be applied or when failure has been returned.

An equation set (possible empty) is in *solved form* if it has the form $\{v_1 = t_1, \ldots, v_n = t_n\}$ and the v_i's are distinct variables which do not occur in the right hand side of any equation (see [LMM88] for further details). That this algorithm terminates and leaves the set in solved form is proved in [LMM88].

Our algorithm for determining satisfiability of a set of equalities and inequalities has two passes. The first pass performs Herbrands unification algorithm with a sixth clause:

> 6) $X \backslash= T$ Skip it

and a slightly changed terminating clause:

The algorithm terminates when no one of the clauses 1 to 5 can be applied or when failure has been returned.

The second pass tests the inequalities for satisfiability. We assume some ordering $\{T_1, ..., T_n\}$ of the elements in the set:

Traverse the set of equations and constraints. For every element in the set, one of the clauses below should be applied:

7) `x = t` If it is an equation, skip it.

8) t_1 `\=` t_2 If it is a constraint, check it:
- If t_1 is an instance of t_2, then halt with failure.
- If t_1 `\=` t_2 is satisfied, i.e. they are not unifiable, then t_1 will always differ from t_2, and t_1 `\=` t_2 can be removed. To check unifiability, use Herbrands algorithm.
- Otherwise, keep t_1 `\=` t_2 and continue.

To check if a term `t` is an instance of `t'`, the following algorithm can be used:

Replace all variables in `t` with new constants. Then use Herbrands algorithm to check if `t` and `t'` are unifiable. If so, `t` is an instance of `t'`, otherwise not.

It is easy to show that the second pass terminates since it is a one pass traversing and the instance procedure uses Herbrands algorithm, which is proved to terminate.

This shows that checking satisfiability of a set of syntactic equalities and inequalities is computable and terminating. Of course there are other, more efficient algorithms. One such is to use unification combined with corouting for checking inequalities in the same manner as corouting can be used to implement `dif/2` in many Prologs, in particular [Smi91] discusses a constraint system which is similar to ours. [LMM88] also treats the solving of systems of equalities and inequalities.

4.2 Algorithm 2 with Constraints

To generalize algorithm 2 to handle constraints the function *mgu* is replaced with a check for satisfiability, and the algorithm starts with an initial constraint set instead of the empty substitution.

4.2.1 Definition

Let the order of the clauses be determined by a list (an ordered set). The heads H and guards G that should be considered are those for which the set $\{H = A\} \cup G \cup \gamma$ is satisfiable, for a given A and a given initial constraint set γ:

$$\{\langle H, G\rangle \mid (H\#G \text{ <= } B) \in \mathcal{D} \text{ and } \{H = A\} \cup G \cup \gamma \text{ is satisfiable}\}$$

Call this set $\mathcal{L}$. Let k denote the cardinality of $\mathcal{L}$, and let γ be the initial set of constraints. Now consider the ordered list $\langle H_1,G_1\rangle, ..., \langle H_k,G_k\rangle$ of $\mathcal{L}$. Let $\mathcal{B}$ be a sum which collects those bodies that are part of the definiens, and define the following algorithm for calculating $suff_{\mathcal{D}}$:

0) $\langle \sigma_0, \mathcal{B}_0 \rangle = \langle \varnothing, \varnothing \rangle$

1) $\langle \sigma_{m+1}, \mathcal{B}_{m+1} \rangle = \langle \sigma_m \cup \{A = H_{m+1}\} \cup G_{m+1}, (B_{m+1} ; \mathcal{B}_m) \rangle$
if $\gamma \cup \sigma_m \cup \{A = H_{m+1}\} \cup G_{m+1}$ is satisfiable

2) $\langle \sigma_{m+1}, \mathcal{B}_{m+1} \rangle = \langle \sigma_m \cup \textit{not}(A = H_{m+1}, G_{m+1}), \mathcal{B}_m \rangle$
if $\gamma \cup \sigma_m \cup \textit{not}(A = H_{m+1}, G_{m+1})$ is satisfiable

4) $\langle \sigma, \mathcal{B} \rangle = \langle \sigma_k, \mathcal{B}_k \rangle$

Note that the step when choosing between 1) and 2) could be nondeterministic, and by always trying 1) first, we get a natural order of the solutions. Also note the use of ***not*** in clause 2), which is indeterministic if the guard is not empty (see the definition of ***not***, section 4.1.2), and one of the possible negations is chosen. By performing a complete search, all possible A-sufficient constraint sets can be generated.

If one compares this algorithm with the corresponding one for substitutions, one could note that the set S and clause 3) has disappeared. This is due to the fact that the constraint system now handles the case when a head H_i is not to contribute positively (i.e. $A = H_i$) in a solution, which was solved with the accumulating set S and clause 3) before. This also means that other clauses whose bodies are not part of the definiens contribute (negatively) to the A-sufficient constraint set. In other words, the algorithm is total in the sense of section 4.1.

4.2.2 Example

1) Consider the definition

```
p(1) <= b1.
p(X)#{X \= 1} <= b2(X).
```

There are two possible `p(Z)`-sufficient constraint sets `{Z = 1}` and `{Z = X, X \= 1}`, and to them correspond the two defining conditions $\langle b_1,$ `{p(Z) = p(1)}`$\rangle$ and $\langle b_2$`(X)`, `{p(Z) = p(X), X \= 1}`$\rangle$ respectively.

4.3 Algorithm 3 with Constraints

As for the second algorithm, the largest difference between algorithm 3 in section 3.3 and this algorithm is that the set S, which incrementally collected the heads which should not be unifiable with A, is removed, and instead of adding heads to S in the second clause of the algorithm, their negation is put in the constraint set.

4.3.1 Definition

Partially evaluate algorithm 2 with respect to a given definition $\mathcal{D}$. The heads and guards that should be considered are all heads and guards in the clauses of the definition. Call this set $\mathcal{L}$. Let k denote the cardinality of $\mathcal{L}$. Now consider the ordered list of pairs $\langle H_1, G_1\rangle, ..., \langle H_k, G_k\rangle$ of $\mathcal{L}$ and define the following algorithm for generating all possible A-sufficient constraint sets:

0) $\langle \sigma_0, \mathcal{B}_0\rangle = \langle \emptyset, \emptyset\rangle$

1) $\langle \sigma_{m+1}, \mathcal{B}_{m+1}\rangle = \langle \sigma_m \cup \{A = H_{m+1}\} \cup G_{m+1}, (B_{m+1} ; \mathcal{B}_m)\rangle$
if $\sigma_m \cup \{A = H_{m+1}\} \cup G_{m+1}$ is satisfiable

2) $\langle \sigma_{m+1}, \mathcal{B}_{m+1}\rangle = \langle \sigma_m \cup \mathit{not}(A = H, G_{m+1}), \mathcal{B}_m\rangle$
if $\sigma_m \cup \mathit{not}(A = H, G_{m+1})$ is satisfiable

4) $\langle \sigma, \mathcal{B}\rangle = \langle \sigma_k, \mathcal{B}_k\rangle$

Number all possible constraint sets σ from 1 to n and let

$$\mathcal{A} = \{D(A, \langle \mathcal{B}_i, \sigma_i\rangle) \mid 1 \leq i \leq n\}$$

where $\mathcal{B}_i$ is the definiens of A and σ_i the A-sufficient constraint set.

That the algorithm computes a total σ is showed by an induction over the heads of the definition. Either $\{A = H\} \cup G$ is in σ, or $\mathit{not}(A = H, G)$ is in σ, for all H, G such that $H \# G \Leftarrow B \in \mathcal{D}$.

4.3.2 Examples

All the examples shows the constraint sets and the new representation without any simplifications.

1) Now it is possible to get answers to negated atoms by a constraint set, which specifies when there is no clause applicable. For example, the definition

```
p(1) <= b1.
```

is compiled into

```
D(p(X), <b1, {p(X) = p(1)}>).
D(p(X), <false, {p(X) \= p(1)}>).
```

and to the query `p(Y) \- false` (which is posing a query 'not `p(Y)`' in GCLA), we get as an answer constraint `p(Y) \= p(1)` (which equals `Y \= 1`).

Negation is one application of the $\mathcal{D}\vdash$ rule, where $\mathit{suff}_{\mathcal{D}}$ is used. There are other cases where this possibility of answering by constraints can be utilized, but negation is one of the most important we have discovered this far. We give further examples of that here.

2) Consider the definition:

```
X = X.
```

This is compiled into

```
D(Z=Y, <true, {(Z=Y) = (X=X)}>).
D(Z=Y, <false, {(Z=Y) \= (X=X)}>).
```

i.e. `Z=Y` is false if `Z=Y` is not an instance of `X=X`, i.e. `Z` is not equal `Y`. This is the same as `dif(X,Y)`, a primitive in some Prologs, which constrains `X` and `Y` not to be equal.

3) Another example is the relation `member/2`,

```
member(E,[E|_]).
member(E,[F|R])#{(F=E) \= (Z=Z)} <= member(E,R).
```

which is compiled into

```
D(member(X,Y), <true, {member(X,Y) = member(E,[E|_])}>).
D(member(X,Y),
  <member(E,R), {member(X,Y) = member(E,[F|R]),
                 (F=E) \= (Z=Z)}>).
D(member(X,Y),
  <false, {member(X,Y) \= member(E,[E|_]),
           member(X,Y) \= member(E,[F|R])}>).
D(member(X,Y),
  <false, {member(X,Y) \= member(E,[E|_]),
           member(X,Y) = member(E,[F|R]),
           (F=E) \= (Z=Z)}>).
```

4) Consider a small database,

```
elephant(dumbo).
elephant(jumbo).
```

Compiling this gives the definiens representation

```
D(elephant(X), <true, {elephant(X) = elephant(dumbo)}>).
D(elephant(X), <true, {elephant(X) = elephant(jumbo)}>).
D(elephant(X),
  <false, {elephant(X) \= elephant(dumbo),
           elephant(X) \= elephant(jumbo)}>).
```

5. Related Work

Since the definiens operation and the notion of A-sufficiency is local to GCLA and Partial inductive definitions (to our knowledge), there is not very much work done elsewhere. However, when incorporating satisfiability of equalities and inequalities, there is a lot of related work in the field of negation (c.f. [MN89, Dra91, Kun87, Wal87, Har91], among others). In our case this is the generation of constraints which corresponds to an empty definiens, i.e. the A-sufficient constraint set to which the definiens operation is empty.

[LMM88] gives a very thorough treatment of substitutions and unifiers of set of equalities and inequalities.

[Smi91] defines U-constraints to universally quantified disequalities, denoted by T_1 <> T_2 where T_1 and/or T_2 can contain universally quantified variables, which is similar to our not-instance-relation `\=`. The difference lies in that in the operation T_1 <> T_2, both T_1 and T_2 can have universally quantified variables, while in the operation T_1 `\=` T_2, all variables in T_2 are universally quantified while all variables in T_1 are existentially quantified. This makes us unable to express the U-constraint `s(?, X) <> Z`, where `?` denotes a universally quantified variable, but makes `\=` easier to implement, and `\=` suffices for our purposes. However, there is a possibility to generalize our relation `\=` into a three-argument relation `\=(Vars, X, Y)`, where *Vars* holds the universally quantified variables, and *X* and *Y* should not be unifiable. The same basic algorithm as in section 4.1.3 can be used, with a the following clause replacing 8):

8) `\=(V,` t_1`,` t_2`)` If it is a constraint, check it:
- If t_1 `\=` t_2 is satisfied, i.e. they are not unifiable, then t_1 will always differ from t_2, and t_1 `\=` t_2 can be removed. To check unifiability, use Herbrands algorithm.
- Replace all variables, which are in *V*, in t_1 with new constants. Call the new term t_1'. Do the same with t_2 forming t_2'. If t_1' and t_2' are unifiable, then t_1 and t_2 will always be unifiable, and the constraint `\=(V,` t_1`,` t_2`)` can never be fulfilled. Halt with failure.
- Otherwise, keep `\=(V,` t_1`,` t_2`)` and continue.

We are then able to express that two terms t_1 and t_2 are unequal, where arbitrary variables in t_1 or t_2 could be universally quantified. For example, the Prolog predicate `dif/2` could be expressed either as `\=([],X,Y)`, or as `\=([Z],p(X,Y),p(Z,Z))`.

[Dra91] gives the notion of SLDFA resolution, which uses constraints of equalities and inequalities. A negated literal L in a goal is solved by finding a set of constraints for which L is finitely failed.

[Wal87] gives a treatment of negation in logic programming with constraints which in much is very similar with [Dra91].

[Har91] defines the completion of clauses on heraditary Harrop (HH) form, and discusses their properties, in particular that the completion is a HH formula itself, and thus is in the language. The completion is defined as:

Let the clauses defining p be the universal closure of

$$p(t_{11}, t_{12}, \ldots, t_{1n}) \Leftarrow B_1.$$
$$\ldots$$
$$p(t_{k1}, t_{k2}, \ldots, t_{kn}) \Leftarrow B_k.$$

Let p^+ be the clause

$$\forall X_1, \ldots, X_n\ p(X_1, \ldots, X_n) \Leftarrow \bigvee_{i=1}^{k} \exists(E_i \,\&\, contr(B_i)))$$

where E_i is $X_1 = t_{i1} \,\&\, \ldots \,\&\, X_n = t_{in}$, $\exists(E_i \,\&\, G_i)$ is the existential closure of all free variables of $E_i \,\&\, G_i$, $1 \le i \le k$, and $X_1, \ldots, X_n$ are new variables not occuring in any G_i. $contr(C)$ replaces all occurrences of $\neg A$ with $A \rightarrow \bot$.

p^- is the clause

$$\forall X_1, \ldots, X_n \bot \Leftarrow p(X_1, \ldots, X_n) \,\&\, \mathop{\&}_{i=1}^{k} \forall(\neg E_i \vee contr\,(fails\,(B_i))).$$

where $fails(C)$ negates the formula C. If there is no clause in the program whose head's name is p, then p^+ is empty and p^- is the clause

$$\forall X_1, \ldots, X_n \bot \Leftarrow p(X_1, \ldots, X_n).$$

The completion of a predicate p is $\{p^+, p^-\}$.

This completion bears close resemblance with the D-representation defined in section 4.3, in that $(\neg E_i \vee contr\,(fails\,(B_i)))$ is a corresponding disjunction to the nondeterministic choice between clauses 1) and 2) in section 4.2 and 4.3.

6. Remarks and Future Work

Note that the second algorithm has the advantage that it can handle dynamic assert in and retract from the definition, and is thus justified for such cases. But for definitions that are not dynamic, the representation calculated by the third algorithm has much better performance.

It should be possible to develop better indexing algorithms for the D-representation than just indexing on the first argument's principal functor, as in most Prolog implementations today. If the '\=' - constraints could be used for indexing purposes, it would reduce the number of choice points generated, since it is often the case that these constraints make the clauses mutually exclusive.

Another interesting generalisation is to develop a constraint language in which the programmer can define his own constraint system. To do this, the properties discussed in section 4 must be fulfilled to guarantee that the definiens operation and the overall GCLA system behaves correctly, but in principle it should be possible. Then the GCLA system should be indexed with the constraint system *CS* in mind, i.e. in the same way as other constraint logic programming languages, which are denoted by CLP(*CS*), and the programmer could define a constraint system that is most suitable for his purposes.

Acknowledgement

The author would like to thank Per Kreuger, Lars-Henrik Eriksson and Lars Hallnäs of the FOPKBS group at SICS for many valuable discussions. The elaborate version \=/3 of \=/2 was especially due to discussions with Per Kreuger. Thanks also to Peter Schroeder-Heister for valuable comments on a draft of this paper. The author would also like to thank the organizers of ELP-92.

References

[Aro90] M. Aronsson, L-H Eriksson, A. Gäredal, L. Hallnäs, P. Olin, The Programming Language GCLA: A Definitional Approach to Logic Programming, New Generation Computing 7(4), pp 381 - 404, 1990

[Aro91] M. Aronsson, *GCLA User's manual*, Technical Report SICS T91:21, 1991

[Aro92a] M. Aronsson, *Methodology and Programming Techniques in GCLAII*, Extensions of Logic Programming: Proceedings of a workshop held at SICS, January 1991, in Springer Lecture Notes in Artificial Intelligence. Also available as SICS Research Report R92:05.

[Aro92b] M.Aronsson, *Implementation Issues in GCLA II*, forthcoming SICS technical report.

[Dra91] W. Drabent, *Constructive Negation by Failed Answers*, Research Report LiTH-IDA-R-91-23, Department of Computer and Information Science, Linköping University, 1991.

[Eri92] Lars-Henrik Eriksson, *A Finitary Version of the Calculus of Partial Inductive Definitions*, Extensions of Logic Programming: Proceedings of a workshop held at SICS, January 1991, in Springer Lecture Notes in Artificial Intelligence. Also available as SICS Research Report R92:08.

[Hal91] L. Hallnäs, *Partial Inductive Definitions*, Theoretical Computer Science 87, pp 115 - 142, 1991.

[HS-H90] L. Hallnäs, P. Schroeder-Heister, *A Proof-Theoretic Approach to Logic Programming. I, Clauses as Rules*, Journal of Logic and Computation vol. 1 no. 2, pp 261 - 283, 1990.

[HS-H91] L. Hallnäs, P. Schroeder-Heister, *A Proof-Theoretic Approach to Logic Programming. II, Programs as Definitions*, Journal of Logic and Computation vol. 1 no. 5, pp 635 - 660, 1991.

[Har91] J. Harland, *A Clausal Form for the Completion of Logic Programs*, Proc. of the International Conference on Logic Programming no. 8, pp 711 - 725, 1991.

[Kre92] P. Kreuger, *GCLAII, A Definitional Approach to Control,*, Extensions of Logic Programming: Proceedings of a workshop held at SICS, January 1991, in Springer Lecture Notes in Artificial Intelligence. Also available as SICS Research Report R92:09.

[Kun87] K. Kunen, *Answer Sets and Negation as Failure*, Proc. of the International Conference on Logic Programming no. 4, pp 219 - 228, MIT Press, 1987.

[LMM88] J-L. Lassez, M.J. Maher, K. Marriott, *Unification Revisited*, in J. Minker, Foundations of Deductive Databases and Logic Programming, Morgan Kaufmann, Los Altos, 1988.

[MN89] J. Maluszynski, T. Näslund, *Fail Substitutions for Negation as Failure*, in Proceedings of the North American Conference on Logic Programming, MIT Press, 1989

[Smi91] D.A. Smith, *Constraint Operations for CLP(FT)*, in Proc. of ICLP 8, MIT Press, 1991.

[Wal87] M. Wallace, *Negation by Constraints: A Sound and Efficient Implementation of Negation in Deductive Databases*, in Proc. of 1987 Symposium on Logic Programming, San Francisco, pp 253 - 2633, 1987

Appendix

This appendix shows a trace of the second example of section 3.2.3. The definition is

```
p(1) <= b1.
p(2) <= b2.
```

and the term A = `p(X)`.

The trace is the following, with the numbered step to the left, and comments to the right:

Answer 1:

0)	$\langle \varepsilon, \emptyset, \emptyset \rangle$	Initial state
1)	$\langle \{X/1\}, \emptyset, \mathtt{b1} \rangle$	Clause 1, indeterministic, i.e. there is a possibility to take clause 2 instead
2)	$\langle \{X/1\}, \emptyset, \mathtt{b1} \rangle$	Clause 3
3)	$\langle \{X/1\}, \mathtt{b1} \rangle$	Clause 4, which gives the final solution

Answer 2:

0)	$\langle \varepsilon, \emptyset, \emptyset \rangle$	Initial state
1)	$\langle \varepsilon, \{\mathtt{p(1)}\}, \emptyset \rangle$	Clause 2, indeterministic, i.e. there is a possibility to take clause 1 instead
2)	$\langle \{X/2\}, \{\mathtt{p(1)}\}, \mathtt{b2} \rangle$	Clause 1
3)	$\langle \{X/2\}, \mathtt{b2} \rangle$	Clause 4, which gives the final solution, where the check $\neg\exists\tau(\tau{=}mgu(\mathtt{p(2)}, \mathtt{p(1)}))$ is satisfied.

Springer-Verlag and the Environment

We at Springer-Verlag firmly believe that an international science publisher has a special obligation to the environment, and our corporate policies consistently reflect this conviction.

We also expect our business partners – paper mills, printers, packaging manufacturers, etc. – to commit themselves to using environmentally friendly materials and production processes.

The paper in this book is made from low- or no-chlorine pulp and is acid free, in conformance with international standards for paper permanency.

Lecture Notes in Artificial Intelligence (LNAI)

Vol. 478: J. van Eijck (Ed.), Logics in AI. Proceedings. 1990. IX, 562 pages. 1991.

Vol. 481: E. Lang, K.-U. Carstensen, G. Simmons, Modelling Spatial Knowledge on a Linguistic Basis. IX, 138 pages. 1991.

Vol. 482: Y. Kodratoff (Ed.), Machine Learning – EWSL-91. Proceedings, 1991. XI, 537 pages. 1991.

Vol. 513: N. M. Mattos, An Approach to Knowledge Base Management. IX, 247 pages. 1991.

Vol. 515: J. P. Martins, M. Reinfrank (Eds.), Truth Maintenance Systems. Proceedings, 1990. VII, 177 pages. 1991.

Vol. 517: K. Nökel, Temporally Distributed Symptoms in Technical Diagnosis. IX, 164 pages. 1991.

Vol. 518: J. G. Williams, Instantiation Theory. VIII, 133 pages. 1991.

Vol. 522: J. Hertzberg (Ed.), European Workshop on Planning. Proceedings, 1991. VII, 121 pages. 1991.

Vol. 535: P. Jorrand, J. Kelemen (Eds.), Fundamentals of Artificial Intelligence Research. Proceedings, 1991. VIII, 255 pages. 1991.

Vol. 541: P. Barahona, L. Moniz Pereira, A. Porto (Eds.), EPIA '91. Proceedings, 1991. VIII, 292 pages. 1991.

Vol. 542: Z. W. Ras, M. Zemankova (Eds.), Methodologies for Intelligent Systems. Proceedings, 1991. X, 644 pages. 1991.

Vol. 543: J. Dix, K. P. Jantke, P. H. Schmitt (Eds.), Nonmonotonic and Inductive Logic. Proceedings, 1990. X, 243 pages. 1991.

Vol. 546: O. Herzog, C.-R. Rollinger (Eds.), Text Understanding in LILOG. XI, 738 pages. 1991.

Vol. 549: E. Ardizzone, S. Gaglio, F. Sorbello (Eds.), Trends in Artificial Intelligence. Proceedings, 1991. XIV, 479 pages. 1991.

Vol. 565: J. D. Becker, I. Eisele, F. W. Mündemann (Eds.), Parallelism, Learning, Evolution. Proceedings, 1989. VIII, 525 pages. 1991.

Vol. 567: H. Boley, M. M. Richter (Eds.), Processing Declarative Kowledge. Proceedings, 1991. XII, 427 pages. 1991.

Vol. 568: H.-J. Bürckert, A Resolution Principle for a Logic with Restricted Quantifiers. X, 116 pages. 1991.

Vol. 587: R. Dale, E. Hovy, D. Rösner, O. Stock (Eds.), Aspects of Automated Natural Language Generation. Proceedings, 1992. VIII, 311 pages. 1992.

Vol. 590: B. Fronhöfer, G. Wrightson (Eds.), Parallelization in Inference Systems. Proceedings, 1990. VIII, 372 pages. 1992.

Vol. 592: A. Voronkov (Ed.), Logic Programming. Proceedings, 1991. IX, 514 pages. 1992.

Vol. 596: L.-H. Eriksson, L. Hallnäs, P. Schroeder-Heister (Eds.), Extensions of Logic Programming. Proceedings, 1991. VII, 369 pages. 1992.

Vol. 597: H. W. Guesgen, J. Hertzberg, A Perspective of Constraint-Based Reasoning. VIII, 123 pages. 1992.

Vol. 599: Th. Wetter, K.-D. Althoff, J. Boose, B. R. Gaines, M. Linster, F. Schmalhofer (Eds.), Current Developments in Knowledge Acquisition - EKAW '92. Proceedings. XIII, 444 pages. 1992.

Vol. 604: F. Belli, F. J. Radermacher (Eds.), Industrial and Engineering Applications of Artificial Intelligence and Expert Systems. Proceedings, 1992. XV, 702 pages. 1992.

Vol. 607: D. Kapur (Ed.), Automated Deduction – CADE-11. Proceedings, 1992. XV, 793 pages. 1992.

Vol. 610: F. von Martial, Coordinating Plans of Autonomous Agents. XII, 246 pages. 1992.

Vol. 611: M. P. Papazoglou, J. Zeleznikow (Eds.), The Next Generation of Information Systems: From Data to Knowledge. VIII, 310 pages. 1992.

Vol. 617: V. Mařík, O. Štěpánková, R. Trappl (Eds.), Advanced Topics in Artificial Intelligence. Proceedings, 1992. IX, 484 pages. 1992.

Vol. 619: D. Pearce, H. Wansing (Eds.), Nonclassical Logics and Information Processing. Proceedings, 1990. VII, 171 pages. 1992.

Vol. 622: F. Schmalhofer, G. Strube, Th. Wetter (Eds.), Contemporary Knowledge Engineering and Cognition. Proceedings, 1991. XII, 258 pages. 1992.

Vol. 624: A. Voronkov (Ed.), Logic Programming and Automated Reasoning. Proceedings, 1992. XIV, 509 pages. 1992.

Vol. 627: J. Pustejovsky, S. Bergler (Eds.), Lexical Semantics and Knowledge Representation. Proceedings, 1991. XII, 381 pages. 1992.

Vol. 633: D. Pearce, G. Wagner (Eds.), Logics in AI. Proceedings. VIII, 410 pages. 1992.

Vol. 636: G. Comyn, N. E. Fuchs, M. J. Ratcliffe (Eds.), Logic Programming in Action. Proceedings, 1992. X, 324 pages. 1992.

Vol. 638: A. F. Rocha, Neural Nets. A Theory for Brains and Machines. XV, 393 pages. 1992.

Vol. 642: K. P. Jantke (Ed.), Analogical and Inductive Inference. Proceedings, 1992. VIII, 319 pages. 1992.

Vol. 659: G. Brewka, K. P. Jantke, P. H. Schmitt (Eds.), Nonmonotonic and Inductive Logic. Proceedings, 1991. VIII, 332 pages. 1993.

Vol. 660: E. Lamma, P. Mello (Eds.), Extensions of Logic Programming. Proceedings, 1992. VIII, 417 pages. 1993.

Lecture Notes in Computer Science

Vol. 621: O. Nurmi, E. Ukkonen (Eds.), Algorithm Theory – SWAT '92. Proceedings. VIII, 434 pages. 1992.

Vol. 622: F. Schmalhofer, G. Strube, Th. Wetter (Eds.), Contemporary Knowledge Engineering and Cognition. Proceedings, 1991. XII, 258 pages. 1992. (Subseries LNAI).

Vol. 623: W. Kuich (Ed.), Automata, Languages and Programming. Proceedings, 1992. XII, 721 pages. 1992.

Vol. 624: A. Voronkov (Ed.), Logic Programming and Automated Reasoning. Proceedings, 1992. XIV, 509 pages. 1992. (Subseries LNAI).

Vol. 625: W. Vogler, Modular Construction and Partial Order Semantics of Petri Nets. IX, 252 pages. 1992.

Vol. 626: E. Börger, G. Jäger, H. Kleine Büning, M. M . Richter (Eds.), Computer Science Logic. Proceedings, 1991. VIII, 428 pages. 1992.

Vol. 628: G. Vosselman, Relational Matching. IX, 190 pages. 1992.

Vol. 629: I. M. Havel, V. Koubek (Eds.), Mathematical Foundations of Computer Science 1992. Proceedings. IX, 521 pages. 1992.

Vol. 630: W. R. Cleaveland (Ed.), CONCUR '92. Proceedings. X, 580 pages. 1992.

Vol. 631: M. Bruynooghe, M. Wirsing (Eds.), Programming Language Implementation and Logic Programming. Proceedings, 1992. XI, 492 pages. 1992.

Vol. 632: H. Kirchner, G. Levi (Eds.), Algebraic and Logic Programming. Proceedings, 1992. IX, 457 pages. 1992.

Vol. 633: D. Pearce, G. Wagner (Eds.), Logics in AI. Proceedings. VIII, 410 pages. 1992. (Subseries LNAI).

Vol. 634: L. Bougé, M. Cosnard, Y. Robert, D. Trystram (Eds.), Parallel Processing: CONPAR 92 – VAPP V. Proceedings. XVII, 853 pages. 1992.

Vol. 635: J. C. Derniame (Ed.), Software Process Technology. Proceedings, 1992. VIII, 253 pages. 1992.

Vol. 636: G. Comyn, N. E. Fuchs, M. J. Ratcliffe (Eds.), Logic Programming in Action. Proceedings, 1992. X, 324 pages. 1992. (Subseries LNAI).

Vol. 637: Y. Bekkers, J. Cohen (Eds.), Memory Management. Proceedings, 1992. XI, 525 pages. 1992.

Vol. 639: A. U. Frank, I. Campari, U. Formentini (Eds.), Theories and Methods of Spatio-Temporal Reasoning in Geographic Space. Proceedings, 1992. XI, 431 pages. 1992.

Vol. 640: C. Sledge (Ed.), Software Engineering Education. Proceedings, 1992. X, 451 pages. 1992.

Vol. 641: U. Kastens, P. Pfahler (Eds.), Compiler Construction. Proceedings, 1992. VIII, 320 pages. 1992.

Vol. 642: K. P. Jantke (Ed.), Analogical and Inductive Inference. Proceedings, 1992. VIII, 319 pages. 1992. (Subseries LNAI).

Vol. 643: A. Habel, Hyperedge Replacement: Grammars and Languages. X, 214 pages. 1992.

Vol. 644: A. Apostolico, M. Crochemore, Z. Galil, U. Manber (Eds.), Combinatorial Pattern Matching. Proceedings, 1992. X, 287 pages. 1992.

Vol. 645: G. Pernul, A M. Tjoa (Eds.), Entity-Relationship Approach – ER '92. Proceedings, 1992. XI, 439 pages, 1992.

Vol. 646: J. Biskup, R. Hull (Eds.), Database Theory – ICDT '92. Proceedings, 1992. IX, 449 pages. 1992.

Vol. 647: A. Segall, S. Zaks (Eds.), Distributed Algorithms. X, 380 pages. 1992.

Vol. 648: Y. Deswarte, G. Eizenberg, J.-J. Quisquater (Eds.), Computer Security – ESORICS 92. Proceedings. XI, 451 pages. 1992.

Vol. 649: A. Pettorossi (Ed.), Meta-Programming in Logic. Proceedings, 1992. XII, 535 pages. 1992.

Vol. 650: T. Ibaraki, Y. Inagaki, K. Iwama, T. Nishizeki, M. Yamashita (Eds.), Algorithms and Computation. Proceedings, 1992. XI, 510 pages. 1992.

Vol. 651: R. Koymans, Specifying Message Passing and Time-Critical Systems with Temporal Logic. IX, 164 pages. 1992.

Vol. 652: R. Shyamasundar (Ed.), Foundations of Software Technology and Theoretical Computer Science. Proceedings, 1992. XIII, 405 pages. 1992.

Vol. 653: A. Bensoussan, J.-P. Verjus (Eds.), Future Tendencies in Computer Science, Control and Applied Mathematics. Proceedings, 1992. XV, 371 pages. 1992.

Vol. 654: A. Nakamura, M. Nivat, A. Saoudi, P. S. P. Wang, K. Inoue (Eds.), Prallel Image Analysis. Proceedings, 1992. VIII, 312 pages. 1992.

Vol. 655: M. Bidoit, C. Choppy (Eds.), Recent Trends in Data Type Specification. X, 344 pages. 1993.

Vol. 656: M. Rusinowitch, J. L. Rémy (Eds.), Conditional Term Rewriting Systems. Proceedings, 1992. XI, 501 pages. 1993.

Vol. 657: E. W. Mayr (Ed.), Graph-Theoretic Concepts in Computer Science. Proceedings, 1992. VIII, 350 pages. 1993.

Vol. 658: R. A. Rueppel (Ed.), Advances in Cryptology – EUROCRYPT '92. Proceedings, 1992. X, 493 pages. 1993.

Vol. 659: G. Brewka, K. P. Jantke, P. H. Schmitt (Eds.), Nonmonotonic and Inductive Logic. Proceedings, 1991. VIII, 332 pages. 1993. (Subseries LNAI).

Vol. 660: E. Lamma, P. Mello (Eds.), Extensions of Logic Programming. Proceedings, 1992. VIII, 417 pages. 1993. (Subseries LNAI).